MW01247079

Where Do We Draw the Line?

Reverend Fred Davis

ISBN 979-8-88616-677-4 (paperback)
ISBN 979-8-88616-678-1 (digital)

Copyright © 2023 by Reverend Fred Davis

All rights reserved. No part of this publication may be reproduced, distributed, or transmitted in any form or by any means, including photocopying, recording, or other electronic or mechanical methods without the prior written permission of the publisher. For permission requests, solicit the publisher via the address below.

Christian Faith Publishing
832 Park Avenue
Meadville, PA 16335
www.christianfaithpublishing.com

Printed in the United States of America

This book is written by Rev. Fred Davis in his own words, in his uneducated style of grammar, and in his own unlearned book-writing skills with no writing knowledge of how to properly write a book. This book should in no way reflect on this wonderful editor or the amazing Christian Faith Publishing.

I want my readers to understand I'm not your average author. In fact, I'm not one at all. I'm just basically trying to get out a message to the world. Just let it be noted that my ignorance and uneducated skills of writing should in no way reflect on this wonderful establishment. This book is solely written by me—Fred Davis—and in my words 100 percent. I hope you can receive God's word and my points and instructions clearly. Thank you, editor, Christian Faith Publishing, and my dear readers. God bless you all.

NOTE: Rev. Fred Davis would like 100 percent of all of (50 percent to LCC, 50 percent to *Minister's Voice* magazine) the proceeds of this book to go to Living Christ Church and Pastor Donahue Green/ Minister James Johnson's "*Ministers Voice* (Church) Magazine."

Foreword

Minister Fred Davis preaches and teaches out of the KJV Bible, and with every fiber of his being...believes the world is in the Last Days, and he believes that the whole Bible is the authentic Word of God. Minister Fred Davis also wants his readers to know that they will receive written text scriptures to where they can cross reference and look up the subjects and topics discussed. This book and topics and thoughts are Minister Fred Davis's and his alone and wants his readers to know, "If you get nothing else out of this book, you'll get the Word of God and you will get Bible scriptures for life today. And it is packed full of God's Holy Word."

Again, opinions and views are solely his and his alone...where you draw the line on life, on death, on warnings from God. His question is, wouldn't a loving God warn his people of great devastations coming on the earth, according to Bible prophecy? Where do we draw the line on the END of the world or on being ready to meet Jesus?

Introduction

"In the beginning was the word and the was with God, and the word was God (Jn. 1–1)." Ever since from the beginning of time, the devil has tried to be God and change what He has said (Gen. 3:1–5) and even used man and women to alter God's Word (Gen. 2–16, 17; Gen. 3–12, 13; Rom. 1–25; Mat. 4:1–10).

In the 1960s' Roe v. Wade, mankind changed God's law from "Thou shalt not kill" to the woman's choice of murdering her unborn child. It's not a choice or a right. It's a human being being murdered. But America, the good ol' USA, the land of the free, has the right to abort, and it doesn't stop there. They are also putting the dead babies in makeup and wearing it on their faces (it's called collagen), a fibrous protein taken from connective fetus tissue, bone, and cartilage. Wow…what a right and choice they have; well, they'll find out on judgment day. What the Bible says in (Hosea 4:6), "My people are destroyed for their lack of knowledge because thou hast rejected knowledge, I will also reject thee, that thou shalt be no priest to me, seeing thou hast forgotten the law of thy God. I will also forget thy children" (KJV). Well, that sounded pretty plain to me. Plus, the Ten Commandments also say, "Thou shalt not kill," and of course, that's why it becomes a "word game" (it's not a baby; it's a fetus.) They say to clear their conscience, fallen into a trap of the devil, it's a human being…and you'll have to deal with murdering your baby for the rest of your life. Pastor after pastor has counseled women who has aborted their babies; many have committed suicide because they can't handle the guilt.

Does God forgive? Yes, absolutely; if we truly repent of our sins, he is faithful and just to forgive us our sins (1 John 1:9) and to cleanse us from all unrighteousness… Also, (Romans 10:9–11).

So you see, man changes the Word of God into a lie so man can have his own choice and live without feeling guilty. Read (Romans 1:25 and Hebrews 11:24, 25). Moses had the choice to live like a king but saw the wrong that was happening to the children of Israel (God's people) that they were so mistreated that he had to decide which side he was on. And Joshua said this in (Joshua 24:15). Also, for you to choose this day who you will serve. Hey, folks, it's God or the devil, heaven or hell. No middle ground. Jesus said, "You're either for me or against me, you'll gather or scatter" (Matt. 12:30, Luke 11:23). You can't be lukewarm; you have to be hot or cold (Rev. 3:15, 16).

I heard my pastor say one day, "You can't be half pregnant. You are, or you're not." So where do we draw the line? It's live right or live wrong, or is it live right or get left? Look back through Bible history. All through it, we read people of God made their decision usually based on right and wrong… As in (Daniel 3, verse 6), "Whosoever doesn't bow to the king's idol will burn" (see verse 3). And in (Exodus 20:5 verse 3, 4) says in the Ten Commandments to not have or make (verse 5) or not to bow down to them. Pretty plain English, even in KJV. (I was a high school dropout, was into drugs in the '60s, and '70s, went back to school ten years later, and got my diploma and still not real bright. I was a C-, D-point average student, yet with the help of the Holy Spirit, God has helped me understand the KJV Bible. So where do we draw the line to obey God's Word or rebel?

(Second Chronicles 7:14) says, "If my people which are called by my name, shall humble themselves and pray and seek my face and turn from their wicked ways, then will I hear from heaven and will forgive their sin and will heal their land."

You may as well cuss a person out as to tell them to repent and get saved. America needs to repent. Ouch… No, that's not a bad word but a good word. Isn't it ironic when you read in every obituary about everyone going to heaven to be with their Lord? But the Bible plainly states in (John 3:3, 5), "We must be born again." We have to repent of our old ways. "If we are in Christ, old things pass away, behold all things are become new" (2 Cor. 5:17). The word *repent* is actually a good word in Greek (*metanoeo* or *metamorpho*), which means a metamorphosis is taking place in the heart and soul, a change. (Romans 12:1–2) says, "Be ye transformed." In (Psalm 51:10), King David said, "Create in me a clean heart of God and renew a right spirit within me."

So if we repented, saved, born again, we are changed. I do not party anymore since I got saved, according to (2 Corinthians 5:17). Since I'm changed, a new creature in Christ, old things are passed away. And now I go to church instead of the bars… Oh sure, there are some that do both, but the Bible says that's a double standard or a hypocrite. (Galatians 5:16 to 21) says people of this nature, arecalled works of the flesh, shall not inherit the kingdom of God. I'm not a Bible scholar but I do understand that this means if you live in sin of this nature, you will not go to heaven!

Jesus said in (Luke 17:32), "Remember Lot's wife, she looked back." Jesus said in (Luke 9:62), "No man having put his hand to the plough (plow) and looks back is fit for the kingdom of God." You'd be surprised of how many people misinterpret the scriptures and just don't get it or don't want to comply to change their life. We can't hang onto the world's way of life and God's, according to the Bible. Then you can even get into the last days and end-time prophecies such as (Mathew 24, 2 Timothy 3, 2 Peter 3, and even 2 Peter 2), which speaks of false prophets and false teachers, etc., even tells of angels that sinned and were cast down to hell. No, not purgatory. Verse 5 tells about the world in the days of Noah also in (Matthew 24:37 to 39), and please note, if anyone, I mean anyone, can speak of these things, I can because God has delivered me from the partying, hippy biker drug life and healed my marriage and turn my life around, took me off drugs, and God took that desire out of my heart to smoke dope and cigarettes and get drunk and get high and chase around and healed my wife's heart and gave her love back for me that I destroyed.

So you see, when I read the Bible telling about those days, I know firsthand, and when I was in school there were four of us long-haired hippies. Now you look, and you're lucky to find four straights (Christians, people living right). Again, 1966 Roe versus Wade, my high school life started spiraling down, and while I'm starting in the drug world, the world is legalizing the killing of innocent babies. As (Isaiah 5:20) says, calling evil good and good evil. People were saying I heard that all my life (2 Pet. 3:3–4). You're repeating yourself, preacher, yes (so did God.) In Matthew, Mark, Luke, John, four gospels, (2 Timothy 3, 2 Peter 2, and 2 Peter 3, and in Revelations 13), we read of the mark of the beast when we are now ready to bring in the microchip and put it in people for the sake of protecting them from identity theft and protect children when they are abducted, etc. And people in these last days are so gullible, they will fall for it.

Point in case, try taking someone's or teenagers' cellphone or computer away from them, so shall it be. When they say in order for you to have access to your phone or computer, you have to have a microchip implanted in your hand. Woe! Better read (Rev. 13) and (Rev. 20:4 to 8). How about reading (2 Corinthians 5:11), "Knowing the terror of the Lord we persuade men." Are you trying to convince people that Jesus is coming? There during the '70s, '80s, '90s, 2000s, there was a good move of God in people. Now forty years after the '70s, you don't hear a lot of it. The days of 9/11 have quieted down. And not to mean in any way to offend anyone, but then the churches was full. People thought, "Are we, as in (Revelations 18), in America, about to be nuked?" But let a few years go by; let me point you to God's Word that man can't do anything about. All the peace talks and negotiating will solve nothing. God teaches we need to repent, which means get right with God or get left behind. People don't want to hear "fear talk" as it makes them uncomfortable; that's why we have millions of ear-tickling, love, encouraging churches that have never or will never teach this stuff of about hell. When, if most people really studied the Bible, we would know we are in the last days; there will be false prophets, false preachers, point in case. Anyone ever hear of Jim Jones (Matt. 24:11) and many, many more over the years? Preachers have fallen from grace; we are not there judge, nor is anyone, mine on this book or my differences of beliefs or biblical views or the way we interpret the bible. Our old pastor said on the fallen preachers, "Be careful not to bad-mouth them because if they repent and get back in good standing with the Lord and you are bad—mouthing them, you are touching God's anointed (Ps. 105:15;

1ˢᵗ Chron. 16–22) and the Bible teaches against that sort of things as very dangerous."

Everyone wants to be accepted and loved. Jesus Christ taught this type of love, showing the example in St. (John 13:1–21). This example of love, even though he was Lord, was to wash all the disciples' feet. In doing this, and Jesus knowing who would deny him (Peter, and who'd betray Him, Judas). Leaving us an example of love and forgiveness. We must forgive others that trespass against us and pray for those that despitefully use and persecute you. And those that fall, we all need to pray for them and the Word of God says we that are spiritual should pray for those that fall, and we are to restore and encourage them. Someone that's drowning doesn't need you to throw them an anchor or anvil, but a life saver, on a rope…and pull them to safety. Followed up with swimming lessons (Phil. 4:3, Gal. 6:1, 2), spiritually speaking: Forgiving others, to that weak swimmer. We all had to learn to crawl before walking, and I had to learn to dog paddle before swimming. And grant it, I was all my life a slow learner. Slow comprehension and, yes, bad in English and a poor speller, but I'm persevering and doing my best; and with the Lord's help, you and I are both gonna make it. Friend, if you fall, remember the little child Jesus spoke of that we must be like in our heart, forgiving, and like a toddler that falls, there is a tenaciousness in that kid that he keeps getting up. And we (the church) need to repent and get back to those old Bible teachings rather than the anvils and anchors bad-mouthing God's anointed (very dangerous).

My wife Brenda was commenting on people taking scripture very lightly. In other words, folks today just seem to think the Bible is just a religious book instead of and rather than being the real authentic Word of God (John 1:1; Matt. 4:4; Heb. 4:12; Luke 6:46). And the Bible is our road map to heaven. But to say it's just a religious book and say or not follow its directions would be a hundred percent sure way to cause that person to not make it to heaven! And there are only two places to go after this life: it's heaven or hell. The Bible tells the reader how to make it to heaven and how to live the way God wants you to live.

If people believe it's just a religious book, then they could ignore the Ten Commandments and all the scriptures that says what sin is and what adultery is. That will send you to hell. So then, people could live the way they did in (Matt 24:37) in Noah's day. Ouch! We are there again, and so history has repeated itself. Wow…true…but make a note: the Bible is very plain if you're living a lie or hypocrite lifestyle. Jesus made it plain to the disciples using the religious guys Pharisees and Sadducees for an example. That religion doesn't save you, a church doesn't save you, a belief or doctrine doesn't save you, only being born again, calling on Jesus, having Christ's blood wash away your sins, confessing your sins to Jesus not a priest or pope or preacher or church but Jesus is the only, I said is the only way, to God (John 14:6; John 3:35; 1 John 1:7, 8, 9; Rom. 10:9–13, 17; Matt. 23). Jesus said if your righteousness doesn't exceed above the Pharisees, you'll in no case enter into the kingdom of heaven (Matt. 5:20). Hello? So where do you draw the line. It's better be straight to Jesus…doing what he said (Lk. 6–46).

Well, no. 1, examine our own selves (Ps. 51:10 to 13; 2nd Cor. 13:5), asking, "How do I line up with the Word Jesus taught?"

No. 2, examine the lifestyle of the Scribes and Pharisees. (They were very, very religious, but Jesus was not in their heart. They constantly were having murder in their heart. Plotting to kill Jesus, lying, scheming, gossiping, framing people, etc., living a hypocrite lifestyle, standing on street corners to look holy while praying out loud so everyone could hear, but inwardly Jesus said they were ravening wolves (Matt. 7:15, Matt. 6:2–5). Most people know that when you start living for God, you don't live for God half-heartedly (Jeremiah 29:13; Psalms 138:1: Psalms 9:1) but with all your heart. Even the Bible says this. When we were partiers, getting drunk, smoking dope, we gave it our all when we partied and when we were sinners. So now that we are saved, we all should give God our whole heart with no reservations.

Oh no. Then you'd be marked as a fanatic. But when Judgment Day comes, you'll wish you had been, but then it'll be too late for people to live for God with their whole heart, mind, and soul (Luke 12:15–21; Matt. 19:16–26). Nothing's worth our soul, especially adultery, sex, and all the time having fights about flirting or spending too much on dope or going out all night, etc. When God healed our marriage and gave love back in my wife's heart, why would I want to destroy that again? Six years of hell was enough in any marriage—oh, there may be a rough spot now and then, but God always helps us through it. Where do you draw the line?

In these end times, the last days before Christ's return, the Bible teaches in (John 16:2, Revelations 2:10). They'll even think they do God service by killing you or putting you in jail but be faithful even unto death, the Bible says. So many people are being persecuted for their walk and beliefs in Jesus Christ especially on the job. Many jobs are for everything on the planet, but God.

While shopping, I heard over the speaker a lady singing, saying, "In this life, anything goes." Does that make it right? No...in fact, it's Bible prophecy coming to pass. Jesus Christ said in the New Testament that in the last days, it'll be as the days of Noah. And as the days of Sodom and Gomorrah, (Matthew 24:37) (repeating myself), it'll be all right. Also in (2 Peter 3:3–14, Luke 9:62, and Luke 17:32), Jesus reminds us of looking back to sin. And Philippians 3:13, 14 says press forward, and in Hebrews 12:1–2, to look to Jesus.

And lay aside the sin that so easily besets us. How many out there that say they are Christians and followers of Christ yet live like a devil? I am so amazed at the people there are in the obituary have said they went to be with the Lord, or went to heaven, died drunk, wow...never read (Galatians 5:15–26, 1 Peter 5:8, 9) doesn't that say be sober, be vigilant (can you be watchful, being drunk, er...a... "No," guess that's why the Bible says all those that live that life don't enter in to heaven (1st Cor. 6:9 to 11).

Then you have the religious that believe the man of God can pray you out of hell after you're dead. WRONG. If you die in your sins, you didn't confess with your mouth the sins you committed, that kind of religion and that kind of man of God is a liar (John 8:21 to; Matthew 23; Romans 3:4 to 23). Where do we draw the line? Right is right. Wrong is wrong. The Bible (KJV) tells us how to live... Again, there is a difference in diving to the ground on purpose or stumbling and falling. God does forgive sin. Don't misunderstand me please (1 John 1:9, 10). If we confess our sins to Jesus, he is faithful and just to forgive our sins and to cleanse US from all unrighteousness. If we say that we have not sinned, we make him a liar and his word (Bible) is not in US. (1st John 2:1, 2) says Jesus is our advocate, propitiation for our sins; Jesus took our place on the cross and died for our sins. (John 3:16, 17, 18) became a curse for us (Gal. 3:13), and we all need to read Galatians 1; the whole chapter says if someone comes to you teaching differently, they are cursed.

Matthew 6:33, Colossians 3:1 say if we are risen with Christ, we should seek those things above; where Christ sits at the right hand of God, set your mind on things above, not on the earth. That's why some Christians are so radical and fanatical. And that (Col. 1:10, KJV) says we are to be (Heb. 11:6) pleasing to God or man (it's left out of some other versions). Our old pastor used to say compare them with KJV, but I say just read KJV. I can understand with God's help. And I was not real bright. Also (Romans 12:1 and 2) says present your bodies a living sacrifice, holy and acceptable unto God, which is your reasonable service. (It is your responsibility.) Read verse 2, "And be not conformed to this world, but be ye transformed by the renewing of your mind that ye may prove what is that good and acceptable and perfect will of God." Read (Luke 21:34, 35, 36), take heed to yourselves lest at any time your hearts be overcharged.

A battery will blow up when it's overcharged! And in these last days, man would not be watching for Jesus Christ's return and second coming while being overly indulging in drunkenness as (Luke 21:34) says. Calling it surfeiting, when I was a drug addict and a drunk, I wasn't thinking of the rapture or even watching for it, and anyone with a brain knows if the law of the land is against you driving drunk, it's because you're not alert enough to stay on the road! So how could that person be watching for Jesus to come in (Luke 21:34–36)?

So many people will say to pacify their conscience in (John 2), Jesus turned the water into wine. And they say one drink is okay, but not for an alcoholic (Heb 12:1–2). So if so many other scriptures tell us to watch, as in (Luke 21:34–36), or be sober and be vigilant—awake, watchful, alert—as in (1 Peter 5:6–8) because your adversary—the enemy of your soul—the devil is a roaring lion and walks about seeking whom he may devour.

Satan wants to make you fall and to destroy you. So again, if everyone's okay and ready, why did (2 Peter 3:17) say, "Beware lest [you = ye] also be led away with your error of the wicked, fall from your own [steadfastness = stability or being fixed firmly on God]." In (Psalm 108:1), the perfect example again is Peter when stepping out of the boat onto the water walking out to Jesus. Then, he took his eyes off Jesus and started sinking (Matt. 14:28–30).

And now because we are in the Last Days, the evilest time of earth's history, this is happening. And yet, ever so many intellects— and yes, even many so-called believers—don't see it! In (Matthew 25), they were all ten Christians or virgins, but only the five that were wise and 100 percent for God, having extra oil filled up plus taking extra oil with them! Or read (Matthew 24:44–51). Wow. And (Luke 21:35): "For as a [snare = a trap] shall it come on All them that dwell on the face of the whole earth." So keep watching for Jesus and stay alert for God! As in (Luke 21-36) Verse 36, "watch ye therefore and pray always." Note: Do you think a drunk is looking for Jesus to return or witnessing to someone to get saved? I don't think so because I was a partier in the '60s and '70s (repeat: finish verse, preacher). And pray always that ye may be accounted worthy to escape all these things that shall come to pass and to stand before the son of man (Jesus).

Years ago, crime was not real bad, but now, it has skyrocketed to an all-time high. And I mean it's everywhere and it used to be, watch out after dark. Now, thugs are hitting and robbing even in the broad daylight. And they used to wear masks, not now, and people are coming out of the closets, and they forget and don't even care what the Bible says. But let a massive tornado rip through a city or a real bad earthquake hit, and bad ones are coming (Revelation 16:18 to 20; Luke 21:11; Luke 21:22). So bad that the Bible says even the mountains are gonna fall flat or move and fall flat (which will cause the water level to rise). Have you ever sat down in half of a bathtub of water? Your body mass raises the water level. The Bible reads on to say every island moved out of their places (Rev. 6:14, Rev. 16:20).

That's one bad earthquake, dude, ten or fifteen or twenty on the Richter scale. Who knows? But we've already been seeing enough come to pass that it's made a believer outta me. Yes, in the Bible, it does say in (2 Timothy 1:7), "For God has not given us the spirit of fear but of power, love and of a sound mind."

Repeat (2 Corinthians 5:11), so why does the Bible say, "knowing therefore the terror of the Lord." We persuade men; is it because he said in the "end of the world, last day chapter"? In (Matthew 24:33–34), it's even at the door and this generation will not pass away till all these things are fulfilled. Now if you know and really believe the Bible and still get drunk, you are not only the stupidest person but are blind according to scripture and will miss heaven (Luke 21:33–36; Gal. 5:21).

Yes, I repeat myself. But come on. Where do you draw the line? The Bible says you can't compromise, yet people do. Hey, I've been a prison minister for eighteen years and pastor of four churches.

I've seen 'em come and go and some live like the devil himself and say they are saved all their lives. Which yes, that's a lie. They haven't changed (according to 2 Corinthians 5:17).

Read (Matthew 25 or Revelations 3:5), or I'll say it again, "Watch therefore and pray" (Luke 21:36). One time, no, don't think so.

But pray ALWAYS that you'll be ready (read it!). Come on, people.

Religions will send you to hell *if* they are teaching false doctrine. The Bible says, "God's people are destroyed for lack of knowledge (wow) and read it in (Hosea 4:6, 2 Timothy 2:15). Apostle Paul wrote, "Study to show yourself approved." A working man needed not to be ashamed, rightly dividing the Word of truth (KJV).

Who gave them permission to change what God said in (Revelations 22, 18–19, Romans 1:25, and Galatians 1:6 to 10)?

Some versions leave out *study*; why is this? They change it. I get so angry when I've studied the word for years and years. And pick up some translation that some have completely removed scripture or altered, changed. Yet (Revelations 22:18–19) says you can't, or you won't make it, yet they do.

(Romans 1:25); (Galatians 1:6 to 10) say they will be accursed.

Oh, it gets better than that. Some anti-Christ, lunatic hairballs that rewrite God's Word into a lie as Paul said in (Romans 1:25) (KJV).

They say God has given them permission with (2 Timothy 3:13 to 17) (in the last days) they forgot what verse 13 says and too stupid to know that the Bible is to correct us. In verses 16 and 17, not that we correct God. Oh, Lord, you didn't really mean "thou shalt not kill" or you didn't really mean "thou shalt not commit adultery" or did you? (Luke 6-46; Exodus 20-13, 14) or thanks for not saying no one can change the scriptures to what they want it to say (Rom. 1-25; Revelation 22:18-19)… Oh, come on, you stupid LIARS! Anti-Christ devils are the only ones that would say that! The Bible is to correct us as in (Luke 6:46). Hear this: only a devil or an Antichrist demon-possessed person would change or alter the Bible! In (Revelation 22:18–19), it's sealed with a curse, and God said not to take away from it or add to it. That's plain to me, but so many devils are changing it and saying we are just clarifying it or making it easier to understand. That's the only Holy Spirit's (Holy Ghost's) job, not theirs (John 14:26).

In Matthew 4, the devil was the one twisting and changing the Word of God into a lie (Rom. 1:25, Matt. 4 verse 3, 5, 6, 8, 9).

No. 1, he tried to trick Jesus into misusing his power.

No. 2, then he tried to trick him into suicide, twisting (Psalm 91:11–12).

No. 3, then tried to trick him into becoming a devil worshipper.

Come on, people, if the devil tried tricking Jesus and twisting God's Word, don't be so blind and gullible (John 14:26).

Many, many will be angry with my book, but it is better to obey God than man (Acts 5:29). Would a real, true Christian really change the Bible? No, no way…so they need to repent, because the Bible says, Jesus said if the blind leads the blind, both will fall in the ditch. Does that mean readers of false Bibles will fall? Yes, but, preacher, what about all those big TV preachers that follow all those other versions? Well, the old saying you heard when you were a kid, if she jumps off a cliff, are you gonna jump too because she did? Don't think so… Yet people forget of the warnings in the last days of all the false doctrines and doctrines of the devil, which the Bible plainly warns us of that and it even says in (Galatians 1:8), "Don't even believe an angel if he tries to give you another gospel."

(Matt. 24): False preachers and false teachers, doctrines of evils (1 Tim. 4:1) Notice in this verse that some shall depart from the faith, as in (John 6:67, 68, 69). So either a devil or someone following a devil would be the only one to change what God himself said! Also notice the last part of (1 Tim. 4:1): "giving heed to seducing spirits and doctrines of devils," and in (verse 2), what are they speaking? "Speaking lies in hypocrisy, they turned to the devil, having their conscience seared with a hot iron." That tells me, when people sear their conscience, which God gave them to keep them right with him so they can walk and live right and follow what God says, if they ignore their conscience, they would easily stray from the true word of God, and be turned toward false doctrines. This is why we should always pray as David did in Psalm—a repenting prayer (Ps. 51:10–12)! And always ask God to create in us a clean heart and a right spirit, etc. Or as Apostle Paul said, "Let this mind be in you, that was in Jesus" (Phil. 2–5). If you are really right in their heart and have the mind of Jesus Christ, you'll even be ready to die for the cause of Jesus Christ. As (Rev. 12:11) tells us, God will then give you an understanding heart, and God sees those who are really sincere and have a made up their minds to follow God 100 percent (Prov. 15:2, 2 Tim. 2:19, Ps. 84:11, Heb. 13:9). Wind of doctrines (Ephesians 4:14), (hello) in (Colossians 2:22, 1 Timothy 1:3, Galatians 1:6 to 10).

Read the whole chapter of Matthew 23. How Jesus reacts to religious Pharisees that change or harp on Jesus not following the Sabbath day.

Yet people today still jump on the same wagon…not even hearing or understanding what Jesus said concerning the Sabbath. Now, I will follow and listen to what Jesus says instead of what religion or churches or some Pharisee devil said. Jesus made it crystal clear in (John 10:25 to 29). And I've worked with some religious folks that really harp on to never get plucked out of his hand. And that gives them license to sin and live like a devil, failing to realize (Revelations

3:5) and (Matthew 25). And like those Pharisees that said they wanted to catch Jesus in his words so they could trap and kill him (Luke 11:52, 54; Mark 12:13). Yet Jesus warned the disciples about the doctrine of the Pharisees, which is hypocrisy. (When people change scripture, they add or take away that's a different doctrine). The Bible is sealed with a curse on anyone that changes it. Why can't people understand it? They want to read something more elaborate. Something more exciting or more meaningful. That is to add to and take away (Rev. 22:18, 19). It just started out. We'll just change the *thee*s and the *thou*s so a non-Christian—a sinner, an unbeliever—can understand the Bible.

This was the wrong motive of altering, rewriting, and changing the Bible into an easier, clearer English Bible designed by a sinner and not by the prophets of God. Wow, people are really stupid! God designed the Bible only for those who follow him 100 percent. The Bible was not designed for evil-minded people, but the loving, intelligent God of the universe designed it that way!

Don't people even have a clue that the same God of heaven that designed and made the human body with cells, blood vessels, bones, muscle tissue, etc.; the vast solar system of the universe, stars, and planets; and the ocean tides operating by the moon's gravity, etc. couldn't have made a simple-to-understand Bible. It wasn't made simple to understand for evil but only for the true followers of Jesus Christ.

An example is the parable (Matthew 13:34, and 35) or (Mark 13:10–12 or Matthew 21:45). Many other scriptures are similar. Some even hated Jesus. Those were the evil-minded type of people who said they can't tell what this man says, as (Matthew 13:10–11) teaches. So nine miles later, the Bible was created for those who are true followers of Jesus Christ.

When people confess their sins and repent of their evil ways and turn from sin and follow Jesus with all their heart, then God gives them an understanding heart. Christians can understand it, not even realizing it's for those who are fully saved, born again, changed, and filled with the Holy Spirit (Ghost) and then the Holy Ghost (John

14:26) will teach, lead, and guide you through the scriptures; but for all these different people, changing God's Word is very wrong.

Hey, some may have meant well, but most are being used by the devil to deceive. Fasting and praying is when a follower of Jesus Christ goes without food and prays continually, and while on the fast, it gives him power with God in the spirit to go against the demonic forces of hell, make him stronger in his faith (as in Jude 20), and to be more sensitive to God's voice; but it's mainly to have power against the devil (Luke 10:19, Acts 1:8). Or evangelists fast so they can be led by God's spirit. But again, Jesus cast out the devil, and he told the disciples this kind goeth not out by fasting and praying. Now if fasting and praying gives Christians power against the devil, and it does, this explains why the devil picked these false prophets, false teachers, false doctrines, and false Bible publishing companies to make Bibles that removed these power scriptures (Mark 9:29, Matt. 17:21). Are people really that blind? Yes, they are! It really amazes me that a doctor will have you fast for a medical test or x-rays and that the whole human race does it...because the doctor said to. Wow. But when God says to fast and the devil comes and whispers in some Antichrist, devil-possessed idiot's ear and says to them, "Go and reprint up a new Bible version and just say they are making it easier to understand by clarifying it by removing the *thees*, *thous*, etc., of course, they won't say they are also taking out scriptures that'll give the child of God power against the devil. Wow. As an example, on a battlefield, it's like firing with blanks against the enemy, yet he's shooting real bullets and missiles at you. Wow, and so it is, living for God (Matt. 24:4–11, Matt. 7:15). Again, (1 Tim. 4:1–2) speaks of the latter times of Last Days. We are there, folks. (Luke 10:19 and Acts 1:8) say that God gives us power over the enemy. Now let's go back to the first part where Jesus is speaking: "Behold I give unto you Power to tread on serpents, and scorpions, and over all the power of the enemy, and nothing shall by any means hurt you." Then (verse 20) says, we are not that the spirits are subject to us but rejoice that our names are written in the Book of Life (Rev. 3:5) in heaven. But my point is, God gives the Christians power against the devil by having them fast and pray, and that's why the devil caused it to be taken out of the newer-version translations! So the Christians in today's generation would be powerless against him. For example, if I gave you a map of a vacant lot that had treasure or ammo and weapons buried in it and your worst enemy erased the information where a bunch of land mines were buried all around the treasure in different spots so you would be blown to pieces and die, how would you react to rushing to the treasure, especially if the warning came from someone you know you trusted? Newer-version translated Bibles are doing just that very thing: leaving out vital information, which would cheat you out of your protection and power against your enemy and cheat you out of a better life. Well, my analogy parable is not as good as Jesus Christ's, but I pray you get my point. God does gives us power, which is "fasting and praying" together, yet they remove it? Maybe they are connected to the food companies or the devil himself. At any case, to alter or remove scripture is wrong! And if the blind leading the blind applies to those that read it and follow those blown-up too, more exciting versions, be careful, reader, about bad-mouthing me on this book. Don't touch God's anointed (1 Chron. 16:22, Ps. 105:15; Isa. 61:1, Luke 4:18).

If you do not agree, that'll be your problem on judgment day, but you've been told and warned. God has had my life programmed out since birth, prison ministry those eighteen years. I've left homeland, families, left everything for the gospel, and God has taken care of me; till he says it's finished for Fred, I'll do what God says, not man (Acts 5–29).

Yes, I'm not at the moment pastoring and do attend a dynamite church, Living Christ Church, with pastors that preach the truth and yes along these lines. Pastor Donahue and Evon Green are not prejudiced and have encouraged me and my wife and they have been there for us, especially these last six years that we've attended there since my on-the-job car wreck following back surgery. And the love of God is on them. And Pastor has made it clear to his church that he follows and reads out from the KJV Bible. We have seen the spirit of God on him so strong. And you feel the spirit of God at Living Christ Church, but not in very many other churches, and I've been to many, especially the ones that teach out of false versions. Their church services are worse than funerals. And I've been to some funerals of a powerhouse preacher that it was like revival service where everyone knew in their hearts that man of God made it. So they were rejoicing in their hearts. And isn't that what it's all about? Making heaven. If this book can turn the light on for one individual, then it's worth it all. My question is WHY? And again, where do we draw the line on people continuing to change God's Word? Pretty soon, it'll be so altered. I heard they're even coming out with a version Bible with street talk in it. I'll repeat myself again. I'm an ex-hippy biker, drug addict. Did about everything, and ashamed to say but God saved me. When I repented, God filled me with the Holy Ghost and his spirit has taught me to understand the scriptures. Why do you think Jesus spoke in parables? So the Pharisees, the religious one with murder and sacrilege and a counterfeit heart couldn't understand because they weren't his sheep. His sheep know his voice (John 10:27). We need to pray for God to fill us with his spirit and ask him for understanding. But to follow a counterfeit recycled version is not of God.

You see, in life, if you are the owner of a busy market and someone passes a few fake counterfeit bills, I've seen them before, you can't hardly tell them (Judas) counterfeit bills apart. Walks like a dog, talks like a dog, looks like a dog...must be a dog, right? Wrong.

The Bible teaches that there will be false doctrines (Matt. 24:11), yet no one warns on them and the ones reading them different version are hooked on them, that they are the authentic Word of God...wrong. It's a counterfeit. And they get mad because you tell them the truth. And then they want to get you or frame you. This is the same attitude the Pharisees and Sadducees and Scribes that were against Jesus. Jesus taught the truth and warned that if they come against me, they'll come against you (Matt. 24:9; Mark 13:13; Luke 21:17; John 15:18, 24, 25; John 17:14–20).

But they (the false Bible version translators) all stated at the very beginning or their retranslations that they were just gonna remove all the *thee*s and the *thou*s to make the Bible easier to understand... And the devil ran with it. And again, I understand, if it would have stopped there. But the devil stuck his foot in and now new versions and retranslations have come out of hell, and I mean some you would have never believe are now using them. So was Jesus wrong in (Matthew 4)? Was Paul wrong when he said what he said in (Galatians 1:8)? If even an angel comes with a different gospel (hello) or in (2 Corinthians 11:14), Satan himself is transformed unto an angel of light.

Wait, it doesn't stop with the devil; read (verse 13) and on in (verse 15). "Therefore, it is no great thing if his MINISTERS also be transformed as the ministers of righteousness whose end shall be according to their works." Come on, folks, where do you draw the line?

Counterfeit is counterfeit; it looks enough like it but lacks authenticity. It is not the real thing (many are fooled).

In (Matthew 4:6), again the devil quotes (Psalm 91:11): To Jesus, yes, he even quotes (verse 12) with a twist and a tempt against on his deity, when Jesus replies in (verse 7 of Matthew 4), "Thou shalt not tempt the Lord thy God." Yes, the devil even has to answer to God (Job 1:7). So the devil was saying to jump off the top of the temple, that the angels will catch him.

So, preacher, you're saying suicide is tempting God? Yes… God is the giver of life. And to take it you're listening to the wrong voice. Paul said in (2 Corinthians 10:5) to cast down imaginations and every high thing that exalteth itself against the knowledge of God and bring into captivity every thought to the obedience of Christ.

The pastor I got saved under taught that if you read a different version, compare it to KJV, but I say why compare it? Just read KJV, period. Folks, I'm making heaven; don't know about you, but if the word is plain and says the blind will lead the blind and both keyword, both—the blind and the one that's blind leading the blind, both fall in the ditch! (Matt. 15:14) The word both is a keyword in the text. Note: I didn't write the Bible verse. If you can't understand that, God help ya, he (Jesus) didn't say they made it to heaven. The whole problem is the devil's using recycled counterfeit versions and taking scripture out of the context. And people are so gullible and blind to it. They are believing the wrong versions, calling 'em translations or anything you want, but they're still counterfeit (Rev. 22:18–19). They are enough truth in them that even the elect is being deceived (Mat. 24:22–24) (God's people are destroyed for their lack of knowledge (Hosea 4–6)). Gee. Could it be because they're not getting nothing but counterfeit?

Moving on, "Ye therefore beloved, seeing ye know these things before, beware lest ye also being led away with the error of the wicked, fall from your own steadfastness" (2 Pet. 3:17). Please note, when Satan twisted in (Matthew 4:6, twisting Psalms 91:11–12), he changes the scripture, leaving out to keep thee in all thy ways and changing it around. So it's not an exact quote; remember taking away and adding to. And even if an angel comes with another gospel (Gal. 1:8 and 2 Cor. 11:13–15), even coming as an angel of light. I'll remind you, friend, the Bible says the devil, Satan, Lucifer was indeed an angel before (Luke 10:18) the serpent in the garden, tempting Adam and Eve. And is still tricking and deceiving people with his lies. But the kick in the pants is, even ministers are falling for it, but even before that, He tried his twisting words on Jesus, and Jesus says, "Thou shalt not tempt the Lord thy God." Yes, probably talking of the suicide, or was it "don't dispute or change my word"? Jesus was probably saying to the devil, "You tricked and lied to Eve by telling her she would be as wise [smart] as God, so don't tempt me with your lies and suicide, devil." Notice here that Jesus said to the devil, "It is written again thou shall not tempt the Lord thy God" (Matt. 4:7). In (John 8:24), Jesus says, "I said therefore unto you, that ye shall die in your sins: for if ye believe not that I am he, ye shall die in your sins." This means we must believe that Jesus is the Son of God and that he came down from above to save the world from their sins (John 8:16–28). Please note that the devil lied at the very beginning to Eve and to Jesus and is still telling people lies today, and he will continue to do so all the way up to the very end of time!

According to (Isaiah 14:12), "How art thou fallen from heaven, O Lucifer son of the morning, how art thou cut down to the ground." WHICH DID WEAKEN THE NATIONS! (Verse 13) (sounds similar to what he told Eve in the garden) (verse 13), for thou hast said in thine heart, I will ascend into heaven, I will exalt, MY THRONE ABOVE the stars of God, I will sit also upon the mount of the congregation in the sides of the North. I will ascend above the heights of the clouds. I will be like the Most High. Remember what the devil said in (Genesis 3:4–5) and told Eve to eat of it. God knows when you eat of it, your eyes will be open, and you'll be as smart as God. Knowing "good and evil," (1) disobeying God's command, (2) lies and says you'll become as God, meaning rebellious like him and kicked out of heaven for listening and following lies. Even as the other angels were (Luke 10:18, Isa. 14:12). Did or did not Jesus say in (John 14:26), "But the comforter, which is the Holy Ghost, whom the father will send in my name"? He shall teach you all things, and bring all things to your remembrance, whatsoever I have said unto you—pretty plain to me (John 16:13)." "How be it, when he, the spirit of truth is come, he will guide you into all truth, for he shall not speak of himself but whatsoever he shall hear that shall he speak. And will show you things to come." It's the Holy Spirit, the Holy Ghost, the Comforter, that's the teacher not the New Translation Version! Would a real Christian rewrite and change, and alter what God already had inspired the original man of God to write and then seal it with a curse and say (Rev. 22:18–19) that whosoever takes away or adds to this book… God will add to him the plagues that are written in the Bible and take away his part out of the "Book of Life." If your name is blotted out and removed out of the "Book of Life," this means you don't go to heaven (Rev. 3:5) only those names that are written in the "Book of Life" will be the only ones that make it into heaven. A lot of people will be shocked and surprised who thought their name was written in the Book of Life, I am speaking about those counterfeit types, those that aren't real for God, living a lie and still hanging on to the old life that God saved them out of (2 Cor. 5:17) or taking the chip (mark of the Beast); let's be real here.

A counterfeit, hypocrite, false believer, Judas-spirited person that lives both for God and the devil is deceived by the devil. This kind of individual is the type that will not totally surrender to God and will not let the old life go; when we truly repent, the old man, the sinner, partier, adulterer leaves and then the spirit of God comes in, and he becomes a new creature in Christ, but we have to surrender to God all the way, letting go of the old life. If a policeman said to a bank robber to drop the weapons, hands up in the air, and the robber drops just one gun but had more weapons in his belt and was planning to draw one on the cop, you get my example, that is not a total surrender to the cop is it. No, but in all reality, the man should have spoken up and not try to hide anything and have his life spared.

The same with God, if we are trying to hide anything, still hanging on to the old ways, this guy was just asking to be killed. These police officers aren't playing games; it's their job and their life is on the line. The same with God; the Bible says he sees all and knows all. He even knew you when you were still in your momma's belly. Wow. So why do people think they can fool God? They can't but some psych their selves out and try to become a good actor to please Mom or their wife; pretenders of this type usually get demon-possessed. You don't play with God's mercy, just like that policeman telling him to fully surrender, and he goes for that hidden gun. Hey, anyone with a brain knows he's dead. And so will he be with God. When a man's name is blotted out of the Book of Life, he will be sent to hell; the Bible calls this the second death, but according to scripture, he burns forever in a new spiritual body that never burns up, "just burns forever" (you won't hear this stuff in those ear-tickling churches).

The good actor type phony Christian, that's not really living for God with all their heart, should really study the words, *diligent, vigilant, sober, watchful, separate,* study the Ten Commandments, Fruits of the Spirit (Gal. 5:22, 23, Gal 5:18–21), works of flesh. So many words people need to look up and study. We're in a lazy generation; again, I know I'm repeating myself, hoping and praying people will get and receive what my point is. In (1 Peter 5:8, 9), it says, be sober, be vigilant because your adversary the devil. As a roaring lion, walketh about seeking whom he may devour. Whom resist steadfast in the faith, knowing that the same afflictions are accomplished in your brethren that are in the world.

In (Hebrew 11:6), the words "diligently seek him" has seem to not be there in a lot of church people. I've pastored and evangelized, and to do this, you must visit many churches to get yourself known to other pastors. This was many, many years ago. So many churches then, and sad to say, are worse today. For clarity, take this example: many, being like you, are at a funeral. But if you compare how God will judge a dead, lifeless church where people just sit and stare compared to a ball game where their team is winning and everyone in the stadium hears them cheering more for their team than for God at church, the Bible says God's a jealous god (Exod. 20:3–5, 34:14; Rev. 2:4–5, 3:1–3, 15–20; John 4:23) and that God desires his people to have a real zeal of enthusiasm from his people to worship him with a whole heart in spirit and truth, not be half-hearted about it or even wish they were at home, watching the game (2 Tim. 3:2–4; Matt. 25-1–13; Jer. 29:13; Ps. 100:1–4, 119:2, 10, Ps. 138:1; Mark 12:30). And according to the last-days prophecy scriptures, this last generation will be and is worse today than the generation of Noah's day. Or as in the gospel song "One Day at a Time." Okay, moving on. When I visited that one particular church and many since, I can say there are many here today that are dead and have no life in them, no enthusiasm, no zeal, and no fire even as (Rev. 3:15–16) says, if you're neither hot or cold but lukewarm in your soul (half-heartedness) and have a lazy spirit, God will spit you out of his mouth. I didn't write the Bible, and that's a different phrase, I admit. But I just read the scriptures, and I do believe that's saying this type of person will not make it to heaven unless he/she repents (Rev. 3:19). Wow! Or as (1 Tim. 5:6) says, "A woman that lives in pleasure is dead while she lives." So this metaphor is saving, (no spiritual life). I visited one, particular church honest, the whole service was the telling of a Christmas movie. Think he said one scripture, I was so sad because there was no FIRE at all. When I was a partier, I let down my hair and gave it my all. Some say I was the life of the party because I got in the thing. Well, when I got saved and delivered from drugs and booze, I read where God is a jealous God and a God that wants your all. God wants to be number 1 in our lives, not second; that's why in the Ten Commandments, in (Exodus 20:3–5, 7), He was saying worship Him alone. Have no other gods before you. Where do we draw the line between what God says he wants us to do right or our wants in what we want to do? Obey. The Bible says to obey is better than sacrifice. This means we draw our line to what God's will is because back then, when people fell short and messed up, they had to offer a sacrifice up to God to cover their sin, so then came the scripture. "It's better to obey than sacrifice (1 Sam. 15:22, Matt. 7:21, 22), but the next verse (1 Sam. 15:23) says for rebellion is the sin of witchcraft and stubbornness is as iniquity and idolatry.

So remembering living for the devil and now serving God, I give God my all. Don't go to bars or parties no more. I've been set free. Sure, I know there are still in churches the tokers, smokers, drinkers, the line walkers, on-the-fence folks. They just need God's persuasion and they'll see it in great tribulation according to the Bible. No, I'm no one's judge, just know what I read in the Word and sees fruit trees with no fruit, it plainly says you can't serve both. Again, repeating myself.

People just don't realize that we need more of God in our lives, not less, to repent; again it's a good word. It seems so many think some holier than thou is rebuking them. No, it simply means to get right with God so we are not left behind to go through the horrible events coming that prophecy warns us about, to draw closer that you can hear the heartbeat of God so to speak. That means that's being really close to God. When a mother nurses her baby, that child can hear it. Jesus said how often he desires to gather his people under his wings as a hen gathers her chicks under her wings and we would not come (Matt. 23:37). He longs for us to cry out to him for forgiveness and he understands even our thoughts when we many times don't know what to say, he will allow his spirit to pray through us, and even teach us how to pray (Matt. 6:5 to 15). This has been confirmed with me in my prayer time. Religion and people that's cold, lukewarm in heart, according to the Bible (Eph. 4:31–32), they must put bitterness away because it will make us ugly in our heart (Heb. 12:15). Bitterness will. Yes, it defiles people. I heard many years ago, a doctor had told someone if they would just forgive those he was so bitter toward, he wouldn't be so sick. Plus, you surely will not go into heaven with hate, unforgiveness, and bitterness in your heart (Matt. 6:14–15; Mark 11:15, Matt. 18:26–35; Gal. 5:15–16, 19–21). Wow, you might want to read verse 21 again. Sometimes, when a mate dies a bad death, the spouse gets bitter against God, but read (verses 22 to 24). This is what'll get you in those pearly gates: love, joy, peace, and longsuffering. But preachers today are bitter people with a road-rage spirit of hate, and bitterness and unforgiveness are everywhere. Yes, it's because they don't give that junk to God. As in (1 Peter 5:7) and as Paul said in (Heb. 12:15), it defiles them, kind of like a rotten potato left among other potatoes: the rot eventually seeps over to them. So why can't people let love overflow, as Jesus said in (Matt. 15:16–20)? but this is what is called agape love (John 15:13) (John 13:3–35), which forgive others and that kind of love only comes from God. But God longs for us to call upon him; even back in the Garden of Eden, it was man's choice to stray away and hide from God's presence. But you see all through time when man was willing to change and turn from his wicked ways (2 Chron. 7:14), that's why Jesus came and died for us. God saw man's animal sacrifice was no longer accepted by God. So Jesus came to die a cruel, hard death, taking our place on the cross, becoming our ultimate sacrifices for our sins.

If you knew me, really knew me, I don't have the intellect to write a book, but don't you see God's given me words. In (Acts 4:13), the Bible says they took knowledge and noticed that the apostles, disciples were ignorant and unlearned, that they weren't very knowledgeable on those things but also noticed they had been with Jesus. Like Moses, whom they put a veil over his face. And please, I'm not trying to compare myself. I'm just an ol' ex-hippy, high school dropout, took ten years later to get my high school diploma, yeah, and that's one of the problems today. Too much pride, people don't want to humble themselves. You don't see any feet-washing services anymore with church folks as we did forty years ago and back in Bible Days (John 13:2 to 17).

This means, we draw our own line to be humble to others, respecting others…even to wash their feet, get rid of our pride, which God hates pride. God wants us to humble ourselves to him and others; we need to apologize to those we've offended, to ask them and God to forgive us is scriptural—also one of the Beatitudes given on the Sermon on the Mount (Matt. 5:3 to 12, Luke 6:27 to 35, and Matt. 7:12). Do unto others as you want them to do unto you. Or some is too proud to confess their shortcomings. Not sins those are under the blood of Jesus, if I choose to mention where God brought me from, that's between me and you, and God and should remain there. And that, too, has become one of the church's problems, but again, you have fruit or works of the flesh; gossip is not fruit. If you're filled with the spirit (Holy Spirit), you're not gonna bad-mouth folks but take 'em to Jesus in prayer, not rebuke them but give them scripture and pray for them; so many times I want to say how many days have you fasted and prayed for that one your bad-mouthing. Do you know God hates gossip and know this that God blesses honest, sincere hearts that do their best (1 Tim. 5:13, 2 Thess. 3:11, 1 Pet. 4:15)? These are gossip scriptures. Gossip also means tattlers, and busy bodies, tail bearers, evil whisperings.

Is sin and brings a reproach against the church, (Gal. 5) speaks against it, but when our heart is right, we will want to pray and ask God to help them, and when we don't, that word *re*, which means get back where you were in your penance with God. So you see repent is a good word because (Revelations 3:5) teaches those that don't repent get blotted out of the book of life. So let's all get to where we need to be with God (Rev. 19:7). And again, if our heart condemns us, God is greater than our heart (1 John 3:20). God gave us a conscience, not to turn a deaf ear to it, which reminds me of the cartoon with the little devil and angel on each shoulder whispering in the ear. God doesn't want us to be prejudiced against others. Again, black people have treated me like gold, and I rented a house from a man from Vietnam; yeah, my brother died in the war there. So I can't and will not be angry with them or be prejudiced to the landlord. He was too young to have served in the Vietnam War; plus, it was not their fault. Being prejudiced is also very, very wrong. Another Vietnam man taught me how to use a hot-melt glue gun properly. And one of my Mexican best friends loaned me his truck and took me and my family in when a job promotion fell through. There are good and bad people of all walks of life. And I have seen Jesus Christ's love in so many at Living Christ Church in Tulare; they don't judge you if you're handicapped, or uneducated, or of a different race.

I have preached, pastored in Oregon, California, Arkansas, Oklahoma, Michigan, and visited all over and this Living Christ's Church in Tulare, California, is probably the best body of believers and best pastor on the entire planet. We thank God for Pastor

Donahue Green Sr. and First Lady Evon, for all your love; you and your wife, and church showed us love before and after my accident, hit-and-run, car wreck, your wife Evon and church. You all truly are men and women of God. And Pastor Donahue Green does preach the truth and does preach from the KJV Bible. A fiery powerhouse anointed man of God that you can still find a Holy Ghost and fire-filled man of God in this evil day. He is still yielding to the Holy Ghost—wow. I've been so blessed and have learned so much from his character and personality and the fantastic man of great integrity. If I ever looked up to anyone, it's this man and his first lady.

Thank you, pastors, for your stand you've took for God. And no, I don't have them on a pedestal. It's just rare that you find one with such class and still unique and yet so full of God. You, wow… at his funerals and the style and collectedness and yielded vessel he is to allow the Holy Ghost to move and flow and use him. And have seen how he detects the wizards and witches and evil spirits. That's a man of prayer and studier of God's Word. Okay, I'll quit on that (but it's true), and I consider them friends, brothers, sisters, and mentors. And I love you, pastors, and everyone at Living Christ Church.

The word says to look to Jesus the author and finisher of our faith. (Hebrews 12:1–2 and in Proverbs 3:5, 6) says, trust in the Lord with all your heart, and lean not to your own understanding. In all your ways acknowledge him, and he will direct your path. So where do we draw the line on looking to Jesus? Again, there are so many macho bad, tuff guys out there who think if I look or turn to Jesus, I'll be looking like a sissy or a whimp. Is that what you are gonna say to God on Judgment Day? I know a lot of tuff guys that live for God, and I never thought for a moment that they were sissies (no way.) Those are lies from Satan; in fact, it'll be opposite. It takes a real man to take a stand for God and tell that old life of sin and the devil to take a hike.

It takes a real man to give your all to live for God with everything in you (Rom. 8:31; Rom. 12:1, 2; Phil. 4:13). It takes a real man to lay down the dope and booze, parties, and wild women and stand up for God and be a real dad to that kid and take them to church and be a good example for once in your life and ask everyone's forgiveness, so he'll have a real hero dad to follow after, instead of some loser drugee making up excuses all the time. Been there, yeah…you are setting a real good example for a kid to pattern his life after… wow. Somewhere, somebody is watching and following your examples that you're living, maybe a nephew, cousin, neighbor, young guy at work… I wrecked one's life. When you stand before God, you will hear, "Good job, you lived for me with all your heart" and that kid that was watching your life, followed your example, he made it too. "Come on in to my heaven, you good and faithful servant," or you'll hear, "you wicked evil, macho, stupid, idiot, full of pride and macho ego, depart from me," and sad to say, the kid followed the example, and he goes to hell with you and others also. Which one of those examples are you? WOW… It's our choice. Want to be in control 100 percent of their life. Seriously, folks, it's coming down to either you believe what the prophets of God wrote, or you don't. The Bible is the inspired Word of God, and I may repeat myself but get over it and learn. The Bible is God's Word and won't return unto him void (Isa. 55:11). He will accomplish what God has intended it to (John 1:1)—if God's gotta send massive earthquakes, cause more sinkholes or sink islands, cause mountains to fall flat (Rev. 16:18–20), or bring back gang wars or different weather patterns (Matt. 24:7–12), people's love will vanish, according to the Bible prophecy. People everywhere are being offended, the prophecy is being fulfilled, and this is that generation that wants to kill one another over anything (John 16:2), but God allows it. And even gang violence is part of it, and so is all the road rage and other things. The love of many waxes cold, and this is part of it, which brings hate in the hearts of people, making them mean and ugly in their hearts and violent. And this is because they have turned away from God, becoming seven times worse than the first (Matt. 12:43–45). God will send them storms, earthquakes, tornados, plagues, nightmare-type famines, and many different weather patterns across the globe. Where one area's flooding and another one's having droughts, come on, people, it's time to wake up cause, all this has already been on the 6:00 o'clock news; everything is now wrapping up and again God help us if we are (Rev. 18) and most believers can see the government has made changes.

And what used to be a "we the people nation" is no longer, and it's time for the anti-Christ identity (mark) "chip." And if you close your eyes to all this, you're not even spiritually thinking. God wants us to remove our carnal blinders and get on our prayer bones as never before. I see things in the spirit that people that are carnally minded according to scripture don't see. They'll think your off the deep end and tag you as a fanatic.

Okay, let 'em. So now what? Don't you know the word? Come on, folks, and smell the coffee and wake up. The last-day prophecies say this. As in the days of Noah, so shall it be, when the son of man comes (Matt. 24:37). Don't you think for one minute that they mocked and ridiculed Noah and his own family began to even question if he was right? Read it, friend. It ain't the gospel according to Fred Davis, fanatic end-time preacher but what thus says the written Word of God and Jesus Christ our soon coming king! I just pray all of this nightmare prophecies come after Jesus comes after us, that we are ready and we'll be in heaven with Jesus when all hell is coming on this earth. It's no time to ignore the horrendous sins and evil in our land. It's no time to ignore the prophecies of the Bible. We are that generations that (Matthew 24) is speaking of and also (2 Timothy 3 and 2 Peter 3).

Too many are wanting, encouraged, and to hear those ear-tickling messages. (God's love, he wouldn't do those things.) Are you reading the same Bible or just stupid and blind? Ouch. No really… read it. God's Word will not return unto him, VOID (Isa. 55:11). I already quoted, but I'll repeat it. I am amazed at so many that look the other way, who stick their head in the sand of who cares, you will when you read (Revelations 3:18, 1 Corinthians 2:14). You have to want to understand the Bible and things of God are because it's spiritually discerned; only people living for God with all their heart are gonna understand God's Word. The Holy Ghost also gives us understanding and brings scripture back to your remembrance when you need it (John 14:26). But please, notice, there is an act of obedience on our part… Even our own DMV laws say that if you are at an intersection (if there's no stop sign), you must yield. That's our problem: no one's yielding to God until something tragic happens! Hello?

But you'll read that about this evil generation. They will yell, blame, and curse God, not knowing the Bible says that God's enemies take his name in vain (Ps. 139:20); and the Bible goes on to say, "And they repented not"! Read it in Rev. 9:20–21). This is the LAST-DAY generation (Matt. 24:33–34)!

Notice John says in (Revelations 3:18), "I counsel thee (you) to buy of me, gold tried in the fire…" These people went through hell on earth just writing and living this gospel. Yet so many don't take the Bible as the authentic Word of God, but it is. You see there is nothing, nothing more valuable than your soul making heaven, the hidden treasure more valuable than gold. Is when man repents and asks for forgiveness of his sins and turns away from the old life of sin and follows Jesus, that's the true gold (Luke 12–21) (Rev. 3–18; Luke 12–34). Then Jesus gives us a white robe and washes away our sins but notice again John says at the last part of verse 18, we must anoint our own eyes and pray that we see things right. Read it: "Draw the line to anoint our eyes, Lord, with eye salve, so that I may see spiritually." (1 Cor. 2:9, 14; Matt. 25:1–13) In these last hours and few days of time we have left, as mentioned in Matt. 24:32–36), your and my eternal destiny all depend on how we see the seriousness and urgency of being and staying ready to go! As in (Matt. 25:1–13, Luke 17-26–27, or Luke 10:38–42), in other words, people were so busy and caught up in everyday life as in Noah's day that they didn't take God's warnings seriously enough just like in 2 Tim. 3:5). And yes, people in this day and time are so busy, and it's just like back then… I say it's just like back then! They were eating, drinking, etc., just going on with everyday life, not taking God seriously or being ready and watching, praying, and seeking God. So many say they are Christians but don't follow the Bible or do what is said in (Luke 6:46). No, again, I'm no one's judge. This preacher is seeing a world ripe for destruction. It's all in the Bible, so why aren't all the ones calling themselves Christians seeing this? I'm thinking they must not read the Bible or just don't believe it.

It all starts happening, if you're in the lukewarm bunch. As in (Revelations 3:15–20), and are so caught up in this world like this preacher friend that was so blessed and comfortable in this life. He told me he could easily live here another one hundred years. That life was so good. Wow.

I shared the prophecies of the Bible and the end-time scriptures, and there was so much friction and disbelief this would happen. Now, those folks in Noah's day probably said the same thing and lived like it too. These are what Jesus was pointing to, cares of this life in the parable of the seeds. But the kick in the pants is, for those caught up in the good life and not even knowing they are the ones God said, he would send strong delusion to them, that they would believe a lie (2 Thess. 2:10 to 12). Come on, folks. Just try kicking up all this in an experiment conversation sometime and look at the looks and attitude you get from those that have ignored the WHOLE BIBLE. You know them. And so do I that go to church on Sunday morning only and think they are doing God a favor and those that don't want to hear the prophecies and hear end-time sermons and hear about hell and Judgment Day, etc., which God's wrath as in (Psalms 78:8, 11, 18, 22, 31, 42, 49, 51), yet the Bible says it'll be worse in our day.

Wow, so, we don't want to be on God's hit list or his bad side. All they want to hear is love, heaven, God's peace, God makes a way. They would have croaked, if they'd have stood in John the Baptist or Apostle Paul's shoes. Why do I see all these things and others don't? "Where do you draw the line on Blindness or Unbelief" in Noah's Day. Their unbelief got them left behind to drown. And they were warned. Today, it's the same way… People just don't want to hear it…or they just don't believe it is gonna happen. And yet, Jesus said it'll be like it was in Noah's Day. Wow (Matt. 24:37–40, 2 Cor. 5:11).

Jesus is more than religion. The Bible says God is Spirit, and we should worship him in spirit and truth. Okay…What's truth? The whole word is truth to neglect parts is deception. Jesus told the woman at the well these things in John 4. And she believed him, yet Jesus told the Pharisees that they erred not knowing the scriptures about not marrying in heaven because we will all be as the angels (non-gender). You'll neither be male or female, Jesus said, you'll be as the angels in (Matthew 22:29, 30). So where do you draw the line on all those type figurines with a cleavage and big breasts if Gabriel looks like that? (I don't think so…) Maybe that's why the Lord told

Moses, no graven images because humans don't have a clue. I don't know, and there are not female angels nowhere in the Bible. They all are non-gender. According to Jesus. Jesus told them they (erred); the word err means in Greek to misunderstand, to make a mistake in believing what is the truth.

"The Bible is the only truth and Jesus Christ is the only way to heaven" (John 14:6) He's the way, the truth, and the life; no man will see God except through Jesus (Mark 12:25, Luke 20:35–36). Again…There is tons of false doctrines and false teaching…even those who AVOID the parts that make people uncomfortable, Jesus said will be punished more severely. According to scripture and I will even throw this at those prosperity types as well, that's the opposite in what the Bible, and Jesus says about what the prophets and apostles preached; it's gonna be as bad, like it was in Jesus's day, they had to go into hiding to go to church at people's houses, the religious Pharisees, like Saul, before he became Paul, was spiritually blind then became physically blind, by Jesus/God because he was persecuting Christians. Killing Stephen and almost got Peter. Hello… Are these blind leaders of the blind false preachers of lies? Are they really reading the same Bible? It's not pick-and-choose buffet of scriptures. (Again, abortion in (Jeremiah 1:5, Psalm 127:3 and 4, Psalm 128:3, Matt. 19:6, Mark 10:6–10.)) God has always intended for reproduction of life with male and female. And he said be fruitful and multiply, to think or believe different is anti-Christ!

"Draw the line straight" to your own convictions not to please others or churches, but God's (Heb. 11:5, 6).

(Second Peter 3:16, 17) is a beware sign, lest you also fall by the same error… Many have been dog bit by not taking heed to the "Beware of dog sign".

"Ye therefore, beloved, seeing ye know these things" before. "Beware" lest ye also, being led away with the error of the wicked, fall from your own steadfastness means fixed in place, steadfast in one's faith unmoveable (1st Cor. 15:58; Ps. 108:1; Ps. 112:7, my heart is fixed).

We are either sold out 100 percent to live for God, or we are not (Josh. 24:15). As for me and my house, we are gonna serve the Lord

(A quote from Pastor Donahue Green, "You can't be half pregnant, either you are or you're not.")

(First Peter 4:17, 18) talks about those that doesn't obey the Gospel (of God). (1 Pet. 4:17, 18) says, that Judgement must begin at the House of God, (but what if the people dont go? or what if the different religious and different Pastors are not obeying God, and warning God's people?) Wow. The whole world, even many of the churches are erasing the line that pertains to the reason Jesus cursed the fig tree, yes, fruitlessness (Matt. 21:18–20 Matt. 3:10 Luke 13:6, 7, 8, 9). When Jesus cursed the fruitless fig tree, it dried up and died. The reason Jesus cursed the fig tree was to demonstrate to the disciples that God wants His people to be fruitful having love…and having the fruit of the spirit.

Most churches are no longer bearing fruit; that's what attracted me to Living Christ Church and Pastor Green's fruit (100 percent pure fruit bearers). The whole purpose and reason Jesus cursed the fig tree was to show the disciples and us that God gets angry at (trees, Christians, us) that are not producing fruit. We are not to be fruitless, but as in (Galatians 5:22), we are to be fruitful naturally and spiritually—having love, joy, peace, longsuffering, putting up with and praying for people, unless your God/or Jesus, which you're not; but the time is coming like when Jesus overthrew the moneychangers' tables. When God can and will send his wrath and anger on people that are not following the Bible that are disobedient; nowadays, it won't be tables he turns over, but great tribulation that will come upon the rebellious generation that rejects Jesus Christ and the Bible, especially on those who have altered and changed what God's Word originally said. And they would have a pastor arrested for such anger and turning tables over and using a whip…wow, that would make some real nasty headlines in the news, amen. And Jesus had anger at the bear fruitless tree that was to demonstrate to all followers of Christ that a Christian should always have something to share out of his/her soul (1 Pet. 3:15) as the tree gives fruit to the eater, so should the Christian, give love, joy, peace, etc. (Gal. 5:15 to 23), or give out evil, like in a witch's black pot of poison potion to ruin the world instead of saving it, as so many protestings spewing out their anger on stores. And his anger at the bearless tree (fruitless) in which that anger, when so doing or turn over the money changer's tables, in such like passages of scriptures today, they'd have a pastor arrested. And are doing so. No longer do Americans have freedom of speech. Everyone's on pins and needles. Ha…and the lukewarm say we are not in the last days.

When Peter spoke of it in (Acts 2:17), which was two thousand years ago, I just heard this preacher say on TV Jesus is coming on Dec. 31, 2015, and today is July 18, 2020. Yes, he lied because the Bible says no one knows (Matt. 24). Even at the door, meaning, you'll know it's close because of all that's going on that lines up with the Bible prophecies. But of a particular day or hour, Jesus Christ said no man will know what day or hour, like the fig tree putting out leaves you'll know summer is coming at the door. But the key scripture is the next one, 34, which says, "This generation shall not pass away till it is all fulfilled." Pretty plain, (verse 36) says, "No man knows the day or hour not even the angels" (that know more than humans) (only God knows). They don't even know. So this preacher was a deceiver and a liar. (Hope he repents.) Hey, dude, don't *PUT DATES* on it. Yes, we are close; yes, it's time, but no one knows that particular day or hour… So don't put dates on it. So many have accused me of using fear tactics yet. So did they back in Bible days, and people laughed at the Noahs, Peters, Pauls types, and anyone that preached prophecy, or end-time, last-day sermons.

When my wife waitressed, she said she dreaded to see the religious crowds that were arrogant and rude, the fruitless ones like Saul, who went to church but no change in heart. Some really showed their fleshly sides. Not being Christlike. And I don't want to sound hypocritical. But I saw a pastor's daughter many years ago push a waitress's hand away—wow, everyone at the table gulped but I'm proud to say, she repented and is back in with the fruitful (Romans 14:12, 13).

Please note: We all have to stay prayed up… Anyone even Peter cutting off the high priest's servant's ear… Wow…ol' Peter must have been having a bad day… More the reason we should always have a repented heart, the Bible was very clear on Peter that he was walking a far off (Mark 14-54) (Mat. 26-56 to 58)…means not close to the Lord, but at a distance, thank God ol' Peter repented because he wrote some real good stuff later on.

According to (Luke 18:1), pray lest you faint. This is why (Luke 18:1), Jesus said to pray, lest you faint… I would say cutting off someone's ear or shoving someone or cussing people out, this is called spiritually fainting or backsliding (walking A-FAR-off, Ps. 27:4) One thing have I desired of the Lord that I will seek after, that I may dwell in the house of the Lord all the days of my life to behold the beauty of the Lord, and to enquire in his temple and as King David said in (Psalms 51:10) asking God to create ("create in him (David) a clean heart, and renew a right spirit within me.").

And I will "Draw my Line to Jesus Christ" (Matt. 6:33).

I'm gonna "Seek ye first the Kingdom of God and his righteousness then all these other things will be added to me." Draw closer to him, friend. You can't get close enough (James 4:7, 8).

Many old folks used to sing the old hymn "Just a Closer Walk with Thee," yet so many walked a far off. "Let's all draw closer to the Lord." We can, no matter what others say or do, we can make it. A preacher lady friend used to sing a song "You can make it." (No matter what's going on you can make it.) Minister Bonnie Morrison sung that song, and it would really lift your spirit. Folks, I believe the closer we get, the more evil the days are getting. So let's walk as close to God in prayer and study our Bibles. She was also one of our mentors, thanks, Bon Bon.

"Draw your line to a closer walk with thee." No matter what others do or say, I'm gonna make it.

Everyone has had nights with no sleep or bad days, or a boss on your back or family rubbing you the wrong way, but we don't take it out on others. This is wrong. That's why Christ said, let your light shine that others may see your good works and glorify God, and again, the only way to keep that kind of glow in your heart and life is like Daniel that prayed three times a day. And the closer we get seems to be the more I have to pray. Not just the taking up the cross daily as scripture teaches but sweet hour of prayer. Continually, I don't see how people make it without it. Don't abort your soul, keep praying.

So what? You already done your devotions this morning, big deal. You have gotten angry since then, or you this or that. I'm gonna keep on going to the throne room of God, even if I get camel knees. Hey, this is my soul; if I gotta repent and like Jesus said 490 times in a day forgive you, come on, people. Pray once. Don't think so. If I gotta keep repenting all day every day is it gonna hurt or kill me? Maybe my flesh needs to die out to carnality; these old religious lies and false doctrines need to be tossed out. Go ahead, you try to enter in heaven with unforgiveness, unbelief, bitterness, anger, malice, strife, junk this world as it hits you with every day. Cast it all on the Lord.

One of the things I want to draw a line to that minister Janeen Goree brings out in the seventh chapter of her book, "What goes wrong on a Sunday morning" is referring to (Daniel 3:15, 18 and Philippians 4:7) and peace of God, which passeth all understanding and shall keep your hearts and minds through Christ Jesus. And she explains that it's God's comforting peace that keeps his people during the troubling times of storms and the trials of this life, using the three Hebrew children for her analogy that we need to have that kind of tenaciousness. And be so determined in our heart and mind. That the things in this life that come our way if on the way to church, school, or the store parking lot or family trials, nothing will separate us from the love of God in Christ Jesus (Rom. 8:31:35, especially 37, 38, 39). In other words, we can draw the line straight to Jesus Christ, he'll never leave us nor forsake us. And God will not allow more to come on us than we can bear, but God will make a way of escape.

We have to develop a deep dependency on Jesus Christ, knowing like a toddler will reach up to the parents' arms as we are in God's. Keep looking to the Lord (1 Cor. 10:13, Heb. 13:5). I kinda added a little to what minister Janeen Goree was saying, but you get my point as God kept them and even Daniel in the lion's den and so on. He'll also keep us as well (Heb. 12:2).

We Are in God's Hand

(Psalm 37:23, 24)

In (Isaiah 55:11, John 8, and Psalm 37:23, 24), the steps of a good man are ordered by the Lord and He delights in his way. Through he falls, he shall not be utterly cast down, for the Lord upholds him in his hand. And God will even make those that worship Satan in Satan's synagogue come and worship God before your feet (Rev. 3:9, Rom. 16:20). Wow.

And the scripture in (Romans 8:2), for the law of the spirit of life in Christ Jesus hath made us free from the law of sin and death. God bent his own law by Jesus dying on the cross for all the world's sins. The price was paid with Christ's blood and life. So because Jesus died, we could make heaven and live forever (1 Cor. 6:20, also read 1 Corinthians 10:13). Jesus is our way of escape (John 14:6). But don't misunderstand as many do. Though Jesus died and freed us from the law of sin and death, this doesn't give us license to kill, murder, abort, etc.

The Bible says there is one God, one lawgiver, one judge, one giver of life. And we are to abide by the laws of the land. As long as they do not conflict with God's Word. That, my friend, is where we better draw the line. People are changing all of it. Laws, Bibles, the government was once instituted for the people by the people well that too has been altered (Ps. 33:12, Ps. 43:1, Ps. 147:20). Read (Psalm 9:17). Nations that forget God, we used to be one nation under God, but are we?

1

Where Does God Draw the Line?

Will God destroy the righteous with the wicked?

But according to (Genesis 18:23–24), God said even ten righteous people he would spare Sodom and Gomorrah. Notice even in the days of Noah, only eight people were saved when the world was being destroyed by flood. There was only eight, but God took them out of the way first and he will us too (1 Pet. 3:20, 2 Pet. 2:5, Gen. 5:29, Matt. 24:37).

Notice there weren't ten righteous in Lot's day (Gen. 18:23 to 32), and there weren't ten righteous in Noah's day. It's only by God's grace America stands; yes, we all know and believe there's more than ten righteous in America, but if you figure the large spectrum, with the amount versus the amount you see, only God knows, but even most animals know when a storm is coming and most believers I know believe and feel it's close. We don't know the day or hour the word says, but we'll know it's close even at the door (Mat. 24:32–33). That's close we know, it's very close. Did I say it's close? We don't know the day or hour the word says, but we'll know it's close even at the door, that's close, we will know, it's close. Did I say it's close, well you can't say nobody told ya. It's CLOSE!

Just stay focused on God; if ya fall short like Peter when he took his eyes off Jesus, looking more at the storm than at Him. Be always repentive. Always be quick to repent if you fall short or think you've sinned... Be repentive quickly.

Note: Many churches and religions teach you to pray once only. I beg your pardon...show me please! The Bible does not teach to pray once, but to be repentive and repetitive as in (Luke 18:1 to 8) (on prayer); it was by her continual coming and Jesus said himself in (verse 7 and 8), "Shall not God avenge his own elect, which cry

2

day and night unto him, though he bear long with them?" So it wasn't "pray just one time." No, it was "pray day and night" (and by her "continual coming" in verse 5). This doesn't sound like one time to me (Col. 2:8, Matt. 15:9, Luke 6:46, 1 Tim. 6:3). And again I'll add, people really crack me up, those that believe that way. Again, they take scripture out of context, follow church doctrine made by man (Acts 5:29), and fail to see why Jesus said to watch and pray so many times if you just pray once, as in (Mark 13:33, Luke 21:36, Matt. 24:41–42, and Matt. 25:13. And again it is mentioned in Luke 21:36 and Luke 18:1) (Luke 18:1) (Luke 18:7 and 8) (Eph. 6:18) to pray always. (Verse 8) of (Luke 18) says God will avenge you speedily, nevertheless when the son of man comes, shall he find faith on the earth. This doesn't mean because I go to God with the same need as so many religions and churches teach; on the contrary, it's the desperate prayer (by a continual coming). Read it a dozen times.

Again, you go ahead with your one prayer, but I'm gonna continue bombarding heaven till my answers come… Oh, but you're not really believing and you're not having faith, oh really. And I say show me in the Bible, that it says to pray Just once, read (Luke 18:1 to 8). Read (Matthew 25:1 to 13) a dozen times. I believe those five foolish virgins quit praying and their spiritual oil ran out—five foolish got left behind, five wise took extra oil with them. I'm gonna keep getting extra oil. Keep having my vessel full and keep praying and praying, and watching, etc., which explains (Luke 21:34, 35, 36); so you read this one, you get this, but I read it's a continual watch and praying always, again (Luke 18:1) that men ought always to pray and not faint. So where do we draw the line on prayer? Is it sin to keep praying? No. Is it lack of faith? No. If so then explain why these scriptures say this and why did Jesus himself prayed twice for the blindman in (Mark 8:24), which said he saw men as trees.

But we are to call those things that aren't as though they were, and I get that (that's faith) and we are to thank God for things he's already supplied (Phil. 4:6, 19). And thank him for hearing your prayers for what you're praying for (I get that, as in John 11:41). But I will draw my line to having a continual praying time. As fishermen, we must keep on casting that prayer to God till his answer comes, praying in Jesus's name and believing we will receive his miracle, just as the fisherman continues casting his lure until he hooks his fish, not giving up but continually doing so. In other words, wouldn't people laugh at a fisherman that went to the lake, put out his boat, cast his fishing lure in the water one time, reeled in his line, and went home? Wow, even in prayer, we're constantly casting my care and prayers up to him as the Bible says, not what some churches say, and not what some religions say, not what people say but as the Bible says. Like in the Old Testament, their continual cries came up to God. I've seen to many miracles and have been one myself.

But I don't condemn those who want to just pray once. Hey, that's your prerogative; it's your choice. We all have to do and follow the Bible and your own heart.

Never try to hide anything or lie to God. He sees all and knows all and is always watching us (Prov. 15:3). And remember, it rains on the just and the unjust (Matt. 5:45). What it all mainly boils down to is that the heart of man needs to draw closer to God.

Why does God use the analogy that Christ is the groom and the church people are the bride of Christ? The Lord wants a relationship with his people as in a marriage (Rev. 19:7).

Religions has messed the whole thing up between God and man. This is my point: there has been nothing more intimate than the relationship between husband and wife or mother and child. God desires a personal, close, loving relationship with his people. God's not a genie to grant your wishes, though He said He'd supply all your needs… When we walk close to someone in a relationship, you are sensitive to their needs and wants many times; you know if something's wrong without even saying a thing, and when there is love both ways, the relationship is prosperous and will be a blessed union. God desires us to love Him. We like it when we are loved, and when we are hugged by our spouse with sweet words of love spoken to us. We feel accepted and loved. God is no different… We need to have that same love effect to God. Many men don't have a clue about intimacy, and sometimes I can just hold my wife's hand and say things like when we first dated over fifty years ago… She says she's still melts, she says with just a kiss and words of love, she's my first love since she was twelve and I was fourteen. Sure, there has been lots of rocky, rough times, but God took us through with His loving hand. And we have a very close love relationship with God as well as each other. We thank Him, and we tell him we love Him. We brag on Him to others—how good God's been to us, many times making a big deal out of it. Usually short of cash to buy the wife flowers, but I don't know what it is about doing that, but when I do, wow, she lights up. Does God light up when you do something out of the ordinary for Him? For Him, not to be seen by others, but something for God from just you to Him. My wife Brenda loves it when I get the guitar and sing a love song to her. What about God? I'm not talking about at church. Yeah, there too, but alone with God, and it doesn't have to be an hour, a few minutes; I know it'd bust God's buttons off. Now, I love it when my wife or my kids or my grandkids sing to me. I love it, and so does God.

So would you call doing this for God a spiritual intimacy with God? Absolutely. Some call it worshipping in truth (John 4:21–24).

My Heart Is Fixed on God

No matter what comes or goes, folks, we've got to have a made-up mind. We are gonna make it to heaven and live for God.

"My heart is fixed, O God, my heart is fixed" (Ps. 57:7, Ps. 108:1).

I will sing and give praise.

How do you draw the line when trouble hits? Are we quick to fold under and run to the bar and get drunk? That's not living for God (Prov. 3:5, 6). That's leaning to our own understanding. We must acknowledge God and stop trying to figure everything out. Quit relying on the arm of the flesh. I'm gonna live for God. If I get my healing today, praise God. If tomorrow, praise God, next month, praise God. You see, my salvation is not based on how God moves for me in my time clock. None of these things Paul said "moves me" (Acts 20:24). Neither do I count my life dear unto myself so that I might finish my course with joy, and the ministry that I have received of the Lord Jesus to testify the gospel of the grace of God. Come on, either we believe this whole thing (Bible) or we don't again. It's not a Bible buffet, pick and choose as so and so many think. Your either in for the long haul or you ain't (Job 13:15). Though God may slay me, yet I will I trust him. BUT I will maintain my own ways before him (Rom. 12:1–3). Read it. Not a quote. We must present ourselves a living sacrifice to him many, many times, especially after my wreck (hit-and-run) and surgery... I didn't feel like praying or reading my Bible or going to church. Back from years ago in the prison ministry in '80s and '90s, there was no one to take your place, you went no matter what. But being 100 percent dedicated, you go where he says and do what he says, fully 100 percent.

Let Every Man Be Fully Persuaded in His Own Mind

(Romans 14:5, Philippians 2:5)

As in (Psalm 9:1), I will praise thee oh Lord with my whole heart… This is one of the problems in our churches today there is only half-heartedness. People don't praise out of their heart. Jesus said they offer honor from their mouth but their heart is far from me (Matt. 15:8).

The day my dad died, I also had a wedding scheduled the same night. They were all so happy, and they didn't know. I'm crying hard on the inside, but I knew they couldn't get no one at the very last minute.

But I've seen my pastor do the same thing. It's your duty and a minister's responsibility to do the right thing, which was good service, especially when you accept the call of duty to be a minister (Rom. 12:1–2).

Either you're in it for everything ya got, or you're not at all. Good with bad, thick, or thin. Are you gonna trust God? If he takes your kid or parents, you can't get bitter and hate God, then expect him to let ya in heaven. It doesn't work like that; we must be like King David and constantly ask God to "create in us a clean heart" O, God, and a lot of that will come when you hide his word (Bible) in your heart. Then your flesh will line up with the spirit of God, but remember, your steering wheel of your life is in your own hand (Ezek. 47:3).

And we can pray the word in our prayers, which gives you spiritual power in your prayers, example (Ps. 51:10–11), create in me a clean heart, oh, God and renew a right spirit within me, etc. Or if it's on an attack from Satan, plead the blood of Jesus over you, quote power scriptures (1 Cor. 10:13; Luke 10:19; Phil. 4:13, 19; Luke 18:27; Matt. 17:19–21; Isa. 54:17; 2 Cor. 10:4–6; Isa. 59:19; Matt. 17:21; Mark 9:29). Satan tried stealing power scriptures like how the NIV and other translations have taken away and added to as written in (Revelations 22:18, 19 and Romans 1:25). When the whole KJV Bible can be used as a sword against the devil. Example: God gave us power scriptures, as in (Matthew 17:21 and Mark 9:29). Jesus said this kind comes forth by nothing but by prayer and fasting. But these verses are removed from some of the other versions and the NIV Bible. Why? The very weapon God gives us to fight off the devil with because the devil comes to steal, kill, and destroy (John 10:10).

So I stay with the KJV Bible that says (in my own words) if you're needing a miracle, fast and pray, so why do these newer versions remove what God said you need to do, which is "fast and pray"? Because the devil knows it'll give you power with God against the devil and help you fight off temptation (and helps you get in the Spirit). Did God give these people permission to alter and change and remove his scriptures (NO!). He didn't! (Read Revelations 22:18, 19 and Romans 1:25.) Would you really change, alter, or even take away, and remove what God said, knowing in those verses God said if you do, God will plague you with the plagues in the Bible. No, but the devil would (Heb. 4:12; 1 Cor. 10:13; 2 Cor. 10:3, 4, 5; Phil. 2:5; 1 Pet. 5:6–9). The KJV Bible is the best to use for weapon scriptures against Satan.

Note: Why would a spirit-filled, born-again Christian remove scriptures that gives you power against an evil devil? He wouldn't! So there is a devil in someone somewhere, tricking people. God gave us weapons through his word. And some devil disguised in sheep skin acting like he's a Christian and gives us a new modern translation that's so much easier to understand ("it's what they say their reason for their deception is") but to be plagued with the plagues in the Bible and to lose your soul is a hard price to pay to deceive people, plus, the Bible says their blood will be on their hands, and if the blind leads the blind, it says both will fall in the ditch! Wow (Matt. 15:14 KJV; Rev. 22:18, 19, read it). You people that want easier versions to understand, that allow (unsaved men) to retranslate your Bible... which you are allowing him/her to take away and ADD too... Don't you see the Bible says that is the Holy Ghost (Holy Spirit's) job... He will lead you and guide you into all truths (Jn. 16:13; Jn. 14:26; Matt. 13:34–35; Luke 8:10) because the Pharisee's hearts were evil and not right with God, so scriptures and parables were hid from them.

God designed it that way, so for man to change it and realter it is sin, and according to (Rom. 1:25, Rev. 22:18 and 19) they will be plagued. Wow, and again reread Matthew 15:14. Again, the Holy Ghost (Holy Spirit) gives us the understanding, not some sinner that's altering God's word (John 14:26). The Holy Spirit will give you understanding! Jesus plainly said the whole reason the religious Pharisees couldn't understand, was because he used parables, that went over their heads, because their hearts wasn't right with God. (Note: The Bible is sealed with a curse, for anyone who takes away or ADDS to it!) Yet foolish people just don't see it. Wow. And they haven't stopped there... Now there's a street version, should I go on... The devil is a liar. People better wake up and learn the Original Bible. This one removed from NIV (Matt. 17:21) because the devil knows it gives the saint power against Him. And remember everyone that serves God has guarding angels and ministering angels (Ps. 91:11; Heb. 1:7, 13, 14; Matt. 18:10), etc.

Oh, yes, angels are real. And I got to get back to my topic. I'm a dirt road preacher as you can see.

This book is 100 percent KJV-based Bible scriptures for the last-day generation church 100 percent opinions, beliefs, thoughts are from the heart and soul of Fred Davis (God-inspired) and not to reflect on any other person. Fred Davis has been a minister of the gospel. For over forty years, cut his teeth on prison ministry for eighteen years, juvenile hall ministry for two and a half years. He did rescue mission one year and pastored ten years and has been an evangelist for nine years overall. Fred Davis preaches the KJV Bible to the last generation and believes. We are in the last hours of time before the return of Jesus Christ and backs it with scripture!

As an evangelist, I have preached and visited many, many churches. In this ol' preacher's opinion, those many churches were not what Bible scriptures teach should be. He uses the Bible as a balance scale and weighs the world on God's holy scale. Fred Davis lives what he preaches. And come from the hardcore hippy-biker drugee, partier pothead lifestyle. And knows on firsthand about the sinner life and is why he related to prisoners for eighteen years, living on both sides of the fence (but now on God's side) Satan's lies vs. God's truth.

NOTE: (Matthew 15:8, 9) sums it up. Where do we draw the line in right and wrong version of Bible worship? So many just mouth service. Hearts are not even in it. Many make themselves. And more into what people say over what the original Word of God says.

"The fool has said in his heart there is no God, corrupt are they, and have done abominable iniquity... There is none that doeth good" (Ps. 53:1, 2).

God looked down from heaven upon the children of men to see if there any that did understand, that did seek God. But that don't give man license to sin just because He don't believe in God. (Now, this was before Jesus's day and before God's outpouring of (Acts 2).)

But the point I was trying to make is, for centuries, man has tried to ease and sear his conscience by telling himself there is no God... An old preacher said once, you'll not find an atheist in a foxhole in the time of war when bombs are dropping all around you, and your comrades are being blown to pieces, hearing screams in other foxholes, that was just motored. But man eases his conscience by saying there's no God, so he can get drunk, rape, kill, party with no fear of being sent to hell. SO he thinks...but that doesn't make it so. Heard a preacher say when he first got saved, a guy approached him with a gun; he was ready to meet God and said so, but the bandit thought he was nuts... Another similar case, another guy with a gun kept telling the bandit he didn't believe he had bullets in it… Pow… The guy found out the hard way that it did.

So we put our faith in God live or die. God's got us…but people who say there is no God (Psalms 14:1; Psalms 53:1–3) are fooling their own self… Pow… Like the gun, it'll be too late (1 Cor. 15:19). God has more to offer than what is in this world. (First Cor. 2:9, Rom. 6:14–18, 23), also see (Romans 6:4–8, 12, 13). But those types say, "Ah, when you're dead, you're dead." It's this life and that's it. Wow. Are they gonna be surprised because they don't believe you must believe to be born again? Again, I say (John 14:6, John 10:1–10, John 3:3, 5, 16, 17, 18, Rom.10:9 to 13, 1ˢᵗ Jn. 1:5 to10).

And then you have those that think they can live like the devil and I see and know many and so many that died without time to pray and call on the Lord Jesus for forgiveness of their sins. I mean, they died drunk, and in a head on, instantly dead on the scene…no time to pray. No, I'm not their judge, but it amazes me reading so many obituaries. Everyone gone to heaven, they say, which is calling Jesus a liar, because he said many are called yet only a few are chosen (Matt. 20:16, Matt. 22:14, John 15:19, 1 Pet. 2:9, Gal. 5:7–26, 1 John 4:1, 2, 5, 6, 7, 8, 15, 1 John 3:11–20, 1 John 1:5–10, 1 John 2:15–18).

Note: This would be one super thick book, if I wrote out every scripture but I give you scripture passages to look up on the subject and some I abbreviated. Some I'll write out. Hey, it's my book! Ha, so where do you draw the line? Many will be by how they feel, but it has to line up according to God's Word. See (verse 7 of Romans 8:7); the word *carnal-minded* is the way partiers and drunks think (verse 7, notice enmity means God's enemy). Oh, they'll say we have plenty of time or I'll repent on my deathbed, or when I'm old and gray, or God understands me, and the real getter is, God made me this way (2 Chron. 7:14), but "the shocker of all shocks to mankind…will be on Judgment Day" (Rom. 8:6).

There will be no second chance after death as so many bimbos think. I had one lady at my work ask me to pray her family member out of hell—ha! When you take that last breath of life and enter into the eternity of God's spirit realm, if you're not what the Bible says, you should be, BORN AGAIN.

Living the life he said, yes, there is no one perfect; all have sinned but not premeditated. Again, there's a big difference in diving and tripping or in a fall. There is a difference in deliberately diving than tripping in a fall. The dive was planned.

But the shock to mankind on Judgment Day will be when God opens the books (Rev. 20:12). The book of remembrance (Mal. 3:16). The book of life in (Revelations 13:8, Revelations 17:8) and the sixty-six books of the Bible—thirty-nine Old Testament, twenty-seven New Testament—but if your name is not in the book of life (Rev. 3:5, Rev. 20:12, Rev. 20:15, Ps. 9:17) and those that forget God, go to hell. Not to mention what God says to those that didn't receive Jesus in their hearts and denied him. And God says (Jesus) I died for you on the cross for nothing, for you, I suffered so you could still party and live like the devil (don't think so) when I (Jesus) died for all that, so you would learn that type of life will send you to hell (Gal. 5:15 to 22). All through the Bible, that word will come back in their face. (How will they escape? The Bible says in (Hebrews 2:1–3), if we neglect so great of salvation.)

And the religious that don't believe in backsliding can't explain (Matt. 25:1–13 and Rev. 3:15 to 20, Rev. 3:5) (John 6:66) (2 Pet. 2:20–22) (Rev. 3:5). And why some see it and understand it, and others don't. Again, many are called and few are chosen. Some just don't want to line up with the Word of God. Therefore, if they are not following God 100 percent with all their heart, then God will not allow them to understand his word, and then he allows them to believe a lie and a strong delusion (2 Thess. 2:10–12). Straight... Draw your line straight; your life must line up straight with God's Word (Matt. 7:13, 14; Ps. 84:11; James 4:17). To Him that knows to do good and does it not...to him that is sin.

So draw your line straight, friend, you've got one chance, one opportunity to make things right with God... You better walk the walk and talk the talk... Just live right so you don't get left behind. Who cares what people say. Let 'em laugh; is being mocked and laughed at worrying you that bad? My soul is worth everything to me…this life, the Bible says is temporary (temporal (2 Corinthians 4:16 to 18, James 4:14), "Life is like a vapor"). You see it on your mirror when taking a shower, turn a vent fan on, or open a window, it's gone… We must draw our line in our life straight to God, because the Bible says, straight is the way (Matt. 7:13, 14, Matt. 3:3 Luke 3:4, John 1:23) There won't be any crookedness with living for God, make his path straight (Matt. 7:13–14) because the way to destruction's wide and easy, full of pleasure-type sins that will destroy you. But to live for God is to deny fleshly lust (Gal. 5:15 to 22). This is where we must walk a straight life and walk and stay close to God. This brings up the thought God's sheep know his voice (John 10:27). And sometimes the shepherd breaks a leg…so that sheep that keeps straying off, so he's not eaten by a pack of hungry wolves. Yes, the Bible says (1 Pet. 5:8–9) the devil comes as a roaring lion, seeking whom he may devour, whom resist steadfast in the faith. You must get violent in your faith and violent against the devil because it's gonna be real fight against spiritual wickedness in high places. We are not to turn to a spirit of road rage against each other; our fight is against the devil (Matt. 4:1–10, 11:12; Eph. 6:10–18; 2 Cor. 10:4–5).

Note: The Bible is a road map to heaven and a guidebook back to life.

We must be Christlike. For years and years, I heard there's too many hypocrites in church, but where else are you gonna find them? There are liars and hypocrites on every job, business, companies, parks, gas stations, and people still go there. And we've seen on the news about scammers scamming people out of their money with phony products that fall apart, cars, houses, belts, meds, surgeries, mesh, things that cause cancers that folks have used, eaten, for years, dietary stuff that later you hear caused cancer. There is a right and a wrong. People doing wrong will reap it on Judgment Day (all for money). That is not worth their soul going to hell for. So many getting caught, scamming people or a product that falls apart…cars, houses, belts, meds that cause cancer. We still chuckle at all the side effects of so many new drugs on the market and some of the side effects on the new drug commercials are worse than the illness.

People will lie and tell you anything to sell a product. Wow. It's amazing, lies in the news, tabloids, and I knew some and even worse many profess to be Christians and lying deceiving people to sell their product. I've pastored in three different states, and when I was a prison minister, I had many ask me about so and so, that they are not what they say they are; they don't live like a Christian… We are not their judge no. 2; the Bible says if we stand or fall, it's to God, not people, though people do watch other people's life's, and this is why everyone needs to live right, and follow Jesus and His word because of them not studying that the Bible teaches these things. This is why the Bible says in (Hosea 4:6). God's people are destroyed for lack of knowledge. And one of those lack of knowledge, that's gonna destroy people of God, according to scripture is them taking God's name in vain. The Bible says that God's enemies take God's name in vain, using the word damn after God's name. It'll send your butt to hell (Ps. 139:20, Exod. 20:7). One of the Ten Commandments and the Bible also says those who forget him (Ps. 9:17). Nations will be sent to hell that forget God.

So would a real Christian flip a bird to God or damn His name knowing He could send you to hell… The Bible says many will come in that day (Judgment Day) saying Lord, Lord (Matt. 7:22, 23), didn't we prophecy in your name, didn't we cast out devils in your name? Hey, folks, a drunk man or partier can't cast out devils. The Bible teaches only those who have fasted and prayed; in other words, this scripture is saying this person once had power with God, to cast out devils, so why didn't he make heaven because he back-slid, or she got bitter, and quit praying only going to church once or twice a month. The disciples were going daily… Wow, today's church people would have a heart attack, saying Sunday morning is good enough, but they'll go paint themselves, sit in the rain, and yell and scream for some guy running for a touchdown with a ball, in his hand when that's just a game but your soul's forever… The same people will call people like me a fanatic because all we want to talk about is heaven, Jesus and the Bible, stuff that's forever through all eternity, football is temporary, no, nothing is wrong with liking it… Just make sure it's not got more of your heart than God does! The

Bible says from the abundance of the heart man speaks. I've been around many Christians when their team won…try working in the Bible or the conversation of the coming of Jesus Christ, etc.

You'll be eaten for lunch, yes, even by Christians…not too many want to discuss it anymore away from church, especially on the job or in public. Many talk the talk at church but not in public, and isn't that what Paul said is being ashamed of the gospel of Christ (Rom. 1:16)? In (Luke 9:26), Jesus said, "For whosoever shall be ashamed of me and my words, of him shall the son of man be ashamed." So if we are ashamed of Jesus, when we stand before him on judgment day, he will be ashamed of us, according to Scripture. Wow, sure sounds like it…heard someone say, you don't have to shove it down their throat…if I was a betting person, I would bet you, if her/his family went to hell, they'd have wished a million times they'd have shoved it down their throat and then some. And what in this world is that individual gonna say to God on Judgment Day about that stupid comment, and this was from a very, very intelligent individual, and the Bible says we are snared by our words.

In one scripture, Jesus said a parable, that was God speaking, "Out of thine own mouth I'll judge you…" (Luke 19:22) and called him wicked for making excuses and you can read about those in (Luke 14:16 to 24) in both of these chapters the people didn't make it. Wow, as in (Matthew 25, Revelation 3:5)—okay, repeating myself.

In any case, there will be a lot of people, multitudes that I would call fence walkers, in the middle, not a fanatic… Sorry, if you are one of them that say people of that church are to fanatical or too religious, you are one that will probably be left behind. I've been shocked at so many so-called Christians, that say the microchip in the hand sounds good to them. Wow… Blind leads the blind. Okay, there are many things, many, many things that people will be left for, but things that take people from God is probably the main one, the Ten Commandments or should say twelve because Jesus added two more, or like in (Luke 18:17–27). Jesus talked in (Luke 12:15–21) about having treasure here and not being rich toward God, so when you are born again and filled with God's Holy Spirit, according to Scripture, that's what makes you prosperous in your soul or rich toward God

(3rd John 2, Rev. 3:18, Luke 12:34). And one other things is real bad and big in churches is fornication and adultery, people shacking up together and going to church. And they are quick to say…don't judge us, wow, read the Ten Commandments, people. Even graven images, false gods, etc. (That's pretty plain to me.) Yet many say they've read the Bible but it's evident they never read (Luke 6:46), yet live like the devil again, we are not their judge; our job is to just pray for them.

Wow. Not allowed to go there. Look, it's plain and simple. We must follow the Bible and the gospel to the best of our ability. No one's gonna stand in your shoes on judgment day. So you better live straight and right and follow the owner's manual. Come on…

So many buy stuff and follow directions to the letter on putting a barbecue grill together, following the owner's manual but have a problem with God's owner's manual on how to make heaven ("The Bible" is God's manual). And so many people making statements, "It's too hard to understand." Yet a stupid, unlearned high school dropout, ten years later got my diploma in the '60s and '70s just about fried my brain with dope and booze. And some say "No way, that can't happen"—been there. Don't believe it. Believe God's Word. A man said to me, "I still party, get high, smoke dope, drink beer, etc., and I'm a Christian. So where's the change as in (2nd Cor. 5:17)"

Like I think, really think, some guy that says he goes to church and still does drugs and gets drunk is a Christian, just because he goes to church, right? Wrong.

That's not Christlike. For one, for two, the word *disciple* means to self-discipline yourself. A follower of Jesus Christ means you will pattern your life. After Christ, I don't see Jesus (taking) and smoking a joint (no way). No, I am not their judge, but Jesus said you will know the tree by (Luke 6:43, Luke 6:44, Luke 13:6) its fruit (Gal. 5:15 to 26). We need to also know the difference between fruit and works, as in (Galatians 5:19) versus (Galatians 5:22 and 23, see verse 24 and 25). People who constantly walk after the flesh live like the rest of the world parties, etc. According to (1 John 2:15 and 16, and Matthew 16:26). Jesus said remember Lot's wife in (Luke 17:32). She looked back to the city of sin, when God sent an angel to bring her out, then she died because (Luke 9:62) the angel said, "Don't look back" (Gen. 19:17), and she looked back in (verse 26), see (Luke 12:21 or Matthew 22:37 and 38). We must love the Lord with all our mind and soul, even if it means letting things go that weight us down (Heb. 12:1 and 2). How valuable is your soul? (Heb. 12, verses 1 and 2), You must get this! Did I say, let things go that pull you down? You better read these, why was the rich man in hell, so determined to bargain with God on Him warning his five brothers to not come there to hell, in (Luke 16:19–31, see verses 27 and 28).

Wow…it'll pay us to be ready and not to have anything in our life to weigh us down or cause us to miss heaven. Notice in verse 31, the Lord said to this bargaining burning rich man (your five brothers have Moses and the prophets preachers, in my words) "if they don't hear them, neither would they hear someone that rose from the dead" (in my words, read it in Luke 16:31).

So our life is our own responsibility, so you better follow the instruction manual (the KJV Bible) and follow Jesus Christ and pray his Holy Spirit changes your heart and mind to think right, so you're not left behind and sent to hell. The Bible even talks about deceivers sent by the devil, like the devil was sent to deceive and trick EVE and ADAM.

Okay, I took a long dirt road on that one, so I hope you got my point. We must be careful, very vigilant, because that tricky ol' devil is sending Delilahs and Bathshebas to trap you into sin. There is so much history and Bible facts and proofs of fallen leaders, so why follow the fallen?

And why lose your soul and get sent to hell? Why should you miss heaven because of others' stupid mistakes? No, you don't have to, so get yourselves in a Bible preaching Church, get grafted into Jesus as (John 15) says, if you're rooted and grounded and grafted into Jesus, you'll bear godly, spiritual fruit love, joy, peace, etc., and you'll make heaven. Again, we must be on guard, be sober and be vigilant, because the devil is as a roaring lion, roaming around seeking someone not on guard and not paying attention, to devour them, but you be steadfast, and unmovable, always abandoning in the faith in the Word of God, and follow Jesus Christ 100 percent.

(In my words, amen. Note: A drunk is not on guard.) Notice, Peter said to be sober and to be vigilant, opposite from being high and drunk. I've been there on both sides of this fence...so don't even try feeding me those lies from hell, "the blind will lead the blind and BOTH WILL FALL IN THE DITCH" (Matt. 15:14) and so will those drunks and partiers that think they'll go to heaven some other way...you've got to go by Jesus Christ (John 14:6, John 10–1, John 10:27). Jesus said His sheep hear his voice.

To him that knows to do good and doesn't do it to him that is sin (James 4:17). I've been there, done that! But I got saved... repented of my sins.

Trying to go forward, no looking back to the wild partying life, pressing forward to heaven (Phil. 3:13 and 14). When you've been on both sides of the fence, and you've learned it the hard way, now you try to help others, not to go down the road of stupid. But I'm trying to direct them all to the STREET called straight (following Jesus Christ). I've been clean and strait for over forty years now. Thank God (Phil. 4:13, Rom. 12:1 and 2, Heb. 12:1 and 2, Rom. 14:5). ((Matt. 6:24), No man can serve two masters. You follow God or the devil.) The way the world lives to party, the drunks, wild lifestyles, was in Noah's day also and is now in ours, and many go to church and go right back to getting stoned after they get out of church. Wow. These are blind people, spiritually blind, and do not know the Bible. Jesus said you are either for me or against me; you'll gather with me or you will scatter (Matt. 12:30). And they are out there by the millions. The preachers calls the worldly casual Christians or the churchgoing partiers say, "Well, Jesus turned the water into wine" (so they can get drunk), not even knowing the spiritual meaning of the (John 2, verses 3 and 4 or 2 Corinthians 5:17, Acts 2:13, Mark 2:22 of John chapter 2:3 and 4) when Jesus turned the water into wine. Notice what Jesus said to Mary when she told him they had no wine for the wedding. She was thinking carnally; Jesus was thinking spiritually (Rom. 8:6): "For to be carnally minded is death, but to be spiritually minded is life and peace." To be carnally minded means to think like a drunk or partier—people that go after anything and everything to get rich by seeking fame, pleasure (1 Tim. 6:4–10), and fortune, and they put God on the shelf to use as a spare tire in case of trouble. But to be spiritually minded means this (Matt. 6:33): "Seek ye first the kingdom of God and his righteousness, then all of these other things shall be added to you." Being spiritually minded, you would also be constantly thinking about winning souls for God. In other words, you'd be trying to get people saved in a sinful world that God's about to destroy again (Matt. 24:37–38). Being spiritually minded is knowing the Bible and the prophecies that tell you that when the world gets like it was in Noah's day (because it is way worse today than it was then), by being spiritually minded, you will want everyone to pray, give their hearts to Jesus Christ, and get saved so they will make heaven concerned about souls that are on the way to hell according to their lifestyles and the scriptures (Mat. 24:48–51, Gal. 5:15–22, Luke 16:19–31). Notice in (verses 27 and 28 of Luke 16) how after this guy's down in hell, he then tries to bargain with God to keep his five brothers out of hell. But then it's too late. We should've warned them earlier, and God said in (verse 31), "If they hear not Moses and the prophets, neither will they [hear] be persuaded, though one rose from the dead" (see 2 Cor. 5:11). (Luke 6:46)—so many called Christians have forgotten this, and John the revelator said in (Rev. 2:4–5) to repent to remember when we left our first love and repent (similar to Rev. 3:3–5 and Rev. 3:15–22).

(1 Cor. 2:14) says, "But the natural man receiveth not the things of the Spirit of God: for they are foolishness unto him: neither can he know them, because they are spiritually discerned." You must want to be spiritually minded because people today are worse than in Noah's day. Go and try to convince the bar crowds; the gamblers; or the pot-smoking, beer-drinking partiers as I did. You can't. They think you're foolish, that it's not cool, or that they'd have to give up all their fun and quit sinning. You see, as it was in Noah's day, so shall it be when Jesus Christ comes back; they were eating, drinking, having sex out of marriage… Oh, excuse me, take a poll of all those divorcees out there. The millions that are out there say, "Why marry?" The trend now is "Let's just live together and try it out first." And so it was in Noah's day; fornication and adultery is at the highest of all time. Conduct a poll, go ahead. You check out all of it: abor-

tions, drugs, the youth watching porn on TV/phones/computers, etc. They can send each other photos on their phones. Hello, people, do you really think this technology was in Noah's day? Come on, folks... Wake up and get spiritually minded. History has come full circle (Matt. 24:33–34). Okay, moving on to the original point I was making about Jesus being spiritually minded to his mother: All she was thinking about was that they were all out of wine for the guests at the wedding, but Jesus said to her, "Woman, what do I have to do with (You) thee? Mine hour is not yet come." What hour? Meaning His hour to die on the cross and rise from the dead and ascend up to heaven to God and send back the Holy Ghost and Fire (the Holy Spirit) that will be inside of you.

The spiritual wine that's a well of water of spiritual life (John 7:37 and 38 and 39) springing up inside you. Also in (John 4:10 to 14), notice (verse 13): If you drink that well of (in my words) physical water (H_2O), you'll still be thirsty, but if you drink Jesus (the Holy Ghost wine) the Living Water, you won't desire the old lifestyle anymore; you won't thirst after the world because Jesus/Holy Ghost satisfies you. The drunks will be real quick to use Jesus turning the water into wine, thinking that it gives them license to sin and get drunk (John 3:19). This is an anti-Christ spirit. That's not what Jesus came to do, Jesus came to save and to deliver and save the soul from hell, to wash him/her clean from their sins (2 Corinthians 5:17). The sins of the old man/and His Old ways of thinking. People forget why God destroyed the world in Noah's Day and in Sodom and Gomorrah (Luke 17:32, Gen. 19:12–26). In (Gen 19:14), the sons-in-law didn't take the two angels' warnings seriously; they weren't indeed even spiritually thinking but were caught up in the sinful lifestyle of the sinful city. And the scripture says, "He seemed as one that mocked." Notice in Lot's days, in Noah's day, and in Jesus Christ's day (Matt. 27:27–31, 9–24; 2 Peter 3:3–14). (Please read it.) And now today, in our day, because of fallen evangelists on TV, pastors everywhere and ministers too have been mocked; and now there's not no respect. The ministry has become a mockery to the world; nothing is holy, sacred, or spiritual anymore; and God is blasphemed on every hand. People forget what the Bible says: that all this will come

(John 16:1–2, Matt. 25:40) (Psalm 9:17) says, "The wicked shall be turned into hell and all the nations that forget God." Also refer to the following verses: (2 Chronicles 7:17; also read verse 14; Heb. 12:1, 2; Psalm 139:20; 2 Peter 2:6; Matthew 10:15, 24:37–39; Jude 7; and Isaiah 13:19). People forget why God destroyed the world in Noah's day even though he said "I give you the rainbow as a promise or a big reminder [in my words]." But that, too, has been distorted by this evil generation! And again I ask, do you think that (like Revelation 18:19 says) America is the NEW Babylon, as in some movies? I've preached this for over forty years, and many have mocked me, even some churches. But it's now coming out on their TV screens. Wow.

It was sex and parties, sex and parties. Have you really looked at our world today, and a real hard look at the movies, the lifestyles of people (2 Tim. 3:4) one of the signs of the last days, and the end of time is men will be lovers of pleasure more than lovers of God (Col. 3:5 to 11, Col. 3:1 to 19, see verse 5 and 6 and see verse 9 and 10). In (Colossians 3:9), God says to put off the old man with his deeds, and (verse 10) says to put on the NEW MAN (also look at 2 Corinthians 5:17). When people get saved and are born again, they are supposed to stop sinning (2 Chron. 7:14) and quit living for the devil. No, I'm not talking about slipping or falling, which I spoke of earlier. People are still hanging on to the old lifestyle, and that's not a total surrender to Jesus Christ. Those types of people will not make it to heaven (Luke 6:46; Gal. 5:19–22; 1 Cor. 6:9–20; Rom. 12:1–2, 8:13; Heb. 12:1–2; 2 Cor. 6:14–17; 2 Pet. 2:4–10). In (2 Pet. 2:4–10), notice how, in (verse 4), God didn't tolerate the angels that sinned but cast them down to hell. So what in the world are people today thinking? That they can keep on continuing to live in sin; go to church on Sunday; and the following Friday night and Saturday night get drunk, rape, steal, kill, party, and fornicate without any change in their life? Again, falling and deliberately diving is different. And, reader friend, you don't answer to me, nor I, you. But on God's judgment day, like no other court hearing, there'll be no escape from God's judgement (Matt. 23:14) (Revelation 20:11–15) (Rev. 14:7) (Rev. 20:4) (Hebrews 12:25) (Hebrews 2:3) (1 Pet. 4:17, 18) (2 Pet. 2:9) and his wrath, and for mankind ignoring God's Word (the Bible), there'll be no excuses accepted. Definitely, there'll be no crooked, lying lawyers (see Luke 11:45–52) to manipulate the system, no. The Bible teaches that everything done in this life will be brought out to the light, even hidden secrets. Again, it just cracks me up how intelligent people really are…concerning all the technology with all types of satellites and surveillance cameras of all kinds. And yet because of man's ignorance and the rocket-science-minded people out there that don't have a clue about any of this prophecy stuff, they don't realize that God had way more of this type technology way back when man was still working on making and inventing the wheel, wow. Please notice that man's evil heart and evil imagination will not change unless he is fully, 100 percent dedicated to God by repentance and that man has eyes full of adultry (2 Pet. 2-14). It's now on prime time commercials advertising some *X*- or-*R*-rated movie, but again, kids can see it (porn) anywhere—on cellphones, computers, T.V. etc.—anytime. And this again was not in Noah's day, but it is in ours; strip clubs and rock concerts, massage parlors, casinos, theaters, etc., was not in Noah's days but it is in ours…on and on from sports, to amusement parks to place after place. There are entire cities that were created for pleasure. You know them as well or better than I do. Yet people will find excuses to ease their conscience, to enjoy them, even if the Bible does forbid them (James 4:17). And being an ex hippy, biker, pot smoker, and druggie, I laugh at all the stupid so-called Christians that make so many excuses to smoke pot, the cause of their pain, now in creams and ointments. Wow, you idiots are gonna have the shock of your life when God reveals all the tricks the devil has tricked you with, but your main problem is you don't know the Bible. And it's because it plainly tells of the devil tricking so many like Adam and Eve, Samson, Aninias and his wife Sappira Achan (and his family), etc. and then the devil comes to try to trick Jesus in (Matt. 4). And the Bible says the devil can even come to you as an angel of light. But again, people are gonna do what they want to do regardless if it's sin or not and will be quick to tell you you're not their judge and, as the devil did to Jesus, twist the Bible scriptures to excuse their sin. Wow. But on Judgement Day, I would advise you to not try those excuses (as in Luke 14) with God or say, "The devil made me do it." But my question is, is your eternal soul really worth having your own way to sin and rebel (James 4:17)?

Read the first three chapters of Revelation again if you really think like this. It says, "Remember where you fell, remember you left him, and so go back and do your first works over again, and repent." Have a devoted time to praying and read God's Word, spending time with God as though your eternal life and soul depended on it…because, friend, IT DOES! And it still amazes me how people will look for any reason or excuse to ease their conscience so they can live in sin. Wow, even though the Bible forbids them, they do it.

We all need to read (Matthew chapter24, and chapter 25) and again (2 Peter chapters 2 and 3). It says God destroyed angels that sinned. Wow, but a way of escape was made for humans… It's JESUS Christ (John 3:16–19). If your a friend with the World in (James 4:4), you are enmity with God, means you're his enemy. Note: We are always to shine our light before all men of the world (Matt. 5:16) and be friendly, nice, etc. but not be part of it or associate with it. We must draw the line here and be separated from the nightlife, partiers, drunks, druggies, and the bright-light-type sinful pleasures (2 Tim. 2:4) (2 Tim. 3:4) that go with the nightlife types that go out to the nightclubs. According to scriptures in the Bible, this is considered sin, and these types of people will not go to heaven (Gal. 5:18–21, 1 Cor. 6:9–10) but will become God's enemy. In (James 4:4), James uses the word *enmity*, which means "God's enemy"… I didn't write the Bible; I just preach from it. And there are many, many more I could write down. For example, (James 4:17) tells us that just knowing to do good and not doing it is sin, and the Bible tells us to be separated from the world and the things of the world (2 Cor. 6:14–17; 1 Cor. 5:11, 3:16–17, 10:20–21; 1 John 2:15–17). Even Jesus Christ taught his disciples that, as in (John 15:18–19), which says, "If you were of the world, the world would love his own, but I have chosen you out of the world, therefore the world hates you." Wow. And (John 16:2) says that "whosoever kills you, will think that he's doing God service [the last half of this scripture is in my words]." But hopefully, you can look these up and read them for yourself because, reader friend, that worldly-living-partier lifestyle will send your butt to hell (according to the Bible). Those people just crack me up on this topic… They are out there all over the world that really believe the devil that's lying to them, like he did to Eve in the garden if Eden and go back to church (2 Pet. 2:22) Peter calls that eating dog vomit. Yeah, sick, huh? Then they redo it again; they go back to the bars again and do it all over again. Friend, the Bible says in (Romans 1:28) that those types of people, God turns into reprobate minds (my words, so read Romans 1:16–32). Being a reprobate means you are no longer controlling your mind. I guess that's why (Matthew 12:43–45) says seven devils come inside you and possess you. Don't play games with God!

As in (Galatians 6:7, 8, 9), be not deceived. God is not mocked for whatsoever a man soweth that shall he also reap (eighth verse): "For he that soweth to his flesh shall of the flesh reap corruption, but he that soweth to the spirit shall of the spirit reap life everlasting." This goes back to what I said earlier about thinking spiritually minded because any ol' dead fish can float down the river, but it takes a self-disciplined life to be read-up and prayed up being alive saint of God, well studied and well exercised in the faith (a Christian disciple) (Romans 12:1, 2) which ables you to swim upstream. Yes, crude analogy, but you get my point. The Bible says to study the Bible to prove yourself to God. You don't have to prove a thing to me or anyone else, just to God. That's why we all will be judged according to what's written in the Bible—because, by golly, if the Bible says that I have to walk upright before God, then so does everyone else. The Bible also says sin is pleasureable for a season see (Heb. 11:25) or like (Prov. 14:12) says, there is a way which seems right to a man but the end there of are the ways of death (James 1:14–15, Heb. 11:25, Rom. 5:12–17), and (Romans 6:23) says, "For the wages of sin is death, but the gift of God is eternal life though Jesus Christ our Lord." Please try and understand that God gave us his Son, Jesus (John 3:16–19). Most everyone has heard it, especially at Christmas. It still gets me that everyone wants to get gifts on Jesus's birthday but that so many don't give God the time of day. Or that everyone wants to have eternal life and go to heaven, but only a few want to go to church. Wow.

I like what Pastor Donahue Green said one day—that everyone wants to have their heavenly home but don't want to go to his earthly home (the house of God, church) (Matt. 6:33, John 14:1–3). And as (verse 9) in (Galatians 6) says, "Let us not be weary in well doing, for in due season we shall reap, if we faint not," which, in my personal opinion, is telling us to keep on doing our best to live for God. And if you make a mistake, be quick to repent, ask forgiveness, and keep on living for God. Don't throw in the towel when you feel you've messed up; that would be considered fainting spiritually (Luke 18:1). When a person physically actually faints, they lose consciousness, passing out for a short time from losing oxygen in the brain or from the loss of blood (which are a couple of ways that some folks blackout physically), but spiritually, it's usually starts from a slackness in the desire to pray, read the Bible, and attend church regularly, losing that desire for God. (Mathew 5:6) says, "Blessed are those that hunger and thirst after righteousness for they shall be filled." When the gas tank of your car is empty and you leave town to go over to the next town, on the way there, you'll run out of gas (your car faints). Living for God is the same way; your spiritual fuel is seeking God in prayer, reading the Bible or listening to it on CD (or now on your Bible app on your cellphone, iPod, etc.), and going and attending a good Bible-preaching church. (Hebrews 10:25)—reread this two or three times… Soak it up, especially the last half of the verse. The Bible plainly says (in my words) we need to go to church the more we see the day approaching. Despite the 9-11 attack and the plague of COVID-19 virus, with millions in an unemployment epidemic and everyone masking up, so many scared out of their skin, people still don't think we're in the end of time and Last Days, as in Mathew 24. Wow, I wonder why. It's because they quit reading the Bible, (which is equivalent to spiritually fainting). Okay, moving on. Let's not faint. Let's reap going heaven because we were faithful in living for God. Those will be the ones that read and make it to heaven, not those that live like the devil and still want to go to heaven. It doesn't work that way (Prov. 21:2, 14:12, 16:25; Deut. 4:29). (Jeremiah 29:13) says, "And ye shall seek me and find me when ye search for me with all your heart." That's when you'll reap and IF WE FAINT NOT (plain to me).

You plant corn, you reap a good crop of corn. You plant stickers, thorns—guess what, you don't reap watermelons (James 4:17).

To him that knows to do good and does it not to him (that) is sin (pretty plain) and don't overlook (verse 4, 5, 6, 7).

But since the beginning of time, people are and have always done what they want to do, regardless of the consequences (verse 7). Submit yourself to God then resist the devil and he will flee from you (James 4:7). People will rebel and do their thing to the end of the world and some will turn to God when they see revelations unfolding. If we somehow could find a way to get through to people, why Jesus cursed the fruitless fig tree, and the tree dried up from the root. We do not want to be cursed or have the wrath of God come on us. Most people know to live right, and it is surprising the magnitude of people, deep down, that really believe there is a God. They just don't want to turn to God and live it, or some are not ready to, and many don't feel like they can because of temptation and loved ones they've seen, that fell off the wagon.

But God's grace is sufficient for you and me.

You'd be surprised how much God can help you overcome. So many I've heard during my prison ministry days say they'll just wait till they know we're entering Great Tribulation days, and then they'll come on board. It sounds to me like they are already believing a lie, that strong delusion Apostle Paul talked about in (2 Thessalonians 2:10–12). It ain't worth chancing, an ol' pastor once said if you can't live for God during the mercy and grace period (now) and then how could they, when the plagues and nightmares of Revelation Days of Great Tribulation are poured out on EARTH, what will people do then. Back to the fruitless tree Jesus cursed, it wasn't even time for fruit yet. Wow, it wasn't even time for fruit to be on it yet. The mind-boggling thing that is trying to be imbedded in the disciples and readers' mind is, we are this tree. And he's making an analogy here that he wants us to bear fruit. And that happens by living for God, reading and following God's Word and with prayer and thanksgiving, but you'll find he rebukes the phony religious (Mat. 23:1 to 12), those not save and born again, esp. the religious Pharisees and scribes, and saducees, (were considered phonies) in the whole 23rd chapter of (Mat. 23) or as in (Luke 12:56) but this is a rebuke to the religious phonies, that were just big actors, which were out to be seen in public, on street corners, making phony prayers, to be seen, Jesus said in (Mat. 23 verse 14) they'd get greater (damnation) (or in my words)=(greater punishment in hell), so this (Luke 20:46-47) chapter tells me that the fake and the phonies, and the false preachers, and false prophets, and yes, even the false followers, (Ephesians 4:14 to 18) will have greater damnation in hell. You won't hear this stuff in those big ear tickeling-rich churches.) so the phony religious people are those like in (Luke 20:46, 47) that are without any fruit of the spirit) as in (Galatian 5:22 to 26) = no love, no faith, no joy, no peace= fruitlessness and sin, but God wants us living in Christ, and Christ living in me, doing what he said to do (Luke 12:21, Luke 6:46).

It Is Written...

(Matthew 4:10) says, "Then saith Jesus to him (Satan) get thee hence (behind me) Satan," for it is written, "Thou shalt worship the Lord thy God, And him only shalt thou serve." Read (verses 1 to 11 of Matthew 4) and see (Luke 10:18, 19).

And it's amazing what you hear from people: excuses and reasons to sin. Now it's pain. So I'm hearing pot's okay, but it's not okay. And you couldn't pay me to go back to that dog vomit lifestyle that God brought me out of. The devil is laying traps for people and they are to blind to see it. So no, it's not okay; it'll send you to hell. I'm an ex-pothead. I know you blind idiots saying it's okay, leading people astray (may God help you); your soul is worth more than getting high. No, it's not, okay, even if it is legalized, (some would say) so big deal, because no, it is a big deal, we are talking about your soul. They also made it legal to drink alcohol, but Google all the people killed by drunk drivers, and then Google, all the scriptures in the Bible that say to be sober (1 Pet. 5:8, 9), be sober, because your adversary the devil, as a roaring lion walks about seeking whom he may devour, and all those scriptures that say, God sends all drunks to hell (Matt. 24:48 to 51, Gal. 5:21, 1 Cor. 6:9, 10). Again, this is why partiers want to change the Bible, but here is a sobering thought, o everyone who gets drunk and gets high and all you pot smokers, it's not the new version Bibles God's gonna judge you out of people (Rev. 20:12, Rom. 2:16).

It's the *Original First Word of God*, that's *the real one*! Man may change the ones here, but on Judgment Day, God'll open His original Bible. Then we'll see man wet his pants, standing before a holy, righteous, very angry God that will send man's soul to hell like a flash of lightning because He changed what God originally said, and He

28

did not call on Jesus and receive Jesus Christ as Lord and Savior. If your name is not in the Book of Life and drunks won't be you will not go into heaven (Rev. 3:5, 20:12–15, 13:8, 17:8, 21:27; Matt. 24:48–51; Luke 10:20; Exod. 32:33; Phil. 4:3; 1 Cor. 6:9–10)! Right now, there is mercy and grace and still time to get saved and give your heart to Jesus Christ, but you better not wait too long, or it could be too late. Today, now, is the accepted time (Rom. 13:11, 2 Cor. 6:2).

And it's obvious they haven't read and studied the Bible, or they would know, just like all the different version Bibles; they haven't read (Romans 1:25, 1 Timothy 4:1), doctrines of devils or (Galatians 1:7) there be some that would pervert the Gospel. (Verse 8) and even if an angel come and preach another gospel unto you let him be accursed. Yet people by the thousands have read these scriptures, and big, well-known ministers and pastors have read (Revelation 22:18, 19) yet they still follow and quote from these doctrine of devil Bibles. And I wrote about this in my other book (Matt. 24:22) if not for the very elects sake no flesh will be saved, just because some famous preacher does it doesn't mean it lines up with God; if a drug dealer gives you a ride and is stopped by a cop; he has twenty keyloes and five guns in the trunk of his car.

Do you think you'll go to jail being an accessory before or after the fact or an accomplice to aiding and being with a felon? Yes, even though you feel you are innocent, and many sometimes are. But please get my point here. Yes, I know I'm repeating myself. Have you got it yet? Read these last three paragraphs again a couple more times. Do you really think you know it all; you may or may not. Don't be stubborn; these last three paragraphs again a couple more times. Do you really think you know it all? You may or you may not. Don't be stubborn. These scriptures I put in my book are out of the Bible; why were they put there? Like (2 Timothy 3:15–17). The scriptures will correct us, not us changing and correcting God's Word, no, the Bible is to reproof us…to correct us, to give us instruction. I still can't believe, so many people following all those different versions and different translation. Hey, some are saying, like this one, this idiot is saying you can take the mark and still make heaven; that's a lie. Another well-known pastor I USED TO LOOK UP TO says the chip is not the mark. That's a lie also. Well, there are some that feel it's okay to get drunk and sleep with a prostitute, more lies these are blind leaders of the blind; that's why the Bible says many are called but only a few chosen. No, I'm not their judge. I'm just saying according to the scriptures, I've written in this book from the Bible, but those deceivers are liars, and Galatians 1 says that they are accursed, so does that mean the people are accursed, so does that mean the people that follow an accursed preacher are cursed as well. Read your Bible; did they not take achan's whole family out and stone them as accomplices? Yes, they did. Wow.

And on and on, it makes you wonder if they have studied scriptures on false doctrines. And if they read (Revelation 22:18–19 and Romans 1:25) at all, or do they just think and believe that the Bible's just a book, instead of it really being the authentic Word of God (probably), and they probably are like the Pharisees and think Jesus was just a teacher, instead of being the Son of God and our Savior and Lord, or why else would they take away and ADD to God's Word or even follow a version Bible that is. Some may not even know, then I pray my book turns on the light. Again, folks, this is the whole reason the Holy Ghost (Holy Spirit) came—to lead us and guide us into all truths, to teach us and give us understanding (John 14:17, 26, 1 Cor, 2:10–16, Acts 1:8) and because these translators are playing God. There's only one God and one Jesus Christ and only one Holy Ghost (Holy Spirit). There is only one God and one mediator between God and man, the man, Christ Jesus: (1ˢᵗ Timothy 2:5–6; Ephesians 4:18).

Especially (Isa. 14, Luke 14, Matt. 4, 2 Cor. 11:3, 14, 15) really explains the devil's tactics, tricks, manipulating schemes to deceive folks (2 Corinthians 11:3 and 4, also read verses 13, 14, 15). And no one is exempt from his tricks like the devil tricked Eve. If the devil tried fooling Jesus Christ, no one else is any different. It's a counterfeit spirit out to trick and deceive people. We all agree that no one when knowing for a fact that a boss was gonna pay you cash in counterfeit bills. Would you really keep working there or accept pay in counterfeit money? No way.

And there are so many that get angry at God for allowing things to happen. Yet like that money, God wants the real thing too. He wants us to be real to him, just like we want our boss to pay us real money instead of counterfeit, not generic or counterfeit but real genuine authentically the real thing. Like living for God and Not being counterfeit or a big show of pretenders or good actor—no, God's wanting us to be real to him and he (God) wants to see real (spiritual fruit) on us...love, joy, peace, not counterfeit or a big show. I've seen 'em and so have you. No, not judging, merely explaining. God wants to see fruit on us...love, joy, peace, longsuffering means to be extra patient with someone that's not as holy as you are, or that struggles in areas no one has arrived yet; there is none righteous no not one. All have sinned and fell short of the glory of God (Rom. 3:10, 23). Things are not always as they appear, example, I have metal implants in my back, and have a lot of pain. I try not to take a lot of pain meds, so I use the hot roll-on ointment, that stuff really smells bad. So I put on extra cologne, and it never fails some wise guy'll say. Wow, you took a bath in you after shave huh? Not knowing I'm trying to cover up the ointment smell. Not trying to attract anyone.

Ol' R. W. Shambock's interpretation of righteousness was "right living." Sure loved that man's preaching!

A particular preacher preached one time on "making a difference," living in sin is the opposite, or do you really honestly buy the fruit that has rotten spots on it or all over it...yuck! No way, but you skip over those and pick out the best ones...come on, folks. Old ways, sinful ways, making ourselves to become like fruit with rotten spots. Just picture, after another country helped us with millions of dollars after major earthquakes and our government was meeting a king or queen from that country, and they bring them some crates of rotten, spotted fruits, with a thank-you card. How do you think the king and queen would respond? Yet you get so many bimbos that think God'll accept them to continue in living their old sinful life after Jesus paid for their souls salvation with his life, so many people are not willing to allow God to change them. When the Bible is very clear on this subject, this is why there are so many translations and so many religions out there; they just say we made it an easier translation for people to understand! And they would more than likely get sent to hell for deceiving people and changing what God said in (Matthew 23:14).

Please note: This is another scripture that's left out of the other versions Bibles. And why do these very intelligent people get mad when you point it out, and they still make even more excuses for their easy-to-understand version Bibles that has scriptures removed and altered, so smart yet so blind. Read it, people. Question, who gave them permission? God didn't! (Rev. 22:18, 19; Rom. 1:25). Again, the people who wrote these New Translation Bibles were not born-again Christians. They are deceivers and counterfeits (2 Tim. 3:13, 2 Pet. 2:4 to 22, 2 Pet. 3:4 to 9, Rev. 22:18, 19) and say God will add a curse to those who takes away or adds to the Bible. So again, the reason is that they can continue to live in sin without feeling guilty or condemned, and the devil's using these blind individuals to take away power scriptures (Matthew 17:21 and Mark 9:29), or like (Philippians 4:13), some versions remove phrases like "through Christ" and replace it with "him" (honest to God, I really believe that's altering God's word—by removing "Jesus Christ" and replacing it with "him"). And mark my words, reader, if you're mocking what I say…you may stand alongside them on Judgement Day! They will be judged by God, not me, and this is not the only one; there are a few scriptures like this that have been removed and altered. (I could write a whole page.) But why did God say in (Revelation 22:18–19) and (Romans 1:25) to not to change, add to, or take away from God's Word? (Mathew 15–14) says they are blind leaders of the blind, and if the blind lead the blind—what does the next part say?—they both will fall into the ditch! (Hello?) And the devil's using these blind individuals to take away power scriptures that give people of God power with God. That's why they are called power scriptures. For example, if the Bible says in (Matthew 18:20, John 14:13–14, and Acts 3:6) Peter prays in Jesus's name or ask anything in Jesus's name, or as in (Acts 4:12), "Neither is there salvation in any other for there is none other name under heaven given among men, where by we must be saved." So again, only a devil would remove a power scripture that gives you a Christian power with God, such as the ones

I gave (I could fill up this whole page), such as the devil coming as an angel of light as in (Galatians 1:6–20) (see verse 8) and also (2 Corinthians 2:11, 11:13–15). Okay, I know I'm repeating myself, but the Bible does say for all of us to do the work of an evangelist (2 Tim. 4:5) and to study. It doesn't say to just read but to study (2 Tim. 2:15). Read it. So why do you think that scripture says that the workman (me and you) "needeth not to be ashamed, rightly dividing the word of truth"? It's because when you stand before God, you'll be ashamed when God explains it all to you. If you're not doing what God says in (Luke 6:45–46) when the devil backs you into a corner of temptation, you better know those power scriptures. As Jesus said to Satan in (Matthew 4) (it is written in verse 7), "Thou shalt not tempt the Lord thy God." And remember, you too can rebuke the devil when he tempts you with suicide as he did to Jesus here, call him a liar, and command all of the devils to back off in Jesus's name, and then you can say, "I plead the blood of Jesus over me," and quote power scriptures like (Luke 10:18–20 and Philipians 4:13, 19).

You see? There is power in the blood of Jesus: it washes our sins away (Eph. 1:7) (Revelation 12:11) (Matt. 26:26, 28, Rev. 1:5, 1 John 1:7), and the devil wants to remove anything that gives you—the Christian followers of Jesus Christ—power with God through Jesus Christ's name and the blood of Jesus and through quoting God's Word. But if it's been altered, then there's no power because now it's not God's Word (Matt. 15:9) but man's recycled version, which is powerless against the devil. Again, I was a prison minister for eighteen and a half years. I came against real devils, so don't even try telling me that truckload of manure of "You're not gonna cast out no devil, saying, 'I cast you out in his name.'" Wrong. It's Jesus Christ, people, Jesus Christ (not in his name, not in him we pray). NO...I am an experienced minister of God, and I'm telling you that in this end time, when nightmare-type earthquakes are about to hit, when they are gonna sink islands and flatten mountains (according to the Bible), and if these next few years, Jesus Tarry's, they are gonna be your worst nightmares. Then according to the Bible (Rev. 6:14, 16:20; Luke 21:6), know the Bible's contents if you really plan on surviving. The devil's not playing games; he wants your soul... because we are seeing the worst protests, fights, and riots. And people are turning on each other like never before. We are the last generation (Matt. 24:33–34), according to the Bible, and you need to know the real Bible. My question on this is, how far will all this go? How many more different versions of the Bible will be made that's NOT from God (Luke 6:46, Matt. 15:9, Col. 2:22, Mark 7:7–13)? Read (Romans 1:16–32), especially (verses 20–25). In (John 6:62, see verse 68). Even back then, man would try and change what God said to Adam and Eve. The devil was the culprit here, clearly, back in the beginning of time and in Jesus's day (Matt. 4). We've discussed already, but there were also others in Jesus's day: the religious actors—those wicked lawyers (even then), evil scribes, and the Pharisees that appeared righteous outwardly only but had an evil heart and were always plotting and scheming to lay traps for Jesus Christ to catch him in his words so they could accuse him and betray him. Now, I don't call these creeps friends. Do you? See (Luke 11:48–54); it's one of those eye-opening/wow chapters like that ol' Peter saying (John 6:68): "Lord, to whom shall we go? [These are my own words.]" You have the words of eternal life, but if man alters them years later, it's not gonna be the words of eternal life from Jesus but what man says. Okay, I've harped on it long enough because those folks that just want to hear just the love messages and just encourage me don't scare me with those going-to-hell sermons or sermons about the end-time, Last Days, how Jesus is coming, etc. Just give me heaven and love sermons. Wow as in (John 3-16), and they don't read (verse 17, 18, and verse 19) that men loved darkness more than light. You better read and follow all of it! It's not a buffet to pick and choose what you want.

So why do people tempt God and hold onto their sinful ways?

Read (Acts 5:39): "But if it be of God, ye cannot overthrow it, lest haply ye be found even to fight against God." According to (Revelation 20:10—15) (specifically, see verse 12), **on judgement day, the whole human race will know** that all this is true, but then it'll be too late for all who made those wrong choices and altered/changed what God said.

Again, as in (Acts 5:39), we do not want to be judged alongside those who rebel against God and those who go against God by scheming, scamming, being underhanded, lying, cheating, etc. as the scribes and Pharisees did in (Mathew 23:23–39), (Mathew 23:14–15), or (Luke 20:47). We must allow God to change us, not us changing

God. Get saved (Rom. 10:9–10, 13; 2 Cor. 5:17; John 3:3, 5; Acts 2:21, 37–41; 1 John 1:6–10). I spoke of these, about not allowing God to change their hearts toward God, but again, they rebel like the Scribes and Pharisees. They knew how to dress and act the part, but Jesus saw right through them and said they were as graves full of dead man's bones full of hypocrisy. Yuck! As in (Matthew 23:27–28), that's pretty plain to me, or even (Hebrews 12:1, 2), telling us to lay aside weights. So let's do what God says and don't change his Word and "don't fight against God." (Acts 5-29) and (Acts 5-39) cause you will lose!

Still on Making a Difference

As I said, I've been a visitor when I evangelized to many different churches. Wow...funeral-type dead, churches having a "form of God but denying the power of God in their church" (2 Tim. 3:5)—all lip-and-mouth service (Matt. 15:8, and 9), you wouldn't even know it was a church if you hadn't saw the building (2 Tim. 3:5), which makes you wonder why they are even going to church if their heart isn't really in going (just a big façade fake front). Now, six years later after I started writing this book, the world is seeing a plague hit with a pandemic that's causing even churches to shut down. Wow, who'd have thought it would happen. Now people wish they would have got up off their hindees and went to church, and just like in the Bible days, folks are gathering at homes for church and Bible studies. Again, history is being repeated; it's wrapping up, folks, and if you don't see it, you are spiritually blind. Pray and ask God to open up your spiritual eyesight (Rev. 3:18).

But I visited this one-of-a-kind, spirit-filled church of power, and this preacher gave some examples; one was when we lift up the Lord by thanking and giving him praise, he will draw all men unto him (John 12-32). And another way is to shine that light in us of God to others. Sometimes you never have to say anything, just showing, kindness, and going out of your way to help someone or allow someone else in the door. First, except at some special security jobs, I won't say where I was yelled at being courteous letting in someone (not now) the world is so bad; people are afraid everyone's gonna steal your identity. Oooh, sounds like the identity chip (666) is coming. Okay, I think that was said already. But we all can still make a big difference in doing what's right and fair and following the Bible.

We are seeing it unfold before our eyes, seeing things that are blowing everyone's mind. We are definitely in the end times— killings, country's testing nuclear bombs, etc. All the beginning of sorrows the Bible says (Matthew 24:4–15) (see verse 8), but even through it all, there is still hope (1 Cor. 15:19). "If in this life only, we have hope in Christ, we are of all men most miserable." But it goes beyond this life to eternal life with Jesus Christ, you see, and it's through Jesus Christ having a one-on-one experience, a personal relationship with our Lord and savior, honoring Him, thanking him for saving you from the depths of sin and hell, Loving and worshipping him out of your heart not lip service, unthankful and dreading to be there attitude, dozing off, wishing this long-winded preacher would shut up, wishing you were watching the ball game attitude. Do you think that's worship? NO, it's not because many people don't even know what true worship is, which is only in spirit and in truth (John 4:21–24). Even living for God makes a difference. And many don't even have a clue on what real, true, out-of-the-depths-of-the-heart-and-soul type of true worship really is (Rom. 3:11). It sure isn't putting on a big showy performance, waving a flag or blowing some ram's horn. It's really amazing, some of the things you see out there, folks, really. God wants you to be real in worshipping and living for him, and when you read (Matthew 23), (John 4), and (Luke 16:23, 20:45–47), Jesus says those Pharisees and scribes (*pretense* meaning a big show or a pretender/actor) are not being real! God wants genuine and real, true worshippers. Now, on Judgement Day, when the devil's phonies are being judged and separated when God divides the goats from the sheep (as in Matthew 25:31–46), I just don't see anyone jumping out of the crowds with a flag, doing a fake performance of worship, when God's throwing all the phonies into hell, as (Matthew 23:14) state. Number 1, a real, true worshipper is first gonna search his heart, asking God to cleanse his heart and soul, making sure nothing's between you and him. I do regardless if I need it or not because the Bible says we've all sinned and come short of the glory of God, and there are none righteous, no, not one (Matt. 5:23–26; Rom. 3:23, 10–11; 1 John 1:8–10). And number 2, what about a doctor that had just finished surgery on a diseased person, his scalpel and tools still bloody, do you really want that doctor to use those instruments on you? I don't think so, yet so many don't have a clue that, that is how God feels about people living in sin with cow-manure spots of sin all over them. And they approach the throne of God with their acting and with their fake praises, making a big showy performance in front of people. So again, would you, standing there in the huge crowd on Judgement Day, seeing God throwing all those Pharisees and Sadducees into hell, really jump out and do a big fake performance that really isn't real, true worship? No...I don't believe anyone with a brain would while wetting their pants before God, yet churches are full of them. Hey...get mad, but I'm telling you the truth. And deep down in your soul, you know it's true. But on that day, those types are gonna really wet their pants when they stand before an angry God. Oh, but preacher God is a God of love (John 3:16–19), mercy, and grace. Yes, he is now, but the Bible teaches that on that day, the Lord will take vengeance on those who didn't obey him (2 Thess. 1:8–10, Matt. 25:30–34, Heb. 2:3, 2 Cor. 5:11). Right now, we are still in the mercy and grace and God's love era, but then on Judgement Day, when all of mankind stands before a holy God, there will be no more time to get right with God (Rev. 22:11–14). So if we really **know all this**, it will make a difference on our worship when we come before God to pray and worship. So those who evidently do not really know the whole Bible (Hosea 4:6, Isa. 5:13). Again, those type that are into yelling more for their team at the ball game than thanking God for food, shelter, health, etc. are not even people who have a personal relationship with God. As I've already stated, that's what really makes the difference.

And the fringe benefits of a true worshipper of God and a true follower is (Psalm 103), chapter 21 and chapter 22 of Revelation's, and (1 Corinthians 15:51–58). The Bible says our eyes haven't seen nor our ears heard, the things God has prepared for us (1 Cor. 2:9). It says neither has entered into the heart of man, the things God's prepared for them that love him. Being a great performer only shows man you're a good actor, but no one, I mean no one can fool God. (John 14) says Jesus went away to prepare a place for all of us that follow him. I look around this old wicked world, and I see some beautiful places. There are places of entertainment some bad, some good, some magnificent places like in the amazon untouched by man, way up in the mountains my brother-in-law, Richard and Fred Hurley, many years ago before my car wreck. We hiked a mile and half down in a canyon. Again, untouched by man, beautiful river and waterfalls, green, plush forest, etc.

So if all these beautiful places God created here on earth are so spectacular here, now, what is this glorious heaven gonna look like, with its streets of pure gold and gates of pearl and walls of jasper and the whole city made of pure gold, like glass (Rev. 21:18, 19, 20, 21). Wow, and it's pure crystal-looking river (Rev. 21:11, Rev. 22:1) a river flowing out of God's throne; wow. And the sea of glass that the saints of God will be standing on before the throne of God and anyone who misses those sights is crazy, and it'll blow anything here on earth out of the water. The Lord has had two thousand years in preparing a place for all of us born-again Christians, and the good news is he's soon to return. According to prophecy and take all who has received him in their hearts home to heaven with Him (John 14:1, 2, 3; John 3; John 3:3, 5; Rom. 10:9, 10, 13; 1 John 1:5–10). When we repent of our sins and ask Jesus Christ to forgive us and come into our hearts and wash our soul clean with his blood and to save our souls, then our name is written down in the Book of Life. Now isn't all of that worth giving him out best true praise and worship? Yeah, it is.

Then, my dear friends, that makes us rapture ready, so we can go to heaven when Jesus comes and gets all his people, then we'll all get to see all those beautiful sights in person that's been prepared for us all, that has called upon his Name (Acts 2:38, 39, 40; Rom. 10:13; Rev. 22:17). It will be worth it all to be ready. Amen... Fringe benefits—some jobs have that, company car, meals, all-expense-paid plane fares, hotel fare, etc., but God's fringe benefits package outweighs 'em all, living forever in a new heavenly body that'll never die or grow old, walking on streets of pure gold, no worries, always having all your needs supplied (Phil. 4:19) Never anyone there to hurt you, rob you, steal from you...no one there to lie to you or accuse you of things you've not done.

Wow, this will be heaven and much, much more. God will wipe away all tears, taking away all things, that hurt, all things that offend, all things that cause pain and sorrow. The Bible is clear, very clear on these things, and all the tears the saint of God have prayed for that prodigal son to come back home and get saved, or that prodigal daughter's life that was such a mess. All those wayward kids and grandkids that need Jesus in their life will someday return to Jesus Christ and our God has written their names in the book of life answering our prayers, so they will enter into those gates of pearl with all of us to see our Lord Jesus that died for us all. That's worth telling folks about, not to mention our testimony (Rev. 12:11). How God changed us from hippy to preacher to God be the glory.

But what about those that are spiritually blind and deaf to God's Word that don't listen at church, or pray, or worship? They just sit and daydream. I know of many. They have been lured by the devil and have gone back to the dog vomit that God brought them out of, some the devil has used to pull others out to smoke dope because of pain, and they will burn in hell too. Ouch…oh, you think God's gonna look the other way. When Jesus died a "painful death on the cross," hello to spiritual blindness, or just plain stupidity?

There are many ways of therapy to help ease pain. The entire world has gone overboard because of pain. I myself have suffered for many years; hot baths or hot showers helps or a bike ride. Sure there's pain while you're doing it, but it does help after. You press through it with prayer but to give place to the devil is very foolish, and he will try anything to trick you into losing your soul for, but wait a minute preacher. You left off the front part of that scripture: (Now that I made my point). It says "Lest Satan should get an advantage of us" for we are not ignorant of his devices. Wow. Yet people still shack up and commit adultery, and quote bible scriptures, and they themselves are breaking the Seventh Commandment, somethings wrong here, they haven't read (Gal. 5:19–21) (1 Cor. 6:9–10) or their double minded, (James 1:8) (James 1:22–25) or people just forget. People soon forget about Adam and Eve, and Achan, Samson and Judas, and in (Acts 5), Annanias and his wife, etc. And how that tricky ol' devil lied and used things and people to deceive them out of heaven. It's so sad that

Jesus himself suffered a horrible, horrible painful death, just so we could make heaven. I just don't see Jesus saying, "Hey, John, can you hold me up a doobie/joint, so I can smoke some pot for this PAIN?" And in (Hebrews 4:15), Jesus knows about pain and temptation (yet without sin)—wow. So don't be deceived; read (Matthew 4). Did Jesus give into the devil's temptations?

No...no way. (Ephesians 4–27) says don't give place to the devil, and these people need to read (2 Corinthians 11:3, 2 Corinthians 11:14–15 and 2 Corinthians 5:11 and Luke 16:19 to 31). The Bible says God will send a strong delusion (2 Thess. 2:10–12) that people will believe a lie and be damned (2 Thess. 2:11, 12) because they didn't believe the truth the Bible, so they'll be damned sent to hell. Wow, pot ain't worth your soul going to hell for. Pray...repent and ask Jesus to forgive you and restore you back before it's too late.

Question: (2 Corinthians 5:11) says, "Knowing therefore the terror of the LORD." We persuade men...is people? Really? Huh? Are people really persuading people today? NO! Maybe some, a few, maybe but most I've seen, again, it's LOVE, LOVE, LOVE. All they want to hear is God is love and encourage me. Preach I can make it, etc. When the world is worse than ever, and there is no persuasions, no warnings. We don't want to offend them; yeah, and the Bible says there blood will be on your hands. If you don't warn (Ezek. 33) them, read it!

Here's another thought before I move on, in the days of Daniel, I read that those evil devils that tricked the king into signing the decree on not praying without permission from the king...most people know the story in (Dan. 6). WOW (Sounds like today, closing down all the churches.) You can't sing, ha. (Watch me!) The devil is a liar!

Okay, at the end of the story of Daniel, we see regrets on the face of the sleepless king and see him taking Daniel out and throwing those evil men and their families into the lion's den. Okay, in (Matthew 23:14), we see there will be more severe torments and more severe punishment to the false phonie, pretenders, and hypocrites. Hey, read it...

We must warn people and try and persuade them. Wow (moving on).

When Things Are Bad, God Is Still God He Has Never and Will Never Change.

He's the same, yesterday, today, and forever (Heb. 13:8, Heb. 12:2). And Jesus loves you so much that he left a paradise in heaven to come to earth to die a hard, cruel death (for you) so when things look bad remember what our Lord went through for us all (John 3:16) paying the price for our salvation (1 Cor. 6:20); thank God, Jesus took our place on the cross, but the Bible says in (1 Peter 5:7), we can call upon Jesus any time, we can cast all our cares of this life on Him because He cares for us, all our Heavy burdens, and all our troubles of this life, we can cast all of our troubles on God. He loves us and desires to help us in our time of need. Then again, don't forget to share the miracle when it comes to others (Ps. 34:15–19, Revelation 12:11).

Those white blank pages in the front of your Bible are great for memory miracles, to look back on things God has done for you.

Remember our best example: Jesus prayed, if it be your will, let this cup (death) pass from me but not my will, thine be done.

People by the droves crumble when they feel their prayers aren't answered as quick as they want. Our lack of faith and lack of patience does not alter the power of God or his miracles. He's the same, yesterday, today, and forever. He changes not. We still gotta keep pressing on. Things ain't gonna always go our way. I think Americans are spoiled rotten; we are still a blessed nation, though the sins of America against God are getting scary especially if you've studied prophecy. But next time, you are in pain or your prayers seem to be unanswered or you're discouraged or you're dragging through life, remember our Lord Jesus dragging his cross, after being beat by all those soldiers mocked and ridiculed Him for doing good.

Dying on the cross was probably a lot worse than the movies and Hollywood portrayed, I'm sure. But Jesus humbled himself and died for us all so we could make heaven. Some versions say we have rooms. I like KJV (mansions). He prepared for us a place in heaven (John 14). Some of the greatest singers and artist that have been on the bestsellers' list are those that we're going through hard fiery troublesome trial of sickness or a battle in life of some kind. Someone said that pressure on coal makes a diamond, crushing roses gives out the best of its fragrance. When life gives you lemons, make lemonade or for Fred, coconut.

Thank you, Jesus, that's what I'm talking about. No, God is still God. No matter what goes on. Don't quit; there is nothing to go back to. Just tie a bigger knot and hang on. God's heard ya. Your answers on the way. As my favorite singer says, there was only one Vestal Goodman and one (Dottie Rambo). And they packed God's anointing even through hard, hard times, and they stayed true to God and in return they were blessed by God's great anointing that separates the greatest from the ordinary. It's the anointing of God that they've carried, that makes the difference between regular talent to the Godsent, extremely anointed, and most people know that type comes from being specially called...or those with a special calling from God, are ones who spend time with God.

What Great Examples You Are

I have seen especially in the church I attend some of the best examples of God's love that I have ever seen in people, beginning with my pastor on down to the deacons, ministers, ushers, deaconesses, sisters and brothers in Christ. Jesus said in (John 15) to continue in my love, and in (verse 9, verse 12), it's Jesus's commandment to love one another and also said in (John 13:35). By this love shall all men know you are my disciple if you have love one to another. And again, the folks at Living Christ Church in Tulare, California, has demonstrated this Christlike love to me and my wife. Some other places we've been, we were not at all treated so well. Oh, we've felt love from a lot of God's people. Just not at this magnitude of extreme, which is that agape, the God kind of love.

The word *agape* is the Greek word for God's kind of love that Jesus was stating that in (John 13:35) that by this agape, God-type love, shall all men know that you're my disciples. By the love you have one toward another. Agape love is not the fondness type the world shows over their favorite dessert, but it's such a deep love down to the soul that you'd lay your life down for them if it came down to it. And Jesus did, by this love they'll know you're my disciple. I have seen this type of love at Living Christ Church. People that sacrifice their personal leisure time to help someone laid up in the hospital, or someone that needs a little help with groceries, etc. I've had my lawn mowed, my truck washed, food and meals brought to me after my surgery. The whole church choir came to my house and sung me some songs...I felt so loved I cried.

This is that agape love; sure, everyone's busy. We live in the busiest time ever. And that's what gets ya. When people lay down their busy schedule to spend a little time to bless someone with stitches up their back, that can't get out. Wow, and Bro. Vance and Bro Shawn hold a special place in my heart when they washed my dirty truck, that I wasn't even able to drive yet. Wow…and many, many, others like Bro. Sye Harris bringing a wheelchair ramp…Pastor Green brought me a hospital bed and wheelchair, and he had Bro. Mike mow my lawn. Wow…

All these and many more, like Sis. Gail make my favorite, a scrath German chocolate cake and especially delivered it with her sweet little mother right to my house, and so many more, sacrificing their time to bless me. Wow…what an impression of God's love these church folks has demonstrated. That's the difference between a regular-fondness-type love than the extreme agape love; you go to the extra mile. There are many, many more. I've seen them show to me and others as well, but any one can say "I love you," but Jesus said they'll "know" you are my disciples by the "love" you show. Wow, what a demonstration of God's love in action. Wow! And let's not forget that big muscle man Bro. Keith Parker that carried my two suits all over the garment district all day long. When the church brotherhood went on the garment district shopping trip down in LA, I tried several times to take them from him (this was a while after my surgery on my back that left me to walk with a cane), but he wouldn't let me. Wow, what love this man of God had; yes, my friends, these folks at Living Christ Church has indeed demonstrated God's true love to me, an old white man that has deserved far worse than all these kind deeds and many more.

Hear me, Christian: Not just words, but this body of believers live what Paul taught (in power and in demonstration, as in 1 Corinthians 2:4).

My speech and my preaching were not with enticing words of man's wisdom, but in demonstration of the Spirit and power. When Christlike folks show love in demonstration, they are indeed demonstrating the power of God's agape love because talk is cheap, but to demonstrate it in action, you then are teaching by example. (WALK the TALK) "Don't Just say you love me…show me that you love me" or in other words… (Practice what you preach) (1st Cor. 9:14) make a difference because I've seen such love and kindness. For about nine years now, I've seen and watched this love of God in action.

These folks have a made-up mind. As Paul said in (Philippians 2:5), let this mind be in you that was also in Christ Jesus (2 Cor. 8:12) When the world shows road rage and a spirit of ugly hate crimes. They the world say the opposite, that hate crimes are ones that don't agree or allow their sin-type lifestyle, opposite of Living Christ Church, which the worlds view is opposite of the love of Christ in those born-again saints of God. God is love, light, and in him is no darkness (1 John 1:5, 6).

Revealed Truths to Know the Mystery of the Kingdom

(Mark 4:9, 10, 11, 12)

In (Matthew 11:25), at that time, Jesus answered and said, I thank you, O Father Lord of heaven and earth because thou hast hid these things from the wise and prudent. And hast revealed them unto babes. (First Corinthians 1:17, 18, 19, verse 20) speaks of the wisdom of this world (which won't get you anywhere with God). (Verse 21) is about foolishness of preaching to save them that believe. And (1 Corinthians 2:1–10, verse 14), but the natural man receives not the things of the Spirit of God, for they are foolishness unto him, neither can he know them, because they are spiritually discerned. You have to want to learn and want to receive with all your heart, those that hunger and thirst after righteousness shall be filled (Matt. 5:6). So you will be taught and filled with knowledge of God's truth, the more you desire it and pray for the Holy Ghost to give you understanding, but there must be an inner hunger and thirst for righteousness means desire to receive and understand God's Word which is truth.

It amazes me that courts still use the Bible to swear you into your oath to tell the truth by laying your hands on the Bible and so, so many still lie. Because deep down, they don't really believe; they are just complying with the court to con and deceive them. But many years ago, most people had a deep inner fear of God, that if you laid your hand on the Bible and lied with an oath to tell the truth, most people fear God if they lied on the Bible. So courts used it to get people to be honest and tell the truth, but nowadays so many lie with an oath, with no fear of God, which is very, very dangerous for his soul. And don't have a clue of the danger of that as in (Rev. 21:8).

If you notice, Jesus used many parables, and it was usually when the religious Pharisees and Sadducees was around, Jesus gave examples and illustrations using parables that those religious anti-Christs couldn't understand, which is a fact that the Bible is fixed to where it's not meant for a devil worshipper or a drunk to understand, but only for those who trust in Jesus Christ as Lord and Savior. This is why people want to alter God's Word, and man again tries to play God, and tries to be the Holy Ghost, which there's only one God, the Bible plainly teaches that the Holy Ghost will teach you the Holy Ghost God's Spirit will explain the scriptures to those that ask for help and when a minister tries explaining to people in His book, that all those retranslations are from devils they get mad at you (come on, people) are they God? No! Did God give them permission to change and rewrite new Bibles. Hello, did He? NO! HE DIDN'T! So why do they get mad at someone that's telling the truth? When the Bible says if anyone takes away or adds to (Rev. 22:18, 19).

Not just to the disciples but all in all, he gave everyone that truly desired with all their heart to learn, an understanding heart, revealing his word. Many remarkable stories, parables that delivered powerful messages. Perfect example is the reaping and sowing (Gal. 6:7 to 9). And it amazes me so many just don't get this one either. Along with (2 Peter 3:3 to 5), you don't mock God. Everyone reaps what you do. There are no exceptions, and it's not all bad things. You do good and you reap good. Some call it karma. Some say what goes around comes around, but the Bible says it's called reap what you sow, good or bad. (It's God's law of life.) The whole reason the whole world especially America, one nation under God (no more). This nation was once so blessed by God, for the stand we took for God. The right way to live and treat people and the way to be a real man of God and other nations saw the difference, but not now; now this sinful nation stands for anything that's sinful. This nation has become a stench in God's nostrils (John 3: 16, 17, 18, 19; Psalms 9:17; 1st Cor. 6:20).

And if it wasn't for America having more than ten righteous, as in (Genesis 18:32). And America would have been destroyed by God, but there (Gen. 19:26, 2 Pet. 2, Rev. 18, 2 Cor. 5:11, 1 Pet. 4:17–18) are more than ten, so why did Jesus Christ mention. Remember lot's wife in (Luke 17:32)? Because she looked back when God delivered her out of the city of sin. Wow. How about USA? (2 Thes. 1:7 to 12) And I'm very sure that the USA is (Rev. 18-100) percent sure.

God gave us five senses that will stay with you even through all eternity, if you go to heaven or hell, you will always have these five senses from this life to the next. And…

Those Five Senses Are Taste, Touch or Feel, See, Hear, Smell

(As in Luke 16:19 to 31)

Then Jesus taught in (Mark 4:9, 10, 11, 12) about the five senses that if you'll notice also the rich man had those five senses in hell (Lk 16: 23 to 28). So somebody please explain why even many, many Christians do not want to even discuss or hear sermons on this, or on the last days (Matt. 24), or on destructions of evil cities, such as (Rev. 18 or Jonah chapter 1, also chapter 3:10; Luke 17:26, 27, 28, 29; Gen. 9:10–11 to 15; Luke 11:29 to 32; 2 Pet. 2:1 to 9); or on this page about hell...which is God's punishment for those who reject Jesus Christ and God's commandments, and for those who rebel against God. If the pastor of the majority of all churches aren't preaching a love message or encourage-me-type sermon.

Then a lot of folks get up and walk out. Wow, this is the ones that Christ talked about in those parables and Paul spoke of those that wanted their ears tickled or encouraged all the time (2 Tim. 4:3, 4), which does explain why so many want the watered-down versions (2 Tim. 4, 3, 4; 1 Tim. 4:1, verse 11 also, to Mark 4:12; Mark 4:11– 12). But in (Mark 4:12), that seeing ye may see and not perceive and hearing they may hearing they may hear and not understand, lest at any time they should be converted. And their sins should be forgiven them. So remember, God gives an understanding heart to them that believe and ask in prayer, really deeply desiring to know and learn

(John 14:26). The Holy Ghost will teach you and bring things to your remembrance what the Lord said to you.

Even in the next life, which we will have those five senses and memory in hell but not in heaven. That is memory of sorrowful things will not be in heaven (Rev. 21:4). For all tears will be wiped away, but in hell, they will remember everything, especially sorrow and every word someone said about Jesus and heaven. Because the Bible says, "Where the worm dies not" (Mark 9:44, 46, 48). Those in hell will remember everything. Every opportunity, every time they could have went to church and missed the special Word God gave the pastor that would have turned them to God. They will hear it over and over, it's not just burning in a new body that will never burn up, but God according to scriptures, God has already previously organized and arranged all of this. In many scriptures like (Ephesians 1:5, Ephesians 1:11, and Romans 8:29–30) say (he has preordained) or predestinated our lives already.

And how so many people just read right over things, sure most of these are referring to those who'll make heaven, and then you read (Luke 16) and all the bargaining and pleading even about his five brothers, so there will be memory and remorse, and it looks like even compassion on the rich man trying to keep those five brothers out of hell—wow. But (verses 29–31) always got me; if they don't hear that man of God, that fanatic preacher, my words or Bible words, say, if they don't hear Moses and the prophets, neither will they (the five brothers) be persuaded if one rose from the dead. (No.) So what do you think God is saying here. Just what I was saying earlier, our technology today, flying jets, rockets, computers (microscopic surgery), cars, tanks, weapons of mass destruction, etc. God had all this technology way before we invented the wheel. Wow. And in many things, sometimes I feel like man tries to play God, but in the end, only God (1st Tim. 2:5) and (the only judge) and the only mediator, Jesus Christ (in my words).

John the revelator says in (Revelations 21:4). For those in heaven: God will wipe away all the tears, meaning taking away troubling thoughts or memories that hurt and bring sorrow, there will be no more sorrow in heaven but, peace, joy, happiness, love, Jesus will give them. And the picture of the rich man in hell looking up, and seeing Lazarus while He was burning in tormented flames of fire (Luke 16:23 and 24).

He could see Lazarus in father Abraham's bosom, it's not purgatory or a holding place as so many of false teachings and religions teach, but a scene of seeing one like a baby cuddled in his father's bosom, peaceful, happy, contented, no worries, no cares, being loved, and taken care of, then there's a scene of the saints of God (Rev. 15:2) all standing on cool water before God's throne that the rich man wants just a drop of water for his tongue. So there is a difference between the two. For example, you want to talk about torment; picture this, this rich guy's burning forever in hell and the whole time he is burning. He looks up begging God for a drop of water while the whole time he's burning, he sees all the Christians standing on a sea of glass in heaven, cooling off their feet, that he's screaming for. Wow. Otherwise, please explain what other purpose would God have for all of the saints of God to stand on the Sea of Glass, that is such a coincidence, that the Sea of Glass is put before the throne of God (which is double torment) (which explains Matt. 23:14). For one it brings other scriptures to pass, such as (Psalms 23:5) (1 Cor. 15:25) or (Romans 16:20) (Luke 20:43) or (Mark 12:36) (Psalms 110:1) (Acts 2:34, 35).

Eternal life after the physical death of the Human body and about eternity in heaven or hell, judgment day, etc. The rich man's thinking was of his wealth. Live for today; who cares about that beggar Lazarus. He faired he constantly prempt in the mirror, maybe all kinds of clothes, etc., but he thought he had plenty of time. And that's the thinking of everyone in the world has today in our day and time, no concern of eternity or thought of seeing God today—oh, but some people are more concerned about a cemetery plot, casket, and their funeral expenses or burial insurance, more than, am I really ready if I died today? Hardly anyone anymore even thinks they will go out of this life by a drunk driver or someone talking on their cellphone while driving kills me today; no, they shove that thought out of their mind. No, they think I won't stand in judgment day before God today. I won't die in my sins today (no), not me. There is plenty of time to call on Jesus to save me (oh, really). The guy on the cell-phone who broke my back when he ran that stoplight, the fireman that cut me out with the jaws of life and said if that guy would have been driving a pick-up truck or a larger car, it would have killed me, because it happened so fast. BAM! It was a shock, there wasn't time to say, "Jesus forgive me of my sins, come into my heart and save my soul." But people all over this evil world think, *Not me, not today, no one knows when our time of death is.* Thank God I was ready, but most people take no thought at all of passing away at any time; no, that's considered negative thinking—any time, all those people from the fires, earthquakes, mass shootings, etc., tornadoes, etc.

Hey, they didn't have a clue this is my day to die or if Jesus came in the rapture; no, all they was thinking about was I've got to go buy this or do this or that, not knowing I'll stand before a holy God today. Am I really, really ready (Rev. 19:7)? So many religions and false teachings have really messed up people (1 Tim. 4:1), especially those positive thinkers, meditation (Col. 2:8 to 23) groups, and cults; people will really be shocked that put their confidence in man, or a priest or a religion, you won't make heaven by confessing your sins to a man. You must confess and pray to Jesus Christ (1 Tim. 2:5; Acts 4:12; John 3:3, 5; Rom. 10:9, 10, 13; Acts 2:21, 38, 39; John 14:6; Heb. 2:3).

I even had a wild conversation with this guy at my job that told me he prayed to a dead captain that was called a holy saint, the Bible teaches against this (Luke 16:19 to 31) one of the Ten Commandments (Exod. 20:3, 4, 5; Heb. 12:2; John14:6; Acts 4:12) and for that other lady that said she was okay, that used God's name in vain, saying damn after his name, needs to read (Exodus 20:7) and (Psalm 139:20) because that's God's enemies that do that according to the Bible, and the Ten Commandments (read it yourself), but having no thought of passing away at any time, no. That's considered negative thinking, but without making preparations with the Lord Jesus Christ (Rom. 10:13, "Whosoever calls on the name of the Lord shall be saved"). Many have called on him at the very last minute, barely making it, but sad to say, not everyone was like that, because the Bible teaches us to be ready all the time. We don't know if Jesus will return before we die nor do we know when we die. But the Bible does say it is appointed that you will, and then the judgment (Heb. 9:27 and 28, Rev. 20:14 and Rev. 21:8). Notice you die once with Jesus in (Hebrews 9:27) and go to heaven.

But those not saved, those that have not been born-again, as in (John 3:3 and 5) and in (Revelations 20:14, and 15), they'll die twice, once in their physical body and again in their heavenly body that they will live forever in and be cast into the Lake of Fire to burn forever and ever. This is the second death (all though it's just called the second death); also see in (Revelations 20:10 and Revelations 14:9, 10, and 11): they burn forever. Wow, that doesn't sound like a party to me, with all your ol beer drinking buddies, as we've heard so many say and then laugh and mock us, but the Christians will be having rest and no more pain, no more sorrow when you read about the things in heaven Jesus has prepared for all his people that follow him. Just makes you want to keep looking for his return. And those who look for him, he shall appear the second time without sin unto salvation (Luke 21:34, 35, 36; Heb. 2:3; Matt. 24:42).

Be ready all the time because if Jesus comes in an hour we think not. What if it was when someone's bad-mouthing their pastor—oops, to him that knows to do good and does it not, that is sin (James 4:17). This is why even this ol' preacher, like Peter, I have to watch my temper and my words...yes...me too. There's none righteous, no, not one (Rom. 3:10). I'll give you some homework. Read and study up on Paul and Nicodemus. They were into religion more than God, but they got saved later on, but God had to blind Paul for three days to wake him up. God had to temporarily take away Paul's (Saul's) eyesight to get his attention, which turned the spiritual light on (Jer. 29:13).

Paul was fulfilling (John 16:2), and he thought because those crazy Jesus followers weren't following his religion, he would perse-cute them and have them done away with. And, reader friend, you may have someone coming against you. God hears your prayers; God knows how to get those who are against us and get their attention (Rom. 8:31), but my point here is, there's hope even for those who are off the deep end, and so religious, and so weird. Yes, Jesus loves them too, they have a soul. God can still save them as he did Paul and Nicodemus, because they can reach ones that we can't. God can save anyone; some just have to have the crap slap out of them to wake em up. Excuse my grammar; don't get self-righteous on me now, and don't tell me you don't hear worse words than mine on TV (amen)— but you get my point.

The rich man never drew a line and weighed out life, death, judgment day. He thought, "If I die in my sins, I'll have plenty of time to call on God. The difference is more than night vs. day. Tormented continually, plus seeing what's going on in heaven (Luke 16:19 to 31), that's pretty clear, which is double the torment. So what do you suppose when Jesus was angry at the religious hypocrites Pharisees that were pretending and acting all holy, judging, arguing, ready to stone him at any time, what was he referring to, their punishment will be greater or worse in hell worse than for others and so in hell, there will be more severe degrees of their torment (Matt. 23:14) Jesus referred to the religious Pharisees, that were into false religion, false doctrine, a big show of false righteousness, and hypocrisy. They were big actors, pretending to be righteous but were full of ungodliness and hypocrisy, Jesus said they were as graves full of dead man's bones. And said they would receive greater punishment, so there must be levels of degrees of punishment in hell (Matt. 23:14, Mark 12:40, Luke 20:47). This is the KJV Bible. So yes, there will be worse levels and different degrees of punishment to the lost and worse levels of pain for the pretender, counterfeits, hypocrite, and phonies than for a regular sinner—wow, do you see that in the scriptures (Matt. 23:14, Mark 12:40, Luke 20:47) notice in (verse 47 of Luke 20) they are putting on a show, or performance, which woule lead people astray is my assumption. So it's no wonder God gives worser punishments because Jesus said, time and time again, and warned against this and said in (Matthew 24:4), Jesus's first warning was, don't let no man deceive you by any means: and this is (again) one reason why God also saves and reveals his word to even stupid, ignorant, unlearned, ex-hippy biker, ex-drugees, ex-high school dropout is able to read and understand the Bible and gave us understanding to, illustrate on judgment day to the wise, intellect, scientific minds, and religious phonies that (even) ignorant people like me and Peter can get saved and learn the Bible (Acts 4:13, 2 Pet. 3:5, 8, 1 Cor. 10:1, 2 Cor. 2:11).

Wow, it's saying they all marveled and took knowledge that these ignorant guys had spent time with Jesus and learned. In (Luke 16), Jesus said in his analogy of the rich man in hell that Abraham was saying to the rich man; remember, back in your life how good you had it, and you weren't even concerned of the beggars. Wow, meeting Lazarus, notice that he used names for examples: Lazarus and Abraham, as the father and leader of all Israel, someone they could relate to, and everyone must have known of Lazarus being a perminate fixture at this particular certain spot by the rich man's gate, just wanting crumbs. And dogs licking his sores.

I heard one preacher say he thought the rich man sicked his dogs on the beggar to scare him off, but God gave him favor with the dogs because it's been said for years there is healing in dog slava (but I'll stick with ointment, ha). All those times of opportunities and chances, you had to get right with God. Plenty of chances and opportunities to get saved and born again. Note what was meant in (Mark 9:44, 46, 48) where the worm dies not. Most pastors believe that's referring to our memory, always remembering those who witnessed to you, those crazy Christian people God put in your life to pray for your soul to be saved, but you mocked them and turned a deaf ear to them, but in hell, those memories will be like maggot worms eating at your mind, reminding you over and over, reminding you of every time you passed up your special opportunity God had set up for you.

Wise Men Still Seek Him

(Matthew 2:1)

An intelligent man named Nicodemus was a ruler of the Sanhedrin Sect of the Pharisee religion. You gotta be pretty smart to have the title or position such as a ruler. And please don't misunderstand my analogies of my self-ignorance. (John 3:3, 5), in verse 1 called Nicodemus a Pharisee, a ruler of the Jews of the synagogue. This Jewish sect was made up of spiritually ignorant people, which (Acts 26:24) you had to have been well studied, who were ignorant of things in the spiritual realm of God, as in (1 Cor. 2:14), but they were very educated, very intelligent in law, and very smart in religious matters of their religion. But they also didn't have a clue about the gifts of the Spirit or of their pride and arrogance and that religion would actually separate them from God, according to (John 4). Jesus said God wants his people to worship him in spirit and in truth. Jesus constantly scolded and rebuked the Pharisees, scribes, and Sadducees for their ugly attitudes and evil hearts. So just because people have degrees in theology and have studied tons of doctrines yet have murder in their hearts, are rapists, etc. Jesus told Nicodemus that he still had to repent, be born again, and be born of the spirit, but as intelligent as he was, he still didn't understand those spiritual terms. So even though an intelligent group of graduates who have studied Greek, Hebrew, etc. and have law degrees out of your ears, it will not get you into heaven, but it's still good to be well studied. Don't misunderstand my point, but they had evil hearts against Jesus that only repentance can solve. But again, being well studied and having a lot of knowledge of law to become a Pharisee in this sect of religion and even Festus the Governor said to Paul, "Much learning has made you mad."

In (Acts 26:24) and in (Acts 26:28), King Agrippa said, "You almost persuade me to be a Christian" to Apostle Paul, and if the king didn't repent, he probably wished he had (amen), which Paul and Nicodemus and even Dr. Luke were very educated men, unlike me, with my bad grammar, and spelling make a real task for my great friends at CFP and <<Note to layout: editor's name here>> I want to say thanks to this great editor cause only God knows how many boo-boos my wonderful editor has fixed. And I sure thank <<Note to layout: Editor's name here>> and the wonderful staff at CFP. Thanks, and God bless you all at CFP for making my book and me and all my bad grammar look good. But most of all, I thank my Lord Jesus for inspiring me.

Yes, wise men still seek the Lord, but you see my point, folks, even the centurion, a ranking officer, Daniel, Solomon, Joseph, okay... Am I out of the doghouse? Just don't want folks to misunderstand my comparisents and examples about me trying to humble myself, even if I say God has really helped me from being so ignorant on issues.

And on the flip side, I've seen people act smarter than they are, some want to put on a big show that they are higher up the ladder than you. Jesus Christ spoke in parables of these types and followed up with God resists those with pride but gives grace to the humble and that God will abase them; it's better for us to try and humble ourselves than God humble us as in (1 Peter 5:5–6, Luke 14:11) and (Luke 18:14) or embarrass you. (First Corinthians 10:12) says, "When you think you stand take heed, lest you fall." I knew someone that thought they were the best singer in the whole universe, and wasn't giving God the credit for her anointing, and so the next time in front of over three thousand people at a convention and God did not anoint this person, and she stumbled all the way through the song and said after the convention was over, I was so embarrassed and vowed to God I will never, ever take your anointing for granted again and will always give God the credit and the glory, and it humbled her to repentance of her pride. Wow, true story, and from then on, many said she sung as good as Vestal Goodman and many compared her to vestal (and remembering Acts 12:23) of King Herod that was eaten of worms after his speech, and he let the people give him the glory instead of God and see the difference in (*Acts 14:11 to 18*). And Jesus Christ himself, practiced what he preached, in (John 13) Jesus humbled hisself down and washed the disciples feet.

These kinds of things are written for us to learn from. The Bible says in (Romans 15:4) not calling saints stupid. Many people have got on to me for this, so please no letters. I've heard it, but also know the word. (Romans 12:3, 1 Corinthians 10:12). We are not to think more highly of ourselves than we ought. And I try to stay humble. The Bible says it's better for us to humble ourselves than to have God humble you. Just go to the gyms, and don't misunderstand me, everyone me included needs to be in better shape but not to where you are arrogant, and you fall into pride and become so full of yourself, that you think you've arrived and are puffed up with so much pride, heading for a fall (1 Cor. 10:12; 1 Tim. 4:7, 8; Matt. 16:26). Nothing is worth losing your soul for (nothing).

When you think you stand take heed lest you fall and (James 4:6–7, 8) the sixth verse explains God resist the proud and gives grace to the humble and then there's all those scriptures on humble yourselves and he'll exalt you in due time, and if you don't (Luke 14:11), he will abase you. Pride goes before a fall. Shall I go on. I've seen them in great power and authority. In high religions, boards of directors. So proud, so full of themselves, and I promised God, that I will remember and stay humble, but if it's call myself stupid or whatever. That's me. I'm not gonna think or act like I'm some high intellect, etc. (Rom. 12:3) first and second verse is good too. Are the gyms and the Pharisee religious types today practicing (Rom. 12:1, 2, 3). "Don't be conformed to this world! No, the world is in the church. It's not like it was thirty years ago. Christian people's standards are not lining up with the Bible today but we need to be transformed by the renewing of our minds (back to Christ, Rev. 3:2 and 3, Rev. 3:15 to 19, Luke 12:15 and 21 and 34, in other words…being rich in our hearts and soul is toward God is really more valuable than having… fame and fortune and millions of dollars), making heaven is way better. Amen.

(Revelations 2:2 to 6, Rom. 12:1 and 2) and presenting our bodies a living sacrifice to God. Oh man, the people in today's world will sacrifice their bodies, and patience in long lines at the amusement parks to ride a two-minute ride. Work out five hours at the gym but will not make themselves go to sun night eve. Church service, oh, too tired because I'll have to make myself go to work in the morning, etc. God could take that job so you'd come to church and pray for another one. "Ouch." The truth will make you free and don't snarl and growl at me. I've worked all night, still went to church, taught class, preached in prison all day (Luke 12:34).

But if your ego is exalted to where you feel, what the Bible calls it puffed up with yourself, we call it pumped. At any case it's pride and goes before a fall, the Bible says, and some get so arrogant, hope they make heaven. Blessings come from our sacrifices we make to God (Rom. 12:1 and 2). Doing things and going the extra mile to help someone in need should make you feel more pumped up for God than that a workout at the gym, which one makes you feel high and mighty. Our flesh needs humbled. I know some humble, buffed guys that have always given God the glory, but I also have seen many brag and boast themselves up on a pedestal. That's very dangerous.

Just remember God needs to get all the glory. Nebuchadnezzar's fate is a good example. God had to humble this arrogant man. He lived like an animal in the woods because he failed to give God credit and glory, and then there's King Herod, and he was eaten of worms. Plus, he touched God's anointed which the Bible says we are not to do (Acts 12:21 to 23, Dan. 4:33).

And there are many, many more, especially in the Old Testament that became arrogant and full of themselves and having an evil heart—so many, many, people in America today. That'll stab you in the back to excel above you. Lie, cheat, steal their way to the top to just find out like the rich man. It was all in vain to become and enemy of God. Instead of being like Moses that left the King's Palace to become a Hebrew slave? What? Wow. Today, he would have been the laugh of the day but (Heb. 11:24–25) says he refused to be called Pharaoh's daughter's son and rather chose to be with the people of God in their affliction, wow. And don't forget Enoch, who in (Hebrews 11:5) had this testimony that he pleased God. Who are you pleasing? The boss. The guys at the gym, the ol' partying crowd. Are you a true Christian or just on Sundays?

I heard a few days ago of some people that go to church and smoke medical pot. Well, I did for years, and God took it away from me. People are being lied to by the devil left and right, the same old lies the devil told Eve. (It's just an apple or whatever it was). In my words, the devil says God does not care—lies, lies. Luke 14 is full of excuses, but when you take your last breath and stand before God, you better not have dope of the devil in ya. Hey, I'm not no one's judge, but God took me out of that mess that I call sin, and these blind hypocrites are telling me it's okay, all lies, I know better cause when I was hooked on that demon dope, I couldn't even think right. Again, the Bible says to those type of people, God will send them strong delusions that they will believe a lie and be damned (means sent to hell). Hello, people (2 Thess. 2:10–12). Read it (Matt. 16:26; Luke 21:34–36; Rom. 11:4; Rom. 14:13). Please note, the Bible calls that a stumbling block, when you act and profess you're a Christian and still continue to live in sin (Heb. 12:1). But God will always have a true faithful follower.

Some today you can't tell the difference from the so-called Christians, that look like hookers, partiers, and bar hoppers. No, we are not their judge. Some I guess it takes longer for God to clean them up. Guess they haven't read those that are partiers and drunks don't go to heaven in (Galatians 5:16 to 22, 1 Corinthians 6:15–16, 1 Corinthians 6:9–11). Read (1 Corinthians 5:5). Wow. God has to let some be turned over to the devil to die. Wow. It's all true. It's the Word of God, that will be quoted back to all those who make up excuses to still sin while going to church. Not realizing they are spitting in God's face and slapping Jesus in the face because he died a horrible death on the cross, to save people from their sins, they may as well been the one using the hammer, nailing those nails in Jesus, anyway. The Bible plainly tells people how to live and how not to live, but again it's all true. Wow. It's true.

So according to the Bible, how do you really "please God with your walk with Him and your lifestyle" (Rom. 14:13; 1 Cor. 8:9, 12; James 4:4; 1 John 3:20, 2:15–16)? The scripture (1 John 2:15–16) plainly says not to love the world nor the things in the world, then over in (Luke 6:46), Jesus Christ said, "Why do you call me Lord, and don't do the things that I've told you to do?" Wow. And again, (Hebrews 11:5–6) says that by faith, Enoch was translated to heaven, and that was before Scotty knew anything about beaming him up. Ha, yeah, they called it in Bible days translating or translated, which sounds like interpreting Spanish to English, but no, it means transporting in the spirit. But Enoch never died because he had this great testimony that he pleased God, so God transported him straight up to heaven. (Read it!) Most people would be surprised at the things that are written in the Bible that they are involved in and are doing, would and that will keep them out of heaven. Oh, but, Minister Fred, I pray and go to church, and believe in God (so do devils) and they tremble, but anyone that's reading the Bible knows these things, or do they? (James 2:19, Gal. 5:15 to 22, Gal. 1:6 to 10, 1 Cor. 6:9–10). Now if we pray, stay repented, walk uprightly before God, live according to God's Word (Bible) and live, doing and hearing what the Bible says.

Personally, I like to put on a Bible on CD while I'm on the treadmill or in the shower; yes, you may not grasp every word, but you're gonna get something and so that's why I play them over and over because faith comes by hearing the Word of God, but we all have to work out our own salvation with fear and trembling (Phil. 2:12). A kind of funny story. I was at my in-laws for a barbecue swim, and their dog sneaked a hotdog and ran. Ha! Everyone laughed except them, naturally, so they kinda scolded the dog because she wouldn't come; the dog's name was Faith. I said use your Bible. They said, "Huh?"

"Yeah," I said, (Romans 10:17) "faith comes by hearing the Word of God" (Rom. 10:17). I think Bob and Barbra wanted to smack me, but we all had a good chuckle. So yes, the Bible says, it's impossible to please God without faith (Heb. 11:6, and you learn also how to live).

Please note, I had a lady that was living with a guy come to me and say, "I pray every day and read my Bible. I feel I am okay." Hey, I'm no one's judge. (I just do my best to follow the Bible, for myself.) Again in (Philippians 2:12) work out your own salvation with fear and trembling because if you are wrong, you'll be the one to pay for all eternity, but if you come to me, asking me, don't get mad at me because I tell you what the Bible says. I didn't write the Bible. But if you want to go to God's heaven, then, my friend, you better clean up your life, get right with Jesus, and knock off the sinful lifestyles (oh well, here comes the excuses). You don't answer to me. You can ask her, "Show me in the Bible," but she can't. Again, Jesus said, "Why call me Lord and don't do what I said?" (Luke 6:46).

I'm just a preacher with a message from God. Where do you draw the line! (On getting in heaven.) You must follow the Bible and be born again, not just repeating a prayer but a repented, changed lifestyle, you changed, when you are born again, just like the scripture says, your spirit man inside you is reborn in the spirit when you repent and ask Jesus Christ's forgiveness of your sins and ask him into your heart, you become a new creature in Christ, old things are passed away behold, all things are become new (in my words) read it (2 Cor. 5:17, John 3:3, 5).

He (Jesus) through the Holy Ghost (Spirit) now comes in you and teaches you, leading and guiding you, and directing you to live right. And God's Spirit would never lead you to do wrong. That old man leaves you according to scripture, and many times we have to make ourselves and there are two in (Romans 6:6 to 16), voices that speak to your mind, God and the devil. If you listen to the devil and continue to party, and go to bed with ones you're not married to and go to bars and nightclubs, etc., that kind of lifestyle according to the Bible that will send you to hell and it's fleshly and carnal, and the Bible says and is called worldly means you are following the world and not God and not pleasing to God. You have to decide and choose between the old life or the new life. Just remember the old life is not pleasing to God and to spend eternity, forever in hell, for years of pleasure; it ain't worth it.

But to live for God and follow the Bible and make heaven will definitely be worth it all, and please don't forget that the Bible also says it's a fearful thing to fall in the hands of the living God. (Hebrews 10:31 and John 14:26, John 14:17, John 16:13)—born of the spirit with Jesus Christ now in you, showing you, teaching you, changing you (in my words). Ever since the beginning of time God has wanted communication and fellowship with mankind, but man in this generation is just too busy; this is why I pray first thing when I roll out of bed. I thank Him for rest, protection, home, etc.

A communication and fellowship with God is not you just covering your list of needs, but loving, worshipping, and thanking him first, for all he's done, many, many things. We just overlook, a beautiful day, seeing flowers, and hearing birds singing, having strength to walk to the bathroom, and not being on a machine to help you go, etc., and God wants us to believe he will supply all our needs (Phil. 4:19) and always pray in Jesus's name, and having a good prayer life. It's not an overnight thing. But it's a personal relationship with God Himself, and you can't be stubborn and rebellious, doing it your way (Matt. 6:33, John 14:6, Matt. 6:10, Luke 18:1 to 8). It's God's way or no way! (Ps. 32:9, 1 Sam. 15:23) stubbornness is as idolatry, and rebellion is as the sin of witchcraft, again. I didn't write the Bible. I just read it and follow it. But you see so many things are wrong that many folks do. Having your fortune read is wrong according to the Bible as in (Acts 16:16–31), and many other scriptures speak against this and witchcraft. Even (Revelation 21:8) says sorcerers also will have their part in the lake of fire. As I said, I didn't write the Bible, but today's Hollywood generation has made it look cool to be a witch and do magic, cast spells, etc. Those who practice and enjoy it need to read the Bible, then you'll be called a bible fanatic. But I'd rather follow the Bible and make it to heaven. Again, God's people are destroyed for their lack of knowledge (Hosea 4:6), but there are also hate groups of these types—those that hate Christian people and don't want to hear what the Bible says. These are those types that want to change it, rewrite it, etc., but again, it's all written in the

Bible. So those who think this is okay, need to read it. How about all the different religions, it's better to line up with the Bible. Read (Galatians 1:6–10). So are you pleasing God or man…or yourself… or family? It's your soul; choose wisely.

Give God thanks and glory first before others. All through the Bible especially in Psalms we are told to give God thanks and give him glory and praise for all he's done. And God sends people and animals our way to help us. I thought of the raven sent to Elijah and the donkey to turn Balaam around, when the donkey spoke with a man's voice to get his attention. And many times, God used objects and angels, and mostly, God uses people to do good deeds to help others, and I am reminded of times of needs in my life where so many came to my rescue, many church folks, Pastor Donahue Green and many from church after my wreck and surgery. So many helped, and we thank God for all of them at Living Christ Church and for their love and prayers and for all they've done. And remember, times years ago when we needed to get relocated to a job up in the mountains, had no money, and my brother-in-law Joel and sister Sharene Beames towed their fifth-wheel trailer up to a camping park for us to live in, that we stayed in for a few months till we were able to rent a house, then he drove way up there to tow it back.

And many others over the years have towed us home and fixed our vehicles, like my ol' buddy Ed Fraizer, and Joel and my wife's brothers William and Richard Hurley, and many times over the years towed us home, and my cousins Jim and Debra Peterson, coming miles and miles just to help us, and Loy and Lois Earles has come to our rescue many times also. Rev. Ray and Gloria Romero took us in when a job transfer fell through and they put up with our faces for a few weeks and even loaned me his truck a time before that, and you say, wow, and the love of God flows through these kindhearted folks is so wonderful so when you see this kinda thing going on, even with someone else, give God thanks, and when you get a special blessings from God, keep your ears tuned to God's voice and you can be used by God to bless someone, yourself, like these good, good friends that's a CHP officer (at church, Danny Aguirre and his wife Lori) have taken us to dinner many, many times just to minister to us. They have such an encouraging spirit about them, and, folks, that is a ministry all by itself just giving someone a meal with a godly conversation, lifting folks spirits up when they are going through a rough time is a ministry indeed, and she's also a minister at our church.

We just say God bless 'em. And everyone like these folks that are used by God, going out of their way to bless others. I think of my sister's husband Joel towing a camping trailer up to the high mountains. Just so we could have a living quarters twice and my wife's brothers, William and Richard many times and Joel when our car broke down. They came miles towing us in and cousin. Jim and my old buddy Ed who spent big bucks on my truck and Mr. Anonymous. So many, many over the years God has used to help and bless us, this total stranger in Oregon where we pastored came to our rescue and helped us we called molly our little guardian angel, but all in all, folks, thank the people, yes, but always give God the glory and thank you as well for "in him we live and move and have our being," (Acts 17:28) it's the Lord that died for us. It's the Lord that saved us; he gave us our talents and abilities, and by his strength, we do this or that, leap over a wall, win a race, defeat the enemy. By his grace are ye saved, lest any man should boast (Eph. 2:8–9).

See, God uses many different people in many different ways, most of all these folks refused to take money for their help. That my friend is God and I thank the Lord for all he's done for me and even helping me kill all these insects, gnats by the thousand, and it seems these little demon gnats are sent from hell to distract my thoughts, cause I know that I know, when you have a thought or a scripture that indeed would help minister to somone, the devil will try to distract you, as with all these gnats from hell, getting my focus on them, which, coincidentally I just preached that in a sermon last Sunday, at our church (Heb. 12:1, 2, 3) for us to look to Jesus, the author and finisher of our faith, (verse 2) (and not to lose our focus, wow) so even as God can use things, so can the devil, and esp. on me, while writing this book. My wife and I have been amazed. At the devil even tries to use distractions on folks, but we are not ignorant to his devices (2 Cor. 2:11, 1 Pet. 5:8, 2 Cor. 11:14, Phil. 4:13, Rom. 8:31

and 37); through Christ we will make it. And be sure extra sure to give him thanks and the glory for everything he does.

Make a big deal out of it, to God and thank him over and over. Really show him appreciation. On the job I worked at for thirty years, they would give special awards when you came up with a job improvement idea or not missing any sick time off, etc. So is God any different? Without others seeing or knowing, give God a special extra extra thanks, make a big deal out of it to him, sometimes while in the rest room, at home. I'll just kneel down and say thank you, God. That I can go pee. Many folks are on dialysis machine or caviters, we forget how blessed we are, and in all honesty, really, we don't thank God enough. Sometimes give a little extra to someone in need or put in the offering basket at church a little extra and say to God, thanks for that miracle.

You do what your heart says. Give your pastor lunch money. We called it a gospel handshake, money in your hand while shaking theirs discreetly…with a whisper, "I love ya, Pastor. Go eat lunch on me." He will light up, I guarantee it. Don't you love these new commercials. Hello, human kindness, where people are shown going out of their way, helping a whale caught in fishing line or people washing crude oil off a baby duck. God bless them, and God said "I love you" when he gave us his Son Jesus to die on the cross so we could live in heaven (John 3:16) and that's the best thing to thank him for. Amen (Luke 10:20) (1 Cor. 6:20).

Where Do We Draw the Line?

Part A

Let's suppose you have a good close friend that had some problems and you took him and his wife in because they were evicted and gave them a place to sleep for a few weeks till they got on their feet, fed them, encouraged them prayed for them, gave them rent money, and they blew it. Then go behind your back and stab you in the back by gossiping about you to another friend of both of you; the other friend comes and spill the beans and gossips about them to you and tells all they said that you said. Where do you draw the line? On that, what do you do? You turn to the Bible and prayer; the Bible says have no more dealings with them but still admonish them as a brother. You still pray for them to get back in fellowship with God. And yes, you forgive them. They have a spending problem.

Champagne, wine desire, on a beer budget, sorry, crude example, but we must know our limits in everything, but you don't need enemies like this, little enough a so-called friend; this is no friend, this is no brother or sister in Christ. They have fallen away from the faith, you continue praying for them, but sever the relationship according to the Bible, and there are many on this (1 Tim. 5:13, Rom. 16:17, 1 Cor. 5:10–13). In (1 Corinthians, see verse 11). The word *railer* means troublemaker—one that brings reproach and insults you / a scoffer / an insulter etc. The Bible classifies them as tattlers and busybodies; it says a few verses down some of these are turn aside after Satan (1 Tim. 5:15) (sounds like they *backslid*). I have

68

many more scripture on gossipers and backsliders that some religions lie but fell away from faith or like (John 6:66) same as backslide and say you can't when the Bible says you can. So I'll believe the Bible over religions; this is why I go to a nondenominational church. I had to many years of that religious nonsense. A man's foes shall be of his own household. And these are now happening all over the world.

People against each other friends that were friends for years betraying each other. Because we are in the end times and last days according to the Bible (Matt. 24:10). We call it "road rage" (Mark 13:12,–13; John 16:2; John 6:66) when people turn away from God they get real ugly inside, real mean and brutal because their heart is not right with God (also in Luke 21:22). These be the days of vengeances (Matthew 7:15, Matthew 10:17 and Matthew 5:44). The Bible says to beware of them that despitefully use you, this is where you draw the line. The Bible says even family will turn on you, yes, even family because we are in the last days. Just before the Lord's return. The devil will use anyone or anything to tear you down. Each time we must look to see what the word teaches about each different situation; each one is different. Remember when Peter confronted Jesus about John (John 21:20–22). Jesus said what is that to you, you follow me and let's not forget the golden rule: do or treat others the way you want to be treated (Matt. 7:12).

And we all reap what we sow (Gal. 6:7–9); these are scriptures. So why didn't these folks follow this? And if you (yes, you) are gossiping and stabbing your good friend that's been so good to you, you must ask them and Jesus for forgiveness and heal your backslidden heart or according to (Galatians 5), you may not make it, many, many scriptures on this. Always forgive others their trespasses 490 times in a day according to scriptures in (Matt. 18:22). But watch out for wolves (false prophets) in sheep clothing, ravening wolves (Matt. 7:15) a mad ravening wolf will kill you. The key word here is *false*; read it. Draw the line. Discern in the spirit. Some, yes, start out right, then something happens they turn back, backslid. Please note: Not everyone that goes to church is a born-again Christian, and not everyone that says that they are a Christian really is one. Jesus said you'll know the tree by their fruit (Matt. 7:16–20), and a true

Christian will be similar to Jesus (Christlike = Christian), having the fruit of the spirit, love, joy, peace, etc. (Gal. 5:22–23).

One of the things I want to point out here is that the reason I say the devil is behind all of this kind of stuff and even translations because he (the devil) came to steal, kill, and to destroy (and cause confusion) but Jesus came to give us life, and that more abundantly, as in John 10:10, in my words). But we have power against the devil through Jesus's name in prayer and in God's Word. And the Blood of Jesus Christ cleanses us from all sin (1 John 1:7). (This is why we don't need some watered-down version) or it's like when you're getting ten gallons of gas and your car spits and sputters down the road, finding out later, seven gallons was an additive—we need real anointed Holy Ghost true KJV words of God. And the original KJV Bible says you can boldly come to the throne of God and ask him for miracles in my words.

Read it (Heb. 4:16, Heb. 13:6). Jesus died for his cause; he died that horrible slow agonizing death on the cross so we could all make heaven and to have a Lord that backs up his word and his promises with him laying down his life on the cross. He backed up his word by doing and showing and demonstrating his love in action, then defying all laws of nature and reality, through the Spirit of God, resurrecting himself up from the grave, and in front of many witnesses, ascends up to heaven, with encouraging words; he'll give us power after the Holy Ghost comes up on us, and as he's ascending up out of their sight, two angels said in (Acts 1:8 to 11) why are ye men of Galilee (which these men are witnesses of his resurrection and ascension), why are you standing here gazing up into heaven, this same Jesus, which you see leaving is coming back to take you, back with him and according to other scriptures, which also says He's coming back to take all those who have called upon his name for salvation is gonna take us all back to heaven with him, and for us to encourage one another with these words (1 Thess. 4:15 to 18, Heb. 9:28, in my words. I shortened some).

Again, I'm not rewriting another Bible, when I brief a scripture or may say it in my words but will always try to give the scripture text to you in parenthesis, so you can read it for yourselves. My book is based out of the KJV. I spiritually suggest you really pray about getting one, at least compare yours with it for a better understanding, but most of all, pray and ask the Holy Ghost to give you an understanding heart. Personally I read a Thompson chain KJV Bible (no opinions, just scripture), but for an evangelist minister, when you look up the numbers at the side of the text, he has done half the work for you, with similar texts scriptures or reference ones.

I love it. (He doesn't add or take away; he just gives scripture.) However, even as our constitution says, "We the people," we all have "rights and freedom of speech for us all," but it seems even that is diminishing. It's been God's grace that has kept us all this far, amen. (But my views and opinions and interpretations of scriptures are mine and mine alone, though I may quote another minister or pastor; my book is on how I personally believe and is not to reflect back on anyone or any organization.

I am my own person. And to any hairball out there that wants to attack me, I stand with God and would strongly advice you as a child of God. I'm a walking, talking miracle, and I'm God's anointed (Ps. 105:15), and furthermore, I am an American-born citizen, and I stand on the constitution and God's Words, claiming my rights to free speech, there are so many devils out there, that seem to think the Christians have no rights, but I'm here to tell you people; if it wasn't for the Christians in America (the USA), would have done been destroyed by God! (Gen. 18:20 to 32, 2 Cor. 5:11, Isa. 64:6). Our righteousness is as filthy rags, but in Christ, we are made righteous by his blood. Christians represents righteousness (2 Thess. 1:8, 2 Pet. 3:7, Rev. 18:5 to 10). No more exports/imports (verses 11 to 23) either by God or our enemies, The USA could become burnt toast! According to (Revelation 18:15, Revelation 18:5–10; 2 Peter 3:10; Zechariah 14:12; and 2 Thessalonians 1:8), there will be no more exports/imports, but we must not fear but stand on God's Word that he will deliver us (Ps. 18:48). So stand on God's Word because I know I'm in his hand (Ps. 37:23, 24) and the constitution that gives you rights as to your freedom of speech, also gives us Christians our rights also, and in fact, you need to go reread the constitution and our history book about why America was founded. It was for the Christians for freedom of religion, etc.

Okay, I got that off my chest; it just chaps my hide that you see so many protesters, not realizing my family and yours fought in wars and died for us all to have freedom and rights, it's not just for one group as so many think. Okay, movin' on, translations and different versions (1 Cor. 14:33). No. 1. God is not the author of confusion. The one thing that I have heard for many, many years from prisoners and new converts, just getting saved and starting out. Ask which Bible do I read there are so many. And more so since I got saved. And they continue to take away and add too. Where will it stop. Well, this group that believes this way wants to remove this or that, or—thee's and thou's etc. etc..

Oh, we don't believe that way, so we want to change it around. Can we call it the new "I don't care what God said" Bible? We'll make up our own version as we go (woe). Sounds like someone making another golden calf idol, as in (Exodus 32:1), in Moses's day, when Moses took too long up on the mountain. Praying to God, so they made their own little god, a golden calf idol to worship instead of the real God. (Read verse 32, 35 of Exod. 32.) Note this: God has been more than merciful to America that we used to be called "ONE nation under GOD"… Wow. It's not anymore (Psalms 9:17), as the Bible says in (Revelations 18:2). USA Babylon has become a habitation for devils where anything goes. History has repeated itself, and prophecies have been fulfilled. Come on, folks, where do you draw the line on the devil taking over our world?

Now, we know the Bible says the devil is the thief that comes to steal, to kill, and to destroy, but Jesus come to give us life and that they might have it more abundantly (John 10:10). He even said my sheep know my voice from (John 10 verses 4, 27, and Revelations 3:20), that says, Jesus speaking, "Behold, I stand at the door and knock, if any man hear my voice and open the door, I will come into him and will sup with him and he with me." I can understand that, but you'd be surprised at those that can't, that have twisted and even have lied to their people of huge church congregations, heard this false preacher on radio and TV with my own ears say God, don't speak to people anymore. That's a lie! When scripture says he does and that he's the same, yesterday, today, and forever. Maybe He has just got away from the Lord so far that, he just can't hear him, but God (Jesus, Holy Ghost) still speaks (according to Revelations 3:20 and John 10:27, and Hebrews 3:7 and 15, and Hebrews 4:7, Revelations 4:1) says God speaks to us, so this false preacher is a liar.

Which is why (1 Timothy 4:1) says, "The Spirit speaketh expressively that in the later times" (maybe us today). Some shall depart from the faith, giving heed to seducing spirits and doctrines of devils (we call it backslid, verse 2) "Speaking what? Lies and hypocrisies…"

So again, I believe the Bible over this TV preacher that's a false prophet. And if God didn't speak to us, no one would get saved and so God is no respect of persons from the beginning to the end, God is and will be the same loving God, saving and convicting people of our sins. And the Bible says all have sinned and come short of the glory of God, and there is none righteous no not one, one of the scriptures that we must look at, it is the devil wants to cause confusion and make the church people look like fools, and religious idiots. But they are not, instead of being a refueling station to go and get revived at and receive godly biblical instruction, which is what the word *Bible* stands for "Basic Instructions Before Leaving Earth" because if you're not following it, you won't make it to heaven (James 1:21, James 4:17, John 10:1, John 14:6).

Well, I know I'm not the brightest candle on the cake, but I do pray and ask God for direction and to give me understanding. But I know that (Rev. 12:9–12). The accuser of the brother is cast down, (Luke 10:18), Jesus said, he saw him, the devil, fall like lightening, and that's fast. (Revelations 12:11) says we overcame him by the blood of the lamb and by the word of our testimony; man looks on the outward appearance, on your figure, looks at your muscles, or the devil tries to make you think you have to have the perfect body and that you have to keep an extreme exercise system going and compete, with everyone. This is carnal thinking of the world and if this is the way you think, you are in the flesh and according to scripture (Rom. 8:13, 1; John 2:15–16; Gal. 5:15–21), bodily exercise profits you little, but godliness is profitable unto all things (1 Tim. 4:8). You need to read this whole chapter because if you're pleasing your flesh your considered worldly and won't make it to heaven.

You better be pleasing to God (Heb. 11:6, 2 Cor. 5:11) and study up on how far is extreme, on satisfying what our flesh wants. (Galatians 2:20 and Galatians 5:24), but then that's man's pride and his puffed-up flesh that Apostle Paul spoke of this in the Bible in (1 Timothy 4:8); this is all called man's pride and being puffed up with themselves in the Bible. People don't want to hear this because everyone wants to do what they want to do, and everyone wants to look good, and we all need a little exercise, but not to an extreme that it's like it's become your god, like it is nowadays. It's all in the Bible, friend, and again, I didn't write the Bible (just talking about it). Seriously, folks, we must be careful with our heart, eyes, ears, and mind in what we feed it, and not to entertain X-rated thoughts or give place to the devil in any way (Matt. 4:1 to 11, Eph. 4:22 to 32, see vs. 27).

Think here for a minute, please. Really take the gyms for an example, or sports or whatever, but mostly things of this type nature where it's a real sacrifice. Yes, our sacrifice is for God (read Romans 12:1–2). I tried lifting weights for a while, and my conscience ate me alive because I know my Bible, and it says God is a jealous God (Exod. 34:14, 20:5; Deut. 6:15) and that we are to put him first (Matt. 6:33). Yet a real bodybuilder usually does at least five to six hours of exercise and all those sets of curls, squats, shoulder shrugs, bench presses, etc. Do they do that much for God? No, I don't think so. Nothing's wrong with it, but if it convicts your conscience as in (1 John 3:20 or in Romans 6:6–23)… I dare ya to read it because it's our soul we are talking about (Matt. 16:26), and you just look around and ask God, to show you, and then, study it out (Google it). The gyms are full, and the churches are empty. (Hello.) These are all written signs of the last days. (Men will be lovers of pleasures more than lovers of God, as in 2 Timothy 3:4–5.) Read (verse 2): For men shall be lovers of their own selves. We are there. People are more concerned about how their body looks than their soul with God. Do they spend an hour in prayer and read the Bible like they do at the gym? I know some that spend hours at the gym. Wow. There are more gyms full of people than full churches that are now empty. (You can ask the editor on this prophetic word, "I wrote this five years ago," now come true!) Yes, sad to say, I'm slow, very slow, with corrections, previews, add-ins, etc., on writing this book, but if I review something I wrote five years ago about churches being closed—wow, not to mention stadiums, ball games, full casinos, full nightclubs and bars, concerts, amusement parks that are all full—I could fill the next two pages on this subject.

We are definitely in the last days because the Bible says these will be the signs of the last days. That bodily exercise profits you little (1 Tim. 4:7 and 8), and that depends on whose eyes you're looking through. The big, buffed guys that died years ago and went to hell because of their pride and big ego would tell you, exercise your mind and spirit more by studying the Bible (2 Tim. 2:15) (James 1:21), which will keep you out of hell (Luke 16:27 to 31). Once you die in your sins your gone. There is no more chances to get your life right. So get the soul and heart right first (now). Pride goes before a fall, the lust of our flesh, a competition-type spirit is carnality and vain. Read verse one of 1 Timothy 4.

Now the spirit speaks expressly that in the latter times some shall depart from the faith giving heed to seducing spirits and doctrines of devils. Speaking lies in hypocrisy, having their conscience seared with a hot iron. We don't overcome the devil by false version Bibles or being religious or being so exercised and being a body builder. Flesh, flesh, flesh—we have been down that road in the 1970s learning karate, lifting weights, constantly checking how high you can kick, looking checking your flexes in the mirror, faster kicks, faster punches, using the nunchucks, sticks, poles, breaking boards, taking speed, pills with cross tops, crank, benies, whites, that help you to have faster reflexes, then working overtime on my reflexes. So much time for what. On a motorcycle on the freeway with some drunk cowboys beside ya, trying to knock the biker and my wife off. Karate and muscles don't do ya any good, especially if we'd have died (that night by those drunk cowboys trying to knock us hippies off my chopper). Back in the 1970s, when I was a hippy biker, I was doing everything there was that's called sin, but my point here is that knowing karate and trying to be a bodybuilder won't help you when someone's trying to knock you off your chopper motorcycle. But spending time with God in prayer as much as I spent working out would get me favor with God or even get me into heaven. It's really just how valuable is your soul to you. Spending hours on a body that's not going to go heaven, huh? Take it easy. Don't misunderstand me. No one's your judge, but when this life is over, if we die or go in the Rapture (1 Thess. 4:16, Rev. 4:1, 1 Cor. 15:50–58), this human body is not going to heaven or hell, just your soul (read 1 Corinthians 15:50). God will give you a new body—a heavenly body—because flesh and blood "will not inherit the Kingdom of God." (Read it: 1 Corinthians 15:50.) Don't be deceived or naïve. All of man's studies, hard work, and efforts in this life's rat race is to help him achieve in this life for retirement etc., or women want to stay more attractive, study books, and try to get a really good education to get a really good job to better themselves in life. But it would be too late. We find out so many folks just didn't make it to that ripe old age to enjoy all the hard work they did for the retirement, though that's most people's goal in life. (Read Luke 12:15, 21 and Matthew 6:19, 20, 33.) Many I went to school with didn't make it. Were they ready to meet God? Only God knows that, but right now, having the time to call on God, if the doctor sends you home with bad news.

If a junkie or drunk or someone on a cellphone didn't see you and hits you head on, and there is no time to call on God, all those muscles and a good looking body won't help you in a head-on crash, but spending that time with God like you spend on your body, being right in your heart and in your soul with God is more important. No, I'm not talking about churches or religions, or opinions, but a one-on-one personal relationship with you and Jesus Christ because when you're in that situation like I was in on the motorcycle because if you're in a wreck, there is not time to pray; it's too quick (been there twice).

So is what the apostle Paul was saying in (1 Timothy 4:8) was that bodily (exercise) is just for the human body (for now) but godly exercise, by learning, reading, studying your Bible (2 Tim. 2:15) in which on the day of judgment you won't stand their feeling like an idiot, that people with lower IQs than you made it in heaven and you were sent in the other direction. Okay, no, you don't go to hell because of high or low IQ, it's if you are born again and living the life and following God's Word.

I've been down a lot of these roads and came so close to death's door. I felt I needed to get the word out that so many are being misled! But honest to God, that's pride and flesh. This body of flesh and blood isn't going into heaven. And people will say, "Yeah, but my grandmother was a short fat little woman of God filled with the holy ghost that prayed over her food and believed God to sanctity it and purify it." And we must do the same. She lived over one hundred years old. Her dad was almost a hundred and four died before his birthday. One of her sons, my uncle, died at 103. He also was a devoted Christian. The Bible tells us the devil will burn in the lake of fire (Rev. 20:10). We must all pray and ask God for constant direction. And always keep our guard up against the devil and his wiles and sly tactics. Is it wrong to work out? No! Hey, everyone could use a little but be careful of pride and being set up for your flesh cause being carnal with your flesh can get you puffed up for a big fall.

And many people, including me, have had an apple out of that bag. And you try to warn others, when you're in your twenties, thirties, and forties, and soon. You are more concerned about your outward appearance, and yes, we all should to a point. Just not to an overboard extreme, but keep a balance so your not to jeopardize your soul (Rom. 12:1 and 2). How far do you go? To many want and desire others to lust over them. As they do others. This is wrong according to the Bible. These are all reasons man has changed the Bible. This one should be called the bodybuilders' new translations. Now you may laugh, but people are changing the Bible to fit their lifestyles. If they are uncomfortable or feeling guilt or shame, they say, let's change it. Like in Moses's day. Make your own God. So you can tell him what to do. And what to write in the let's make our own version and our own God, out of gold (Deut. 11:4 to 8, Numbers 16:30–32, Exod. 32:1–33, Acts. 7:40–41); they even offered sacrifices to it and ticked off God by saying this idol delivered us out of

Egypt bondage. Maybe those were the ones when the bad earthquake hit, and the ground opened up and swallowed them alive.

You don't want to make God mad. You need to read that story in its entirety. From (Exodus 32:1–35 and Deuteronomy 11:4–8, Numbers 16:32). I believe that's why the devil has tried so hard to get the Bibles changed. The ones that get me are the enhanced, magnified ones, which is adding too…oh, watch out. Why do people get upset? Well, folks, on judgment day. We all know and those that added and took away have to stand before God and answer why they listen to the devil as in (Matthew 4:3, 5, 6, 8, 9) yet. Since the garden in the beginning to the end the devil still lies and tricks and deceives people and they get mad when you try and warn them. If you ask me, this world is way, way worse now than then, and if God got ticked off at them, then what about our generation today that's killing millions and millions of babies just so women can have a choice? That's so messed up. God ought to put sinkholes at every abortion clinic there is, and I'll bet you, then, they'd think twice about their choice. Oh sure, I know there are many, many other groups just as bad with evil people that rob, steal, kill, rape, traffic drugs and sex, etc. And **God** has been very patient and **has already forewarned us all in the Bible in (Matthew 24:37–42)**. Yes, I repeat myself, and so does the Bible. Wow, do you think that with all the warnings and repetitions, people will get it? No, just a few are chosen, though many are called (Matt. 22:14) Wow. But…

Does it or does it not say whoever takes away or adds to. (Revelations 20:18, 19; 2 Timothy 3:15–17), that the scripture is to correct you not you're to correct God and rewrite his word (Romans 1:25) (John 17:17) (2nd Tim. 3:16) this scripture does not give man permission to change and alter God's word (as so many think). No, but it means, the Bible will correct and change us, and instruct us on how to live right, so we all can be pleasing to God, and be ready and make it to heaven (John 14:6) (John 8:32) (john 16:13). But that the man of God may be perfect, thoroughly furnished unto all good works. The word will correct you, make you wise, convict you of wrong behavior, direct you to salvation to Jesus Christ. The author and finisher of our faith. Todays, church's sound almost like in the days of Moses, up in the mountain too long so they made up their own golden calf God and their own Bibles (2 Cor. 11:3), but I fear, lest by any means, as the serpent beguiled Eve through his subtlety (2 Cor. 11:3 KJV) (tricks, lies, craftiness, subtilty). So through his subtlety, your minds should be corrupted from the simplicity that is in Christ, (verse 4) goes with (Galatians 1:6, 7, 8, 9). (If anyone preaches another gospel, they will be cursed, okay.)

You see, if the devil can get us to believe a false version and get us all sidetracked. Then he'll bring in doctrines of devils and according to scripture (1 Tim. 4:1 and Thess. 2:10, 11, 12) they'll be left behind and go through the "Mark of the Beast 666 (chip)," etc., believe a lie and be damned (2 Thess. 2:7 to 12; Rev. 13) being damned doesn't mean going to heaven no. But going to hell is what being damned means.

You don't hear this kinda of stuff in those mega ear-tickling churches.

When's the last, last time ya heard the megachurches preach on hell, (Luke 16 or Matthew 24), on the end time or in the days of Noah, etc. And let me add and say this, if and I say if God allows the next generation to come, I say, God, help us. Because this is the worst generation ever that has ever been on earth, I was even in the hippy era, yes, in the '60s and '70s was bad, but here we are now in the year 2022 when drive-by shootings and schools becoming targets, gangs having their new members' initiation to kill someone or commit some gruesome act. And the courts and lawyers get them back on the streets, yes. I still pray for their salvation and hope the whole world gets saved and born again.

But again, according to scripture the things happening. Now, according to the Bible is the last generation and I could go on and on from the cults to music (demonic music) to the drugs, them legalizing pot. Oh my, talk about a blind generation and a bunch of the stupidest people passing these laws. And yes, I've heard the misquoting scripture about the herbs God gave us, for the use. That's taking scripture out of context. Read it right. I was a pothead, in the '60s and '70s, I'll be the first to say it was wrong then and it's wrong now.

(James 4:17) K.J.V. bible says: "Therefore to him that knows, to do good, and does it not to him it is sin."

When man was born as a baby, he starts trying to get his way. And so many let the kid have his/her way to keep him happy or keep the peace. They allow the child to grow up having their way. And it's worse today than ever. The movies, phone sex, computer sex, porn. We are worse today than in the days of Noah. I am shocked at some that really think the world will go another one hundred years. No, I don't think so. Nor do I believe God is gonna apologize to Noah. As one preacher stated, God said his word will not return unto him void (Isa. 55:11). A quote from the Prophet Isaiah. Note: So if God's Word is God's Word and won't return back to him, void, why do we get mad and want to change what he said? Cause (Psalms 119:89) says forever O Lord thy word is settled in heaven. So what is the answer to this sin sick epidemic world. It's believe on the Lord Jesus Christ have and keep a repented heart, (Rev. 2:5) twenty-four hours a day, seven days a week and pray (2 Chron. 7:14). If my people which are called by my name, shall humble themselves and pray and seek my face and turn from their wicked ways: then will I hear from heaven and will forgive their sin and heal their land. Now that's having a repented heart, when you turn form your wicked ways, (and follow Jesus).

Note: Notice the scripture said to humble themselves, but this is the worst and most rebellious generation ever and it's those rebellious evil types generations that usually has to have God humble them to repentance (2nd Chronicles 7:14) and as (Ps. 51:10 to 17). But people are so full of pride and many don't fill they need to repent because they feel like they are good people and do good deeds. But the Bible also says to turn from our wicked ways (2nd Chronicles 7:14); yet they can't, except they call on Jesus to save and change them. As in (2 Corinthians 5:17), then they become a new creature in Christ and old things pass away behold all things become new. Only when we are willing to accept Jesus. And willing for him to change us. No, America will not change! The Bible says many are called, but only few are chosen. Tag me doomsday preacher, I don't really care. I must speak the truth and that is I believe with every fiber of my being we are (America, the USA, once a nation under God). Are the back slidden nation of the great whore Babylon (Rev. 18) is USA, and God will allow it to become desolate because of the sin.

It is only the Christians that are here that has kept away God's wrath this far. And I believe the rapture (caught up) catching away of the church is very, very near, no we don't know what day or hour, but I'm not stupid or blind. I can see scripture unfolding before my eyes. And cannot believe some so-called Bible scholars that have bought into the idea of all the devil sent truth robbed version Bibles, and God ain't lost, so why do they read the lost books of the Bible? God doesn't need some hairball non-Christian Bible college seminar student that's studied in Greek and Hebrew scrolls to interpret the KJV.

No man, all we need is the in filling of the Holy Ghost to give us our own divine revelation like he said he would do. If it was good enough at the day of Pentecost, it's good enough for the people in 1611, when the bible was originally transcribed from Greek and Hebrew scrolls by King James, into the Kings english, and from its original tongues, which is written in the front of the authentic—King James Version Bibles. And you can google and research most of this as I have, but if this gospel of Jesus Christ was good enough for the disciples and folks clear back in King James day…it's good enough for me today. We just need to pray till the glory comes down on us, praying with all your heart. And pray for God to have mercy on us all. Yes, I believe the return of the Lord may even come before this book is out in print. It is possible but no one knows the day or hour. As I read last day prophecies in (Matthew 24), I look at (verse 28). And realize all the dead dry unmoved.

Funeral-type churches I have visited, are so, so dead and am reminded of (verse 28): you have never seen an eagle act like a buzzard. You study them, and they catch live rabbits; the eagle can swoop down on them at 90 mph before that dude even realizes he needs to run. He's dinner. No, that verse is speaking about spiritual things concerning the dead dry church as in (2 Timothy 3:5; Revelations 2:4, 5; and Revelations 3:2 to 5 and Revelations 3:15 to 22), deep down some feel they need to go to church but no power is there. And even some I know of, sin, has even entered, which is a dangerous thing for people to attend God's house unmoved, untouched by the Spirit of God, and we are in those days of eagle Christians, when so many eagle Christians want to soar above in the spirit as in (Isaiah 40:31), which also goes along with (Luke 24:49; Acts 1:2–5, 2:16–40, 2:37–40; and Joel 2:28–32)

Yet there is so much carnality and flesh operating in churches today. They are so spiritually dead see (John 3:3–12) (Matt. 22:32) (Luke 9:60) (John 2:24, 25) (James 2:26) (Luke 9:60) "Jesus said let the dead bury their dead: but go thou and preach the kingdom of God." You see this is physically impossible, but it's a spiritual phrase, that really simply means. Let those that act spiritual, that are spiritually dead in their soul and are not really true Christians and are not really truly saved and born again = those like the Nicolations, that act holy but aren't (as in Rev. 2:15 see verse 6) (Lk. 20:46) (Matt. 23:5) (see verse 27) let the spiritually dead bury their dead like the meaning of what the prodigal son's dad said, my son was dead (spiritually) now he's alive (spiritually) = he got saved, and became born again (John 3:35) (1 Cor. 2:14). We must think spiritually minded as in (Philip 2:5 and John 6:63)…it is the spirit that quickens the flesh profits nothing! The words I speak, are spirit and life, (the words I speak are spirit and life) (John 6:63). But the carnal, the spiritually dead type, do not let the spirit move in the church or their life. This is why Jesus, John and Paul refers to them as dead, (again spiritually speaking). As in (Rom. 8:11) see verses (1 to 11) esp. (verse 5 and 6 of Rom. 8) also read (verse 13). So according to scriptures that is a dead body and a D-E-A-D carcase (Luke 17:37) (John 3:12) (and 1 Cor. 2:14) as in the K.J.V. Bible or as in (Luke 17:37) where the body is. Please note: the reason why the newer version aren't spiritually meaning (case in point). I googled all of this, and some hairball version pops up talking about corpses and vultures, proving my point. This is when the educated mind of intellects that takes away from spiritual words (Rev. 22:18, 19) (Philip 2:5) (1 Cor. 2:14) (John 6:63) (Rom. 8:6) cause their not thinking spiritually, so they want to re-write the bible, (which is wrong, very wrong and will be plagued for it). Again: Jesus was referring to the Pharisee actors, acting like Christians and compared them to dead people burying their dead, spiritually speaking, dead in their soul, and dead in their thinking. Jesus also referred in the last days, to the spiritually dead, the Pharisees and scribes which were big phonies, big actors, he called them dead = spiritually, dead, and finally, the dead body of believers the dead church where the eagle Christians will be at church also. As I already quoted in (Mat. 24:28) = "for where so ever the carcase is = (dead body-dead church) (the church is a body of believers) is, there will be eagles = spirit filled Christians be gathered together," Note = remember in (Mat. 18:20) for where two or three are gathered together in my name = (Jesus), there am I in the midst. (where)? At the same church where those spiritually dead Christians are, (Rev. 2:2 to 5) (Rev. 3:15 to 19) (Mat. 25:1 to 13) (spirit filled) can still serve God even around the spiritually dead ones, that's what (Mat 24:28) means!!! Again, a dead body, = is a dead church, not an actual corpse, it's a spiritual meaning: (again,) because, and eagle don't eat like a buzzard, but an eagle Christian is already soaring in his soul, so you'll have to continually go to church the more you see the day approaching, as in (Hebrew 10:25) so dead, or alive: Eagle Christians which is gonna go to church, and he will also feed his/her own self at home, with reading the bible, hearing Christian music, hearing Preachers on TV or CD, and hearing bible on CD etc. etc. building up your faith. As in (Jude 20), But once again, without the spirit there is no life. (James 2:26) (Romans 8-9 to 11)… But ye are not in the flesh, but in the spirit, if so be that the **spirit** of God dwell in you. **Now if any man have not the spirit of Christ**, he is **none of his**. (Read verse 11) **"But if the spirit of him (God) that raised up Jesus from the dead dwell in you, he (God) that raised up Christ from the dead, shall also quicken your mortal bodies by his spirit that dwells in you."** (in my words…look it up) (also read) (John 3-3 to 5) esp. (the 5th verse) (but in verse 3) Jesus said to Nicodemus, you must be born again, and then in (verse 5) Jesus answered, verily, verily, I say unto you, except a man be born of water (be baptized), and of the spirit, (filled with the Holy Ghost), he cannot enter into the kingdom of God. (in my words, look it up) (I didn't write the bible) but you see once again, this is why there are so many different version bibles and so many different churches, cause people disagree, or should I say want it there way, (this ain't burger king dude) on judgement day everyone will find out the whole truth, but then it'll be to late for the stubborn and rebellious ones who disagree, (again) I'm an ex-hippy biker pot head from the 60's and 70's, and I understand it, (WOE…back up Fred) oh, excuse me, after, I got saved and filled with the Holy Ghost, the Holy Spirit of God quicken this ol ignorant (Acts 4–13) ex hippy biker, and he Holy Ghost (spirit) gave me understanding, (Sorry I must give him the credit) (John 14–26). But the eagle would be as the ones in (Acts 2) but not as a buzzard. And yes, there were dead, so-called Christians there then even as today, (see Matthew 8:22). The Lord used the Pharisees, in speaking of a powerless church of religious Pharisees, spiritually dead that are spectators and not true worshippers, can we be a participator in adversities? Where do we draw the line on bad reports?

As we walk with Christ, it's a win-win situation with the Lord. When we live for God, if you're told you've got cancer or a divorce, etc., no matter what the case may be, if you get bitter against God, then comes hate and resentment, will this kind of attitude go into heaven? No! No! And No! (Always stay prayed up.) David said in (Psalm 51:10), "Create in me a clean heart…" Read (verses 11, 12) also. And in (Acts 2:37–39), the people asked Peter what must we do, Peter said in verse (38, 39, 40) repent (again, this is a good word) meaning for us to ask the Lord for forgiveness (Rom. 10:9, 10). And as David said in the (Psalms 51:10), we have to ask God to create in us that clean heart and renew a right spirit in us because an evil heart and an ugly spirit will send you to hell. It's a win-win deal with God, if you're healed, you win, if you die you win because you go to heaven, so staying right with God is a win-win situation, so guard your heart from bitterness because bitter people can't be a true worshipper. We must worship God in spirit and truth (John 4:23). So be a participator, not spectators. God desires all those to worship him in spirit and in truth (John 4:24). Did you notice in (verse 23), God the father seeks (looks) for those that worship Him in *spirit* and in truth being real.

We must participate, we must worship him in spirit and truth. There can't be any fake, no phonies, no acting—we must be genuine, authentic, 100 percent—real in our worship. God inhabits the praises of Israel (his people, us too…we are grafted in Psalm 22:3; John 15:4, 5; Romans 11:23 and 24). And all those followers that didn't really hear the words of Christ, makes you wonder what purpose was the Pharisees, except to give Jesus and his followers trouble (just constant trouble), which Jesus refers to as dead (spiritually dead) and was saying these spiritually dead Pharisees, and the other spiritually dead actors, that just pretend to be religious and Holy should bury the physically dead. So now when you read it you can understand, when Christ was saying in (Matthew 8:22), you'll get it that he was saying let those spiritually dead pretenders bury the physical dead bodies.

And when you enter a church where there is no life and there is nothing but a bunch of actors, no move of the spirit, so it is dead. A dead body is a dead carcass in (Matthew 24:28, Luke 17:37), but this body, of supposed-to-be believers. But if you really do (John 4:23) believe you'll worship in spirit and truth (John 4:23), not having a form of godliness as in (2nd Tim. 3 verse 5) or (in my words) being a great actor, or a great pretender. This is why Jesus always rebuked the Pharisees, he saw right through them in (Matthew 23:27) he said they were as graves full of dead man's bones (in my words). When the spirit of the Lord hovers over a church and sees life he abides there, but no one wants to hang around a dead body, no life, no out of the heart singing, or praise, no thanking God for supplying your needs. Just motionless and dead. I ride bikes with my grandkids, a lot, one day we were riding down the street a few houses from my house, in the street was a dead squirrel, my seven-year-old grandson Alan goes and makes a sign RIP (*rest in peace*) and puts it on the dead squirrel. It was so funny, but he was so sincere, and I wondered does God feel that way when people just sit like a bump on a log, in church, when the spirit of God is moving from God, I heard two different preachers with a same type of message, and that is to tell people that God's gonna destroy them unless they repent and get right with God.

Does God really watch us (Prov. 15:3) or does he receive our prayers (while we just sit there, or does God watch how bored folks are and really tag them. Yes, and when people halfheartedly praise the Lord, oh, you don't see the actual physical sign or mark on their head but you sure read about it in scriptures (Rev, 3:16) (see verses 15–19 in Rev. 3) (Mat. 25:1 to 13) hearts, (Rev. 3:15, 16) that God has tagged and marked those (Gen. 4:15) who are lukewarm in their hearts that Jesus and God also has said in his word, Jesus knows those who are his (2 Tim. 2:19 to 21), and he even said he places a seal of approval, on those that are his (Rev. 7:3) and sealed them in their foreheads (wow, 2 Tim. 2:19).

Please note, God gives everyone plenty of time, and opportunities to get right with him, many God has to send bad things to them to try and turn them back to him. Now if you'll read the story of Jonah in the book of Jonah chapter 1, verse 2 and 3. You'll find that Jonah ran from God and disobeyed what God wanted him to do (to go tell the city of Nineveh to repent and turn to God or else be destroyed, so he jumps on a ship to take him to a city name Tarshish, which is going in the opposite direction, I haven't heard a lot of comments on this, when Jonah ran from God six hundred miles in the opposite direction, when the whale swallowed ol' Jonah, did you realize that the whale traveled from Tarshish (Joppa area) is about five thousand six hundred and sixty six miles from Nineveh where God told the whale to go and barf him up. Wow. That's really something.

That whales obey God, but man runs away from God and rebels—wow. But as for me, I'll travel by bus, plane, or my truck. Thank you, Jesus, but couldn't you just hear some ol' guy in Nineveh say, "Hey, bro. Jonah, how did you get here? Well, I took a whale 5,666 miles, kicking back in his belly…Ha. Wow. Then I took a hot puke bath…yuck…yes," and then he was now ready to obey God. But before he gets swallowed by the whale he runs from God and hops on a boat going the other way (to a city called Tarshish), and so God rocks the boat by sending him a very bad storm, the storm was so bad everyone on board begin to question, "What have we done to make God so mad at us?" And then Jonah fessed up and said, "It's me God's after me, if you throw me overboard the storm will stop, and you'll all live," so our stormy problems do affect others, don't they? Yes, they do (if God's behind them). Now the main thing I want to point out here about Jonah is, he had the same opportunity as Noah, the difference here is called obedience. Jonah disobeys God, and Noah obeys God…each one was assigned a task to go and warn *people* to get right *with God* (repented) or God would destroy them.

So God does send storms, and many other types of warnings, to turn us to him, wow, this type sermons isn't heard preached anymore. No, you might offend someone. But on judgment day…folks'll need a lot of depends diapers because of the shock, they'll wet their pants when man stands alone before an angry God for all those who disobeyed God, and rebelled, they'll be No bargaining or begging then (Luke 16:19 to 31, Heb. 10:31, 2 Cor. 5:11, 2 Thess. 1:7 to 10). For now, we are under grace, love, and forgiveness, but on Judgment Day, for those who rebelled, just read the Bible story of Moses, who warned Pharaoh, and all the warnings, chances, and opportunities God gave to Pharaoh when God was telling Pharaoh to let God's people go. God gave him chance after chance after chance. God was way more patient, tolerant, and lenient than most of us would ever be. God is long suffering. This word is taken from the Greek word *makrothumia*, which means "very patient," and that's the very thing, God tells us, we need. We have need of patience that, after we've done the will of God, we might receive the promise (Heb. 10:36). This reminds me of kind of a funny story of my Aunt Eva Dean Peterson. On one Sunday, when her pastor was being a little long winded, she said, "The Lord told Pharaoh to let my people go." Ha. I think she was hungry. But man, on judgment day will not have no excuses, though. (Luke 14) tells of many, but God gives mankind more time than man gives to others (as in Matthew 18:23–35 and Mark 14:21). Jesus is saying it would be better to have never been born than to betray Jesus by refusing to follow Jesus (in my words) because Jesus gave his life on the cross so you and the rest of the world could be saved. And to reject his perfect plan of salvation is to slap God in the face (in my words). (But read these: (John 3:16–19, 1 Corinthians 6:20, and John 10:18)). So yes, God does still warn people, and God does give people chances and plenty of opportunities to turn to Him and get right, and get saved. (Romans 10:13) says, "For whosoever shall call up on the name of the Lord shall be saved." And in (Revelations 3:20) says, "Behold I stand at the door and knock:

if any man (or woman) hears my voice, and opens the door, I will come into him, and will sup with him and he with me." You have the doorknob; you have to open your heart's door, and you invite Jesus into your heart, and into your life and ask Jesus to save your soul; when you ask, he will come into your heart. Don't try to figure it out how it works or will I become a fanatic? Just obey God's Word and pray to Jesus Christ, and God, and ask him to forgive you of your sins...; it's not rocket science, then ask God to have the Holy Spirit to teach you how to understand and learn the Bible (start in the New Testament). I always passed over all of the begats which means Jacob had a son name Joseph (Mat. 1:16) (in my words) (begat means: a man and women had a baby).

It may sound crazy, but our old head prison minister, Rev. Joe Avery, always told the guys (inmates) to start reading in St. John's gospel first because it's the main book on salvation and Romans, and then read Matthew, and work your way through to revelation. But the decision has to be yours with a made-up mind. Then everything else God designed to fall into place. Living the Christian life was the best decision I ever made. Oh, it wasn't easy, but I made up in my mind, like Jonah. I got tired of running, and deep down, I knew God wanted me to turn to him. But one of the Great things about it. When a problem arises we can take it to our God through Jesus Christ, and he goes to God for us as our mediator the Bible says (1 Tim. 2:5): unlike the world, people that are of this world, sinners, partiers, drunks, etc., can't make heaven unless they repent of their sins. And being all alone explains why they are so miserable and turn to booze instead of turning to God.

These same type examples are told by Jesus Christ in the New Testament, the examples he gave he called them parables (like the dead squirrel, I saw an opportunity to explain to my Grandson Alan, about looking both ways when crossing the street). The crazy squirrel didn't have a clue like a lot of hookers and partiers; they got one thing on their minds; it's not God. No, that last part I didn't say to my seven-year-old grandson, just the part of the squirrel not looking both ways, so he won't end up like the dead squirrel; he has a bad habit of making U-turns on the street without looking, so I was using that as an analogy or parable to explain SAFE bike riding keeps you alive! And so does living for God, and when it is your time to go, you'll be ready, and isn't making it to heaven gonna be worth it all at the END.

All this talk of death, I just wonder how many people have read (1 Corinthians 5:5); it amazes me that so many read right over stuff and don't even try to research it, and study it out; well, for one, they're in a hurry, just to get their one chapter read, so they can start their day. But this text, some may ask, would a loving God really turn a person that's not saved over to Satan; the answer is yes, please reread the scripture again. God would answer a mother, grandmother, grandpa's and Dad's prayer for their prodigal son's salvation (Luke 15:11 to 32, for such was I), but God would rather see our physical body die and before that one dies that moms praying for, he calls on Jesus, it's called death bed repentance…And many stubborn mule headed sons have been saved over the years.

Note (Psalm 32:9, 2 Peter 3:5), but even if it means someone going to the grave/by dying, and repenting and getting saved, at the very last moment, even on their deathbed shows us that God is a merciful God because it's not God's will for anyone to perish this means to be lost for all eternity forever in hell, but God wants all people everywhere to turn to Him, and come to repentance (2 Pet. 3:9, In my words, 1 Cor. 5:5) but it's smart to not wait to the last minute, just for the fact that many have died instantly so fast, with no time to even think or even time to pray. I know, when I was in my hit and run car wreck, there's no time to pray so be ready all the time (Matt. 24:42, Luke 21:36).

So watch ye therefore and pray always that you may be accounted worthly to escape all these things that shall come to pass, and to stand before the son of the man (Jesus) (Mat. 12:12 to 17) and again this was the reason he (Jesus) spoke in parables. So the evil religious Pharisees and Scribes, and those wicked religious leaders wouldn't understand his parables, Jesus stated in these verse, that God doesn't want evil followers, esp. Evil righteous, religious but were evil in their hearts, so Jesus spoke in parable (read it) (see Mat. 13-15) and Jesus even knew their thoughts, in Matthew 22:18, Matthew 9:4 and knew who would betray him (and kill him, Matt. 26:21, John 13:11), but these evil men were so full of hate, they could not hear or even get the message Jesus tried to teach them, because their hearts were evil (Matt. 9:4, Matt. 15:19, 1 Cor. 2:14, John 12:37 to 43, Matt. 17:22 and 23, John 17:14–23) because according to Jesus and scripture you must be changed and born again to a repented life before God gives us an understanding heart (John 3:3 to 5) (Romans 10:9, 10, 13) (2nd Cor. 5:17) (1st Cor. 2:14) and a light of understanding would turn on in the heart and soul of a born-again believer.

(First Corinthians 2:14) states, "But the natural man = (sinner) receives not the things of the Spirit of God: for they are foolish unto him; neither can he know them, because they are spiritually discerned. As in (Matthew 16:20–26, as in Matthew 17:1–7, or as in Mark 9:2–10), in these verses of Scripture, even the disciples didn't have a clue about Jesus rising up from the dead or why Jesus's body and his clothes were white and glistening as the light on the Mount of Transfiguration when Jesus was trying to show them what his supernatural, spiritual body would look like after he rises from the dead because he had the power of being the son of God to raise himself up after three days from the dead (John 10:18). But they just couldn't comprehend spiritual things yet (1 Cor. 2:14). Sometimes the light doesn't come on in the soul of man till he's trapped in a burning building or in a car submerged under water and pinned in. Then he gets spiritual quick and calls out to the Lord, with a sincere cry. Forgetting about religion and stuff that distracts the heart. All that is number one then is getting my heart right with my creator and thinking of those I'll leave behind.

This was my thoughts in 1977 when I called on the Lord, I tried it my way—the world's way—without God in my life. I didn't care anymore about being macho, I'm gonna die here, don't want to go out in a blaze of glory as the wacked out macho guys in the movies that die a fool's death without God. The Bible says the fool has said in his heart there is no God (Psalms 14:1 to 4)! And when he dies and on resurrection day, "Surprise" and chick tracts really brings this out, and so many more great examples as well. I passed many out to inmates during those eighteen years of prison ministry.

Anyway, back to (Matthew 16:21), Jesus began to try to explain to the disciples of the coming event time, of when he lays down his life in (John 3:16–18; Matthew 16:22), etc. But old Peter was thinking carnally because Peter wasn't all the way in yet, but as the scriptures teach in (Matthew 26:58), Peter was following Jesus a far off…and wanted to see the end.

Again, Peter was following, and if you notice in the next scripture (Matt. 16:23), now Jesus was actually speaking now to Satan, though he's confronting Peter. He is indeed speaking to Satan that was speaking in Peter's ear. And Jesus knew it, so Jesus speaks directly to the source, which is the one we seem to listen to his lies when we think carnally minded. Jesus was trying to address the main point, which was that he was going to suffer at the cross and die a cruel death and rise from the dead, but ol' Peter wasn't thinking spiritually minded. And he listened to the devil, and that's why Jesus rebukes Satan. No one likes a rebuke, then kapow, Jesus nails him, but actually he's coming against Satan that Peter's listening to.

Now note: Jesus says at the end of this text (verse 28 of Matt. 16), they'll be some here that won't taste of death (well, it's the year 2022) Peter's still in his grave. What about that, preacher? Glad you ask (Matt. 17:1). Keep reading through the next chapter. Jesus knew they were not completely converted yet, so he fulfills his word. (Remember God's Word won't return unto him void) (Isaiah 55:11). So notice Jesus didn't have all the group go with him up into the mountain, just Peter, James, and John. And all heaven came down and wow, wish I'd have been there, ya see Peter was getting his light turned on to see Jesus in his glorified body, as he'll be on judgment day, and resurrection day and then appears Moses and Elijah, wow. Peter's still thinking carnally but wants to focus spiritually.

And again, he puts his foot in his mouth, saying, "Hey let's make three tabernacles, one for you, Lord, one for Moses, and one for Elijah." He was so scared not knowing what to say, and God comes over in a cloud saying (Matt. 17:5). Listen to my son, whom I am well pleased with, hear ye him. Wow. When God himself says, you ain't listening. Wow, man, since the beginning of time has always and is still trying to figure it all out and tries to change it all and man wants it all his way. I just looked up a scripture on Google, and it gave fifty-five different versions. Wow, which one is right? Again, where do we draw the line on changing, taking away, and adding to God's Word (Rev. 22:18–19, Rom. 1:25)? Yeah, I know, I may still repeat it again! So at times God sends a stop sign or in this case a cloud with a voice coming out of it. And in Moses's day, a bush that fire was in it, yet it did not burn up, cause that fire was God himself, and a voice of God speaking out of the bush to Moses. When we need to just call on the Lord and ask for forgiveness of all our sinful ways and ask for direction especially through his word. And pray for the Holy Spirit to teach us and give us understanding and lead and guide us and fill us with his spirit and friend he will. Moving on to (verse 9) still in (Matthew 17) notice Jesus told them not to tell anyone of the vision, which was an easy way to explain to them, the world or sinners, (1 Corinthians 2:14) will not understand spiritual things, in other words, they'll be like on the day of Pentecost. (Acts 2:13. They'll be thinking your drunk or flipped out.) In (Matthew 7:6), maybe that's why Jesus said "don't cast your pearls before swine [pigs]" which would mean, you don't allow pigs to play with a ten thousand dollar necklace, No, —because they don't know how to appreciate such beautiful pearls. Jesus said they'll turn and rend you (they will viciously trample over your treasure and attack you and tear you up, especially boars, which can be very dangerously vicious, cruel, and violent, not understanding your treasure). Jesus was using this analogy to explain the importance of comparing something that's a treasure and something that's very expensive, sacred, and holy. Dogs in those days weren't pets; they ran in packs like the wild boars, so what's the most valuable thing in your life? It should be your soul (Matt. 6:19–21, Mark 8:34–38). (Read Mark 8 please and see verse 37.) Yet like the man trying to show and display his most valuable treasure to dogs or pigs, they just don't understand the value of the treasure. Whose fault will it be if your soul is sent to hell? It's yours and yours alone! No blame game, your soul is your responsibility—period. People today are so much like this guy displaying the pearls: no clue. Look, friend, you have just one chance in life to get right with God. This book may be yours, and there is nothing more valuable or important than your soul making it to heaven. If you died in a head-on car wreck because some idiot was texting on his phone and you went to hell (hello…it used to be drunks, but now you gotta watch out for people on the phone, wow). And people slack a lot in praying and searching out what the Bible says about the conditions on making it to heaven. No matter what a church or religion says, people are not going to heaven just because they are a good, moral person. No, ya see, most people don't have a clue (Gal. 4:10, 5:16–26; Rom. 1:16–32; Matt. 24:42–51, Luke 21:34–36 1 Cor. 6:9–11). There are many scriptures that teach you how.

People that are not saved and are not born again, and are not Christians, just don't understand a spiritual touch and move of God, but it's in the Bible when God's spirit was poured out on people (Acts 2) they that received him, were changed and felt God's touch, kinda like your standing out in the backyard and someone walks up with a bucket of water and dumps it on ya, you will definitely feel it and it changes your dry body into a wet body; when folks are filled with God's Spirit and filled with the Holy Ghost and fire (Matt. 3:11). It's a spiritual fire that burns off the old sinful ways and makes you new (2 Cor. 5:17). There comes not only a touch that you feel but a change within the soul, God takes out all the junk, and the crappy way of thinking, excuse my term, but the old man is crucified with Christ (spiritually speaking). The old man is born again, in spirit, changed, becoming a new creation in Christ, old things are passed away, behold all things are become new (2 Cor. 5:17) Those that go to church and still party and drink and stay the same way, they weren't really born again, there wasn't a change in their soul, so don't tell me that if someone makes a huge bomb fire, with logs, kindling, gas, in your living room in your house, even for just one minute, there would be a change in your living room in your house, and so it is with God's Spirit, He does not tolerate the world-type partying lifestyle; it's all through the Bible.

The fornication, adultery, drunks, etc., is not a changed life. I've seen them, shacking up partiers, even having the Mr. Cool Attitude, with the earring, cool walk and cool talk, do you really think God's gonna let that prideful, worldly lustful spirit in his heaven, you better go read the Bible, I've been on both sides of this fence, I've came from that old vomit worldly lifestyle, and don't tell me I'm not your judge. No, I'm not, but I am the guy God told to write this book and to set your tail straight, you are told in the Bible, to lay down and lay aside those weights and the sins that beset you (Heb. 12:1 and 2) or pulls you down, try swimming across shark infested waters with dumbbells strap around your waist—well, preacher, you'd be crazy to even try that. Hello…yeah, you'd probably drown before you got ate. It's the same way trying to make heaven while living the partier, drunkard, or drugee lifestyle, you can't live both ways (1 Cor. 3:16 and 17) (1 Cor. 6:9, 10) (Matt. 24:42–51) (Matt. 6:24) (Luke 6:13) (1 John 2:15, 16) (James 4:4) (Rom. 6:16–22).

Again, my pastor said a woman's pregnant or she's not, cause you can't be half pregnant, and your a Christian or you're not! You have to follow the Bible and be born again! (John 3:3 and 5, John 14:6). Read (Hebrews 12:1, 2; Romans 12:1, 2, 3; Galatians 5:15 to 22; 1 Corinthians 3:17; 2 Corinthians 13:5; Galatians 2:20; 1 Corinthians 6:9, 10; 2 Corinthians 5:11; Romans 6:6 to 16; 2 Corinthians 6:16; John 14:17). Read them: Just remember this analogy when someone tells you you can live in sin, party, get drunk, commit adultery, and still go to heaven without God changing you…*which is a lie*! (Read Matthew 7:13 to 24, Luke 6:46).

Sad, but very true. See (Matthew 7:21): "Not everyone that says 'Lord Lord' shall enter into the kingdom of Heaven, but he that does the will of my father which is in Heaven." So in other words, not everyone who calls him Lord will make it to heaven. God knows those who are his (2 Timothy 2:19). Yes, I was also going 90mph in life. Partying like there was no judgment day. Enjoying the now, doing whatever you want, no matter what the consequences which is the way the world is now all over, what makes a man a man is it muscles, some think so, but not so, or that you fight good, having a black belt, no, or being a playboy, and getting lots of women. No, or because you've grown a full beard since your teens. No, or having a real hairy chest, no, being that hero that's a tuff comrade that saved a half dozen wounded comrades in his unit, no (but that is good) but no. SO my mother-in-law told her sons go into the military, it'll make a man out of ya. No, it'll make ya tuffer. Yes, but no, because theirs woman soldiers that are still women—oops, still no. So what makes a guy a real man? It's simple, making a stand for God, it takes a real man to take a stand to live right, and teach his kids to live right, and takes his family to church and learn about God, and turn away from temptation, and sin, which is unlike that whimp that slaps his wife or girlfriend, around, that's a real tuff guy, that'll burn in hell, but it's the man that will live right and a real man will follow the Bible, I love the way one of chick tracts puts it in the "sissy." About Jesus turning the other cheek because if Jesus hit back with all that power of God inside him, it would have probably wiped out the whole world.

But I'm reminded of so many that God helped that were small in stature but mighty in God, David against Goliath, Daniel, Samson, Joshua, Moses, Gideon, King Jehoshaphat, etc., more and more, men of God that took a stand for God. Those are real men, and this also applies to controlling wives. Do they really think God approves of that? No, he doesn't; it's all in the Bible (1 Pet. 3:1). And this was the condition of the whole world in the days of Noah's DAYS, and in Jezebel's DAY and Pilate's wife in (Matthew 27:19), yes, I'm repeating myself again. Where do we draw the line between God's way and the devil's way, or your way? No, sorry. It's gotta be God's way, or you don't go up…

Anything goes if you're on the devil's side of the line, the world's identification system, which the Bible speaks of is now coming in, no one will have access to their phones, iPads, or anything ran by computer unless you have the chip in your hand that's now in your cards, etc. So because everyone, including most Christians, are so caught up in the world system of computers, will not let go of their phones, etc., even cars have a computer, your meters, everything is run by computer except you, and you are next and it is here, very soon it'll be mandatory, and if you buck up against it, and rebel, guess what, your marked as a traitor, come on, folks. We are there; the convenience of not carrying a purse or wallet ever again will be a blinder to a lot, but the word says if you take the MARK-666 the microchip you are doomed to hell, according to the Bible. And this is why the changing the Bibles has been going on. Don't you know they are putting out another one, right. Now, and are ready already to get rid of the fanatics that preach against the mark of the beast…666, etc. See my book *Is the Chip, the mark of the Beast 666* by Rev. Fred Davis.

The Bible says they speak good of evil and speak evil against good. Come on, folks, we are that generation that all this is coming to pass in. The Lord said, when you see it coming in, this generation won't pass away till it's all fulfilled. I just pray the light of Jesus gets turn on in people's hearts before it's too late. We must draw the line between the rights and wrongs and pray for God to gives us spiritual discernment. They are already arresting people who take a stand, this is wrong. This nation was founded on free speech, freedom of choice, etc. To take away a right of Christian's choice is wrong and evil. (Matthew 18:6) says whosoever shall offend one of these little ones who believe in me; it were better for him that a millstone would be hanged about his neck and that he was drowned in the depth of the sea (Matt. 18:6).

The Bible says also not to touch God's anointed (Ps. 105:15) and do his prophets no harm. That's pretty plain but again. Just like when they came and killed Jesus. They want to kill you too. Like Jesus said (John 16:2) they'll think their doing God a favor by killing you. Look at John the Baptist killed cause of a vow to a dancing young girl that pleased King Herod.

In (Matthew 14:4), John the Baptist, told King Herod it's not lawful for you to have his brother's wife. The woman told her daughter to behead John in (Matthew 14:8 to 10) (see verse 4 to verse 8). So here are two scriptures in the Bible that even a king and a governor had a controlling wife (Matt. 14:8 and Matt. 27:19) (and sad to say, I've seen them even in many churches, ouch). In (Matthew 27:19), Pilate's wife said don't have anything to do with Jesus, we are told not to follow old wives' fables, but exercise thy self to godliness (1 Tim. 4:7). So where did these controlling wives draw the line between right and wrong and between good and evil or between God and the devil. I would say their choices they made were wrong and evil, but they chose to go against God and the Bible. (Hebrews 11:24 and 25) says Moses made a choice to not be the step son of Pharaoh's daughter because they did evil, even if it meant, suffering with the people of God because he saw and knew Pharaoh was wrong and he was mistreating the people of God, and Moses did not want any part of it because he knew in his heart Pharaoh was wrong (in my words).

If a man driving down the road and he just robbed a bank and stopped and gave you a ride, and the cops surrounded the car and arrested the driver; guess what, the law says, you get arrested too because you are called an accessory or an accomplice to the crime, even though you're really truly innocent. Moses did not want any part of Pharaoh's sins. Because to be evil, God would not have used and blessed Moses's life, the way he did. A lot of people today would have chosen the power and the fame and fortune of being heir to Pharaoh over serving God, not even looking at the eternal side of heaven or hell. We are here just a season, a short time/versus an eternal life with God in heaven forever, but remember life here is short, but eternal life is forever. Have you really ever wondered what Heaven is really like, streets of gold, gates of pearl, (1st Cor. 2:9).

Question? What is a season? It's like springtime, but at the end of spring's season is harvest time, when farmers, "gather up their crops," taking them out of the field, that was once a place of toiling and hard work. Now, bringing those many ripe fruits and veggies into the master's house, sounds almost like the rapture. Moses, choosing rather to suffer afflictions with the people of God, than to enjoy the pleasures of sin for a season. Also notice in (verse 24 of Heb. 11) (once he became old enough, he refused to be called the son of Pharaoh's daughter.) Wow, what a choice and that marked him, but he made his choice and forsook Egypt (verse 26, 27) and left the lifestyle of the riches, treasures of the palace life and left with the people of God, everyone I think knows that story of the Ten Commandments, yet in the depth of its contents it does not soak in because if it did this old wicked world would be ready for God's wrath and judgment, which if God doesn't shorten the days soon there will not be any flesh saved (Matt. 24:22). This scripture in Matthew paints an ugly picture in those verses and those who have studied prophecy know, it's gonna be much, much worse especially with our modern technology we have today. No, please don't misunderstand. Please, some technology is great.

I love watching the gospel music programs on TV and my favorite Preacher Bishop Jakes (next to my pastor, Donahae Green) at Living Christ Church, Tulare, CA. And heard him say, when preaching about Moses that people do good when their seeking God for something but when bad things come, with some folks they get what they want from God, and then they are gone! Just use God like a spare tire. Yes, even back in the days of Moses people backslid, while Moses was up with God on the mountain, the people down in the valley naked and lying about it, worshipping a golden calf. Wow, and 666, the devil's number. (John 6:66) tells about backsliders in Jesus Christ's day. Where do we draw the line? God has blessed America beyond all other nations and I don't know the percentage but probably half of USA has turn their back on God and according to scripture, he can turn us over to our enemy. This was once a nation that was founded on God.

And on our money is printed, "IN GOD WE TRUST," and there are devils trying to remove that, like the Ten Commandments, and other Christian artifacts. When we were little kids would say one nation under God in our pledge of allegiance and had religious release hour for the Christian kids. But we have forgotten the scripture that's in (Psalm 9:17) says, "The wicked shall be turned into hell and all the nations that forget God." Wow, hard stuff, preacher, yet if our son was to die, like my brother did in Vietnam.

And the memorial building that had his name on the plaque wrong and they couldn't even get his name right, they put Alvin instead of Alan, yet he died for our freedom—sad, yes, we forgave him. I went around and around with them over it. And he stated it was too much money to change it. That he'd have to change the whole thing. It's one whole unit. I said that's not right or fair. But it's having our name in God's book of life, that's the most important thing. God wants us to keep our hearts renewed with him daily (2nd Cor. 4:16). Sure, some feel that God's not gonna disown you. And again, that's where we have to know what the Bible says (Matt. 25).

Ten virgins means, all ten were born-again Christians and five made it to heaven, and five got left behind (Rev. 3:5, John 6:66).

Some religions teach that this can't happen, but that's false doctrine because the Bible says that you can (backslide) (1 Tim. 4:1) (John 6:66) (Rom. 1:25–32) (2 Pet. 2:1) (Jude 1:4), I've got two pages of scriptures on the subject, that says there were back-sliders even in Jesus's day, that turned back, so I'll believe the Bible over religions or some false doctrine. I've known many over the years being a prison minister and pastor and worked with many. The five that was left behind were not prepared to meet Jesus (see verses 8, 9, 10, 11 in Matthew 25:1 to 13: they ran out of oil). This was an analogy God is telling the church to be ready, like the first three chapters of Revelation's is warnings to the church people, not to be lukewarm (but be hot) or like Paul said to Timothy, in 2 Timothy 3:5 having a form of godliness, but deny the power thereof, from such turn away (wow, power means filled with Holy Ghost and fire). And there is many that'll still spread their lies and false doctrine and say the opposite, but remember, all of this Jesus, told us in Matthew 24:4, 10, 11, 24, 48. Read it.

And in many of his parables guess that's why the Bible says for us all to work out our own salvation, many, many are gonna be shocked like those five foolish, that ran out of oil. Anyone knows even in your car, a full tank of gas is not gonna last you a year. Come on, folks, when we see the gauge is low, that means you must put out an effort, even if you don't feel like it and get some GAS. Hello, or on being full, and being ready and making it because your full, so you don't run out. The emphasis here is to keep your tank full, this is sometimes hard to do with your car, and your soul, but some folks especially with their car, run real low on money to get a full tank but I'm referring to the soul not our cars but, spiritually speaking, this subject is for all those many people who are not fully dedicated to God 100 percent or I should say spirit-filled. Many think they're okay, just going to church once in a while, but if that was the case, my car is more religious than a lot of people because there's sure a lot of people out there that think you don't have to be, but church doesn't save people. Again, it's having a personal relationship with our Lord Jesus. If I just came home to see my wife once or twice a month like some people go to church once or twice a month, or even pray to God just in emergency cases only.

Do you think a wife would stay married to someone like that, or just call her and say hi. I love you, but never being there, not ever showing love just saying it, and have no feelings behind those words, when your there you just sit there, looking like you don't want to be there, a wife would not like it, nor would God like it neither, and so many, many people are this way to God at church, this was those five foolish in Matthew 25 no desire, no effort just there, just enough gas to get you by, some wishing they were at the game or somewhere else. People do not realize God's always looking down and listening. He knows all and sees all, and if you really study these five foolish ones in Matthew 25, do you wonder why Jesus used the word *foolish*? If you missed heaven as they did, then you would be very foolish, no, stupid! So be like the five wise that were full in their lamps (soul) and ready...and they even took an extra container that was also full. Wow, that's wisdom (Matthew 25:1–13—read this, please). (Proverbs 15:3, John 6:64, Luke 6:8, John 13:11; John 1:10, Psalm 53:1–3; Psalm 14:1–4) then these five foolish was knocking at the door (Matt. 25:1–13) (Rev. 3:8) (John 15:18–20), that Jesus already shut, and he wasn't gonna open it again, their opportunity was gone, or I could get into those left behind in Noah's Day, pounding on the boat as the water rose higher and higher, screaming, we believe you now, we're done laughing at you (John 15:20) (2 Pet. 2:5). But it's too late on having a full tank of (John 7:37, 38) (John 4:10–14) in your soul, after the Rapture of the church. Then it'll be too late to try getting a full tank of spiritual gas (which is a spiritual metaphor, spiritually speaking) to repent and get prayed up (Rev. 22:11) because the days coming when *bam*...Jesus returns, and (Revelation 22:11) will be fulfilled. Everyone will still be as they are, no time to repent or change anymore (Matt. 7:21–23), and that's why the Bible says call on him while there's still time because like the ten virgins, the five that were full of God (Matt. 25:1–13) and even that extra full container of fuel must represent being like Daniel, who was praying three times a day. And this means being ready and being right in your heart with God, ready and prepared to meet the Lord (Matt. 25:4, 1 Cor. 9:27, and notice Matthew 24:36, 37). That it'll be the same way when Jesus comes.

The five foolish went to buy more oil cause their oil was burn up. They didn't take extra like the five wise did and wanted to borrow some of their oil. This being-out-of-oil thing with the five foolish means everything else in this life was more important than their soul (2 Tim. 3:4, 5) or spending time in prayer with God. People today do this with their car; they try to make it across town on empty (Matt. 6:33) (Acts 1:8) (Acts 1:5) (Acts 2:4) (John 7:37, 38) (Acts 19:1–6). When they know the gas gauge says they're on empty (and these newer cars even have an alarm and a blinking light) and keep ignoring it, someone's gonna be stranded. Oh, running out of gas in your car is not too bad. You just need to call someone on your cellphone. But what trouble that causes. But if your soul is out of spiritual gas, meaning you're unsaved or not prayed up to full capacity / to being full where there's no room for any kind of manure or junk of this life to get in. You see, the five wise were full and filled up, and if something else tried creeping into their hearts, they just hosed it out with the extra container (staying full), not letting their heart grow cold or lukewarm. Sure, the foolish ones will call you a fanatic, but it'll be the fanatic Daniels that make it to heaven (Rev. 2:2–5, 3:3–5, 15–20)! And hear me, mocker, if you are that one who mocks those fired-up fanatics, you better reread (Matthew 25:8–13) and those other ones a few more times because those five foolish ones were left behind. Wow, you see your soul should be number one priority meaning in this parable is your being ready in your heart as in (Luke 21:34–36) pray always that you may be accounted worthy to escape. All these things, yet, religions teach just pray once, like those five foolish groups etc. (Mat. 25 and Luke 21:34–36). Don't listen to anyone that rewrites the Bible or some religion (Gal. 1:7–9). Don't let anyone deceive you. "Be Ready" I pray every day and ask the Lord's forgiveness of anything and try to keep a constant repented heart. Yes, there are people that preach the opposite. Where do you draw the line, and is the scripture (Revelations 3:5) referring to those? I believe so. People try to explain away the scriptures that are for the very purpose of warning to the soul but America once was a Christian nation, one nation under God.

It isn't anymore. It has become so evil, so bad, it's getting pretty scary here. And as it was stated earlier, let a tornado or bad earthquake come or some horrific ordeal happen and it's oh, God, please help us, yet where is honoring Him (God) all the rest of the time? And people don't know the scripture that talks about these things yet if you point them out, folks get mad, most Americans don't even want to be warned. They've seen so many phonies and counterfeits. They've been turned off, yet they know and watch the clerks at stores and banks hold up the dollars to check it for counterfeit yet. They still use money to buy things. Even so we should still be a Christian nation and pray to God when things are going well.

Have you ever saw in a movie where people are trapped in a room of a sunken ship and when they are rescued, they always go to a bar and celebrate instead of going to church and thanking God, oh preacher that's just a movie is it really? No, that is the way America really is. And you mention it. Oh, you are negative or to extreme. What if God said that next time, when disaster hits them. Wow. Come on. "Where does America draw the line (Matt. 24:43–51)? So again why does the Bible say to watch and pray always that you may be accounted worthy to escape all these things that shall come to pass and to stand before the son of man (Jesus).

The Bible says to warn them (1 Thess. 5:14). And this book is mine. And it's main goal is to warn the world. To wake up and get right with God. Are we really (Rev. 18) if we are that nation in (Rev. 18). God help us! When God destroys this wicked evil nation, or that nation gets nuked. Again, my question is, is this (Rev. 18) America? I say, yes, it is! Read the whole chapter, five times and everywhere you see whore, in your mind say America. Then tell me, (in Rev. 18) (Zechariah 14-12) (2nd Pet. 3-10) (2nd Thes. 1-8, 9) will America be nuked, or will that be an asteroid or a meteor sent from God himself. At any case, it gets destroyed cause of its sins. And God told Noah, if the world got that bad again it would be destroyed by fire next time not water, hello. Did he or did he not? And are we there again or not if you say we are (not) you are a liar.

And don't know the truth of the Bible (1 Thess. 5:3) (2 Cor. 4:4) (2 Thess. 2:10, 11 and 12). And anyone can see that this ol world is more eviler and wicked that it ever has been before (John 12:40). God is ready to destroy this evil world again. Hey, call me Noah Jr. I don't care. I gotta tell the truth and deep down in your guts and heart you know it to. And just like in those days of Noah (Luke 17:27–30) (Matt. 24:38–51). They were eating and drinking etc. (means) they were continuing on with life as always with no change, as in (Rev. 22:11). No one wants to hear it cause that cramps their fun, what? Or lifestyle, what? Or makes them uncomfortable, what? Are you telling me (2 Tim. 3:1, 2, 3, 4, 5, 8) is coming to pass, in the last days they will be lovers of pleasures more than God. Yep, verse 9 says, they'll proceed no further (verse 7) says, corrupt minds (verse 10) they've fully known the scriptures, doctrines manner of life (purpose) some people are so stupid. They think the whole reason for life is so they can have sex with anyone, and not be married, and they think the whole reason for life is to party, enjoy, have fun, ignore God or many go to church but yet dread going. This was the same way they thought in Noah's day when the flood came and took them all away (Matt. 24:39) and in Moses's day when the earthquake opened (Num. 16:32) the ground and swallowed them all. (Read it: Numbers 26:10.) Please take not here in the last word in (verse 10 of Numbers 26). The word sign, these things shall be an example of they became a sign, and many other places in the Bible that says, these were written (for a sign or for examples) for those after or later that would live ungodly (1 Cor. 10:11) (2 Pet. 2:5 and 6) (Matt. 12: 39, 40, 41) and many many more, also see (Matt. 13:17). What about when you see the world get like it was back then? That generation will not pass away till all of these things are fulfilled. (Matt. 24:34), (See vs. 37, 38, 39 in Matt. 24)

And their hearts are not in going to church or in seeking God or people don't have no more vision or no desire to worship and bow the head and thank God for their food, they are ashamed that someone will laugh at them, Jesus said, if you are ashamed of me before man, I'll be ashamed of you before Jesus' angels (Luke 9:26). Pretty plain, God's people perish for their lack of knowledge, yet if you went running into some of the places of entertainment, stadiums, bars, casinos, etc., and screamed the thing Noah did. They'd lock you up, right, and that's what Jesus was saying, we are there again folks. In a type of evil time, "Where do you draw the line." True, no one knows the day or hour but he said you'll know it's near (Matt. 24:29–39) by the signs of the times and it'll even be at the door, I have never saw the world this bad. The terrorist, etc., yet the world continues in her sin. No change, until disaster hits, folks, this is no fairy tale, Jesus is coming, those watching and praying will go back with him.

Jesus gave the disciples instructions on what to look for...and said these signs will be a sign to you, in which, when you see these things (Matt. 24) And Apostle Paul said some, and John and Peter, in (2 Pet. 2 and 2 Pet. 3, Rev. 13, Rev. 14 is the anti-Christ. Remember Matthew 25). You say you believe (James 2:19) says, the devils also believe and tremble (because they know judgment day is coming for them). In (Revelations 12:12), "The devil is come down unto you, having great wrath because he knows that he has a short time." A short time to deceive people, a short time to trick and manipulate unlearned victims to do his dirty work, and there are multitudes that desires to do evil, right now there are a lot of people all over this evil world that are full of the devil.

And in these evil times and with these types of evil people are mentioned all through the Bible are those that will miss the rapture, and they will be here when all hell breaks loose on this evil world, and I don't really get the part about the hateful birds, unless it's like one commentary wrote and said, it was used as a metaphor, so to excuse his unbelief, and I will point out to you in case you refer to them with scriptures to search in commentaries for better understanding I say...beware, again (Matt. 7:21) says, not everyone that says Lord, Lord will enter in. So many that write commentaries are excusing the unbelievable so please do not dismiss what I said, until you too have researched all those hateful birds that America has imported. There are a lot of ten different species in America. Again unless the verse in (Revelation 18) means, something different than that America has imported birds like those in New York Zoo, which are imported from Europe and Africa. These birds are called starlings and secretary birds, which are invasive species, and those birds in many zoos such as eagles, hawks, or cassowaries can be most aggressive. But there are so many different breeds and species that you'd run out of paper in describing them all, but I am sure John the Revelator in (Revelation 18) was referring to all those that America has imported at the huge zoos in many of the large state zoos. And yes, they are in huge cages, which John was also stating. You can Google it for yourself, but my point is that when this (Revelation 18) thing happens, if it's America or whoever. But I believe it's the USA because, case in point, everything that the chapter describes is in America! Wow. And we have that technology to wipe out a nation in one hour's time (see Zechariah 14:12 and also Revelation 18:9–10, 17–19). But the kick-in-the-teeth scripture is verse 24, where it says that in her (the nation/evil city) was found the blood of prophets and saints (in my words), which are Christians, preachers, and pastors. Yes, America, has had many men of God murdered, so, yes, this sounds like America, and where is it that everyone in every country wants to come and live in? (The land of the free, U.S.A) I rest my case. Wow, but back to the men of God slain and the blood of saints, it's been in the news for years, and not it's the schools. Wow, then God'll say, "Touch not my anointed" (Ps. 105:15) and take it personally, according to (Matthew 25:40–46). Remember in (Acts 9:1–5) when Saul was persecuting the church people? (Verse 5) is saying that you're persecuting me to Saul, Jesus said when you or someone persecutes God's people (read it). When Jesus spoke out of the bright light, in (Acts 9:4) and said Saul why are you persecuting me, Jesus was taking it personal. So when evil people come against you, they are, come, n at a child of God, remember (Matthew 25:40). Jesus said when you've done it to one of the least of these, you done it unto me. Wow. So God takes it personally when evil people go against his people. So which side are you on (Ps. 124)? But again, we don't want to be here when all hell is breaking loose in this world, as Scripture says. In (Revelations 18:2), but I believe the Bible is the true Word of God, and these prophesies are now coming to pass, and this is why God's wrath will soon be poured out, and yes, you'll always hear those unbelievers saying…I don't believe in all that ____ ____ stuff…

105

oh…but you will, but just like in Noah's Day…Then it'll be too late for a revival then and for all those scoffers who need to repent, according to (2 Peter 3:3 to 7. Read 1 Peter 4:17 and 18; Hebrews 3:10–13; Hebrews 2:3; Hebrews 4:1; 2 Corinthians 6:2). Please read all these scriptures, I took the time to look them up, please, you'll be glad you did. I'd like to challenge you to Read (Luke 16:19–31) esp. see (verse 27, 28, 29) says he was tormented so bad, he asks Father Abraham to warn his five brothers not to go to hell, and burn forever and end up there like he did (verse 28). Plus it's also written to give your heart a stirring (Romans 15:4) (2 Tim. 3:16, 17).

For many, tomorrow will not come, for they will be gone…The Bible says today is the day to call on Jesus, and repent and ask for his forgiveness. Tomorrow, no one has a promise they'll still be here, or the Lord could come in an hour we think not (Luke 12:40).

So while it's called today, come and get saved. If judgment begins at church first, then those that stay away from church or those bored, and not listening to the pastor's sermon, that is supposed to check your conscience when you hear the Bible preached and conviction grips your heart and leads you to give your heart to Jesus (my words of 1 Pet. 4:17–18).

Ya, see friend it's too late for those fallen angels that are now called demons (2 Pet. 2:4). But not for us. We can call on the Lord today. Today is the day of salvation. Stay ready. Don't let anyone trick or deceive you, stay ready. So they call you an extremist or fanatic, big deal. I'm gonna make it and with all the road rage spirits where people everywhere are provoking bullying people not just at school. But on the job everywhere in the stores in the parking lots, there is bad evil spirits in the land. And the intent of man's heart is continually wicked (Jer. 17:9, Gen. 6:5), so much violence in our world, where kids are carrying guns to school not just the ones that are wacked out cause of abusive parents but kids that are tired of being bullied and it's on the job, etc., people everywhere are getting concealed gun permits so they can protect themselves. And many are even carrying guns without the permits. Why? Many say the world is still safe! If there are church shootings and people living in fear, where can a Christian go to church and feel safe. And (1 Thessalonians 5:3) always got me, on peace and safety, but where can you go to feel safe?

Can you go to church, if churches continue to be burned up and shot up. Yes, the Bible says, God has not given us a spirit of fear, but of power, and of love and of a sound mind (2 Tim. 1:7). The days are here like in the days of old. People are gathering at homes because of fear and the pandemic (plague), to have church safely, but at church or home, God is with us (Ps. 27:1 to 6), and it's just about time for Jesus to come, according to (Matt. 24:22, Luke 21:22 to 28, Rom. 9:28) and all these signs that we see and read of in the Bible. (Matthew 24:42) says, we may not know the exact hour, but we know by the Bible and signs. No…we may not feel safe anywhere, but the Bible says, in (Romans 8:31), if God be for us who can be against us? I've preached, if God got Noah's family out safely, and Lot's family out safely, etc., then he will get us out also, amen.

And you can Google any one of these topics to check on my research (KJV) prophecy is very exciting to study because it's all over two-thousand-year-old writings, coming to pass in our generation. And again, according to scriptures, when you see these things in your generation, unfolding. That's the last generation (Matt. 24:33; Matt. 24:34, Luke 21:28, 32, in my words). Please make note, those who have prayed and ask Jesus Christ for forgiveness of their sins don't have to fear. It's the ones left behind; they'll live in the nightmares of all time. The worst ones are in (Revelations 6:14, Revelations 16:20, Revelations 9:10, Revelations 8:11). People left behind will see mountains fall flat, islands fled away, water all plagued with worm-wood, giant locusts with scorpion type stingers in their tails, will give you (five months of pain). Yes, it'll pay us all TO BE READY to meet the Lord… So where do you draw the line if all of this Bible proph-ecy is true for this generation? Well, it is true! And it'll pay everyone in the whole world to be ready, and our technology with chemical warfare especially nuclear, could be very well be our own destruction, with some of the hotheaded dictator idiots running other countries especially the communist ones. At any case, again, if it's God that's just fed up with mankind's sins, or our own ignorance, at any case it's a very scary time, and this is the day and hour that'll pay us all to be ready and right with God.

When our leaders quit praying in the White house. Oh, that would offend those who follow idols. Like I said. We have come full circle and our world is about to come to be what no one has ever seen such devastation that the Bible says is coming, again like (Rev. 18, Zech. 14:12) which sounds like nuclear or one angry God (Rev. 8:10–11) or a meteor shower, or stars falling on the waters, plaguing the water supply which is called wormwood (Rev. 8:11). "But I read Jesus is coming when you see these things going on. Are you looking for him? Watch, he said He'll come at an hour we think not. Wow. Again, the question…is the world really safe? Really? When the leaders of our nation no longer pray in the white house as our four fathers did. Hear these quotes, from President Lincoln said, "I believe the Bible is the best gift God has ever given to mankind." And the first President George Washington said, "It is impossible to rightly govern the world without God and the Bible. Don't let anyone claiming to be a true American patriot, if they attempt to separate religion from politics." Quote, unquote (sounds like 2 Chron. 7:14; Ps. 119:139; Ps. 9:17; Ps. 86:9–13; Ps 51:1–15).

Yet that's exactly what's going on. Again (2 Cor. 5:11) knowing the terror of the Lord we persuaded men or do we (Really?) Tell me one, most of the so-called preachers on TV scream, "Send me more money" than they warn people of "Great Tribulation" Last Days, etc. "Oh that would offend my wealthy tithers…er…a…yeah, you just keep preaching your ear tickling sermons of encouragement while the world is sliding down to hell all around you. And these types will be punished worse than anyone (Matt. 23:14, Mark 12:40, see verse 46 of Luke 20:47). Bet you they don't preach these scriptures either, or on the subject of verse 4 of (2 Tim. 4:3, 4) just for prophecy's sake I wrote out a list of about two pages or so of movies that are out, that are fictional, or fables, magical and fantasies, etc., that are out of Hollywood, and they have made millions from them but I was amazed at all I knew, and there are still so many more, we in America have become prophetic in this evil generation, according to (2 Tim. 4:3 and 4) just on this subject alone.

Try your own experiment, and see for yourself, go ahead, and name them off...you'll be amazed, at those you know, then maybe you to will see America is fulfilling prophecy of fables, fiction, horror, evil, corrupt even sinful ones that are gruesome, death from hell movies and these are all of today's so called Hero's and role models. And it's sad to say kids pattern their life after them, yet some other ones fun-type and some are very entertaining...but you get my point. No one can tell me Bible scriptures aren't coming to pass and being fulfilled, yes, they are especially on this subject. Even at amusement parks...with the magic stuff...and fantasies, etc., and (2 Thessalonians 2:9–12; Acts 20:31; Ezekiel 33:3–9 Colossians 1:28, 2 Corinthians 5:11).

All these scriptures say for us to warn people (Col. 2:8), and I wouldn't want to stand in any person's shoes that don't warn folks and tell them what the Bible says on the End of the World, Last Days, and the return of Jesus, etc. The Bible is very strict on this with warnings to the Believers"! I heard someone say she was witnessing to someone, in front of someone, else and was rebuked for it, "Saying you don't have to shove it down people's throats," wow. On Judgement Day if those don't make it to heaven, Those words will bite back hard. It's in the word or haven't you read (Ezekiel 33 or 2 Corinthians 5:11).

See (Matthew 24:14, Acts 1:8, Acts 22:15, Acts 20:31), and I dare ya to read them. Not many people witness today. And yet, we are closer than ever before. Hey, we are too busy. I was out washing my truck one day when a solar guy walking door to door yelled, "How are ya?" And I said, "Blessed." Well, he wanted to know what that meant (a preacher's trap run, ha, like an ant to sugar). I said, "Well, I almost died a couple of times, and I'm alive. I called on Jesus to save my soul, and now that we are in the Last Days and the time is ready for Jesus to return [Matt. 24:32–34] for his people, hey, I'm ready to go." And he was trying to edge his self away, ha. Well, he can't say I didn't try to tell him. Are you blessed? If you're born again and have asked Jesus Christ to forgive you of your sins, then you are blessed. Just having your name written in the Book of Life makes you blessed. Oh, I could've moaned about my woes, but everyone's got some kind of trouble. But we are still blessed just by being ready to go with Jesus. Amen. Again, we are too busy, and so were the people in Noah's day. (Only eight made it out [2 Pet. 2:5]). We don't have time, we've gotta text Joe…oh, I can't say that, they didn't have cell phones in Noah's Day. No way. But wouldn't they freak out to see how far we've come, with our technology, it even freaks me out. But the sad part about it, is, a lot of it distracts our youth, and many adults, and what's even worse, is, the youth can click on porn sites with the click of a finger, and other ungodly stuff, that was sin in my old party'n days, and, yes it is still sin today.

Kids today can enter into a life of sin, with the touch of a finger, and no one even knows, except God, wow…Reminds me of a "New Book" coming out, called (Matthew 24:22). "Unless God shortens the days no flesh will be saved. If the six o'clock news announcer, said, an asteroid was on collision course with earth I wonder how many would take time to pray then. Or be to buzy on their computers or TVs or football games, etc., you mean, oh, come on, people, I just hope this book gets on the shelf before the rapture but you may say…God knows my heart and I'm a good person. The sad thing: (Matthew 25 and Genesis 9 and Matthew 24:38, 39). Please read these two scriptures, "As it was (then) in Noah's Day, so shall it be…" (When?) When Jesus comes back. Yet I just believe they were probably beating down the door of the ship (ark).

Screaming we believe you now as the water level was up to their chins holding their babies above water as that chick publications track shows, excellent job! Jack, and God who inspired these men of God to write tracts and the Bibles (2 Tim. 3:16) and we pray that people will read, learn and follow them in Jesus's name. But it's sad to say…those devils Hollywood movie making telling lies and showing events about Noah, in these Hollywood movies that are not true nor even what the Bible says, this is adding too and taking away. This again is why it's good to read the King James Version Bible, so you'll know the truth. I understand they want to enhance the film and make it more exciting, but they are teaching lies to our kids.

So where do we draw the line to Hollywood devils already making some movies of superhero comic book heroes, some getting unfit for kids? To watch is one thing, but when the jerks in Hollywood start producing all these wanna-be Bible movies, that are full of lies, they are just asking for the wrath of God to be poured out on them (according to scriptures). The Bible is very clear on this, if God sent a lot of bad earthquakes or huge asteroids (something only God sends), and take out some of these Hollywood studios, I wonder if that would tell them, when they take a Bible story out of context, out of the Bible and ADD lies (makes God very angry) and distorting the truth of the Bible, then our children see these lies and believe them thinking that's what the Bible really says (Rom. 1:25 to 32) which tells us about these kinds of liars, which is a lie from hell and the Bible says again, they'll burn hotter in hell (Matt. 23:14) plus and the plagues in (Revelations 22:18, 19) will be added to them.

And they've taken away the truth from Bible stories in the Bible that plainly says, God will turn them over to a reprobate mind (Rom. 1:25 to 28) and take away their name out of the Book of Life. This is not a game, to destroy a Bible story, adding lies, and to distort our biblical history. This is so wrong (Rev. 3:5). There are many more scriptures to back up what I'm saying. And I believe that we are entering that time and era, that God's wrath is about to be unleashed and poured out upon the Earth, and people will probably get upset at me, so be it, again if America is (Rev. 18) may God help us. People have taken God's mercy and grace for granted. When a sacred Bible movie is no longer sacred, no, God will soon get these evil rebellious people's attention (Isa. 55:11).

So God has the right, and will send them strong delusions (Thess. 2:10–12) and severe judgment (and 2 Pet. 2:1–22). If God didn't spare angels that sinned (Verse 4), what will become of man that ignores God's gift (John 3:16–18) because the price was paid (1 Cor. 6:20). For all mankind when Jesus died on the cross, but that too has been distorted, by religions and false Bibles, we are definitely in the Last Days (Matt. 24:4, 11; 1 Tim. 4:1–2 and 2 Tim. 4:3–4; Col. 2:8). And we the people in America need to pray and get this nation back to God before God's wrath and anger is poured out, yes, I believe we are (Rev. 18). And not what many scholars say. It seems like everyone wants to come here to the USA because of freedom, and jobs, etc. Some come for merchandise, many countries do not have all the things the USA provides, and America is still the most blessed nation on the planet, next to Israel of course.

But it's because of people's prayers, and our parents, and grand-parents, and theirs before them, had good godly Christian morals, and lived for God. Again, that's what our forefathers stood for our whole nation was founded on "In God We Trust"....And God blessed and prospered us, but America has turned her back on God...And it's been by God's mercy and grace...We've not been destroyed already. Products and jobs, music and all those things (cars) = chariots, etc., oh, sure, other countries produce and manufactured these things also. But America is known as a female nation...America ah...she's a beautiful and free, freedom, to serve the devil or God. Your choice yeah right.

Do we really understand the word? Choice or freedom, *Webster's Dictionary* says *freedom* is, the state or quality of being free, independence, liberty, being able to move, without hindrance or restraints, being able to choose, released from imprisonment, etc. The Bible says whom the son (Jesus) has set free he is free indeed which is the opposite of bondage (People all over the world especially in USA the land of the free) probably have more people in bondage to drugs, porn, affairs, sins of all types, I believe the USA (probably) has more prisons than any other country in the world. And they are full, yet we are called the land of the free. But sad to say there are more peo-ple bound and hooked on drugs and alcohol, and many other things roaming the streets, than those in prison, yes, I speak from experi-ence, but I've been clean and free for over forty years...Hey don't clap or pat me on the back, give God the glory. The Lord did my change whom the son has set free, they are free indeed (John 8:36).

So why are so many people bound...this is the land of the free, and this was a Christian nation, or it used to be one nation under God...but sad to say it's not now anymore...It's become a nation of bondage. A habitation of devils because this nation has turned its back on God, but we can return to him, and ask forgiveness, and truly repent of our sins, then you and I will be free. There are born-again men and women in prison, that are more free-er than most walking the streets. Cause they found Jesus (2 Chron. 7:14). If my people, which are called by my name (Christians), shall humble themselves, and pray, and seek my face, and turn from their wicked ways, then will I hear from heaven, and will forgive their sin, and will heal their land ("real true freedom is living for God").

Choice, Joshua said, you choose this day whom you will serve (Josh. 24:15, Isa. 58:6; John 8:32, Heb. 11:25). So you see even God himself will have a leg to stand on as the old saying goes, his word, will be thrown in everyone's face that don't make it and tries to offer excuses for the way they've lived today. (I was hooked on dope, cigarettes, booze, running around with different women, etc.) People say oh I can't quit this or that. You weren't born that way and you can quit! (Philippians 4:13) says, I can do all things through Christ which strengthens me.) And to say you can't is calling God a liar…I was hooked. When Jesus saves.

He changes you (2 Cor. 5:17). We are a new creature, old things pass away behold all things become new. That's why Jesus Christ called it being born again. Once your spirit man gets connected with God's spirit through Jesus Christ. Through you repenting. And asking forgiveness of your sins. The new man (the spirit man comes inside you) called the Holy Ghost or Holy Spirit and he changes you. But he does the molding and change in you. Like a potter does to the clay (Jer. 18:1–6, Rom. 9:20–22). If we ask him to help us change, he will. And many others also have, and he delivered them and now they to are free. But it has to be your own choice…choose wisely… And soon. Things are wrapping up (According to scripture) when you take an old car and completely restore it, it has now become restored new. It's been put back to its original new state as it was in, when it was first created. Wow…and you know that's God's transforming power.

Won't you allow God to restore your broken life today (in Romans 10:9, 10, 13) (1 John 1:6–10). It's really simple, all you have to do is bow your head, and pray and ask Jesus Christ to come into your heart, and save your soul admit, and confess your sins to Jesus, saying Lord Jesus. Please forgive me of all my sins, for Lord I have sinned. Come into my heart and save my soul, and I receive you now into my heart in Jesus name. Thank you for saving my soul, Amen, simple but affective. The beauty of serving God, is, he is the same, yesterday, today, and forever (Heb. 13:8) and He's a No respect of person's God (Rom. 2:11, Col. 3:25). In other words, God has no favorites, we all reap what we sow (Galatians 6:7, 8, 9) but my point is God healed my wife's heart and gave her love back for me. God restored my marriage, that my drug-ee, hippy-biker life-style destroyed. And he can for you, if you're both willing, and both willing to give up that partying lifestyle, and go to a Bible preaching church and live for God and give Him the steering wheel of your life. Then by you allowing him to restore and remold you like a potter remakes his pottery out of clay (Jer. 18:1, 2, 3; Rom. 9:20–23), taking out those bad lumps…and maybe an area that needs some extra pounding on, or reshaping, or if you're real dry…he might ADD some water to soften you to where he can mold you, and if you've never been hosed out by the Holy Ghost. Just ask God to allow the Holy Ghost in Jesus's name to hose you out, clean inside your heart and soul, and to fill you up with his spirit: (John 7:37–39; 2 Cor. 5:17) And ask him to take out anything that's not pleasing to God, please read these scriptures (Psalms 51:9 to 17) (1 John 1:6 to 10), and as the potter does to the clay, ask him to remold you and shape you into that NEW creature in Christ Jesus.

Because you don't know what you've been missing, I must have cried like a baby when praying to God, what seem to be hours…and I just pleaded guilty and felt so clean and restored. I thanked him as I poured out my heart (Ps. 62:8, Phil. 4:6), and my wife did also, we knew we had to give it all to God, and as He hosed us out with his Holy Ghost water hose, Wow God healed us (John 4:13, 14, 28, 29; John 7:37–39). Wow…but there must first be a willing mind on your part with "both of you" (Rom. 14:4, 5; Phil. 2:5; 2 Cor. 8:12). And you must ask Jesus to forgive you as well as you forgive each other (Matt. 6:14 and 15) and mean it. Pray, and stand on God's Word, and his promises cause with God all things are possible and believe God and his Word (Mark 10:27, Matt. 19:26, Luke 18:27, Mark 9:23).

You've been changed, and reborn, and God will make you both new again, and restore you with a new fresh love, and when disagreement arises, take them to Jesus, and if you feel you need counseling…most pastors are good marriage counselors. If you're gonna live for God, keep everything Christian…even your marriage counselors. Amen. Keep the Lord in your life and marriage…be quick to say you're sorry and mean it. Also be quick to repent to God…Forgive others and watch the blessings roll in. Many things in life God allows to test you…but not everything is a test. We live in a mean world, fighting mean devils along our way. Learn and use Bible Scriptures as you would a sword against a wolf coming at you, if you feel you are under an attack by the devil, quote Scriptures (Eph. 6:10 to 18, Heb. 4:12, Luke 10:19, Isa. 59:19, Isa. 58:6, Isa. 54:17, Phil. 4:13–19). Your defense against the devil is in the Lord and in his Word and praying in Jesus…name, telling the devil, you are still under and washed by the blood of Jesus and the blood of Jesus has washed away your sins (Rev. 1:5).

As in (Rev. 12:11), so because our sins are covered by the blood of Jesus, we give him praise…and in Thanksgiving with the songs of thanksgiving and praise (read Acts 16:16 to 25) when going through a hard time, a thankful heart, God is well pleased with, also you can rebuke the devil and tell him to flee in Jesus's name, and Plead the Blood of Jesus over you and anoint you and your home (Exod. 12:7) and your family with olive oil (which represents the blood of Jesus) (Exodus 12:13) (1 John 1:7). Don't ever let down your guard, we are warring against an angry devil (1 Pet. 5:5–9, Rev. 12:9–12) and remember. "The gates of hell Will Not prevail against God's people (Matt. 16:18–19; Ps. 91:1–16; 2 Chron. 20:15–17, 21, 22).

Many times we need to put it in God's hands, and allow God to work it out, and at times God wants us to have a dependence on him (Matt. 6:23–33) if we have give him our heart, he'll take care of us, and restore our lives; he can redo, and restore us again to NEW, being "redone" ("born again") is the biblical term for humans restoration, of the soul restored back to God. So let the master mechanic, potter remold you back to the original state that God intended, Born of the spirit.

It's your choice. I was one of them. My moma could tell you stories. And she is one of the first ones I had to go to; and ask her to forgive me of being the Bratt kid I was, yes, I was also a prodigal son, and because of all mom and grand ma's prayers…for me, then, and gave up the partier druggie pot smoking hippie lifestyle, after I gave my heart to God, and ask Jesus Christ to come into my heart, and save my soul, and change me, and heal me, and my marriage. And He did, after years of running, from God, after going through all the hell-ish life, or like Jonah that ran from God Type, or as a prodigal hippy biker idiot that I was, then I got saved. Thank God, for mom and grand ma's prayers.

You need to read the story of the prodigal son in (Luke 15:11–32). This story, no doubt was written for me: But I had to discipline myself, and make myself…live right (Heb. 12:1) (Rom. 12:1–2).

To stay out of falling back into the old lifestyle, that Luke describes as a pigpen life. You must learn and quote the Bible scriptures, like bullets at your enemy the devil. Once you learn how to memorize and quote them to the devil as Jesus did to the devil in (Matthew 4, Hebrew 4:12, 1 Corinthians 10:13, 2 Corinthians 10:3–5), remember the devil twisted God's Words to Adam and Eve, and to Jesus and he will to you also, be vigilant on your guard, remember, it's a new life, and God gives us spiritual ammo. Don't be naïve like Eve was in (2nd Cor. 11:3; Gen. 3:1 to 6) and in (2 Corinthians 11:–15) or again, when that lying devil tries making you doubt, quote those faith texts and power scriptures to him, like Jesus did in Matthew 4, and like when the devil came to Eve saying "Oh God didn't really mean you can't eat of that tree because God knows that when you eat of "that tree"…you will become as smart as God knowing good and evil" and so gullible Eve, listened to that lying devil, and lost out with God…to disobey God…and obey a devil, right there, she should have known she was messing up. This is why the Bible teaches to try or test the Spirits (1 John 4:1) to see if they are of God or don't forget, not everything that happens is from the devil (James 1:2–6).

And don't think because strange things happen, that your all alone, or in the Twilight Zone, no, all Christians go through trying times (1 Pet. 4:12) Even as our parents and grandparents did and those back before them, in Bible days. As in (2 Corinthians 4:8–9; 2 Thessalonians 1:4 to 10; 2 Tim. 3:11–12). Just remember we want to always bounce back, and shine bright (Rom. 8:18 and Job 23:10 and 1 Pet. 1:7) for God, as Job said, when God has tried me I'll come forth as Gold. (Just think about God asking the devil to test you) like he did Job. In (Job. 1:8–10), God was bragging about you—or I mean Job to the devil, on how spiritually and tuff you are in the spirit, now check out what the devil said back to God in Job 1:10, "Hast not thou" (God) made and Hedge about him, Psalm 91:1, 2, a covering of protection.

They persevered in prayer for me, so I must carry on their heritage of my mother and grandmother's, praying for my children and grandchildren. I remember back in my trucking days…I'd get a call from either one of them at different times, on a bad no sleep night… tired, a long shift, and many miles of dosing…power drinks and coffee-d out with…many times, having lots of close calls to having a wreck and being, real fatigued, my mom or grandma would call and say I was up in the middle of the night. I had you on my heart and I prayed for you…Wow, what a hero legend my mom and grandma Peterson was to me. If I can learn and be half the prayer warrior they were and have that mountain moving faith, thanks God for those great memories of them both. "Lessons learned today, makes you a legend, later in life," to your family. (Wow.) Thank God.

I remember growing up with mom quoting scripture when she stepped on a nail sticking out of a board, she quoted (Ezekiel 16:6), "And when I passed by thee, and saw thee polluted in thine own blood, I said unto thee when thou was in thy blood, live, yea. I said unto thee when thou was in thy blood, live." The scripture repeats itself, and it speaks life to the one bleeding, my mother and grandma would quote this about three times and pray when someone was bleeding, a wise guy type, told me one time, she said that's talking about a woman's minstrel cycle…I commented back and said, wow for generations my family has used it coupled with faith and prayer to stop bleeding that scripture is speaking life and yes I to noticed like dozens of other repetitive verses in the Bible, it to repeats itself… with a purpose of faith and life inside the word.

Go with what you learn, and don't allow others to dampen your faith. I learned as a kid, watching my brothers, both of them lose fingers, and God healed them as mom and uncle Edward and family gather around the bed and prayed and read that scripture, while Uncle Ed taped the finger on a an ice cream stick, wow…There was so much faith in that room that day, and so many more miracles and even though I was that prodigal son in my rebellious teenage life and strayed away from God, God brought me back because of mom and Grandma's tenacious prayers, never giving up on that prodigal son. Thank you, Jesus. And Reader friend, if you never had a problem, how would you know God's the same deliverer for you (Heb. 13:8, Heb. 11:39–40). And just like those Faith Hero's in the Bible and in our life, we too, can be one for those following our examples of faith. But remember, if Daniel had not been thrown into the lion's den… we today wouldn't know God can deliver Daniel from lions, Moses from the Red Sea, the three Hebrew boys in the fire furnace, etc.

The words *love* and *forgiveness* Jesus told Peter (Matt. 18:21, 22) 70×7 = 490 times we must forgive others that trespass against us, Jesus didn't say we had to agree with the trespass or situation but forgive, as in (Luke 6:37; Matthew 18:35; Matthew 6:14–15, story in Matthew 18:23–35) love covers a multitude of sins. First Peter 4:8 charity is the definition of love. My wife is the perfect example of love to forgive me of all the cheating, lying, etc., and take me back. She is the most caring person and submissive wife on earth in my eyes. She still loved me when I was a creep in those hippy biker drug scene days, I treated her like dirt, and she forgave me. We can preach God's love behind the pulpit in church but if we've not forgiven others then (1 Cor. 13:1), We are just a bunch of noise; (1 John 4:20–21; 1 John 1:8–10) God will not forgive us unless we forgive others (Matt. 6:14, 15).

And we would become a liar. God's Word will always come back in our face and marriages if both man and wife would love and forgive as my wife did. Your marriage would also be healed and blessed. But it takes work, and both in love and forgiveness and agreement.

Just ask Brenda Davis, my mother is done gone to be with Jesus but yes, I put her through hell too. And I'm thankful to God she forgave me and got to see Jesus save me before she passed. I've heard stories of some that it came later. And your heart goes out to them, them dying, not seeing 'em saved. But the whole thing of this type of love is first from God. (John 3:16) and agape love that is so strong you give your only son to not just die for someone but to suffer an agony hard, treacherous type cruel death and seeing it is so bad you have to look away. And the whole time all this is going on you (God) had the power to stop it but knew it had to be done, and the whole time through the whole ordeal the so-called religious rulers were mocking him and spitting on him. And you God had power to even wipe them all out but you allowed it all to go on. So man could be saved… Wow…that is love. That's a God kind of love, called agape love.

(Psalm 37:23–24). The steps of a good man are ordered by the Lord and he delighteth in his way. (That's the ones that follow the Bible and Jesus and living like he said to live) (verse 24), Though he falls, he shall not be utterly cast down. For the Lord upholds him with his hand. In big time wrestling they have a thing called taking a dive, which is basically saying a wrestler or a boxer acts like he's falling, when it's really a dive. You dive in the pool, it's doing a going down motion on purpose this scripture is speaking of a real fall, trip, a mistake you messed up cause of a situation that was not premeditated or planned. And any true repentance when you are truly sorry. God says he's faithful and just and will forgive our sins, but we have to ask for forgiveness and be willing to turn from our sin. **If I was still getting drunk and smoking dope and saying, and professing I'm saved and born again. Yet there's no change of the heart, I would be a liar**, Jesus said when the inside of the cup and platter is washed clean that the outside is gonna get clean also, but, who in the world out there is gonna wanna drink out of a cup if someone only washed the outside of it. When some of us cups has been dirty for a long time and need to be hosed out boiled out, soap and scrubbed inside and out, spiritually speaking that only Jesus Christ and the Holy Ghost can do, but know this if you're a compromiser or in the middle or on the fence (people not claiming to be on either side should be careful): God'll spit you out or knock you off into hell (Rev. 2:4–5, Rev. 3:2–5, Rev. 3:15–20). Hot or cold means no lukewarm or no one in the middle (no one being on the fence). You're either on God's side or the devil's, not in between (1 Cor. 10:21; Luke 6:46, 11:23; Matt. 12:30)! Read 2 Timothy 3:5. People want to go to heaven, but they'll stay away from the spirit-filled fanatics (who have the power of God and the Holy Ghost and fire-filled saints of God [Acts 1:8, Matt. 3:11]). This is why the Bible is very, very specific here on this issue, and the Lord has said that Spirit-filled saints of God should not associate with those unbelievers or, as the KJV says, (2 Cor. 6:14) Don't be be unequally yoked together. As these next scriptures say, like an old pastor once explained it, you don't hook up a team of oxen to pull a plow if one's really large while the other is really small or hook up two mules together; you must use a mule with a horse because two stubborn mules fight.

    2 Corinthians 6:14, 16, 17,
    1 Corinthians 3:16–17
    Ephesians 5:3
    Ephesians 5:26–27; Ephesians 4:26–27
    1 Corinthians 6:9–11
    Romans 9:20–22
    1 Thessalonians 4:4–8
    John 12:46–48
    Romans 8:5–11
    1 Corinthians 6:16–20
    Ephesians 3:17
    John 14:15–17
    2 Timothy 1:12–14

The Bible teaches God will not dwell in an unclean vessel, but when we've ask for his (Jesus) forgiveness and ask him to save us from all our sins and to cleanse us from all our unrighteousness. And ask for the Lord to fill us with his spirit, then the Holy Ghost and fire comes in the clean heart and saves our soul. Christ refers to a point in one's life, where, when you get saved that our spiritual house is the soul of man is cleansed, swept and garnished def (to furnish, to protect, decorate, adorn) as in (Luke 11:25 see verse 35 or Luke 12:21) even describe being so full of God your rich in God (John 15:1–10), (verse 4), the branch has to be connected to the vine in order to bear fruit, even so we must be in Christ and Christ in us. In order to produce the fruit called love as in (Galatians 5:22), God takes the old wine bottle (you are the bottle) and makes it new, before he puts his spirit (the new wine) in the new bottle, that's renewed by accepting Jesus Christ into our life (Mark 2:22, 2 Cor. 5:17, Acts 2:13, John 2:4).

Note: Most people that don't want to fully change and follow Jesus 100 percent and those that still want to get drunk and say they are saved. Do not understand these scriptures. That when we get saved and we are becoming new, penance, or penitent being sorry for your sins, sorrow for wrong doing or wrong living, remorse.

They'll say not now (Matt. 24:43–51; Gal. 5:16–21 or 1 Pet. 4:7; 1 Pet 5:8–9; 1 Thess. 5:6, 8; Luke 21:34–36). But when we repent asking Jesus to forgive us and to save our souls...then we become that "New Creature in Jesus Christ," that Apostle Paul spoke of in (2 Corinthians 5:17), we are a new vessel now ready for God's Holy Ghost New Wine. This explains that God doesn't put his New Wine His Holy Ghost/spirit into that old drunken partier, No that's an Old bottle that old partier must become born again, become a New Creature in Christ (John 3:3, 5; Rom. 10:9, 10, 13). Note: the heart of man must be converted to God as a little child (Mat. 19:14) for such is the Kingdom of God, and being in your heart as, the innocence of a toddler, this is why (John 3:3, 5) says we must be born again, in our heart.) But only to the committed, sincere, and the ones who are serious enough to seek God with their whole heart (Ps. 119:2, Ps. 119:34, 1 Thess. 5:23, Ps. 139:23, Jer. 29:13).

When in all honestly, the Bible teaches that Jesus, in turning the water into wine, when he said, in the verses (John 2:4), he's actually referring to his hour to go to the cross, die, go to the grave, rise from the dead, go up to heaven and send back the Holy Ghost, which is that new wine that fills the inside of the new bottle—you. After you've been saved (born again), after you're clean/renewed, and after praying and asking forgiveness of all your sins, that makes you the NEW "BOTTLE," and now you're ready to be filled with God's new wine—the infilling of the Holy Ghost (spirit), which means our old, human nature is changed when we repent of our sins. Because like an old wineskin in those days, it would crack and bust, leaking out all the new wine, which would be a great loss. This analogy is mentioned in (Mark 2:22, 2 Corinthians 5:17, Acts 2:13, and John 2:4). So God puts his new wine into new bottles. So many wonder why they are not filled with God's Spirit; it's because they are not becoming new in Christ. They are still living the old life, old ways to stubborn (Ps. 32:8, 9) to allow God to change you are usually the ones that say your judging them and are the ones that are still hanging on to their old life, and don't want to change their old ways… Many scriptures say you can't do this, even Jesus himself said don't do that (1ˢᵗ Cor. 6:9, 10) (Gal. 5:10 to 22) (1ˢᵗ Cor. 6:15 to 20) (1ˢᵗ Cor. 10:21). He said you'll hate the one or lose the other, you will gather or scatter (Matt. 12:30, Luke 11:23, 1 Cor. 10:21, 1 King 18:21, Luke 16:13, Luke 9:62, Luke 17:32, Matt. 6:24, Rev. 19:7)she made herself ready…as in (Rom. 12:1, 2) (Heb. 12:1) and only then, when one has truly repented of their sins and turned away from their old ways and have ask Jesus to forgive them and ask him to change them, and cleanse and save their soul…then God will fill them up with his Holy Spirit, in (John 15), Jesus explains it.

And in (John 7:37–39), then he will fill your cup of your soul to overflow. So God only fills repented, changed people, with his spirit, that have ask forgiveness of their sins. Then they are clean and ready in their souls to have God's spirit come in them. Reminds me back when I was a kid when they gave school field trips to the soda pop factory and they used old glass bottles, that were scalded in boiling hot water before putting in the soda pop because they'd be sued and run out of business if they put it in dirty bottles. God's that way too. He's a holy righteous God, and he's very strict on putting his spirit in some dirty old pot smoking long haired filthy talking hippy biker… Ha. (Like I was.) He had to save me first and clean up my filthy heart and filthy mouth and sinful ways.

As I said, there are many that think they can still get drunk and smoke dope and make heaven. (That's unrighteousness.) And that's wrong, and that's a lie from the devil, again that's the same kind of thinking that got Eve kicked out of the Garden of Eden. Now if God allowed pot smoking Christians to go into heaven (and I know some) God would be a liar… "God's not a liar" nor is he gonna apologize to Adam and Eve. He's not a hypocrite either! God's Word will not return to him void (Isa. 55:11) and God said let every man be a liar and let God be true (Rom. 3:4). Now, this is a deceiving spirit, and Anti-Christians as in (2 Thessalonians 2:9–12), that the Bible says God will allow those kind of people that don't want to change to be deceived because they don't wanna hear the truth in the Bible, they just (want to do what they want to) and they want to keep on sinning and follow the devil and will become reprobate minded and believe a lie and be damned. According to the Bible because unrighteousness will NOT enter into heaven: don't be deceived, God is not mocked, whatsoever man or a (woman) sows that he shall also reap (Gal. 6:7–9). All this is in the Bible!

The Bible says for us to submit to God (first) then resist the devil and he will flee. Draw nigh (near) to God and he will draw near to you (James 4:7, 8). Seek ye first the kingdom of God and his righteous then all these other things will be added unto you (Matt. 6:33; 1 Pet. 5:5–9). God resists the proud, of this generation because it is so full of pride, and many are taught, be proud, stand up, and don't let no one downgrade or bad-mouth you, be proud, don't let anyone bully you, fightback, don't be a sissy, stand-up for yourself, be a man, yet Jesus (the Bible says) (Isa. 53:7) (Acts 8:32) was as a sheep before the slaughter. Jesus taught and lived the opposite of (so-called buffed proud tuff guys today.) So puffed up from working out six hours at the gym. (Wow.) Yet the Bible says that profits little to a man (1 Tim. 4:7–8). And if the church could get as many people that are in the gyms, wow, God would probably faint. Yet.

The buffed pride that comes from that workout is the opposite of what the Bible teaches…Oh they'll get in your face and call you fat boy. You need to work out. Sure and do some, but that like anything else can be addicting. And I was doing good till I broke my back but let's look at the whole spirit of it all, what does a man give in exchange for his soul, you don't answer to me, nor I to you, but my dear friend you will answer to God for how you live and if you are puffed up with your body, car, house, smarts, money, job, etc. "It's the thinking your better attitude (Your puffed up pride) that will keep you out of heaven." You don't find Jesus, coming off the cross, kicking some guys butt with a karate round house kick, no, he was like a lamb, a sheep needs a shepherd, and a sheep dog for protection: They are not fighters. Nor are they violent, vicious, rude, arrogant, nor are they full of pride, they are not mean to other sheep, nor do they envy one another.

It is amazing how the sheep mind their own business. They just eat and sleep and follow the shepherd, go where he says wow. So many have said a Christian, like the sheep. Is a sissy. (Really.) Let's use the chick tract example on the sissy. I highly recommend you read it. Okay. Let's say you are Jesus. You have all the power God does. Lightning bolts, thunder, stop winds, part oceans, walk on water, walk in fires, glow like lightning and let's not forget walking through walls, and raising up people from the dead back to life again. With all that power Jesus had in him, he had to turn the other cheek, but he also wanted to demonstrate a God kind of love to mankind, by laying down His life on a cross for all mankind, for all generations to come (John 3:16–18, 1 Cor. 6:20, 1 John 3:16, John 10:17–18). So you had to turn the other cheek because you knew you already had power to call fire down like on Sodom and Gomorrah, so knowing, you have all that power in you, naturally you'd turn the other cheek, the problem was those idiots, that hit Jesus, pulled out his beard, beat him with a cat of nine tails (whip with glass, bone, sharp metal in the strands) and the carrying the cross, nailing him to the cross, the crown of thorns smashed on his head, the mockery, the spitting in His face, the towel over the face then slapping him, saying, Prophecy. Who slapped you (Luke 22:64). Wow, just doing that to a regular human being is so, so wrong, but as chick tract says he's the Godman, with all that power, Jesus had to turn the cheek. "As a lamb, before his shearers" (Isa. 53:7).

Wow. So the Bible says, He didn't say a word. Knowing He had power. And that they all would stand in shock before him on that Great day of Judgment Day. Wow. So that next time your all puffed up with your bad self. With muscles, smarts, riches, etc.

And catch yourself looking down your nose, at some fat Christian. Remember the sheep and, with the same Judgment. You judge with, God'll judge you (Mat. 7:2) (Rom. 2:1), myself included. (No one is exempt.) Jesus was sheeplike, we should be sheeplike, not looks (but attitude) A lot of people are gonna stand in shock. On Judgment Day, with their bad self especially in church. You see more wolf type and more of the world on people in most churches today. And don't get me started on the body piercings and all that mess. When I came to Christ, with the help of the Lord, He took all that worldly junk, I laid it all down (Phil. 4:13) and some cost me big bucks, again I've been on both sides of that fence being Mr. Cool, and Mr. Bad. Just a wannabe (Phil. 3:8) you gotta count that kinda loss like Paul said, as poop, if Jesus laid down his life the least I can do is lay a side those weights that hinder my walk with Christ and lay down things that bring a reproach to God and lay down things that would darken my light (Heb. 12:1, 2; Phil. 2:5; Matt. 5:14–16).

Plus, if we teach others wrong by living a sinful hypocrite life, or like the pot smoking Christians, that are a stumbling block to some ex-drugee, I believe (Matthew 23:14) would be them, and (Romans 14:13, Romans 12:1 to 3). You all go ahead knowing we are so close to the return of Christ, go ahead...Live like the world, Not! You better let anything and everything that's worldly go. And follow Jesus Christ examples, even he said do as I do. My old pastor, said years before the T-shirts came out WWJD, "What would Jesus do? Is your answer to anything in life. Turning the other check. No sin or guile was found in him and one of the problems of this world over the years has been too much pride and arrogance and wrong teaching.

Many called but a few chosen he (Jesus) said, to be meek. Pride goes before a fall...oh I've even been mocked by preachers, even after my traffic accident. Folks not knowing the long-term plan of God for my life, and was even accused of going over board, Thank God, God's my judge. We all reap what we sow. And when the Bible says not to touch God's anointed (1st Chronicles 16:22) and (Psalms 105:15), buddy you better be careful of bad mouthing them that's God anointed man or woman of God, because of that's very dangerous with God. Maybe that's why the Bible says (1 Pet. 4:17–18)

Judgment must first begin at the house of God and if it first begins at us, what shall the end be of them that don't obey the gospel of God, = the BIBLE (Gospel, life and preaching of Jesus, verse 18) and if the righteous scarcely be saved, where shall the ungodly and the sinner appear?

I'm sure you've noticed, out of all the animals, Jesus picks the one that can't defend himself that we the Christian are supposed to be like, meek and lowly. And have to depend upon the shepherd for protection, wow. That blows a lot of people out of the water! Some folks seem to forget about the sheep type Christians that are suppose be humble and meek, and even forget that pride goes before destruction. And a haughty spirit before a fall, or take heed when you think you stand, lest you fall, and please don't forget God resists the proud, that must mean your BAAAAAAAD...Ha. But he gives grace to the humble (James 4:6, 7, 8; Prov. 16:18; 1 Cor. 10:12; Heb. 4:1 and 11). As in (Matthew 6:33), when you submit your life to God first, then...

You see that takes the controls of your life out of your hands and puts them in God's hands—so he can direct our path (Prov. 3:5 and 6). And like real sheep. We must depend on the shepherd (Jesus, God) to protect us from our enemies. God is faithful; there has no temptation taken you, but such is common to man, but God is faithful, who will not suffer (Allow) you to be tempted above that ye are able: but will with the temptation also make a way to escape, that ye may be able to bear it (1 Cor. 10:13, verse 20 to 22). I want pot smoking Christians to read (1 Corinthians 10 verse 20–22; James 4:17; Luke 6:46). Are we gonna provoke God to jealousy. We cannot drink the cup of the Lord and the cup of devils. Ye cannot be partakers of the Lord's table and of the table of devils. "Where do you draw the line" on compromise, in school they teach, the world, the macho man, we don't want to be looked at as weak or as wimpy. Again, this goes back to pride. We forget, the Bible teaches to be a separated people, apart from the rest of the world, we don't want to appear as weak and wimpy. As I said already, this is the way of the world (1 John 2:15).

Love not the world, neither the things that are in the world. If any man loves the world, the love of the father is not in him. Wow, I know some, one said he wished he could live here another hundred years. He had it is so good, and he loved his Ranch, and the outdoors, etc. Yes, God made the world, but those who are saved are looking for our savior to return for us to take us to a better place, and everyone hasn't had life so great, many, many have struggled in life and are looking for that blessed hope where in dwells righteousness. You see if you're content here why look there (Heb. 11:39–40, see Heb. 11:10 to 16). These are all simple, basic teachings of Christ. "They will know you are my disciple by the love you have one toward another" (John 13:35).

It is very, very crucial how we draw the line of right and wrong in this life. We have one opportunity in life and when life is stopped, by an accident or by natural causes or however we go out into eternity to meet God. We will want to number 1 most of all be 100 percent ready. Again, the Bible tells of the rich man in Luke 16:19. Looking up into heaven but those in heaven will not see in hell for that would be sorrow and the Bible says they'll be no more sorrow and I'm sure you've heard over the years, where someone's love one's died, and they'd say oh I really feel like they are watching over is. No, that sounds real good, but no, it's impossible according to scripture, again that would be more sorrow for them, and once you get to heaven all tears are wiped away, and there will be no more sorrow (Rev. 21:4) (Rev. 15:2). There will be Saints standing on the sea of glass could this possibly be a two-way mirror glass with water on top side standing cooling feet of saints and sinners lost forever in hell, looking up, and seeing the saints of God through it, standing on water…Cooling their feet, standing on what the rich man in hell wants for his tongue in (Luke 16:23–24, Rev. 15:2).

This is all going on, as people that were saved standing on water. On the sea of glass. At the same time people underneath in hell are looking up. "Are you seeing this?" Read (Luke 16 and Rev. 15). And people are partying like they were going to just be excused from all this, only if they repent before Jesus returns for his people. Read (Matthew 25); in fact, Jesus told many examples, in his parables, I've already covered some. Wow, while they are burning in hell and looking up into heaven and seeing loved ones, and even the preacher and might say, hey, ain't that the preacher or look there's, oh John, that looks like grandma that first told me of Jesus. Eyes not seen, nor ears heard (1 Cor. 2:9). It will be worth it to be ready!

(Second Tim. 1:7) says for God has not given us a spirit of fear but of power and love and of a sound mind. I have heard so many preachers preach on love, love, love, hey, love is good and one of the reasons God so loved the world was so we could be saved and make heaven and not go to hell. Spiritual churches preach on hell, or 666, or last days, or the return of Christ and great tribulation warnings that the Bible is so clear on preaching and warning folks to be ready. Yes. Love sermons are great, but if a child wonders in the street. Is there not a parent on this earth that's going to warn and teach them, of the dangers. Yes, so why are so many churches just teaching love only. And leave out the warnings (Ezek. 33:1–6). Sounds like people's blood will be on a lot of preachers' hands, there has to be a balance, or as on a battery, a negative post, and a positive post. It's the Word of God. Yes, there is both! But you'll never hear that from the ear ticklers. But have you notice that society will warn the public of swift dangerous waters and even post warning signs "No Trespassing" "Danger Stay Out" "No Swimming," etc., even have it put on the six o'clock eve, news. Wow…And yet millions die every day around the world and go out into eternity, with or without God, only God knows.

But if you've done any kind of traveling or watch the world news, its sins and crimes are worse now than ever before in the history of this wicked earth, and if you say it's not, you are a liar, and don't know the Bible at all, nor can see the signs of the times because it's time for it to all wrap up according to prophecy…(Rev. 6:12 to 17 and Rev. 20:9) this was to happen to those that were deceived by the devil, that missed the Rapture, and the Return of Jesus Christ. (See verse 10, 1 Pet. 3:20, Luke 21:20 to 36, Matt. 24:15, Matt. 24:29 to 44) and it's all wrapping up folks. I don't understand why so many that say they are Christians, and especially those who say they are ministers and don't see this (2 Tim. 3:5). Again, like the one pastor that told about a movie all through his sermon, I think he read one scripture we had visited there to hear our grandkids sing in the children's choir. Wow...what a disappointment his lukewarm Hollywood sermon was, I don't believe that was from God at all, but whom am I (Romans 14:4).

If he stands or falls it's to God, not me. It's by God's grace any of us are saved. Yes, we need to pray God to revive and restore him. Amen. And even though we are in the LAST DAYS, God still pours out his spirit on his people, and still uses people to bless others. Now what's the chances of you getting this book, at the same time new plagues, homelessness, and crazy ridiculous attacks on the president, etc., is all this a coincidence? No! "Absolutely No"! Read (Revelations 21:7 to 9). It's all prophecy! (Read Matthew 24:34) Wow. A coincidence (No) better think again! It's any time now...so get READY... or stay ready! "Get right so you don't get left"!

And one of the things I wanted to note where we draw the line on things, I wanted to give a pat on the back to minister Ray and Gloria Romero, they loaned us their truck and took us in at a hard time in our life when a promotion fell through. We gave our landlords notice we were transferring out of town. The landlord rented the house out, since we gave him notice that my job was transferring me, and then my job transfer fell through, and now, we had nowhere to go. And this has happened twice, and the love that came from people, even a boss, Romero (a different Romero) who worked me some extra time to where I could move. People that God spoke to, that helped in different ways but I wanted to pat them on the back.

So others would know, good deeds don't go unnoticed. Even in the last days and God will reward those who blessed us. Because when there is nowhere to go, and Bob and Barbara Clark also took us in, and Joel and Sharene Beames, loaned us their travel trailer and Jim and Debra Peterson gave us aid, and help and finances and also Molly Cox and Pastor Donahue Green and First Lady Evon Green at different times. And during some of my surgeries my daughter Melanie and Floyd cooking, etc., and my granddaughter, Trinity and grandsons Josh and Alan came and did many odd jobs. And also helped my wife and so many more folks, I'm sure, and please forgive me if I failed to mention any others, of your kindness too, and acts of love also to us, I tried to remember everyone, and I pray that God will bless you all (hundredfold back to you)! These folks all came to our rescue and helped us, running us around, helping with things only a woman and man of God could know and do.

And taking us in and showing God's love, wow. Going out of their way, miles, I'll never be able to repay their kindness. And acts of love. Thanks to all of you. And thank you, Jesus, for using Pastor Green and Minister James Johnson to confirm my book and Bishop Jakes also. Wow, confirmations amazes me, even in a Bible study. Putting the fiery bush that Moses stood before, and they preached on this on this very topic at the time I'm writing it in my book. Wow, confirmation or what? (Preachers look for confirmations) When I knew they didn't know that I was putting the fiery bush and this explanation also in my book, wow. And bishop Jakes several times mentioning drawing a line between prayer "Wow" he said you associate success with money, draw a line between hope for the prayer which drawing the line part was conformation on my book, thanks bishop.

And thank you, Jesus, for letting these men of God confirm my book to me. I've been blessed by his ministry. And my pastors of course more. And can honestly say so even though I minister for over forty years because even though I've been a pastor, of four different churches, and eighteen and a half years of prison ministry cause (No one knows it all! I have learned and gleaned from this man of God. Cause you still learn more, but you have to always be moldable and teachable, I've seen some that thought they knew it all. They were unteachable, and headed for a fall. I think of this lady at our church, she's about my age Debra Epps went back to school last year and got her doctrine degree, wow...she and her husband Willard are so humble and full of love...And full of God so we can learn if we are teachable and applicable, and moldable.... Even as the clay is in the potter's hands...so is this lady in God's... And this lady packs the anointing "of the Holy Ghost" in her singing and preaching.

I can honestly say I have gleaned and learned from her ministry. And I have received from God through these techniques and manner these men and women of God has released in the spirit. I have watched their style and godly manner and the unique fashion they use and methods, with great anointing gifted by the Holy Ghost which only he can give. Pastor's funerals are so classically done with such pride and elegance with a touch of cool in the spirit, if I am aloud to phrase it that way. Even as you get older and more mature, you still don't know everything there is to know, and if you do ever get to that place that's where the Holy Spirit will back off from teaching you, but as long as we all stay humble, and appliable in the potter's hand (Jer. 18:1 to 6, Rom. 9:20–21). He will continue to teach, mold and instruct us no matter how old we get. I knew a man in his late eighties said he had just learned something new. So we never get to old to learn. The Bible says, we will still bring forth fruit in our old age (Ps. 92:14). And I too have learnt from these men of God, so, "Draw the line, straight and directly to God, and always allow him to teach and instruct you (1 Thess. 2:4, John 16:13, John 14:17 and 26).

Where Do You Draw the Line?

The Bible and Jesus was very clear on how we are to live, from the "beatitudes or the sermon on the mount." straight talk to ones that plan on making it to heaven. Just saying someone made it, or to merely ease others conscience or grief, we are taught by the Lord Jesus and apostles, we must be born again (John 3:3, 5). Jesus said in (Matthew 7:13, 14) enter in at the strait gate (John 14:6) Jesus said he is the way. Jesus said, he was the door, for you to go through. (John 10:1, 7) and (Rev. 3:20) continued at (Matthew 7:13–14). For wide is the gate and broad is the way, that leads to destruction and many there be which go in there at. (Vs. 14) because strait is the gate and narrow is the way which leads to life and few there be that find it. (Folks that's pretty plain, that it's stating just a few is gonna make it into heaven.

So in the scriptures, it doesn't say just because somebody says so and so passed on, even though they've been a good moral, giving, good deed doing, never hurt anybody. Never done anybody wrong kinda person. That doesn't get them in through the pearly gates, you must be born again and had to have ask Jesus Christ to forgive you of all your sins and come into your heart and save your soul. Confess with your mouth to Jesus Christ not man or religion. Turning from your old ways. And begin following Jesus Christ and read and follow Jesus and live according to what the Bible says especially The New Testament and (verse 15), tells us to watch out and beware of false prophets who are in appearance like a sheep but inside they are like a wolf, not just a wolf but a ravening wolf, the kind that would rip you apart (Matt. 7:15).

Pretty plain to me. Where do we draw the line? This world today, some preach so many things. I want to hear lot of scripture.

Myself personally, I want to hear a lot of scriptures, more than someone's stories. We are living in the day and age, that many different opinions and beliefs results in many different religions and many different versions of the Bible. What in this world are all those people gonna say on judgment day? When the Lord asks, why did you change my words, didn't you read that the devil was the one in the very beginning (that changed what I said) when the devil was trying to deceive Adam and Eve, in (Gen. 3), then later in Matthew 4 with Jesus. Yes, the Bible says we all have to work out our own salvation with fear and trembling (Phil. 2:12), but the only thing is that too many versions has been distorted by the anti-fear groups and anti-Christ movement some years back, but there are two types of fears, 1.) a godly respectful fear or 2.) the fear of man and what people think, or even a third fear, 3.) to have a fear of torment which is a spirit from hell (Luke 21:26, Matt. 10:28, 2 Tim. 1:7, 1 John 4:18, Jude 12, Phil. 2:12, Jude 23) just like there are two different spirits that man listens to, God or the devil.

So no matter what comes or goes, we should always try our best to keep a godly fear, and try our best to pray and ask the Holy Ghost to give you understanding of his word, again when I go to church, I want to hear a lot of Bible scriptures (Rom. 10:17). Faith comes by hearing and hearing by the Word of God equals The Bible. And it's impossible to please (God) Him, *without Faith*! (Heb. 11:6, in my words, read it) because He that comes to God, must believe that He is a rewarder of them that diligently (working hard to put out an effort to seek him. Are you getting this?). If you plan on making it to heaven, you must have faith to please GOD! Faith according to *Webster's Dictionary* is to believe/a belief in a Christian religion…To urge, be convinced, to persuade, unquestioning belief in God. To trust in, or have confidence in… We just need to draw the line to where scripture is in it.

Is our scripture life, our weapons, stories are good when kept in their place, but it's the word, "The Bible" that'll keep you when things around you crumble, the Bible is again our weapon (Heb. 4:12, 2 Cor. 10:4–5; Eph. 6:10–18; Ps. 119:11; Ps. 119:105; Matt. 4:4; Rev. 3:22) and anyone taking notes on the subject of repeating…I have a huge list in the back of my Bible on different scriptures on repeats in the Bible, I wrote, after a certain sister at church rebuked me one time for repeating myself, this one's for her. (Look up Revelations 2:7, Revelations 2:11, Revelations 2:17, Revelations 2:29, Revelations 3:6, Revelations 3:13, Revelations 3:22, and Revelations 13:9.) (All say He that has an ear, let him hear what the spirit says to the church.) Some are worded a little differently than others, but then are people really listening and hearing the Word of God? It's no wonder the devil is trying to destroy and water it down…"Because it's your weapon against him," and it's also a road map, with directions on how to make it to heaven. If you don't use and follow it, you don't make it. That's a fact! because for one spirits don't back down to what was seen on a movie but knowing, and learning and quoting scriptures in our prayers, even to ourselves for encouragement, it'll keep us (Ps. 124:2) if it had not been the Lord who was on our side when men rose up against us:

"So shall they fear the name of the Lord from the west and his glory from the rising of the sun when the enemy shall come in like a flood, the spirit of the Lord shall lift up a standard against him" (Isa. 59:19). That's telling me as long as I serve and live for God he's got me in his hand (Ps. 37:24) and when it seems I'm surrounded by problems of this life or when the devils been pouncing on me the Lord will lift up a barrier against him (the devil, the enemy, Isa. 59:19). Those that are in Christ are protected and are taught in the Bible such as Daniel in the Lion's Den, three Hebrews in the fiery furnace. At our times of our lion's den in our trials, we constantly wonder why God? Why are you allowing this? Yet we read how God delivered Daniel said, and Daniel said "God has sent his angel, and he has shut the lion's mouth and they have not hurt me." Yes, we can quote scriptures in our prayers. And shut the lion's mouth, prayer, yes prayer goes with quoting those scriptures.

Praying in Jesus's name and trying with all the faith we can to believe, but when we question God that brings in disbelief and doubt. And that according to scripture frustrates God. Gospel-Christian music plays a big part in helping a Christian Live a successful Christian Life, and this is even told in scripture (Eph. 5:19) which is told by most ministers to encourage folks. It helps ya on your walk with God, I had to lay down the Rock and Roll, now it's Gospel music is better for the soul. Yeah, we know Fred. You've been on both sides of that their fence pilgrim. HA. Just makes ya wanna go slap yer ol' mule…HA…What? you don't have one…okay…stop the presses, go get one, we'll wait…HA.

Hey, I maybe a fanatic for God, but I'm not dead…I still got a sense of humor. Okay, I'll quit, Hey…It's my book…okay. And I hope God don't never get upset or frustrated at ol' Fred, cause I've got a truck-load of Humor in me, had an ol' Gal meet me in the back of the First Church I pastored on what God could turn us into, of all things poop a pillar of salt, fish food, or food for lions or even burnt at the steak and she snarled at me in this real cranky voice and said as she stormed out the door, saying, Pastor Fred, Levitty has no place in the House of God…and away she stomped, I looked at my wife and said, well. Guess we won't see her no more, about two weeks later she invited us over for dinner, HA guess her conscience was bothering her…HA. But I wasn't trying to be funny…the sermon just came out that way, it was on Jonah and the whale, and I explained how my dad caught this catfish, we had put in it this floating net stringer, and it was real windy and the water was real choppy, the fish barfed up his lunch from a day or two ago…this tiny perch he ate he was bleached completely white, no markings and no scales, it was bleached off, I said the acids in his belly just about dissolved him and explained to the church, after you eat corn or especially nuts, a day or two you notice it…it passes through ya.

Quick, well my point was your digestive system sends acid to dissolve your food and Jonah was like that cat fish's, lunch, Jonah was in The Whales belly three days (Matt. 12:40) before he prayed, and was puked up (Jonah 2:10) Notice the analogy, that God intended, so it would be more effective to Nineveh so if Jonah look like that, catfish's lunch of a bleached white leprosy-looking-small type perch, bleached from the stomach acids…and was almost dissolved into fish poop. I read in one commentary by Warren Wiersbe that stated, God was after Jonah to get him right with God, so Jonah could deliver the message to Nineveh, and God wanted Jonah to repent, as well as the Ninevites, because God even loved those vicious Ninevites as well as Jonah. One commentary said the whale wasn't a whale, but a huge fish, but Jesus Christ in (Matthew 12:40) said Jonah was three days and three nights in the whale's belly...so I'll believe Jesus, over anyone else, at any case, if they strain their food through their teeth or not, as some say, and some say whale's don't eat people, but the fact remains, and the point here is, God prepared it for the very purpose, of swallowing Jonah, and it was a swift swimmer, and swam the distance from Tarshish/Joppa area to Nineveh, as I said earlier, one commentary said it was over 5,666 miles by boat and another one said, as the crow flies about 2,500 miles plus the six hundred extra miles that he went in the opposite direction.

At any case, Jonah traveled all that way in the belly of a whale, Wow... That whale was really moving to make that distance in three days, but I'll stick to flying by jet, thank you. Amen. Again, for a whale to travel and to be so accurate and precise to where he needed to spit Jonah out at...it was the exact the precised place that God had intended the whale to spit Jonah out at, is so amazing, but unlike man, the whale was obeying the voice of his creator. I always wondered why Jonah took three days to pray and God must have kept him in a sack of air, cause you'd a thought he would have ran out of oxygen, but again, it was all orchestrated by God. This ol' boy, Fred would have been calling on God before I was in his mouth... but God draws man's heart to him, according to the Bible, it says, in (John 6:44). So God must have not dealt with his heart till the third day...giving the whale traveling time, Wow, traveled by whale, was their seatbelts in there...Ha.

I read this other one that I looked up, that said, he thought Jonah took time to clean up on the way (Yeah, right). like Jonah had money, and a suitcase of clothes with him...Ha. What a lie. The whole point of this amazing story was, again, that the whales acids bleached him, and half dissolved his clothes and hair, for a more effectiveness on the Ninevites...Amen, well, go read the story yourself and pray for God to explain it to you...moving on and God said, "Now, I said go warn the people of Nineveh, if they don't get saved and turn from their sinful ways," etc. Then (God) said I will destroy them…but what I said that everyone laughed at was, I said, it was a good thing Jonah prayed when he did, after three days, he could have been whale poop if he had not obeyed God's voice, but once Jonah finally prayed and quit running from God, and obeyed and did what God said for him to do, then God took care of Jonah, but many times like with Jonah running away from God, God sends some stop signs, and wake-up calls, and attention getters, yes, God knows just how to wake us up out of this is my life kind of thinking, and I'm an adult now and I'll live like I want to, you ain't my boss, you can't tell me what to do, not knowing that rebellion is the sin of witchcraft (Sam. 15:23 Jer. 28:16, 1). Hey, Jonah, can you explain this to today's stubborn mule headed generation that, God'll get their attention even the hard way, welcome to the school of hard knocks, been there, done that, cause God's gonna smack you a good one… you may as well just give up, especially if someone's pray-n for ya. So we must keep on believing if not today then tomorrow.

Just don't stop believing, God told Paul his grace is sufficient for him (you) and God won't allow more on us than what you can bear, but will make a way of escape (1 Cor. 10:13). It's scripture that'll help you through. Like, (Ps. 119:105) thy word is a lamp unto my feet and a light unto my path. My sisters (Lana and Sharene) can tell you some stories, way before my prodigal son days, as a kid, our Christian mother used the Bible, quoting it especially in times of trouble or emergency, she even prayed for cars, washer, etc. It flowed out of her but she always prayed in Jesus's name for everything she prayed for (John 14:13–14) The Bible scriptures would flow out of her mouth (Ps. 119:11) because it was planted deep in her soul by her mother and so on. Like the times like, when I fell on a Curtin Rod, but for me doctors who could afford them. So Mom prayed. We saw a lot of miracles. Mom put a compress of wash cloths on my wound, and call for her Bible, and prayed while holding the compress against my leg.

We just couldn't afford a doctor, so mom would read (Ezekiel 16:6), three times while praying, and it stopped the bleeding, when my two brothers cut off their finger. My Uncle Ed was over and he got a popsicle stick and tape it to my brother's finger, and mom and the family and uncle Edward gathered in prayer around mom's bed and quoted that word and prayed the glory of God down on my brother, and a few hours later. It looked like his finger had been stitched up by a doctor. (Dr. Jesus Christ) Amen. So that same word (Bible) that God spoke light into existence with, will also keep us in our life, being a light to our path (Ps. 119:105 and Ps. 119:89 or Ps. 119:11). "Forever O Lord, thy word is settled in heaven. Thy word have I hid in mine heart. That I might not sin against thee. So the line here is a dependency upon God's Word that will keep us in check with God (Rom. 8:1), there is therefore now, no condemnation to them that are in Christ Jesus, who walk not after the flesh but after the spirit. So if you are living in your flesh 100 percent of the time your gonna constantly feel under the condemning finger of your conscience and hammered by the devil but if you're in Christ then you're not under condemnation, but skip down to (Rom. 8:11).

But if the spirit of him that raised up Jesus from the dead, dwell in you, he that raised up Christ from the dead shall also quicken your mortal bodies by his spirit that dwelleth in you. His spirit and his word hid in your heart will keep you in check. The Bible says in (Daniel 6:3) that Daniel was preferred above the other presidents and princess because of an excellent spirit that was in him and the king thought to set him over the whole realm. Now no one is perfect, the Bible plainly teaches, there is none righteous no not one (Rom. 3:10). The only ones that are even close is those that have that excellent spirit in them, are those that have the Holy Spirit so it's not by any ones works, but it's that gift of the Holy Spirit and it's a whosoever will let him come (Rev. 22:17, Ps. 37:37). Mark the perfect man and behold the upright for the end of that man is peace.

Wow, to have been in Daniel's shoes, animals sense when someone is evil like those evil guys that tricked Daniel, and deceived the king, with their evil petition, but those bad evil men and their families were ate up by the lions. So they reaped what they sowed. (Daniel 6:24). Plus. (First Chronicles 16:22 and Psalm 105:15) says, don't touch God's anointed prophets and don't do no harm to them. Well, these evil devils were doing that and more, sounds like people at my place of work. Wow, don't care who you stab in the back, as long as you get promoted up the latter of success, lie, cheat, steal, scheme, plot, plan your way to hell... I mean, well you get my point, our day is worse than Daniels, we've all seen it, but we bind and rebuke these devils in Jesus's name, Lord we pray you deliver them and open their eyes to see, they are attacking your anointed people of God, and open their eyes to the truth of God.

Show them the way to you in Jesus's name. Amen. And these at my work were of a different religion, like those religious Pharisees that constantly attack Jesus, blinded by religion and too stupid to even realize the very one their attacking could save their soul, and take them to heaven. Because people that's right in their heart don't attack others, but it was because they want to get drunk, and cheat on their wives, etc., and Jesus stood against that, and so did I...thus bringing on their attacks of Hate (Matt. 5:11, 12; John 15:20, 21; John 5:16; Ps. 35:7, 8; Luke 11:53, 54; Ps. 141:8 to 10; Ps. 9:15; Prov. 11:5 and 6; John 10:12 and 13). Again, God does not want religious people, but he wants people that will be obedient (Luke 6:46) to him and his word (Bible) and God wants to have a one-on-one personal relationship with each one of us, and that we will confess our sins to Jesus Christ (not to a man...or Idol, or a dead saint (1 Tim. 2:5). We have only one mediator between God and man, that's Jesus Christ! (Heb. 12:24) My point is this, according to scripture, God takes it personal, when an evil hearted, mean spirited person comes against a preacher or prophet of God or even an ordinary Christian that lives for God.

Like those in (Acts 9), Saul was killing Christians cause the 6th commandment says not to kill and these bright Pharisees was suppose to know the mosaic law, and ten commandments, and, the Lord took it personally, saying, why are you persecuting me. Well, the Lord, saved Saul who later was named Paul and as a punishment and a wake-up call, God made (Saul) Paul blind. (Saul later changed his name to Paul, if you were confused there.) Anyway, the Lord blinded him for three days. Then used a devoted man of God named Annanias to lay hands on him, and he was healed, then the spiritual and physical eyes of Paul were opened. So God does use situations many times, to call people into ministry or saved them from God destroying them for attacking his anointed people. Like in (Acts.

139

5:39), "But if it be of God, you cannot overthrow it, lest happily you be found even to fight against God." And this is the thing that people don't realize, that a religion can get you destroyed by God, so we need to be sure, and know that we know, that we know, in who we believe. Number 1, God's not gonna tell you to throw people to the lions, and number 2, that pride of power, will also get God mad at you, because it plainly says, all power belongs to God (Rom. 13:1 and 2 and Ps. 62:11) (1 Pet. 5:11, to 13) (Matt. 28:18 to 20) and the attitude behind people of evil power are usually destroyed and sent to hell, it's all written in the Bible, wicked king after wicked King, like even Jezebel after the Prophet Elijah, the dogs ate her, just like it was prophesied, because she came against God's anointed prophet Elijah.

So live for God. He's got your back. Good always prevails over evil. Even if Daniel had been the lions' breakfast, he would have still it made it to heaven, but for the sake of the reader knowing, God still delivers from lions and other things and also punishes those who go against his prophets (Acts 5:39; 2 Pet. 2:7, 9, 3:3–10)! Wow... But again, he would have still made heaven but the Bible teaches, God's face is against those who commit evil (Ps. 34:16), which explains (Rev. 6:16 and 17). And again you may feel many times in your life, like your about to be eaten alive in your own lion's den of your situations but know this, if Daniel was never in his Lion's den, he and us would not ever know God still delivers from Lion's dens and he is the same yesterday, today and forever (Heb. 13:5 to 8 see verse 6). About five years ago I was face to face with two cougars and believe you me. You want God's undivided attention, in wrecks, earthquakes, tornado's (knowing) you can call on God, knowing your on his side of the line, makes all the difference but remember others that watch in Daniels case even the kings and the same with the three Hebrew children.

As with you, others are watching your life, how you come through, your lion's den or fiery furnace. And will be witnessed to by how we did on the Lord's side of the line. When God delivered us. Some folks God wants us to witness to, others, God just wants us to be a light around them. There are many people that you just can't get through to, it is gonna take an act of God to convince and show some. And of course even back in the days of Christ, he told us even then, that there were those who just don't want to hear it and will not believe (John 16:2, Luke 11:49 and 50, Luke 21:12 see verse 13). Two different times. I tried talking about how the Lord changed my life, by witnessing to them about the Lord and the Bible both times, to two different carpet cleaning companies. We got to talking, one was real bitter over the death of his mother. The next time, we had one other cleaner in to shampoo, this guy had been in a half a dozen different religions and had studied the Coran (Eph. 4:14–18, Gal. 1:7–9, 1 Tim. 1:3, 1 Tim. 4:1).

Eastern mysticism, Hindu, and one of the ones, was the lost books of the Bible and another one was Islam, and another one was some weird religion where Samuel was supposed to be a God and had an affair with Eve. What kinda of stuff are people getting into and believe a lie and be damned. The Bible says in (2 Thessalonians 2:10, 11, 12) and one other man said He still smokes pot, and he enjoys studying about all types of religions (And I saw a red flag) just listening to him, He didn't sound convinced of any. But he was doing all kinds of mind games, but He's about to get possessed of the devil. And I feel like He was just messing with me. There will be (1 Tim. 4:1, doctrines of devils), and they will depart from the faith (backslide), giving heed to seducing spirits and doctrines of devils. People are blind, and gullible.

They don't want to hear the truth. Just junk, fables, lies, etc. And so much fiction, etc. (verse 2, speaking lies in hypocrisy, having their conscience seared with a hot iron.) I remember the cowboy movies, where the tuff cowboy was snake bit. And made a cut and sucked out the poison, and seared the wound shut with a branding iron. (Yeah, right.) Ha. But you get the point, Apostle Paul was saying, that people sear their conscience. And that's so true today.

So many people don't seem to even have a conscience. They kill and rob you without blinking an eye. This guy reminded you in ways that he acted, kind of, like the man (legion) In (Mark 5:9–15), after Jesus was done with the naked man who was in the graveyard, cutting himself, Jesus cast the devils out of him. And he was sitting, calm, and had clothes on, and in his right mind. Wow. And God wants to restore and deliver every troubled, hurting person on earth. They just need to call on Jesus. And ask Jesus to forgive them and he will (1 John 1:7 to 9, Rom. 10:13, Rom. 10:9–10, John 3:3–5). Then the being born of the spirit process begins. And God starts restoring mind, body, and soul. I want to make a point that I should have made back in the story of Jonah. The Bible says in many places, and one is in the Old Testament (Jonah 3:10) that God repented of the evil he was gonna do to that wicked city of Nineveh (if they didn't repent). so my point is, what I was saying about that was that we need to also, always be repentive (24–7) because if God himself repented, wow…are we exempt? No, no, no…no matter how good or righteous or holy we think we are, and I don't care who you think you are, if God repents, then so should you, and me! Amen, yes, amen! Because there are many people in our world today, because of drugs and running from God, they end up like this man (full of devils).

This man's mind was so full of lies and false doctrine, he was almost reprobate in the mind (legion) come to my thoughts. Once he was delivered, and was in his right mind, why I seem to always get to witness to ones off the deep end. All I can think of, on that is I'll plant the seed. God's gotta send him someone more knowledgeable on wicked, occults, and false doctrines, as it says in (Galatians 1:6 to 10, 1 Timothy 4:1 and 2, Colossians 2:8, 1 Timothy 1:3 and 4, Ephesians 4:14, Hebrews 13:9, 2 Timothy 4:3 and 4, 1 Corinthians 3:6). So someone else can water the seed I planted in his heart. Wow, I finally got to add before his ninety-five mystical religion comments and said, I'll settle for the KJV Bible and Jesus Christ, two hours. Later he cleans my carpet…whew…This is why, I try to tell people be careful what you listen to and read, learn the Bible. I would pick different topics usually on prophecy, coming of Christ, etc., each time.

Here comes a false doctrine, wow, this guy was so brain washed and deceived. But again, the Bible teaches in the last days, this will happen. Like those that believe you can kill a multitude of people and yourself too and become an emperor in heaven: talk about lies and false doctrine. Many people like this guy that cleaned my carpet, was so brain washed from so many false doctrines, and believing you can kill others and without repenting of it, and he was killed also, and really believed he'd still make heaven, overlooking, scriptures like (James 4:17 and Romans 6:12, 13, 14, 15, 16, 19, 23; 1 John 1:5 to 10; Hebrews 10:26; Romans 6:1 and 2; Hebrews 12:25; 2 Corinthians 5:17; Proverb 15:32). For he that refuses instruction, despises his own soul (Isa. 5:13–24, Isa 6:9–13, 2 Chron. 7:14, Matt. 18:23–35, Matt. 24:48–51—wow—or 2 Cor. 5:11, 1 Cor. 10:21 and 22) and even (Matthew 4:5–7) and, most of all, (Luke 6:46).

But to even think like some of those cults, that you can murder someone, and die while committing it, and believe you'll still go to heaven without repenting, and they think they'll become an emperor or king type over a certain part of heaven is 100 percent lies and false doctrine. This is that strong delusion, in (2 Thessalonians 2:10–12), to believe a lie and then be damned (They get sent to hell) It just ain't worth it. Wow. Is those folks deceived? "What was it about thou shalt not kill, didn't they understand? Again, the 6th command of the ten commandments in (Exodus 20:13) says, "Thou shalt not kill"!!! Understand this, the devil doesn't care who he tricks and deceives, he's doomed and wants to take as many as he can, with him (Rev. 12:10–12; Rev. 20:10 to 15; 2 Cor. 11:3 and verses 13, 14, and 15; John 8:44).

The scripture in (Matthew 25:41) says in the last of the verse "The everlasting fire, was prepared for the devil and His angels: hell or lake of fire (Rev. 20:10 to 15, And the devil that deceived them was cast into the LAKE OF FIRE and Brimstones) where the beast (Anti-Christ dictator, in my words) and the false prophet are, and shall be tormented day, and night, forever and ever (vs. 15). And whosoever was not found written in the Book of Life, was cast into the Lake of FIRE. There are millions of people today that think God was lying about hell. Wrong! For it is impossible for God to lie (Heb. 6:18, Titus 1:2) And yes, hell was originally made for the devil and his angels (Matt. 25:41, Isa. 5:14). The Bible says, hell has gotten larger is it because of more people that are living in sin today? Cause (Ps. 9:17) says, "The Wicked shall be turned into hell, and *all the nations* that *forget GOD*." So always remember God and thank him for everything. But the sad part of it all is (Luke 16:23) while being in hell burning, you're also seeing everyone in heaven, and everything that's a happy life, and all those who told you about Jesus dying for your sins, standing on the sea of Glass (standing on water, cooling their feet, Rev. 15:2) Are you serious? While they are burning forever in their heavenly eternal body, that will never die again and seeing their loved ones, and friends, singing, walking around on water, and walking on the streets of Gold, seeing everything in heaven while burning in hell forever.

Wow, but you see…as of right now, everyone on this earth has the same opportunity and privilege to call on Jesus Christ for salvation, until that heavenly trumpet sounds, there is still time, to say, Jesus, I've sinned, forgive me of all my sins and come into my heart and save me, in Jesus's name. I receive you into my heart as my Lord and Savior. Thank you for dying on the cross for my sins. Thank you for saving me in Jesus's name, amen (John 3:3, 5; Rom. 10:9, 10, 13; 1 John 1:5 to 10). So simple to just believe and call upon his name. So always remember God and thank him for everything, especially for his Son Jesus (John.3:16–19; Luke 16:23, 24). So as we read these verses in (Luke 16:23 and 24), we can understand that God still wants people to still know that there is indeed a real hell, and people do suffer and burn in torment there forever… And frankly, I'm so sick and tired, of all these religious drunks, that say God is a God of love, He wouldn't send anyone to hell (Oh no, oh really…) you send yourself, for not following the Bible, and God just helps you get there, because you rejected God's Word and His Son Jesus Christ! Why is it in the KJV Bible (Luke 16:19 to 31) it's an actual real live place and live event, cause He used names, Lazarus, and Moses! And even in (Revelations 20:10 to 15) the Antichrist world dictator is sent there and (Revelations 14:9 to 11).

So again why does the KJV Bible say this? And you won't hear this in the mega churches, and they won't tell you about prophecy or end time events now happening or about hell, and they won't explain that the Bible teaches that in hell the five senses are still working in full operation touch, see, hear, taste and smell and you're in the new heavenly body as well, that will never ever die which could have been living up in heaven forever, living in paradise, but instead, that rich man, along with others, got tricked by the devil and so there they'll burn, forever looking up into heaven, seeing everyone they know, and just hoping like he did in (Luke 16, verse 28), that those still alive back on earth won't come to that Horrible place. Where you burn forever, unlike those in heaven, but you will burn forever while looking into heaven forever, wow, they don't preach that in them ear ticking love churches. But it's the true Word of God. Yes (John 3:16–19) preachers of the love churches just stick with (John 3:16) And fail to cover the other three verses, but you go ahead and read them.

There always should be a balance. Yes, God is a God of love. Yes, that's why God sent Jesus to die a horrible death on the cross with all the mockers and persecutors, etc. But don't leave out "Why He Died" And what the next three verses say! Nobody likes what's in the last part of (John 3:18 and 19). In Romans 8:1, those that are in Christ aren't condemned... The word condemn in the original Greek says the word *Kri-no*, which means damned...Sentenced, and judged) The scripture says The rich man already noticed in (Luke 16:27–28). But He's concerned about his five brothers so his memory is working good and, also being very thirsty, the rich man in hell begging God to cool his tongue with just a drop of water, in (Luke 16:24), so this scripture tells me even a new heavenly body, will crave water, when burning in intensive heat, this means this spiritual body God gives to all that goes to heaven and hell. The ones in hell will be feeling and seeing, experiencing pain and agonizing and even memory as in (verse 25), many scholars believe this is what the scripture means where the worm dies not. Your memory always eating at your mind.

Remembering and seeing those in heaven that tried to warn you about hell, and that the return of the Lord was near. But the world and wealth blinded the eyes and mind and he thought he had plenty of time. But those that go to heaven, will not see into hell because that would be sorrow. Plus, God will want those in hell to see those in heaven having a fantastic time forever throughout all eternity (1 Cor. 2:9). Eyes not seen, nor ear heard, neither has entered into heart of man, the things God has prepared for them that love him (Rev.

21:4). And God shall wipe away all tears from their eyes (maybe bad memories) and there shall be no more death, neither sorrow (told you). Nor crying, neither shall there be any more pain. (Wow.) For the former things are passed away.

So in heaven it'll be worth it all but in hell. People will live with regret, and pain and agony forever. Non-stop torments forever (Luke 16:23, 24) (Rev. 14:10, Rev. 14:11) and (Rev. 20:10 to 15)! Are you seeing any of this in your spirit, when you read Luke 16, and the rich man was tormented forever (Rev. 14:11). See verse 13, This is the opposite for the Christian (vs. 12) says) and again (verse 13). The Christian receives rest from their labors and (vs. 11) says those sinners that received the "Mark of the Beast," (or in my words) = (the micro-chip) burn forever, and "the smoke of their torment ascends up forever, and ever. Ya know that doesn't sound like a party to me, as I've heard so many of those spineless, mocking, sinning backslidders say, and…they won't be smoking no medical marijuana for their pain either. It'll be the nightmares of all nightmares, it'll pay us all to pray and stay ready to go be with Jesus (Rev. 20:10 to 15) and again both type people receive a heavenly body (Christians and sinners), and those who go to hell, cause the sinners are gonna burn forever and ever…but the saints, the believers, the born-again Christians that are blood bought saints of God, hallelujah!

Are all gonna have a new heaven body (as in, Mark 16:12, Luke 9:29) and no one I know, has ever commented on this one of Jesus, (taking on another form), as in (Daniel 3:25) (John 6:62) where Jesus comments, "what and if ye see the son of man ascend up where he was before?" (Acts 1:9, 10, 11) Wow Read (1 Cor. 15:50–56). But when our molecular structure of our human fleshly body is completely changed from our flesh form of blood and bone and skin, and changed into that heavenly spiritual body, as Jesus showed and demonstrated in the fiery furnace, or as in (Luke 24:31) and on the Mount of transfiguration (Matt. 17:2) (Mark 9:3), then and only then, will God's people finally fully grasp the full understanding of that heavenly body's form and power of it's true effectiveness against the elements etc. etc. (1 Cor. 15:54), as in (Daniel 3:25) Wow. (Phil. 3:21, 1 Cor. 15:44, 2 Cor. 5:2, 1 Cor. 15:50–58) see (vs. 55–57, Rev.

21:1–4). former things are passed away (Isa. 25:8 and 1 Cor. 15:54). Death is swallowed up in victory for the Christian. Thank God, if you recall reading about Jesus Christ's Transfiguration. Jesus showed the disciples (his resurrection power and his spiritual heavenly body, with Moses and Elijah (Luke 9:29–36) I really honestly believe when the disciples saw all of this supernatural stuff going on, they had to be very freaked out, because if a person isn't in the spirit, thinking spiritually because our flesh just don't comprehend spiritual manifestations, according to (1 Corinthians 2:14). In our day and time, someone would have probably said, okay, who slipped me a mickey. Amen (Col. 3:4, 1 Thess. 4:13 to 18, 1 John 3:2–3).

They saw his glorified state, and heard him say that he would die and rise again, for the sins of the world...but the demonstration of his transfiguration: on Jesus demonstrating his power over life and death (as in, John 11:23–44, Luke 9:29 to 36, Matt. 17:2–3) to transform his earthly body into his heavenly body. Wow. Would have been something to see. Again, up on the mountain of Transfiguration, Jesus's demonstration went right over the top of the disciples head and they saw Jesus's power over death and life...that supernatural power over life and death...with Moses and Elijah there also, either you believe it or you don't. Remember (John 20:24–25) ol' doubting Thomas said unless I put my finger into the print of the nails, and put my hand into Jesus' side I won't believe, but Peter, James and John saw the transfiguration, and was still wondering about it, if it was for real, and I might caution you skeptics, you must truly believe it all...or be left behind!

As my pastor, Donahve Green has stated so many times, you can't be half pregnant, you are or you ain't. Don't you waver, as the man told Jesus Christ when Jesus was praying for him, Lord, help mine unbelief (Mark 9:23–24). And I also like, where Jesus said, "What if you see me ascend back up where I was before" (John 6:62, John 17:5) Wow (Heb. 12:1–2) Look to Jesus...Remember we need to keep our eyes on Jesus, and walk as close as you can, and quit worrying about what people say. I am amazed at so many that stay out of church, some come when it's convenient, wow, and they are expecting for God to let their lukewarm butts in his heaven (They need to read, Rev. chapter 2 and chapter 3) (Matt. 25). Lukewarm casual worldly so-called saints, don't make it, except they repent, of their deeds, and return to their first love. Not my words, I didn't write the Bible, though I did paraphrase for you wise guys that wanna fuss at me (Just go read those two chapters for yourself.) on the promises of God and read them out of KJV.

Again, we have the promises of God, that he's gonna provide for us as heirs (Rom. 8:9–17) and let's not forget that promise of a mansion, in heaven (John 14:1–3) KJV and he said he (Jesus) would come again and get us (that believe in him) and again, receive our new heavenly body, and take us back with him, to a prepared heavenly home. But back to my main point here is whether you choose heaven or hell, the new body you will get will be a supernatural heavenly body that will never die, in heaven or hell. These bodies is an eternal body, that the Christian will need it to travel through outer space through to another dimensional time zone to where heaven is at, traveling at warp speed of light through to the eternal time zone, that's in the third heaven (2 Cor. 12:2), which is in another dimension somewhere in the universe, if it's through a black hole, or a worm hole in deep space, or if it's just up where the twenty-two-thousand-mile atmosphere line separates, outer space from our blue sky, only God knows, but one thing is for sure that we learn from the Bible, and that is, flesh and blood (see verse 50 of 1 Cor. 15). The human fleshly body can't go into it (1 Cor. 15:53–54) see (verses 51 and 52).

This body will be changed to a spiritual body (not a ghost) a ghost doesn't eat fruit, as in (Revelations 22:2). Also read (1 Corinthians 15:50) again. Flesh and blood can't enter into heaven period. You must be changed…as Jesus told Nicodemus in (John 3:1 to 5), you must be born again…changed, that supernatural happening thing that takes place in your soul when you repent and get saved. It's like a rocket fuel for the Christian, because, when Jesus returns for all us Christians, that we call the rapture of the church the catching away caught up, to meet the Lord in the air, again, this old human body is not going, but within a twinkle of an eye (1 Cor. 15:52) at the last trump ("We'll be changed"). Notice it folks, at the last trump of that trumpet blast (1 Thess. 4:16, 1 Cor. 15:52) so that tells me there is gonna be more than one (blast of the trumpet) and then this corruptible old flesh is gonna be changed in the twinkle of an eye, "that's quicker than a blink or a wink," at any case, it'll be fast (verse 52) and the dead in Christ will rise first, then we (Christians that are alive and remain, will be caught up with our Lord, and will be changed into our new heavenly body, to meet our Lord, and will be caught up together in the air, to be *with our Lord* (1 Thess. 4:17) Hallelujah. Wow…

Again, though people in hell have that same heavenly body that will not disintegrate (burn up) cause God's Word don't lie. But that heavenly body was feeling pain from the fire and he (the rich man in hell, Luke 16:23) saw Lazarus (He was seeing the dead Christian beggar) that sat begging at his front gate, in heaven the whole time, so then he realizing after his talk with the Lord. Hey, don't let my five brothers come into this place of torment, let that guy come back from the dead and scare them straight (Luke 16:27–28). So they'll make heaven, but it's not that easy. The Lord said no. They have Moses and the Prophets. If they won't hear them or (in my words=preachers Roman 10:14 "how will they hear without a preacher") preachers then they would not be persuaded (2 Cor. 5:11) though one rose from the dead. They'd probably think or they'd say they've been drugged or was dreaming, etc. (in my words).

It's sad, this is not preached from very few pulpits, especially the mega churches. I preached. This very subject in Arkansas and afterwards the pastor came up and apologized to the church. It was a huge and wealthy type of church that had big pillars out front. Well-to-do folks. All those from that church, if they don't make it to heaven, their blood will be on that pastor's hands (Ezek. 3:18–21, Ezek. 33:6, to 8, Matt. 23:14). This pastor was wrong. I think He was afraid some wealthy parishioners would get mad and leave and he'd lose money. Not thinking about, was God offended at him? (Ezek. 33:6, Heb. 10:31, 2 Cor. 5:11) Their blood will be on that Pastor's hands, according to scripture and Jesus Christ, he even said it'll be more tolerable for the city of Nineveh (Matt. 12:41–42) also (verses 39, 40). Remember in (John 2:13–16, 1 Pet. 4:17–18) that Jesus drove out the money changers out of church with a whip over money and their animals, and I was trying to save souls out of hell...oh yes...God was very ticked off with this false shepherd, and it was very obvious.

Note: (Verse 41 of Matt. 12) a city that God was ready to destroy and they repented and so when God saw their hearts and lives were changed, he spared them and did not destroy them, yes, he changed his mind. So this story of Moses and the prophets, was told to the rich man in hell. Even though this kinda of message may not be preached anymore, it's so far, still in a lot of Bibles. But the devil is trying to change those cause since the beginning of time, he's tried to change what God has said. Taking away, and adding to and no one sees this going on, just amazes me.

Where Do We Draw the Line?

It is evident, everyone says and thinks they are going to heaven. Yet. Jesus said, many are called yet only a few are chosen, why? Our life-styles maybe (Heb. 11:25, Heb. 11:5–6), Moses chose to live with the people of God even though it meant being persecuted, he chose God over the world. He could have been living like a king. If our life is not pleasing to God or doing and following his word (Bible) we will not make it. Some people live double life's, and play the harlot life becoming a hypocrite, which is a stink in God's nostrils, however, those that live a uncompromised life which deny those ungodly lusts of the flesh, are a sweet smelling savor to God. I smelt a homeless mans stinky body odor, that was a Christian, that had a kind heart in living for God, which gave off a-real-good attitude, which that is a smelling fragrance to God. Some folks have criticized me with a ugly attitude…over the years, on me having on way too much musk cologne, not knowing of my circumstance of having metal implants in my back, and I was using (stinky muscle) roll-on-ointment, at the time, so I put on extra cologne to mask the stinky ointment smell and many people do that spiritually. Speaking by putting on a big act to cover their sins, but only the blood of Jesus can cover up our sins (Isa. 1:18) (1 John 1:7) (Rev. 1:5) amen. But for Moses. It got rough, for Daniel it got rough, for the three Hebrew children it got rough, etc. We may have some rough times but we have God to turn to for help. The evil people of the world do not! This false pastor was out for the money…not trusting in God, not believing God'll take care of him, as in (Matthew 6:33) or (Philippians 4:19) and worrying about people more than a message sent by God. Jesus taught this in his parables in (Luke 12:15–34). Read it. So many inmates even people I have pastored and worked with on the job over those thirty-five years, have said they don't believe the whole Bible. Some have admitted they feel more love should be preached, less damnation, more blessings, more prosperity, more about heaven.

This is the whole reason the people way back then made the Golden Calf and all the other idols and some lied and said their idol fell down from Jupiter, the great goddess Diana (Acts 19:24, 35) ha. Or saying it jumped out of the fire, what a joke. People make something with their own hands and then bow down and pray to it. Wow, and they call me stupid. (Exodus 32:24, see vs. 4 and 8) is what really angered God, they lied and said the Golden Calf that came out of the Fire was the god that brought them out of Egypt bondage, when God heard that and saw them worship and sacrifice to it, it angered God (verse 8). This is the kind of thing that has caused the wrath of God on people for centuries. Yet it still continues.

Even today, let's see what was it that was said to that man in hell. They have Moses and the prophets let your brothers hear what they have to say, but again did they? No, are they today, hearing preachers? No…some, but people are turning a deaf ear. At the most crucial and most critical time of the world, last days. End time generation when everything's about to unfold. You wonder will people really keep waiting, till islands sink and mountains all fall flat like Revelations says. What is gonna bring that end time revival, Jesus said he'll return as a thief in the night. Christ also was saying for us to keep watching that if the man of the house had been watching, he wouldn't of got his valuables stolen. This is an analogy of the return of Christ, coming back to get his people, he said those that watch and pray will be ready to go with him to heaven (Luke 21:34–36, Matt. 24:42–51).

Our soul is priceless and more valuable than stuff (Luke 12:15 to 21). So Jesus Christ is so plain to illustrate this type of example, that one certain young lady told me, that this kinda talk always depressed her, for the real Christian that is ready to go and watching and praying like Jesus said, it's a joyful time, to hear its almost time to go to heaven, to have a new body, to live forever. All the negative, last days, end time, scriptures just connect the positive with negative and you have power. If the positive post, on your car battery doesn't have ground or a negative post. There is no power, and it is so in the spiritual realm as well. Such as the forces of Good and evil. There has always been a balance, between man and the devil, and that's God. These trues in the Bible just point the way, that we are just a little closer to Christ's return and the whole reason this little lady always got upset at these topics is because she was not living right and her conscience was checking her and made her very uncomfortable. And yet, let her trade places with the rich man in hell for one minute, and we all know she would change her way of thinking at the blink of an eye. The Bible says, on the day of judgment day, the books will be opened (sixty-six Books of the Bible) and the book of life (Rev. 20:12) were the books that were opened, and in (Mal. 3:16). A book of remembrance, also which most Bible teachers and preachers believe, it's a history, dictation record of your life, from birth to death.

And so many so-called Christians that don't want to hear or discuss these issues because they are like the young lady, it makes them uncomfortable which is good. Anyway, our modern technology is amazing when you really see how advanced we are from the days of chariots and bows and arrows. Now jets, precision radar guided missiles that can take out a city or nation. In one hour (Rev, 18:10–19), man can now, destroy a nation or city in one hour time, when back in Bible days, this type warfare and technology was not even heard of as in (Rev. 18), man or soldier can with radar guided missiles, taken out a city in one hour's time (as in Rev. 18:10–19) especially if it's nuclear, and it just amazes me that I read and see this unfolding in scripture and so many others don't, because if you ask these editors, about my penmanship and spelling, etc. They'll tell you of all the corrections they make. (God bless them all.) Cassy, and pastor Vincent Damiano other names here please if there are others that have corrected all my booboos.

Just ask them, they'll tell ya that I'm not real bright. Just like the pen in my hand, allowing the Lord to use me to write, as bad and sloppy and misspelled as it is. (WA-LA.) God's grace keeps us going, without the Lord directing us all where would we be. So if you do read something that turns the light on, give the Lord the credit, always give God the glory in everything (And these wonderful folks at CFP) Honest to God, these people and God, definitely make me look good. We can open a locked car door by a satellite. We can turn the church lights on by cell phone at home, we can talk on a wireless device to someone around the world. Yet before man ever invented the phone Christians had wireless communication with God called Prayer. Yet most of us never really use it (it's called prayer) until they're trapped in a burning building or in a car wreck in a river with the car filling up with water. Oh yes. And the wireless connection is working well.

Oh, God, please help us. We'll go to church, get me out of this one, I promise, but where's that connection when everything is going well. God still wants to talk, and we are too busy, yes. We go to church, sometimes their body is there, but the mind is on this or that. And not on God. So why do people go to church? Saints are supposed to go there to pray, seek God, worship and receive a word from the man of God. When God is wanting a real thank-you. I love you Lord. I lift my hands to surrender a praise to you. Not just mouthing words or stuff but out of my heart and soul. Saying thank you, Lord, for my Christian heritage. And giving me a praying mama and a praying grandma, as in (2 Timothy 1:9) (see verse 5 to verse 9), (Rom. 8:29). Just the thought of God knowing us before we are in the womb or before we were even conceived is a mind-boggling issue that only a believer that has been forgiven is gonna understand. This is why abortion is so wrong. So are we blind, spiritually speaking? (Matt. 11:25; John 9:39 to 41; Jer. 1:5; Isa. 49:1 to 5; James 4:17; Isa. 43:7; Isa. 44:2, 24; Gal. 1:15; Ps. 71:6; Matt. 13:13 to 15, many people back then didn't see or understand the parables, etc. (Amos 1:13).

And years, and years ago people sneered at Hitler's sins of that great slaughter of all the Jews, yet America has aborted over 250 million babies since 1973, for women's rights and choice, wow, and yet there are scriptures saying God will hold man accountable, and if God plagued kings and kingdoms that did a lot less than America's sins is America exempt from God's wrath, or again is America that nuked nation in (Rev. 18). I believe it is, and God will make an example of her, and to the rest of the world as well, according to the Bible… Oh that's just your interpretation preacher, oh, is it is it really… Are you positively sure? Well. Would you stake your life on it? Well, you're wrong. God did it in Noah's Day, and in Lot's Day, and in Moses Day, and almost in Jonah's Day for a lot less, than America's sins but Nineveh repented, and was spared…So don't tell me, cause I've studied my Bible…Call me Noah Jr., doomsday preacher. I don't really care, I'm telling you, the Authentic Word of God, the Gospel truth, and deep down, you know it too.

Your problem is you're too comfortable in this world and you have rebelled and have been blinded by it…ever see the nose blind commercial. Ha (Rom. 8:6–10, Job 33:4, Job 1:21, Gen. 2:7, Ps. 36:9, John 1:1 to 3). God's the giver of life. God's the giver of life and that spirit of rebellion of choice and my right, will definitely send down a soul to hell but yes, even that can be forgiven through a repented heart to Jesus, cause the scriptures teach his blood cleanses us from all our sins, if we have confessed them to Jesus (1 John 1:7, 8, 9, 10; Rom. 10:9, 10). But rebellion again, started at the beginning of creation, in the garden, brought in by the devil himself. Tricking Adam and Eve, and is even still tricking people today, you have the right to your choice, the devil says. It's your body, go ahead and murder that unborn baby. It's just a fetus the devil says, and Jesus said the devil is a liar, and was a murderer from the Beginning (John 8:44). And is still going on in those who are not in Christ. And Paul taught in (Romans 8) we even battle with thoughts of carnality, it's a real job to make our flesh line up with the spirit (1 Cor. 2:14, Matt. 26:41). That's why it's so crucially important that the followers of Christ learn, quote and use the scriptures as a sword in your prayer life. Against the devil. Draw that line between right and wrong. Your young people especially in the Bible colleges and Christian's Universities that are there to learn and become ministers of the gospel. And from a survey, recent poll taken, several Christian Universities reported many abortions, to keep mom and Dad from finding out that they've been sinning, committing fornication with a boyfriend minister. Wow (pouring gas on the fire).

When they are supposed to be studying to be a minister. Wow, what are they gonna preach, How to murder an unborn baby, or the Bible College is a rendezvous getaway to secretly have sex. Oops. Some bodies sins found them out. What if one of those aborted babies was supposed to be another Billy Gram or Moses type or even president, what will God say on Judgment Day cause God gave life and they took it because it's their right. Wow…Hope they don't tell God that on Judgment Day, cause it's a slap in the face to God, and a sin against God, but thanks to Jesus dying on the Cross. His blood will wash the sin and shame of it all away. And heal and restore. That my friend is called miracle favor with God, it's God's mercy, and a loving God that's overflowing with grace. By the Truck loads. When we all rightly deserve a death sentence, he gave us mercy and grace. But we all had better be more concerned about the eyes watching us from heaven (Prov. 15:3). Come on, grow up.

What in this world are these people thinking? When I heard that on that Christian family program I was so moved. Hearing Christian couples by the multitudes that were (LUKE 6:46, 1 Thess. 5:22, 2 Pet. 2:2, Isa. 5:20, James 4:17) having sex, then aborting the babies, we're not just talking about one Christian University here, but many, and I'm sure you can Google it, but my point here is, what are they going to a Christian University for? To become ministers, and they've already committed two evil sins, and the report on this program was mind boggling, to hear that they were pastor's kids, number 1, they didn't learn much at home, number 2, then they smear the family name, number 3, they sinned against God, and themselves and their families and the University, and what are they gonna preach? Wow, yes, God's a forgiving God, but (Heb. 10:26) slaps ya right in the face, and along with the next twelve verses also, wow, but we are not talking about a handful of people here, we are definitely in the Last Days, and for sure this must be the Last Generation of this evil world (Isa. 5:20, Matt. 24:33, to 39). This kind of thinking and life-style was why God destroyed the world in Noah's Day (and we are there again), but notice (verse 39). They knew not. No clue, but they weren't going to the Christian University to become a minister either, but to please Mom and Dad, and so this would make our day worse than Noah's Day. Amen.

Guess they didn't read (Luke 6:46), while they were at the Christian University. Wow. And I just pray in Jesus's name that God will help them to study, and learn the Bible and its contents that are going in one ear and out the other, but they should have read (Philippians 2:5) just going to Bible College to please Dad or to get a job as a well-paid pastor, as I heard one minister college student say at a big dinner I was attending: And He also said, no. 1 it's just a subject as Math or English to him, he said, and besides that it's easy work and good pay if you get a big church, wow, I was shocked, I said, so you're not interested in souls being saved? And you're not interested in teaching your church people the gospel and instructing them on how to make heaven? He said with a snap in his voice, "Well, No" he replied. He replied, it's the best, and easiest cushy job there is. Wow.

I was shocked, my mouth dropped open, I felt so ashamed for him, cause, he didn't have a clue, I don't feel the guy was even saved (No, Not judging, the Bible says in (1 John 4:1 (KJV)) try the spirits and that was a self-gain all the way, kind of spirit, nothing for God at all. Wow. And this was the same attitude with those "getting pregnant and aborting in Christian universities so Mom and Dad don't find out" kind of attitude. Wow, forget what God thinks; of course, you've gotta be saved to think about what God thinks. Again, to go to a Christian College, and all these people, are just thinking it's just a subject, or some topic to major in.

Wow, not even believing any of the Bible, are you readers seeing this, by the thousands, maybe millions since 1973, come on, folks, and you don't think America is about to be destroyed by God. You better reread your Bible (especially in Rev. 18) and ask the Holy Ghost (Spirit) to show you. But to them, it's just classes to get their degree, a subject, something to major in, something to make pastor Dad proud of them. Wow. Really? Again, to them their heart really isn't in living for God. They don't have a clue, it's just an Education, or degree, or they would restrain themselves from each other, because if you are truly God called. As in (Col. 3:5 and 6), you'd discipline yourself and so could you University students, please reread (verse

6, and verse 1 and 2 up to verse 10)? Wow, are Bible students doing this? (Luke 6:46). No…I'm not their judge, because if they stand or fall it's to his own master, God. (Rom. 14:4, Heb. 10:31, Heb. 12:1 and 2 and 3), but again, for those of you that think I'm judging. I've said already, I had a Christian mother and a Christian Grandmother before my hippy biker lifestyle, did drugs, having affairs, etc.

No, not proud of it, but I've lived on both sides of this fence, I know what I'm talking about, been there, done that. And I'm telling ya God does forgive, and it took me years. And a lot of eating crow as the saying goes to get back right with God, and now I'm trying with all my heart to help all of you prodigal sons and daughters out there, to swallow your pride, as I did, and as (Luke 15) tells us to humble yourselves before God and (James 4:6, 7 and 8; 1 Peter 5:5 to 9). As a Christian friend I would like to say to you, if your the one all this is hitting you in the face. Please, while there is still time, go now, to your parents and God ask them to forgive you (admit your sins (Rom 10:9, 10), instead of angering God more, by adding more fuel on the fire, and allow God the time to change and mold you (2 Cor. 5:17, Rom. 9:21, Jer. 18:1, 2 Cor. 5:17, Rom. 9:21, Jer. 18:1 to 6). A disciple means: one that is self-disciplined for the cause of Christ and according to many back in the Bible Days, according to (Matt. 19:12) says Jesus stated, some that couldn't constrain themselves, they made themselves Eunuchs, for the kingdom of heaven's sake (in my words, but you can read it, I briefed it up).

Anyway the question still remains, what does a man give in exchange for his/her soul (Matt. 16:26). And again, the last half of (James 1:27) tells us to keep ourselves unspotted from the world. You have to make yourself stay away from bad music, bad movies, bad company, etc. (1 Cor. 15:33), this is why someone that's put in jail for too many traffic violations, he starts hanging around with the wrong crowd and he can't help that, he has no choice, in the matter, being locked up with them, usually he comes out worse than when he went in, because of the bad environment he is in, etc. (Rom. 12:1–2, 1 Pet. 4, 1–2, Matt. 5:28), which applies both ways (men or women) I've never seen a day where women are checking out means butts, and again you see it everywhere, even in church it's not just men anymore, and we could get deeper, but I'm sure you get my point on lust. As in (Romans 1:27, etc., or 2 Peter 2:4 to 10, 1 John 2:15, 16, 17). Some folks just don't get, that part in the Bible that says we must obey God's Word in order to make it into heaven (Luke 6:46, John 14:23, Heb. 2:3, 2 Thess. 1:8, Rev. 22:14) But some folks just don't get it, and they follow the way the rest of the world lives… Example, many think cause Mr. Rock and roller, or miss Hollywood star and singer calls themselves Christians and got arrested for drunk driving…Hello…Yes… I know, again, I'm not their judge, that's why I don't use real names, but parables and examples to make you a point, that anyone can say there a car, cause they sleep in the garage, and wear hub cap earrings, and tie a carabarator around their neck and makes sounds like a car, hey, sounds like, looks like, stays in the garage like, he even calls hisself a car, come on, folks, that don't make him a car, no more than all these drunk stars and partying singers that are making Gospel recordings, one even confessed on an interview that she wasn't a Christian, it's to make Mom happy… Many have since I was a kid, but just because people that live like a devil say they are a Christian, that don't make them one!

A Christian means Christ-like (John 13:35) by this shall all men know that ye are my disciples, if ye have love, one to another. Living like the Bible says and this ol' world is no way living like the Bible says, because this is the days of vengeance (LUKE 21:22) but God said in (Hebrew 10:30, Romans 12:19), vengeance belongs to God, and He will repay and in (2 Thess. 2:8, 2 Thess. 1:8 and 9) in flaming fire taking vengeance on them that (don't know Him (God)) "Wow." And if you want to live like the partying rock in roll drunk…, etc., if you do, you are the stupidest on the earth, cause if we are saying we are followers of Christ, and still live like the devil and the world, the Bible teaches, we are a liar and God's Word is not in us (1 John 1:5 to 10). What did (James 1:27) mean for us to be unspotted, from the world, if I'm on my way to a wedding, and I have on my new tux, and I come by your house, and you are painting it, I'm not gonna grab a paint brush and start helping, no matter how much of a bad time you give me, or all the beer you can drink paint party as I've seen in the old partying days, No, because I would spot up my tux, I would stay away even as God has told his people to stay ready and watch, as in my analogy, and as (James 1:27) points out stay unspotted from the world (1 Thess. 5:22–23; Rom. 12:2; 1 John 2:15; James 4:4; Col. 3:1, 2; Luke 21:34, 35, 36; Matt. 24:42 to 51) how can you watch and pray if you're partying and getting drunk? (You can't.) I've been there, you can't, you'll get left behind, that's the devils voice, you'll get spots on ya. From the world's paint can, but most of all rebellious people learn the hard way.

But according to Scriptures, when we see all these kinda things, that is a sign of the end time, and Last Day generation. It's all in the Bible, read it (Matt. 24; Matt. 25; Luke 12; Luke 21; 2 Tim. 3; 2 Pet. 3; Rom. 12:1, 2; Rom. 1:16 to 32; 2 Pet. 2) and there's much, much more, Google it. And read it. Especially (Amos 8:11) about a famine that's here today. And (Hosea 4:6) that God's own people are destroyed for lack of knowledge. And (Hebrews 10:31), (Colossians 3:5) tells us to mortify your members. A disciple is one who follows the Lord and disciplines themselves, and keeps themselves unspotted from the world (James 1:27, Rom. 12:1–2, 1 Pet. 4:1–2, Phil. 2:5). But let this mind be in you which was also in Christ Jesus, so what was in our Lord's mind, we know he came to die on the cross so we all could be saved, and he lived and taught the gospel, he healed the sick and raised the dead. He gave two more commandments in (Matthew 22:37 to 40), about loving God with all our heart and love our neighbor as ourselves.

Wow, I guess this one's left out of the newer versions, because this generation is lovers of their own self. Oh, that's in (2 Timothy 3:2), the Last Day Chapter. And lovers of pleasure more than lovers of God or deny ourselves our family time, recreational time, etc., and staying in prison all day to tell the inmates about Jesus on Father's Day. Wow, that'd be denying yourself, or leaving your home, and your good paying job, and leave all your kinfolks, and journey off to a distant land to pastor a church, where you were treated like, well I better not say that, but it devastated you, for all you sacrificed and it was nothing like you thought, young preacher friend, you better know that you know, you are God called and really pray and wait on God's Fully 100 percent direction, but God still opened other doors because we stayed faithful too him. And kept a tender heart before him. But we learned a lot, many by not leaning to our own understanding but trusting in God (Prov. 3:5, 6) that he would lead, guide, direct us, and provide for us as long as we lived for him (Matt. 6:33; Phil. 4:13, 19; 1 Cor. 10:13).

And we knew his ears was hearing us (Ps. 34:4 to 7, to 15, 18, 19) And even though people you came to help, turn against you, we knew we were in God's big hands (John 10:27, 28, 29; Ps. 37:23, 24, 25; Isa. 58:9 to 14) and when some (not all) rose up against us, we stood, knowing God's on our side (Ps. 124:2 and Ps. 118:6) and we stood on God's Word, that no weapon formed against us would prosper (Isa. 54:17) and God's Word would not return back to him void, but it will accomplish that which God pleases (Isa. 55:11, put in my words) but know this, when you set out to do God's work, and people that aren't living for God oppose you and come against you, I've seen with my own eyes, God removed them (literally) and other times I felt God say, time to move on. But everytime and every place we put God first, and lived for Him with our whole hearts, and God has always provided for us a way out, and with provisions (1 Cor. 10:13, Phil. 4:19) until Jesus returns, we are gonna have to stand on God's Word, living it and quoting it, even as if our very life depended on it because it does. And remember (Gen. 50:20) After Joseph revealed his self to his brothers, he said, you thought it for evil against me but God meant it for good (in my words), so we need to quote that to the devil, along with (Rom. 8:28 to 39). Okay, but God is still in control, and he is still a God of mercy. And God will still forgive a repented heart. Always, I mean always keep a tender humble repentive heart to God, and don't ever be too proud to say I'm sorry, I was wrong, forgive me. As (John 8) Jesus taught mercy and forgiveness. But he also said in (verse 11), go and sin no more.

And the main purpose of a minister learning the Bible is so you'll be able to instruct others on how to make heaven, and stay away from sin and temptation, to show them directions of the life of a Christian, to follow the Bible that's a road map for the Believer, to direct lost souls, and give them keys to the kingdom (2 Tim. 2:15, 1 Pet. 3:15, 1 Pet. 4:17–18) which is our weapon against the devil and a road map to heaven, even the Ten Commandments teach us. The life of Moses, when he came down from getting the Ten Commandments to see all those blind misguided people naked, committing adultery and fornication, were so wrong and caught in the act and what's even worse they turned from worshipping God to worship a golden calf.

Read what happened to them. Oh, preacher don't be a fanatic, we are under Grace, yeah, well tell about the time Peter confronted Ananias and Sapphira that when God killed them for lying to God, in (Acts 5:1–10), but they didn't even read, (2 Timothy 3:15–17 or 2 Timothy 4:18) you folks better get repented and get back under the blood of Jesus, Jesus said (Luke 17:32) remember lot's wife. What about it, she didn't draw a line between right and wrong but looked back to the city of sin that God destroyed and was plainly warned by the angel not to look back. Yet people by the thousands are looking back and going back, because of false teaching and false religions, false doctrines = false Bibles (2 Tim. 4:3–5, 1 Tim. 4:1–2, Col. 2:8, 22, Matthew 24:24, Heb. 13:9, Col. 3:1 to 6) with some trues but with twisted or removed key scriptures that's in the KJV Bible gives power to the believers (Matt. 17:21, 1 Cor. 7:9).

Such as scriptures on fasting or better to marry than to burn, some translations have left these two verses and many more. Out of the other version Bibles (this is wrong) and according to (Rev. 22:18, 19) those people will be plagued, and their names will be blotted out of the Book of Life (Rev. 3:5). Now are you sure you want to follow someone that rewritten and changed the Bible that's cursed by God, WOW…if you do you are stupid and have no spiritual discernment at all. I don't care who you are. The Bible is sealed…God's not given anyone permission to change it. On "Knowing" the devil comes to steal, kill and to destroy, but Jesus came to give life and that more abundantly (Matt. 4:1 to 10, John 10:10) Note: These two scriptures have been altered and changed in many different version Bibles… Why? Cause the devil's behind it…to misguide people, so they'll have no power with God, in (Matthew 17:21 and 1 Corinthians 7:9) in the KJV Bible, means those that commit adultery will burn in hell, And the devil wants Folks To Burn and not know, so false versions are created…plain and simple (Rev. 22:18, 19; Luke 21:33; Matt. 5:18; Isa. 55:11; and many, many more).

I have two full pages in my Bible…from the versions, like the N.I.V. that scriptures that are "Completely removed," or altered, and changed (which is against God). Some they left completely out, well according to (Matt. 4:6, the devil twists and leaves out scripture (Ps. 91:11, only a devil will leave out scripture). Such as better to marry than to burn. Some of these lying devils that retranslated these New version Bibles that are deceiving people and the new one that is now coming out is worse than them all (Rom. 1:25).

Today, many people want something easy rather than study it out, many of the New Version Bible, are leading people astray of course this is prophecy for told in the last days, many of which, I just wrote, and there are many more. And people will believe a lie and be damned (2 Thess. 2:10–12). It'll pay a saint of God, to pray about what version they read and follow. I heard an ol' preacher say always compare them to KJV. And I said, just read KJV, problem solved. The newer version says you'll burn with lust in your heart, no, it means if you commit adultery you'll burn in hell (You'll go to heaven or hell: Gal. 5:19–21; 1 Cor. 6:9, 10, 11; 2 Pet. 2). If God threw out angels that sinned and destroyed the world in the days of Noah and destroyed Sodom and Gomorrah (2 Pet. 2:4 to 8 and 2 Pet. 3:3, to 10). Do you think he will tolerate ours? God gives us a list in (1 Corinthians 6:9, 10) and in (Galatians 5:19 to 21), that plainly says, if you do things it's talking about, you will not inherit the kingdom of God. Drunkenness, murders, witchcraft, idolatry, hatred, adultery, fornication, etc. You can read it.

Where do you draw the line to God saying don't do that? Please note: Those who wrote scriptures in the Bible, were men of God, moved on by the spirit of God in what to write down…And they prayed over these writings: even as "Pastor Fred Davis" and many others has prayed over "This Book I'm Writing"…which also gives Bible Scriptures, to help people learn. Do you believe God heard the prayers of all those people, I do, and God has also heard my prayers for my books also, 100 percent (Ps. 34:15) If you get nothing else out of my books, you will get plenty of God's Word.

So it's better to marry than to burn, living in sin you will not go to heaven (Gal. 5:19–21). There is heaven and hell, if you don't make heaven, Hell-o. But these religions and new doctrines that want to deceive people into thinking it's not gonna send them to hell and more worried about what mom and dad are gonna think than God (Rev. 12:11). The Bible says, and they (the church people, Christians) overcame him (the devil) by the blood, of the Lamb (Of God) (Jesus Christ), and by the word of their testimony, and they loved not their own lives unto the death (in my words). And I ask you friend if it came down to it, would you be willing to lay down your life as the scriptures say, for the cause of Christ? I've known many over the years, they couldn't even sacrifice their evening time to get out of their recliners to come to evening church service, so how could they ever be a martyr for Christ, The scripture I quoted didn't say you had to, but just-wants you to-be willing (cause they love God more than their own life, just in case you didn't (see Rev. 12:11).

You need to read (Romans 12:1 and 2, John 15:13, Matthew 22:37 to 40, John 14:23, 24, John 21:15, 16, 17). Talk about your repeats. Wow, you have probably already asked yourself why does this (preacher/author) repeat himself for? And I ask you, why did Jesus ask Peter three times here in (John 21:15 to 17), "Do you love me?" (John 13:15 and 35, John 14:15) Jesus was saying in these scriptures if you love me you'll do what I say (Luke 6:46) and keep my commandments (Matt. 10:37, 38, 2 Cor. 4:11, Matt. 10:28, Mark 8:35 or John 12:25), but we must love God with all our soul, love God with all our heart, and with all our mind, but most of all this ones (Mark 12:29, 30, 31). Come on, people, (Gal. 5:16:21), plainly states the ones that do such things will not inherit the kingdom of God. And (1 Corinthians 6:9, 10, 11).

In the days of Moses when the curse of the first born was sent (Exod. 11:1 to Exod. 12:7, 13). Speaks of putting the lambs blood on your door to protect the ones in the house from the plague, and the death angel will see the lambs blood, he will pass over, but today, in our day and time, Jesus is our lamb. And we apply Jesus's blood to the door posts of our heart, when we are saved and born again (John 3:3, 5, 1 Cor. 5:7, John 1:29, 1 Pet. 1:19, Heb. 9:12 to 28,

Rev. 1:5, 1 John 1:7) and Jesus's blood washes us from all our sins (in my words).

The word teaches us that Jesus Christ became that sacrificed lamb for us. And his blood will wash away all our sins, they were told while the death angel was coming to stay in the house that has the lamb's blood on it. That was their covering of protection for those who obey God's command. And now things are changed just a little, but the same principle applies. Stay under the blood of Christ. Don't be deceived by religions and false doctrines that say your always saved. That only a devil is gonna tell you. (Matt. 25) again, tells of the ten virgins, five that were wise and spiritual full of oil and even extra oil...5 foolish ran out of oil, all ten were virgins, pure ready to become the bride—bride of Christ. Five went in, five got left out (Rev. 3:5) (John 6:66), name blotted out of the book of life (John 6:66). Hello, well guess that once saved always saved didn't apply here. My own dad believed this lie. Cause of wrong religious teachings and false doctrine of man's beliefs, wrong rewritten version Bibles that have been changed, taken away from and added too.

And again, even a lot of the big, well-known preachers are following them. They are wrong too! Don't you even read it, that even the very elect (Matt. 24:22). The very elect can be deceived, read (Romans 1:20–30, verse 20), says man will be without excuse (Vs. 21?) says when they knew God they didn't glorify him as God. Sounds like (2 Tim. 3:5, Having a form of Godliness but deny the power thereof.) They don't want to be marked as a fanatic or tongue talking Bible Quoting Holy Roller. Wow. Sounds like my church. I'm no one's judge, that's why I put out so much scripture, you bad-mouth me all you want, but if this is all Bible Truths, then people have to line up with the Bible not me. Read the scripture for yourself. This is why there are so many versions (Rom. 1:25) Man don't like what God originally said so he'll change it just a little, then the next version added a little, and on and on. Now, some street version, Gomorrah Versions. Hello, people, where does it stop (in hell).

Ouch. Just read Luke 16. The Bible says for people not to think they stand (in other words, don't act like your perfect and have never made a mistake.) or you may fall. Or in (Romans 12:3), for a man not to think more highly of himself than he ought to think, but to think soberly. (Wow.) So Paul is saying, don't think like a drunk would, wow. Because this is my soul, and we only have one shot, at eternity, it's forever dude, and if you're wrong, you'll pay HARD, FOREVER, and EVER, choose wisely...Pray hard, ask God to fill you with his spirit because, according to (Rom. 8:26) Likewise the spirit also helps our infirmities for) we don't know how to pray as we ought, but the spirit itself makes intercession for us, with groanings which cannot be uttered. So Paul is saying our human mind doesn't know the right way to pray, like if a whole family were killed, except a mother, at home, you would not know how to pray for such a tragic event, but the Holy Spirit would know how to pray *through us* and gives us the right words to say for such a tragic event, but the Holy Spirit would, I don't know about you but on major issues of this sort, I want God's spirit in me, to pray through me like water through a hose. When God's spirit directs our prayers and our thoughts, He checks our hearts, and deals with our conscience, and it should even be the same way with praying as well as reading his word, you can't rely on cult members like Jim Jones bunch to instruct you, but know this that the Bible says the comforter the Holy Ghost will lead you, and guide you, and the Bibles says in (Matthew 5:18). Not one Jot, or one title will pass from the law till all be fulfilled. (In my words, you can read it.) Those people changing the Bible don't have a clue, it's sealed with a curse (Gal. 1:7, 8, 9; Rev. 22:18, 19), but I know God'll tell everyone on Judgment Day, that many were deceived by false versions, and I am doing my best to turn the light on. Again, no one has permission to take away or add to God's Word! (Rom. 1:25) Where is the line being drawn on deception. How far is man gonna go with these lies. Are we gonna follow the Jim Jones Crowds? Well, they killed themselves and well, God's not gonna disown us so let's follow their evil wrong twisted false example.

Not! I'm not jumping off the cliff because some back slider did, oh wait John 666 (anti-Christ number) read it, you that say you can't backslide (1. Cor. 10:12) so why does it say you can fall? Where do we draw the line on this and those that say just pray one time or you don't have faith? What about Jesus when praying for the guy who saw men? As trees, was Jesus wrong cause, yes, he prayed twice (Mark. 8:22, 24, 25, 1 Thess. 5:17, Luke 21:34, 35, 36) pray always. Luke 18:5, 7 by her continual coming) Daniel prayed three times a day, in (Daniel 6:10). So like Paul praying three times (2 Cor. 12:7, 8, 9) was Paul faithless. No. Not at all, but being taught through an infirmity of God's love and grace, that God will help us regardless of any situation and through your difficult time that others will see how God helped you through it. I've seen God heal me many times of many things, then some had surgery on. This is why we are not to judge someone. (Because after the surgery I witnessed to other patients, Rom. 8:28, Acts 1:8.)

God always has a reason for any situation he allows you to be put in, he also allows a way of escape (1 Cor. 10:13). Just because they didn't get healed the first time around prayer, maybe like with Jesus praying the second time for the blind man or three or four, but don't give up and hey, maybe I gave up to soon too on the surgery, but man wasn't in my shoes of pain, night after night, oh it is so easy to mock or point the finger, yet we all gotta reap from all that nonsense, believe me I learned and reaped it myself. So draw your line saint of God and don't let people persuade you with religion or doctrine. Depend 100 percent on the Holy Ghost, to lead you, God wants us to depend on him for direction, to lead, guide and direct our path through the word (Prov. 3:5, 6) (Ps. 37:23). Don't get mad, but pray, seek God for the truth ask him what's right and to help you discern in the spirit, to fill you with the holy ghost and fire (Matt. 3:11).

Those of you that mock the speaking in tongues, and mock those that jump and run, and raise their hands and praise the Lord in those fanatic Holy Roller churches. Well, if you are those that yell for your favorite sports team. I would do some research on God being a jealous God. And even study those first three of the Ten Commandments, and (Matthew 6:33), etc. If I wrote all the scriptures just on this topic. I'd have to write another book on it. But I'm telling you the truth. These that mock, as in (2 Pet. 3:3–5), paint themselves at ball games, scream, jump, wave banners, stand out in the rain, snow, heat, and cheer on their team. For a stupid

Ball game. And not for a God that died on a cross for your soul, to keep your butt outta hell! Huh? I wouldn't want to be in those shoes on Judgment Day. No, I'm not saying sports are wrong. Only of mockers who mock church folks as in (Galatians 6:7, Jude 18, 2 Pet. 3:3, 5) and do the same thing or worse, for a GAME, painting themselves, yelling, etc. Wouldn't that be a hypocrite, and like God blinding (Saul Paul) could those that are scoffers and mockers be in danger of God's wrath? God's Word is very plain (especially in Ps. 78, Ps. 107) How these same type people forgot that God delivered them out of Egypt Bondage, they forgot all the miracles God did for them, other things occupied their mind, wow, sounds like people today (Acts 2:13). Other people mock cause they don't fully understand God's spiritual out pouring, or God's Word because they don't (1 Cor. 2:14). think spiritually (Rom. 8:6, 7).

In (Acts 2:11), so many today, and for years, have bad-mouthed, the Holy Ghost tongues, etc. But if they would read what those tongues were saying in (Acts 2:11), even then there was mockers, sent by Satan, and these men that were mocking the apostles and the other men there, because the mockers hearts were not in worshipping God, saying these men are full of new wine (calling them drunks, Acts 2:11 and 13) but God wants his people to know that when God does those kind of miracles, because God wants our reverence, and a thankful heart, not mockery or unbelief (1. Cor. 2:14) God wants to pour out his spirit on all of his people (Acts 2:17), but they have to want it (John 7:37, 38; Matt. 5:6)... Then, you're supposed to thank him, and remember them outpourings of God's spirit speaking through those apostles (Acts 2:11, notice verse 4) that they were all filled and spoke in tongues, for you that don't believe, you need to pray Lord help my unbelief...and if this is real for today and it is, fill me with the Holy Ghost and fire in Jesus's name, cause you see, God is no respect of persons (Acts 10:34 to 48).

You just need more faith, and believe, and quit listening to un-believers, but God was speaking through these men of God in different languages, about the wonders of God or as the scripture says in (Acts 2:11) "the wonderful works of God" (that could have been) about the times God parted the ocean, and took children of Israel through the ocean, to the other side, or it could have been about saving Daniel out of the lion's den, or saving David from the Giant, or taking the three Hebrew boys out of the Fire Furnace...etc. But my point here is it wasn't a bunch of gibberish as many mockers think, especially when it is foretold in other books in the Bible at different periods of time. God put the word out on that day of Pentecost, when other nationalities were all by coincidence, gathered together in the same room, to hear God speak about the wonderful works of God in their own language that they were born in (wow). Coincidence...I don't think so... It was God's plan and God ordained (Rom. 8:29, 30). And man that badmouths it is in danger of God's wrath! If this is you, you need to do some serious soul searching and some serious praying to God for understanding things of the Spirit (1 Cor. 2:14).

Once that Holy Ghost and fire comes in, then the teacher, which is the Holy Ghost, will teach you and lead you into all truths, and guide you. He will explain spiritual things to you. And give you an understanding, concerning the Bible because the Holy Spirit will quicken your mind and your mortal body by his spirit that dwells in you (Rom. 8:11). Note: The Phrase...Holy Ghost and Fire is as in (Matthew 3:11), God uses Holy Ghost fire that will purify, when raw meat is put on fire, it changes the texture of the meat from RAW to cooked...a metamorphosis stage takes place, and change (inside and out) takes place, anything that fire gets on changes the structure of the thing, applied fire properly, and used with authority and intelligence as cooking or, as in a welder's cutting torch, cutting out a designed piece of metal to make a horse-shoe or a sword (till its red hot), and to make knives, etc. The metal must be heated till it's structure is red hot, then beat it to form it, then dipped in water to temper it, to make it stronger! So many Bible verses mention water and fire usually speaking of being in the spirit, or baptism, or even the Holy Ghost as in (John 7:37, 38, 39). Fire is hot which purifies, concerning the fire of the Holy Ghost, if you read, about internal structure of God himself, his structure of his body...That powerful force is indeed fire.

Read (Heb. 12:29: "For God is a consuming fire" (okay long dirt road) to explain, that when the fire of God's spirit gets inside man, there will be a change in him. Purifying your soul, spirit, and heart and mind, to where you will be yielding to God, and will be teachable allowing the Holy Spirit to remold you (as you the clay are moldable to God the potter.) And once the clay is formed to satisfaction, then, yes, back in the fire you go. The clay was marred in the Potter's hand (Jer. 18:4, Rom. 9:20 to 22), so he can remold it, and take out those bad lumps that might cause a leak in your cup. Folks God just wants us to be yielding to him as soft clay is in a potter's hand, moldable, easy to work with, so what's the process if it is too hard and has lumps in the clay us, so you soak it in the water, and work with it, are you set in your ways, are you yielding yourself to God or do you need God to hose you inside and out with his Holy Ghost water, as in (John 4:14, John 7:37, 38, 39) because when your dry and hard in your heart you're not moldable, as the hard clay, but a stubborn, and rebellious heart, the Bible notes this is as the sin of witchcraft. Wow.

(First Sam. 15:23) but God is a God full of love and compassion, and wants to encourage you and touch your heart and minister to the depths of your soul, He loves you, he knows how hard things have been for you, and he said he loves you more than the sparrows, and your more valuable than the birds and God feeds and takes care of all the birds (Matt. 6:25, 26) in the world (Matt. 10:29 to 31) God longs for you to call on him, and cast all your cares upon him, for he cares for you (1 Pet. 5:7), but read the previous (verse 6), humble yourselves therefore under the mighty hand of God, that he may exalt you in due time. If you're humbled before the Lord, then God can mold and shape you. I've seen people that have been through deaths of loved ones, or through a bad divorce, can sometimes make people hard and bitter in their heart, becoming what the Bible calls them a stiff neck people (Acts 7:51, Please note here, the word resist) in (Acts 7:51).

The Bible says they, as their fathers did also resist the Holy Ghost. Wow, so man's brain has always gotten in God's way...God has always wanted to bless man, but again his macho pride and brain has always tried to figure everything out, or they listen to a so-called friend, that detours them away from getting blessed by God. Please focus here, and hear me, "Getting filled with the Holy Ghost when I got saved, was the best thing that ever happen to me in my whole life" (Exod. 32:9). And once we realize it we need to repent and ask Jesus to have the Holy Ghost hose us out, because God usually destroyed these types, but since Jesus came in and took our place on the cross, now God allows those type situations, such as floods or fires or some great storm to come so we will call up on him, then God can touch us, and start the softening of your heart as the clay sitting in the bowl of water. Many people get mad at a pastor at a funeral, for giving an alter call, but some pastors have what the Bible calls discernment, this type of pastor is full of God's spirit, and being led by the Holy Ghost, and this pastor is seeing that this individual is not gonna ever come to church any other time, and their heart right now is being soften by the grief of losing this loved one, so no matter if you agree or not, this is the perfect time for God to save this person's soul, and if you still disagree, read (Luke 16:19 to 31). God will do what he has to, to keep people out of hell, and to get people ready to meet Jesus. Personally, I admire a pastor that gives alter calls at funerals, hope I go in the rapture, but if the Lord tarries and I happen to go by the way of the grave, then I say to my pastor or whoever is doing mine, take your liberty, go for it, by all means, give an alter call, you have my permission. What an honor that would be that someone would get saved and turn their life over to Jesus Christ at my Funeral, Wow, I would be deeply honored, so people that are offended in this are not right in their own heart with God. Cause even the rich man burning in hell didn't want his brothers to come there and burn. Wow. Some folks are just not thinking spiritually minded (Phil. 2:5, 1 Cor. 2:14). This is the whole reason Jesus died on the Cross. Amen. Anyway, back to the clay, the Bible uses the word marred as in (Jer. 18:4), which in the original Hebrew is *shaw-Khath*, which means "ruin, waste, perish, spill, lose, mar," but in the Potter's hand it's restored back to where the Potter begins.

The restoration process, as I already discussed, when the Potter "God" uses his Holy Ghost with fire that spiritually burns off any type of spiritual germs, or demonic organisms or spiritual bacteria that tries to infect the soul of man spiritually speaking, the fire of

God that purifies the heart, soul mind and spirit to conform you to him, to transform you into the new creature in Christ. (Rom. 12:1, 2, 3; 2 Cor. 5:17), but a rebellious heart is like (Ps. 32:9). God's face is against stubborn rebellious people. No doubt America is (Rev. 18). Waiting for her destruction by God, because of the sins and rebellion and those that once served him and now turned their back on him. Once one nation under God, was once our purpose of life. Now a back-slidden nation. And it's those that are still living for God, that has kept back God's wrath (Gen. 18:24, 26; Matt. 24:22; 1 Thess. 5:9, 19.) You see those that rely on their own understanding, or even rely on mankind to teach them to learn about that which is against God's Word. We should always ask and pray for God to direct us (Prov. 3:5, 6). Even in the prayer Jesus taught, lead us not into temptation. And deliver us from evil. That covers a lot of ground (Matt. 6:9, 10, 11, 12, 13, 14, 15). We must forgive others their trespasses against us, the Bible says vengeance is God's and he will repay them for their evil and for touching God's anointed. People just do not realize this dangerous area of mockery and ones that are so blind allowing the devil to use them against you. The Bible says in (2 Pet. 3:3, 4, 5), they are willing ignorant, hey, I'm first to admit, I know I'm not the brightest individual. Don't claim to be. And inside I chuckle at people that stand up and brag and carry on, yet, the Bible says we are to follow Christ examples, he was not a proud braggadocious person, but humbled himself, washed feet (John 13:14, 15).

And Jesus said, I've left you an example, (verse 15), to follow, he said turn the other cheek. I've had ministers come at me to fight me right in church two different times and I've seen God take out people after a word from the Lord was given out. God does not and will not put up with people going against his anointed preachers or even the saints of God are his anointed ones, blood bought child of God, watch out devil, you're trespassing on Holy ground. That is where we stand with Jesus Christ in our hearts, knowing if God be for me who can be against me (Rom. 8:31). And so many times we need to just shut up and let God be God and let him fight our battles like 2 Chron. 20:15) "This battle is not yours, but God's. Stop worrying what the enemy is trying to do to us and get back on the

Holy ground. Prayer bones and give God back the steering wheel of your life cause only God can fight those enemies that have us out numbered or that stand nine feet tall or are in such high-ranking power of authority where you have no say. (Oh yes, you do.) In God, our father who art in heaven, hollowed be thy name. Acknowledge our Lord, give him praise, present your request with thanksgiving and be careful for nothing Paul says (in Philip 4:6, 7), Jesus said why take ye thought for the morrow (Matt. 6: 27–33) and look back at (verse 26).

He takes care of all the birds, my pastor said once, if a man that was a millionaire had to take care and feed all the birds in the world alone, not counting other animals just birds. In one day, He would be broke, yet God feeds them every day. And Jesus goes on to say, for your heavenly father knows our need, even before we ask (Matt. 6:8) and (verse 33) tell us to seek first the kingdom of God and his righteousness and all these other things shall be added unto you, and (Philippians 4:19), God'll supply all your need. So seeking God in prayer Paul said, do it with thanksgiving, in (Philippians 4:6), try it.

That's what Jesus was saying when he mentioned his righteousness. The psalmist said enter his courts (his presence) with praise. Just begin with thanking him with what you are deep down really thankful for, my mother and grandma bombing heaven with prayers to God for my soul is one I use and God healing my marriage giving back love in my wife's heart that I destroyed and our home, family, truck, etc. Prayers that God answered my prayers for new tires, I prayed for finances—etc., and the Bibles says God is a spirit so those that worship him must worship him in spirit and in truth. So be honest in your worship. And as long as we are honest and sincere. God always looks on our heart, so seeing God looking on our heart, we should always have a repented heart, and a thankful one too. We can't hide anything, yes we all know people that try or think they are, but God's they're judge not us, but those that followed, God and God's Word, will automatically bring God's ears down to their prayers (Ps. 34:15; Ps. 51:10–17; Ps. 57:7; 1 Sam 16:7). How do we draw the line before a holy and righteous God, who knows of our coming in and our going out of this life? He knows us better than we know ourselves. The Bible says in (James 4:14), our life is like a vapor, it's here, and then gone. It's what we've done for God during the little time we have in this life, that's gonna count on Judgment day when those deeds that were recorded, and the words such as you've done to the least of these, you've done it to me, enter into the joy of the Lord thou good and faithful servant.

Or you'll hear, depart from me into everlasting torment, for I never knew you, thou wicked and slothful servant, for such as you did not do to the least of these you did it not to me (Matt. 25:31 to 46). So it's like when Jesus (Acts 9) was scolding Saul (Paul) for persecuting his disciples, hauling them away to imprisonment them, and having the Christians all put to death which would end Christianity, so God takes it personal when Bad people come against his anointed men and women of God (Ps. 105:15). God knows our thoughts and the intents of our heart. The Bible says God even knows our thoughts and intents of our heart. And God has looked down upon man and saw that his heart and thoughts were continually wicked (Ps. 94:11, Matt. 9:4, Luke 5:22, Luke 6:8, Gen. 6:5, Prov. 15:3). This is why, when we enter into his presence, we should always have a repentive heart and thank him for his mercy and grace he has had on us.

Don't let the devil rob God of being thanked (Ps. 100:4 and Phil. 4:6). We send thank-you cards to people that have done favors or good deeds to us, for gifts, etc. We should always thank God for the gifts he has given us, his son Jesus, the Holy Ghost, the word, freedom, and things, etc., our home, food, etc. (John 11:41) even Jesus thanked God for hearing him pray before he called Lazarus back to life. But in our case, we should always clear the pathway of any sin in our heart and life, always have a repented heart, heard someone say one time they never sin. What a lie, just their self-righteousness alone is sin, always cleanse yourself with a prayer of asking Jesus to forgive you of any sin in your heart, then thank him for everything you can think of.

The Scribes and Pharisees and the religious zealots in Christ's days paraded around acting all Holy and was rebuked by the Lord in (Matthew 23). It doesn't hurt a thing, to repent. Yet people get so bent out of shape, why, just do it, my view is eating or drinking out of something that came out of the dishwasher after being washed, and still has some gunk on it. I don't want to use it, how about you. Hello, where do you draw the line on tables being clean at a restaurant if there's a dirty table and clean table left which do you pick, both empty. There's extra silverware on the table one set looks dirty the other clean, are you gonna go ahead and eat with the dirty looking silver-ware, or reach over at the other empty table and get the clean set?

Do you think God's any different? Where do we draw the line on settling? We seem to think God is gonna accept our yummy dinner of praise, when our silverware of our heart is got some bitterness toward someone on it, so what's in our heart is like the silverware in a restaurant. We want to eat with clean utensils and God wants us praising him with a clean heart. Not having bitterness or hatred toward someone, and praising God with a dirty heart. So we should always first ask forgiveness of any sin then, give thanks and praise to God, but clean out the spots and gunk first (Matt. 5:23, 24; Matt. 6:33; Ps. 51:10, 11, 12, 13, 17; Ps. 57:7; Matt. 15:18, 19; Luke 12:34). The Lord said, make it right then come and do your offering to God. It takes just a minute to change to a clean fork or wash it again, it doesn't kill us. Get over it. It's better to be right and be accepted by God than to be rejected because of stubbornness and pride which that too is sin. (Read Deut. 21:18–23 or Deut. 9:27 or 1 Sam. 15:23.)

For rebellion is as the sin of witchcraft and stubbornness is as iniquity and idolatry. Because thou hast rejected the word of the Lord, he hath also rejected thee from being king. Pretty plain right. I personally do not even care to stand there and talk to people that have an ugly attitude or if someone is so bull headed and so stubborn to even hear you talk I will usually walk away or let them have their say and if it is one sided, then leave. And so are you and is God any different to us, if we harden our heart and stiffen our neck and turn a deaf ear. Then God don't listen to our praise. Some folks think that God will hear them regardless, not so (Ps. 66:18). But if we have a repentive heart especially even if we feel we are okay and say like King David.

175

Saying: Search me and know my heart, to God (Ps. 139:23, 24) So what is a hypocrite? Webster's dictionary says, it's an actor, a pretender, one who pretends to be what he is not, one who pretends to be better than he is.

My pastor, Donahue Green, said, most folks say they're only at church but, they are at the store, and they are at the restaurant, and the gas station, and people still go there, but they just use that, as an excuse to stay home from church, and Jesus said it also, and I also agree, good word pastor, thank you, Jesus (Luke 14:16 to 24), everyone should read that (verse 24) especially if you play a lot of hooky from church, and make a lot of excuses, now, make a note here my reader friend. Don't mistake a reason, such as taking someone to ER or having the diarrhea, I've to stayed home for such causes, those are reasons, not excuses. There is a difference, but it all goes back to the heart, if your heart is right with God, and you are sold out to live for him 100 percent, then you'll serve him and be at church and even live like the Bible says when you're in public…but those real hypocrites, they are good actors at church, but the Bible says their sins will find them out (Numbers 32:33) (Isa. 59:2). And in (Ps. 51:10), King David ask God to create a clean heart in him, a heart that is renewed, makes him have a right kind of spirit that God will accept.

This is that repentive clean heart (1 John 3:20–21). Now that is someone with a clear conscience that God can put back on his potter's wheel and remold and shape and take out those lumps of bitterness or dryness, he can redip us back in his bucket of love and restore our soul. Wow. What love God has for us, (1 John 3:1–16). You see when the people of God walk up right before the Lord and don't try to hide things from God, as Adam and Eve did (Gen. 3:10), walk up right before the Lord and don't try (hiding anything), he knows all anyway. Yet many do. So let's "Draw the line," on walking up right before the Lord, knowing he'll not with hold. No good thing from them that walk uprightly (Ps. 84:11). Meaning being right in our hearts before the Lord (1 John 3:19, 20, 21, 22; 1 John 4:6), heard my pastor say it's not a smorgee buffet where you can pick and choose what you want. The Bible is clear with scriptures that tell us right ways to live and the things that are wrong. Yet it amazes me the people out there that you see live like the world, and live like the devil himself, and think the Bibles not meaning them, or some just don't care or even read it. May be that's why (Hos. 4:6).

The Bible says, God's people are destroyed for their lack of knowledge, wow... So this is the meaning of (Rom. 8:1). (First John 3:20) says, "For if our Heart (conscience) condemns us, God is greater than our heart, and knoweth all things." God gives us our conscience to keep us in line, so what Paul and John are touching on here, are when folks are walking in God, we will not feel that condemning spirit hammering us, but we'll have confidence in knowing we are reading our Bibles and seeking God, when we are doing all God has informed us to do which the Bible says it's our duty...it's our responsibility as a born-again Christian, to put on our spiritual armor on each day, by reading the Bible and praying, etc., then we have the armor on as in (Eph. 6) and we have assurance and not condemnation. Yes, I repeat myself, those that are in, Christ Jesus and are not walking after the flesh but are walking after the spirit, are not under condemnation, wow. That was a long dirt road out of the way explanation.

But the Bible says to teach with simplicity. Keep it simple and again, the parables and the examples are for our learning (Rom. 15:4; Rom. 16:17, 18; Rom. 12:8; 2 Cor. 11:3). And let us also be aware that the devil as a roaring lion that wants to devour us (1 Pet. 5:8). To (devour) us, simply means, the devil wants to destroy and annihilate anyone that's a Christian. And the devils tactics are so severe, that most people don't even think about it or even have a clue, that the devils the one using someone or your enemy is not the clerk at the store) or something against them, Satan will use anything, or anyone, the Bible says, we are not ignorant of the devil's devices, or his tactics, and he can even appear as an angel of light (2 Cor. 2:11).

Acting Holy (2 Tim. 3:5, 2 Cor. 11:13, 14, 15) but remember some people that are not all the way in living for God...Those are usually the ones the devil will try to use against you...but you have to get it in your spirit, they are not your enemy, the devil is your enemy. He'll just use anything or anyone against you and usually it's someone that does not know the Bible, or even people that are into religion and false doctrine, that comes against people of God. And his darkness does not like the light of Christ. And that's why Paul said in (2 Corinthians 11:3), lest by any means, as the serpent (the devil) beguiled Eve through his subtility (trickery...cunning, crafty) so your minds should be corrupted from the simplicity that is in Christ.) It's not complicated, it's simple folks.

The Bible says the devils the author of confusion (And He's the one) behind all misunderstandings, and this is really huge in our day and offenses (Matt. 24:10). The devil tries to make folks think it's too hard to be a Christian...No, it's the opposite...The way of the transgressor is hard (Prov. 13:15, I've heard R. W. Shambock quote). We have God to turn to, as King Jehoshaphat (2 Chron. 20) heard God say, when he was surrounded by three armies...This battle is the Lord's (James 4:7, 8, 1 Pet. 5:7). And as Paul taught again in (2 Corinthians 11:3) the devil is using tactics that you just don't think about. These tiny little flying insect demons has definitely been distracting me (in the eyes, up the nose, buzzing my face). Since, I've been writing this book, gnats from hell have pestered me, and I know in my soul the devil is trying to distract my train of thought: I smashed some in my dictionary and trinity my granddaughter with a paper scraping it off the page, it ended up being a joke, with a note wrote on the page, this was the spot of a dead distracting Gnat.

Anyway, she got a big kick out of it, I was just thrilled I smashed the little devil. But you get the point. So your focus is on the stupid bug from hell. And even more kept coming to where, you stop and kill. Finally found a big bowl of fruit they were after. Lest Satan get advantage of us but we are not ignorant of his devices (tools, Eph. 4:26, 27; 2 Cor. 2:11). And one of my favorites, "When the enemy shall come in like the flood the spirit of the Lord will lift up a standard against him." Praise the Lord for (Isa. 59:19) and even the first verse, God's hand is not shortened, that it cannot save, neither his ear heavy, that it cannot hear. Wow don't read (verse 2). So when man sin's and don't repent of it, that sin separates us from God. And (Isa. 59:2), your iniquities have separated you from you and your God, and because of your sins God has hid his face from you that he will not hear. And in (Heb. 9) and (Rom. 6:1–16) when man would sin and bring an animal's blood sacrifice to the priest to offer to God for his sins (Heb. 9:7 to 14).

Man would continue to live in sin, and the Bible says, we should not continue to live in sin, but that sin (Rom. 6 Verse 14) shall not have dominion over you (Verse 23) for the wages of sin is death, but the gift of God is eternal life through Jesus Christ our Lord. And (Rom. 10:13) says whosoever calls on the name of the Lord shall be saved. Sin and rebellion, disobedience is, our old man nature and is the whole reason Jesus came and died on the cross, cause the high priests sacrificed lamb. God was no longer accepting because man thought he could still bring a lamb to sacrifice for his sins, so he could be reconciled back to God but God was no longer accepting man's offering for sin, because man would continue to live in sin (Heb. 10:10, 11, 12, 13, 14, 17, 18, 19) So God sends Jesus Christ his only son to be the final ultimate sacrifice for the whole world, to be a sacrificed lamb, on the cross, for us all. So this is why Jesus, laid down his life on the cross for man, so we all could be saved, and have the fellowship back with God (John 3:16). So Jesus became the bridge between God and man, to bring us back together again. And leaves it up to man to choose. Choose Jesus, call on him while it's called today, and confess your sins to Jesus Christ, and not to man (1st Timothy 2:5, 2 Cor. 6:2).

When you pray, confess your sins to Jesus (1 John1:7 to 10) and ask him to forgive you and cleanse you from all your iniquities, and come into your heart, and save me, and heal your soul and restore your life today (Ps. 51:10–12), and say, I received you Lord Jesus into my heart and I thank you, Lord, for saving my soul, thank you, Lord, for dying on the cross and shedding your blood to wash away all my sins. Thank you, Jesus, then tell someone, you received Jesus Christ, and got saved (Luke 22:32, Acts 1:8). And pray for God to keep us from going back to our old ways, the Bible calls it, going back to the dog vomit that God brought you out of, this is what God thinks of someone getting saved, and turning back to their old ways (2 Pet. 2:20–22, Luke 9:62).

And to go back to party'n and getting drunk, etc., is called friendship (Gal 5:19–21, James 4:4, 1 Cor. 5:11) with the world, and thus making you an enemy of God because that's why Jesus died so if you continue in sin, you may as well say damn after his name, cause your soul will be (Ps. 9:17, Ps. 139:20, Heb. 9:7, 12, 13, 14, 15, 22, 26, 27, 28 (Heb. 10:10–11) So to go back to live in sin is to curse God, because God made a perfect way for man to be saved, through his son Jesus, and so the scripture (2 Cor. 5:17) says, therefore if any man be in Christ: He is a new creature, old things are passed away behold all things becomes new. So when Jesus comes into someone's life and truly saves them that have truly repented. He changes them into a new creation, but again. We must be appliable as the clay is in the potter's hands and allow him to mold and change us. The whole problem with the whole wide world is, no one wants to change. They want to continue living in sin. But you can't according to the Bible (2 Chron 7:14 and Matt. 6:24). Sure, everyone messes up now and then, I always say, be quick to repent, now again, there is a difference between diving in a pool and tripping and falling in one. But to go back and live back in sin, your deliberately asking to get devil possessed. Yes, the Bible says, you'll be seven times worse, the devil will come in and your seven times worse (Matt. 12:43–45).

So it's very dangerous to turn back from God. You have to understand God's point of view. God allowed his only son Jesus to die on a cross, and suffer an agonizing death for us all, so we could make heaven, and for us to reject Jesus and go back to our old life is a slap in the face to God and is an unforgiveable sin called Blaspheming the Holy Ghost (Luke 12:10). And that's why people become devil possessed, which is also why witchcraft, wizards, Palm Readers, and Physics all are against God, this is an opposite spirit, it's called an anti-Christ spirit from hell, Read (Acts. 16:16 to 25) once Paul cast out the devil out of a physic, she had no power. These people become the enemies of God, and God cast the devil out of heaven (Rev. 12:10, 12; Luke 10:18; Isa. 14:12 to 16) and to choose to leave God and get involved with the devils work (Eph. 4:27), you're asking to become devil possessed (2 Cor. 2:11).

And it's no wonder there is such a warfare going on. I am so amazed at so many Christians that don't even have a clue on palm readers, and horoscopes, etc. Most of the ones that don't have a clue are the casual ones that aren't sold out to God, who just go to church when they are in the mood…and it's obvious when you hear them talk about psychic readings that they've never read (Acts 16:16 to 25), like the one that told a preacher name Apostle Paul things about him, then Paul casts the devil out of her and she lost her ability to tell her psychic fortune telling and foreseeing from the devil since the devil was cast out of her, it is a spirit of divination and is from hell, as said in (2 Corinthians 11:14, 1 John 4:1, Isa. 5:20, 2 John 7, Rev. 20:3 and 8, Luke 11:24 to 26, Rev. 16:13, to 15, Isa. 14:12 to 16), Hollywood has glamorized the devils work and twisted it, as in (Matthew 4) so the youth of this world would be sucked into believing the devil's lies and be damned (2 Thess. 2:12, Mark 16:15 to 17). This is why the Christian that is living for God 100 percent reads their Bible and prays every day, putting on the Armor of God so he can have that power to stand against the devil (Eph. 6:11, Luke 10:19, 20).

That's why the Bible teaches us that in the last days we need to wake up and be on our guard, to stay vigilant as in (1 Pet. 5:8) and (Luke 21:34, 35, 36) And according to scriptures on the end time and last days (Matt. 24:33, 34) we are that last generation that all hell is gonna be unleashed upon (Rev. 12:12) (just remember Luke 10:19) (Luke 21:22, Mat. 24:4–51, Rev. 16:18–21 see verse 2 to verse 8). This is when, as (Luke 21:6) and (Revelation 16:20) tell us, that big, huge earthquake will happen, which is what scientists have been talking about for years. It's one where islands will be moved or sunk and where mountains will fall flat, and (Luke 21:6) says, "Not one stone will be upon another, that shall not be thrown down." Wow, now that's gotta be the "Big One." Amen. Wow. I hope the Rapture of the church is taken up before then. I believe it will. Sorry to bust your bubble but the world has been caught up in too much pleasures, work and education and exercise, and have taken their eyes off prophecy of the End Time…people everywhere in every state and country are hoping and praying things are gonna get better…I'm sad to say it's Not! Not according to the Bible prophecy, when you see the things now going on, happen…that's the signs of the Last generation…I've been preaching this message for thirty forty years. We're it…can anyone show me different, No, and the Bible says, when you see it get like this (like Noah's Day) (HA) we've past him up long time ago, people are so…so in denial…and have watched way too much TV and the devil has used Hollywood's movies to desensitize us for way too long.

But with businesses, restaurants, factories, etc., closing, etc., so many out of work, folks are panicking, some are seeing we are at the closing hours, but according to (2 Thess. 2:10, 11, 12) Folks are falling for the devils lies and are believing his strong delusions. Let's ask for the Lord Jesus forgiveness and to anoint our eyes that we can see and watch for Jesus to come back any time now (Rev. 3:18). When he says, in (Rev. 4:1), come up here and verse 2 immediately—not fifty more years, not ten, but *immediately*…if you don't see these, we'll pray more for your spiritual eyesight (Acts 17:27). For God to open up and fill your soul with his spirit…check and examine your soul. And I am so amazed at so many, many Christians and ministers, that are so blind and are saying it's gonna get better, all you folks need to repent of your lies! From Noah to now, show me in the Bible. Please, where does it say that? You can't (cause it doesn't, but it shows you the opposite [2 Tim. 3:1–13])! It'll be as bad or worse than Noah's day (water versus fire) (Jude 7, 2 Thess. 1:7–9, Mark 6:11, Luke 10:12, Matt. 24:19, Rev. 9:1–21). I dare ya to read all these because all those who don't go back with Jesus when he comes for his people will experience the worst nightmares of all time. It pays us all to be ready. And all this is just what I've been saying for forty years, and many may call me Noeh JR. I don't care, or an exstreamest fanatic, by some, but who cares, the Bible says it in (Matthew 24:32, 33, 24 and verses 36, 37, 38; Luke 21:7 to 36; 2 Tim. 3:1 to 5; 2 Pet. 3:3 to 5; 2 Pet. 2:1 to 22). Read 'em and you want to talk of earthquakes, the big one is coming…for sure very soon, read (Luke 21:6, Rev. 16:20, Rev. 11:13), hope us Christians are outta here and are with Jesus then, okay you get my point, but you can if you pray, you can really see evil distractions, and again the devil is using Hollywood, in making movies glamorizing the devil's work and power in movies, and in music, and the world is blindly taking it hook, line, and sinker.

The devil is making it all exciting and as with Adam and Eve, it's pleasant to the eyes (Gen. 3:6, 2 Cor. 11:3, And they lost out with God and was throwed out of the Garden of paradise/Eden (Luke 13:27, 28) (1 Cor. 10:21 and 22, 2 Cor. 2:11, John 10:10) and according to scripture God looked (Prov. 15:3, Acts 17:27, Ps. 14:2, Isa. 55:6, Ps. 53:2 and 3, Ps. 102:19) down from heaven, and saw he had to do something in order to save his creation to save us from destruction, I believe God drew that line straight to Jesus and knew Jesus had to become that sacrificed lamb but instead of it being on a sacrificing alter it was on an old rugged cross to become the ultimate sacrifice for all mankind. It was the most slow, agonizing, and torturous death. He took our place, he that knew no sin become sin for us (2 Cor. 5:21, Phil. 2:8).

And in Moses's day when the lambs blood were applied on the door post of their houses when the death angel saw the blood he passed over that house, so it is when we apply Christ's blood by asking Jesus to forgive us of all our sins, his blood washes us clean from all our sins by us repenting, that applies the lamb of God's blood of Jesus to our door post of our hearts. And when God looks down and is ready to execute judgment on those sinners on earth and sees the blood of Jesus Christ applied to our hearts, thanks to Jesus shedding his precious blood on the cross. John 8. Tells a time in the morning the religious Scribes and Pharisees brought a woman taken in the very act of adultery. And we all have wondered for years what Jesus was writing in the dirt with his finger (John 8).

Brings to life the story of a woman brought to Jesus, that was taken in adultery, Jesus used his finger, drawing a line, or writing a name in the dirt, or the time, date, scripture, about adultery, pointing out the man or men who committed adultery with her. Though we don't really know for sure, exactly what it was that he wrote in the dirt but whatever Jesus wrote in the dirt, convicted all those men (1st John 3:20, 21). And they dropped their rocks that they were going to stone her with. And left (Matt. 9:4, Matt. 12:25, Matt. 15:19). Jesus also said, "You that is without sin, cast the first stone at her. So with whatever he wrote, they left, feeling conviction of their sins" (1st John 3:20, 21; John 8:9) which drew a guilty conscience of. A line pointing the one out, the man taken in adultery with her or days and times that others was with her, or text verses of scripture, and I've wondered about the scripture that says Jesus even knew their thoughts (Matt. 9:4, Matt. 12:25) and said out of the heart comes evil thoughts (Matt. 15:19).

Wow. And the whole time Jesus knew their thoughts: But the part that really gets ya about this is in (John 8:5) their quoting Moses's law, that commands us to stone her but in those same ten laws of commandments it also says not to commit adultery, and it also says, not to lie or kill. Wow, makes you wonder, but the scripture's plain they were trying to trap Jesus, so much for religious Pharisees and Scribes. The lesson here was, you take care of your own sins, you live for God, and don't Judge someone else (John 21:20, 21, 22, 23) (Matt. 7:1–5). And in (John 8 verse 6, 8), Jesus stoops down as though he didn't hear them and wrote something on the ground, cause the Bible says they were tempting or trying to provoke him into passing judgment on her, so they could turn it back around on him, so they would have something to trap him with. Note this reader, the Bible says Jesus was without spot, Jesus was without blemish (A spotless lamb of God) They couldn't and didn't find anything against him. So they brought in false accusers, liars, and even Pilate admitted, he's done nothing worthy of death, and he washes his hands of it all (Matthew 27:24). (in Luke 23:10 see verse 25, Mark 15:3, Mark 14:55, 56, 57, 58, 59) (Even the Chief Priest accused him, Wow… so much for being a man of God) wow…to pass judgment to try and put someone innocent to death. But the Bible says in (Mark 15:10 Matt. 27:18) for Jesus knew that the chief priests had delivered him for envy (wow).

I, too, worked with a man like these religious Pharisees, and he laid a trap for me too. I think he was trying to get me fired or embarrass me so I would quit. But in front of the other guy and in front of the employee I held out my hand out and apologized asking for forgiveness, not allowing the devil to run with that situation (Eph. 4:26, 27). I said I didn't mean anything bad about it, so forgive me, and everyone stood there with their mouths wide open.

So we can be as wise as a serpent and harmless as a dove (Matt. 10:16) and don't let the devil have an inch of space (Eph. 4:27; 2 Cor. 2:11) But through that little scheme of the devil's I learned a lesson, that we need to always be willing to humble ourselves and ask forgiveness, even though that trap was deliberately set up by the devil, we must always...I'm saying "ALWAYS Be Vigilant," because the devil is out to get us especially even when we feel we are in the right, and especially when we feel we are innocent, and didn't do anything wrong, I mean I was the victim here, but I swallowed my pride, cause I knew this devil had set me up, with the smerk on his face, you could read his mind... "What are ya gonna do now preacher." Blow them away with love and kindness and forgiveness freak 'em out and leave them speechless, knowing his judgment day is coming, and my conscience is clear and isn't that what Jesus would do...Amen (Rom. 16:20; 1 Pet. 5:8, 9; Isa. 59:19; Isa. 54:17; Rev. 12:12) (1 Pet. 5:8, 9 and Rev. 12:11) but back to Jesus writing in the dirt, I believe the word teaches that man does truly reap what they sow (Gal. 6:7 to 9), and that the evil will be exposed to the light of God (Ephesians 5:13, Eph. 4:11 to 20, John 3:19 to 21, Luke 16:8) and the scripture that always griped my heart, was (Matthew 25:30 to 46) when Jesus said for such as you have done to the least of these, you have done it unto me.

Wow, sounds like when Jesus was rebuking Saul in (Acts 9) for persecuting his people. And then he blinds him to get his attention. Wow. I'm trying to get back to Jesus writing in the dirt...for Jesus to know these evil so-called religious leaders thoughts and write whatever he wrote in the dirt, started a spirit of conviction in their hearts, then Jesus gets up, and says, you that's without sin, throw the first stone or be first to throw a stone at her. And stoops down and writes some more in the dirt. So if it was sins they committed or with what he wrote the second time, wiped out their conscience, being convicted in their heart, they dropped their rocks and left. Then Jesus ask the woman was anyone there to accuse her and she said no man Lord. Jesus told her. Neither do I condemn you, go and sin no more. He didn't say your lifestyle was okay. (Verse 11, in John 8) so in your opinion reader who do you think out of the three groups of people were the evilest, it was a trap and a set-up. And I've seen this kind in our days as well. Those counterfeits were worse than the woman and she knows who the man with her was probably one of them. Again, it was all a trap but it was prevented because (John 8:12) "Jesus is the light of the world."

Jesus was explaining in (Matthew 23:13), (Matt. 23:14) that those who are hypocrites and do evil, don't make it in to heaven, plus their damnation in hell will be greater. Wow, in my words, and like the rich man in hell in (Luke 16:19 to 31 in verse 21), the beggar name Lazarus desired to be fed from crumbs that fell from the rich man's table. Wow. And I have known some and lived by people that had two and three freezers full of food and a bedroom full of shelves full of food, and their neighbor had none, and when they died... most of it was freezer burnt, and was throwed in the trash, I heard someone say, they could have fed many in the family and even neighbors too, but instead, they hoared it, and it went bad. A lot of older folks from the depression days, hoared food, in fear of going back to the days of depression. And so it was with those Pharisees, not even knowing Jesus was explaining about hypocrites, and thieves that steal poor widows houses, and for a big show pray long prayers, and Jesus said they'd receive greater damnation. Wow (in my words, read it).

In (Matthew 23:14), (Mark 12:40), (Luke 20:47) says, those Scribes and Pharisees and hypocrites would receive greater damnation. So there will be levels, degrees of punishments. But the flip side of that coin says back in (Luke 20:35, 36), those that will be accounted worthy, are gonna be equal to the angels. So for those that are the real true Christian followers of Jesus Christ that will be accounted worthy are those that, take heed to their selves not causing trouble, not getting drunk, watching and being careful not to be snared with the cares of this life and pray always. That you may be accounted worthy to escape all these things that shall come to pass (end time, last day stuff.) And to stand before the son of man Jesus Christ, (Luke 21:34, 35, 36). This is pretty plain, yet so many religious people say different views and rewrite the scriptures. Well, I'm most assured those will be alongside the Scribes, Pharisees, and hypocrites because they lied too and tried to change and stop Jesus.

The Word of God is **not** written to argue over, or bring confusion but to deliver souls from hell, to point the way to heaven and to direct us to be full of Jesus and the Holy Ghost and fire. People you worked with say, people you pastored say, they wondered what the Bible really means, and so many are confused, and saying which Bible, which Baptism which name, I'd say I follow the oldest, the KJV And I myself baptize in both ways which is right (Matt. 28:19) (Acts 2:38) which I do both, saying, upon your confession in the name of the Lord Jesus Christ. I now baptized you in the name of the Father, son and Holy Ghost…IN JESUS NAME.

Many people are divided into different sects of religions, but Jesus said baptize in the name of the Father, Son, and Holy Ghost in (Matthew 28:19) and the disciples taught in (Acts 2:38, 39) to be baptized in Jesus's name, so even as my pastor done, so do I, I do both as he did because it makes sense, and it gets rid of all confusion. I say upon your confession in the name of our Lord Jesus Christ I now baptize you in the name of the Father, and the Son, and in the Holy Ghost in Jesus's name (and under they go.) to stop all the controversies. I do both. And don't anyone dare say anything. People was the same way in Jesus Christ's day. You see here is another perfect example of these devil minded religious chief priests, (in vs. 10 of John 12) wanting to put Lazarus to death again, wow, talk about idiots, don't these blind devils have any brains, common sense tells ya, if Jesus Christ raised up Lazarus once, he could do it again, and what in the world is a chief priest that his power and authority has gone to his head, not love,…but wanting to murder Lazarus, so people wouldn't believe on Jesus…wow how evil can you get.

That's like those blind religious people today that are using car bombs to murder people, so they'll become an Emperor in heaven, wow…talk about false teaching and blind and being deceived into believing a lie, they over looked… "Thou shall not kill" (Exod. 20:13) oh yes I think they follow a different Bible. He said they strain at a Gnat and swallow a camel. Wow (Matt. 23:24) make a mountain out of a moles hill. I wonder if people even pray and ask the comforter, the Holy Ghost to lead, them, and guide them, and teach and explain to them. No instead they go to some recycled version, some guy that's not even saved rewrote (Rev. 22:18–19, Rom. 1:25) cause a real Christian is not gonna, no way change what God said. You'll see God judge them, your gonna stand there on Judgment day and see, and all the people that were misled by them. You'll see it. Yet when I was pastoring, so many confused, which one, who's right, how do we know for sure?

Again, if we are full of the Holy Ghost and fire, he will direct us and God has always and will always want to show you the way, but you have to give him the steering wheel of your life (John 12:10, 11, 12; John 16:13; Matt. 6:33; Matt. 11:28; Prov. 3:5, 6; Deut. 6:5; Ps. 119:2; Jer. 29:13; 2 Chron. 7:14; Rom. 6:12 to 16). Allow him to teach you and allow the Holy Ghost and fire to give you an understanding heart. I was a C and D and sometimes F student, And was a high school dropout. And ten years later, I went back to adult school and received my diploma, and wished I would have stayed in school, and so you see, I'm not a very intelligent person, nor do I claim to act like I'm a Bible scholar or some spiritual genius professor, cause I'm not, I have seen so much pride and arrogance on so many that are. We can have a spiritual boldness and take our stand for God, submitting ourselves to God, then resist the devil and he will flee, attitude, but not a rooster arrogance that we think we are God's only child on earth kinda thinking, that's a carnal trap of the devil but relying 100 percent on the Lord, allowing his spirit to explain to our spirit. The word or phrase being born again.

You are a babe in Christ. A dependency of a baby in life. Looks to his mother, she feeds, changes, nurtures, teaches. Again: this is why Jesus referred to Nicodemus in (John 3:1–8), notice in (verse 9), Nicodemus is questioning Jesus, this is a ruler of the Sanhedrin Sect. A ruler of the Pharisees...very intelligent. Yet when an old stupid hippy biker drug addict was sent home to die after a second Opion doctor at Kawaeah Delta Hospital in 1977. I knew and told the doctor I can't die. I'll go to hell. The doctor said sounds like you need to go talk to a preacher and the light came on. And then I knew I needed to get saved. But it doesn't take a degree to know that, nor did I have to have some institute, or man teach me, I got a Bible, went to church, and attended Sunday school. And I learnt by reading, searching, etc., and putting out an effort (Heb. 11:6) while diligently, and trying my best. I felt since I really believed I was gonna die, so I needed to get all I could get from God and I see now, forty-three some odd years later, I can see God allowed that to get me serious enough to persevere as in (Eph. 6:10 to 18), cause when there is a desperateness in us, as there was in the woman with the issue of blood (in Luke 8:43–48 and Mark 5:24–34), notice, the bible didn't say…go touch Jesus', clothers, and you'll be healed, (see verse 28 of Mark 5) and (Matthew 9:21) she said within herself…if I may but touch his garment, I shall be whole, wow, so this was her faith (Heb. 11:6), and determination, and a-act of desperation, we can get to a determination to get a move of God in our life. As is seen in the Bible, in (Hebrews 11:5–6), we must also have faith in God. And the Bible says that this woman with the issue of blood spent all she had on doctors…so when doctors are no help…but she grew worse, this creates a stirring in the soul to believe or know your dying, oh sure, there are some real mule headed stubborn donkey's out there (I'm trying to say it nicely) Ha. Or too much pride or they get bitter and mad at God.

But we must wake up outta that kind of stink-n think…and wake up to the fact, if you die in your sins…Hell-o (yes it's hell you go) and I always believed in God and heaven and hell, I was just too busy partying to think about it, but when your too sick to party or when you're dying, it's time to do something, I said get off your…I said "It's time to do something," don't just sit there pray. Call on God, He loves you. Anyway, I prayed and asking the Holy Ghost to teach me. And he did. When we get saved, it's almost like we become a child looking to our mother (God) being born again, having a total dependency on God, as the baby does its mother. And God knows that we need to souly depend on him 100 percent and there becomes a special bond between them. And so when we are born again in the spirit getting saved. We look to Jesus the author and finisher of our faith (Heb. 12:2). God wants us to have a bond, connections in the spirit with him and he wants us to cry out to him for understanding of his holy scriptures, parables that even in Christ's day. That the religious Pharisees and Scribes that constantly wanting to kill him. They couldn't understand the parables or the mystery of the kingdom of heaven, (Mark 4:11), (as in Mat. 13:1 to 53), (Rom. 11:16:25).

The Bible says, in (1 Corinthians 2:14), but the natural man receives not the things of the spirit, for they are foolish unto him: Neither can he know them, because they are spiritually discerned. It's plain and simple. You have to want it so bad. To learn, to understand, you pray and ask God to teach you. In other words, there has to be a inner hunger and thirst for understanding, then according to scripture, God will fill you and give you an understanding heart, but know this. God has never and will never give an understanding to someone that lives like a devil and shacks up in adultery, fornicates, gets drunk, following the rest of the world, but we are to be dedicated and consecrated to live for God 100 percent, with all your heart, then my friend, God hears that spiritually discerned prayer, and gives you his spirit of understanding, but you won't get it from a university, it only comes from the Holy Ghost, and given to those that hunger and thirst after righteousness (Matt. 5:6).

So this is why the natural man or someone not saved (1 Co. 2:14), and not born again, can't receive understanding of the Bible and this is why so many want to rewrite it. But again. A real true Christian is not gonna rewrite it. Cause those that rewrite the Bible that it plainly says it's sealed with a curse to anyone who adds to it or takes away from it (Rev. 22:18, 19). So who is this person listening too. Read Matthew 4. The devil is the one that changes and twists scriptures, and takes away scriptures and adds to the Bible, and the devil, since Adam and Eve, all the way up to Jesus, then up to us has tried re-writing the Bible and wanted to change what God has said (Romans 1:25), and anyone else the devil can trick, he will surely try. Here's your secret weapon against the devil (Heb. 4:12, Eph. 6:10 to 18) and each time the devil came to attack Jesus, he quotes the Bible, as Jesus was swinging a two-edged sword at the devil (in Matthew 4). Which after Jesus had fasted, Jesus used his sword of the spirit which is the Word of God, for this is a spiritual warfare, which takes spiritual weapons, to fight against the devil (Eph. 6:10 to 18).

But a point I need to make here is, there are many scriptures people need to read on "the Mystery or Mysteries of the Kingdom" like (Romans 16:25) and especially (Matthew 13:10, 11), which explains what I'm saying here...Even Jesus explained to the disciples, the main reason he spoke and taught in parables, was to keep the hypocrite Pharisee types that weren't really a follower of God, from understanding it, cause it was designed that way ever since the world began, and it's been kept secret ever since (Rom. 16:25) and the Bible was written for God's people, and it has many different functions, but the main one is, it's a weapon for the saint against the devil. And this was the case in Matthew 4, and we must follow Jesus's examples, as he also said in (John 13:15). Read it. And look it up or Google... All those other scriptures on mystery (And) in the KJV Bible. The Thomson Chain is my favorite, with reference numbers that compares it with similar texts on the side margin, works good for preparing sermons, but the main problem with the modern man giving his views and rewriting by altering, changing, adding to, and taking away from the Bible, thus changing it, is he is adding the **plagues** in the book of Revelation in the Bible to himself, according to (Revelation 22:18–19). And God will take out his name from / blot out his name in the Book of Life (Rev. 3:5, 22:18–19; Rom. 1:25–32)...wow. Read it! And adding the plagues to his life? Wow. So again...would a real, true born-again Christian following Jesus with all his heart willingly change, alter, add to, or take away from the Bible? No...absolutely no! And jeopardize his soul? No way! Again, these people are playing God because this again is the Holy Ghost's (the Spirit) job, not man's (John 14:26). Otherwise, there would be confusion and contradictions, which would imply God is confused. But he is not, and God's not a contradictor or liar (Heb. 6:18, Titus 1:2, Num. 23:19).

In (1 Corinthians 2:14) Paul is speaking, hearing and receiving what God wants to teach his people, but if our heart and mind are corrupted and we've not become born again and repent of our sins, then we are not gonna understand scripture, because scripture is spiritual knowledge verse 14. But the natural man, meaning the guy that's not following God 100 percent is not a repented born-again believer. And receives not the things of the spirit of God for they are foolishness unto him neither can he know them, because they are spiritually discerned. So when we seek ye first, the kingdom of God and his righteousness. All these other things shall be added to us (Matt. 6:33), but we have to want it and ask him for understanding. And it is so sad that there is, so many that are following false doctrines and counterfeit versions. And again written by people that are not even saved, okay now…back to the garden, from the beginning of time the devil has changed what God told Eve. And is still doing it.

And people are gullible and lazy. Not seeking the Lord for understanding so, they turn to something written more easily to understand but once again. In (Rev. 22:18, 19), I don't care if a blooming angel pops in front of you with a recycled version. (Gal. 1:7, 8, 9, 10) says, let him be accursed, you can't take away or add too. So even the big important holier than thou high and mighty intelligent TV preachers that want to sell you their new modern translation version. Hello, even if an angel…yet so many just except it. Where is the discernment of God's people?

I know people get mad at this. Just like when I got a spanking when I was a kid. Sure, I got mad and under my breath said things that after I grew up, I regretted.

Well, all people, both small and great (Rev. 20:11–15), will stand naked and alone on Judgement Day before one angry God that will judge those who have rewritten and changed his Word; and on that day of judgement of all mankind, there won't be the merciful Lord of love anymore, and no, but his fierce wrath will send all those who rejected Jesus and rejected the real Holy Bible to hell then on to the lake of fire (Rev. 20:15, 19:20, 21:8; Matt. 23:14). Right now is the time of grace and mercy before the Rapture of the church, when Jesus returns for those watching for his return (Luke 21:34–36). It'll be those that will go to heaven with Jesus (Heb. 9:26–28, 11:6). "The word diligently seek him" means to make an effort or to be constant and persistent in doing something. Again, it'll be those putting out an effort to watch and pray (Luke 21:36) that will go back to heaven with Jesus Christ when he returns for his bride (adorned wife-to-be) (Rev. 19:7). In the phrase "His wife has made herself ready," the wife is us; the church is the bride of Christ, which is his wife. Yes, men too. No, it's not a perverted thing. It's spiritually speaking, but on that day of the Lord's return, when we all stand before our maker, then we'll all know that God's Word was designed to change us. And to help us to be corrected and get instruction in righteousness that the man of God may be perfect thoroughly furnished unto all good works (2 Tim. 3:5:17), we should not be like the devil, and mislead Eve in the garden of Eden, saying, "Oh God didn't really mean, you can't eat of that tree, it'll make you wise. You'll be as smart as God. So the devil has twisted the truth from the beginning of creation. He's been a thief and a liar and will always be a thief and liar (John 8:44). Okay, I've repeated myself, maybe I should change my title. I've noticed when we babysit the grandkids, sometimes they are so preoccupied with TV or games. Many times you have to get their attention. Some differ but you tell em three or four times finally it soaks in. Notice verse 7 of 2 Timothy 3. I just wondered over the years, since Christian Bible universities has been established...how many, "really" had a deep hunger and thirst to learn the Bible, or was they there for Dad or for a hoping for a TV ministry in the spotlight wrong reason for a Job, kind of thinking. This last-day chapter of 2 Timothy 3:7 sure sounds like our world today, in our day and time where people by the thousands or millions are getting all kinds of doctorates and degrees from studying their brains out, trying to accumulate that biblical knowledge like those scribes and Pharisees that, again, were unlike me. They were very intelligent, but they lacked that spiritual knowledge and spiritual hunger that only comes from the Holy Ghost, and they could not receive him (Holy Ghost) because they couldn't see him as in John 14:7, Matthew 13:13, Luke 8:10, and 1 Corinthians 2:14 because, let's face it, not everyone that goes to a Bible university goes to learn how to win souls for God or how to preach the gospel and prophecies. No, because I know some myself who are doing it for money, a great job, and fame. Wow, okay, another repeat. Moving on...

Yes, they are out there by the thousands. Again, you don't have to have a degree to ask God for him to give you a deep hunger for God's Word to learn it. Just a voice, to ask God to put it in your heart (a right spirit) and a hunger to learn (Ps. 51:10 to 13, Matt. 5:6, John 16:13) so to begin to learn, it must first be in the heart, then, we must call on the Holy Ghost to fill us with his spirit in Jesus's name cause the Holy Ghost is the teacher and then ask the Holy Ghost to lead and guide you through the scriptures, and ask him to give you understanding…and you'll be amazed, if you are really sincere unlike the evil men in (2 Timothy 3:7, 8). Ever learning and never able to come to the knowledge of the truth. Verse 8, men of corrupt minds. Resisting the truth. Reprobate concerning the faith. To me this is a personal walk with me and my Lord Jesus. It's not a religion or belief, but it's having a personal relationship with God/Jesus Christ.

I want all I can get in the spirit and there's no way I would think of ever rearranging, or changing, or try to say or take away from what God is trying to tell his people. Get ready, folks, things are wrapping up. Keep your guard up, the false doctrines and false teachers are out there. It's all signs of the last days. I believe we are the last generation according to (Matt. 24). And please note: it was always the religious Pharisee anti-Christ type, that always tried to kill and attack, and try to trap Jesus. (They were religious) not saved, and not born-again believers, and many of them Jesus called devils (in John 8:44–45), but in (Matt. 12:34) (Matt. 23:33) and (John 8:44, 45) and (Rev. 12:9) (even as in Gen. 3) some of these scriptures say serpents, = or vipers = devils…or satan but the religious types, can cover a large vast area of many beliefs, some as ridiculous as praying to a rock (Acts 19:34–35). How foolish to say this rock-made-idol named Diana fell down from Jupiter or to say the golden calf idol in Moses's day jumped out of the fire. Regarding the latter, they lied, breaking four of the ten commandments by making it, worshipping it, lying about it, and committing adultery. Wow, so (Leviticus 26:1, 2 Chronicles 7:17, 19, 20 also see verse 14 and Deuteronomy 4:28) didn't sink into their ears. Wow… It was told fifty-three times (and in Exodus 31:18, 20:3–5). God told Moses in the Ten Commandments, but at any case, these men was sent and used by the devil, to come against Jesus Christ.

But I want to get back to what I said on it's a personal relationship with me and my Lord, not religion, but, fellowshipping with my Adopted Father, and we can't lean to our own understanding (Prov. 3:5, 6) We have to depend on the Holy Ghost. Again, it's my personal relationship with the Lord. My Lord and I have a bond between us. The KJV Bible in (Ps. 23) explains it good.

> The Lord is **MY** shepherd, **I** shall not want, He maketh **ME** to lie down in green pastures, he leadth **ME** beside the still waters, He restoreth **MY** soul; he leadeth **ME** in the paths of righteousness for his name sake. Yea, though **I** walk through the valley of shadow of death **I** will fear no evil, for thou art with **ME**; (Thy rod and thy staff they comfort me). Thou preparest a table before **Me** in the presence of mine enemies: Thou anointest my head with oil: my cup runneth over. Surely goodness and mercy shall follow me all the days of my life: and **I** will dwell in the house of the Lord forever.

And you see now, it's a personal walk relationship with "me and my Lord"…did you notice all of the Me's and the I's and my's (it's personal) okay you got it. Well, I think we should be like ol' Peter that said, Lord I'll lay down my life for you, a lot of people out there wouldn't, they would say, No…This is just a religion, that's the attitude those folks had when moses took to long up on the mountain, and so they made a golden calf idol, and worshipped it, and had wild sex orgies, but the worshipping an idol that they just made and, saying it brought them out of Egypt instead of God is what really angered God so bad…That God sent a real powerful earthquake where the ground opened up and swallowed them. A religion is what this really is to most folks that aren't really into living for God…it's not just going to church, but it's having a personal relationship with God. If relationships in marriages was like most folks that (just) go to church once a month with no real personal experience with our Lord, Wow, try just getting married and drop by once a week or once a month or just call when you're wanting sex kind of attitude, saying, Can I drop by for half hour? A marriage with no commitment, with no involvement, with no relationship, with no one-on-one communication, that type of marriage just will not work.

They'll be divorced in no time, and it's the same with God. God's not gonna give his Holy Spirit or his understanding of his holy word to just anyone, just like the marriage, God wants a devoted servant, that will serve him, and honor him, and one who will truly live for him, and be faithful to him, and spend time with him, and love him, and sing to him, and thank him for everything he's done for you. I thank my wife for the meals she cooked, etc., and I don't just say I love you.

I demonstrate and express my love, we communicate, and I also love and commune with my Lord, cause it's a personal relationship. It's a relationship with a created being loving and worshipping their creator, and when you really know him as Lord, and knowing he left heaven to die for me, suffered for me, through all he did…how can we not love him, or be willing to lay down your life like Peter said…That is deep love for your God. Question: How could an idol that they just made answer prayers, provide water, food, etc. When they just made it…it can't move, how can it provide? But my God in heaven can, as the rest of (Psalm 23) continues to say: in the last half of (verse 5), "Thou Anointest MY head with oil; MY cup runneth over, Surely goodness and mercy shall follow ME all the days of MY life. And I will dwell in the house of the Lord forever. I like the scriptures that tells us that Jesus is dwelling in us" (John 14:20, 1 Cor. 3:16, John 14:17, John 17:23, Gal. 2:20, Rom. 8:9 and 11, 2 Cor. 6:16, Eph. 3:17).

The Lord is our provider, our teacher, our leader, our comforter, our source of strength. When we feel weak or faint, he'll strengthen us. He is a restorer, when our victory, and our strength is low, he leads us to green pastures, not to a dried up wilted, not fit to eat pastures, but green. Well-watered and flourishing. And so on, my point is this…that the Twenty-Third chapter of Psalms is God plainly saying He'll be a provider for those he shepherds, and a well of water to make you flourish to the depths of the soul (John 4:13, 14; John 7:37, 38, 39). When we are thirsty, he gives us his living water. As in (John 4, John 7:37, 38, 39). The woman at the well, said after Jesus read her life like a book. She said, "Come see a man that told me all things I ever did. Is not this the Christ? Do you see, it was personalized, so greatly that she left her water pot and went into the city to tell everyone how Jesus Christ changed her life. When you've been touched by the Lord, to a change in your life.

When the Lord really truly delivers you from a lifestyle. You must and want to tell everyone how it all happened and how Jesus saved you. And then comes the badmouthers badmouthing you, always provoking you, calling you a fanatic, or religious freak, or saying. Don't go around, Fred, all Fred wants to talk about is the Bible or how Jesus saved Him, wow what a religious fanatic, amen. God knows our going out and our coming in (Isa. 37:28, Ps. 139:7 to 10), even if we make our bed in hell or ascend up to heaven, cause God knew us when we were in our sins. He knew us when we were in our mother's womb. And this is why abortion is so wrong. If the Bible really is true and it is, The Bible plainly says, God knew us and formed us in our mother's womb (Jer. 1:5) says, that he sanctified Jeremiah and ordained him to be a prophet from the womb, wow… or what about (Isa. 49:1).

The Lord has called me from my mother's womb. Wow, so if God called a prophet or minister from the womb and the mother aborts the baby, and killing the calling of God that was on that baby (wow), which is killing and murdering her unborn baby…Thank God Mary didn't abort Jesus or my mother abort me. This is so wrong…It's not a right or a choice, it's murder, and on Judgment Day those people will stand before God, wow…What will they say if their aborted baby was a prophet or minister like these scriptures say, ouch or how about (Gal. 1:15 and 16, Ps. 71:6, Isa. 44:2, Isa. 44:24) and there are many more scriptures. I question that, or have they even read the Bible especially Gal. 5:21) All this (Matt. 19:16, 17, 18, 19) Jesus was telling this young man how to have eternal life, and how to make it to heaven (see verse 18) "Thou shalt do no murder" Quote, unquote! Also see, the sixth command of the Ten Commandments (Exod. 20:13) Please make note, and notice, in *Webster's Dictionary*, it also states, that the Ten Commandments are ten laws, given to Moses by God. And I have given you scriptures in the Old Testament, and the New Testament, out of the King James Version Bible, and even out of Websters Dictionary. Folks, God is not gonna mislead his people. God wants everyone to make heaven, and everyone thinks they are going…but the Bible says that everyone is not going…The Bible says in (Matthew 22:14, Matt. 20:16, Matt. 25:11, 12), that many are called, but only a few chosen.

The Bible says in (John 10:11) Jesus is the shepherd of the sheep. Jesus wants to lead and guide us, and wants to give us the "Holy Ghost" where we can hear our Lord's voice, see (John 10:27) This verse says, his sheep hear his voice, but if you are stubborn and rebellious and break the Ten Commandments and don't follow God's Word, then you're not his sheep! So how do you expect to make heaven, just because some priest or religion says you can? You better follow what Jesus said and forget the others. Amen. In John 4 Jesus told this woman at the well if you knew who it was that was asking you for a drink of this water. And if you knew the gift of God, you would have asked me for a drink.

Here's the difference between the spiritual from the natural and I would have given you a spiritual drink of living water. My words, again I'm not writing another Bible. The woman to me sounds like she's being a wise guy. And says I got the bucket (in my words) the well is deep. And you don't have the bucket, how are you gonna give me a drink. Carnal thinking of H_2O physical water, when Jesus is referring to the spirit, the living water, which is the opposite of the physical H_2O, liquid compound of hydrogen and oxygen that we physically drink to quench the physical body's thirst (John 4:13, 14) but this scripture passage is referring to the difference between body and soul. But just like our physical body has to have (H_2O) our soul/spirit man has to have the spiritual thirst quenched, as well as the soul craves and hungers for that spiritual drink from the Holy Ghost well that only God gives to those who truly desires it, and asks for it, as this woman at the well in (John 4:15).

But if you study our history, you'll find man over the years since time begin, man has tried filling that void in his soul with parties, sex, booze, drugs, crime, wild lifestyles, trying and doing anything and everything that's exciting, and tries filling that void with wealth and riches, no matter what the richest people on earth can get, it's not enough…they're never satisfied, nor are they ever happy, nor content. There's always an empty void spot. Why? Because God Almighty designed the human soul to have an empty void place in it, so that it was designed just for himself to fill it. Wow, and nothing else, absolutely nothing else can satisfy that inner soul's hunger and thirst for righteousness, but God's spirit the Holy Ghost infilling of himself!

Now John the Baptist said in (Matthew 3:11 and 12) that Jesus will baptize you after you repent (ask forgiveness of your sins) and then when you ask in Jesus name for the Holy Ghost to fill you with his spirit in Jesus name—always ask **in Jesus name** when you pray then Jesus will baptize you with the Holy Ghost and fire (in my words)…Now, a lot of people get confused, here, cause he's submerging folks underwater to baptize them and says you'll receive the Holy Ghost and Fire but it's speaking about spiritual fire, the Holy Ghost Holy Spirit of God. (Heb. 12:29) says, God is a consuming fire, and when his spirit comes into a person's soul, it changes them, God will not remain inside someone taking drugs or getting drunk, he'll either burn those desires for sin out of ya, or he will leave. No man can serve God and the devil. And isn't it odd, that Jesus says this scripture just before telling of the rich man in hell. In (Luke 16:13), you can't serve two masters (Matt. 6:24; Rom. 8:9, 11; John 4:22, 23, 24; Eph. 3:17; 1 Cor. 3:16, 17; 1 Cor. 6:15 to 19). Again, Jesus was referring to the spirit of the living water THE Holy Ghost infilling because when you drink the H_2O you're still thirsty an hour later.

But that Holy Ghost living water satisfies deep down to the soul, takes away the crave to get drunk, etc. This is why I've said along with dozens of the other fanatic preachers out there, people that are into some religions that are still drinking beer, we saw a beer truck out in front of a certain religious church, and our mouths fell open, and I said I wonder what type Bible that priest was teaching from, cause it sure wasn't KJV because (Galatians 5:21; 1 Corinthians 6:9–11, 5:11; Romans 13:13; Luke 21:34–36, and Mathew 24: 42–51). Google and look up all the verses in the KJV Bible and find scriptures on "being **sober**," especially ones with the phrase "watch and pray, and **be sober**." You see, it's hard enough to even watch while you're out on the road when your drunk. How do you think you can watch for Jesus's return while you're drunk or even pray drunk? You can't! Been there, done that. Again, I've been on both sides of the fence… hello. So what will that priest say to God on Judgment Day of all those he led astray…and what if someone that gets drunk at that false church, gets in a car wreck and kills someone, that false prophet will give an account to God and our Law will probably send them to jail (Matt. 24:11). So this is not God (read these and see). Because whosoever drinks of this water will still be thirsty again. Verse (John 4:13, 14). Cause, again, God would be a liar if he allowed you to get drunk, when so many scriptures say you can't, and still go to heaven. So it's man's misunderstandings, God will have multitudes of people like myself, that have got off of the Booze and dope, and got filled with God's spirit, which is a million times better, with no hang-over: and (God's not even a liar) also again…this living water really satisfies your thirst.

Which brings a change of heart, mind, and soul. This is why if the church you're going to says it's okay to still get drunk and has a beer truck drop off cases of beer. That is a false prophet and a deceiver, and you better get out of that church of lies, and search and find one that's spirit-filled, and preaches out of the KJV Bible.

Again, these type people, churches, and priest's and religion are blind, and they use (John 2) where Jesus turn the water into wine at a wedding. Note: nowhere in the Bible does it say God said it's okay to get drunk, one glass of fresh made wine, will not get anyone drunk! It's not been time enough for a fermented process to take place, so it wasn't much more than grape juice, which is like a light table wine, besides if the Lord made a fermented wine wouldn't that be kind of hypocritical and we know Jesus was no hypocrite. Amen. So when many scriptures says you can't make heaven if you get drunk, but as I said earlier, if you read the fourth verse in John 2) you'll see when Mary said in verse 3 they have no wine, listen to Jesus's reply…Now, people that aren't real true Christians think what Paul calls (carnal thinking) the way the dopers and partiers and drunks think…but Jesus and most Christians think spiritually minded (Phil. 2:5, 1 Cor.

2:14) or the natural carnal mind versus the spiritual mind (read Romans 8:6, 7, 8) Now notice (John 2:4) and see what Jesus said, "Jesus said unto her, woman what do I have to do with thee (you)? Mine hour is not yet come." Now, Jesus was saying it's not my hour… what hour? His hour, was the only thing and only reason he come to earth to die for the sins of the world (not to encourage drinking and getting drunk [John 3:16–21]). But Jesus Christ's number one goal and purpose was to come and be born of a pure virgin, live a pure holy life, performing and demonstrating miracles, and show and illustrate that he was God's son and had the power to heal and raise the dead. And he even showed it and demonstrated it on the Mount of Transfiguration that he had power over death, so when he died on the cross, and rose, ascending up to heaven, it also encouraged his followers and those that were Christians not to fear death. But again, his hour, which he was speaking to Mary about, hadn't yet come; it wasn't his time to die yet… Notice this scripture: "Jesus saith unto her woman, what do I have to do with thee [you]? Mine hour is not yet come." It wasn't Jesus Christ's hour to die on the cross yet… It wasn't Jesus Christ's hour to resurrect up from the dead yet…and it wasn't time for him to ascend up to heaven yet. And it wasn't time to send back the comforter—the Holy Ghost—yet. **This was the hour Jesus was talking to his mother, Mary, about**, and it was not about turning the water in to wine to make the world think it's okay to get drunk. Hello, no, it was so he could save the world from their sins! So now every time you hear some wise idiot say, "It's okay to drink booze because Jesus turned the water into wine," you can reply, "It wasn't Jesus Christ's hour yet." Amen… As in Acts 2:13, people that were spectators, those who were just standing by, watching the outpouring of God's spirit on those true worshipping disciples and followers of Jesus Christ (again, see 2nd Chronicles 7:14) (Acts 2:13 to 15), those Pharisee spectators that were badmouthing the Holy Ghost outpouring said these men were full of **new wine**, not understanding it… They didn't understand because they were carnal, and they were not even saved and were not born again (Mark 2:22, 2 Cor. 5:17). Plus, their hearts were evil and not right with God (2 Chron. 7:14), and God only fills a repented heart (Ps. 51:10–17)!

Again, God took that as an insult to the spirit (Matt. 12:31–32, Gal. 6:7) because Jesus taught all of this in (John 3, 14:26, 15, and 16) of being born again to going away and sending back the comforter, which is the new wine/comforter/Holy Ghost infilling that made the disciples appear drunk in the Spirit (Acts 2:13). Again, the people said and they called it the New Wine…because those that received the Holy Ghost acted drunk. Now, also (Mark 2:22) was telling us (in my words) that God's not gonna put his Holy Ghost (Spirit) New wine (into an old bottle=someone that's not been saved or born again, 2nd Cor. 5-17), but must be changed from an old bottle, but he puts his new wine Holy Spirit into new bottles… (2 Cor. 5:17, in my words, Read these for yourself).

Nowhere in the Bible does it say that God fills drunks with his spirit that are drunks, no way, cause they must be saved and born again, and become changed in their heart and mind, then God, fills that new bottle (Mark 2:22 and 2 Cor. 5:17, Rom. 10:9, 10, 13, 1st John 1:5–10) That's repented and changed. Again, according to (Rom. 1:25) this is why, even back in Moses Day…they lie and changed what God said, even clear back to the devil lying to Eve. (Man, I repeat myself. So people like this that rewrite Bibles aren't really God's real followers but deceivers, and the Bible warns in the Last Days this will happen (I just try to explain it to you). Jesus said in (Matthew 3:10; Matthew 7:15 to 23 but see verses 17 to 20) especially; (Matthew 12:33; Luke 6:44, 45 and 46) and still smoke cigarettes, pot, get drunk, party and listen to their rock and roll. I myself question, "Where is the change on that tree?" (2 Cor. 5:17). We are good branch spiritually speaking, grafted in a good vine, or a good tree, bringing forth good fruit (John 15:4 and 5) (Rom. 11:21 to 25) (Luke 6:45), and (2 Corinthians 5-17) says, "Therefore if any man be in Christ, he is a **new creature**: old things are passed away, behold all things are become **new.**" When I gave my heart, life, mind, and soul to God and asked Jesus to come into my heart and save my soul, Jesus kicked out the old Fred, saved me, and remolded me (as in Jeremiah 18:1–6 and Romans 9:20–28). As God the potter took me as clay, he removed the bad lumps of drug use and of the rock and roll and put in my heart God's Christian gospel music. So when you see drunks smoking, cussing, taking drugs, drinking booze, and committing adultery, don't tell me that's a Christian just because they go to church because I will call you a liar and them hypocrites as well. According to the Bible, a Christian is Christlike. I don't see Jesus smoking medical marijuana or cigarettes, sleeping with someone they're not married to, committing adultery with someone they are not married to, etc. Hello, where's the change? Where's the NEW creature in Christ? Did the old things pass away? So many liars still hang on to the old life that the Bible says God'll bring us out of, and like Peter said in (2 Peter 2:20–22), the dog has turned back to his vomit (Luke 9:62, 17:32). Yes, here, people are referred to as a dog, an in other places, man's called a tree, branch, wolf, sheep, fish, viper, or blind leaders of the blind. Some are called clay, a vessel or utensil, a cup and platter, etc. This is why so many want to rewrite the Bible—because they like getting drunk and taking dope (1 John 2:15–16). They want to hang on to God and the world, but a real, true Christian will be the one that's **pliable clay in God** the potter's hands... This is a Christian metaphor, or analogy-type-parable type of explanation. We must and will always allow him to remold us and remake us all into a **new creation** to become Christlike, which is to be Christian. And again, the Bible says that, I quote again, you will know them by the fruit that they bear (John 15:1–14, Matt. 7:16). And this is why on Judgment Day, God will open all those (sixty-six books of the real Bible) and judge people from the real word of God, which he originally said in the beginning before man started changing it! That is why now, Jesus is using the analogy of fruit trees.

So when you see people that's supposed to of gotten saved, born again and spirit-filled.

Rewrite the Bible, go back to the bars, still token on a doobie, smoking marijuana, and still smoking cigarettes and cussing...no. Not talking about someone falling I explained that earlier. There's a difference in diving and falling, the lord forgives our falls. I know there's a growing process and maturing in God, but it's like this text reads, once giving a drink of the spiritual water, the spiritual man requires spiritual food and drink, word and prayer. And there is nothing in this life, I mean nothing that compares to a Holy Ghost gusher hosing out feeling, that only the Holy Ghost can give a boo-hooen snott slinging time in God's presence, when you have been hosed out by the Holy Ghost, wow taste and see. Don't knock it, there's nothing that can compare to it, until you've tasted it. No drugs, no booze, no feeling like it, when the Holy Ghost flushes out your soul. You don't want the old life's junk, the hangovers, etc., that goes with it, like fights, getting into fights over someone flirting or dancing with you or your spouse, I sure don't want back in that mess no more. Not after tasting the Holy Ghost New heavenly Wine infilling, so why do some go back to the old lifestyles. Bars and parties, etc. It has to be either lack of understanding or false teaching, and the Bible says in the Last generation, there would be false prophets, and many false teachers (Matt. 24:11, Matt. 24:24, Mark 13:22, 2 Cor. 11:13, 14, 15, 2 Pet. 2:1, 1 John 4:5).

Some go back to the parties and the bars because they didn't get that living water hosed outness from God. There has to be a fully dedicated heart, mind and 100 percent yielding to the Lord, then we go away so touched by God we feel we're gonna bust if we don't share it with someone like that woman at the well with Jesus in John 4, saying, "Come see a man (in John 4:28, 29)." Come see a man who told me all I ever did. When you are eating out at a restaurant and order something no one else at the table did and it is so fantastic, better than you ever ate before, the first thing that comes out of your mouth is "hey, wow." You gotta taste this, it's the best I've ever eaten, and you want and offer them a bite, giving them just a taste to see how good it is. Sounds like (Ps. 34:8, O-taste and see that the Lord is good) So even the psalmist is saying, try the Lord, you'll see the Christian life is fantastic. Oh everyone has a need or problem, now, and then, but isn't it great that the Bible teaches, we can take it to the Lord in prayer, and cast all our cares on him for he cares for us (1 Pet. 5:7).

Because in the old life as a partier, you were stuck in the miry mud with all your troubles on your own shoulder and knowing you're living in sin. But come on over to the winning side. We're following Jesus. Hallelujah. Oh sure. People will call you a fanatic like they have me. But you see it's their loss. They are so bound by their foolish stinking pride, if they would just yield themselves to

God long enough and pray, and say, God, if this Holy Ghost, Holy .
spirit infilling stuff is like what this ol' preacher Fred says. Fill me up
and run my souls cup to overflow, give me that Holy Ghost well of
springing up water that Jesus told the woman at the well in (John
4:14) and (Jn, 7:37–38) Oh. I feel the spirit of God, while the tears
are streaming down my face. Hallelujah! You just have to lift up your
hands, and say thank you, God, thank you, Jesus, for the price you
paid on the cross for my sins.

Thank you for saving me, thank you for that praying grandma,
and praying mother you gave me, when those times before I was a
Christian, when I was almost killed in the seventies coming home
so drunk, I couldn't even stay on the road, taking the back roads
home, so many times you spared me (God), and all the time, Mom
and grandma were bombing heaven, praying for this crazy ol' hippy-biker's soul. As I do for mine and you don't think this fanatic has
something to thank my God about, just like the missionary asking
this ol' Indian chief what God has done for him. The ol' chief took a
caterpillar worm and laid it on a leaf, and set the edges on fire, then
took the caterpillar out of the leaf, just before it burned up and held
him high and said this is what God has done for me Hallelujah. God
has been so merciful to us all. America is still a good taste to people
who want to come here and live because they see freedom, and a better life. Some may have heard, some may have visited, and saw, but if
all America would just get back to living for God as our forefathers,
they'd see freedom and blessings from God on America again, like no
one's seen before, America has been a blessed nation because of God's
mercy and grace.

That's why I'm such a fanatic (cause I've seen it.). I'm not religious as so many Carnal Christians think and say "your off the deep
end Fred." Why? Doesn't people want to go where the Holy Ghost
and fire and the outpouring of God is. Well, for one. They'd have to
line up with the Bible, for 2. They are hanging on to the flesh and
I've seen so many preachers would not leave the security of a job and
home life to go off to a distant land to preach. Well, that was your
thing, preacher, I still hold no reservations. I'm in this for the long
haul. And I have put my walk with my mouth. And I practice what I

preach, we've got to seek God on our own. Again, it's a personal walk with the Lord. And if we are 100 percent sold out for God, he will flood your soul, just ask.

We need more of God, he will flood your soul, just ask. We need more of God in this end-time, more more more sinkholes all over, ground caving in, terrorist, crime, identity thefts (I believe the plagues of Revelation is *now* coming on this evil world like the one in China, and it's spreading fast all over the globe). And according to the Bible, it tells us that worse things than that, are coming, on a evil generation, or, and in (Matthew 24:33, 34), when you *see* these kind of things *happen* (that generation will not pass away till it all is fulfilled in my words) *Wow*. Read it, but evil men will be getting worse and worse, the Bible says in (2 Timothy 3:13, Eph. 5:6, Rom. 1:18, John 3:36). And this explains why our generation has been building *more and* more prisons, than ever before in the History of Mankind! What are you saying preacher, that this generation is worse than when God destroyed the world in Noah's day? Yes! (2 Pet. 2:4, 5, 6; Mark 13:30; Luke 21:31 to 36; see vss. 32; Luke 21:22, 23). Need more cops. No, we need revival, outpourings of God's Spirit. More upper room type outpourings. Come on, folks, that (Acts 2:16 to 22) was not the end, but Peter was just exhorting on what the prophet Joel said about God's great outpouring of his spirit, (Acts 2:16–27) in the last days that he'd save souls, (see verse 21)...of those who called on his name = (Jesus) and had prophesied of the things that are coming on the last generation—us.

We are the ones in (Matt. 24, 2 Tim. 3, 2 Pet. 3) is talking about when you see these things, that this generation will not pass away till all is fulfilled (Matt. 24:34). It's this generation and if you think God's gonna permit this world to keep murdering and aborting babies. Note: All through the Bible, we are told, God creates life, but our generation is the only one in the history of time, that man / doctors / scientist have tried to be God and create life = in test tubes, implants from embroils, and from sperm banks etc. and people think this is ok with God, no, it's not, again, this is the Generation of God's wrath, because man tries to be God (Gen. 1:1) (Colossians 1:16) (Genesis 2:7). There is only one giver of life, one God, one Creator, one Mediator,...and that's God / Jesus Christ (James 4:12) (Prov. 16:4) and God knew you, when you were in your mother's womb. So if God created life, and you take it. "You are a murderer," and a thief, stealing and killing what God created, the Bible says, there is only one law giver, only one God and one creator. According to the Book of (James 4:12–17) in the KJV New Testament, in the Old Testament (Jer. 1:5, Isa. 44:2 and 24, Job 31:15, Ps. 22:9, Isa. 49:5 and 15, Gal. 1:15, Gen. 25:23). Twins were in Rebekah's womb, two nations, one was Jacob, later named Israel by an angel, becoming the nation of Israel.

I know I have mentioned all this earlier, but listen to my point, please, if God would have allowed abortion, even back in Old Testament days. All hope would be gone for all creation. And even if God hadn't created woman to repopulate and become pregnant, life would have stopped, people would have grew old and life would have stopped...God had life preplanned, preordained, predestined (Rom. 8:29, 30) from the beginning of time and this is why God made male and female. (Read Romans 1.) The whole chapter. It's clear to me (Gen. 32:28). If these twins had of been aborted then the nation of Israel would have never existed, and all of those people, plus, Mary and Jesus Christ who was born there in Bethlehem of Israel, would never have existed, thus leaving us to die in our sins.

But thank God that the devil in Jane Roe vs. Wade in 1973 didn't start abortion back in Bible days, because this was meant for the Last Days prophesies...over 60,000,069 (over sixty million) babies abortions worldwide since (1973 Roe vs Wade) 54 million in the USA and many preachers do not believe (Rev. 18) is America, this subject alone is enough for God to destroy America, oh yes, regardless of what others say...you read Rev. 18 a few times and pray and ask God to show you. Take it a step further you that believe abortion is your choice and think it's your right, you do like my wife and I did...and Google this, you too will be horrified and if you're not... "You are a devil" and dead in your soul. The research they tell on these poor fetuses and the horror of the after effects, the morbid things done with the baby body parts...and some, even the tissue sent to become the collagen used in women's makeup, wow...they abort the babies then wear it on their faces… There are real devils out, just wanting to deceive you into believing a lie (2 Thess. 1:10–12, 1 Pet. 5:8–9, Gal. 6:7–8, 1 Cor. 6:9–10). Isn't it mind-boggling that this is the very first thing Jesus said in (Matthew 24:4) to the disciples when they asked him what would be the sign of the Last Days: "And Jesus answered and said unto them, take heed that no man deceive you"? Wow, you could fill this whole page with scriptures on this topic. Yet many, many women will tell you they don't care what's in their makeup as long as it makes them look pretty. Some not really knowing. So don't tell me God is not gonna destroy America, because he is!

People all over the world were outraged over Hitler, and the Holocaust, but the 6 million Jews killed, and the five hundred thousand others killed in the concentration camps, or all those babies slaughtered by King Herod when he was looking for and trying to kill Baby Jesus, none of those horrifying events that angered people, and God even compares to all those murdered aborted babies since 1973: "These evil murdering people behind this will not escape the wrath of God." And those in other ordeals that are hooded and masked in robberies, killings, thefts, etc., hasn't got a clue of God watching and recording all their evil deeds for Judgment day. Man has evolved so far with his technology, man is so smart today with so many inventions, and yet no clue about God's knowledge versus man's technology and knowledge since the stone age has developed so great, with microscopic surgery, to the satellites giving the capability to spy, or investigate or ability to find, etc.

Man's intelligence has skyrocketed mankind has exceled and has surpassed extremely far beyond those days of the horse and chariot days and don't even get me started on the new robots that look like humans and drones, and clonings, etc. and now to flying cars, etc… from travel, to weapons, and even our modern way of life, such as the outdoor farmers market to inside shopping at the grocery store, from paying with money, to paying with a card. And we all know how far we have progressed to. Now, since the chariot days to now having jets and rocket missiles, when we can now snuff out a city with a missile and spy with the satellites. God had this technology when man was still making the wheel. Yet man still thinks he's indestructible with his technology. And doesn't have a clue we are about to be anni- hilated by God (Rev. 18) because of our sins, a force they have no power against, cause the Bible has foretold these type things). When the world gets like it was in Noah's Day and we are worse now than we were then, and God will destroy the world again because as it was told to Noah, and even told by Jesus Christ in (Matthew 24:37)...

Yes, sorry to say we are there again...This is that generation, and don't get mad at me, I'm just the messenger: I didn't write the Bible prophecies, I'm just explaining them. And I know many minis- ters that disagree but that's their prerogative cause there were people in Noah's day that didn't believe as well, but for us, we'll just pray and stay ready. Amen. (Matt. 25:10, Luke 21:34, 35, 36) because when God does destroy the world again, we all wanta be ready cause it'll all happen fast (Matt. 24:42 to 51) but back then they were wicked and evil but they didn't kill 60 million babies, and there wasn't 2,220,300 (million) inmates in 1,719 state prisons and 102 Federal Prisons this is not counting all the juvenile halls and work farms and road camp facilities and boys prison ranch's like I worked at for almost a year, so if Noah's Day had all that plus all the gangs, plus all the porch pirates, and scammers, identity thefts and crooked lawyers, crooked companies, crooked law enforcement (rapes, sex trafficking) shall I continue on and fill ten more pages on crime, porn, etc., because I could just Google all this, search it out, check it for yourself...

Study out the last days, see if Noah had any of this, and the end time prophecies, etc., don't just sit there and take my word, or sit there and mock me, I wouldn't do that if I were you (Ps. 105:15, 2 Pet. 3:3 to 5) because God takes care of me (Ps. 105:15) And please don't be offended by my words, please, but Google this stuff, look it up in the Bible, I'm not a false prophet, I'm telling you the truth (John 8:32) and read the Ten Commandments again, okay, moving on...If I've offended you, please forgive me, I just want to knock the blinders off people and turn a light on, I don't ever mean to offend anyone. But I again, didn't write the Bible, I'm just a messenger send- ing out a message, a wake-up call, which was also the name of my Radio Broadcast back in 2000, wonder if anyone woke-up, most people are set in there ways...like I was partying all night long until tragedies woke me up. So if its nuclear like my dream/nightmare I had, or if God sends meteors big balls of fire on our world, again ending life as we know it, will people believe then?...like in Noah's Day, after the "Door was shut"...And water was up to their chin, holding their babies up saying save our babies, please help us, were not laughing and mocking you anymore...

Please help us, Noah...we believe you now, no doubt that was a horrifying day, because God shut that huge door and Noah could not open it, and sad to say, they heard all those people crying and screaming till they sailed away or the people drowned, it's very, very sad that mankind then would rather die in sin than repent and even now in our day, people still hasn't changed their sinful ways, our world is back to that same old type of thinking, and acting worse now than in Noah's Day...though progress and technology in modern conveniences have improved a 100 percent better life than then but sin has also progressed to be worse now than in Noah's Day (read it yourself).

Don't stick your head in the sand (2 Tim. 2:15, Matt. 24:38, 39). So ask yourself why hasn't Minister Fred went back to the hippy life, to all that partying lifestyle because God showed me all of this and cause I believe that we are there and Bible prophecy is true cause if I didn't really, deep down believe all this was true in the Bible, I'd probably be back to partying, but I'm sold out for Jesus, I tried both lives and I choose to follow Jesus, cause I see it all wrapping up. And as my Pastor Donahue Green says after his sermon, "I rest my case..."

The first four chapters of revelations is to the church. God is trying to get the church revived, but so many churches, have people that need to grow up, and quit finding faults cause there is no perfect church, cause there is no perfect people, but many such babies, crying and jealousy and envy, malice, strife. In the church of God, the devil comes in trying to trick and deceive. But I'll tell ya, if America is Rev. 18. God help us and last night the wife and I was watching all those reports that showed homes, cars, buildings falling all over the USA in sinkholes, where the ground was just caving in cause lack of water and most of them was because of the type of soil. After it had been dried inside. And I wondered about the San Andreus Fault line down Calif. Coast line, things are wrapping up folks, when you read end time stuff like islands sinking and mountains falling flat (in Rev. 16:20, Rev. 11:12, Luke 21:6).

Wow, I was amazed as I watched those news reports on all the sinkholes on the east coast. (Not to mention, the volcanos in Hawaii, and they are saying now, on the Geyser's at yellow stone National Park is volcanic, and has tunnel chambers, going into other states, and they stated many scientists believe when the Big One Hits, it will be centered in yellow stone and will also effect other states as well from the tunnels. Wow, this could be (Rev. 16:18, 20; Rev. 6:14; Luke 21:11; Matt. 24:7) there was a great earthquake, so mighty and so great (Rev. 16:18 and 19) and the Great city was divided into three parts, Wow. That's a huge earthquake and the cities of the nation fell, and great Babylon came in remembrance before God, to give her the cup of wine of his fierceness of his wrath. (Rev. 16:20) And every island fled away, and every mountain were not found.

Wow, this would be the Big one for sure (Rev. 16:18, 19, so great, not since men were on the earth the Bible says. And scientists have been predicting the Big Earth Quake for years) And if that San Andreas Fault Line down the Calif. Coast line caves off into the ocean, and possibly fulfilling scriptures on Bible prophecy that (Rev. 16:18, 19, 20) is referring to it would make a lot of sense, if it's the same prophecy?, do you think people will wake up and call on God then (according to, Rev. 6:14, 15 and Rev. 6:16–17) and when you read (Rev. 9:20, 21). And they still didn't repent which this could have been those people had already taken the chip, 666 mark of the Beast, and knew they were already doomed, otherwise why would they call out to the rocks to fall on them to hide them from God, unless they already read the Bible, in (Rev. 6:15, 16 and 17) and didn't really believe it then, but now after, it's too late, wow... but just like (Matt. 24:38, 39) says, as in Noeha's day, = the people didn't listen then either, they just laughed and mocked ol-Noeha just like today (in my words). I believe that there is multitudes of people that deep down they really believe in God, but they just haven't ever been ready to fully sell-out all the way to God, for many number of reasons, but some just don't want to be a hypocrite, or make a commitment and let go of the partying type of lifestyle. But, folks, it's time to get on the boat. Amen (Mark 8:34 to 38) (Hebrews 3:15) (Matthew 25:1 to 13) because when the door is shut, it's shut for all eternity (2nd Cor. 6:2) (Rev. 3:20).

Because the big one is coming…and frankly I feel Jesus is coming first and sooner than that. Yes. It's sad many will wait until it's too late or till meteors and stars fall as in (Rev. 6:13, Rev. 8:10, 12), but for the people living for God he's got us in his great big hand and according to scripture He'll take us out of here before earth is destroyed again.…wow…But the Earthquakes (will be for sure) worse than ever before knocking down mountains into the ocean raising the water level, sinking islands, plagues so bad and they cry for the rocks to fall on them to hide them from the face of God… And yet people still wouldn't repent of their sins…wow…And they call me stupid…wow These people are blind and stupid! And it's sad to say I know some like that, because pleasure and sin—blinds the soul of man. Wow…Makes me want to stay ready (with everything in me). Makes you want to be ready and stay ready!

No time for nonsense, everything as we know in life is about to change. According to prophecies in revelation's it's gonna be worse than Noah's day…and worse than ever before since the beginning of time. But it all, tells me, we are closer to the return of Jesus Christ than ever before. The love of many will wax cold (Matt. 24:12, which is last day prophecy sounds like today to me.) We are there (Matt. 24:10) says and many will be offended, we are there, wars and rumors of wars, earth quakes, pestilence, deceases, plagues, evil people, killings, prejudice, haters of those that do good, lovers of pleasures more than lovers of God (2 Tim. 3:1 to 5) children disobeying their parents (yes, I was one of them) on and on. They are now passing out the mark of the beast 666. We are there and if I read my Bible correctly, and if all these things are going on now and they are. And I read the Lord will return before this dictator anti-Christ passes out the identification chip. Mark of the beast. Read it for yourself (2 Thess. 2:3 to 13), carefully read over and over (verse 7, 8; 7) only he (God) will let until he be taken out of the way which is the Spirit of God. (That's in your heart.)

So the spirit of God in our hearts is called up to heaven (1. Thess. 4:13:18, Rev. 4:1, 2, 1 Thess. 5:9). God had not appointed us to wrath= great tribulation= God's wrath poured out on the children of disobedience (Colossians 3:6) (Romans 1:18) (Rev. 6:16, 17). So the Lord will catch us up out of here and then the anti-Christ dictator will force those left behind to take the microchip mark of the beast 666, but I still don't get those volunteering right now.) Okay, another repeat, but bear with me please. Note: They have started volunteering already, people were on the six o'clock news taking the microchip in the hand. (See my book is the chip the mark of the Beast, 666.) Yes, it is. They were opening doors with their chip in their hand and buying a candy bar out of a candy machine with the chip in their hand. Key word is-IN. They injected it in the hand of a CEO of a large company, to encourage employees to do also as well. Now it is time, in this life, for this prophecy, and it is now in our life time coming to pass now a two-thousand-year-old prophecy," "Now" it is here, did I say, NOW, it is here! Yes, I did! (Just checking.) So then, according to scripture, Jesus, should be coming any time. Yes, no one knows the exact day or hour (Matt. 24:36) but Jesus said you'll know it's close to the door, by the signs of the time. Well, if that microchip deal and the weather, volcanoes, earthquakes, crime, no value on life, especially of little babies, etc. Now going on in the world, if that doesn't turn the light on for you, telling you, Jesus is coming.

Then you need some strong o-glasses, and anoint your eyes with eye salve, and ask God to show you (Matt. 24, 1 Thess. 5:9). God's not appointed us to wrath, God's wrath is Great Tribulation. This is Great Tribulation stuff. In other words (1 Cor. 10:13), God's gonna make a way of escape for his people. God's people will not go through God's wrath—the days of God's vengeance on earth when God's wrath will be poured out on the earth on all those who missed the return of Jesus Christ (2 Thess. 1:7–10; Matt. 24:1–22, 24:27–39, 24:1–13). Then the wrath of God is called Great Tribulation. If the pandemic isn't a plague, then what is it? According to Scripture, plagues are God's wrath, especially ones of this magnitude like in Moses's day when God was trying to get the wicked Pharaoh's attention, and it took ten warning plagues to finally wake him up. I just wonder how many will the sleeping USA get? Or the whole world. Do you think the pandemic is a plague or a warning from God? I do! Some friends used to sing that old gospel song "Plenty of Time" by Connie Smith, wow (Google it or look it up on YouTube, I dare ya). So if there is still plenty of time, then someone please explain the pandemic, road rage, sex trafficking, drugs, porn, full prisons, and people taking the microchip in their hand (*in*—that's a keyword; this is happening in our day, and it's being injected inside the hand [Rev. 14:9–11]). Wow, and people just sweep it under the rug… Oh, take a chill pill, preacher, and no one believes we are in the Last Days. Wow, because of pleasure, phones, TV, sports, entertainment, love life, and fun, they'll call you a negative thinker. They'll say, "You're discouraging me," "You're bringing me down," "No, we don't want to read (2 Timothy 3 and 2 Peter 3)," etc. Again, this generation has come full circle. I know I'm reading the Bible correctly. I see it. Why don't others? Are you reading the Bible correctly? So then Jesus could come any time Now. You can now compare the Bible prophecies with the daily newspaper. Robberies in broad daylight. It isn't safe even in the daytime anymore, wow, wait a minute, that to is told, when they cry "peace and safety" then sudden destruction (1 Thess. 5:3) then the Lord is about to come. (Matt. 24:31–33). I hope we all make it, God save our families and friends, in Jesus's name and help people to see my points and get a better understanding of the closeness we are to Christ's return. And help them to draw the line straight between the devil and you Lord Jesus to be on God's side of the line in Jesus's name.

Note: in this day and time and even in Christ's day where people love pleasures, more than God (2 Tim. 3:4) where politics are more important to them than God, where sports, TV, entertainment, fun pleasure, anything and everything Is more important than God. Until a tornado or hurricane, or fire or flood, or volcano, etc., takes it all away. Sure, a lot of very good people lost their all. And had to start over, I know what it's all about to start all over. It's hard, and I pray, God help them all. But my point is about good people, even good, nice people, stray, according to scripture, but even the last few verses of (Matthew 24:42, 43, 44) says: if the good man of the house had known in what watch the thief would come, he would have watched and would not have suffered his house to be broken up also in (1st Thes. 5:2) the Bible says, the day of the Lord so cometh as a thief in the night. Also see, (2nd Peter 3-1) (Rev. 3-3) (Revelation 16-15) it's spiritually speaking about how a real life like thief comes, he comes in the night when your asleep or gone, you don't know he even comes till afterwards then it's to late, this is the analogy of Jesus' coming back for his people, he's coming as a thief in the night, (1st Thes. 5-2) (2nd Peter 3-10) (Mat. 24-43) (Luke 12-39) and so many people are so busy partying and getting drunk, they are not watching when Jesus comes like a thief in the night, as in (Luke 21-34 to 36) you have to be sober to watch, there are even people that are so ugly in their hearts cause of authority type on their job or put in a position that's gone to their head, I know many, I read a bumper sticker that read, "it's hard to soar with eagles when you work with so many turkeys," ha. But truthfully when you study about Jesus, he never exalted his self but preached and taught the opposite, yes it's sad when you see the puffed up people looking down their noses at ya even in churches it's sad to say I've seen them so puffed up with pride with all their muscular physiques, and all their multitudes of degrees, and awards of being well learned in other docterines, and don't misunderstand me please, all that's good if they can stay humble, and not get puffed-up with pride, cause then that's when you fall and become prideful and arrogant with a naughty spirit (Proverbs 16-18) (1st Cor. 10-12) (1st Cor. 13-4) (Romans 12-3) (Acts 4-13) some of these people have forgotten Jesus was written about, that he was humble as a sheep before his shearers (Act 8-32) (Isa. 53-7), he was a King of Kings and Lord of Lords, yet he bowed down and humbled his self before his disciples and washed their feet (John 13-3 to 15) (see verse 35). Does anyone out there think you could go and visit some king or president, or even some stuff shirt siminar scholar or some buffed up with pride body builder, or some intellect scholar with all kinds of degrees, would you see any of them bow down and wash your feet, (no way)... I've been in meetings over the years and said I thought we should have some old fashion feet washing service.

Also read (Philippians 2:2 to 10) (see verse 5 and verse 7) (wow) you ought a heard all the excuses, ha, you want to see a revival, some have said, yet they are to proud to get down and wash feet like Jesus did in (John 13), see (verse 15) that Jesus said he left us an **example** for us to also do and follow, and (35) says…by this shall all men know you are my disciples, if you have love one toward another. (Hell-o) **WOW**…and people wonder why there's no revival today. So back when the thief came, the good man of the House would not have suffered the loss though that doesn't apply to storms. My point is many good folks think because they are good, they donate to their favorite charities, they volunteer to help as a cook at a rescue center or mission or help at food give away, hospital, etc. (This saves no one spiritually from their sins.)

Good deeds will not save you. You must be born again (John 3:3, 5). And I'm repeating myself. But there are many in the world I have known, that don't believe you have to follow God and the Bible. And I feel for them. But again, according to scripture, God sends the devastations to many, to get them to turn to Him. And it also says, it rains on the just and the unjust, and nobody knows why so many things, that happens to folks, including me, but God is always got the answer. Again, and if we do die, we have a better place to go to (John 14:1 to 4). Many people do not want to make wave's especially when it's time to take a stand for what's right or for God. This is one of the reasons I know that I know, judgment is coming from God. I've seen people pleasers in so many crooked factory businesses. Everyone looks the other way.

One in particular I quit, and I stood in the face of that boss and said this kind of stuff is wrong and gave my two weeks' notice, and was told, you can go right now, and I did with no regrets. Notice I was told, you can go right now. That Boss, knew I was a pastor then, my small church then, Just took in enough to pay the bills many times I had to take out of my own pocket to pay bills of the church, I have my own to pay as well, so I've always worked a second job as well as pastoring, which cuts into study time, and visitation or God forbid a funeral or wedding: most folks don't have a clue about it, *they just think* the pastor magically gets his bills and the churches paid. From his magic money tree. Ha. That would be nice, but usually a small church pastor sacrifices his hind end off, at both ends, working two jobs, and no one has a clue. But again, you try to do what's right, as all servants of God Do good, to plant good seeds.

You'll see, especially If it is like the corn type seeds (wow…study that one out or The Golden Rule as Jesus taught (Matt. 7:12) it really works usually, bad treatment from others is a lot of times from people who think they are better than others, or people in authority and it's gone to their head, or those that are really gifted or very talented. At any case I've seen many, many reap good and bad (Gal. 6:7, 8, 9; James 4:17). Think on this reader friend, when you die, what kind of eulogy will be said of you at your funeral. Now is a good time to start planting good memories of yourself…And if you are sincere about it…start it like King David did in prayer, as in (Ps. 51), once our heart is right with God…The rest will follow, then ask God for help on it. But be real, not hypocritical. I heard a preacher tell a eulogy about a rich hit man, his brother was paying the pastor $10,000 to say he was a good godly saint…So the pastor agreed to do it. At the funeral, the pastor said Joe was a no-good thief and a liar, murdering bum/drunken tramp, that would steal dead flies from a blind spider, but next to his lying thieving brother Frank here, he was a good ol' godly Saint. HA. Wow…So plant good memories, ask God to always check you, I've had to go and apologize to people many, many times, don't be to puffed up or to proud to say I was wrong, and I'm sorry… Forgive me…God blesses a humble heart. Anyway, where do we draw the line pleasing God, more than pleasing man, humbled people pleases God (1 Pet. 5:5; James 4:6, see verses 7:10; Heb. 11:24, 25; Galatians 1:10; Acts 5:29)? For if I yet pleased man, I should not be the servant of Christ and we ought to obey God rather than man. That is what turned me on to the church called Living Christ Church in Tulare, Ca. If there was a church that pleased God, this is it. Oh, I'm sure there are a few problems in all churches because no one is perfect but after we resigned our church. We shopped around, and our minister friend Ray said I must visit the church he attended. And it's been about nine years now.

And man, these folks know how to have church, and they have all showed the love of Christ and the pastor preaches what God tells him to. He fasts and prays for God's perfect will and for the right words to give, Pastor Donahue and Evon Green are indeed sent by God (And in my book) "the best pastors on the planet. This man of God holds nothing back; he gives it his all and really flows in the spirit. And he is very sensitive to the spirit of God and has casted out many devils since I've been there and is not a man pleaser but a God pleaser. And this man follows the Bible, and walks the walk, and walks the talk, and lives what he preaches. And preaches against sin, and probably steps on a few toes. And he is definitely respected for it. We all need to hear the truth from the Bible. And at Living Christ Church, you get the truth. After resigning my church, we looked and looked for a church where anointed preaching was and a man of God preached the whole word without compromise and yes step on our toes.

And delivers anointed messages from God with love and with power. Thank you, Pastor Donahue Green and First Lady Evon Green for your stand, you're a rare but chosen vessel that allows God to move and flow through him, you won't misunderstand this man of God, cause it's very obvious this man's full of God, and he loves people but in love preaches the 100 percent Word of God, and that is rare, most of the mega churches do not, in fear of people. Any way I've covered this already but wanted to pat the man of God on the back. No not kissing up, as they say on the job places. I'm my own person with my own integrity and have been persecuted for God on the job. At many companies and not meaning to run myself righteousness up on a flag pole (1 Cor. 1:28 and 29 verse 26 to 29). Just making a point that we all are about to face this era in life where it's about the rubber meeting the road and you better thank God if you have a man of God, that fasts and prays for a word from God to give you, a lot of those out there like I mentioned earlier are ear ticklers (2 Tim. 4:3, 4, 5; 2 Pet. 3:16, 17; Rom. 8:8; Rom. 15:3 and 4; 1 Cor. 1:17 to 28; 1 Cor. 2:4, 5).

We need more men of God like this, that preaches it all. But it's good to be encouraged but it is a time to draw closer to God, and a time to be more sensitive to God's Spirit, and to God's time clock in this prophetic day we are living in, people have been desensitized by the media, movies, sports, music, friends, and just plain-o flat out unbelief, that we are actually in the Last Days, and *this is why God has to allow the things of those great devastation type scriptures to start unfolding is to get people's attention* and because people have been spiritually rocked to sleep by the devil, and social media, and sin is now vastly worldwide spread with just the flick of a button on phones, iPads, computers, TVs, and even children can now get access to porn, etc., and ungodly stuff that desensitizes their soul and spirit, people especially the youth don't and won't listen to the Gospel preached or prophecy, unless they are extremely awakened, and have God to turn on the light, by some horrific catastrophic event type nightmare situation to happen on earth and it is sad to say that it takes tornadoes, earthquakes, etc., to get people to pray but if you've studied prophecy, then you too would know, according to the end time prophecies, earth is about to embark on such a nightmare type events written in the end time prophecy scriptures.

And this is not preached from church pulpits because of their lukewarm souls (Rev. 3:15 to 20, Rev. 2:2 to 16) nor do people want to hear it…Everyone wants to be encouraged, and to have their ears tickled (2nd Tim. 4:34), which is also end time prophecy, which I have already covered, but you may ask what needs to take place to prevent this, people need to be revived, we need revival like never before (and God will do what he has to, to get people ready), especially when they don't want to pray and get saved and those that are saved but if people have a praying mother or grandma praying for you to get saved like I did (I had both) you may as well give up to God now, it'll save ya a lot of butt kick ns. From God later, and those that are saved need to draw closer than ever before to God with all their hearts (Matt. 12:40, 41; 2 Chron. 7:14; Rev. 2:4, 5; people just don't see it) so this last scripture says unless we repent…God will remove the candlestick (which is the light of our salvation) which explains (Rev. 3:5) getting your name blotted out of the Book of Life, which happens to those who stray, that so many false religions teach the opposite.

But I believe God's Word (KJV). (It's our soul, and eternity, I'm talking about and you better stay repented, and stay right with God so you aren't left. (Gal. 5:16 to 21, 1 Cor. 6:9, 10) And there are many other scriptures that warns you, that will keep you out of heaven sin, and disobedience, and these are not being preached on from a lot of church pulpits (Why?). So many of these Pastors today are people pleasing pastors (So do we draw the line to) want to please the people, or God? (Gal. 1:10, Heb. 11:6) So to be like Enoch (verse 5) having a great testimony, or reputation that you pleased God with the way you live your life for God, and so much, that God don't even let you die...instead he just beams you up to heaven. Wow... and so living a life opposite of that is in sin, and disobeying God's commandments and disobeying God's Word is a good way to get on God's hit list of his wrath. The Bible is really firm on this (so if you read. Eph. 5:6).

Some pastors that don't warn their flocks are not true shepherds, and God "will" send His wrath down on them for disobeying God! (Ezek. 33) Yes...Pastors will be judged for not preaching the whole truth (Ps. 25:4, 5, 1 Thess. 5:14, 2 Pet. 3:17, Heb. 12:25, Gal. 1:10) plainly says if I please men, then I won't be the servant of Christ. Wow, I preach the Word of God. And I had a pastor in Arkansas, apologize to his congregation afterwards, I was shocked, it was a good message, he was an ear tickler type, and no doubt, probably never ever stepped on any toes of his wealthy parishioners, in fear of losing those high dollar tithers, which this type of pastor, won't make heaven anyway according to scripture, but in fact would be considered another judas, loving money more than people's souls. Jesus said it would have been better that he'd never been born (Matt. 26:24, Luke 12:34, Luke 12:21) than to betray the son of God, wow, so the price Jesus paid for these souls with his life on the Cross, was just cast to the dirt (1 Cor. 6:20) (Matt. 26:11), and this Judas pastor was only concerned about his money (Mark 14:5–7) and (John 12:4–6) (see verse 6) (1 Tim. 6:10).

Jesus will say for such as you done it not to the least of these (Matt. 25:41 to 46) or will he say depart from me, I never knew you or will we hear him say... "Enter into the joy of the Lord, thou good and faithful servant" (Matt. 25:23, Matt. 12:30, Luke 6:46). Wow. I assure you there will be great multitudes of people, that will say on that day, Lord, we prayed in your name, and casted out devils in your name (Matt. 7:22–23 and Matt. 25:41) and Jesus will say, "I never knew you, depart from me, you that work-iniquity. Wow, so somebody backslid or what. You have to have a good relationship with God to cast out a devil, so somewhere along the way. These folks turned back away from God (John 6:66) (Heb. 4:11) and (1 Tim. 4:1) (2 Pet. 2:21–22) losing their spiritual power and favor with God (Luke 9:62) but then rewards and eternity comes, they forget they backslid, and expect God to still reward them for back when they worked for God, no sorry, it doesn't work like that, you have to stay on God's boat all the way to the other side. You can't put your hand to the plow and look back (Luke 9:62). You've got to go all the way, that's why Jesus said remember, Lot's wife, she looked back, and died (Luke 17:32) She didn't make it. We can't be two faced or dou-bled-minded (James 1:8).

But we must put on the mind of Christ (Phil. 2:5) 'cause we can't eat at God's table and the devils table (1 Cor. 10:21–22) but I believe, since Jesus said, depart from me I never knew you, they had to of backslid, as in (John 6:66). So you can't turn away or stay away from God, and then on Judgment day remind Him of all the things you done for him (Matt. 7:22–23). Even though you turned away and went back to the Dog vomit life that (2 Pet. 2:20–22) He saved you out of. Wow, what a slap in God's face is that. Will he say go away, or will we hear the Lord say? Enter in thou good and faithful servant (Matt. 25:23) or "depart from me, I never knew you" So to turn back, and turn away from God is to say out of one's heart, my fun, my pleasure, everything about my lifestyle has no room for you God (1 Pet. 2:21 to 24; Luke 13:27, 28; Matt. 25:41). So then God says, then, when you leave this life and wouldn't give me time of day and you lived your life without worshipping me, why would I let you into my heaven, that I prepared for my people (John 14:1–4), you lived your life without me, go I never knew you, you chose, to live the way you wanted, to not including me, so I will in return not include you, in my new heaven that I've prepared for those who love and follow me, so depart from me, I never knew (Matt. 7:23, Matt. 16:26) you, ouch.

But this will be the hard words to hear to millions that mistakenly thought they would just be accepted into heaven because they've been a good person. This is a delusion, but, if your name is blotted out of the Book of Life as in (Rev. 3:5), your doomed. And hearing the words "Depart from me," will echo in the sinner's mind and soul forever. How horrifying is that? Because it's only those that ask for Jesus Christ's forgiveness of all their sins and ask him to come into their hearts and save their soul, turning from their ways and follow Jesus. That'll make it in (1 John 1:7–9; John 3:3, 5; Rom. 10:9–10; Rom. 10:13; Luke 6:46; Matt. 7:21, 22, 23). This, even this Jesus experienced on the cross while suffering in pain and torturous death, and feeling all alone and people denying that they know him in fear of being crucified with him, so before he dies, when he takes all the sins of the whole world upon him, and God the father even looks away, so Jesus would experience, the feeling of isolation from his own father, that (Heb. 2:18 and Heb. 4:15) shows us, and through this, Jesus seeing God the father turn away, not looking on Him when he took all the sins of the world on him, Jesus cried Eli-Eli, la' ma sa-bach' tha-ni? (Matt. 27:46). That is to say, "My God, my God, why has thou forsaken me [because God looked away from Jesus, and all the sins, Jesus took upon him from man]?"

So Jesus had indeed experienced the worst death, and isolation from God, plus taking our sins upon him, to die for us all, so we all could make it to heaven. For those that call upon him for salvation and repent and turn from their wicked ways (2 Chron. 7:14). So you see why God will pour out his wrath on those who reject Jesus Christ. Everyone has the same opportunity to ask Jesus to forgive them. And most people that pay big bucks for something and it ends up being no good, most all people would exchange it or demand a refund (2 Cor. 5:21) says for he (God) made him (Jesus) to be sin for us, who knew no sin, that we might be made the righteousness of God in him (1 Cor. 6:20) says (for ye are bought with a price, And that was paid for with his life, so Jesus paid our way to heaven And God has the right to get mad at those who reject Jesus. Just like we would if we paid hundreds of thousands of dollars for a house that caved in a sinkhole, everything was a loss. We all would want a refund. Is God any different?

God wants what he paid for with his son's life, the highest price, of all time. "Don't ever think you aren't worth anything. We've heard parents say that growing up. Some neighbor, friend, wife tell her loser husband that lost his job, or got arrested, but don't ever think your worthless. No matter what anybody says, you were worth Jesus Christ dying for, that God so loved (you, the world) that he gave his only begotten son, that whosoever (that's you) believes in him (Jesus), should not perish, but have everlasting life (John 3:16). So make God proud, live right, pray, ask forgiveness from God and even others. Through God you can change (Phil. 4:13, Fred did) anyone can. Amen (Phil. 4:13–19), so can you with the Lord's help. You can (Matt. 6:33). Each day seek God daily. Then you too'll hear those words, "Enter into the joy of the Lord, thou Good and faithful servant." And Jesus felt alone, he said in his word, he was tempted in all points as we are yet without sin, Heb. 4:15, Heb. 2:18 and Jesus cried from the cross. (Matthew 27:46). Eli Eli, la ma sa bach tha ni? That is to say my God, my God, why hast thou forsaken me?

So you see, my friend, you will know when you're in pain and hurting all night and feel all alone, know Jesus has also gone through this so he can relate to your situations, forsaken, alone suffering even betrayal sold out by his own disciple, mocked, spit on, slapped, beard pulled, beat, whipped, stabbed, nails in his feet and hands, crown of thorns, then made to carry the cross to his place to die at. Oh, dear friend, he done and allowed all this so you could be saved and make heaven. This is why, there will be the day of wrath from God on those that reject Jesus Christ. I was so angry at our hometown memorial of my brother Crpl. Alan Eunice Davis that gave his life in the army (in the Vietnam War) and dies so we could have freedom and the memorial building had his name printed as Alvin (wrong) yes, I had to repent, but I was not a Christian then! But thank God the wall got my brother's name right, and other Vietnam war soldiers names right. So you see we get upset when it's us. Do we think God doesn't have feelings or gets upset when he (God) feels his son (Jesus)

223

died for nothing. (John 3:16) says, God so loved the world (so much) that he gave us his son (Repeat) God loved us, the world so much, he was willing to die. A suffering type death to show us how much he loves us. And it goes right over people's heads. It doesn't even soak in. In (John 10:18), Jesus said, "No man takes my life from me, but I lay it down of myself, I have power to lay it down, and I have power to take it again, this commandment have I received of my father."

I admired Mel Gibson's movie the *Passion of Christ*. And even Mr. Gibson wanted people to see the in-depth of the death of Christ. Although I felt he should have empathized more on the reason (Why) Jesus died, and to also explain the plan of salvation, and have a man of God praying with someone, leading them to Christ in prayer, allowing someone in the movie to get saved. And I am not talking about any religion or church, but someone praying with someone in a sinner's prayer because churches and religions just give doctrines and beliefs, but a prayer takes you to the throne of God. And that is eternal. People don't care God gave his only son (John 3:16, 17, 18). Some think it's just a story, someday they'll know…oopps…it'll be too late then! But the wrath of God will not be taken out on the true believer (1. Thess. 5:9) because God delivered Noah, and Lot, and Moses and the children of Israel all escaped God's wrath and so will those who follow Jesus and live for him, after those who received Jesus Christ as Lord and savior and follow the Bible. Example of (Luke 16:23) you must notice here one is burning in hell, and one is in "The Arms of Abraham…in heaven." Wow is (Ps. 23:5) but again not all will follow Jesus and the Bible, which explains why (Matt. 25:32, 33) was written. Jesus will gather together all nations and divide them as a shepherd separates the goats from the sheep. Goats on the left, sheep on the right (Ps. 78:52, Matt. 10:16).

So if the followers of Christ are considered sheep and he is gonna separate the sheep from the goats. Why is there cult religions that represents goats? It has to be lack of knowledge (Hos. 4:6). Again, the sheep are on the right side and the goats are separated to the left. Verse 34 of (Matt. 25:32 to 34). Then the king says unto them on the right hand. Come ye blessed of my father, inherit the kingdom prepared for you from the foundation of the world. The

Bible is clear and to the point. People who don't want to change their life and follow Jesus Christ are considered goats, according to scriptures. But this is merely a biblical analogy, that Jesus used and he called them parables, to explain an examples or certain situations to them. And again, this is the reason Jesus said he would send back (the comforter the Holy Ghoset The Holy Spirit) that when he got to heaven he would send back the Holy Ghost, that would come inside the believer and teach, lead, and guide him through the scriptures, giving him understanding (so man would not have to teach you.) Because to what seems to be a mystery of the *thee*s and *thou*s, and parables, to many people, they just don't get it when others that are fully 100 percent dedicated to God who don't still party and don't get drunk, don't drink anymore and don't smoke anymore till their eyes turn red, and they are not rubbing shoulders with the world, when all through the New Testament it says not too, and yet many scriptures such as these mysteries, are giving understanding to the believers by the Holy Ghost.

But one thing is for sure that's all through the Bible, evil, cruel, wicked, mockery, murderous hateful spirited type's will not make it. (Gal. 5:15–26). But the Bible says whosoever calls on the Lord Jesus, shall be saved. As in (Romans 10:9, 10, 13; Revelations 22:17; Revelations 21:6; 1 Corinthians 2:12). It's a free gift of God, salvation (John 3:16; Rom. 5:15 to 19; Rom. 6:22; John 4:10; Acts 2:38, 39; Rom. 6:23; Eph. 2:8; Heb. 6:4).

So you see salvation is a gift, when you receive Jesus Christ in your heart, when you repent and get saved he comes in after we ask him to save and cleanse our hearts from sin, which is getting our soul washed out from the filthy way we used to live in sin, partying and getting drunk, cussing and chasing around, and committing adultery and fornication, etc. (Rev. 1:5, 1 John 1:7) and it's sad to say, many in the churches today are still shacking up and living in adultery (Exod. 20:14) which is one of the Ten Commandments. Sad to say. They have a real shocking awaking coming. They won't make heaven. (Gal. 5:17–22, Eph. 5:18, 1 Cor. 6:9–10, 1 Cor. 5:11) is anybody really that blind and stupid, what's the point of getting saved, if you are gonna keep living in sin, you may as well go sell your soul to the devil, you're going to hell anyway. No, I don't really want you to do that, but try to understand my point, God ain't playing games here, get your butt right or get left. Why is it you can tell someone rules to the Game shows on TV that pay the Big Bucks and they get it and do it. (Is that called selective hearing?)

But tell them what the Bible says on how to make heaven. But they just don't get it. So once our soul and heart has asked forgiveness of all the old man ways, the scripture says Jesus comes into the clean garnished heart dwelling place and makes us a new creation in Christ (2 Cor. 5:17). This is why you can't follow religion, some will not teach this, some want you to confess your sins to man. Not so, but to Christ (1 Tim. 2:5, Acts 4:12). Like one that says in the Bible, call no man on the earth father (Matt. 23:9) Yet many churches and families do (Rom 10:9, 10, 13) And then again, I'm speaking about what the Bible says, and not what man's religions and churches say. This is the whole reason everyone needs to read the first four chapters of revelation (Rom. 10:9, 10, 13; John 3:3, 5; Rom. 8:9, 10, 11, 14, 17).

Yes, it is a gift, but like a plane ticket gift, it'll change your destination, even though it's a gift, you still must have to be at the airport at the right airlines, and right time, at the right gate, and be ready and board that plane, there are conditions that are your responsibilities, rules, and regulations to go to heaven or if traveling by airplane to some other state or country. Just because someone gave you a free ticket doesn't magically put you there. Come on, folks, there are preparations on our part to go and travel anywhere, are you taking clothes, suitcases, shoes, and undees, etc. Again the time clock of your departure is extremely important, very important to arrive early.

Because your gate could be on the other side of the airport, if you've ever flown out of Dallas, you understand. And spiritually speaking, staying ready in your soul is not much different, being ready, staying ready. Watch God's time clock in the prophecy scriptures, knowing, now is the time, any time now, and those dummies that say Jesus delays his coming and eat and drink with the drunkards, Jesus said I will come in a day and in an hour they are not aware of (Matt. 24:36) (Mark 13:32) (Mat. 24:44) (Luke 12:40–46) (Matt. 24:48 to 50). Back to having your ticket to your plane some may decide to throw their ticket away…in other words people have given up on God, cause of misunderstandings, offenses, jealousy, etc. And say they miss the old life and go back to it, going back to their old ways. People are throwing it away cause someone in church upset them, or someone died, or misunderstandings, offences, jealousy, envies, sin of turning back to their old ways.

And you can, some think you can't but I believe the Bible over people and it says you can go back to your old ways and become seven times worse than before, but tell that to those religious folks (2 Pet. 2:21–22 and Matt. 12:43–45) when a man is saved and born again as in (John 3:3, 5 and Matthew 18:3, 4,) we must be converted into the same type spirit and innocence of a little child, our spirit man becomes reborn in spirit, when we repent and ask Jesus Christ into our hearts and ask him to forgive us of our sins! But to return back to our old ways is so blasphemous, and a slap in the face to God. Yet so many do and become seven times worse than they was before they got saved (Matt. 12:43–45) This is the generation, more wicked than in Noah's Day, and according to (Matt. 24) The God of heaven will soon destroy this earth again, but, there will be seven years of sorrow, and half of that is called Great Tribulation three and a half years, which will be hell on earth (see my book (is the chip 666) and my other book (Matt. 24:22, Unless God shortens the days no flesh will be saved!)

Oh yes, friends, we may not know the exact day. But Jesus said you'll know your close by the signs of the times (Matt. 24:32–43). And this all explains the man legion (Luke 8:30) and Hollywood is on dangerous grounds with God with all their ungodly movies, I've seen previews of some, and they are worse now than in my old hippy days, for sure worse than Noah's day. So beware friends, stay close to God, like a sheep to his shepherd, things are wrapping up. Which explains the man legion who must have kept going back and forth, or how about those that haven't (Rom. 11:4). God will let people go back and live for the devil. Yes, you heard right, God never has and never will force anyone to live for him and it's what thus says the Word of God. (John 6:66) again says many of his disciples. DISCIPLES = followers of Jesus Christ, but these ex-followers went back cause their heart wasn't truly right with God and walked no more with him (as in John 6:66). Isn't it weird and peculiar, that John would write the scripture text number of the chapter and verse, to be the same number as the mark of the beast 666 (chapter 6, verse 66) "an anti-Christ" = "A Backslidder."

Wow, are you seeing this. And over the forty-some years I've preached, I've heard so many of certain religions that just want to argue and say God's not gonna disown ya or leave ya, Ha. If you are that backslidder, you are deceived and too stupid to just read and understand what I just wrote; the backslider walked away from God! He turned away…God paid the price (1 Cor. 6:20) for your salvation, why would he walk away? He'll take a backslider back, if he truly repents. God loves them (John 3:16, 17, 18, 19). The sin in it, is, the lie, that the backslider says he's still saved, which is calling God and God's Word-a-lie, and the Bible says you can't hang on to both, the worldly life of sin and living for the devil and still say your saved…that's a lie (2 Cor. 2:11, 1 Cor. 6:9 to 20, 2 Cor. 5:17, 1 Cor. 10:21) Which I covered already! They quit. Living for god (Matt. 11:28 to 30, 1 Pet. 5:6 to 9) God's a loving and forgiving God, and will take anyone back, with stretched out hands (the word "who-so-ever") means anyone can call upon the name of the Lord shall be saved. And his name is Jesus Christ, amen. (Again, those scriptures are, John 6:66, 1 Tim. 4:1, 1 John 2:19, Rev. 2:4, 5) And there are still people that think the opposite. I love what peter said in John 6:68, after Jesus said are you gonna go away also in verse 67.

Wow, Peter says Lord to whom shall we go? You have the words to eternal life (Rev. 3:20). Behold, I stand at the door and knock. If any man hears my voice and open the door, I will come into him and will sup with him. And he with me. No. 1 The doorknob is on your side of the door. He has power to force it open, but he is a gentleman and wants it to always be our choice to follow him. Our decision, we have to decide and draw our own choice's line to God or to the way of the world or the way of God. "How do we draw the line." To live like the world does is to anger God, that would be throwing your ticket away. To go back to that sinful life would be throwing your ticket away…To those who don't follow the Bible would be throwing your ticket away.

Again as Peter said Jesus has the words to eternal life, and to reject Jesus and the Bible, that's throwing away your ticket to heaven: Recognizing the one behind a misunderstanding, or blaming a person for something, instead of seeing that the Bible says it's the devil that comes to steal, kill and to destroy (John 10:10; 1 Pet. 5:8, 9; Rev. 12:10, 11, 12). And even though we see that the devil as the accuser of the brother and is come down to you with great wrath, because he knows he has a short time, see (verse 11) says, they (we, you, and me) overcame him (the devil) by the blood of the Lamb, and by the word of their testimony (our, your confession in Jesus Christ) and they loved *NOT* their lives unto the death. If the rulers of this world take my head, and my life for refusing the New World order, such as refusing to be chipped as in (Rev. 20:4, Rev. 13:16), in my words. I choose to follow Jesus Christ and the written Word of God (The KJV Bible).

I have lived both lives and have been on both sides of the fence. And I chose to follow Jesus. And his word and yes, there are many, many opinions, beliefs, views, religions, but it's up to us as individuals to choose. I prayed and asked the Lord to direct me (Prov. 3:5, 6), you have the steering wheel and the doorknob, you can't blame Mama and Daddy. They will not stand in your shoes on judgment day. You must decide, then once you choose, it is very important to keep praying, reading the Bible, start with KJV in the New Testament, four gospels, first the life of Christ, then work your way through, the New Testament first, you were just born again, not to sound offensive but according to scripture, you become a babe in Christ, and the New Testament is considered milk of the word the Basics of learning the Christian walk, becoming a follower, and a disciple of Jesus Christ.

As a real baby can't chew a steak when he's a few months old, so is a new born-again believer, so you now begin to study the New Testament first, then go to the old and always pray and ask the Holy Ghost to give you understanding (John 14:26, 1 Cor. 2:13–14), when you desire to know and learn, you develop a inner discernment, a deep hunger to understand, when that hunger for spiritual knowledge comes inside you, then your hearts cry is, feed me Lord, reveal your word down in the depths of my soul, fill me with your word and spirit. Then get ready, Jesus, through the Holy Ghost will give you both barrels (hallelujah). A good secret (Key) to stay in good standing with God is always keep the communication lines open and clear. In other words, keep a repented heart always (as in Ps. 51:10, 11, 12, 13:17).

Note: Psalms is also good with the New Testament, which is the way the little pocket New Testaments are set up (always). Keep a clear honest conscience before God if you feel you've sinned, get it under the blood of Jesus. And if there is an offense, nip it. Pray, ask them also for forgiveness (Matt. 5:23–24) (also see verse 42) (Matt. 18:21–22) (Eph. 4:32) (Matt. 6:14–15). The Greek word katallage which means, reconciliation, as in (Rom. 5:10–11) or (Matt. 18:15–19) or (Rom. 11:15–23) (2 Cor. 5:17–19). We must forgive, if we want power to agree (Eph. 2:8). But always pray, ask the Lord in Jesus's name to forgive you, of any and all sin and teach you, asking the Holy Ghost to lead you and guide you into all truths, scripture. And thank him for hearing your prayers and supplying all your needs.

And having this kind of attitude and desiring to be taught and wanting to learn. God is faithful, (1 Cor. 10:13, Rom. 8:11, John 14:26, John 15:6, 7). Wow. God does really love us all. Remember the devil's the accuser of the brethren and the author of confusion. And does not want us to understand. Yes, there is a battle, a fight against evil. Against the devil and he brings the bad thoughts to our mind. And tries to trick us with anything he can, and Jesus said the devil is the father of liars. Scriptures teach that if the devil himself has appeared to some as an angel of light, don't marvel, if he does come with false ministries, false religions, etc. (2 Cor. 2:11, 2 Cor. 11:3, 2 Cor. 11:13–15). So don't be surprised, when you see them on TV appearing as an evangelist of God, but they are just after your money. You wonder, would they ever preach to prisoners for free. And buy Bibles out of their own pockets to give to a prisoner? Probably not but those Judas's will beg for our Christian grandma's last dollar! And yes. The Bible warns us about them (2 Tim. 3:5–6, Col. 2:8, Matt. 7:15).

I think I already mention about the pastor in Arkansas that called me a liar and said (Matt. 7:15) wasn't in the Bible, I let him have his say. It was at his house. Rather than argue, we left but I showed my wife at my home and said, here it is (Matt. 7:15). False prophets which come to you in sheep's clothing but inwardly are ravening wolves. And I saw on YouTube a preacher that has made a ministry out of downing them by name, my old pastor said many years ago if the man your naming, repents, then you are touching God's anointing, which God forbids (Ps. 105:15). So preacher friend don't use names, we are no one's judge, we have a beam in our own eye. So how can we see to take a speck out of someone else's. And we are not their judge. That's God's job. That's why Jesus said let the weeds and the wheat grow together. And on judgment day, God'll have his angels separate them, the tares weeds on one side (to burn) and (Matthew 13:30) wheat Christians, are gathered into God's Barn heaven. And that includes me as well (Rom. 14:4; John 21:20, 21, 22).

Jesus called those religious Pharisees, Hypocrites, but if you noticed, he never mentioned their names, as in the story ("The Rich man") he just referred to him as ("the rich man") and didn't use a name, but however, Jesus did use Lazarus's name in (Luke 16:19, 20) because it's okay to brag on, and use Lazarus as a testimony, so others will follow a good pattern and make heaven, but he kept it as a whole unit (Plural, A Group, This isn't a personal war against each other). But "The war is against the devil," And your pastor is not the enemy...The devil is the enemy. Please note this: The devil wants to keep the church from having that spiritual bond of agreement between fellow Christians, cause he (the devil) knows, the church folks has power in agreement to get prayers answered so this is why he causes division and misunderstandings to try and break that yoke of agreement (Matt. 18:19, 20; Rev. 12:12). The devil is come down having great wrath because he knows he has a short time (Matthew 8:29).) wow...Yet a lot of churches don't even see it, and the world sure don't either! God blinded (Saul) who later was named Paul, God took care of him, and got him converted to Christianity. If Paul would have been in our day, He would have been run out of town by those who want to take God's place as judge, jury, and executioner.

231

Jesus told Peter, when Peter was so caught up with John leaning on Jesus chest (John 21:20–22), well. What about John, what's he gonna do. Jesus said, what's it to ya? You follow me, ha. Yeah, what is that to you, you follow me, hey. Big-eyed preacher, follow Jesus, and Jesus also said, if your eye offends you. Pluck it out. Ouch, our ministry should never be to destroy, but to save the lost and I would like to ask that minister that has made his ministry on destroying other ministries. So you need to read (Romans 14:4) and read (John 21:20–22) (Psalms 105:15) where Jesus said, What's that to you, you follow me...How many days did you spend fasting and praying for them?...ouch. If God saved Paul, when he was killing Christians, then God can also turn on the light to others, and always remember, people don't answer to you, but they'll answer to God. Amen.

Jesus constantly rebuked those Scribes and Pharisees that paraded around in ceremonial robes acting all holier than thou, Jesus called them hypocrites because they didn't live the right kinda life. They went to church and lived like a devil and no doubt as in (John 8 and Acts 7:54 to 60). Many go to all different type churches. And there are many people that don't go to church but watch those that do. And those that aren't really living for God. Just going, out of guilt or family obligation, or attend it for entertainment. These all are seen by others that think they are the real deal and judge the rest of the church by those bad examples. These religious men that listened to the devil, stoned Stephen while he was calling on God, (verse 59 of Acts 7), These blind men were so caught up in religion. They forgot the Bible and commandments that says for us not to kill, but again even back then people, seem to think they are judge, jury and executioner. I used to, but God showed me he's God.

He doesn't need my help; he's been God for thousands of years before I was born, and he don't need my help now. Just to be a witness with my Christian walk, to be a light in a dark world. Not a judge but we must live like Jesus said Christian (being Christ-like) The Bible says, he was like a lamb (harmless). We must forgive, if we want God to forgive us. We must forgive others or he won't forgive us all our trespasses: 7×70 490 times a day (Matt. 18:21–22) but if you read the rest of (Matt. 18 chapter, verse 23 to verse 35) it's pretty plain. Which it does sound like the same spirit and attitude those religious Pharisees and Scribes had.

So where do we draw the line? On religion. Church or religion won't save anyone) it's about having a personal relationship with Jesus Christ. *Webster's Dictionary* definition of religion is "a system of religious beliefs a belief in a divine, a belief, in a creator of the universe, etc." (And then it goes on to talk about religions of idol worship, etc.) But my point is a religion is a basic belief in something people want to bow down to, and worship. Many are indeed wrong but I'm not their judge. Again, but in Jesus's day, there were those that were, but if you didn't follow their religion, you were considered a babbler (1 Tim. 6:20, 21; Acts 17:18; 2 Tim. 2:16) or blasphemer, but, I myself, I'm gonna follow God, Jesus, and the Holy Ghost, and the KJV Bible. We all have to choose, what we believe.

Note: The world, the boozers, partiers, all tag, all church goers as religious but Jesus doesn't want religious people. Just saved, born-again believers, not religious, those religious guys were all the time coming against Christ. And Jesus was always rebuking them for being devils and being evil, and being hypocrites. So their being religious didn't save them. Nor just because people goes to church mean they get to go to heaven, again: they have to be saved and born again and following Jesus not religion, and read and follow the Bible 100 percent (even as I've said before, John 3:3 and 5, Rom. 10:9, 10, 13, 1 John 1:6, 7, 8, 9, 10). If we read (Matthew 25) and study it (Rev. 2:4–6, Rev. 3:5, 15–22), You gotta be full of God. Let's all get the facts straight and get a better understanding. What the people of today's world thinks a religious person is, and what Jesus Christ calls religious, are two completely different types. The one that people today call religious, they really mean fanatics, holy rollers, over board extremists, but it was these types, that think that we are fanatics that came to our church begging for you to pray for (So-in-so) that was dying in the hospital. The tagging was not so important then, and so when someone is between life and death and needing a miracle, a fanatic is the one they call on for prayer.

Wow, but in Jesus's day those religious guys that he called religious, were evil, self-centered, out for self-gain, and parading around in long robes (Acting) Holy, praying long prayers, on the street corners but most of all they came against Jesus, constantly provoking Jesus, and hindering the Gospel, Jesus called them children of the devil, and if you read the KJV (Matt. 23) the whole chapter is a rebuke to them. And they were so blind, they didn't even realize they were touching God's anointed son (Ps. 105:15) And the devil was using them against the work of the Gospel. And what about us, do we bad-mouth people that are doing God's work, or are we helping God get souls saved or are we hindering God, are we putting tags on people cause we are jealous that they are being used by God and we aren't. It's the life change, being born again, becoming a new creature in Christ, Jesus. (John 3:3, 5, 2 Cor. 5:17).

Allowing Jesus Christ to transform and change our heart and mind, our way of thinking is now become to the pleasing of God, learning and following scripture (Heb. 11:5–6). (The true definition of a Christian) is being Christ-like, loving, forgiving, not being a troublemaker but healing, performing, and doing God's work, as Jesus himself did. A follower of Jesus Christ, and his teachings, preaching and teaching the Gospel. Being God's example of a believer. I am so amazed at many so-called Christians = Christlike people of what we are supposed to reflect the image of Christ's love, cause ya can't be prejudiced and make heaven, but soldiers at time of war, or if you're a police officer, etc. Otherwise you can't kill people (and kill people) and make heaven (unless you're a) soldier at a time of war. You can't hate someone because his skin is a different color that's sin, that's being prejudiced, and it's sin. How does folks expect to get along in heaven if they can't get along here. (The Bible tells us all this!) No wonder the devil is trying to change the Bible so much, and cause chaos and confusion, with all different translations and different version Bibles (Rev. 22:18–19, Rom. 1:25). Why? Since Adam and Eve, the devil's been lying to folks. Yes, I'm repeating myself. (Gen. 3:1–5, Matt. 4:1–11)

We just have to remember, how I live here, will determine how I'll be judged there in heaven. We must do our best, to watch and pray, read and follow the Bible to our best of our ability and don't be blind and gullible knowing our adversary is the devil (1 Pet. 5:8–9) as a roaring lion he is seeking whom he may devour. He's out to try and deceive. And destroy anything and anyone who follows Christ. The Bible says to try the spirits to see if they are of God. It's not meaning join 'em but test them, check them with scripture, draw your line on your spiritual scale. Pray, line 'em up in prayer, asking the holy spirit to give you a discerning heart. One of the problems is most people anymore believe anything that. Anybody is giving them the benefit of the doubt. Well, maybe we're imagining things. I've seen real devil possessed people come into church and even prophecy and I knew one for years, not judging, but knew, oh sure.

If I know anyone that ever was full of the devil, she was and anyone can be delivered, and get the devil cast out of them, even her, but they gotta want to be delivered, and set free, this one was a performing demon, that came into our church, and put on a big performance, wow, what a act and then went right back out to prostitution (2 Pet. 2:20–22; 2 Cor. 11:13–15). That's not born again, not changed and delivered, 2 Cor. 5:17 repeat. Yes again, just hope with all my repeats, folks get it.

Yes, the Word says there is none righteous, no not one. We have all sinned and come short of the Glory of God (1 John 1:10, Rom. 3:23, 2 Pet. 2:4).

Note: God (Rom. 3:23) didn't put up with the angels that sinned, but cast them down to hell, and God sure won't tolerate it with us either. Read (2 Pet. 2:4–9). Wow…But that's being a fanatic for God, so why…Do people who deep down in their soul, that really believe and know about God and heaven and hell, and yet don't live for God 100 percent (but maybe just 51 percent) kinda on the fence, halfway type, yet if they feel they are dying. When they receive a very bad report from the doctor, then they want to get right with God, but, before the doctor's report. God wasn't even important enough to worship and live for, just on Easter and Christmas and Mother's Day or rare occasion, to do God a favor and make an appearance now and then, gee, this sounds like the Pharisees, or this sounds like being lukewarm to me (Rev. 3:15–19, 2:3–5) because lukewarm isn't hot or cold. It's being on the fence. It's in between. It's in the middle. It's neither for God or for the devil—lukewarm. Notice I said…I believe what the Bible says and this book is based on the KJV but I believe what the Bible (KJV) says, that the drunks, partiers, those who practice, sorcery, and witchcraft, evil workers of darkness, and idol worshippers, will not inherit the Kingdom of God (Gal. 5, Rev. 21:8, Rev. 18:23, Rev. 9:20–21, 1 Cor. 10:20–28, 1 Cor. 6:9–11) and for people that are reading this book and are doing what I've written, I will say to you, I did not write the Bible. I'm just merely saying and repeating what it says but I'm not the one you're really mad at, it's God you're mad at. I to was mad, cause before I got saved, I liked to party, and do those things God and the Bible condemns, but I also knew deep down, when I heard the doctor say I was gonna die, I had to let all that junk go, if I was gonna make heaven. And you know it too. Is getting your way really worth losing your soul forever in hell?

Really, you have a decision. (Yes, you have a decision to make! God or the devil, heaven or hell, to follow the truth, or live and follow lies and deception. No middle ground. You're all the way in or you're not, imagine, someone with one foot on a boat and one on the dock, and the boat is leaving, come on now. That's these same types of people we've been teaching about here, this is why, Jesus called them sinners, and they must be saved. So let's say this guy with one foot on the boat, and with the other one on the dock, and the boat is leaving and he can't swim, or…how far do ya go to revive someone? Spiritually speaking (spiritual CPR).

Note: In real life, if someone was drowning, you'd give them CPR. But in the Spirit spiritually speaking…There is a whole world of people drowning in their sins.) Ha. Wow, then he's gonna need, CPR, the sinners of the world, need spiritual CPR. That means they would need God's, cardiopulmonary Resuscitation (Gen. 2:7 and John 20:22) which when God truly saves, he breathes his breath of life into them, spiritually speaking, then begins a new breath of spiritual life and this is what John was saying in (John 3:3–5) being reborn. Again, a spiritual birth, but like my pastor Donahue Green has said, like being pregnant, you are or you're not. And soon it'll show outwardly and inwardly. There will be evidence you are. Wow, a great analogy pastor especially the part where he said, you can't be half pregnant, you are, or you're not!

But the true Christian, that truly lives for God 100 percent, wants everyone I mean all people everywhere to be saved, and according to the Bible if you don't want to do anything to try and convince people that they need Jesus (2 Cor. 5:11), even when family and friends call them a fanatic or say they are being too religious. And we are fanatics and are shoving it down people's throats. But when you read (Luke 16:19 to 31, especially verse 29). Wow (Luke 6:46 to 49) Jesus saying "why do you call me Lord, Lord, and don't do what I said to do?" Wow… What are these people gonna say on Judgment Day (Luke 14:16 to 24)? Notice what the verse 24 says "For I say unto you, that NONE of those men which were bidden shall taste of my supper."

None of those that were invited, that made excuses are going to the marriage supper of the Lamb! They will not go to heaven (in other words) to make excuses to God…when you could actually come and be there…you won't go into the marriage supper of the Lamb (heaven), which is the biggest event of all time ever. If you miss that, you're doomed to hell (Rev. 19:6 to 9). Notice verse 7, the bride wife of Jesus' wife. The wife has made herself ready (the keyword here is *made*). The Christian made herself ready (Rom. 12:1, 2; Heb. 12:1, 2). The disciples of the Lord, you and I must deny and self-discipline ourselves, disciples, followers of Christ. The wife of the Lamb the Christians (are you seeing this in scripture?) I don't mean to question anyone's mentality of intelligence, so please don't misunderstand my trying and teaching with simplicity (Rom. 12:8, 2 Cor. 11:3) as apostle Paul and Jesus Christ said to do. I see key words in scripture that almost seem to jump off the page, and at times I feel I need to break them down for a clearer understanding.

And God forgive me if I sound like I am contradicting myself (cause I'm not!) (Cause we know the main teaching of the Bible is from the Holy Ghost, (John 14:26)) I never want to contradict what I say or try to take the Holy Spirit's place, cause that's the Holy Ghost's job is giving you a clearer understanding (John 16:13), I pray that you just see my points and views. Amen. Again, the wife has made herself ready to meet the Lord(Revelation 19:17), wow (also see, ten virgins in (Matthew 25), brides to be). (Acts 1:8, 2 Cor. 5:11) says for us to witness and warn and to persuade people, and (Matt. 24:44) (Matt. 25:10) (Mark 13:30 to 37, Rev. 19:7) say, for all of us to watch and pray and be ready, but (Luke 14:16 to 24) says they all made excuses, saying...I married a wife, so I can't come...wow, hen pecked already...People even in Jesus day made excuses... Half of the chapter of (Luke 14) is on excuses, well again that won't fly on Judgment Day. When (Luke 16:27, 28), the rich man will stand and judge them (Notice he said to testify, to witness, and according to what Jesus said in (Luke 16:29 and Matthew 12:39 to 41).

So we don't have Moses and those same prophets today, like they had, back then, we call them ministers and pastors, and us pastors and those of us that still witness for Jesus, are doing a great work, for God inviting folks to church, and according to Jesus those people like in Jonah's Day that he warned according to (Matt. 12:39 to 41) will have the people in Jonah's Day rise up in Judgment against those today, that don't witness for God, or invite people to church, Wow, and now people want to go to church and can't cause of the pandemic plague and in (Luke 16:27, 28, 29), which is one of the main reasons Jesus Christ died on the cross, and is the no. 1 reason why the Christians are supposed to *witness* to the un-saved people, which is to keep them "OUT OF HELL," but they won't know if we don't warn them, or as the rich man in hell said, AGAIN (2 Cor. 5:11 is to persuade them) or in (Luke 16:28) to testify (witness) to them. (Acts 1:8) says you'll receive power after the Holy Ghost has come upon you (to witness) (this is in my words, so read it). This power isn't for fame or recognition of the saint, no. It's to take away your fleshly, carnal fear of what you think that man thinks, and this power takes away the fear of man. This power of the Holy Ghost is to give you a fuel of boldness to be an effective example and witness of God's love so you may share what the Bible says. Just as Paul wrote in (2 Corinthians 5:11), it is to persuade people to get on the boat that's about to sail again. God wants his people to witness to people like the brothers of the rich man in hell so they don't end up there in hell, in that place of torment, and there is only one way to stay out of hell, it's JESUS (Acts 4:12, John 14:6) And I must point out to everyone that thinks that your so intelligent, or you know more than me, and you believe that I don't know what I'm talking about (Acts 4:13).

Like my old friend thought, *how could dumb Fred teach ME? He doesn't know!* Even those in hell from our day that went to hell, they'll judge you if you don't want to witness to people, and according to (Matt. 12:41) says, the people of Nineveh that God was gonna destroy, will rise in Judgment with this generation…Hello…" Are you understanding the words that are coming out of my mouth," There are many, many, many more scriptures on this subject, but I must move on. If you read the four gospels and the New Testament, place after place tells of more of this, so those who refuse to witness will have many, many that will rise in judgment to accuse you on Judgment Day for not obeying what Jesus said.

And on Judgment Day the Bible=66 books of the Bible and the Book of Remembrance (Malachi 3:16) (and the Book of Life) will be opened (according to Rev. 20:12) And I saw the dead small and great, stand before God, and the books were opened (thirty-nine books of the Old Testament, and twenty-seven books in the New Testament equals sixty-six books of the Bible) and another book was opened which is the Book of Life, and the dead was judged out of those things which were written in the books, according to their works. Wow (I've heard people for years say the opposite.) So they that don't want to witness and those that have that, "I don't have to do nothing for God attitude type spirit" saying, "don't tell me to testify and witness to people," and they say "I don't believe I have to shove it down their throat attitude is definitely a spirit of rebellion! It is not a Christlike spirit of love or a I don't want to see any people go to hell attitude. No, so this is called a spirit of Anti-Christ or an opposite Spirit, or as (2 Tim. 3:5) says (it's a form of godliness but deny the power thereof) but again this rebellious attitude toward being a witness for Jesus Christ is not the spirit of God (but it is an Anti-Christ Spirit, a rebellious spirit) working in the children of disobedience (Eph. 2:2, Eph. 5:6, Col. 3:1 to 6) and according to the Bible…How about (Mal. 3:16) When the Book of Remembrance is opened… Wow…Are you telling me, that our lives are being recorded…oh yeah…you have been for years and you have no idea (1 Cor. 2:9).

God had the technology we have now, way back when man was inventing the wheel, and way, way more, we all would wet our pants if we really knew how much, and how powerful God really is, people seem to think they are dealing with a mild meek God, oh sure, your God is full of love and because of his son Jesus dying, he showed His love, and mercy and grace, abounds but that rebellious spirit in man, and woman, God has tolerated, long enough, but because Jesus died on the cross and paid the price for our sins, and his time clock of mercy and grace of getting in the door is on the last hour (Matt. 25:10) and signs of the times are wrapping up...God has dealt a merciful hand to man, and has been very patient with man's disobedience and rebellious ways. God has warned mankind for centuries, and God's Word is now unfolding and being fulfilled... If man misses the boats door shutting, cause it's about to sail, it's his own fault. God is saying get on the boat, come...

Today is your day to getting our names put in the Book of Life. If you haven't ask him to come into your heart yet and save your soul in other words you need to get saved now...so get your name written in the Book of Life, before the door is shut and before Jesus takes us out of here, when you repent, it means when you turn away from your sins, leave your old ways of living in sin, and turn your life over to Jesus, asking him to come into your heart and save you and, asking him to forgive you of all your sins, and ask for his help to understand the Bible and ask him to give you a desire to read it (or as the Bible says it: a hunger and thirst for righteousness.) Then He will, and then write your name in the Book of Life.

And despite what some religions teach, lies and false doctrine and they say you can't back slide, They lie, cause if you read (Rev. 3:5); it says: "He that overcometh, the same shall be clothed in white rainment, and will not "Blot out" his name out of the Book of Life, but I will confess his name before my father, and before his angels. Question: why does it say, to him that overcomes (if you're always saved) if you are like those religions that say "once saved always saved"? Hello...yet it plainly says to him that overcomes. ("You must overcome" or get blotted out.) Not to mention (John 6:66 and Matthew 25) Now I'm thinking one for sure way to get your name blotted out is to think that the chip isn't the mark of the Beast but it is and then take it, no. Don't you dare? You'd damn your soul forever.

Many will be deceived in the last days the Bible says in (Matthew 24 and 2 Thess. 2:8, 9, 10, 11, 12). They'll believe a lie, a strong delusion being damned in hell forever, lost for all eternity: And be damned cause if you are following a false doctrine, you will believe a lie, and reap the destruction according to (2 Thess. 2:10, 11, 12 and 2 Pet. 2:1 to 9, 1 Tim. 4:1, 2) which means (sent to hell) is the meaning of being damned. According to (Luke 16:19 to 31, and Rev. 21:8 and Rev. 20:11 to 15) Again, I believe that the rich man and the other people in hell will judge all those following false doctrine as in (Galatians 1:6 to 10, Luke 16:27, 28). Again if we took a real serious look into Hell, we would want to do more than just shine our light to family or there is something definitely wrong with your heart to not want to try and prevent, especially a family member from going to hell. Amen.) Read "The Letter" Christian tract, by chick publication, it explains my point perfectly of (Luke 16:19 to 31). In (1st Cor. 13:12, Rev. 3:18, Matthew 15:6, Mark 7:13, Romans 3:3, Romans 4:14, Romans 9:6 and Galatians 3:17 and Galatians 5:4), all talk about people's traditions or they make the faith of God ineffective, or they make the promise of God, or the Word of God of none effect.

God wants us all to be effected by the Bible, and by the testimony of some drunk that got saved, but some folks just aren't into living for God with their whole heart (Ps. 119:10, 11), which, this too, a sinner can see a half-heartedness, which makes the Gospel of Jesus Christ of none effect. The Bible says: "You've made it of none effect, by your tradition (by not following what the Bible says to do. Luke 6:46) But on the contrary the Bible says, "to tell everyone" which is why the Holy Ghost gives us power to be an effective witness (Acts 1:8, 2 Tim. 1:7) God has not given us a spirit of fear, but of power, and of love and of a sound mind. Thank God. He gives us power through Jesus's name, and through his word (Eph. 6:10, Luke 10:19, Phil. 4:13), through the Holy Spirit, and through the blood of Jesus (Rev. 12:11). But most of all, after the Holy Ghost has come upon you, you shall receive power (Acts 1:8) to be a witness for Jesus Christ because it's the devil that tries to put the fear and excuses in you, but we have the power to shake that off, and power to stand up for Jesus Christ, and let the world know…Jesus died to save you…and he's coming back to take us who are ready and born again back with him to heaven (1 Thess. 4:13 to 18) see verse 18, wherefore comfort one another with these words (Mark. 16:15–18; 1 Cor. 1:17–18; Rom. 3:2, 3; Rom. 9:6; Gal. 3:17; and Galatians 5:4; 1 Thess. 5:14). Let us remember, just as we want to go to heaven and hear those sweet words in (Matthew 25:21).

Enter into the joy of the Lord, thou Good and faithful servant even so we want to hear that, we should also want others to hear it also. Enter in thy Good and faithful servant…what? "Serve-ant"… does that mean we have to serve Jesus *here on earth*, by witnessing, and that's why, Jesus says, enter into (heaven) the joy of the Lord thy good and Faithful "SERVANT" (Matt. 25:21). And everyone knows what that word *servant means* (hello) or do they? Some people act as if God is telling them to rob a bank, no…just hell, Rob hell, keep people from going there, by telling them about Jesus, witness/ testifying!

Isn't everyone that's saved, called a servant? In Luke 16:29, why did God say let those five brothers hear Moses and the prophets, couldn't they just, sit and do nothing, Don't you have to be a good faithful servant in going out and putting an effort into witnessing in (Rev. 20:12 and 13 and Matthew 16:27), didn't both those two verses say they were judged according to their works (Rev. 20:12, 13 and Matthew 25:21) (yes…it sure does) so people that just go to church and that's it…they don't do anything at all for God (Just sit and) don't even put out an effort, they will be judged (well read it) or Google it, Google being judged, by God for works, Google about that lazy guy that buried his talent and did nothing in (Matthew 25:25 to 30): wow…or the opposite, the women at the well, that carried that big ol' water pot on her head all the way out of town to Jacob's well, where Jesus sat on it. She went to get water in John 4 and after Jesus got done with her and she got saved. (Read verse 28, 29.)

She left her water pot, after walking all that way for water…She left the water pot there to go tell the men back in the city, come see a man that told me all I ever did, when you are really saved and born again, you'll leave the "pot"—wow, I did too! And share Jesus with others...and witness how he delivered you, that you've been changed (2nd Cor. 5:17), and been born again, your happy now, and your now on your way to heaven, instead of fearing you'd die in your sins and split hell wide open, could it be that one of the reasons so many folks do not want to witness and tell people about Jesus is that they are still empty or that they didn't truly repent and get saved (John 4:28–29)? Or do they still have weights in their life (Heb. 12:1–2; 2 Cor. 5:17, 2 Chron. 7:14)? But when I got saved, I gave it all up. I felt like a dump truck of bricks was taken off me, and I cried like a baby when Jesus saved my soul. I felt so clean inside my soul (Rev. 12:11). But you may say, but I don't feel that way... Well, "Jump in," "taste and see," that the Lord is good (Ps. 34:8).

Keep praying (press, push) rebuke the devil in Jesus's name to back off...make more of an effort...try harder, ask the Lord to fill you up with his spirit, don't give up...begin to thank him for everything, and I thanked God over and over for my mother and grandma for all the prayers they prayed for me, and when you feel God lift off that truck load of bricks off you, then you'll feel like you'll bust if you don't tell and share it with someone and when you've cried out to God for help for your broken marriage, and to take you off drugs, etc. And when the load's lifted, tell someone and you'll be like the woman at the well...hey come see Jesus...look I'm alive...look... I'm off the dope.

Look what Jesus did for me, He healed my body. He healed my marriage...wow, how can people just sit on this...when the Bible says the rocks'll cry out in our place? (Hello!) In my book, I really feel people who keep quiet, I question their salvation, go tell someone (Luke 22:32) Jesus told Peter "When you are converted (saved and born again) strengthen your brother (testify witness) (or minister to him) (Acts 1:8, Mark 16:15). It's all written in the Bible, I read it and repented of my sins and ask Jesus to forgive me, and he did...I told mom first, then, hitchhikers, and people in parks, prisoners, and past out chick gospel tracts everywhere and Jack Chick has done the leg work for us, it's all in the tract, how to pray, etc. He gives these little life examples, that are great. I love "the Sissy" and "the Bull" and

"This is your Life" and "Somebody Goofed," but "the letter" is my most favorite and "Hi there" and "the sissy." (You can order online at www.chick.com or call chick publications at 909-987-0771). I highly recommend these from over eighteen years of experience in Prison Ministry, this works, as I said Jack Chick has done all the leg work for you. Just hand one to someone or put it on the restaurant table or in the bathroom (on the toilet paper holder), people like to read there. HA.

And it's the easiest way to witness. And you are sowing seeds into the kingdom of heaven. No, chick publications didn't ask me to say that, it's a God sent tool for evangelizing the world, and in most other languages also and hearing those words enter in thou good and faithful servant will be worth it all, and excuse me, if a wealthy man had a maid that never did anything... She would probably be fired and lose her job. So when people get saved, and don't tell anyone, don't witness, don't do anything...Hello...Read the four gospels... And tell me Jesus is saying this stuff. Don't you see that's the whole reason God will call his saints and say enter into the joy of the Lord thou good and faithful servant? Cause a servant is one who serves (look it up) and works for the Lord, do you really think he suffered and died on the cross, I mean really suffered, going through everything he did, so you can just sit on your lazy hypocrite butt of doing nothing, but shine your lukewarm light to a dying, sinning going to hell world. Then go read (Matthew 24:24–30) or (Luke 17:10 and read Luke 16:19—31) again and read (Luke 16:29) says they (the five brothers) have Moses and the prophets, let them hear them. What if I told you that you, yes you, are the only Moses or prophet Christians folks will hear or the only witness some folks are gonna listen to...well are ya saying anything to anyone? Well, are ya?...Huh? Then pretend the rich man is your child, brother, or sister and that no one wants to share or witness the good news of the gospel, which is Jesus still saves souls from going to hell.

Wow, are you gonna tell God you're faithful in witnessing for him and you're a faithful servant working for the kingdom of heaven and winning souls for God? If you really believe he will believe your faithful, when you just sit but if you are, then praise the Lord. Folks there is not a whole lot of time left, and if your Bible tells you like mine says when they are receiving a chip in their hand and people don't think we are close to Jesus's coming, wow, the world's about to have the shock of their life very soon now. God's gonna let all those go into heaven that have worked hard at witnessing and did their best at trying to win souls for God (and let it be noted) you can't make anyone turn to Jesus, but we are commanded to witness and give them a testimony, in so doing we plant a seed in their heart then God sends someone else by to water the witnessed seed that you planted...then many times God allows some type situation to happen to cause them to get a light turned on by having the seed in their heart to germinate, and bring forth the increase (1 Cor. 3:6, 7, 8, 9). And only Judgment Day will tell us it all in detail.

And we all know deep down in our heart if we are slacking on witnessing for God, remember the phrase Jesus said night comes when no man can work, well with our modern-day technology I have worked a few years on the night shift in factories and drove a mail truck for thirty years and twenty of that was on nights...but you see that scripture phrase Jesus was not talking about night time on our secular carnal Job's (John 9:4, John 3:19, 20, 21) No, but Jesus was talking about the evil days of darkness, that the times of the Last Days, that are gonna be so wicked and evil darkness, which we are now entering into, as in Noah's Day, so evil of a time, that good is evil spoken of: and they call evil good (Isa. 5:20, Rom. 13:11 to 14, 2 Pet. 2:2, John 16:2, John 3:19) Just channel surf on your TV channels...Wow.

You'll get your eyes burnt, so much evil by the flick of your remote button, so many movies with killings, rapes, gangs, thieves, adulterous affairs. Wow, sounds like real life and all this crap, Hollywood calls good entertainment...magic, sorcery, witchcraft, demon possessed people hacking up people, people rising up from the dead, walking out of their graves, killing other people, eating people that only a devil would make this stuff, and just try and find something decent to watch, so don't tell me this bull manure is entertainment cause it ain't and the language is so bad it's no wonder little children are cussing out their teachers and talking worse than sailors, and these producers in Hollywood will answer to God for it. Wow, I see a world that is about to be destroyed by God (and kids want to copycat them.) And man calls them "good movies." No, it's sin! (And we'll pay for it) in more ways than money. Wow. (God knows our hearts and what we watch) and Thank God (Prov. 15:3).

We still have old reruns and old clean comedies to watch, and yes we can still control what we watch, but the selection of all the bad movies are out numbering the good ones (by ninety-five to five) so my conclusion is God's not waiting for another Noah to come, No because the warning was given (again by Jesus Christ himself, and Apostle Paul, and Peter) and those folks that can't see it, are blinded by it, and they are way too caught up in it, to even realize the damage done to kids (Luke 17:32) and our government officials and law enforcement can't see it or figure it out either, why they are building more and more juvenile detentions and more prisons... and now legalizing some crimes that in my generation, it was called crimes then, and then a felony and is still sin according to the Bible, and illegal to me, and because of lack of space and prisons being overrun and overcrowded, these idiots that are making the new laws and our so-called leaders today are letting out criminals with their crooked lawyers to let them commit more crimes, and you to ask... where does it all stop? When God says it's finished, and that's it, and then here comes the plagues, and the wrath of God, and all hell is gonna come down and hit earth bad and according to the Bible (that says, Luke 21:6) there will not be one stone left on top of another... wow, that shall not be thrown down, that's the Big One, so when the enormous earthquakes hit and mountains are falling flat (Rev. 16:18 to 21) wow, and islands are all gone, and people still cursed God and would not repent of their sins.

Because they love that kind of life (John 3:19; Rev. 16:8, 9; Rev. 16:11; Rev. 9:20, 21). And you better believe this old preacher, and these Bible scriptures are now coming to pass, including the micro-chip mark of the beast 666, sure a lot of people say that chop isn't the mark of the beast, but read (Mat. 24:4) (see verse 3) (2 Thess. 2:3). This was the first thing Jesus said to watch out for...don't let no man deceive you...kinda like the Jim Jones crowd. Note: The scripture in

(Rev. 19:20) plainly says the guy which is the Anti-christ/the Beast/ the false prophet which had deceived them into taking the mark of the beast…(in my words…again people are saying, the chip ain't the mark, which is being deceived.) Read (Rev. 19:20) again (Rev. 13:16 to 18, Rev. 14:9 to 11, Rev. 19:20, Rev. 20:4) that people is now already getting. And the rest is coming also. Wow, I'm telling ya, the world is about to have the shock of their life very soon now, when God starts the three and a half years of Great Tribulation (Rev. 11:2 and 3, Rev. 12:14, which to me it seems like it has already started with the chip 666, or about to any time) The world has been bad and very evil for years, but nothing like today, we are for sure the Last Generation, and again those who have been de-sensitized by movies and are rubbing elbows with the world will soon be surprised when they are left behind to go through Great Tribulation (Luke 21:26) and this is why I stress so hard on telling folks to witness and win souls. There won't be no angels giving you a second chance, and if you'll notice the scripture on it (in Rev. 22:11) and (Rev. 19:7) (1 Cor. 15:52) says at the Last Trump…so there must be more than one trumpet blast! But (1 Thess. 4:16) just says with the trump of God. (At any case) once that trumpet of God sounds, it'll be too late to witness, because people will be in a worldwide panic, especially those who knew the Bible but just couldn't leave the sinful life alone enough to turn to God 100 percent (Rev. 3:15 to 22, Rev. 2:4, 5 (Rev. 3:5, 2 Tim. 3:5, "See—Luke 16:27 to 31, Luke 24:47, 48, Ephesians 5:16, Hebrews 10:25, Mat. 24:15, Mat. 24:33).

But those that worked hard witnessing, and passing out Gospel tracts, etc., those saints of God will receive their reward on Judgment Day, when rewards are handed down (Rev. 22:12, Matt. 5:12, Luke 6:22 and 23 and vs. 35, Rev. 2:10), so you that don't believe you have to witness to sinners about making heaven, when the Bible says you do because God wants you to win souls for the kingdom of heaven, and this is why God had you buy this book. And the Bible says "Everyone will give an account of his/her life on Judgment Day, when your life's recordings are played back. Wow, and if you're left here, you'll wish a million times you'd done what the Bible says (Luke 6:46), and stayed ready (1 Tim. 4:12 and 13, Luke 21:31 to 36) And most believers believe there's a real devil, well (Rev. 12:10) calls him the accuser of the brethren and He will be there in God's courtroom on Judgment Day…pointing his ugly accusing finger at everyone, especially at those who have not received Jesus as Lord and Savior. So it is good to remember who is the real enemy and know who is the real accuser of the brother/sister. (I even have to remind myself also) But mostly that accusing devil will rub everyone's nose in, for not listening to those who tried to warn ya of the end time, and tell ya about Jesus because let's face it not everyone wants to hear about it, until it's too late (Luke 16:27 to 31).

Then it's "TOO LATE!" Kinda like the drunk busted for DUI because he was caught, he has regrets…and excuses, but right now there is still time for everyone…to call on the Lord Jesus to save their soul. Did you ever wonder about all the people in Noah's Day that didn't make it, they mocked him, and laughed at him, but God wiped the smirks off their faces when they started treading water. They were also day after day many people mocking Jesus, and he also reminded people in his day of Noah's Day and warned future generations, to take heed of when the world becomes that evil again (Matt. 24:37, okay, another repeat.) But wait NOAH preached the same message DAY AFTER DAY for years (2 Pet. 2:4 and 5) says, Noah was a preacher of righteousness in (verse 5), but in (Gen. 6:3), we read that God's spirit will not always strive with man, and (verse 5) and God saw that the wickedness of man was great in the earth, and that every imagination of the thoughts of his heart was only evil continually. (Sounds like today!) But please, please see (2 Peter 2:6–7). God gave the rainbow in (Genesis 9:13–15). Notice it's a sign of a promise (as I discussed earlier). God said that the rainbow was a promise that he wouldn't destroy the world again with a flood of water, but in (2 Peter 2:6–7) (2 Peter 3:6–7) (2 Peter 1:3–4), it's reminding the reader that by that same word, which is saying, "They are kept in store, reserved unto fire, against the day of judgement and perdition of ungodly men," God's gonna have one huge BBQ (in my own words) (2 Thess. 1:7–10). Read it at least a couple of times. I see flaming fire taking vengeance on those that know not God. Wow, see verse 10 about how our testimony was believed and since our generation is way worse (than in Noah's day), which probably is the reason Apostle Paul wrote for us to "cast down imaginations and every high thing that exalts itself AGAINST THE KNOWLEDGE OF GOD, and bringing into captivity every thought to the obedience of Christ" (2 Cor. 10:5). Wow, so we can control our thinking and thoughts. My ol' pastor used to say, it becomes sin when you continue to think and dwell on it and entertain the lustful thought (Eph. 4:27).

When lust is conceived, it brings forth sin, and then death (James 1:14, 15), paraphrased in my words, (Rom. 1:27, Gal. 5:16, 17, 1 John 2:16, 17). And another one of Paul's writings in (1 Corinthians 11:28) and (2 Corinthians 13:5). Both say, we should "EXAMINE" ourselves…so why would Paul say that? I believe that our flesh wants to control us, we have to make our eyes turn away and let our spirit man be in control over our being, and always be yielding to God and listening to his small still voice that checks our heart (1st Kings 19:11–13) (Acts 17:27–28, Phil. 1:6, Phil. 2:5). This voice of God said "this is my son (Jesus) hear him" (in my words) (Matt. 17:1–6) (Acts 9:3–4) (Mark 9:7) (1st Jn. 3:20–21) (see verse 5). So talking and thinking like Jesus…will help us to be ready. Judge ourselves, so we'll not be judged (1 Cor. 11:31). And everyone who's name is not in the Book of Life, doesn't go to heaven. A lot of people really think they're going! But the Bible says, if they didn't follow God's Word, and Jesus's, they will not enter in. Again, I'm not writing another Bible, nor am I trying to say things it does not say. I try and give text scriptures where you can look them up for yourself.

This world is so full of hypocrites in all walks of life, and if anybody out there really thinks you can do nothing and make heaven you are blind and stupid. Look up duty. Look up sluggard, consider the ant (Proverbs 6:6–8). God wants us to be a fruitful tree for him…I believe I've discussed the fruitless tree already, and why Jesus cursed it…It wasn't doing anything it was just there existing…No fruit, not being fruitful and not multiplying = (win souls is one way.) Are you fruitful for Jesus (read John 15, In Act 2:11). Study out the upper room and why God poured out his spirit. One of the things people don't even see is, they were saying God's done wonderful works and saying it in different languages out of those that were there, and that most amazing part about it, was all those men were all born in different dialects that other men were born at, and it wasn't a bunch of gibberish, but speaking about the different wonderful works of God in different languages and it could have been about how God took Daniel out of the Lion's den or it could have been about God parting the ocean for Moses…etc., but the Word is plural… (meaning more than one).

What was the wonderful works of God, that God wanted all those people in all languages to know, I'll tell ya (John 3:16) was probably one, or maybe (Rom. 10:13) whosoever calls on the name of the Lord shall be saved. At any case, whatever it was, it was so important enough to say it in all languages, but more important than that, God poured out his spirit on all the men that day, letting everyone know that when you wait on God, and seek God with two or three or more, there God is in the midst of you (Matt. 18:20) for where two or three are gathered together in my (Jesus) name, there am I in the midst of them. (Wow, Make note of, Luke 24:53, these disciples of Jesus Christ) were continually in the temple, praising and blessing God. Amen.

Many people I know from on the job or an old acquaintance, say they don't feel they need to go to church, well this was one that shows that the disciples were continually in the temple praising and blessing God. (Notice in Luke 24:53 that word continually.) Also read (Heb. 10:25), as you see the day approaching: (Notice that many scriptures give secret keys or little gold nuggets, such as going to church and gathering together…and I believe the Bible is saying in this text that we should continue to gather together to have church, the more we see the days are getting closer to the coming of Jesus (plagues or not). Cause, even if we are wearing masks or not, or standing twenty feet apart, it's the being in God's presence together in Jesus' name, is what God is trying to tell us all, but if it's seeking God at home alone or gathering as in (Matt. 18:20), and (John 17:11 to 20) (Luke 24:48, 49) (Acts 2:1) together in unity. That's my interpretation of (Heb. 10:25) and I like (1 Pet. 4:17, 18) which also explains why the devil tries to keep so many people out of church, cause that's where we hear the Bible preached, and judgment must begin at church first!

(Read it.) and there is many more, like how will you hear to build up your faith, so without a preacher, How will they hear? (See verse 14 of Romans 10:13, 14, 15, 16, 17) and many more like (Psalms 23:6, Ps. 122:1 or Ps. 84:4, Luke 4:16); it was Jesus's custom to go to church, some of us need a new custom or a new desire (Ps. 27:4) and there are many, many more on church attendance. But I've made my point. So don't let nothing stop you from seeking God. Even at home, cause now we are seeing people to afraid to go, so afraid they'll catch a plague or disease, so for sure, we are indeed the last generation (Matt. 24:33, 34).

I've said many times, God has kept us protected, clothed, and kept a roof over our heads, and gives us food to eat, God deserves thanks and praise not just from your mouth, but we need to love him out of our heart. As Paul said in (Romans 15:11) to Laud him all you people. Praise him with a song, from out of your heart and soul, I like to remember back when my mom and grandma was still alive, come home and hearing them in their own little upper room prayer meetings, have-ing their praise and thanking God songs a going and hearing them woo-ing and saying "Thank you, Lord, for watching over my kids" "Thank you, Lord, for supplying all our needs." Hallelujah, you are worthy to be praised." I mean there was a thankful spirit coming out of their soul. It wasn't a being bored attitude like young folks today. Well, I'll lift my hands to God I guess, or for a second I wonder what time it is, or I gotta go get things done, this is boring (No, mom and grand ma Peterson took out time for God out of their busy lives, from out of their heart and soul) and not just praying for their needs, but thanking God for things that he's already done…making a big deal about them to him in praise and thanksgiving and worshipping him with some hallelujah…and saying we love you Lord…we praise you Jesus…hallelujah (This generation now, don't know or do much of this it's little quickie micro-wave-instant-drive-through thanks, oh…yeah…Hey, thanks, Lord, see ya later… Wow…Just Jesus dying on the cross deserves a lot more thanks than we could ever give him.

In fact, you can't in no way ever praise him or thank him enough or even repent enough and what about all those promises you made to God, when you said "Help me...Get me out of this one Lord... and I promise I'll go to church, and live right...oh...are you surprised that I knew? The Bible says God knew you when you were in your mama's belly...Wow, and unlike people, God keeps his promises...so we do owe him thanks and praises, Hey, so, go in your bedroom (every day) and shut the door, like the movie *The War Room*, an excellent film by the way, where she had converted her closet into her "war-prayer room" getting alone with God, and sure you can tell him all about your troubles...He knew before you spoke them (Matt. 6:8), but, call out to him, and ask him to run your spiritual cup to overflow, and just say, hose me out Lord in Jesus's name, then think in your mind of all your miracles and think of all the things that you are most thankful for, and then, now begin thanking him for them all, and don't quench or hold back the tears...let God hose you out...then give him his hallelujahs and sing songs to Him like "Thank You, Lord, for saving my soul," etc. MAKE a big deal out of it to Him. He deserves your best praise...Amen...unload your cares and troubles, with thanksgiving (1 Pete. 5:7, Phil. 4:6), for my eyes, legs, health. I can feed myself, and hear, and see, thank you, Jesus... most of all for dying on the Cross for my sins...okay. And also, we can ask Jesus to forgive us of anything in our life that's not pleasing to him. You get the picture.

Now, that's the attitude the disciples had in the upper room prayer meeting, when God poured out his spirit on them and hosed them out, as in (Acts 3:19), (John 7:37 to 39), (John 4:14) and, in (Acts 2, Luke 24:53), the spirit, so we never want to take a do nothing for God attitude or act bored in church...we should always come into church with a thankful heart and ready to yield ourself to God, and roll out of bed with a thankful heart with an attitude of praise to God. Then when your next need arises, God'll know you'll be thankful and thank him for supplying all your needs (Phil. 4:19, Matt. 6:33). I like the example in the parable of the talents: in (Matthew 25:21) where the man was told by the Lord ("Well done, thou good and faithful servant, you have been faithful over a few things, I will make you ruler over many things, enter thou into the joy of thy Lord.) For those who have been faithful and are living for God, and witnessing for him as the Bible says, and staying away from the partying, sinful lifestyle living as in (Luke 15 and Luke 21:34, 35, 36), etc., and doing right, to hear the words enter in, will be music to our ears.

But those who lived in sin, partying, committing all kinds of sin, never turning away from it, never calling on Jesus to SAVE their soul, will hear, "Depart from me, you that worked iniquity, I never knew you (Matt. 7:23) will be saddest words anyone could ever hear, to be lost in hell forever. So my reader friend if you don't know Jesus, don't wait too long to pray and call on him. Read the rest of the verses of the talents in (verses 24, 25, 26 of Matthew 25) and even (Matthew 25:8) the text scriptures both show the man that buried and hid his talent (money) and the five virgins that were called foolish cause they were empty, no desire, no extra oil, not praying, just empty…when you really live for God with all your heart, it's gonna show on your countenance, just like Daniel that prayed three times a day in (Dan. 6:3), the Bible says he was preferred above all the others, because of the excellent spirit in him (in my words) Wow. Question? How do people expect Jesus to let them in heaven when they can't get out of their recliners to go to church, but can go anywhere else any time.

So the bottom line here…is when we put out and make an effort…to pray…and give God the proper thanks and praise that's past due to him…some people show more affection to their pets than to our Lord, and he died to save our soul from going to hell. Wow. A disciple is self-discipline and there is requirements of being faithful stewards according to the Bible, and faithful servants of God (Google it), such as witnessing (1 Cor. 4:2; Luke 9:23; Luke 24:53; Luke 10:1, 2; Acts 1:8) and inviting people to church, doing our devotions, visiting the sick, praying and reading the Bible, etc., attending church (Acts 2:46, 47; Luke 24:53). Faithfully (notice many of those scriptures says the disciples went to church daily) not just Sunday mornings, but they all went daily to all services, so when you can go, go, because once you start playing hooky because you're too tired… then it's easier to stay home all the time, what if Jesus said I'm too tired to answer your prayers, ouch...or I'm too tired to die on the cross...remember (Rev. 2:4, 5; Rev. 3:15 to 20) you don't wanna be like (Matt. 25) the five foolish they didn't want to go either...so push (I make myself go. We all get tired. A disciple is well disciplined, and far too many people just don't know and aren't even aware of (Hos. 4:6, Matt. 20:16, Rom. 12:1 and 2 and Matthew 7:21, 22, 23, Luke 6:46) that God will use these scriptures and many more on Judgment Day, we all have times of just being to exhausted, but I'm not referring to that, as I am of folks that have just lost their hunger and thirst for righteousness, and have no desire in serving or seeking God at all, or no more push left in them, yet, there is always a push if someone was giving away a family inheritance and their name was at the top of the list, or free tickets to a raffle and they won, or someone was buying them a steak dinner, etc. It's really about where is our most important priorities of this life at?

So as the scriptures say...where your treasure is there will your heart be also (Luke 12:34) but if people can't push and make themselves go to church, why would God even let them in heaven? Also, this is a sign of one that has lost their first love. Backslid in their heart and is equal to (Matthew 25:8), five foolish virgins that ran out of desire. I mean oil (Rev. 2:4, 5 and Rev. 3:5 and Rev. 3:15 to 22) we must have a desire for God's house, for being in God's presence, to thank Him, to show love to him, to worship him, and when God has performed miracles (Again: we should always give God thanks for it), we've learnt from the Bible we are to tell others, also, but I don't see much of any of this anymore. Why? Because we are in the Last Days (Titus 1:16). Many today just say they are a Christian (Matt. 23:3, Mark 7:6, 7, 8; Matt. 24:12; 2 Thess. 2:3).

But many people don't know the difference between ceremonialism and having a form of Godliness (2 Tim. 3:5) being religious like the Pharisees or the deeds of the Nicolaitanes that God hates (Rev. 2:6) also the Bible says in (Rev. 3:13 to 20 and see verse 14), that's to the church of Laodiceans see (Rev. 2:6 and 2:15) (2nd Tim. 3:5) keywords to notice are deeds and doctrines of the Laodiceans as (in Rev. 3:14 to 20) and the Nicolairtans in (Rev. 2:1 to 6)...about them being lukewarm (in the middle) not on God's side or the devils or not totally to God, just in neutral concerning God. Wow, this is today's way of most so-called Christians, but people today don't even realize scriptures in the Bible are being fulfilled, example, try getting a church group together, to have church in 2022, now do you think that's what (Matt. 10:28) (Rev. 2:10) means. I do, wow, this world is no longer fit for Christians…saints are saying come quickly Lord Jesus.

In (Matthew 24:11 and Matthew 24:24), some start being curious, reading false doctrines (1 Tim. 4:1). When a person backslides the Bible says they become seven times worse and cause of Guilt, they get hateful, and mean, now, if this person, had the calling to be a minister or prophet (on their life), and something devastating happened and he turned away from God, but still reads the Bible, but refused to surrender back to God 100 percent, this guy would most likely become a false prophet or false preacher (And get into studying false doctrines) and usually it all starts gradually, from getting offended about something, and it escalates, and, because of bitterness against God, then they'll start missing church services, and pretty soon they've lost the desire to go, but they still feel the tug in ministry (Rom. 11:29, says) the gifts and the callings of God are without repentance. In other words, there will be people that were called to preach the Gospel, and never pursued it, some died and may have went to hell according to scripture, and felt the calling all their life, and did nothing…about it, these types are usually ones that become the false prophets, and false ministers, I've known some over the years (some have come back to God) but, a lot of them was in jail, when I was in prison ministry and I've seen people that strayed away from the truth, being so hungry for something new and different, and they got into cult type doctrines (1 Tim. 4:1) I don't understand why they want to leave the eternal words of Jesus Christ.

Just to know or learn something different that no one else knows I guess (Acts 17:21, John 6:66–68). Even in Jesus's Day, people turned away from the truth, then Jesus asked the twelve disciples, "will you also go away?" but in vs. 68. Peter said, "where shall we go" (Jesus) has the words of eternal life. In (Galatians 3:13) Christ redeemed us form the curse of the law. But only for believers, for those who are in Christ, because, Jesus became a curse in our place, on the cross. Because according to the Bible, those that have not asked Jesus Christ to forgive them of their sins and come into their hearts and save their souls. They are still under the curse of the law. If you read back in Moses Day when they killed the sacrificed lamb, and applied the lamb's blood over the door post of their houses, when the death angel came, he saw the blood and passed on over them.

Jesus became our eternal sacrifice lamb when he shed his blood on the cross, but we have to apply his blood to our heart by asking him to forgive us of all our sins, and wash us clean with his blood. This also removes the curse of the law, for without our confession to Jesus Christ there is no remission of sins (Matt. 26:28, Eph. 1:7, Heb. 9:22, Acts. 2:38–39, Rev. 1:5, 1 John 1:6–10, Exod. 12:7–13, Rom. 10:9–10, Col. 1:14). So the blood of Jesus, and the repentance by confessing our sins to Jesus Christ takes the curse away from us, but know this, there is no other way to redeem us! (Gal. 4:4 to 7, Heb. 9:12–28) Now the word (Ichabod) is a cursed name meaning: God has departed (1 Sam. 4:21–22) For the Ark of God was captured because of sin, the only other way would be to blaspheme against the Holy Ghost (Mark 3:28, 29 and 30) in which many Bible scholars believe, this is rejecting Jesus Christ, because he's the only way to heaven (John 14:6) so to reject him is to damn your soul! And when God puts the word Ichabod over a door, he has departed from them but (verse 30) plainly says, they said he (Jesus) had an unclean spirit, wow.

The Bible says: it's a fearful thing to fall into the hands of a living God (Heb. 10:31) and because we have been a blessed nation, cause of all the Christian grandparents, and forefathers that lived for God before us, we've been a blessed nation, but since the '60s this nation's went to the sewer, this younger generation has no respect and lives like the devil himself, as I said before, if not for God's protecting hand of mercy and grace on America, this nation would have done been burnt toast, and it's because of the amount of Christians that are here with God's grace and mercy that's spared America's destruction, and I believe when the rapture and the return of Jesus Christ returns for all of us Christians, all hell will break lose on this evil world, and I really believe it'll start with America (Rev. 18) and God help those who are not ready, and get left cause people today that haven't studied prophecy and the book of Revelation, in the Bible, don't have a clue what's coming on this EARTH, but if (Rev. 18) is the USA and I believe it is, it's burnt toast, according to (Rev. 18) It'll be wiped out in one hour's time, according to (Rev. 18:10 to 19) and this generation is so caught up in electronics and our modern-day technology they won't even see it coming. If there was ever a blind nation of people it's the USA! America is called a female country (Rev. 18:19) says she is made desolate in one hour. When have you ever seen the world have the knowledge enough to destroy a nation in an hour's time. Not till now. She was also called a whore and verse 9 says she committed fornication with the kings of the earth (Rev. 19:2 see verse 3 "Her Smoke," the second verse) called her a great whore, USA was once a Christian nation (Ps. 9:17, Deut. 6:12) USA is a considered a whore nation cause of (Exod. 20:3 and 4) cause America has turned to everything but God! *Webster's Dictionary* definition of whore is considered the same as a prostitute to commit fornication with a whore (spiritually speaking). The Bible is very clear on physical fornication/adultery and spiritual fornication as in (Romans 1:23–24 and Jude 7). People all over are…leaving God (Rom. 1:18) speaks about the wrath of God is revealed from heaven against all ungodliness and unrightousness of men…and in (verse 25) says they changed the truth of God into a lie…Wow. And leaving God and turning to a false god, that is, idols made with hands, for example. Many have turned to them for centuries, and most people that don't study the Bible haven't got a clue about what the Bible says on the subject or their fate even as 1 Corinthians 10:5–11 says the Ten Commandments and many other scriptures, and especially in the first four chapters of Revelation, because those first four chapters are telling the church people to return to their first love (which is Christ). Please understand that the church is considered spiritually the Bride of Christ A Pure Virgin, ready for marriage, when a nation's people turn to false gods the Bible classifies that as, God's people committing spiritual adultery. A whore nation: so many scriptures on this (Rev. 17:5). And many will experience it because of unbelief and stubbornness, God gives everyone chance after chance, opportunity after opportunity to get back right with God. The Bible says, unlike us, having no patience with people, "God is long suffering" I mean he's looooooong suffering. Did I say long, I want you to get this.

Are you always short with people, quick tempered with them, they don't get right fast enough for you. Well, God's long in patience (For now) And is giving mankind plenty of time to get themselves right with him, but listen (The way I read) According to this ol' preacher, the way I interpret God's time clock of prophecy, and yes I know, no one knows the day or hour, but the Bible says in (Matthew 24:33 and 36 and 42). That we'll know we are close by all the signs, and if you don't see it's any time now, by people already taking the chip in the hand that was on the news, you are double blind, physically and spiritually, then you need to read (Matthew 15:14, Rev. 3:17 and 18), to pray and ask God to anoint your eyes, that you can see spiritually, "you have not, cause you ask not" (James 4:2). Pray for understanding of prophecy too. We are there, any time now. Again, I'm not saying a date or hour, no man knows, and those that say dates are false prophets, which would mean they've backslid, even though they are God's called to be a preacher or Prophet are usually the most Hateful and evil of all because deep down, they know they blew it. They want to get back with God, I see a name backslider has been written over their door. But don't sell 'em out completely, God restored Peter... God is able to Heal anyone who turns from their wicked ways, calling on Jesus (2 Chron. 7:14). But they have to quit living in sin, and turn or burn, it's do, or die, swim or drown (James 4:17) Come on, people, Nuclear war is about to Happen,... And all hell has been Hitting Earth in so many different places, and not Just America... But earth, God wants us to quit the nitpicking and bickering. God is trying to get people saved and this kind of nonsense makes Christians look like fools... "Grow up" get right or you'll get left! This is not a game...you could get killed by a drunk driver, etc., and with this here kind of crap and garbage, and manure type stinkin', thinkin' in your heart, with hate and unforgiveness toward others, you'd split hell wide open.

We have to forgive others even as Jesus Christ has forgiven us (Matt. 6:15) but 70×7 in a day, we must forgive over and over (Matt. 18:22) Draw the line…be a separated spirit-filled child of the living God, And walk in love and forgiveness 70×7 a day… Love your neighbor as yourself, then you will hear those words of our Lord say, "enter in thou good and faithful servant in to the joy of the Lord and it will be worth it all, and to be ready to meet the Lord. Yes, this ol' Preacher really repeats himself in this Book…yet, I've noticed especially in the New Testament, four gospels lots of topics are also repeated (I made a whole list like the whole chapter of (Ps. 118:1–4, Ps. 136 whole chapter) Wow (John 21:15–19) and about thirty or more repeats on a post note, so repeats are good. But some things are different, like the Prodigal son is not repeated in (Luke 15:11–32), love (vs. 17, He woke up, and came to his senses), which does give hope to the one who falls into sin which he tells himself to get up, and get back to his father's house,…and notice the father doesn't cast him out cause he blew all his hard earned money, but showed him love with hugs, and his Dad put a ring on his finger (the sign of sonship), and a robe on him, and shoes on his feet…Wow (makes you wonder no shoes) so this Dad is representing our heavenly father, forgiving us when we've strayed away.

No matter how far we've strayed, the Father still hugs us and forgives us, but he still expects us to mortify our flesh and keep our body and mind under subjection to the Lord. (Col. 3:5, 6, 1 Cor. 9:27, Phil. 2:5, Rom. 12:1 and 2, James 4:7), even to the point that we may have to discipline ourselves and make ourselves and push ourselves to do right…even make ourselves go to church when we would rather kick back and watch TV and stay home. That's a true disciple that is self-disciplined. Amen! (Col. 3:1 to 10, Rom. 12:1, 2) even though we look and smell like pig crap from the pigpen, and he accepts us back into the family.

Please note, the humbleness and repented heart in Luke 15:21. Wow, today, most dads would disown their son, but if the son could only see through the eyes of God and know Dad loves him, with all his heart, with tears streaming down his face, saying come on home son, we still love you, all is forgiven, and like Dad that forgives and welcomes his prodigal son home, with hugs and kisses, and so does God, when we humble ourselves and pray and ask him for forgiveness, he restores our soul (Ps. 23:3).

And God says I forgive you, now get up and get back to your father's house (Don't go back to the pigpen) stay close to me so I can complete the healing in your hurting heart. I will heal all those broken places, and do a restoring down to the depths of your soul, and I will put back in you what the devil stole then. And the father also calls for his hired employees to cook a big meal, saying, my lost son has been found and has come back home, and if you are backslidden in your heart, know (this, that) Jesus loves and forgives you and takes you back, That's why Jesus died for you, to show you he loves and forgives you, the price has been paid at the Cross when Jesus laid down his life, so you could live your life, in heaven (2 Pet 3:12, 13, 14, notice verse 9) it's not God's will that anyone perish, but that all should come to repentance and come back to God, with a simple I'm sorry God, Jesus forgive me, I'm sorry, of my sins, And I say it with tears friend, Get up, try again, this time you can make it, don't you see, all heaven wants you to win, so gather all your courage together and make a final stand, cause I know through Jesus you can make it this time, and get your ears tuned to listening to the right voice.

Don't give your ear, to the voice of Satan, learn the difference between the two voices that speak to your mind. Actually three, counting your own voice or thoughts, and God's and the devils. The devil won't tell you to do good, and God won't tell you to do evil (Luke 10:19, 2 Cor. 10:4, 5, 2 Cor. 11:3, Eph. 6:10–18, Rom. 6:12 to 18, Matt. 4:1 to 11), weigh things out...what would Jesus do? What does the Bible say about it. Now, you can get other opinions... As I did, praying a devil out of my church, where I pastored and a well-known famous TV preacher, I was talking to, said I should go and bring him back, I said no way, I prayed him out, so even the ones that seem to be high up the ladder in God, may not have discernment of spirits, cause this guy was full of the devil, that we prayed out. So you have to pray yourself, and be led by God.

I prayed that trouble making devil out, why in the world would I want to bring back a devil that disrupting services and bringing in confusion and dividing the flock of God's people, No, you see, that tells ya. Not everyone that gives you advice is right all the time, so pray, examine it with the Bible, and let the Lord direct you, I was discussing repeating myself, wow, long dirt road hey... I'm a dirt road preacher. I ask a pastor, why I did that. He said, there's folks that live down these dirt roads. Amen, well so many things in the Bible that are indeed repetitive, Even the disciples, repeated things they heard from Jesus, and sometimes it's an ouch, when Jesus fed the five thousand, He demonstrated the power of God, and increased the faith of his followers. Many, many things, examples, scriptures, Phrases, texts, were repeated to teach and instruct the disciples and all followers from generation to generation, because Jesus is the same, yesterday, today, and forever (Heb. 13:8, 2 Pet. 3:7, 1 Pet. 5:9, 1 Tim. 4:12, Gal. 6:7, 8, 9).

We all having our own situations in life, some worse than others, some it seems good though life, to some life seems better, but let's face it... Some people born in poverty had life worse or harder than someone born in a wealthy home, but we've all heard stories of faith instilled in folks, especially poverty-stricken folks. Because many had to depend on God for provisions (myself included, Matt. 5:45) And it does rain on the just as it also does on the unjust. Some seem so prosperous in life, without any problems, but the word teaches it rains on the just and the unjust. Same God over all. I can't explain why some are born with a birth defect and others seem so healthy and prosperous in life. Many times things and situations happen for a reason (read Rom. 8:28 to 39), cause each time I try to compare life events with scripture, some feels it's a dog eat dog world and its kill or be killed, but that kinda think is the way the sinful world, and the terrorist types thinks, or they say do what you gotta do to survive, wow...you've heard it, we've all heard it.

But things spoken by macho Nachos, yeah, yeah, Macho proud tuff guys that thinks these bodies are going into eternal life "wrong"! Bodily exercise profited little. Again, repeating myself. We may all need enough exercise to help us, but some get to puffed up with pride, like some do with money, jobs, success and soon, when we leave this life...you're not gonna take anything with you...most

Pastors say, when preaching on dying, when someone passes away, you'll never see a U-haul movers truck or trailer behind the hearst... you are not gonna take anything with you...body, muscles, or slender figure, money, fame, nothing is going... Naked you came into this world, and naked you will leave it (Job 1:21). It's what you do with your soul not your money, or your body, but most of these folks probably never read (1ˢᵗ Tim. 4:8, 1ˢᵗ Cor. 15:50, Luke 12:4 to 21, see verse 34 and Revelation 21:27) this earthly body so many people really work hard on it getting it buffed and in shape, when all the time it's gonna be changed into a heavenly body, I've watched on google and Youtube the before's and after's and gotten a kick out of all these body builders and glamorous women stars back in the 1970s and 80s seen them flex their muscles and figures, and worked so hard for years and now 40–50 years later...Age has crept upon on all of them, they've lacked off their work outs, and lost their looks and lost their huge muscular physiques. Now they've got wrinkles and have big bellies, wow, and now there are so many women stars lost theirs also. Now after plastic surgeries and botox injections etc. trying to restore what they messed up. They look now worse than ever, when the bible plainly says life is like a vapor...Read (James 4:14 to 16) but the soul of man will live forever in heaven or hell, and many have already departed this life, and only God knows if they made it to heaven, cause this body is not going to heaven or hell, just the soul. I've known some, that work out at the gym six hours a day (1 Tim. 4:8) Wow, do they put that kind of time in studying the Bible? Wow, like that body is going to heaven. "Don't think so." And people's success in life won't either or failure in life, we place such a value on things, even above our souls when the Bible says what does a man give in exchange for his soul (Matt. 16:26, Mark 8:37) Being concerned is very important, but some folks think going to church is like just having a place to go to, or think they are doing God a favour, or make themselves cause it's right to go, but their heart isn't even in going, etc., when they put their flesh under submission, which is what (Rom. 12:1, 2) says: but it is so very important especially at this end time closing hour, that our hearts and minds draw as close to the spirit of God as we can, and our minds should be on God, as much as possible and I've wondered how many people that go to church really truly believe in God, because when you look out over the crowd, many folks are there in body only.

Back when I Pastored, especially when I would have a guest speaker, I'd look out over the crowd and see different one's drawing, or talking in-a-lengthy-conversation, which is very rude, and some, just thumbing through pages, and many times you see people talking which is very rude not only to the poor speaker that spent time in prayer and studying and preparing the message, but most of all they are being rude to God, and, are distracting those sitting behind them also and they are even neglecting their own soul, cause that could be the very word from God, that would get you through the next Day, when trouble comes. This reminds me of the gospel tract "This is your life" by Jack Chick Publications, and how God recorded their life from birth to Death, but you can't help but wonder why do these people come to church? When you know your guest speaker has spent time studying and praying for the right message, don't these people know this minister can see that they are bored, and they are not even into the spirit of it all, but more important. They must not even believe in God, because he's recording them for Judgment Day.

And they don't even know it. This subject would make a good book, "God's watching you" or "smile your on God's satellite camera." Ha. And you mention that to someone, and they'll give you a look of disbelief and yet, today we humans have this surveillance technology, and yet, God had this and more before man was ever created. Thousands and thousands of years ago. And look how long it's taken us to get here. Wow. Yet the Bible says, God even knew you when you were in your mother's womb and now with our modern advanced technology ___ the doctor can look inside the womb to see what sex the baby is ____ (Jer. 1:5 and Isa. 44:2). And people still think abortions okay. Wrong it's murder. But that too will be revealed on Judgment Day.

And people won't hide from all God's recorded info. And everyone's mouth will fall open in surprise, I like standing over ants, or a bug out on the drive way and say you don't have a clue I'm watching you, I could smash you into eternity, but I'll let you live. Wow,

God could snuff us out Just like that cause everyone's so busy, not even saying thank you, Lord, for the breath I breathe today, thank you for my life today. For my existence, and well-being, and people in church could pray, "LORD, I'm day dreaming, away from this preacher's sermon, please, help me focus, and stay alert, in Jesus's name, and that to would even be recorded also. Wow, so if we are trying, Judgment Day will look a lot better for us on God's satellite camera, amen (Eccl. 12:14, Numb. 32:23, Luke 12:2). Nothing is hidden from God, he see's everything (Prov. 15:3). People Just don't think spiritually minded: Nor realize that the very sermon your pastor or evangelist has prayed and studied for, may be the very thing you'll need to get you through the next day, especially if that was the day that trouble came, because, I have seen such cases over the years, and have heard powerful testimonies, yet, if folks aren't listening and are preoccupied. Then they miss the answer that God is trying to speak into their lives.

Yes, I've seen it many times myself, sitting, and hearing a particular sermon, and tell the wife, after church many times, that sermon, would have been a good message for so and so to hear, but they aren't here to hear or they left early. Wow, and even when I was a pastor, God would give me a word for a particular person and others would say that was straight to them, this is why God's Word says, God's Word will NOT return unto Him VOID (Isa. 55:11). It shall accomplish, that which I (God) Please, and it shall prosper in the thing where to I (God) sent it. Wow, and also why the word is the answer and it says it is. In many scriptures, and that is the mystery of the Gospel. You can even read it one year and the very next year you read the same thing and it jumps out at you. And you say, wow, I've read this before, but this time.

Wow, look what this is saying, "God has designed it to work that way," it's the spirit of God on paper, and is gonna do what God's own mouth has spoken to man to write. It's like some folks are so antsy, and restless, and maybe because they aren't living right and sometimes the Bible verses seem to step on folks, toes, and making them restless and feel so uneasy. I've experienced it before myself, before I was saved, and I thought, how did this preacher know this about me, not knowing half the church was thinking the same thing about themselves. This is the mystery of the Gospel, and the Word of God will convict you, and stir you (James 1:21) says. It's the engrafted word that's able to save your soul (Eph. 5:26) and John 15:3 Ye are clean through the word (Bible, Ps. 119:11) Thy word have I hid in my heart that I might not sin against thee (God) And so knowing the Bible, we'll know if this and that is wrong and people that do such don't make heaven, etc. (James 4:17).

So if the Bible even says (God's own people (perish are destroyed for their lack of knowledge, Hos. 4:6) I'm thinking people had best wake up and study and learn the Bible, when I can read stuff that sounds like an all-out nuclear war in scripture, and I've mentioned these type things to folks that supposedly are Christians, and they say, they've never heard of it. Wow. That amazes me. And frankly I keep feeling like earth is gonna be hit with a bad meteor shower similar to the one that wiped out Sodom and Gomorrah, and the feeling keeps getting stronger. Other prophecy ministers say they feel it too. And people are so busy in their minds, they gotta do this, gotta do that… when no one knows what tomorrow holds… Sometimes you want to scream in their ears…Get ready… Jesus is coming. A few years back we were at the beach one day, there were people lined up, sitting up and down the pier and on the beach with their iPods phones and tablets. Missing life. We came to see to beach, and we love it. We are old school. I guess, but life is just passing them by.

They don't realize how short life really is. And you want to tell them, but they don't hear you. But if someone put an article on media, saying next Sunday morning a millionaire was giving away a million dollars at church, plus a new car is being given as a door prize, and trips, cruises, etc. But you have to be there to win. Do you think they would get that message? Ha. I think for the first time since 911 the church would be packed out. So money, and pleasure, and things are worth more to this generation than there soul (2 Tim. 3:1–5) is definitely talking about this generation (especially vs. 3). Are you hearing anything at all! (when I was in the hospital I saw people that many didn't ever get visitors) Some when they did, it was very short…at thanks giving day meal and even other meals I try to always thank the Lord for my health, and strength… God has blessed us with, food, roof, over our heads, only God knows how many times we are spared from drunk drivers, drive-bys and wow, cellphones are causing more wrecks than drunks…Actually, it's the driver not the phone…so hang up and drive, drivers texting on their phones while driving are causing wrecks everywhere, one crashed in to me and broke my back, and I had to have surgery…calls can wait.

There are men who get so evil and have no conscience at all… and they will not repent (Rev. 9:21). Folks don't text and drive) (oh, that'll never happen to me…"wanna bet" not really…. It's now becoming the number 1 cause of accidents, and deaths in car wrecks, It is now very, very, scary out on the streets and highways…especially at the holidays time of year People are so distracted by their phones, to die for a phone call or text message, or to cause an innocent by stander in a crosswalk or little child to be maimed for life or killed, it ain't worth it folks, the call can wait…come on, people, it can wait, or pull over. Imagine this…you're texting while driving and you caused a death of someone that was unsaved, wasn't ready to step into eternity…wow, or killed a mother that was the only parent to a child. Where do we draw the line on a life's value? How valuable is their soul? You see in my case, this joker had no license and had no insurance and hit and ran and left me lying there screaming and didn't care if I was alive or dead.

Just thinking of his own self, after cops arrested him, all he could say was if that van hadn't been in my way… I'd have kept on going! Wow, other lives are meaningless to others and after surgery and a year of therapy and recoup time, off the walker now on a cane, yes, getting around better, but have permanent nerve damage in my left foot, swelling in right leg…and the feeling of the huge butcher's knife, stuck in my back, where the eight screws, two rods, and two bone cages are from my back surgery (24:7) and all this dude got was a year in jail, and left me with a life that is so different, to just get in my truck is such a challenge and a real chore.

And he is back out on the street to do it to someone else, yes, I forgave him, Just wanted to paint you the reader a picture, of what texting while driving can do to some innocent guy, I was working on the job, making a left turn on a green arrow, doing my job, and this guy doing 55 mph and didn't even see me. Why? The only good thing that came out of it, was I started writing books, and going with my pastor doing visitation, and praying for others worse than myself, and believe me. I now have more compassion for others that are hurting. So now we understand (Rom. 8:28). A real picture that a year in jail versus a life of nerve damage and handicapped pain, a whole changed way of life for me (so he can text and drive again.) Somethings in life, don't seem fair or even right.

And the victims get the aftereffects, but know this and you listen good. Reaping and sowing, what goes around, comes around, you can plant good seeds and you'll reap good corn, or potatoes, but if you plant thorns and stickers, guess what that's what you'll get. Thousands, maybe millions of people are being ugly mean and nasty to everyone. Never in my life have I seen a generation of so many evil people. Worse than any generations ever before, road rage at an all-time high. Drive by's not even concerned about innocent people could be hit and killed, that's not fair to them. This generation is so full of themselves, Identity thieves, scammers, people stealing UPS packages, people breaking in homes in the broad daylight, I heard and saw on the evening news, where sad low life creeps broke into homes of forest fire evacuees, wow…when you think you've heard it all…of demon possessed low life devils, wow…what I classify them right up there with the church burners.

Amen…and the concealed weapons are at the highest, everyone wanting protection, hey, just watch the news for a few weeks, and see every day someone's murdered, terrorist, and thieves arrested, now, even cops, yesterday in the news were two different towns, two different policemen were arrested for sex crimes, yes, cops, wow, people in all walks of life are tempted by the devil, and it's worse now than ever before, but back to the road rage, I heard a preacher say: it's evil spirits that were released out of the bottomless pit (Rev. 9:1 to 12) and we are even seeing devil possessed ministers as in (Rev. 16:13) and (Matt. 24:11), because crime is at an all-time high everywhere, prisons are so full, they are building more, and filling them and they are releasing the non-violent offenders to make room for the very violent offenders, now if this type attitudes is from thousands of demons unleashed from the bottomless pit. Then we have entered the tribulation period. Which would explain the road rage extreme violent behavior everywhere, and all hell will be soon hitting Earth, that will be a lot worse than Noah's Day, and God has warned us in the Bible when we see that it is that bad, God's wrath will be poured out, on earth, and we are there, we need to pray more than ever before (see, Rev. 9:20, 21) and what gets me, is, Hollywood will turn right around after some gruesome act of violence, and make a Hit Movie out of the crime...and even turn the killer into a Hero because the days are so evil (John 3:19) and man loves darkness more than light, and loves evil more than good, and (again) most of the kid's superhero's are being on the dark side anymore.

Man is proud of his sins (Romans 1:18 to 32) (2nd Tim. 3:13) (John 3) (James 4:16, 17) (Isa. 5:20), and wants the Christians to embrace his sin cause man don't want to accept what God said that He'd destroy mankind again (Matt. 24:37 to 39). See Rev. 9:20–21 and read that they would not repent of (Rev. 16:11, 2 Pet. 3:9, 2 Cor. 7:10, Luke 24:47). There's the problem, no remorse no repentance which goes back to "Reaping and Sowing" or "what goes around comes around (Gal. 6:7, 8, 9) because it's one of God's Natural Laws of Life, when you plant bad seed you reap (bad crop from bad seeds) even though you repent, you still have to reap it, but though you are repented of it, God's mercy is extended and will help you to reap mercifully with grace added to it. Been there done that... your repeating yourself Preacher, yeah...should probably change the title to "repeat." Oh well, I'm also a real life example of reaping and sowing and that's both side of the coin...And I have reaped the bad since 1977, and all those years planting bad seeds and then after I got saved in Oct, of 1977, I started the next year in Prison Ministry with a brother from my church, and planted those good seeds for the next eighteen years, and the two years of Juvenile Hall Ministry, and two years in rescue mission ministry...And then pastored for about eight years and was a criminal counselor for a year, so since 1977 I've planted good seeds traveling miles from Calif to Michigan, to mo.

To Arkansas to Oregon, preaching and pastoring, all for the Kingdom of God, and as my old Pastor Cleo Roberts used to say, "God is keeping the books," and God does record our lives from birth to death...As I said earlier, and we should always give God the glory in anything we do, especially when you plant seeds in God's ground, and if I went into detail, some may think I'm running my deeds, and righteousness up a flag pole of recognition, but not so (just explaining...) An am now starting to reap the harvest of those good seeds I've been planting for a little over forty years now of ministry and we reap the ultimate return harvest when we get to heaven, but I've seen many, reap before they've departed, and I have been to some of those godly saints funerals that indeed was like a revival service, and celebration cause everyone knew without a doubt they were soul winners, and finished their course and they have kept the faith (2 Tim. 4:7, And finished their labors victoriously, and that they had completed and fulfilled their calling, Now absent from their body (in heaven) they are present with our Lord, 2 Cor. 5:8, in my words). (Hallelujah.) Seeing these great men and women of faith stand through all that just encourages my socks off.

Victorious labor, that they had completed and fulfilled their calling, now absent from the body is to be present with the Lord... hallelujah.... Praise the Lord, it'll be worth it all, when we get to the other side if we've been faithful in a little we'll be blessed with a lot, the Bible says, so my friend look to Jesus the author and finisher of your faith. (Heb. 12:2), and if you fall short, ask the Lord to forgive ya, get back up, and try it again, with everything you got...you can make it, as a lady preacher sings about, three of these ladies have battled, over the years, Laura, Peggy, Bonnie, sung "you can make it" and Sis. Debra Epps and watched the battle through cancer and you still sung and encouraged people even though you were in the battle of your life, what an awesome testimony and great example you all are to me and all of us. Wow, your song, words of wisdom and encouragement, seeing you battle and carry that load and still sing and have joy in your heart, and shine your light through it all, and many others that were a rock and pillar to me, over the years, we have all had ups and downs highs and lows in life, and again, when your finally through it, it'll be worth it all to make it to the other side, and for many it's the pressure against the chunk of coal that transformed it in to the diamond… Lord, I hope and pray, folks can look beyond me being a chunk of Coal right now and see later (1 Pet. 4:12, 1 Pet 5:5 to 11, 1 Pet. 1:7, Job 23:10) down the road on after coming through some horrific (Matt. 5:14, 16) ordeal…And still standing for God, seeing and knowing God was the one who brought you through it when the finished product once passed through the pressures of this life and through the fiery trial we will be changed in the twinkle of an eye (1 Cor. 15:51, 52), and when this corruption has put on incorruption and this mortal shall have put on immortality (then shall be brought to pass the saying that is written, death is swallowed up in victory, o—death where is thy sting, o-grave, where is thy victory? (1 Cor. 15:53, 54, 55; Rev. 21:4).

So the pressures and trials and problems in this life, puts us to praying to God for help, and God, draws us closer to him and prepares our souls for heaven, cause if things didn't ever happen, then many folks wouldn't pray…So because pressure is applied to us chunks of coal, we become a diamond in Christ (Phil. 4:13; 2 Cor. 5:17; James 4:7, 8; Matt. 6:33; 1 Pet. 5:6, 7, 8, 9) casting all your cares upon Him for He cares for you. Knowing we can call upon God at any time because his ears are open to our cry. (Ps. 34:17 and verse 19) says, "Many are the afflictions of the righteous, "But the Lord delivers ("you") Him-her out of them all. Again, the things, the trials, battles and struggles in life (2 Cor. 12:7) those thorns in the flesh Apostle Paul spoke of, will help you one day become that Pillar and that Rock, that Diamond, that light House to some lost ship, alone out there in a sea of trouble…And they see you with your burning bright light (Matt. 5:14, 16) you being a lighthouse for God) because when you've already been through those (2 Cor. 12:7 to 9, Thorns in the flesh) as fiery trials in (1st Peter. 4:12 to 19)… And received a passing grade from God, and you've moved up to the next higher level of a light house (spiritually speaking, Matt. 5:14, 16) you'll burn your light bright for those other troubled ships out there on the troubled sea of life, battered by the waves of despair… And they see your light of Hope on (Rev. 12:11). They overcame him (the devil) by the blood of the Lamb (Jesus) and by the Word of their Testimony: And they loved not their lives unto the Death (John 3:3, 5 and Rom. 10:9, 10 and 2 Cor. 5:17) means it's by Jesus's blood that washes away our sins when we pray, and repent and we tell others by witnessing how Jesus saved us...Because, we are many times the only church, the only Bible, the only Jesus some people are gonna ever see according to the Bible: sure the world calls people like us fanatics, but according to the Bible...in (Rev. 2 and Rev. 3 and Matt. 25) it's the fanatics, that are the ones who make heaven, the lukewarm, and those not all the way in are like the foolish virgins in Matthew 25 that wasn't full, was the ones that got left behind.

It's the full ones, that are filled up with God. When the cancer doctor at UCLA said cancer is in your throat...The old Fred would have went berserk, and when you keep standing for God, He will help you through it (Phil. 4:13, 19) And that encourages others, but even if you do die...making heaven is worth it all. So stand strong for God in the Power of His might (Eph. 6:10, 1 Cor. 15:52–55, Rom. 16:20) and the God of peace shall burse Satan under your feet (S-H-O-R-T-L-Y.)...under your feet...ones that have gone on over to be with Jesus (God will put Satan under your feet, Rom. 16:20) you that are true believers in Christ, God'll even make your enemies worship God at your feet (Rev. 3:9, 10) (Psalms 23:5), and I believe that even people that sabotaged the work of the Lord, church burners, and people that have persecuted ministers and ministries, these sabotagers will face the Judgment of God (Rev. 20:14, 15; Rev. 20:11–13; Matt. 23:23–28; Heb. 2:3; Jude verse 15 to verse 19, Luke 11:52; Luke 16:19 to 31, Acts 5:39) if all mankind could just look in through God's eyes, and see into hell, those that have already died and went to hell that hindered the work of God, somewhere even religious folks, that were blinded by religion, Jesus rebuked them one after another in (Matthew 23).

I don't believe any of them made heaven. Do you? Are we hindering or helping God? Because if anyone is a troublemaker and hindering the work of God and given people of God (other Christians) and ministers, and pastors fits or trouble or a bad time, according to the Bible, they won't make it into heaven, but are full of the devil

(1 Cor. 9:12, Gal. 5:7, Acts 5:38, 39, Phil. 3:17 to 20, Matt. 25:41, 2 Pet. 2:4, James 4:17, 2 Thess. 1:8, 9, 1 Tim. 5:11 to 15, 1 Cor. 15:24 to 27) says Christ is gonna put all our enemies under our feet. (God'll bruise Satan under your feet (Rom. 16:20, Rev. 3:9) And (1 Corinthians 15:24 to 27) says Christ is gonna put all our enemies under his (Jesus) feet. Wow (hallelujah) sickness, Disease, death, foes, of all types, if it came against you, and you're a born-again child of God, believer in Christ. He (Jesus) will put all those things, hurts, disappointments, evil people, etc. Under your feet (I believe that is also hell talking about hell under your feet when standing on the sea of glass (Rev. 15:2, Luke 16:23) People in hell looking up into heaven as in the story of the Rich man in hell, looking up in (Luke 16:19–31), and again this would be double the punishment, while burning forever, and seeing those who tried to tell you about Jesus, standing on water on "The Sea of Glass" otherwise someone explain in (Rev. 15:2). The purpose of water mingled with fire, if it's not like a two-way mirror of a layer of water overlapping the fire of hell, in which those in hell seeing into heaven, but those in heaven just seeing their own reflection (it's my own interpretation) not trying to add to the Bible…that's what I see, where the rich man in hell… according to (Luke 16:19–31) where the rich man in hell looked up into heaven (in other words, he was under everyone in heaven's feet).

Even (Rev. 15:2) people in hell get to see those fanatic Christians standing on the sea of glass. On water, while they are begging God for a drink of what those Christians are standing on. Wow, does God know how to slap your enemy or what? (Luke 18:17 and 8, Rom. 12:19, Heb. 10:30, 31) That's why the Bible says that you're not to be an A-venger, "Avenge not yourselves," don't pay back evil for evil" (1 Thess. 5:22 and 23, 1 Pet. 3:9, 1 Thess. 5:15) God'll take care of them (for it's written "Vengeance is mine and I (God) will repay saith the Lord) (Heb. 10:30) (2 Thess. 1:8, Luke 21:22, Rom. 12:19) I just put one-half of the scripture, but you can look it up and if we allow God to fight our battles then we'll stay out of Jail. Yes, people still lie on you because they have lied on Jesus, and so they'll lie on you and me. Just remember God's the avenger, some scriptures I've written out all of it, and some I just brief it or just write the text, hope you look them up. Sorry, but it's already a big book the way it is.

(First Cor. 15:26) says the last enemy that shall be destroyed is death, Isn't it amazing that several times it says enemies are gonna be put under our feet? Wow and (1 Corinthians 2:9 says). But as it is written, eyes has not seen, nor ears heard, neither have entered into the heart of man, the things which God hath prepared for them that love him. (1st Cor. 2:9) to those who are not looking for Jesus Christ's Return (The Rapture) you will indeed miss so, so much… not just missing heaven, but the journey, and the change over, and all the Splendor of it all, in between. (Isa. 64:4), just what little we read in scripture we know God's been preparing now for those who believe in him, follow him, and received him as Lord and savior, have a place in heaven (John 14:1 to 6, and according to the scripture's time clock, it is very soon.) we don't know exactly what day or hour (Matt. 25:13) but we know it's close (Matt. 24:50, Matt. 24:36).

Please note (Matthew 24:33): DOORS, so close that it is even at the time DOOR…or the door, but DOORS…yes (repeat) (Rev. 3:20). I stand at the DOOR (that's at your heart's door, Jesus is knocking for you to let him in your life (heart). Oh…yeah, but (Matt. 24:33) DOORS (Matt. 16:28) some'll not taste death (one door, 1 Thess. 4:13, 14, 15, 16, 17, 18) Notice (verse 15) those that are alive (we, saints of God) and remain, unto (or until) the coming of the Lord, still at door, number 1, verse 17) we'll be caught up, in the clouds, to meet the Lord in the air: (this is the door number 2) going through a different dimension, comparing text to text (1 Cor. 15:46, verse 45, verse 52, 53), which will be another door of changing the natural body in to the spiritual (type of metamorphose transformations) of the physical human cell structure of this fleshly body could in no way… No how travel through space, through time at the speed of light, without burning up…when passing up through outer spaces atmosphere.

So this door, as spoken of in (Rev. 4:1, verse 2) immediately. I was in the spirit, a throne, was set in heaven, notice, immediately… or, in (1 Cor. 15:52) says. In a "moment of a twinkling of an eye" used (half of scripture, Note: you can Google it). Wow…too long to put in my book, but briefly, a twinkle is faster than a blink or a wink. A twinkle is about 26.6666667 mm so we double that to 53.3333334. This is the distance light must travel. A blink is at 300 to 400 milliseconds or three-tenths or four-tenths of a second. So yes, when you blink that's really fast, so knowing the twinkle of an eye is faster than a blink, wow it will be a super-fast, quick pass through from one physical state to the spirit state… A metamorphose state but not only in our physical human body that changes into our new spiritual heavenly body…but we will travel through another dimension at the speed of light, which is again the reason for a heavenly body, and this change and the passing through this dimensional door is all gonna happen in the twinkle of an eye. It's the Word of God (1 Cor. 15:52).

And this dimensional door where God's dimensional area is, only a spiritual heavenly body that's supernatural could travel at the speed of light, and even enter into the supernatural presence of God (Notice in verse 21 in Exodus 33:20 to 23, thou shalt stand upon a rock = that rock is Jesus = 1 Cor. 13:12) only with that heavenly body will saints of God be able to enter through that door into the presence of God Almighty. God told Moses in (Exodus 33:20) (you can't see my face and live) but, there is a place by me (and in verse 21) (where you can stand on a rock = Jesus) Now, (Psalms 91:1–4) calls it a secret place, that if you dwell there (in my words you'll be under the protection of his wings). (Read it) but most folks don't even comprehend or even think of all this stuff, but God is a force, he's a supernatural being, Paul said he was a consuming fire (Heb. 12:29). Wow. Again, so this human body has to change into a heavenly supernatural body that could only exist, live and be there, only if it was changed = being born again = (John 3:3, 5). We are taught in school…that is, in outer space in deep space there is no oxygen, no breathable air for this human body. Once passed through the upper atmosphere, there would have to be some type of breathable device or you would Die… Naturally… Unless, God designs a body that's a supernatural body…that's changed to a heavenly body that's able to withstand, all the atmospheric heat and withstand the force, and pressure that would burn up a human body. And according to scriptures this change over takes place in a moment of time, quicker than a blink of an eye (called a twinkle.) Now that's fast (1 Cor. 15:50 to 58).

We all have to experience a super natural change… Wow… Are you getting this…. Our heavenly father has had this designed way before we ever thought of making a wheel. Wow… And has revealed it to us through his word by his spirit. Even since Jesus Christ's Day has been a long time ago, example being, see how Jesus changed his physical molecular body structure before the disciples, into a glistening spiritual heavenly body in Matthew 17:2 and Mark 9:2 and 3 and comparing (Luke 9:29, 30, 31) Jesus and Moses and Elijah were all three in white glistering (glory glowing) heavenly bodies, and notice (verse 31) Moses and Elijah was speaking about when he's gonna die (but I want to point out it was a spiritual demonstration) that was showing the disciples the new heavenly bodies and also to reassure them of Jesus's death and resurrection that would result in a new heavenly body, but if you are a real studier of God's Word, then you know things are wrapping up…and getting closer every day, and again, ones that don't see it, are too caught up in this life, And folks there in (2 Timothy 4:5).

Note: scripture tells us to do the work of an evangelist, which there is a difference, in rushing through a quick chapter, rather than each verse by verse, and sometimes rereading a verse or even looking up a similar one comparing it, and even looking up meanings of a particular word in the dictionary or concordance. Oh that takes too long…but that's doing the study's of an Evangelist. Yes, it does take longer…that's why when you grow in God, a bowl of cereal scriptures, don't feed ya full, or get you through the day, you need some meat of the word and especially if you're preaching this service today. You'll be glad you studied like an Evangelist, cause the Bible also says to always be ready to give an answer to every man that asks you a reason of hope in you (in my words, in 1 Pet. 3:15, Plus, you receive more in your own soul) back when I used to drive for a living, I had a cassette and CD player in my truck and played Bible on tape/CD, and I would rewind that tape button so many times, over and over… we need to get the Word of God down deep in our souls so when things happen, such as it did with Jesus, when he was confronted by the devil to tempt/test/and try him in (Matthew 4:1 to 11)... As Jesus spoke the sharp two-edged sword of the Word to him, even as we must also "Speak the Word." Amen. It's not about competitiveness nor how quick we read; it's about whether or not you received anything from the Lord into your heart from what you read. Cause when something pops-up in life, you'll need some ammo to shoot back at the devil cause from the abundance of the heart the mouth speaks what's put in it, and thy word have I hid in my heart that I will not sin against thee (Matt. 12:34, Ps. 119:11).

Plus, faith comes by hearing the word (Rom. 10:17). Some folks just read a quick chapter so they can ease their conscience and say I read my Bible today... Yet the Bible says to STUDY (2 Tim. 2:15, "to show thy self approved unto God) a workman that needed not to be ashamed rightly dividing the word of truth. But studying the Bible doesn't mean we are to change or rewrite the Bible, but it's saying: You are to learn God's Word and your (John 8:47, Matt. 24:35, Luke 9:44, Rev. 3:8, John 5:24, Rom. 10:17, Matt. 7:24, 25, James 1:22, verse 21) NOT to change what God said (Rom. 1:25) the main function and reason for the Holy Ghost is to give the Christian followers (John 14:26)-understanding, the Holy Ghost gives the understanding. Not man rewording the Bible. Or to speed real quick through scripture... No...but study...Try comparing, and looking up the meaning of words, see if Mathew's version goes along with Mark's or Luke's (some do) look the words up in dictionary and up in the Greek...oh, it does take longer to study...yet, texting, games...relaxing in front of the TV does to! I'll be honest, I've always enjoyed Bible and New Testament on CD when you take a drive, many, many, many, times to get the juice of the thing, like Shambock said to a guy one time, why do you keep chewing on the steak...if you get what I mean when you really get into something...it's gonna get in you.

I think a lot of times people get over confident in themselves, and feel oh I don't have to put that much time in it, people has really bragged on my wife's flowers and the TLC she gives them, they have to naturally grow and blossom, and so does our spirit man. I think it is so neat when some preacher has been spending extra time in prayer and study and dumps a full load of a gospel dinner on ya, and you really received a gold nugget or a spiritual steak. And it shows, it really shows, but more than giving out to others, we feed ourselves by studying God's Word, and it will nourish our own souls as well, and then next time we read it we even get new meanings, also because this is part of the mystery that the Bible speaks of in so many scriptures.

We remember that we read this last year but I see something different in that same scripture this year, but when man alters it, he takes away the spiritual insight and the true meaning of it. And according to (Rev. 22:18–19) plagues will be added to those people. God has sealed his holy word with a curse to people that change it. That's pretty plain speech to me, yet, you see so many different versions that are adding to and taking away. But they don't answer to me, but we are seeing some starting to hit America now, but just like rereading the same scriptures again and get a different meaning, it's all a mystery. (Just Google it.) The "mystery" of when you reread the Bible verses again the next year, many times, you see something different or new, and you scratch your head, saying wow, I read this a dozen times, It was just a few days ago, I told this very concept to my wife on another scripture, it's one of the amazing things of God's Word... And that's what some preacher's mean when speaking of getting gold nuggets on having an appetite for God's Word (Matt. 5:6) Even a little baby will let you know when He's hungry...Are you crying out to God to feed your soul or to give you a hunger or new desire for a new appetite for God's Word?... Another thing is, many times we feel guilty, cause, It's like a kid that's been snacking before dinner, and mom has been working, and cooking making a big meal especially if company is over, and little Freddie doesn't have an appetite, cause that little bug has been spoiling his dinner (well pastor has been praying and preparing a spiritual meal for you), er...a...I mean, moms (Ha) gonna get her feelings hurt if you're not hungry... Hurt, cause she spent a lot of time preparing that meal...and yes, Pastor's get discouraged too when they see people preoccupied in their seat thumbing through their Bibles, or texting...or talking... yes I'm repeating myself.

Pastor spends time to give you ammo, or a spiritual meal) So do you have an appetite to hear what thus says the Word of God, or are you bored too. Well, are you? Then pray and ask God for a new hunger. The Bible says, you have not cause you ask not (James 4:2) so "Ask," don't just sit there empty (Matt. 5:6) We are on a battlefield for God...you are God's gun, the enemy is the devil, the bullets are the scriptures in the Bible, there has to be an effort on our part to put the bullets in our gun (Reading/studying the Bible) and to quote them is firing them spiritual lock and load bullets scriptures at the devil as in Matthew 4 Jesus telling the devil what the Bible says, quoting that Bible with the right scriptures to fit the right situations...but using blanks, you'd be dead on a real battlefield, shooting blanks don't kill no body (spiritually speaking) Hope you get my analogy: Prayer goes with quoting scriptures using your mouth like a sword to speak the Bible (I dare ya to read Revelation 19:15; Hebrews 4:12; Matt. 8:8), also pleading the Blood of Jesus...And saying I rebuke you devil in Jesus's name with some authority...we get neighbor dogs pooping in our yard...And I'll charge out the door waving my cane hitting the steel screen DOOR...saying with authority...Get outta here...And they leave. Many times, I've told the Lord I need something from your word Lord, and other times the spiritual appetite just wasn't there, So then you pray, Lord created in me a clean heart, Restore the joy of the Lord (one church we pastored at that time to preach, the youth would go out into the kitchen and have a doughnut, not realizing what (James 1:21–22) says, or they weren't even concerned that would hurt Pastor's feelings, when he spent so much time getting the sermon and they leave just to visit over a doughnut. The doughnut won't save your soul but the word will. And it was obvious they didn't want to hear it. When they should have been praying for a new hunger for God's Word. No desire no care of life spiritually and should say, give me a new hunger Lord and thirst for righteousness, those that hunger and thirst after righteousness shall be filled (Matt. 5:6, Matt. 6:33) and already discussed (John 4, John 7:37, 38) living water that satisfies the thirstiness of a man's soul, and not meaning to confuse anyone on different analogies, the Bible, the word is a lamp to our feet, it directs us, or its food for the soul (a gold nugget, make you rich in God, Luke 12:21) it's a weapon, a sword (Heb. 4:12) to fight against temptation and against the devil as in (Matthew 4) where Jesus quotes scripture to the devil, it's a key to unlock secret locks in the spirit, Jesus told peter he would give him keys to the kingdom (Matt. 16:19, Luke 11:52, Rev. 1:18, Matt. 6:19, 20, 21) so it's just not mere words on paper that someone stuck in a book and called it a Bible, No, it's your weapon (sword, Heb. 4:12) and your keys to heaven cause if you don't follow and live your life according to the Bible…then you don't make heaven (period) Jesus said he's the way, the truth, and the life no man comes to the father but through Jesus. (John 14:6, Jesus is the word.) He's the Living word (John 1:1, 2) see (John 1:14) and the word was made flesh, and dwelt among us,) this all can keep on going so deep…and I think my point is made clear, you need the life Necessities of things to survive in life, and the same principles applies spiritually… Plus there are real devils, real false doctrines, and in a jungle, you would need real weapons for protection…and in the spirit, your sword is the word, A weapon, quoting the Bible scriptures in your prayers, quoting it to temptation, etc. (1 Cor. 2:14), so like in our natural life and in our spiritual Life, we have to do what we have to do to survive.

The Bible and prayer, praying in the holy ghost (Jude 20) and praying in Jesus's name quoting those particular key verse scriptures for the particular situations, and (doors) and keys to unlock some doors and other scripture in (Rev. 4:1 and Rev. 3:8), we should always be obedient to God and go through doors that he opens to leading someone to God in prayer, that God has put before us open doors no man can shut. (Rev. 3:8), opportunities, to lead someone to Christ, Door to God's ear is always open to hear your cry. (PS: 34:15:19, Rom. 10:13 Joel 2:32, Acts. 2:21, Acts 2:38, 39, keys secrets Ps. 91:1), He that dwelleth in the secret place because you see, when you dwell in the presence of the Lord he's gonna empower you with your spiritual bullets for your gun, or God will fight the battle for you as he did for King Jehoshaphat in (2 Chron. 20:15 to 18) when God told him, God would fight his battle…wow…case in point, all God ask King Jehoshaphat and his people to do was sing praise songs to God…Wow. And God took care of King Jehoshaphat's enemies, all three armies God killed, plus gave the people of God their treasures. On knowing that the devil that has aggravated and came against God's people, God will burn all his enemies in the Lake of Fire forever, and the devil's first on the list (Rev. 20:10), and it's all biblical, case in point, all he ask King Jehoshaphat to do was sing songs of praise and God took care of all the enemies...other times God helped them fight by directing the stone to the head of the Giant for David, or protected Daniel while he was in with some killer lions...but before the lion's den, he prayed three times a day... that's being in the secret place (example, if I'm out at the park with my grandkid, and he's right beside me and up walks a vicious killer dog trying to get my grandkids hot dog.

That dog is gonna have to go through me to get my Grandkid, when it comes down to this type of situation, even someone else's kid, are you gonna stand there and watch a kid be tore up, don't think so...Is God any different? (Matt. 7:11, Matt. 6:33) so you to are protected in God's presence (secret place, Psalms 91:1; Exod. 33:17 to 22) see (vs. 21, another key) Praying in the name of Jesus

(John 14:13, 14) and (Acts 3:1 to 16, see verses 6 and 16) (1 John 5:13–15) (John 15:16) (Jn. 16:23). It's Jesus who died on the cross and rose from the dead, etc. And it's the name of Jesus the Bible says (devils believe and tremble at) so we mentioning the (James 2:19) name of Jesus can make the devil tremble, guess Satan knows that Jesus is gonna be the one that fries him (Rev 20:10; Matt. 8:28, 29; Matt. 25:41; Rev. 20:4; Matt. 8:29) says, "Art thou come here to torment us before the time." So yes, the devil knows his time is short too. (Rev. 12:12) but verse 11 we can stand on, "And they (Christians) overcame him (Satan) by the blood of the lamb (Jesus), and by the word of their testimony.

And loved not their loves unto the death. The word of our testimony is, we knelt at an altar and repented, and called on Jesus for salvation, believing he died on the cross for all my sins, and rose the third day, ascended up to heaven and is soon to return for us believers, and we take him at his word when he said whosoever calls on the name of our Lord Jesus will be saved (John 3:3, 5) (Romans 10:13) (Rom. 10:9, 10) (Joel 2:32) (Acts 2:21). Amen. And Jesus told the disciples, and all the followers of Christ, that they could ask anything in his name (John 14:12 and 13) (Luke 18:27) Notice He that believes on me in (verse 12)…the works that I do shall he do also: (John 15:7, Mark 9:38–40) Jesus and the Bible says, in (Matthew 16:18–19) and (Revelation 1:18) we are the church, and the Gates of hell shall not prevail against us, And the Lord told Peter, He is given the keys of the Kingdom of heaven…(in my words you can read it) to the Church, = The followers of Jesus Christ have been given many door keys, tools, abilities, gifts and power through the blood of Jesus, Power in agreement, Power By Praying in the name of Jesus, power by Praying in the Spirit, Power over Death and hell, Jesus has given us keys over all these through (Luke 10:19) his blood and his name to escape death by calling upon Jesus.

Keys to the kingdom of heaven is one with our mouth key (Rom. 10:9, 10, 1 John 1:6 to 10) by praying and asking forgiveness this is called (the key of repentance) with the mouth confession is made unto Salvation and this gets your name written in the Book of Life (Rev. 3:5) with that same key…Also keeps you from eternal Death, which is hell and the Lake of Fire (which is called the Second Death, (Rev. 20:14, Rev. 21:8, 1 Cor. 5:5, 1 Cor. 6:9, 10, 11). Now the well-known late pastor, Adrian Rogers, once said, if you're born twice, flesh and blood birth, and then you become born-again equals spiritual birth (John 3:3, you only die once.) But if you're born once, your gonna die Twice (meaning: you never got saved, born again spiritually) Which if you do die twice, physically, and spiritually, you'll wish you'd never been born at all (Mark 14:21). Anyway the Bible says death has no dominion on the Lord and the Christians (Rom. 6:9 to 23, 1 Cor. 15:26) says, and the last enemy that shall be destroyed is death (1 Cor. 15:54, 55).

From the very beginning of time when man gave up the dominion in the Garden of Eden, that God gave him, when man yielded to sin, and gave place to the devil (Eph. 4:27) in the garden of Eden, and then the devil stole man's dominional power of authority (Gen. 3:1 to 7) at the cross when Jesus died, God gave back that dominion of authority to man that Adam and Eve lost, (Gen. 1: 26 to 28, Luke 10:19, 1 Cor. 15:45 to 58) but at the cross, after Jesus was born as a man, yet still part God (I like what chick publications says Jesus was the God-man.) Wow, and so Jesus dukes it out with the devil, and at the cross, Jesus paying the price for our sins and our salvation with his life (1 Cor. 6:20) took back all authority for man, but this kind of dominion only comes back to man through salvation from Jesus Christ, when we repent and give ourselves back to God through Jesus Christ, it only comes to those who have called upon his name. And to those he makes them the Sons of God (John 1:12) (1 John 3:2) (Rom. 8:14) (Gal. 3:26). When we are born again through repentance, Jesus writes our name in the Book of Life, giving us back that power of authority in fellowship, and dominion with God as Adam had before he sinned. I want to clarify a big misunderstanding in many religions, where many people misunderstand the phrase ("Come as you are") this only applies when you first come to God, then after salvation, through repentance, then comes a spiritual growing process of learning the basics, to read the Bible and pray and grow up spiritually. But the phrase has been over the years, misleading folks to think that they can still live in their sins (not so), or that folks that, just because they go to church, they'll have that power and authority (not so, Phil. 4:13) the word (through) is used, water that goes through a piece of pipe to give you water, but that pipe (you) has to be connected to the water source (converted to it, as in John 15:4 to 7 see verse 5) that says, without me = (Jesus) you can do nothing (see again Philip 4:13) (2 Tim. 2:19) says, we must depart from iniquity, which is what was in our old life before we ask Jesus to save us from all our sins, according to (2 Cor. 5:17) We are a new creature (creation) in Christ, old things pass away, behold all things are become new.

We have to be willing to (depart) from sin and (leave it alone) so that phrase that says (come as you are) is just until you get saved.... then there is supposed to be a change within your heart and soul. And even as your physical body from a child grows up into an adult, and so should your spiritual man also grow up and matures in the things of God (1 Cor. 2:14, John 15:5). I know many that still live and do things that's sin, there has been no change (Rom. 14:4 verse 5, 1 Cor. 10:12), but I'm not their judge, but this has become a false doctrine in many religions, as also the phrase ("once saved always saved") this is a lie and false doctrine. And is a religion, not Bible scripture, or then explain why the Bible says in so many scriptures for the saint of God to "watch and pray" and be ready for you know not what hour your Lord comes...or (Luke 21:34, 35, 36, Matt. 25, Rev. 3:5, 1 Cor. 6:9, 10, 11), etc. So why watch and pray if you're once saved, always ready? Or why does (Rev. 3:5) say names will or can be blotted out of the Book of life? And why did Jesus say daily take up your cross and follow him (Jesus, Luke 9:23) why daily if you're once saved, always saved? Follow the Bible and Jesus, not Religion!

Anyway, my dad was in that religion. But came out of it at the last of his life. Thank God, but this is why Jesus and the Bible warns us to be aware of false doctrines, and false prophets (Matt. 24:4 to 15) and false religions. I can give many more scriptures, but again this is why the Bible says, God's own people are destroyed for their lack of knowledge (Hos. 4:6) and again it says for us to study (2 Tim. 2:15) but that is left up to each individual, as turning away from sin is. And this is why so many are on the defensive side when it's mentioned, because they want to live in sin (John 3:18 to 21, Rom. 1:16 to 32, 1 John 3:20, 1 John 1:6) I can give many more on both subjects, the Word of God is gonna judge man, on Judgment Day (not me) and this is why so many want to change the Bible, to ease their conscience, but man can't change the original Bible in heaven, that he will be judged out of on Judgment Day (Rev. 20:12, Malachi 3:16, Rev. 3:5, 1 Cor. 11:28 and 31; and 2 Cor. 13:5).

Study that word *reprobate*, cause if you try hanging on to the life of sin and try hanging on to God at the same time, he'll turn you over to a reprobate mind, if you are refusing to change (Rom. 1:28, Read it, 1 Cor. 10:21, 22), etc. In fact if you read the whole first chapter of Romans and the tenth chapter of First Corinthians when God destroyed those in Moses day, when God gave Moses the Ten Commandments in (Exod. 20) and (Numbers 16:30 to 32) when all those evil men were swallowed by a *massive* earthquake, when the ground opened up. And in our world even today, we are seeing the same attitude and evil spirit in men and women as it says in (Romans 1:26, 27), it's a $23 billion dollar-industry worldwide in adult sex toys...Hello, planet Earth...you have forgotten the days of Noah and the days of Moses, and the man named Lot of Sodom and Gomorrah in (Genesis 19) and (Luke 17:32). But to all who truly repent, and change with the help of God (Phil. 4:13) you can do all things through Christ which strengthens you.

And so the key of our mouth calling on God through Jesus Christ our Lord, and his blood washes away all our trespasses and sins (Isa. 1:16, 17, 18, 19, 1 John 1:5 to 10, Rom. 10:9, 10). So as the old Gospel Hymn said, "There is Power in the Blood" (And weapons, armor, strength, and salvation, etc. And Jesus's Blood washes away our sins (Rev. 1:5, Rev. 7:14, Mark 16:16 and 17 and Rev. 12:11 and 1 John 1:7, Col. 1:14) cause as we now see the Revelation plagues unfolding (Matt. 24:21), todays'll be worse than Moses day! (the blood key) washes away our sins...and the mouth key asks forgiveness of our sins (Isa. 1:16, 17, 18, 19, 1 John 1:6, 7, 8, 9, 10, verse 7) his blood cleanses us...from all sin. There are doors, keys, tools, weapons, armor, power, strength, salvation, grace, mercy, shelter, protection...etc.

But the best one is Jesus Christ's blood, that washes away all our sins, but also I have been in many dangerous situations and I started pleading the blood of Jesus over us, as in the days of Moses with the blood put over the door, so when (Col. 1:14, Gal. 2:20, Eph. 2:8) the death angel would see the blood (Exod. 12:7 to 13) He would see the blood applied and he'd pass over people's homes of those with the blood on their door, and now Jesus's blood is applied to the door post of our heart when we repent and get saved, the blood of Jesus Christ cleanses us from all sin (1 John 1:7, Exod. 12:12, 13) So we could say the Blood of Jesus is a preservative, to preserve us, and save our souls (John 1:29, Jesus was called the Lamb of God, which takes away the sin of the world, used one-half scriptures) So in Moses's Day they used a spotless real live lamb (1 Pet. 1:19, Heb. 9:7 and 9:22 see verse 28), and after God saw that the sins of man were worse than ever (Prov. 15:3) He had to save his creation and make a way to remove man's sins (Phil. 2:6 and 8). So God took on the form of (Phil. 2:7) a human man (1 Cor. 15:47) and laid down his life on an old rugged cross and became a sacrificed human lamb, which He was the ultimate sacrificed lamb one-half human and one-half God, to demonstrate his love for all humanity for all generations to come, so God could say, "I gave my only son to die for you, so you can receive me (Jesus) into your life and make heaven." John 3:16 and Eph. 2:8, 9 says, "For by grace are (ye/we) saved through faith: and that not of yourselves it's a gift of God.

Not of works, lest any man should boast. But there are little secrets and pointers to stay ready, and that is like the song… "Just a closer walk with thee." So where do you draw the line on just how close do we walk to the Lord? (As a lamb would to the shepherd when wolves were nearby.) With praying, and studying the word, and using it as your spiritual weapons, always guarding and protecting your hearts, from tricks and lies, and traps of the devil…according to Job, the first two chapters it's clear the devil is having to ask permission to set these traps. And God does allow it to happen: but he also gives us the equipment, weapons, power, strength, tools keys, and protection, to overcome him (but we must stay under the blood of Jesus and stay within that realm of his presence, (1 Cor. 10:13), God'll take care of us) "There hath no temptation taken you but such as is common to man: but God is faithful, who will not suffer (allow) you to be tempted above that ye are able: but will with the temptation also make a way of escape, that ye may be able to bear it (1 Cor. 10:13, Hebrews 2:3).

We must remember Peter's example, he was doing fine stepping out of the boat in faith knowing he was with Jesus walking on the water which was the only man except Jesus to ever walk on water (Eph. 6:10). And you know the story. He took his eyes and mind off Jesus and looked at the storm, and waves and sunk. Please notice the passage of scripture in (Matthew 14:30), "When he saw the boisterous wind, he was afraid, and begging to sink, he cried, saying, Lord, save me!" Now this little example may have happened just to teach saints of God a lesson in, keeping your eyes and mind on the Lord even though you feel your 100 percent right with God, and your right next to him as Peter was, and you are doing so good, "Hey, I'm walking on the water, defying the laws of Gravity" but doesn't the Bible say in (1 Corinthians 10:12), "Wherefore let him that thinks he stands take heed, lest he fall." We must always be alert, so we can be right next to the Lord and still fall short but I've always preached be quick to repent, like Peter did, right off he called on the Lord, always be quick to repent. We gotta swallow our pride and just do it. Get back in the realm of God's presence and protection.

No, Peter didn't commit no great sin, he was just being taught in order to step out into your measure of faith, you must keep focused on Jesus, which is the author and finisher of our faith (Heb. 12:2) "Stay focused in this evil day, where any kind of wind may distract your attention (Ephesian 4:14) and (James 1:6) even a wind of doctrine, that word (Boisterous) (in Matt. 14:30) means, violent, rough, turbulent storm (it wasn't just a big wave) I'm reminded of Jesus, when he called Lazarus back to life in (John 11:41–43). Jesus thanked God for hearing him, wow (We too can follow that same example of thankfulness) rather than whine-N about it…Thank God for hearing your prayers, and everything you have, ears to hear the birds, and those great old time gospel singers that I have playing, The Happy Goodmans and KennyHinson. Wow, they are just about my most favorite singers, and I'm so so thankful I can hear them and my cousin Jim Peterson and my wife Brenda Davis can sing right up there with the best of them, and my son's no. 1, Sgt. Fred D. Davis Jr.) and many at my church thanks God, for my ears, and eyes, and arms, etc. I had a pulled muscle in my right shoulder and for about a week I had lost use of my right arm, and it sure makes you thankful when you get use of it again.

We just take things in life for granted. I had made a little list of things God fixed and answered and tacked it up on my prayer bulletin board with my three sheets of prayer lists, and I try every day to remind myself to thank God for all those answered prayers, and try to remember the older I get, post notes really work and I love those sticky notes I have 'em everywhere. Draw your line to what works, for you, but don't forget to thank God. Amen. I believe part of Jesus's examples he taught the disciples and us is having a thankful heart, as Apostle Paul also did in (Ephesians 5:19, 20; Colossians 3:16, 17; Psalm 107:1; Psalm 118:1; Psalm 118:29; Psalm 136:1; Psalm 136:26; Ps. 136:3). All say, give thanks to the Lord…Wow, talk about your repeats, if you're making notes…HA. But good ones. Anyway have a thankful heart, and follow up any and all prayers with thanksgiving, Thanking him for answering your prayers (give God thanks for hearing our prayers even as Jesus did in John 11:41), miracles, etc., also praise, and sing him songs of adoration because God inhabits the praises of his people (Israel, Ps. 22:3) have you ever went out of your way to do a good deed for someone and they walk away…and didn't say thank-you. Kind of a slap in the face (right) God deserves more than a thank-you and more than our worship… some just mouth words that are not from the heart…God wants your whole heart 100 percent…then if a tragic situation occurs, we can call on him, without guilt knowing with all assurance that God's got us in his hand, and He will never leave us or forsaken us (Ps. 37:24, Heb. 13:5).

Now, knowing the Bible teaches all this, the only way for the hand of God to be away from us…would be if we turned back to live in sin again (Heb. 3:12; Heb. 2:1–3; Ps. 34:16; Ps. 37:9; Prov. 8:36; Isa. 1:4 to 20; Isa. 5:20 to 25; Isa. 3:9, see verses 17 to 26 esp. 20, 21, 23) Wow sounds like today; (Rom. 6:23; Heb. 2:1, 2, 3; 2 Pet. 2:1, 2, 3, 4, 5, 6; Luke 9:62; Matt. 5:28; Luke 17:32). Only this time, in Luke 17:32, you have to research it, and see what Jesus is referring to, saying remember Lot's wife. She didn't have the heart like Peter had, to walk close to the Lord. Sin and pleasure and fun, something back in the "Sin City of Sodom and Gomorrah" had her attention, so bad, she ignored the warning from the angel, not to look back," oops.

And she perished along with that evil city. I heard an ol' Preacher say once, "You can take the people out of Sodom and Gomorrah/the city of sin," "but it takes a Big God to get Sodom and Gomorrah out of the people!" Wow (John 3:18, 19, 20, 2 Thess. 2:10, 11, 12) cause they love the darkness lifestyle, more than the light of Jesus Christ than to live right, This is one of the signs of the Last Generation, Loving Pleasures more than God, That's today's generation, by the Billions: we must not take the warnings from God so lightly! What does a man give in exchange for his soul? If you lose your soul by dying in your sins, if your rebellious ways don't change, you could be lost forever, people worry about dying but it's not giving up this body and this life that you should be concerned about, you may live to be 90 or 100 or 120, but your soul's life in hell or heaven is gonna be forever, throughout all eternity, forever and ever, with God or in hell, the choice is ours right now, choose wisely but, "Being concerned of where one spends eternity, that sounds like what the world should be thinking of," And drawing their line to calling upon "Jesus Christ to save their souls," but Sodom and Gomorrah's evil history is now again being "repeated again, which if you reread history.

It was just before it was destroyed by an Angry God. So don't mess around and lose that time God gives you to get right, cause despite what many religions teach, the Bible says, "God's spirit will NOT ALWAYS STRIVE WITH MAN (Gen. 6:3). "Now" is the accepted time... "Now" is the day of salvation. Before it's too late (2 Cor. 6:2 and Heb. 3:7, 13, 2 Cor. 4:16) Because...you and I have no promise of tomorrow, but the question is "Does God know your name"...Is your name written down in the Lambs Book of Life? If you have prayed the "sinners prayer and have accepted Jesus Christ into your heart as Lord and savior then God knows your Name," and that reminds me of a true story that I heard a Gospel singing Group called (The Rochester Family Singers). If I can tell it correctly, one of them told a true story of some ministers traveling with them, and the part of the area they were in, was right behind a drug Lord and his gang, and the gang was stopping car after car and beating each driver to death, and these singers and ministers gave their testimony how they had the song playing on the CD player... "He knows my Name"...and someone had hit the replay button, and the song kept replaying over and over... Now, when these gangs came to their car they heard... "He knows my name"... Playing, and took their hand back off of the Door handle, and went to the next car...and the cops were approaching, as the family rolled out of their car into the nearby ditch, to roll-away from all the flying bullets... As they ducked down with their family and minister friends, they could still hear that song on replay... "He knows my name." Wow (I cried) Wow, and none of the Christian folks were hurt... Just shook-up and thankful... hallelujah. Thank you, Jesus... Wow... "What a protecting hand of God." Or what? Wow... Where do you draw your line to God knowing your Name? So then once you see and know God delivered them all (Heb. 13:8) We know Jesus Christ is the same yesterday, today, and forever (Luke 11:32, Gen. 19:26).

Back when God delivered lots family out of Sodom, and Gomorrah, when lots wife looked back and was destroyed, and right after the angel told them all not to look back... This is what (Luke 17:32 means, Ps. 9:17, Deut. 6:12) her heart had to be on someone back in that evil place of sin, which wasn't worth losing your life and soul for (Matt. 16:26, Luke 9:62) Even people that sabotage other people's work (I have known some) will be like lots wife, which to me they are deliberately drawing there line to deceive and destroy their own soul (James 4:17, 2 Thess. 2:10, 11, 12), kinda like the price gouging in times of disaster which is against man's and God's Laws or hording in a crisis time such as the plague that has hit this world, oh, society cleans it up nice and saying it real pretty, calling it a virus because they haven't studied prophecies of God's wrath in Revelation's...Just like abortion, calling it a fetus, and ease (sear) their conscience...it's a human life, it's a baby, and it's murder, you think the virus plague is bad, it ain't nothing compared to the nightmares in Revelation's that's coming on this Earth, Islands sinking caused by massive earthquakes, and meteor showers burning up two-thirds of the Earth, to the giant flying plague of insects with stingers in their tails like scorpions...People we need to pray like never before. Well, while we're on this subject, where do you draw the line to the devils in the pharmaceutical companies, and the high prices on the urgent important type medicines that are so ridiculously priced so high that only the wealthy can afford them, I'm telling you these devils will stand in Judgment, And will answer to a God that my Bible says will avenge his very elect (Luke 18:7, 8; Matt. 25:40 to 46); All these devils have on their mind is money, not on helping others.

Sure there are some generic brands, and thank God for them, but there are many that are price gouging deliberately because of high demand for the product, this is wrong. Now come on, folks, if I can see that this evil act of price gouging is wrong.... Don't you think God sees it too! (Proverbs 15:3) Yes, He does! (Heb. 10:30, 31; Rom. 12:19; 2 Thess. 1:8; Heb. 2:3; 1 Thess. 4:3 to 18; see verse

12, James 4:17; Matt. 25:40; Rom. 14:12). "So then everyone shall give an account of himself to God.") As in (2 Corinthians 5:10, 11), They should read this one for sure. Verse 10 says, "For we must all appear before the judgment seat of Christ; that everyone may receive the things done in his body, according to that he hath done, whether it be good or bad." Wow, see what I mean (see verse 11). "Knowing therefore the terror of the LORD, we persuade men, but we are made manifest unto God, and I trust also are made manifest in your con-science.") So those two verses are very plain to me in my KJV Bible, so if a stupid high school drop-out ex-hippy biker drug addict that went back to school and got my diploma ten years later, can under-stand this, with the help of the Holy Ghost directing and teaching me, and giving me understanding, then what about all these intelli-gent scientific minded pharmaceutical companies, that are smarter, that will definitely stand in judgment for ripping off poor people, oh yes, they will not escape God's wrath! (Read it!) And any other of those liar companies that lie on their phony commercials on TV, some I tried, and I called them thieves and liars, the Bible says in Rev. 21:8 that all liars will burn (Read it, SORCERERS in Rev. 21:8). Wow…there's a lot more that our society calls good and accepts and they say it's okay, that the Bible says it's sin.

But back to Lot's wife looking back to her destruction and disobeying the angel's word from God. Again, it's the same as the Bible…which is God's Road map to heaven, and his Authentic Rule Book, and His Divine set of instructions to the letter how man is to live, and to self-discipline his self, but man chooses to disobey like lots wife, and even in (Acts 5:1 to 11) concerning lying (They both died.) but again we see in scripture the importance of conducting ourselves right, and following God's Word. It is very crucial in this evil day and hour that we do so.

But Lot's wife's fleshly desires had over powered her conscience, and her remembering what the angel told her, because her heart wasn't right with God, nor was her desires on God…but back in the city of sin, where God took her out of before he destroyed it, This is why Jesus died, was so his blood would cover our sin…what a slap in the face to God, for people to say…as those religious folks

I worked with, after they chewed me up and spit me out, this one certain Pharisees said to me, that even after he was saved and born again, that his religions says he could still go back out and get drunk, kill, rape, steal, and if he was shot and killed while doing all this that he would still make heaven, this folks is the kind of deception the Anti-Christ will bring in, this type of strong delusion and is deception, and one of the first signs of the last days Jesus Christ spoke of in Matthew 24:4 was take heed that no man deceive you.) This man that I worked with was definitely 100 percent deceived and was believing a lie (Gal. 6:7, 8, 9, 1 Tim. 4:1, Matt. 25:1 to 13, Heb. 2:3, Matt. 15:14, Gal. 5:16–22, Heb. 4:1, Luke 9:62, Heb. 10:38, Gal. 1:6–10, John 6:63–66) that's pretty plain to me, but what about Jesus saying, in (Matthew 7:21–23, Luke 6:46).

The guy at work was saying he could still do evil and make heaven, yet, Jesus says these guys in Matthew 7 are doing good by casting out devils, and did many wonderful works but somewhere they fell back into their old ways of sinful living, because Jesus said He told them in verse 21 not everyone that says Lord, Lord, shall enter into the Kingdom of heaven, but only those that does the will of his father in heaven. Is killing, raping, stealing, God's will. No way, that's plain to me, but Jesus adds more, saying in verse 22 even though you do great things. Jesus can still say depart from me, you that work and do iniquity equals sin in verse 23; yes, the Bible does say if we sin we have an advocate with the Father, yes, Jesus in (1 John 2:1, 2) is our mediator, but the Bible also says in (Heb. 10:26) if we sin willfully after that we have received the knowledge of the truth, there remains no more sacrifice for sins. (Wow, read it! Which means premeditated.) You planned it out and did it.

Wow, yeah, again, this man is in a false religion, that's also into false doctrines, that says you can commit those evil sins and you'll still be going into heaven, Lies, this is a deceiving spirit from hell, making them believe lies from hell, strong delusions, etc. (2 Thess. 2:10, 11, 12). And living for God is not easy…in fact Jesus even told us and the disciples (in John 16:2) that the time will come that those who kill you will think they are doing God service (my words, read it, Wow) And that people that are Christians, = us followers of Jesus

Christ…would be persecuted, he didn't say how, and I'm sure this kind of talk rubs people the wrong way…but we all have to work out our own salvation with fear and trembling (Phil. 2:12) but Bro. Fred, doesn't the Bible say God hasn't gave us the Spirit of fear (2 Tim. 1:7).

Yes, but you can Google all the different types of fears good and bad…but between us, when you really read the alternatives if we had to lay down our life for the Gospel of Christ, cause missing heaven and going to hell after reading (Luke 16:19 to 31) And seeing up into heaven while you are burning is not my idea of a good choice, I choose to follow Jesus…We have to weigh it all…ALL…ALL out… is there really anything worth missing heaven for…anything really? No, No, No, Nothing, so what, so what if we get some type of persecution, I guarantee you making heaven will be worth it all, even if you was a million-air and had to give it all up for God…or as the disciples were martyrs, as (Rev. 20:4, Matt. 14:10, Rev. 17:6, Acts 22:20, Rev. 2:13, 14, Acts 12:1, 2) what denomination or Religion do you think this is? God doesn't want people that's into Religions! God wants his-self to be in people (John 4:14, John 4:23, 24, John 15:4 to 7), He wants a personal relationship with all of us (Rom. 8:9, Rev. 2:6 to 16, Rom. 8:11).

So study out those verses and look at the same Pharisees and Sadducees, and Scribes and the Nicolaitanes in (verse 15 of Rev. 2). Just study the first three chapters of Revelation's And you'll see in these closing days, hours, before (Rev. 4:1) Jesus calling his people up to heaven: Jesus plainly tells us there will be no lukewarm, or people standing in the middle, or on the fence (in my words) you'll either be hot (spirit-filled) or cold (sinners, in my words, read the first three chapters of revelation over and over. You see if we are martyrs for Jesus Christ, we would just step out of this human shell called a body and step into our new heavenly body (1 Thess. 4:16, 17–18, 1 Cor. 15:50 to 54, Col. 3:4, Matt. 22:30, 1 Cor. 15:44, Phil. 3:21, Luke 9:29, 30, 31) So we see according to scripture, we will have a new heavenly body, that will live forever, as I previously stated… and Jesus said to watch and pray (Luke 21:34, 35, 36) and Jesus said we'll know he's about to come when you see all the things spoken of in (Matthew 24)…Come on, people, look around you…yes I'm repeating myself again…but really (look around). "Do you really, really, really, really think things are gonna get better…I see an evil world that's became so bad the Bible has said, God will destroy it and the Bible is definitely being fulfilled, and if you are so blind and so caught up in this evil life in this evil world that you can't see it (Rev. 3:18) you better read about Lots wife again (in Luke 17:32 and Gen. 19:26, Luke 9:26) cause you to just might get left behind but God still forgives a repented heart.

And He wants you to be informed, and comparing the Bible's Prophecy, Last Days, End Time info. With today's evening news, many people just want to stick their heads in the sand when these subjects are mentioned…As I've said before and no one wants to talk about it. The subject of the End of the World, Last Days (Matt. 24), The Rapture, or like my Book that's out on the markets… "Is the chip the mark of the Beast 666." (Yes, it is.) All this stuff is warnings—signs that the Bible, Jesus/God has said in the Bible that we are to watch for. And Jesus also said it'll be like a thief/ or burglar that comes in the night and you are caught off guard because you were asleep (means not alert, or not watching, not ready, I'm just explaining what the Bible says folks). Do people today really compare the news with the Bible, no, I've pastored four churches and I say, no, they don't…AS I said, you'd be shocked in knowing of all the people that say they are Christians, and couldn't even tell you where Bible verses, are or what's in the news or of the severe magnitude of events that line up w/Bible Prophecy and things happening, weather events, destruction devastated sites that's been in the news that lines up with Bible prophecies, and to interview multitudes of people who are Christians, that blindly think the world will continue on for another hundred years…wouldn't that be calling the Bible and God a lie, but then that too is also Bible Prophecy, and Peter said they'll even say, we've heard that all our life (2 Pet. 3:3 to 5) I too have had people on the Job say (We've heard that all our life), saying scripture to me, and not even knowing they were quoting ol' Peter, but the text scripture in vs. 5 says that "For this they are willingly ignorant of…" Wow, and I'd say, yes, that too is in the Bible.

Wow...You see it was this same way in Noah's Day (Matt. 24:37). A lot of people just go to work, eat, sleep, some go to church, and don't really listen, they are bored, go just out of tradition or obligation, or to please someone, but most folks are so caught up in doing what thrills and excites them, they miss all the signs of the time. I'm talking about all the crooked lawyers, I've even been the victim, and crooked companies, scammers, crooked workers comp. But today, everywhere there are millions of liars, just watch the commercials on TV, salespeople, especially will tell you anything to make a sale, and lie like the devil himself. Liars come in all walks of life, we all need to repent, and tell the truth, and it's not just fishermen, ha.

If everyone knew they were gonna die in the next hour especially with the virus plague going on, and knew the Bible says all liars are gonna burn in the lake of fire (Rev. 21:8) I think they'd pray, but the good news is we can repent and ask now for Jesus to come in our hearts, and ask for forgiveness...And yes I told this once before, that the Bible says: We have a mediator, Jesus Christ, that we can go to God, we can go to him when we have fallen short, and at those times we messed up (Heb. 12:24, 1 Tim. 2:5, Rom. 10:9 and 10, 13). God/Jesus is long suffering the Bibles says, He wants us to bring him all our cares and problems, but we have to ask him, he paid the price on the cross already, you just gotta take the baseball bat away from the accuser (the devil, Rev. 12:10) And also you need to forgive yourself. Some folks help the devil beat themselves over past mistakes. (1 Peter 5:7) says for is to cast all our cares on him (Jesus), cause he cares for (us) you. So forgive yourself, and others, cause many are sick cause they don't forgive and even doctor's say that if many people would just forgive, and pray—and let all the bitterness out, and let the past go, they wouldn't be half as sick as they are. So, forgive and ask God for help, and confirm it with your doctor, some folks even see Christian doctors.

And I thank God for my good doctors, though as I said, there are crooks and liars in all walks of life, and all types of thieves, identity thieves, etc., thieves of all kinds, robbers, killers, gangs, drug lords, drug dealers, extortioners, embezzlers (crime is at an all-time high) I was a prison minister for eighteen years, and I can't tell you, of all the prisoners that get out, and come right back in again cause there is too many to count…they are hooked on crime and sin and it takes a miracle for them to change. And I could go a lot deeper on all this: They are building more and more and more prisons (why). I've already told you (because man's heart is continually wicked (Matt. 15:19–20, Gen. 6:5 to 17, Matt. 24:37 to 39, Jer. 17:9–10, Ps. 9:17) and this type of generation of people as we are discussing is the last generation according to the Bible's end time prophecy.

But people, even so-called Christians, just don't want to hear it, or don't even believe it, because they like this evil world of darkness and sin and corruption: I'm telling you the truth (John 8:32) and the truth shall make you free. Jesus Christ himself said man loved darkness more than light because his deeds are evil (John 3:19 to 21, Rom. 12:1, 2, 3). This is my point on deception: on (Matt. 24:4) Jesus said, let no man deceive you. This was the first thing he said when he started discussing the "Last Days" subject. *Webster's Dictionary* says, someone that misleads, or causes a person to believe what is not true, to be false, or betray them, lie or cause someone to believe an illusion or even fraud them with tricks.

This sounds like the devil himself, or even sounds like the scriptures (2 Thess. 2:10, 11, 12, John 10:10, 2 John 7, Gal. 6:7, 1 Cor. 6:9, 10, 2 Cor. 3:13, Rev. 18:23, Rev. 2:4 and 5) "The Bride the Church, Believers, Christians are caught up in the rapture of the saints." The light or candle stick (Matt. 5:14 to 16) when you are saved, and Jesus is the light, his spirit comes in you when you repent of your sins and when people see you, your countenance of your face is lite up as when they ask Moses to cover his face with a vail, cause people that live in sin gets convicted of their sinful dark lifestyle, and if you'll notice a lot of Hollywood movies are using a lot of dead, evil, gruesome and dark, or darkness, devilish…they think it's cool…and some have been killed in car wrecks, and some have died of aids, and cancer, etc., but the point here is God is light and in him is NO DARKNESS AT ALL (1 John 1:5) And being evil is not cool, nor will it go to heaven! Nor will those who walk in darkness go to heaven! (John 8:12, Rev. 21:27, John 3:19, Titus 1:16) Wow… sounds like today's Hollywood Christians. Now I'm not their Judge, cause all have sinned, and they don't answer to me. I'm just saying the scriptures that points to them in prophecy of these chapters of the last days (2 Tim. 3) (Matt.24) (2 Pet. 3) (Heb. 12) (1 Cor. 6) (Rom. 1) (2 Pet. 2) (Rom. 13:12, 13 and 14, Matt. 6:23, Eph. 5:5 to 11, see vs. 8) Again (1 John 1:5, There is no darkness in God or in heaven (Rev. 22:5 and 1 Cor. 4:5, 2 Cor. 4:6; 2 Cor. 6:14) and there is many, many more scriptures on this, but hopefully you see my point. The Bible is our road map and rule book to heaven, and Jesus is the door, if you don't follow the Bible and Jesus, the Bible says you will not go into heaven! There is a huge lie and false doctrine out there, that says many paths lead to heaven, this a lie and false doctrine (John 14:6, John 10:1 and verse 9, Luke 9:23 to 26, John 8:12, Rev. 20:10, 1 Cor. 15:33, Luke 21:8).

And this Pharisee I worked with that professed he was a Christian but told a lie after lie, and he believed he could do any-thing he wanted, murder, rape, steal, and if he was shot and killed in the process while doing it, like I said earlier, He really believed and thought he'd still go to heaven (this is a lie and false doctrine, Ezek. 18:20, 1 John 1:6 to 10, 1 John 3:6 to 8, 1 John 5:18) according to (Matthew 4:6, 7; 2 Thess. 2:10, 11, 12; 1 Tim. 4:1, 2; 2 Tim. 3:13; Heb. 10:26; Rom. 6:12 to 16; Matt. 15:14; Matt. 23:36, 37, 38, 39; Eph. 4:18–32). Why did Jesus say sin no more lest a worse thing come upon you (John 5:14; John 8:11; Rom. 6:1, 2 to 6; Rom. 6:14, 15, 16; Rom. 8:1, 4; 1 John 3:4, 8, 9; Isa. 5:20; 1 Thess. 5:22; 1 Thess. 5:15; 2 Tim. 3:13; 2 Pet. 2:22; 2 Cor. 5:17; Rev 2:2, 4, 5; Rev. 3:2, 3, 4, 5; Rev. 3:15 to 19).

Please note: why is there the word *repent* used so many times, I count sixty-five times just in the New Testament... Wow. And seven in the first three chapters of Revelation, which is a warning to the church...and it is told to the church...hello, people, come on... scripture after scripture to the "church"... "to repent" I don't want to be standing anywhere near some liar...that say, they can still commit Sin and Still make it, I'm not talking about falling, but Deliberately Diving into, there is a DIFFERENCE! Again I've repeated myself (Rom. 6:13, 14, 15, 16). In (Romans 6:15), what then? "Shall we keep on sinning because we got saved and are now under grace? God forbid, Paul said. And again, Jesus told several people, one was the woman taken in adultery. In (John 8, verse 11), "Go, and sin no more." Wow, so how many people are suckered in to this wise guy that I worked with false doctrine.

Yes, that, too, is one of the last day signs is false preachers, and false prophets, people causing offenses, and that guy was, one also, I tried to give him scripture, all he kept saying was God will not disown you, yet, Jesus said it'd been better that Judas was never born than to betray him (Mark 14:21). But maybe that's why the Bible says for each one of us to work out our own salvation with fear and trembling (Phil. 2:12) cause if we are wrong, we will stand in God's Judgment alone, and we can't blame no one, and no one will take your place in judgment, Jesus already paid the price so everyone can make heaven, but sad to say many will not, because of stubborn self-will and rebellion, wanting their own way. Then they will hear. "Surprise. You were wrong." You didn't follow the Bible, there will be weeping and Gnashing of teeth (Luke 16:19–31 see vs. 24, Luke 13:27–28) it'll be sheer horror, looking into hell and seeing into heaven the whole time they are there in hell. (Look at verse 28 of Luke 13), if you remember me telling you of the rich man in hell and seeing into heaven, seeing Abraham and Lazarus in (Luke 16:23) and in (Rev. 15:2). People standing on water, now read (Luke 13:28) wow, are you seeing it. Scripture repeats itself before Jesus tells of the rich man in hell. Wow. Gnashing and Gnawing their teeth for pain, yet that eternal body will never burn up, but will feel fire forever (2 Cor. 5:11, Matt. 24:51, Luke 13:27–28).

In the Old Testament (Isa. 5:13) says: God's people are gone into captivity, because they have no knowledge (half of the verse). In (Isa. 5:14), The Bible says: hell has enlarged itself.) Is it because more people are into churches and religions more than Jesus Christ? I am so amazed at the great multitudes of different religions, out there. Oh no, you don't dare disqualify or dishonor them, no. Never meaning to, downgrade or insult anyone. Honest, every human being on earth has the right to who or what they worship, in America (No matter how wrong they are) we are not their judge. Myself I follow Jesus (and that's my right, and the KJV Bible and Biblical History has come full circle.

The time has come all the way around again, to where evil is being spoken of as good, and good is evil spoken of (Isa. 5:20, Eph. 5:11, 12). And there is nowhere in the Bible, where God has said to go ahead and continue to live in sin, deep down in everyone's heart most everyone knows right from wrong (Matt. 22:37, 38, 39, 40) Minister R. W. Shambock used to say that the word righteousness meant in (1 Corinthians 15, verse 34) meant right living cause everyone knows right from wrong (James 4:17). It's just that we are in the last days, and this is one of the signs, man would rather disobey God, and again it's like the many different version translation Bibles, it's all rebellion, and disobedience (Please don't hang up keep reading) and even your famous TV preachers are willfully, I said willingly... willfully following them, using them, etc., when again the KJV Bible says in (Rev. 22:18–19), you can't take away or add too.

My question is (listen up, you know it all preachers) the Bible says, plagues will be added to those taking away or adding to, I wonder, if that also applies to those using them in their ministry also (Matt. 15:14). Do people really read that scripture? Yes, I believe also, cause in our law even though you were not actually committing a robbery, but you were with them in the car, that makes you an accomplice. Yes, that's the law, so wouldn't that also apply here. Yes it would Yes it would, again, the Magnified version Bibles are adding too, the Newer Translations which both types take a way and add too, but the newer ones, are condensing, which definitely are removing complete verses, who gave them permission, God sure didn't (Rom. 1:25) Not in (Galatians 1:6–10) it tells us that if any one comes with another gospel they will be ACCURSED. This word means, if you take away or add to God's Word the Bible plainly says, those people will be cursed with the plagues that's in the Bible! Is a light coming on here? Hello...yet no one sees this (Matt. 5:18).

We were discussing earlier, don't let anyone, No one, deceive you (Matt. 24:4). Some idiot that's full of the devil comes along and rewrites the Bible and says, we are just removing the thees and the thous and are making it easier to understand, it's just like when the devil told Eve, oh God didn't really mean don't eat or touch it, cause God knows when you do your eyes'll be open and you'll be as smart as God (Gen. 3:1 to 7, 2nd Cor. 11:3, 2nd Cor. 2:11, 2nd Cor. 11:13 to 15 see verse 14) (in my words) listen these people and the devil are trying to take the Holy Spirit's Place (Job)...Read (John 14:26) again read Galatians 1:6 to 10, John 14:16, 17 and (John 16:13, 2 Cor. 11:14 and 15, Matt. 4:5, 6, 7) see (Verse 6) It's not... Our place to rewrite, add or change God's Word, or even explain it, that's the Holy Spirit's job. (John 14:26 and in Matthew 4:3, 6, 8, 9, in verse 6). The devil's quoting (Ps. 91:11 and 12) twisting it. When the devil tries tricking even Jesus with a twisted scripture, as he did to Eve in the Garden do you really think you are exempt.

Jesus said the truth will make you free (John 8:32 and Jesus said each time to the devil) "It's written" (verse 4 of Matthew 4:4) Man shall not live by bread alone, but by every word that proceeds out of the mouth of God. Jesus said in verse 7, it's written again "Thou shalt not tempt the Lord thy God" (meaning, we are not to commit suicide), which is tempting and provoking God, cause he is the Giver of life. In verse 9, the devil was even trying to trick Jesus into becoming a devil worshipper, but notice what Jesus replied, Get thee hence (in my words, he's saying, get outta here) Satan: "For it is written, Thou shalt worship the Lord thy God, and him only shalt thou serve. (Notice the words here which is a command = Thou shalt) a commandment in (Exod. 20:3 to 5) one of the Ten Commandments to have no other gods before you. Also notice the words "to serve only God" (Isa. 14:13, 14; see verse 12, serve only God). In (Isa. 14:13, 14, Luke 10:18), Jesus said, I saw Satan as lightning fall from heaven cause the devil said he would exalt himself above God, what a liar, and He's still trying today, and he's still trying to trick and deceive people with twisted version Bibles (once again) only a devil-or-a devil possessed person, only a reprobate person would attempt to rewrite and change what God said (a real Christian wouldn't) cause it's...very, very dangerous (Gal. 1:6 to 10) And God'll add all of the plagues that are written in this book, to their lives, and we are seeing the beginning of the end now, and anyone with any brains can see the world has enter into a real nightmare plague era but again, this ain't nothing compared to the vials of God's wrath that's told of in Revelation's in the Bible prophecies that God is about to, and gonna pour out on the Earth, that is still yet to come, God's showed me in my prayer time, and my pastor has also said for months, something big was coming, and told the church folks to put back and store up.

I have preached about Noah, and the end of the world sermons for forty years now, and many has thought I was off my rocker, but again, while praying I was seeing God's time clock winding down, wondering in my heart if people were gonna see it as a wakeup call, that God was saying it's time to get on the boat of God (no, I don't know, day or hour) before God raptures out the church people, don't you think He would send something to happen to open people's eyes to see that it's time to get woke-up and ready to meet God/Jesus (1 Thess. 4:13 to 18) No, I don't know if it's on a Tuesday or a Thursday (Matt. 24:36) or when Jesus is coming, if it's morning, night, or at noon, but I can see many are just sweeping it under the rug as if it's just a twenty-four-hour bug, and think it will pass, so many people are in denial when it comes to prophecy of great devastation, or God's Judgment, cause it's real scary or depressing, or to negative, but if you really pray and ask God to show you, he will, people back in the olden days thought before the flood was upon the Earth, the people then thought, Noah was off the deep end, and they all perished, they mocked him, just like they mock preachers today, we've come full circle folks (Matt. 24:32 to 39) see the last part of verse 39 says: so shall also the coming of the son of man = (Jesus) be see (Matt. 24:48–50) but many just don't see it, or believe it, and don't want to hear it, and that to is told in the Bible (2 Pet. 3:3, 5). But as bad as it seems, like (Ps. 91) this still don't compare to God's wrath that is still yet to come on the Earth (Rev. 6:12 to 17). Some say we've had eclipses before, yes, and some folks say we've had a blood moon before, yes, but not with tons of falling stars which is a definite sign in (verse 13 of Revelation 6, Matthew 24:29), so be careful on hearing people say that has already happened, cause there are those who try and de-sense-itize those prophecies, so people will be caught off guard. (Read it, Rev. 6:12 to 17, Mat. 24:29 see verse 22.) It's all in sequential order, carefully read it over and over… "as a fig tree

casteth her untimely figs, when she is shaken of a mighty wind."
(Wow.) That's telling me when that Eclipse comes showing a blood
moon, it'll be followed up with a bunch of falling stars, like figs falling by a mighty wind. (Hello, read it again, do you ever pray when
you read prophecies? Time to start! When God pours out those vials
of his wrath on a sinful world that has rejected his son Jesus Christ
(Rev. 15:1 to 7, Rev. 16:1 to 19, Rev. 19:15, Ps. 91:1). Now I heard
one lady say to her kid, Oh the old Bible scriptures were just stories,
and not real. What a lie, wonder what she thinks now...or when
she stands before God on judgement day. Another lady said when
my best friend died, before he died she said, if that was her she'd be
beating down the church door, too late, it's closed up.

But seriously folks in your own opinion, what would you do if
you was God, to show people to tell them, and giving them warning
after warnings, signs after signs (2 Tim. 3, Matt. 24, Col. 1:28, 2
Cor. 5:11) trying to warn the world when you see these things, like
wars and rumors or wars (Matt. 24:6, Luke 21:10 to 12) pestilences
plagues, earthquakes are coming as mankind has never ever seen,
with great devastation, never seen before, so great, Islands pass away,
mountains fall flat. Wow...what would that register on the richer
scale, it'd probably bust it (Rev. 6:14 to 17, Rev. 16:18 to 21) And
man will not be able to escape (Heb. 2:3). But it's according to the
Bible, not minister Fred Davis, and God will also remove and blot
out names out of the *Book of Life* (Rev. 3:5) (Psalm 69:28) (Exodus
32:33) *because* many will turn back to their old sinful pleasures (2
Pet. 2:22) as lots wife did (Luke 17:32, 2 Pet. 2:1 to 8) and that blows
some religions out of the water, read it. (Rev. 3:5, Luke 21:22 to 36,
see verse 22 drive-bys and road rage, see verse 25 and tell me we've
not seen crazy stuff going on in the world and in the sky and worse
to come, and that leads me to verse 26.) People will be dying from
heart attacks, for fear of looking at things coming on the Earth, but
if people want to stick their head in the sand, that's their choice, but
I'm living for Jesus Christ, and looking for his soon return.

Back to (Galatians 1:6 to 10), read it a few times, along with
these other ones, the Bible is like todays newspapers, when you look
at every other thing that gets affected by it, when a plague is active,

it affects jobs, education, people panic and the hording begins, etc. And I do believe they very could begin marshal law with the military. But I hope not. So God has the right to start the tribulation period. And He will also remove their name out of the Book of Life that took away from God's Word making it a false version bible. And their name will be blotted out of the Book of Life forever (Rev. 22:18, 19; Rev. 3:5; Rom. 1:25 to 32). And yet people keep reading them, why? Some appear to be smart; I just want to fly over in a helicopter with a loudspeaker and say, "Follow the old King James Version" and pray and ask the Holy Spirit for understanding... Don't be cursed... Don't be blind, and don't be led by the spiritually blind"! That's plain to me *Webster's Dictionary* says, *accursed* means to pronounce a curse upon, or be excommunicated, or to be cursed, or damnable, look up that word, when you're damned, means sent to hell, Now, you still want to Read and follow these new retranslated versions, yeah, I know there will still be the blind leading the blind, and they'll still follow them, but if they read this book after me breaking it down, for them, wow...it ain't my fault, believe me there is a Jezebel-Demon-Seducing Spirit in our land, deceiving multitudes of people, and there is a strong spirit of rebellion in our land, study that one out, it's as the sin of witchcraft.

Wow (Acts 16:16, 17; 1 Sam. 15:23; Gal. 5:20; verse 21; 2 Chron. 33:6)? Read these scriptures and (Ps. 78; Rev. 22:18, 19; 2 Cor. 5:11; 2 Thess. 1:8, 9; Jude 7) and my question is, do you really want to tick off a God who could melt you right off your skeleton (Zechariah 14:12) could be a nuclear missile, or one angry God, and worse than that, he could send people's soul to hell forever. Yes, that's why Jesus died on the cross for our sins so we can make heaven (John 3:16; John 10:17, 18; 1 Cor. 6:20) but you must follow his rule book the Bible, and in it we all are told how to live, act, and conduct ourselves, Jesus said to take up our cross daily, and follow him, and pray to him every day, cause we always fall short in some way, cause there is no perfect person (Rom. 3:10), but those that are close to being perfect, like Daniel was, He prayed three times a day, and was a very good man of God, but even Daniel wasn't 100 percent perfect cause he was still human.

And the Bible says there is none righteous no not one (Perfect) (Holy) (Rom. 3:10, Matt. 19:21) People that think they are, haven't done this (Matt. 19:21, 1 Pet. 4:17, 18, Matt. 23:27, 28, Luke 13:24 to 28). Yeah, so they will be cursed by God, with plagues added to them, then sent to hell, and marked as one practicing witchcraft. Wow "So don't take from God's book or mine…" I'm just the messenger delivering his message. Wow, so these smart doctors and theologians, of different doctrines, are gonna be held as accomplices by God. Wow with all those curses and plagues added to their lives, and they won't listen to an uneducated ministers warnings.

Because they are so full of pride themselves, and think they're way up the high ladder of self-knowledge (1 Cor. 10:12) like those Jews and Pharisees that rebuked the blindman that was healed in (John 9:34) (see verse 16 and 18), when they said, you were born altogether in sin, and you are trying to teach us. Ooooh, they were puffed up religious prideful, unteachable, schooled in the spirit of the Nicolations and Sanhedrin sect or what. Why don't people listen. And they want to get and give more of an in-depth revelation to people new stuff, new information, new things that no one else knows about (Acts 17:21) something that's new that they themselves will appear to people to be more knowledgeable and deeper, and more of a spiritual intellect than anyone else, this is a self-exaltation spirit (Acts 12:21 to 23) (that's an anti-Christ spirit, 1 John 2:18, 1 John 4:3 and 5, 2 John 7, Gal. 1:6 to 10) To bring in and teach something new or a new interpretation, or a new doctrine of new revelation is wrong, living for God is not about people that's so puffed up with their self-pride, and all their self-gained accomplishments, no, but God is love (1 Cor. 13) Jesus is love (John 3:16).

Remember, Jesus came as a lamb among wolves, and humbled himself to death and to others. (Hey, great idea, let's all have an old-fashioned feet washing service) I've been in those services, wow. It's very humbling (John 13:4 to 17) and you pray for them while washing their feet (see verse 35). Serving God is not a competition expo on saints trying to outstudy each other or who can achieve the highest honors, no, it's about recognizing where the world has come to, and about how much time is there left to win souls for God and recognizing to work while it's still day because even though, the days are evil, it's recognizing souls are dying and being lost without God and without being born again (John 3:3, 5) it's all about the harvest (Luke 10:2) is white (RIPE) the field the world, it is riper than ever before, it's time for us all to keep a repented heart, and ask the Lord to create in us that broken contrite heart and a right spirit (Ps. 51:10 to 17) this means us humbling ourselves before God and each other! (2 Chron. 7:14, Matt. 18:4, 1 Pet. 5:5 to 9, Luke 10:27) according to (Gal. 1:6 to 10) because that would just anger God (Col. 3:6) and besides, what's wrong with the old original gospel in the KJV it was good enough for Mom and grandma, and it's good enough for me, Lord help my repeats soak in these people's hearts and minds down into their spirit, turn that heavenly light on, let them see that I'm telling them the truth, in Jesus's name (1 Cor. 9:12 to 17, 1 Cor. 9:27, 1 Cor. 15:34, Heb. 12:1, 2).

My point on this is, we must all work out or own salvation with fear and trembling and don't let others deceive you with false doctrines or new revelations (Matt. 24:4 and 11, Phil. 2:12, 1 Tim. 1:3, Eph. 4:14, 1 Tim. 4:1). Or doctrines of men, or doctrines of devils. Because the Bible says the devil can come to you as an angel of light and his (Satan's) minister's can also appear as a minister of righteousness (2 Cor. 11:15, also see:, 2 Cor. 11:13 and 14 and 2 Cor. 11:3) that explains how Satan tricked even Eve, which was deceived by the tricky cunningness of the devil (called subtilty) lies, deception, craftyness and false, and counterfeit doctrines that's not real (with the same type delusions that the anti-Christ will use to deceive people (2 Thess. 2:9 to 13) into taking the chip/mark of the beast 666) he used that same craftiness on Eve and Adam, and many others down through the ages, of Bible history, to steal, kill and destroy (John 10:10) but Jesus came to give us life, and a more abundant life. (In my words, 1 Cor. 2:9, John 14:1, 2, 3.) Don't let the devil cheat you out of what God's prepared for you, study, and learn (2 Tim. 2:15) God's Word for yourself, cause you'll stand before God alone on Judgment Day...and you can see by lookin around, and by comparing the way the world is now to how the Bible says it'll be in the last days...are you gonna depend on some fruit cake type doctrine,

I'm following Jesus and the KJV. And God has nowhere in the Bible said to continue in sin...no...but he did say, sin no more! (John 8:11, John 5:14, Heb. 12:1 and 2) lest a worse thing come on ya...So is it really okay to go back to that dog vomit life, that God brought you out of....No, I don't think so...Yes "God" destroyed Sodom and Gomorrah (2 Pet. 2:6) Notice the word "ensample" (which means the same word as "example"...the verse is saying, God made them examples to those after, that would live ungodly!) so when you give people a word of warning, as I have many times used these scriptures explaining God gave us those examples to teach us, to warn us not to live like that, and said in (Matthew 10:14 and 15), if they don't hear and receive YOUR WORDS of warning (my words) when you leave, shake off the dust off your feet because it'll be more tolerable for Sodom and Gomorrah on Judgment Day than for them! "WOW" (read it and Romans 8:29, 30, Jude 7) God made examples out of the angels that sinned (2 Pet.   2:4) and then with the people in Noah's day then in Lot's day with Sodom and Gomorrah then in the days of Moses with the Earth opening up and swallowing them for their rebellion and sins, in (Numbers 16:30, 31, 32), and people today really think God is gonna look the other way with them.

WOW...but again (2 Pet. 2:5, 6, 7, 8; Matt. 10:14, 15; Rom. 8:29, 30; Jude 7; 2 Pet. 2:5, 6, 7, 8) and the world in the days of NOAH, because of their evil sins, and again God would have destroyed the city of Nineveh, but they repented from the king on down to the beggars. So God spared them from destruction because, There was a change deep within their hearts, because they truly repented (2 Cor. 5:17). Please, please, please, read (verse 28 of Luke 11:29 to 32, Luke 11:29 to 32, verse 32) saying the men of Nineveh shall rise in judgment against this generation...Wow, and I believe many others also will stand in judgment, including those evil doctors and nurses at the abortion clinics, and the women who had abortions that did not repent of it, for killing and murdering all the aborted fetuses (babies that were murdered by crooked killer doctors 61,054,786 babies to be exact go back to 1970 it was 8,329,844.7 by planned parenthood. Before it became legal or those in back alley black market Home Slaughter make shift clinics in the '50s and '60s

305

up to Roe verses Wade and up till now even more now than this I'm sure, Google it yourself.

They'll give you a few different amounts, both are unhuman/ in human to destroy a human Baby, they call it a fetus to ease their conscience, and again, it's like the plague today, they feel they should nice it up, with a nice name, and call it a virus (but Google the word plague). yes, I understand keeping down the panic of people, and I also believe most folks with a brain or Bible knowledge has already figured it out. And again, the aborted baby is a real human being, and all those responsible for all those deaths and murders, will stand before one angry God on Judgment Day. It really gets me, the way they turn it all around, and throw a bloody fit and say "Save the spotted owl" "Save the whales" "Save these poor abused cats and dogs" but abort the fetuses... Wow... Yes, I'm repeating myself... And those of you that get mad at me and my views, I have my constitutional right of free speech, the same as you and if you're mad, you better check your heart with God, because I'll give you a dozen scriptures to voice my views on the subject, cause I know my Bible! Do you really think God is gonna sweep all those innocent deaths under the Rug... I don't think so... Is there anyone that is that blind of God's laws and commandments, and calling the Baby a Fetus to justify it, and try to take away the guilt (ok) Now, the flip side, to those mothers that have not committed suicide, I know there's been many that's thought about it... And that's not the answer, because we serve a big loving God, He died for your sins...and he will help you, if you call upon him, and repent of your sins, and ask him to forgive you in Jesus's name, and he will (Rom. 10:13) whosoever calls on the name of the Lord shall be save...then pray for a healing in your mind.

Then you need to forgive yourself, and once you've done both, when the devil comes reminding you of your sin...tell him their under the blood of Jesus...because when you confess your sins to Jesus, he is just and faithful to cleanse and forgive you of all your sins (1 John 1:9). And the Bible teaches that the accuser (the devil) that accuses us all before God day and night. In (Rev. 12:10), 11 but verse11 tells us, we overcome that lying accuser devil, by the blood of the Lamb (Jesus), and by the word of our testimony when I repented and confessed my sins (Rom. 10:9 and 10) and prayed the sinners prayer, asking for forgiveness, and gave my heart to Jesus Christ, and lay aside all those weights that beset me (Heb. 12:1 and 2) and became a born-again new believer, a new creature in Christ and old things (in my words) passed away.

All things became new. Jesus changed my life 100 percent (John 3:3, 5, 2 Cor. 5:17, Ps. 51:10, 11, 12, 1 John 1:5 to 10) And this is why we have to know the scriptures, to quote them at the devil as Jesus did in Matthew 4, etc. And Luke 10:19 and Ephesians 6:10 to 18 and Philippians 4:13 and 19, Romans 8:13. God is just waiting on you to get right with him, then he'll help you overcome, but you must take the first step, and confess, repent, and ask him to cleanse you, and save you. He's waiting on you... Then when this subject comes up you won't be on the offensive side because you'll know you've been forgiven. And this applies to all of us, yes, us, preachers as well, we must all walk and talk the talk, and live it as well (1 Cor. 9:27). Always be quick to repent.

Again, I'm just the messenger, yeah, I've seen people get mad at the evening news guy, He's just telling the News or Weather... He's not causing it. (HA.) But back on the New Technology. That's being used wrong, God gave them the knowledge for good. If the city Nineveh is gonna rise in Judgment as I said, who's to say all those babies murdered in USA won't also, they sure could, and people have just swept it under the rug, oh it's just a fetus, and then they put the stem cells and tissues in women's make-up…oh yeah…Judgment Day is coming to America and again, I believe USA is (Rev. 18) okay…Repeats (Matt. 12:41)…if they would have continued living the way they was, scripture teaches us that God would have destroyed them. So we go back to the same old song and dance here. So if God is gonna allow us to go back and continue in sin then God would be made a Liar, and would have destroyed all those people for nothing in the Days of Noah and in the Days of Sodom and Gommorrah, and now he would be a Hypocrite God.

No way God Is not a liar! God is not a hypocrite! (Rom. 3:4, Titus 1:2, Isa. 55:11, Luke 21:33, 2 Pet. 3:11, 1 Thess. 5:22, 1 Pet. 4:2, 1 Thess. 4:3 to 17) did that scripture (1 Thess. 5:22) say, abstain from fornication. Yes, it does my friendly Reader, How do you draw the line" IN God's Word with these scriptures, in (Luke 14:16 to 24) This is what I call the excuses chapter. Where people make excuses to get out of going and attending this great super, and invited many… and the text clearly Points out this represents the resurrection of the just (in Verse 14) but all the people in verse 18, they all made excuses and verse 24 says: none of them will even taste of MY SUPPER, and you'll be amazed at those who still say…the opposite. People are gonna do what they want to do…Even if they have to make excuses to stay out of church. That explains why you need to Read (Rev. 22:11).

So the Lord in this scenario is saying those who made excuses will not make it or even taste of it. Wow, now, this doesn't apply to a reason, God understands reasons, like someone that hits your car on the way. By the time the police report was done, church was over. This type of situation's out of your hands, and considered as a (reason) why you weren't there. But those people in (Luke 14) were just making an excuse. (A reason is different than an excuse.) So this is one of the reasons for people writing their own version Bibles, they should name them "The Rebellion versions, or some might say God don't mean, oh really? Can we really just live any ol' way we want? No…we can't, but who was the very first one in this world to say, "Oh, God didn't really mean 'Don't eat of that tree,' because God knows that it'll make you as wise as God"? Yes, it was the devil lying to Eve (Gen. 3:4–7, 2 Cor. 2:11, 1 Pet. 5:8). Wow. Read it (1 John 3:20). And if the Bible condemns them, they'll write their own Bible that permits them to live anyway they want. Read Romans 1:25, who changed the truth of God into a lie (Note: I wrote only one-half the text…You can read it if you want to), That's pretty plain.

That whole chapter sounds like the world Today. Some, are like the counterfeit bills, and it has enough of the real one in it, to make it look like the real authentic bill, but counterfeit is counterfeit, and when you're dealing with preachers, prophets, followers of Jesus Christ they better be real, or like a counterfeit dollar bill, it's only good to start fires with. Yes, there are idiots out there, that will risk their freedom, and go to prison, just like those that risk their souls on going to hell, Jesus Christ said in (Mark 12:40), they'd have greater damnation, and in (Matthew 23:14) also. In fact, the whole Twenty-Third chapter of Matthew is a rebuke to the counterfeit Pharisees, Scribes, and Sadducees, and God would save them too, if they dropped the form of Godliness (2 Tim. 3:5) and hypocrisy, and repented of their counterfeit lifestyle. (Which is just a big show. Titus 1:16 and Ps. 94:11, Matt. 9:4, Prov. 15:3, but they don't have no power with God, 2 Tim. 3:5) (Just) having a form of godliness, but denying the power there of, from such turn away.

And so like the counterfeit bills, the Phony Pharisee-type Christians, put on a big act, but they deny that Holy Ghost power of God which would make them straighten up their life and follow him 100 percent and would make them live right! But cause they are phonies and don't fear God and they don't want it, so instead they become good actors, counterfeits, but if you're spirit-filled, the Lord will reveal them to you, I've seen many, like the counterfeit bills they are lacking the authentic-ness, strips, and chips and colors that the new bills have, they are now making it hard to counter fit, and creating a new special authentic look...And for the Christian, that's why the Lord gave us the out-pouring of his spirit in the upper room, in (Acts 2) and to give them Christians everywhere, as many that will receive him, to you and your children and all that are a far off, as many as the Lord will call. Read (Acts 2:38, 39). The Holy Ghost'll give you Power to stand (Lk 10:19) In this evil Generation, he's our perseverance, he'll keep us, from going bad (Jude 20, Ps. 23:3 he restores my soul).

One of the reasons God wants to empower you by infilling you with the Holy Ghost is so you'll have power to stand in the evil day against the devil (Eph. 6:10 to 18) and God will also help you when evil people come against you, but most of all he uses his Holy Spirit to preserve and keep you, and he will teach you, and lead you through the Bible, and let's not forget (Rom. 8:26, Jude 20) that says, many times we don't know how to pray as we ought, so God's Holy Spirit will pray through us as in (Acts 2: John 14:16, 17 and John 14:26 and John 15:26 and John 16:7, John 16:13) all speak of the Holy Ghost (Spirit) as being the "Comforter." There is a blanket called a comforter that keeps you warm but this is (not the same) but the Holy Ghost Comforter will minister to your spirit, and encourage you in a way that no human being can because he penetrates deep into the heart and soul, even as God's Word says in Heb. 4:12 and the comforter can uplift you (Jude 20) and build you up when you're down, or discouraged, or sorrowing over some loved one that passed away, he soothes the grieving heart to the place that the Bible says he gives you a peace that passes all understanding (Phil. 4:7, like when I went in for throat cancer surgery, been there, done that, Wow…that was the peace of God) and he can hose you out and make you feel so clean in your soul, that just makes you love everybody, and gives you love for others that you never had before or restore that love, like God did to my wife for me when I was a hippy-biker drug-ee.

God healed my wife's heart…and he can do the same for you. I mean like back when the disciples were beat and put in prison for their faith, etc., as in (Acts 12, Acts 16:16 to 30, Acts 5:18 to 42, Rev. 2:10, Rev. 12:11). No one knows what tomorrow holds, or what things the Christians will endure before Jesus Christ's return, so we need all of God we can get. It's not a church or religion (thing) but it's a personal relationship with the Lord Jesus Christ and being (John 3:3 and 5 born again) born of the water and filled with the Holy Ghost and fire. Not meaning to be offensive by any means, but if you do not understand spiritual talk as (1 Cor. 2:14) says, you need to first search your heart, ask yourself, what is my number 1 priority, cars, sports, work, fun, pleasure, etc., well, God should be number 1 and serving and living for Jesus should be no. 1 priority, when we die or go in the rapture, there will be a Judgment Day, and if you were more into sports than God…or other things…Wow… like those who paint themselves at ball games and stand in the rain, or hunters, fishermen (No there is nothing wrong with any of those things) but if you're more into things more than God, most of these types, laugh at a fanatic like me that raises his hands to God, and sing songs to God, yet, they are bored when they go to church, or are not sincere at all unless they need something…but when there's a touchdown…wooo, wooo…go…go…go…Yee-haw…we scored… or at their favorite concert everyone's raising hands but for the band, or that favorite song…Hey, I've been on both sides of this fence, but if you die you are instantly gonna stand before a holy God and you will give an account for how you live your life, and the time you give God versus all the time you spent doing your thing.

You better be listening…many of you, have made promises to God, and haven't kept yours…but you're quick to remind God of what he said he would do for his people…are you really his…really? Read (Luke 12:15 to 21 and see vs. 31 Matt. 6:33) says seek ye first to the kingdom of God, and his righteousness and all these things shall be added unto you, or (Luke 12:34 to 40, Matt. 24:42 to 51) or if you still think it's okay to party and get drunk and take drugs, and still go to church making God a mockery and slapping him in the face with an evil lifestyle, when God plainly said in the Bible we must change and come out away from the evil lifestyles of the world and (be ye separated from them, 2 Cor. 6:17) Make note here, I've seen many over the years that would make excuses and twist scriptures to ease their conscience, such as (Rom. 3:10, 23) All have sinned, and there's none righteous, these are both true, but that doesn't give anyone a permission slip from God to keep living in sin! (Romans 6:23) (For the wages of sin is death but the gift of God is eternal life through Jesus Christ our Lord.) (Rom. 6:1, verse 2, Heb. 12:1 and 2, Heb. 2:3, James 4:7 and 8 to 17, Rom. 6:12 to 17; Rom. 6:13; Eph. 4:27) you would be deliberately asking for God to turn you over to a reprobate mind (2 Tim. 3:8, Rom. 1:28, 2 Cor. 13:5). Again, there is no middle ground, you're either for God or against God, and the Bible says, you can't live a double life, or you'll become God's enemy. Google that word, enemies of God, (Psalms 139:20) say: God's enemies take God's name in vain, I know many who say the word dam after God's name…which is in vain, or what is enmity with God mean? In (James 4:4), it means and says if you are a friend of this world, you're an enemy of God. (Wow.) That's pretty plain and in (1 John 2:15, 16) also.

Life in this life is very short (James 4:14), compared to the next life that you go to after this one, it's heaven or hell and it is forever, and the Bible is plain, if you're a friend of this world, you're an enemy of God (God won't let his enemies in heaven). Hello, it's forever for

311

all eternity in hell or heaven, and you won't make heaven just because you want to go to heaven, you must be born again and live a separated life and follow the Bible. I know a lot of people that live like a devil and really want to go to heaven but they still follow the world's lifestyles, partying, sex out of marriage, etc.

There is no change in their life. And they are very quick to say, don't judge me…who are you to judge me…but on judgement day according to the bible they'll say, why didn't somebody warn us. Hell-o…ha. Just in case it didn't soak in yet, this book is a warning. (Rom. 8:6, 7, 8; 2 Cor. 5:17; Luke 6:46; Eph. 5:11, 12; 1 Cor. 9:27; 1 Cor. 10:21, 22; Gal. 5:15 to 22; 1 Cor. 6:9, 10; Matt. 24:37 to 51; and Matt. 25:1 to 13.) I could fill this page with many, many more scriptures and don't scoff or mock me please. People just don't realize because of movies, etc., and many companies and businesses have meetings with alcohol, this is also wrong. You must draw the line and be on God's side if you really plan on making heaven. It won't be because you want to go, it'll be by your choice to be willing to change and follow Jesus and his word, and live a godly lifestyle.

Again, going to church or putting on a big performance, and acting the part won't get you in heaven either (we must be true). Religions and churches won't save you either (John 3:3 to 5, Rom. 10:9, 10 and 13, Acts 2:38, 39) And you don't know when you'll die, one idiot told me, he'll call on God when he's old and gray, died in a car wreck, and another one said, well if I go to hell we'll have one big party…really? Wow…are people really that dumb? That's why (Rom. 12:1 and 2) explains to us, we have to discipline ourselves, and make ourselves, to many people are looking for an easy way. It all starts with a made up mind (Phil. 2:5) and then God will start helping you (Phil. 4:13 and 19, Phil. 1:6, Ps. 37:23 to 25).

But the Bible says be willing to even die for the cause of Christ (Mark 13:12, 13; John 16:2, 3; Matt. 10:21, 22; Rev. 12:11; Mark 16:15 to 18; John 12:24 to 27; Matt. 26:41; 2 Cor. 8–12; 1 Cor. 9:16, 17; 1 Cor. 15:19; Acts 20:24; Rom. 8:6). But you will have to stay Prayed up my friend to have this kind of courage, then how will you draw the line between "Life and Death."? (Phil. 1:21 to 23) 21. For me to live is Christ, and to die is gain. 23. For I am in a strait

Betwixt (between) two, having a desire to depart, and to be with Christ: which is far better… According to how I interpret scriptures, this (physical body life) is just a dressing room compared to eternal life in heaven, or Damned to hell for eternity, and if you take the chip (mark of the beast) you'll be going against God and become a counterfeit to him and he will send you to hell (Rev. 13:16, 17; Rev. 15:2; Rev. 14: 9 to 11; Rev. 16:2; Rev. 19:20; Rev. 20:4).

Yes, this is very scary…but it is finally here, and they are now giving out the microchip 666 mark of the Beast, I recorded it on the six o'clock news, wow, and people swept it under the rug in disbelief. It's all volunteer for now, just don't volunteer, but I say to you (Again) don't take it, this isn't a joke or game, you can't back out, once you've completed this process, you'll be damned forever. Unless you cut off the hand. But could you? They are about to distribute it. (Again…I repeat, do not take it.) Don't believe any lies, pray, pray, pray, God gives you courage, and strength to stand in, this evil day.

Even if they take your life (Don't take it.) You'll be Tagged as a terrorist or rebel going against the government monetary system, but this is taught to us, that the last Generation would go through. Why would the writer of James, in James 1:2 Say to the brothers, count it all joy, when you fall into diver's temptations. (Different types) because I personally get frustrated, and I don't think I've ever seen in my forty-two years of ministry, seeing anyone jump up and down, screaming yippee, hurray, hallelujah another trial, another test of my faith is come, even if (James 1:2, does say, count it all joy) when you enter into diver temptations, I know deep down, things happen for my good (Rom. 8:28) but I still don't get happy about it, nor do I celebrate. Ha. But seriously, when I get in deep thought, and knowing what the Bible says about the prophecies are unfolding and coming, knowing so many, that I am related to, and so many I've worked with, people I know, don't have a clue, and you try to warn or explain, they get mad or don't want to be around you, this breaks my heart.

Because I know the outcome Because God has already foretold how it all is gonna come out in the end. People need so desperately to Read the Bible especially The parts of Prophecies that are now unfolding in our day. Those Days when we had the little testing times of Anger or lack of patience, are a thing of the past, when God was trying to teach us how to Grow-up in God, are now behind us, and the things coming on the Earth are gonna be much more severe than a test of your Faith or a resistance of your flesh, compared to different ones Fighting for their very existence, but we have to remember other Bible Scriptures that will give us Hope in God like (Phil. 4:13 and 19, 1 Cor. 10:13, Ps. 107:8, 13, 15, 19, 21, 22, 28, 31, Acts 2:11, Isa. 46:9, Josh. 4:2 to 7, Ps. 105:5) Remembering is one of the reasons God told Joshua to have one man out of each of the twelve tribes of Israel to bring a stone and make a memorial monument out of twelve stones, was (Heb. 10:32) because, God has wanted mankind down through the ages *to remember* all the miracles and things God has done from the days of creation till now, things, and miracles in your life, and mine, I wrote them answered prayers in the blank white pages in the front of my Bible.

And on a yellow post note of some recent answered prayers on my bulletin board. To remind me to thank God, and to remind me that "God (Jesus) is the same yesterday today and FOREVER! (Heb. 13:8) Cause down through the years you can read place after place where man wavered in his faith, and forgot when God took them out of their troubles, from giants, and took out of fires and parting the ocean, to lion's dens, to three armies coming from all sides with no way out, and God delivered them with a song...A song? Yes, a song of praise to God (2 Chron. 20:15 to 25) plus three days of gathering treasures, because the people of God chose to obey and sing instead of fight (also Acts 16:16 to 25) But again God has gotten angry with people that forgot the miracle working power of God, even in Jesus's day (Matt. 16:8 to 10) so let's remember what God has done even if it is making a note, or a monument, so let's be like Joshua, make those piles of stones as a marker, or place of remembrance, when I get the extra money, I want to have a shiny stone bench made with some engravings of my miracles on it...on a landscape with boulders, etc., but for now it's post notes: and it does remind me to thank God for all my miracles. Amen. (Because we must remember!) but we are not to just remember...but to give Him thanks, praise, songs and

314

worship Him for your miracles. Amen (1 Cor. 10:13, Rom. 15:11, Laud him all you people) (Praise the Lord with a song of praise) But we must see and get it in our spirits that this last generation is now here and where do we draw the line to nightmare weather conditions that some are still coming that are called Plagues in the Bible... Again, don't forget God can still protect his people (Ps. 91:1 to 10) Key words here is those who *abide* or *dwell in the secret place* your prayer closet, to keep trusting God, keep believing, and read the whole chapter of (Heb. 11) Keep up your faith by quoting scriptures of faith and miracles, and praying in Jesus's name, and stay under (the blood of Jesus) and keep pleading the blood of Jesus over your situation, and you, and always keep a repented heart, keeping a clear pathway from you to God (Rev. 9:20, Heb. 11:5–6).

Now (Rev. 15:1 to 7, which are the seven last plagues) (Rev. 15:1 God's wrath) the seven last plagues (Hopefully the church will be gone), cause "God's not appointed us to wrath." (1 Thess. 5:9) But God's wrath will be bringing in weather formations like we've never seen before, life will start changing as we've never seen, and things are about to turn very nasty before people can say, "*Baruch haba beshem Adonai* [Hebrew]," which means "Blessed is he who comes in the name of the Lord," or say, "Come quickly, Lord Jesus." As of yet, people have not started crying out for the Lord to come quickly as in Revelation 22:22 and in Matthew 23:39, so it's gonna have to get really bad before most folks would get out of their comfort zone to pray a desperate prayer of this nature... And it's all wrapping up, according to prophecy scriptures, meteors or solar flares from the sun that even our own scientists have been predicting for awhile now, that (Rev. 16:8–9) will come into our Atmosphere hitting the Earth and sea (verse 8) men are scorched with fire from the sun (must be solar flares off the sun, verse 9) And people blasphemed God and still would not repent. Wow, and the Bible says, stars from heaven will Fall, which some scientist would classify them as asteroids or meteors (A great big meteor or star), at any case, the prophecy in (Rev. 8:10–11) calls one, worm-wood, that will mess up our water supply and rivers, and in (Rev. 8:10–11) it sounds like a great mountain burning with fire falling out of the sky into the sea (This, in my thoughts could cause a Tsunami) or tidal waves, Depending on the size, but to me, the word "great" is considered enormous especially a mountain is huge, and where or what coast line, how close to land, and how far out (Rev. 16:18, down to verse 21) we don't know, it's so huge of an earthquake it splits the earth apart dividing the great city into three parts (verse 19 of Rev. 16 says) and in (Luke 21:6) says, one stone will not be left upon another that will not be thrown down...wow... that's one big earthquake, but we are not to give into a spirit of fear, because God has not given us the spirit of fear, but of power, and love and of a sound mind (2 Tim. 1:7) and the only way to keep fear out of your heart in such a horrific event would be having a very close walk with God. Amen (Isa. 26:3).

Or as (Luke 21:26) says men's heart fail them for fear for looking after those things coming on the earth. Wow... But we are to channel that fear into faith, knowing if we are serving God, and our sins are forgiven, and if they aren't, stop sinning and repent... Get under the Blood of Jesus, but know Christian friend, no one knows just how much will happen before Jesus comes, but be ready and stay ready... Most of this is called the Wrath of God, that's coming on the sinners and rebellious disobedient anti-Christ followers, and this period of time is called Great Tribulation, in which Christians are not supposed to go through.

But come on, folks, is there anyone of you that really knows when all this is coming? No, no one does. And is anyone crying out for Jesus to come, no, but Jesus said as it was in Noah's Day...so shall it be in ours, in my words...we are there, Jesus went on to say it's even at the doors. (Notice D-O-O-R-S.) Plural, more than one (Matt. 24:33). Is anyone of you now crying out for Jesus to come and take us to heaven (Matt. 23:39) to come and take us out of here... No...everyone is to comfortable, so something has got to start making them call him, He said he'll return then. In (Rev. 8:7) speaks of some intense heat that burns up one-third of the trees and all the green grass was burnt up. (Wow.) But if you will notice at the beginning of some of these chapters in Revelation it'll say "The Wrath of God" (Like Rev. 15:1 or Rev. 16:1; Rev. 16:19; Rev. 19:15) in (verse 2 of Rev. 15) at the time of God's wrath the saints of God are in Heaven standing on the sea of Glass. And most of all of it would have all been prevented if man would have just repented, and turn his life over to God (Rev. 2:4 and 5, Rev. 3:2 to 5, Rev. 3:15 to 20, Rom. 10:13, Rev. 16:15) but (Rev. 15:1, Rev. 16:1, To me is Great Tribulation) as in (Rev. 15:1) or it'll say "Plague" or both.

Now (Rev. 16:1 and 2) It says the wrath of God is poured out on those who took the mark of the beast! (A Plague of sores), grevous sores (very severe, critical, dreadful, terrible, and awful, according to Google's dictionary): This plague of sores came upon all those who took the mark/666. God's wrath is because these people chose to follow a counterfeit devil dictator, over God's son that died on a cross for their sins…so rejecting God's salvation Plan is a slap in God's Face. Break man's law you go to jail, break God's laws and go to hell. Hey, it rhymes. No…it's no joking matter… No, it is rejecting God's plan…we've read about it for years and years…since we were kids. And now with man's own technology, man hangs his own self. Wow… We are seeing it unfold…yet people still don't get it. But personally, I'm in agreement with my old pastor that said… I don't believe God will let the righteous suffer with the unrighteous, no, when Abraham was interceding in prayer for his Nephew Lot, God told him he would take him out of the city.

Before he burned up Sodom and Gomorrah, and he did, and he delivered Noah, and he delivered Jonah, and Moses, and Daniel, so are we any different? No… Amen, He will deliver us out too, so pray. We need to pray for our loved ones to get saved, because folks, I'll be saying, and praying, "Come and get us, Lord Jesus…come quickly…" (Rev. 22:20) because this wicked ol-world is growing more wicked and more evil everyday, and people that are born again believers will not be waiting much longer on calling for the Lord to come and get us before all hell breaks loose on Earth (Rev. 3:11, Rev. 22:20, Matt. 23:39, Acts 1:11, Heb. 10:37, Rev. 22:7 and 12) say, I come quickly, but if you'll notice this has been written after every-thing else was written, no, that doesn't say or mean that everything has to take place before Jesus Christ returns for us Christians. Let's look at (Matthew 23:39): For I say unto you, you shall not see me henceforth, till you shall say, "Blessed is he that comes in the Name of the Lord"…most people are caught up in stuff, computer, TV, sports, games, phones, iPads, jobs, etc. (2 Tim. 3:1 to 4). The Lord told us The Signs of the Times in Matthew 24 to watch and pray… We have stepped into a new era, and in this preacher's opinion, we are Ripe for the Picking… And yes, no one knows the exact day or hour, but Jesus said You'll know we are close by the signs of the time, and we are close, again things are happening so bad in some places people indeed have said They felt like it was the End of the world… I agree, I believe it has started the cycle of the Tribulation Period.

And if we were to categorize every detail I'm afraid we'd fill up A whole Tablet. But you must realize as I mentioned a few pages back, many folks think these crazy Events of weird goings on are testing times of the Christians, not so, but we are entering into Tribulation or we've been in it already, at any case, No one Knows exactly, The Day or hour, This is true, but if you study Prophecy, you'll know when you see All of these things Hitting everywhere…come on, people, wish it was just getting us prepared for the next level…and is it the Rapture.? A few trials and tests of our Faith as (James 1:2) I'd be counting it all joy…or even three and four. The trying of my patience, and four goes on to say let Patience have her perfect work that you may be perfect. And entire wanting nothing…oh, that can't be talking to this generation, cause it's the give me, give me People. But we indeed are gonna Need something really Tuff down in our souls if the Lord tarries much longer. All these things should have been building up our Faith, that takes us into the next level, and the Bible says in (Heb. 10:36).

That ye have need of patience, that after ye have done the will of God ye might receive the promise. What promise? The comforter the Holy Ghost was a promise, Jesus gave us another promise he'd soon return to get all of us to take us all back to heaven with him, and in (John 14), he said he prepared a place for us, and it's taken two thousand years, so it's gonna be great. That's another promise, so I guess that's why we have need of patience (Heb. 10:36) says for ye have need of patience, that after ye have done the will of God ye might receive the promise. God wants us to allow him ample time to move in our situation, but this generation is spoilt rotten: when we've been raised on microwave ovens, fast food. Some people have heart attacks cause the traffic lights don't change fast enough or the drive-thru burger joint is taking to long, so yes a lack of patience this generation is definitely in need of patience.

Hup-om-o-e, a Greek word, meaning, endurance, or to wait patiently, as in (Luke 24:49 or Heb. 10:36 or James 1:4 or Luke 21:19), or even in the Old Testament (Isa. 40:31, Ps. 37:7) or a Hebrew word, QA-VAH (Ps. 40:1) to expect faith, or to wait patiently…believing…but not meaning to say to ever pray for patience, because patience brings tribulations, and life itself brings enough struggles without praying for patience. So once our life and faith has been tested and tried, as Job said, in the book of (Job 23:10) Job said when he (God) has tried me, I shall come forth as Gold (in my words); he was a real trooper for God (Ps. 37:37). Mark the perfect man and behold the upright for the end of that man is peace. So all of the rough necks, macho, trouble makers, are the opposite of a peace maker, amen. (A peacemaker means a person who makes peace) And this is a fruit of the spirit. Found in Galatians 5:22–23, but the opposite of worldly people, and the opposite of a brawler, or a partier, or people that stir up trouble (James 3:14–18, Rom. 8:6, Isa. 26:3, Titus 3:2, Heb. 12:14).

And this opposite attitude is called "works of the flesh," in the Bible. People that kill, take out revenge on others (Luke 21:22), murderers, drunks, adulterers, etc. These type people are not going to heaven unless they repent. These are found in (Galatians 5:15–22) works of the flesh, means what it says. Fruit of the spirit comes into people that repent and those who give their heart to Jesus Christ. (James 3:18) says, "The fruit of righteousness is sown in peace of them that make peace) wow, That was my symbol in the hippy days my cousin Jim and I would go around with the two fingers held up, yelling peace, with ol' Sam and Eugene, We were the opposite, before Christ came in our hearts trying to be cool.

I had luggage with it on it. But Jesus said the peace he gives us is not the same as the peace that the world gives (John 14:27) Because, like I said the world has a different view of peace than God's peace, God's peace is not a cool symbol, or settling down and quiet time from war not, a calmness after a storm, no, God's peace, Jesus was speaking about in (John 14:27) is not what the world understands as peace (John 16:33) God's peace is different from the world, cause in the world you'll have tribulation) but Jesus overcame the world cause, he is peace, love, and joy (Gal. 5:22, It's also a fruit of the spirit) And his peace passes all understanding (Phil. 4:7) but his peace is a spiritual peace, an inner peace that flowed from the blood on the cross (Col. 1:20, into our souls when we were born again and repented and confessed our sins to Jesus Christ and he keeps us in that peace supernaturally, when our minds is stayed (kept) on him (Isa. 26:3). When I was wheeled into the surgery room at the cancer center at UCLA, there was a spirit of peace that came over me, and my good friend, Sis. Lanet was there praying and driving us and comforting my wife.

And just knowing that I was in good hands with Dr. Berke, and God, and there was another set of hands that you couldn't see, that was calming my troubled heart, an assurance that God was guiding this throat cancer surgeon's hands, God was giving me a deep inner peace, somehow I knew, I was gonna be fine, it was three years ago the day before my birthday, and folks were sad for me but I was looking at it from a different point of view, thinking what a neat birthday present from God, taking away that throat cancer, so I thank my God and Dr. Berke and all his staff at UCLA and the sweet birthday song from a little sweet nurse that brought in the birthday cupcake. Wow, God bless 'em all.

And now three years later, I am still CANCER-FREE...Thank God! To God be the glory, thank you, Jesus, and praise the Lord.

To the Hippy in the '60s and '70s, Peace Was Just a Cool Symbol

Painted on the side of my suitcase, we had Christians tell us those are broken upside-down crosses. Well, it was peace to a bunch of partying hippies, but in all reality it wasn't. We didn't know peace till we found Jesus Christ, then we knew real peace. Anyway, this kinda "perfect peace" is what the rest of the whole world needs, and believe me, the worse the world gets in crime and the road rage, which is an evil spirit from hell, that gets a hold of people in a hurry. They need this inner peace that only comes from God.

And we all need it now more than ever before, but the scary part about it is, when they cry peace and safety? Then sudden destruction comes (1 Thess. 5:3, but if everyone turned to Jesus. There would be no need for sudden destruction, but God has to use whatever means he can to get people on board, because God's boat is about to sail, according to all the signs written in the Bible prophecies, even Christians that are true believers that are physically blind, can tell you from the brail Bible, they read, we are close to the coming of Jesus Christ's return, oh, no one knows the exact day or hour, but again, we know by the signs of the time. And believe me the worse the world gets. Is when now we need peace now more than ever before. Peace in our heart that passes all understanding because there are times in our Christian walk we have to tap into that spirit of peace, especially when times of aggravation or times of chaos.

When one thing after another is going on, when it's one of those kinda days that seems to come on you, especially when everything has gone wrong. That's when we need to tap into that spirit of peace, in our prayer (Matt. 6:6) closet, our quiet place, our secret place

(Ps. 91:1) and take a chill pill of his peace because when all hell has broken loose on top of you, you have got to yield yourself to God. Picture a bucking horse, and the cowboy trying to put a saddle on him. Now, I saw an Indian one time lead that bucking horse down to a pond, up to his waist, the horse calmed down, knowing he'd drink a lot of water, and he was able to subdue the will of the horse. Once we get that spiritual water from Jesus Christ (John 7:37–38, John 4:13–14) by our yielding our will to God then he satisfies the thirsting of our soul, with that sweet holy spirit that floods in us like a gushing geyser out of our belly from deep within, satisfying all longings, quenching that inner thirst. (Hallelujah.) And better felt than telt (told). Amen.

No booze, no dope, nothing can match or come close to that inner hosing out cleansing that the Holy Ghost gives you when he floods your soul. (What?) You've never experienced this? Hey, if you really believe in the Bible and in Jesus Christ, then all you have to do is start praying and asking in Jesus's name (Luke 11:13), by saying, Lord, if this is real then show me, and teach me, and Lord fill me with your Holy Spirit also as your word says, your no respect of persons, fill me Lord to over flow, give me that gusher, of the Holy Ghost water from out of my belly. (John 7:37–38) take away any unbelief in Jesus's name, fill me Lord, run my cup over, get ready. Keep asking, keep believing, you'll get it (Act. 2:38–39, it's for you.) I love it, when God hoses me out. Many, many times when thanking God, the Holy Ghost hit me, when I've been in prayer, and always thank God for hearing your prayer. (Like Jesus did in John 11:41, and I would thank God for a praying Mom and a praying grandma, that prayed many prayers for me, I would tap into the Holy Ghost out pouring of his spirit, by yielding my spirit to him, and by focusing on the things that really touches my heart and my soul and the things that I am most thankful for more than anything else in the world.

Which is my family, my wife, kids, grandkids, great grandkids, my mom, and my sisters, grandma's prayers, etc., but most of all my salvation and I would thank God for his mercy and grace that he had on me and thank you Jesus for paying the price on the cross (for my salvation) when he laid down his life and died, so I could live, and God sent us good Christian friends to pray for us and witness to us, to get us saved…Thank God for Denver and Bonnie, and Frank Williams, and many more. And Bam, the flood gates opened and the Holy Ghost hosed me out.

And you can't buy this hosed out feeling in a bottle of booze, or in drugs, or in a water pipe of pot, there is nothing on Earth that can compare to the in-filling of the Holy Ghost…and isn't it weird that God would take an ol-ex-hippy biker drug addict and save him and clean him up and fill him with his spirit, and have him explain to people the difference, cause this ol-ex-hippy biker has been on both sides of this fence, and there is *NO* comparison, none! When you have tasted that Holy Ghost wine, that is like gushing a gushing geyser well springing up in you, you'll never want the old physical wine, or dope, or booze, the old worldly life stops. When you've been filled with God's spirit, nothing on Earth can compare, amen! I'm living proof.

And when tragedy happens, I've got my Lord Jesus to turn to (and again a partier doesn't know how to pray). but in the Bible in Romans 8:26 says God's spirit will pray through us (in my words.) cause so many times in life things happen, and it's how we respond to these things that will show God how much more tests or trials we need to pass to move on to the next levels. I don't believe everything that happens in life is a test or trial because some things in life are unpreventable, but we must recognize when the devil is behind some, or God allows some at either case God's watching how we handle ourselves, if we quote and stand on his word, or throw a fit like a little child and lose our temper. We must remember God's eyes sees everything (Prov. 15:3, Ps. 33:18–19) And not just the evil things, but as the song goes, "His eye is on the sparrow, and I know he watches me" (hallelujah, Matt. 10:29–31) Though some things happen because of our misunderstandings, which brings in frustrations, anger, which makes the other person draw the wrong conclusion, cause The Bible says: God is not the author of confusion! (The devil is.) (1ˢᵗ Cor. 14:33) (Rev. 12:10 to 12) (2ⁿᵈ Cor. 2:11) (James 3:16) So if there is chaos and confusion, we know the devil is behind it because the Bible says in John 10:10 the thief (the devil) comes to steal, kill, and to destroy (but) I (Jesus) come that they might have life, and that they might have it more abundantly (in my words).

You see from the beginning of time, Jesus knew and said (John 6:64, Rev. 12:10). The devil has been known as the accuser of the brethren, and that he was a thief, and a liar, and a murderer (John 8:44, 1. Pet. 5:8–9; 2 Cor. 2:11, 2 Cor. 11:13–15) And so if there is chaos and confusion (James 3:15–16) and it brings every evil work and usually it's caused by the devil, but not always, such as, in the time of king Jehoshaphat, when he prayed to God for help, being surrounded by three different armies (that I already previously said earlier) that God had told this king to have his people to lay down their weapons, and sing songs of praise to God...which would take some huge faith and take some major trusting in God for deliverance, you see this is what I've been trying to drill into my readers, that you can't rely on what the natural mind thinks (1 Cor. 2:14, Prov. 3:5–6) We must walk in the spirit, and rely on God's ultimate divine direction, by *having the mind of Christ on* (Phil. 2:5).

Because friend, this ol' world's existence is just about over, and again, so many are so wrapped up in it they commit suicide when the stock market crashes or goes down, and I would challenge sports god worshippers, that eat, drink, and sleep sports, you need to read (John 15:1–19, John 18:36), No nothing's wrong with sports, if you're not consumed with it, but like anything else can become like a god, 1 John 2:15–17) I had to get out of learning kung fu, I got consumed with it eat, drink, and sleep it, and watched every Bruce Lee and Chuck Norris movie, and spent so much time at it, had three sets of nunchucks, a long pole, stacks of boards to break, kicking seven feet, four karate kicks, etc., it consumed me.

God called me to preached not fight (John 18:36) after saving my soul, it begin to bother me, cause in my soul I felt like I was another type of Noah, and that I needed and did preach the last days and end of the world to, prisoners for eighteen and a half years, then started pastoring, okay, already covered this, but you must search out your own heart and soul, you must pray and ask God is this (_____, okay, you fill in the blank.) Has this become a god to me, am I so involved, and consumed, and sucked into this

world's system that I make up excuses for it. Do I pray, like I do this
(_____)? (or spend as much time to read the Bible?) Am I
really living for God as much as this (_____? John 3:12).

Is this considered of the world? Worldly lifestyle, or is it really of
God. According to (2 Timothy 3:1–5 or 1 John 2:15–16, Phil. 2:12);
you see Moses could have excelled up the money ladder having the
treasures of Egypt, but he chose to be with the people of God, even if
it meant to suffer with them (Heb. 11:24–25) this is the opposite of
the lifestyles of the rich and worldly (Jn. 17:14, 15, 6) (Matt. 6:20–
21), yeah, everyone wants to become famous, but then Jesus always
said in Matthew 16:20, Luke 5:14, Phil. 2:5–10. Don't tell anyone
until his mission was completed, and he was always humble as a
lamb (1 Pet. 5:5–6) (2 Chron. 7:14) and he was even called the lamb
of God. Again, these are opposites of the way the people of this evil
world live today, and many (2 Cor. 6:14–17, Rom. 12:2, Col. 3:1–2)
of them will kill you for a dollar or, stab you in the back for your job,
or for a promotion, or party till the sun comes up…then beg God to
help them at the toilet, while puke-n their party up and saying…oh
help me Lord, never. Again Lord, baah…yet…the following week-
end here they go again, they forgot their last toilet experience, wow.

Or live like the devil, and have a tragic event happen, an then
think he's supposed to rescue them. Wow…but this is the way of
worldly want-a-be Christians…Try to live, with one foot in the
world, and one in the church (or on the fence, Rev. 3:15, 16).

I really wonder if all the ones I know that shack up in adultery
and talk Bible and church kinda talk, and are always thanking the
Lord, yet don't have a clue what (Gal. 5:15–22) says (Jun. 8:1–11)
or (Matt. 24:37–51) (1 Cor. 6:14–17) or (Matt. 25) or (Heb. 12:1)
or (Rom. 12:1 and 2) or those that go to church, and post all their
wild lifestyle sins on line. Not knowing they embarrassing everyong
who knows them (James 1:8) K.J.V. Bible calls this being double
minded, they can't really decide whose side their on God's or the
devils (1 Cor. 10:21–22) but if you read these scriptures they plainly
say, these types don't make Heaven. No…not judging…just saying
what's in the Bible…wow. This should not be (James 1:8) a worldly
Christian is those who still party, and go to bars, clubs, casinos, drink

booze, do drugs and live in adultery and fornication etc. (1 Cor. 5:11), and think it's okay, etc. With no change in the heart, as (2 Cor. 5:17) says. It's all in the Bible. I know (been there done that) but back to life's tests and trials of life. One of the best things of being a true born-again believer (is you know where you're going and) when something arises you can take it to God in prayer, and know without a doubt God hears your prayers (Ps. 34:15–19, Luke 18:1–8), but not the sinner (Psalm 66:18) (1 Cor. 5:9–11), but after we pass one of life's trials, we feel encouraged, so draw your line to Jesus (on being set free/or still living in bondage, 2 Tim. 3:5, John 3:19, Rom. 8:11 to 16, Gal. 5:1, John 8:32 and 36, John 14:6, Matt. 24:48–51, Matt. 24:37–39) and the old partier crowds don't make heaven (Luke 6:46).

As in (Luke 21:34–36; 1 Corinthians 6:9–10; Ephesians 5:18), again everyone has to repent of their sins, and ask forgiveness from Jesus Christ/God (John 14:6 John 10:1 and 9) in order to make heaven, everyone reaps, good and bad. So just plant good seeds and even plant extra good seeds and my dear brothers and sisters, then you get to reap good. It is so sad all those years of ministry. I have seen people especially inmates, get out and come back in again, get out again and come back, over and over. And I would preach the word along those lines.

Stay away from the old crowds, stay away from the old ways. (2 Cor. 5:17), we are become new. All things pass away, behold, all things are become new. We are a new creature in Jesus Christ (2 Cor. 5:17). Old things pass away, behold all things become new. (But People that want to hang around the old partying crowds, they will NOT spiritually survive. (Read these, 1 Cor. 5:9–11, Luke 6:46, 2 Thess. 3:14–15) And everyone will reap what they sow. People that want to hang around the old life stomping grounds, and the old partying crowds will not spiritually survive. Apostle Paul said, come out and be separated from them, (2 Cor. 6:17).

Pretty plain to me, I stopped associating with the old partiers, they were still coming to my house with Dope, I had to tell them I don't party anymore, one of my dealers said he was a Christian, and he said he went to church and still partied, Ha, I said you must be reading a different version Bible than I read, cause there will be a change in a person when they become born again, and repent of their sins, and God's not gonna put his spirit (his spiritual new (Mark 2:22, 2 Cor. 5:17) wine) inside you, and you are called an old wine bottle before your saved (spiritually speaking) but new wine is put into a new wine bottle, spiritually speaking: (Mark 2:22, 2 Cor. 5:17) but there must be a change take place, in our soul, a transition, or a transformation a Greek-word called a metamorphosis takes place in the soul, and heart of someone that repents before a spiritual—metamorphosis state or process begins in the spirit of someone who truly repents as the caterpillar worm transforms into a beautiful butterfly…And just like there is a process of time in the change-over from the old to the new, even so when someone truly repents, there is a *transformational change within the* heart and soul…oh you may look the same physically (outwardly) on the outside, but in the soul there is a change, this (2 Corinthians 5:17).

Moses spent so much time with God, it showed on the countenance of his face, in fact it was so lit up, that the people were convicted of their sins, from the glow on Moses face, and the people wanted to cover up Moses's face with a vail, instead of repenting (wow, 2 Cor. 3:13–16) You must see (verse 16) "the vail is taken away, it's done away with…in Christ" When we turn to live 100 percent for Jesus… there will be a change in your heart, soul and countenance (God makes the change in us) this is why (John 16:2) and unlike those opposite, none saved religious Pharisees that were always attacking Jesus, and always trying to trick him and set traps for him is because they weren't saved, but just religious, and that don't get anyone into heaven (and being around a real saint of God, bugs them bad, but) I must say, I am so amazed what so-called wannabe Christians say on Facebook (no, I'm not into all that) just see stuff pop up when using my wife's phone) and just commenting…but I am so amazed how people want to fuss and argue and give place to the devil, over demonstrations and protests and politics, wow, are they all gonna be shocked and surprised on judgment day, cause all that non-sense the Bible says is carnal and worldly and of the flesh, according to (Rom. 8 and Gal. 5:15–22) and will not, I said will not…enter into heaven, but you go ahead and get sucked into to all that crap of the devil, and of the world (1 John 2:15) you go ahead, it'll take you straight to hell—in a heartbeat, and the Bible says so, and Jesus said you'll know they are my disciples by the LOVE you have one toward another. (John 13:35) What I saw on the news, at those protests and demonstrations "wasn't the love of Jesus" No, no, no (and someone else said) the terrorists groups send in their trouble makers to bust the windows and burn police cars and loot stores, etc., destroy businesses, etc., this could be true, we'll find out on judgment day, but again, a true born-again Christian cannot behave this way, and make heaven! But again, this just tells me the more I hear it that we are for sure in the last days, but if you study prophecy and history, then you too will also know, "the Lord is about to come" amen.

It's getting close and things are wrapping up! (Exod. 34:33–35) you mean like in the days of Moses, when there's a place by God even when there are plagues everywhere, we can still be in our secret place by God. According to the Bible (Psalm 91:1) and (Exodus 33:20, 21) (Romans 10:17) (Psalms 46:1–11). So we to cover our face in time of plagues; but Moses covered his people didn't want to see God's residue of the presence of God still on Moses face, reminds me back when I was a welder, you'd lift your welding head gear, that protected your eyes and face, to check your welding bead and the heat from the hot metal and the flash to start, at the end of the day made you look sun burnt of a plague is preacher, giving your face a type of glow, but unlike Moses, a face being in front of the mighty fire—force of God, as in (Heb. 12:29) (Exodus 33:20–23) which also explains the glistering of Jesus countenance on the mount of Transfiguration in (Luke 9:29). I believe Moses was actually reflecting God's presence even as you face under the sun when laying unprotected out on the beach all day (setting sun burnt). So people still wanting to live in their sin, didn't want to see anything that looked-like or that reflected God, (John 8:9) (1 John 3:20). So when we leave our prayer room should we cover our face like they did Moses, no, his whole face they wanted all of it covered, because even in the end of the world (in Rev. 6:16) the Bible says, Man will cry out for the rocks and mountains to fall on them *and hide them from* God, people who want to party and commit adultery, etc., And deep down know to do right (James 4:17) don't want to see a real spirit-filled Christian (again) it bugs them.

Because a rebellious spirit is in these men, and they will feel such shame, that they would rather hide from, and ran from God, cause of guilt, gee, sounds like when Adam and Eve hid from God after they disobeyed God and sinned. (Gen. 3:8) And this is the ("**proud of my sin generation**,") the ("**no shame generation**,") I'm out of the closet with no fear generation, with a who cares generation, and a rebellious disobedient generation as never before that never accepted or believed when God destroyed the world in Noah's and Lot's generation (Matt. 24:37–39) And no matter if anyone believes it or not…"The cycle of the last days has begun." The King James version Bible says: Apostle Paul told us in (2 Corinthians 6:14–17), (1 Corinthians 6:9–10) to come out and be separated from them, so what does the word repent mean, *Webster's Dictionary*, says *repent* means…to feel sorry for one's sins, or feel remorse, or for wrong doings, or be contrite over one's errors, sins, etc. (See Penitent) Question: Is our soul worth losing it over anything or, getting our own way? Is anything worth losing our soul for? How valuable is it to you? (Matt. 16:22–26; Rom. 12:1–2; Heb. 12:1–2; Luke 21:34 to 36, as in Luke 13:3–5, 15:7–10, 10:13; 2 Pet. 3:9; Acts 2:38–39, 3:19; Rev. 2:5, 20:15).

And whosoever was not found written in the Book of Life was cast into the Lake of Fire. So when a person "Truly Repents" and ask Jesus to forgive them of all their sins, and asks him to come into their heart and save their soul, there'll be a change, then their name is written in the Book of Life, see (Rev. 3:5; Luke 10:19–21; John 3:3–5; Rom. 10:9, 10, 13, 17; 1 John 1:6–10; Ps. 51:10–13, 17) So why did Jesus die for our sins? God was tired of man going right back out into sin again, after the Priests offered a Lamb, and took his sins to God, as (2 Pet. 2:20–22) God refused to accept animal sacrifices anymore, so Jesus, became the ultimate sacrificed Lamb of God. (John 3:16–19, John 1:29) so why did Jesus die if he knew man was not gonna change and get saved?

Because He knew there would be a lot that would get saved, and God always has to have a leg to stand on, and that leg is called LOVE, and man will be un-excusable on Judgment Day (Heb. 10:26, Rom.

1:20, 1 Cor. 6:20, 1 Cor. 7:23) God paid the price for our sins, with his son Jesus, and gave us great examples, and parables, like the Prodigal son, in (Luke 15:11–32 and Luke 16:19 to 31) that tells of the rich man that went to hell because he loved hisself and his wealth more than God, and Luke gives and overall view of heaven and hell, to help man think, of (Matthew 6:24 or Luke 12:15, Luke 12:21, Matt. 16:26). And again there has to be a change in the heart, we must reflect Christ and our life must turn from sin or you will go to hell. (Gal. 5:19–22).

Man must make the decision and decide which one he will follow, God or the devil, or follow the way of this world, or the way of heaven, many, many, that I've known some over the years, that think they can do both, "Not so," according to (1 Cor. 10:21, John 15:19, John 17:14 to 16, 2 Cor. 6:14–18 see verse 17) And the first three chapters of Revelation is a very strong message to the church, that they too better line up their lives with God's Word, and John says we must not be lukewarm or on the fence or in the middle, in my words God wants us Hot or Cold for him. (Rev. 3:15 to 22, Rev. 2:4 and 5)

And between God's way and the devil's way. But I saw prisoner after prisoner like a yoyo back and forth, this went on for the whole eighteen years of my prison ministry, some changed and some got out and got in church and started over. Some, but so, so many would say, "Hey, preacher, remember me?" and like all those prisoners that would get out and get put right back in again, cause they couldn't lay down the old ways and the old lifestyle and follow Jesus 100 percent, and so here they come back to jail/prison again, you have to lay down the dope, parties, booze, etc.

If you keep hanging on to them, you'll end up in jail or hell. God don't mess with people that's not serious with him, God will let you do what you want to even if it costs you, your home, your marriage, your job, and your freedom, and even your soul, and I heard many say, hey, preacher remember me, from the jail or The Juvenile Hall, to the prison, yeah, hey…if you had listened then and stuck with Jesus you wouldn't be here today, many I knew, got out and came right back, very, very sad.

This went on for eighteen and a half years, so I then started pastoring. People just don't realize without God's protecting hand, you are open prey for the devil. Question?…So I ask you, what's in the middle of hot and cold mean? Warm-right, but John the Revelator said God wants us spiritually, Hot or Cold not lukewarm. (in Rev. 3:15–16) (God'll spit you out of his mouth, spiritually/metaphoricly speaking). Luke warm people=half hearted for God, will not make it to heaven!!! But thanks to Jesus I've seen many change and reform (self included) I've been clean since 1977, but it wasn't through some rehab clinic or some Therapy Ranch, no it was 100 percent Jesus (Phil. 4:13) I can do all things through Christ that strengthens me. He changed me and he can you too. You just gotta be willing. (Matt. 26:41, 2 Cor. 8:12, Phil. 2:5) With God's help someday you could be a pastor or a singer or a famous writer/author… There is a book on the market that will bless your socks off, entitled ("Life Without Limits" by Nick Vujicic, it sounds like voyages) He's from Australia, and a fantastic preacher, with a fantastic personality and sense of humor, you'll love his video, also on CD or Google it, or YouTube it.

I promise ya you'll love this guy. He is very, very inspiring. This guy is excelling in life, and you can see on his countenance he spends time with God. Look at Moses, he did not feel like he was qualified to be a speaker for God, because he stuttered (Isa. 28:1; Exodus 4:10 to 13; Rom. 8:30, 31) but as we all read, he became a great prophet of God, but the part that got me was (Heb. 11:24–25 and Luke 18:27). The part that says Moses chose afflictions with the people of God, than to enjoy the pleasures of sin for a season (life is short), so we must live for God and do what he says, Moses could have lived as a King, but chose to follow God and lead people of God, and in the process of it all, we read God always provided a way, and showed how God can use not only obedient people, but also things, such as a rod to perform miracles, thus leaving us monumental legends of great heroes of the faith, and Moses became one of the greatest leaders of all time.

We all mess up from time to time but we are quick to ask God to forgive us, With God's help I have done my best to be a living example, but again like many, I to many, many times have fell short over the years, we must get up, pray, and ask for forgiveness and go on living for God again, and always be quick to repent, keep our faults, mistakes, and sins under the blood of Jesus (1 John 1:6–10). If we are quick to repent God will forgive our sins. But the real secret is to keep living right or start living right, just don't stay down when you do fall short and ignore the holier than thou folks that that act like they've never messed up (Rom. 3:23, 1 Cor. 10:12–13). And don't forget to forgive others and forgive yourself also. (Just do it.) Walk in love and forgiveness (John 13:35). (Mark 11:25–26) We can all change and do right and do better, we all can change for the better. (Phil. 4:13) I did in 1977 and it's been a daily walk, till now, till Jesus comes, I'll be quick to repent when I fall short, but the main secret is, to stay away from the temptation, if you're living right, and going to church, and following the Bible, God's gonna bless you and protect you and give you new friends (that are also Christians) and a new life, behold all things become (New) (2 Cor. 5:17 and 2 Chron. 7:14) Just ask Fred or my wife Brenda, if God didn't change me, and heal her broken heart (1 Cor. 10:13, Luke 4:18). And even when pastoring those that wouldn't leave the old crowds alone, and leave their old ways alone, it wasn't long, and those that couldn't leave those old crowds alone were right back out there party-ing again, and back in jail they go...Another DUI.

Wow, it's sad to say but sometimes we have to learn things in life the hard way, which helps us to grow up and learn...but most convicts miss watching their kids growing up...miss their kids baseball games, and teaching them how to drive, etc., and all life's memories...No mom, no Dad, how sad. All because they weren't willing to turn to God and live right. And sad to say that the majority of convicts kids end up in prison as well, even sadder. 2.7 million kids have a parent in jail or prison. One in twenty-eight children have a parent in prison. (In 1991 mothers-in prison-with children, has increased 131 percent since 1991 to 2007) Wow, and crime is still rising so I Googled an update, since I started this book in 2015. This bad cycle has to stop and in my opinion, a law needs to be passed, for all inmates to be rehabilitated.

I made up my mind, die, sink or swim, I was gonna change with God's help. (2 Cor. 8:12, Phil. 2:5, Rom. 14:5, Matt. 26:41) but people that's not willing to turn to God and they're not willing to let God change them, end up, right back to living in that same old manure lifestyle again, Yes, I do plead and warn them, but they went right back out there doing the same old manure lifestyle again. (2 Pet. 2:21–22), Isn't it peculiar that God chose a dog vomiting, and turning back and eating it, to show us how sick God thinks of us going back to our old lifestyle is. Wow! But remember (Luke 15:20–24) God'll always welcome you back with hugs and kisses as I would to mine "But too many make bad choices." (Bad choices.) Which reaps you a bad life and usually an early grave when man turns away from God, and refuses to let God change him as the Prophet Jeremiah said about the clay on the potter's wheel (Jer. 18:1–6, Rom. 9:20–24), and goes back to his old lifestyle of living.

The Bible says you become seven times worse than the first (Matt. 12:43–45) HELL-O people, most folks don't realize that there are false doctrines out there that teach lies, false religions, as in (Matthew 24:11, 1 Tim. 4:1 and 2, 2 Tim. 3:13 to 15, 2 Pet. 2:13) and yes the Jim Jones type pastors spreading their lies and writing false Bibles, that have removed the major important stuff that'll help arm the new Christians with spiritual ammo, to fight off devils, that like the real Jim Jones deceived almost a thousand followers, with his phony, false doctrine, but none of them would listen to the original Bible truths, they didn't believe you could backslide, now they are dead, and only God knows if they made it to heaven or not. (Matt. 15:14) Again (2 Thess. 2:9–12) warns about those that follow false doctrines, and Jesus and the apostles warned of false doctrines (1 Tim. 4:1) and of backsliders and those departing from the faith (Matt. 15:9; Mark 7:7–8; Heb. 13:9; Mark 13:22–23) means, us Christians are the elect, which are the repented saints of God who have ask Jesus to forgive us of all our sins…also see (Matt. 24:22, Matt. 24:12) someone please Explain (Matthew 25:1–4; Revelations 3:5, Revelations 2:4–5; John 6:66; 2 Peter 2:20 to 22; Hosea 11:7, Proverbs 14:14; Luke 9:62; 1 Timothy 5:12–15).

Please note here, gossipers tattlers tattletale busy bodies tale bearers; which are all gossipers which are all backsliders…according to (verse 12 and 13) of 1 Timothy 5; 1 Timothy 6:20–21; Hebrews 3:12. You just Google how many times the Bible says to repent (Question? Why does the Bible say in all those many, many scriptures for us…all to repent) if we are all okay, then why does the Bible say repent and say it so many times?? Hello! And for someone to contradict Jesus and the Bible or say God's Word doesn't say it and it does, then they make the Word of God of non-effect or a lie (Isa. 55:11, Mark 7:13, 1ˢᵗ Cor. 1:17,18, Rom. 3:3, Gal. 5:4, Again, altering and changing what God said (Rom. 1:25, Mark 7:13, Luke 14:24) ouch or (Luke 18:34), and look up the word backslider and repent (or Google it); I said to the churches…God is warning and pleading for who? Yes, cranky ol-self-righteous, stiff necked can't tell me to repent backslidden church members to get revived, and it's talking to all of us…yes, me included, we've gotta be pure before Jesus takes us to heaven folks.

Again repent is not a bad word, but a good word, All through the first three chapters of Revelation chapter 2 and 3 the Lord speaks to the backsliders, and the lukewarm churches pleading with them to come back, and repent, and do their first works over again, and to get back to spending ample time with God. He warns and he pleads, so only a devil would say the opposite, that would keep people feeling that they are okay, staying in a backslidden condition, and that would cause them to miss the rapture of the church (Matt. 25:1 to 14) explains it, perfect, so the false religions and false doctrines that teach you can't backslide are liars and are (Matt. 15:14) blind leading the blind and both will fall in the ditch. (Read it.) And it is false doctrine, to teach you can't backslide cause I personally have known many in the prison ministry that became devil possessed, cause they turned back from God, and become seven times worse, as in (Matthew 12:45) because God ain't playing games here, this isn't no social country club or some group of fraternity-acting students learning how to worship frogs, no, God HAS gave warnings, and explained throughout scripture of these things and again, because man wants his own way religion and his own doctrine his own way, he changes the real true doctrine of God into a lie. (Rom. 1:25, Rev. 22:18–19) So where do we draw the line on false doctrines? Man will believe and follow what he wants to but a man of God that's wanting to please God (Heb. 11:6) and is after God's own heart, he will allow the Holy Spirit to fill him with his spirit and the Holy Ghost will teach you all those things and reveal the truth to you. (John 14:26, in my words). Again: just be sincere in your heart and ask him to teach you, pray in Jesus's name, and ask God am I telling you the truth, he'll show you. Look up these scriptures and see.

Then you will know why there are so many prisons and they are full and running over, and our stupid idiot leaders that run our country, are letting them out of prison, instead of making a huge facility and start rehabilitating them, and train them, and make it a law that they have to pass the rehabilitating classes before they are released back into society, wow, but no, we have criminals in our government that get wealthy off crime, and nobody sees it (I know a few things) did I say I was a prison minister for eighteen years and a criminal counselor for one year…yes, I did…I sure did, I saw a lot, and learned a lot in the classes I had to take. I had to study the same book that the prison gards studied, which is called "The games criminals play".

Are you getting any of this? Our world is gotten so wicked, because of false doctrines, false teachers, and false religions and false hypocrite leaders in our government, so it's true they are releasing un-rehabilitated convicts back out into society, but the answer is to change a very wicked world back to a peaceful one, that believes in God, and get our nation back to the standards and godly morals that our forefathers had when this great country was founded on (in God we trust), but they don't want to for two reasons (history has come full circle) no. 1, because man loves darkness and a evil life more than a righteous one (Rom. 1:16 to 32), because their heart is not right with God. (John 3:19) So because man chose to follow evil, God will send more plagues and more earthquakes as man has never seen (Matt. 24:7, Luke 21:6, Rev. 6:12 to 14) notice in (verse 17 of Rev. 6). "The day of his (God's) wrath is come." This is speaking of the time of great tribulation (see Matt. 24:21) (God's wrath, 1

Thess. 5:9) but this is not for the true Christian, this is the time of God's wrath to be poured out on all those who have rejected Jesus Christ. F.Y.I. scripture places that say "and they repented not"... means, they reject Jesus and God's plan of salvation (Heb. 2:3) such as (Rev. 16:9) or (Rev. 2:21–22) (Rev. 11:18, Rev. 14:10, verse 9 and 19, Rev. 15:1 to 7, Rev. 16:1 and 19, Rev. 19:15, Please, look these up and read them all, And stay and keep prayed up) don't listen to anyone saying anything different. (Gal. 1:6 to 12) (Rev. 16:18–21) and God'll destroy this earth again as God told the disciples and Noah (Matt. 24:37–39, see verse 34) Now don't tell me you've not seen people price g-o-u-g-e seen (price gouging), on the News, and all the hording of toilet paper, etc., and items people have needed, so this is just the beginning of Tribulation according to the Bible, just wait seven more years (three and a half + three and half = seven years total, 3 and half Tribulation and 3 and half Great Tribulation) = (7 years, Matt. 24:21 to 29, Rev. 11:2–7) notice the prophecy scriptures before (verse 21 of Matthew 24, it's bad then, but when it says great tribulation, it escalates) and compare it with what (Luke 21:22–28) when you see all these things...in (Matt. 24:33) but in Luke 21:28 says, "When these things come to pass, then look up," and (Luke 21:22), "These be the days of vengeance" as we can see "but notice the last part of that verse, that all things which are written maybe fulfilled" and see (Luke 21:23) glad to say we are there, but thank God, he said to lift up your head your redemption draws near (in my words, Jesus is about to come) and again when you read about God's wrath, which is great tribulation, we the church folks according to scripture are gonna be out of here in the rapture, amen (1 Thess. 5:9). God has not appointed us to wrath but we had best to be ready and right with God and be rapture ready cause it's gonna happen any time now, are you watchin? Are you staying prayed up? And ready to go? Don't get caught up in whose side are you on debates about protests, everyone's fussin and fighting over race, religion, politics, etc., the devil is tricking a lot of people.

Sure, we have to take a stand, in a godly manner. In (John 18:36), remember Jesus said if my kingdom was of this world, then, then, then my servants would fight. (Hello!) Also remember, Jesus told James and John when they wanted to call fire down on a city cause they didn't agree or accept them, and in (Luke 9:54, 55), Jesus questioned what manner of spirit they are of, in vs. 55, because Jesus came to die and to save man from his sins. (vs. 56) and again Jesus came as a Lamb, not a pack of raving maniac mob protestors busting and destroying people's property, killing and looting, again, that's works of the flesh and is carnal and will make you miss heaven (a devil's trap, 2 Cor. 2:11; 2 Cor. 11:14–15; Gal. 5:15–22) again, do you know what manner of spirit you are of? So many blind so-called Christians don't even have a clue on the flesh and carnal thinking verses being spiritually minded (Phil. 2:5) and fruit of the spirit (Gal. 5:22 to 26), etc., a lot worse than this, it's all in the Bible (just read it).

If Tribulation has indeed started, then friend if so, you all need to do some serious soul searching, and (2 Cor. 13:5) we should all pray for God to revel his word of the prophecies of the Bible to our heart, cause all hell is about to break loose on this earth! Yes, it has started, according to Bible prophesy. You have never in your life saw people beginning to take ID chips in their hand, yes or no? (Come on, let's be real) Can you think of the worse time in the history of this earth, that compares to now, from Noah's day till now, Moses day is the closest only time that may have been worse, or Noah's day…but his day was a swifter destruction, but for years in the Bible, God has warned mankind, yes, he has! Now, if man continues to sweep all this pandemic covid/monkey pox—stuff under the rug, and say it's just a disease like the measles, or the mumps, not realizing it's a plague, (so what's next?) prophecy time has come as in those ten plagues in Moses day, and the world is now way worse today than back then. Makes you wonder if people have even read (Matt. 24:7), and (Matt. 24:21–22) and (Luke 21:11) or as (Rev. 16:20–21) (Rev. 9:3–6) and it's not just a bad case, they are saying…Oh really, there were the same type (2 Pet. 3:3–5) of blind idiots in Noah's day in (Gen. 6, Matt. 24:37–39, 2 Pet. 2:4–6), until the water was up to their chin, then they quit laughing and (2 Pet. 3:3–5) mocking that old preacher Noah (2 Pet. 2:5) but it was too late, God shut the door (Gen. 7:16) compared to (Rev. 3:8) Now, you can turn a deaf ear like they did, and go through all the hell, of the great tribulation that's coming, that the Bible says will be worse than any other time, a time when the great grievous sores that's put on man (Rev. 16:2) and man cries out for pain and wants to die and can't, and a time when man's thirsty and wants to drink water, but it's all plagued, with wormwood (Rev. 8:11, Rev. 16:4) and it became blood, and all the way to the very END of the world. (Rev. 16:9–11) The Bible teaches man will still not believe (Rev. 9:20; 21, Rev. 2:21, 22) or repent of his sins. (And they call me dumb, 2 Pet. 3:3–5, Feel free to Google any of this.)

In KJV Bible (2 Pet. 3:9, Matt. 11:20–24, Matt. 10:33), you see there are all walks of life, and all types of people, smart, dumb, ex-cons, ex-drunks, ex-drugees, people of all kinds turning their lives over to Jesus Christ, God has turned the light on, The Bible says people that were taught as a child about God, and when they are older they can't get away from that teaching they got. (in my words, Prov. 22:6, 1 Cor. 2:14, Ps. 27:4 to 11, Prov. 12:15, Prov. 14:12, Ps. 51:10–13, 17) but many are waking up spiritually speaking, and coming back to God. Okay, I've gotta get back to the point of the backslider and that is anyone, I said anyone, can call on the Lord Jesus Christ for salvations and repent and ask for forgiveness of their sins.

And the verse in (Matthew 12:43–45), he said it'll be even to this wicked generation, people backsliding and becoming seven times worse, but he didn't say that it would be impossible to be saved, just seven times worse, but when you're dealing with spirits/devils, of this sort, a person needs it cast out, I've seen people come up to my pastor wanting to be saved, but they needed the devils cast out, I've seen it many times, but the INDIVIDUAL must have the inner hunger to be saved, and really want to be delivered, and many have been, and I've seen some, as I said earlier, go right back out to the pig pen (partier friends or shack up lovers), etc., and here came back the seven more devils (Matt. 12:45) and many say that they don't believe that stuff, that's their prerogative, but the Bible says it, so I believe it.

Plus, I've seen it! Because that verse says when you backslide seven more devils come in you. But some people have to learn the hard way. Though I've wondered why some keep going after the same kind of characters, or same people, and I hate to use this term.

But some, you'd think they had the word "losers wanted" tattooed on their foreheads, Wow, yes, I was one also, but I've been saved and delivered, again, just ask I've been with my sweet wife, Brenda, since 1971, and forty-two years clean and sober, and still cancer free, oh, I didn't tell you that all those years smokin Dope and smokin cigarettes and partying gave me cancer of the throat, and it took a change of life, for God to get it all out of me, but it's all gone, thank you, Jesus, and Dr. Berke at UCLA. Thank you for everyone that prayed for me.

Especially Pastor Green, and Living Christ church, my family, friends, and neighbors. But that was reaping on my part, from my old lifestyle, it took a while, but I reaped it, but the good news is, God gave me mercy and grace when I totally surrendered my life to my Lord Jesus (hallelujah, to God be the Glory.) Anyway, I knew of people attracted to this type, I counted about twenty total from one lady. She just kept going after one loser type, after another loser, they had no job, no car, no home, no life, nothing, just a body and a partier, lifestyle, twenty different ones, what in this world was she looking for, then I heard it. She wanted one just like her daddy, wow, she thought in some twisted way that her dad was a cool dude? No, the loser, got saved and became a preacher, she was looking for the before guy, the cool loser type, the sinner, the BC guy, the dad-like boyfriend before Christ. She wanted the old guy that wasn't saved... but after she saw her dad become a preacher...sometime down the road, God turn her light on, and she saw a spirit-filled changed man and saw that a winner is way better than a loser.

I know many and some not just two or three or four but twenty and still continuing after that type. Once you become saved you are entitled to God's best. We have to pray and ask for direction and try the spirit of God, wait upon God, I've seen lonely people, desperate people make the same choice over and over. If you added up the mistakes of times of jumping the gun, then, it blowing up in your face, that time and all the other times, and added those up, the time you spent getting and leaving those losers, it would be less time if she would have just prayed and waited on God to send the right one. But people are too impatient and don't want to wait on God. (Isa. 40:31). But we have to pray and ask in Jesus's name for the right direction, and try the spirits, the Bible says, to see if they are of God (1 John 4:1). Don't believe them, but try them (Pray, ask God) line them up with the Bible, if they don't line up with God's Word then you don't want them. (2 Cor. 6:14) cause the Bible says, for us not to be yoked together with unbelievers, or don't be unequally yoked together (means joined together or connected in marriage) The Bible and Jesus said, you'll know them by their fruit, sooner or later if you wait long enough good fruit will produce, or evil bad, fruit, or even no fruit, Jesus said corrupt fruit can't grow on a good tree. (Matt. 7:17–23, Luke 6:43–44) nor a bad tree will not produce good fruit, so the tree is known by its fruit (Matt. 12:33) This is where some preachers call themselves fruit inspectors, watching, and waiting to see how some act under pressure or when rough times come, or if they throw in the towel over minute (my-noot) situations, etc., some people crumble under pressure, and others may be a little spoilt rotten in always having it their way.

Hey, it's God's way or no way, so many think they're going to heaven and they can't even keep the Ten Commandments, I thought I was in the twilight zone, when I got saved, it was like I was having to learn all over again. And there was a lot that I did learn and one was controlling my temper, I needed more teachings on waiting on God, so yes, being born again is what it says, your relearning how to live for God, and learning how to make heaven, and learning things that *are* sin, and you learn that the Bible is your weapon against temptation, as in Matthew 4, and it'll become your best friend and your comfort in hard times, as well as encouragement in low times that Book of Psalms blessed me in many low times in my life.

I think I mentioned, I also have noted in the back of my Bible the times in those low times that a particular scripture I WAS directed to by the Holy Ghost, flooded my eyes with tears, so God knows what you need that will pick you up. You just gotta wait on him and trust him to do it. Just tell him, like you would your DAD (ABBA FATHER) Lord, I feel down today, I could sure use a word from you Lord. Boom. Once, I'm driving down the freeway and someone put it on a billboard just what I needed. Once I saw a cow standing on the back of another cow with a paint brush writing eat more chicken (from chic filet) I laughed for an hour. And that was just what I needed (Prov. 17:22) but back to my point on waiting on God, sometimes it's nerve racking, but if we learn to channel that in our prayers, and look up scriptures on it, or anything you go through, there are many helpful scriptures to get you through it.

My cousin Jim was having a real battle giving up smokes and he didn't want to appear or live a hypocrite life, so he's really praying about it, and he was in a battle, God told this ol' preacher to give him the scripture (1 Cor. 10:13) that says: "There hath (has) no temptation taken you but such as is common to man: but God is faithful, who will not suffer you to be tempted above that ye are able; but will with the temptation also make a way of escape, that ye may be able to bear it." And it did, he quit with God's help, and he quoted that scripture dozens of times, and I think it's been around forty years now and no booze no smoking now for forty years, wow, and he had it bad. So the scripture in (Philippians 4:13) is true.

We can do all things through Christ which strengthen s us. God gives us that promise that he'll never leave us nor forsake us, he'll go with us to the end of the world. And so we know from God's Word in any situation, God's got our back, and no one wants or even likes to wait, at a long traffic light or being the last one at the doctor's office waiting room, when you were first, etc. but then that's why it's called a waiting room, right ha.

But on some major important matters such as marriage, or a house, etc. Pray, pray, wait, wait, wait on God's divine direction. Marriage for example, this is for the rest of your life, you need to know that you know (you know.) I've seen so many, rush in, and in a few weeks or few months…single again, and it's sad but, sometimes with a child on the way, cause many times that you tell them no, or let's wait a little longer because your waiting and trying the Spirit, as those scriptures I quoted, say, about the trees (in time), especially fruit trees, they'll bloom and bear fruit and (some don't), The Bible says, they'll be used for fire wood (John 15:6) (Matt. 3:10) cause those that don't bear fruit'll be fire wood…wow…isn't that referring to us, His followers?, and I know, I've had some fruitless trees, yes, cause we should have taken care of it before I moved there, cause it didn't even make very good fire wood. But humans are a little different, but Jesus compared life to many examples, such as the trees, spiritually speaking.

God wants our soul to be prosperous as a flourishing fruit tree. Other times the Bible compares us as if we are old dry hard clay in (Jeremiah 18:1–6) and (Romans 9:20–23), saying we need to go down to the Potter's house and hear the word of the Lord, in my words) but think of ourselves unlike the *fruitless* tree that *wasn't* fertilized (Luke 13:6–9), cultivated, and water, never bared fruit (is fire wood) But the clay, that's represents you also, on the Potter's wheel, and (ol Potter God) takes out the bad lumps that might cause a leak, so the clay (you) allows God ample time to mold and shape your life, so down the road when your being rubbed the wrong way, you won't spring a leak, cause God the Potter already put in you his word, and took out that bad lump, when he had you on his wheel (read Isaiah 40:31). Give God the time to mold you and shape you, so stay on God's potter's wheel, then you have to keep praying and looking unto Jesus the author and finisher of our faith and he will provide, cause wouldn't you rather have what God has for you, rather that you searching and picking the wrong one again? Amen (Heb. 12:2). God will honor your perseverance, and your patience, and Faith… but don't settle for losers, God's got so much better for ya, especially if you're feeling desperate or lonely (don't be in weariness to settle for just anyone, Gal. 6:9, Rom. 8:31, Matt. 19:26, Matt. 6:33). Stand on God's Word (Rev. 3:8). God can open doors no man can close (1 Pet. 5:8–9). It's all sad to see, and your heart goes out to them.

But I guess some have to learn the hard way. Yes, some will always have to learn the hard way, then you see people blame God (Ps. 78:8; Ps. 74:18, Ps. 139:20; Heb. 12:15; Eph. 4:26, 27; Isa. 40:31) waiting on and giving God our time, and doing our devotions which is our duty…And giving extra praise and thanksgiving to God for his dessert. (Rom. 12:1 and 2, Gen. 8:20, 21, Please note here on this text about Noah) And see (verse 21), notice, even in such a horrific time, Noah still offered thanks up to God (Phil. 4:18). Come on, people, it's no time to crumble, we can't fold under it's die, sink, or swim, we've come to far, we've got hell to shun, and heaven to gain (Phil. 1:21) to live is Christ, and to die is gain... Jesus is about to come according to what I see in the prophesies, it's no time to lose hope. (Romans 15:4, Romans 5:1 to 9 see verses 2, 3, 4, 5, 1st Cor. 15:9, 1st Peter 1:12, 13, 2 Cor. 2:14 and 15, Heb. 13:15–16) I love sweets, after I eat a meal, and so does God, thanking Him, and praising him out of your heart is, worshipping the Lord in spirit and truth is a sweet dessert to him. (Ps. 22:3, Luke 17:10). (Phil. 4:6, 7) But they that wait on the Lord, shall renew their strength. They shall mount up with wings as eagles, they shall run and not be weary and they shall walk and not faint (Isa. 40:31).

So we all need that peace of God and we all need to wait on God for a wife or husband or to buy something. Pray and ask the Lord to direct your path each day (Prov. 3:4–6) even in small matters, that later may turn into a nightmare type situation, this is why it is very important to read the Bible and pray each day. This is called your devotion time, when you take your needs to God, and pray for others also. And give God thanks, praise, and worship, and be thankful even for small things. God wants more thankfulness than just your little quickie prayer of thanks over your food. Give him proper time, because you sure want him to take time out for you when something arises. Then (Rom. 8:1) we will not feel condemned or feel guilty and then you can stand knowing we have given God our quality time in prayer and Bible reading, then you can go to God in faith, and confidence knowing we have done our duty in what God commanded us to do, and that's also putting bullets in our spiritual gun and gas in our tank, now we can come to the throne of God boldly with our needs on our list. (Heb. 4:16, Phil. 4:19, Matt. 6:33) and being strong in the Lord and in the power of his might (Eph. 6:10) being strong, in knowing His word, that says, he'll never leave you or he'll never forsake you.

When you know that you know, God's got you in his big hands... You can't help but to give him thanks and praise, when you see people that's not as blessed as you are, give God thanks for your legs, eyes, ears, roof over your head..., etc. And for your freedom, many I've known over the years God kept them from going to prison... Thank him for it... There are things I thank him for all the time, and one is, for all the prayers my mom and Grandma prayed for me, etc. (God loves a thankful people), and when you give God quality time in prayer and reading your Bible which is putting spiritual bullets in your spiritual gun, being ready for anything the devil may throw at you. (Rom. 12:1–2, 2 Cor. 10:4–5, Phil. 4:19, Eph. 6:10–18) because we all need to be ready for anything the devil throws at us. And we've heard it preached that we need to put on the whole armor of God, but the point I wanted to make was in (Eph. 6:10) that verse 10 says to be strong in the Lord, and in the power of his might, you see we are no match for the devil in our own strength, but if you are starting your day with prayer and reading the Bible each day, that's putting on the whole armor of God, and always keeping your hearts clean washing your spiritual garment by asking forgiveness of any sin, keep a clear communication line open between you and God, and his blood'll cleanse you from all your sins (1 John 1:5 to 10). Be a servant to him and he'll be a God to you, just do it.

And when you read the Bible, believe his words that you read, the passages, stories, prophecies…all of it is for us. Don't be like Eve and Sarai, for when God says something, he may take a while; it's on his time clock, not ours, and we get it when he gives it. Sometimes he's slow answering for a reason, but stay faithful and believe that he will, come through, he will. Sarai had some doubt and thought she'd help God, I've seen it in church folks today, he's not fast enough to suit us. Well, you know the story (Gen. 16) she gave Abraham her hand maid and said, here, give me children through her cause Sarai was not being patient enough to wait on God. Yes, it was a long time, but the whole point of that particular Bible story was God wanted to show them and us, and all God's people down through the ages of time, that God's still a miracle working God, and the God of impossible situations, and even though your old, and past the age of fertility, God proves to all generations, that He's a God of miracles, as we also saw with Moses, and Daniel, Samson, Gideon, David and so many more, And me, and you. (God has always stuck to his word.) He is Jehovah Jireh (My Provider) (Gen. 22:13–14) yes, God took his time on this and he had his purpose and reason for it, to show and teach others, valuable lessons in believing God will move.

Because God can even do the impossible, like parting the oceans or keeping a lion's mouth shut, and using this kind of Bible information to increase our faith and then, we'll know God'll help us also, out of our own lion's dens, and through impossible situations, but that knowledge has to be put in us by our own self-discipline, and devotional time. Some of you don't even have a devotional time to get the word in your soul, cause to many folks depend totally on their pastor to give them spiritual food for their souls…And yes, we do need that spiritual food from our Pastor, but that's good for Sunday and mid-week night service but we must also feed our own souls daily ourselves. The rest of the week. This is when you mature in God. I was witnessing to a man of a different religion at work, sharing a particular scripture, and he said his priest told him to let him worry about what the Bible says: If that's true both will fall in the ditch, because the Bible says we all must work our own salvation with fear and trembling: (Phil. 2:12, Phil. 1:6, Matt. 24:4, 2 Thess. 2:3, Matt. 15:14, 1 Tim. 2:5) And the Bible says let no man deceive you by any means, so where do you (we) draw the line for a dependency on a man, priest, pastors, chaplains, etc., people by the millions will stand on Judgment Day, and give an account for their sins, to God for confessing their sins to a man, cause they depend on a man to take their sins to God, this is very wrong. (This is religion), we have one mediator between God and man, that's Jesus Christ (1 Tim. 2:5) but preacher, this has been going on for years, so has idol worship, but God gave Moses the Ten Commandments and the first one says, Thou shalt not have *no* other gods before me, (Exod. 20:3 and 4 and 5) and the second one says, Thou shalt not make any graven images, and the third one) says Thou shalt not take the name of the Lord thy God in vain.

Now this guy not only prays to some priest, but Mary, and a soldier that died, and a statue, and you discuss it, he gets mad. And it's all in the Bible, and it's in the Ten Commandments so why did God take five scriptures (in Exodus 20:1 to 5) He took (five verses) to explain, that you can't make them, or pray to them, or bow down to them. Yet they do, wow, and he calls me dumb, and he breaks the third one using God's name in vain. (Exodus 20:7) says not to take

God's name in vain, and this is the third commandment of the Ten Commandments of God. Similarly, Psalm 139:20 and 9:17 say that God's enemies takes God's name in vain. You can read them—two different scriptures, one commandment, and the other stating that only God's enemies take his name in vain. Wow... (using the word *damn* or *dammit*) after his Holy name. Another time, this one lady asked me to pray her aunt out of hell (this, too, is religion), cause the Bible says if you didn't get saved by confessing your sins to Jesus Christ you go to hell.

I didn't write the Bible! I'm just a preacher bringing the message! Yes, it is people's right to choose and follow their own religion: But I dare them to say that to God on Judgment Day...wow... Yeah, that phrase has been so abused over the years..."I know my rights," or I have the right...yes, they do, and God will let anyone do what they very well please, to do, but there are consequences to anything, that's against God. Just read Luke 16:19 to 31 but by then it's too late. Look folks you've got one opportunity and only one time in this life, to get right with God, wouldn't it look absurd for some preacher sprinkling oil over plots at the cemetery saying I forgive you of all of your sins, go on to heaven in my name I pray. Wow.

And I'm sure there are some wackos out there that would believe such nonsense, but the Bible teaches if you die in your sins (that's it) your doomed forever in hell forever, wow, so why in the world do you think preachers and pastors preach peoples ears off for years and years warning them, to call on Jesus Christ today, and be born again, and ask Jesus into their hearts and ask Jesus Christ to forgive them of all their sins. (Rom. 10:9, 10, 13, John 3:3, 5, 1 John 1:5 to 10, Acts 2:38, 39) Tomorrow is promised to no one (Heb. 3, verse 12:13, 15, 2 Cor. 4:16) This is the day of Salvation, Today (2 Cor. 6:2), God wants us to call on him today to read and study the Bible each day, and to live each day for God as if there was No Tomorrow! This is the beginning of wisdom, and this is when you *begin* to mature in God.

When you ask God through the Holy Spirit in Jesus's name to check your heart when you mess up or fall sort, he will check your spirit and convict you, then it starts bugging you...so, call on Jesus in prayer, and confess your mess ups, and ask Jesus to forgive you, and get back up, and forgive your (Ps. 51:10–12; 1 John 1:6–10; Rom. 10:9, 10, 13) self, just get in a habit even if you have to get up an extra half hour earlier, but always start your day with prayer, and read some Bible verses, I've got up late before, and always carried my pocket New Testament with me so at lunch or at my bathroom break, or when I waited to switch loads with the other driver back when I worked (retired now.) So I could either read at home or on break, or at the restroom, or there were days when I was in a hurry or time just gets away from me, that's when I'll put on a Bible CD and while I'm driving or showering I'm hearing the word, building up my faith (Rom. 10:17) And you that are filled with the Holy Ghost, can pray in the spirit which will also build up your most holy faith (Jude 20) because we need faith to please God, cause it's impossible to please God without it. (Heb. 11:6 and Ps. 119:11) says: Thy word have I hid in my heart that I might not sin against thee (God and James 1:21) teaches us that the word is able to save your souls.

It directs you, encourages you in Psalms, and in the four gospels it gives you the basic instructions, examples, and parables, and teaches you the pattern of how to pray, and live the right way. So if a person don't read the Bible and pray, the Bible says he becomes unfruitful and spiritually speaking, the Bible calls and classifies you as a tree, or a branch, and says if we aren't bearing fruit, love, joy, peace, long suffering, gentleness, goodness, faith, meekness, temperance (Gal. 5:22–23) So if we don't bear fruit, Jesus had before cursed the fruitless fig tree that he was looking for fruit on it, and didn't find any. SO we know and remember when Jesus had once cursed the fruitless tree and the tree died, wow cause according to scripture (again) we are supposed to bear fruit, and we do not want God to curse us. Amen. (Matt. 21:18–20, John 15:6) says it is cast into a fire, and burned wow. Don't mean to sound self-righteous but my point is: The Bible book store sells cheap daily devotional guide books. Or you can make your own Bible chart but don't neglect your spirit man inside you, I saw many times, when a hard day of trouble came, that word was reminded in my soul, and because I was prayed up, my spirit man was conducting himself properly as a gentleman saint and not getting in the carnal flesh, taking out vengeance, and fight the battle, thus keeping me right with him (God), and keeping me out of trouble with officials (Ps. 119:11).

But there would be so much less crime in the world and less incidents if people sought first the kingdom of God and his righteousness, then all these other things would be added to you. (Matt. 6:33) Again, the word has to be put in us, by our self, in order for it to come out of our heart! Just like your car, when you keep putting in gas, it gets you where you are going, but stop putting it in, try driving your car out of state, passing up all the Gas stations, you'll soon be on the roadside, your spirit man is no different (Matt. 25). This is why so many Christians and yes ministers too, are bad-mouthed by the public, oh did you see so and so, or on the news (even worse), it was reported today at 2:00 p.m. That brother Decon lost his temper in the checkout line at the local grocery store, and punch out the cashier, all because we neglect out spirit man to give him spiritual nourishment, and fuel for the soul. Amen. This is all up to you, it's up to each individual (Luke 10:38–42), I'm reminded of Steven Curtis Chapman's song my son used to sing "You know better than that" and weren't you thankful that you spent time in prayer when your miracle came on the Holy Ghost quickening your memory. (John 14:26), in reading that word and the holy ghost brought that back to your memory but the word has to be in you before the Holy Ghost can bring it back out of you, at a crucial time when you need it.

He has reminded me of spiritual things including scriptures and even some things I forgot to do He'll remind me. And again it's all up to us, cause God's not gonna send down armed angels with shot guns, saying, now you back away from the TV and lay down that phone, and get your Bible, and you go pray right now…Ha. But seriously folks the Bible says in (Romans 12:1 and 2), "I beseech you therefore, brethren, by the mercies of God, that ye present your bodies a living sacrifice, Holy, acceptable unto God, which is your reasonable service." (It is our responsibility (Luke 17:10). It's our duty.) You can read the verse for yourself, and to many, it may seem to be a sacrifice to take out time out of their busy schedule, to pray and read their Bible, but at the end of time, we'll be glad we did. No…God lets us do it our way…but he tells us in his word, in Philippians 2:12

WHERE DO WE DRAW THE LINE?

says for us to work out our own salvation with fear and trembling: Do you wonder about that, but didn't God say in (2 Timothy 1:7) he's not gave us the spirit of fear....yes, but we are to work out is to put out an effort, and if you've studied the Bible, it tells us people will be held accountable for how everyone lived their life.

And again...God loves us...so he sends us his spirit, the comforter, to help us. But we need to know that, having a little fear will keep us in check with God. There is a godly fear that is different from a Spirit of fear (that one's a demon). but (Luke 21:26) is someone who has not obeyed God (Heb. 4:1) and this is what partiers and drunks don't have...which is a fear of God, and to be concerned enough about your soul, that you stay right in your heart and follow the Bible, which partiers and drunks do not do as in 1 Corinthians 6:9, 10, 11 and Galatians 5:15–22, Matt. 24:48 to 51, Luke 21:34 to 36, Notice, 1 Thess. 5:6 and 8 and 1 Pet. 4:7 and 1 Pet. 5:8) all say to watch and be sober...and the word (vigilant, means to be awake and alert and watchful.) And I ask you, have you really ever seen a drunk or doped up drug addict be sober, alert, watchful, no! Once again: This man has lived on both sides of this fence. I know from experience, no you can't! and we are seeing prophecy of the Last Days unfold before our eyes, and some have a heart attack, and this is why God has told us in (Luke 21:26 to 36, 2 Cor. 5:11) that knowing the terror of the Lord, we persuade men so we all can make heaven, so we aren't left behind to go through Great Tribulation.

But in that scripture (2 Cor. 5:11) Please Note: I put those last two scriptures in my words to explain the meaning: Some people don't want to witness or shove God down peoples throat, they need to read: (2 Cor. 5:11) But as I was trying to explain, but was running out of page. The Days of Great Tribulation, are Days of Sheer hell on Earth that's coming on the earth, when God's wrath and God's judgment and deep anger and fury will be poured out on the evil people on EARTH, it will be sheer terror as no man has ever seen before (2 Cor. 5:11 is saying) And these blind stupid idiots, that are so slack in their soul, yet very smart in business, don't have a clue, when they say Christians aren't supposed to shove the Bible down their throats, yet, according to scripture, if Christians fail, and don't warn others, their

349

blood will be on their hands, and it's that kind of attitude that will make people miss the rapture. All through the scriptures, the Bible says for us to warn, and to witness, and to win souls for Christ (Acts 1:8, Luke 10:19, Phil. 4:13) Jesus said to the twelve disciples and seventy more to go and witness by two's. And he gave us the comforter the Holy Ghost to give us power to witness. He even said at the time you need him, cause the Holy Ghost will speak through you and give you words to say, as (Rom. 8:26 and Jude 20, 21, 22 verse 23) says, Others save with fear pulling them out of the fire (what fire?, hell) if someone don't witness to someone they might just end up in hell, and those who don't will not make heaven. (Luke 6:46) why call ye me Lord, Lord and do not do the things I say (John 10:27) my sheep hear my voice (Matt. 10:16, I send you forth as sheep among wolves, Acts. 1:8) this is why most people don't want to get out of their easy chair, and witness, like Jesus said the people that go to hell will stand in Judgment against those who don't want to witness for Jesus Christ (in my words), Jesus wasn't making a request, but a command (Matt. 22:37–38) that's loving God with all your heart, and with all your soul, and all your mind (Matt. 22:36–40), and doing what you can, even if it's just handing out-a-Gospel tract, or pamphlet to some lost soul.

Doing something's better than doing nothing. It is your duty as a Christian. (Luke 17:10) or why did (Acts 1:8, Luke 10:19) Jesus sent the twelve disciples and the seventy also out by two's to witness, and to tell people that the kingdom of God is at hand (Matt. 10:5 to 7, Luke 10:1 to 3) how much more toward the End of the world are we to be witnesses. (Acts 1:8, Rev. 12:11, Heb. 10:25). And the more, as you see the day approaching only used one-half text and that day is definitely approaching, so much that (Matt. 24:22, Speaking of the Last Days) says, and except those days should be shorten, there should no flesh be saved, but for the Elects sake (born-again Christians) Those days shall be shortened. Wow, so when God's wrath is poured out on earth, you will not want to be here with all those who rejected Jesus Christ and those that refuse to witness will be numbered with them and those that rejected Jesus Christ (John 12:48) will be judged by the Bible. (In my words, Read it), because Jesus laid down his life on the cross to pay the price for man's sins…And then the sins (1 Cor. 6:20) of man has him so blinded in his pleasures he don't see, like as in Noah's Days and Sodom and Gomorrah's Day, man has become worse and so God has warned man, and God saw he better make a way of escape for man, so he sends his only Son Jesus Christ to die a horrible agonizing death, taking man's place as a sacrificed lamb. And the people that know, but just couldn't live for God, are probably some of the ones whose hearts fail them for fear, for looking after the things coming on the Earth (Luke 21:26) plagues, mountains falling flat, islands sinking (Rev. 16:18 to 21, There are people that are on those islands), and stars, meteors and asteroids (which some are around 490 miles in diameter) huge balls of fire don't want to be here when those kind are hitting the earth (Rev. 6:13) and according to scripture, they will fall from outer space to earth, big balls of fire, as falling stars, or asteroids, or meteor showers, as in Rev. 8:8 to 11 describes it as a great mountain burning with fire, big balls of fire this big would explain the scripture (Rev. 8:9, Rev. 16:3) that says every living creature/soul in the sea died, so the huge asteroids heated up the water and probably boiled all the fish to death. Wow. These big balls of fire falling out of the sky on the sea. Wow and (Rev. 16:8, 9) and the fourth angel poured out his vial upon the sun and power was given to him to scorch men with fire (Verse 9) And men were scorched with great heat, and blasphemed the name of God, which had power over these *plagues* and they repented not to give him glory. (Also see): (Ps. 139:20, Exod. 20:7) These Sinners have already rejected the Lord, now there gonna add gas on the fire, by blaspheming and cursing God's name.

Wow (And they call me dumb, Rom. 15:4) For whatsoever things were written a foretime were written for our learning, that we through patience and comfort of the scriptures might have hope. (Hope to stay ready.) If it's like some scientist has said already years ago, about solar flares breaking loose from the sun NASA's scientist's Kusano said there could even be solar storms, from the solar flares, back in 2013 he said this same type hit earth back in 1859 on September 1 so this kind of thing has happen before on a lower scale, or even as these scriptures teach, at any case it'll pay us all to be ready to meet the Lord. Amen, cause balls of fire-meteor showers, etc., is not my idea of living. No, in fact this could very well be where one-third part of the earth is burned up. I dare you to (Google) the sun's solar flares that's breaking off of the sun, you'll be amazed. Then read the prophecy that's coming in (Rev. 16:8–9). Wow.

But after this, there's not a lot of men left on earth. If a third of earth's men had died just from this plague alone, from the sun's solar flare, meteors, etc. (according to Revelation 9:18), it would've only left two-thirds of men on earth. Wow. There is so much more Horrific Days coming…See my book, "(Matt. 24:22)," for more horrific details in Revelation…On those who took the mark 666, etc. And don't forget those beastlike insects, which sounds like a science fiction movie has come to life—these scorpion-type locusts that the Bible mentions in (Revelation 9:2—11) have stingers in their tails like scorpions, that hurt men five months (Rev. 9:10) And water will be diseased and plagued and some water turns into blood, and will not be drinkable…And the Bible says and man still would not repent of his sins…but cursed God…wow…does that make any sense? (2 Cor. 5:11) and knowing the terror of the Lord, we persuade men. And a lot of people don't know there is a good Samaritan law in most states, if you see someone in an emergency situation on the highway and you pass by and keep going…you can be fined or even imprisoned, so not to mention, its human decency, so at least call everyone you know, but again I question ones experience with the Lord (the fruit of the spirit, etc.) and everything of what I've been discussing in the Bible, like the good Samaritan Law, do people really really think they will escape God's judgment because they didn't witness a warning to at least their own family, and friends (2 Cor. 5:11). Oh you have no idea what's ahead for those type of wanna-be Christians that just want to go to heaven, but don't want to witness and tell others out of fear, that they would be rejected or marked as a fanatic.

Wow, I know of many…And they'll bite your head off…Now is that the fruit of the Spirit (Gal. 5:22–24) No that's not Christ-like. (Everyone has to make themselves line up with the Bible, and (Philippians 2:12) says, to work out your own salvation with fear and trembling. Yes…even preachers, or do we?) maybe that's why the

Bible says for everyone to do the work of an evangelist. (2 Tim. 4:5) (they have to study, and be prepared for their next service, the evangelist, knowing the church people is dependent on him for a word from God. Because those who don't make themselves study. Do for sure, need something from God, according to scripture, God'll keep tugging at our conscience to seek him and draw closer.

Okay, moving on. Where do we draw the line on having equivalent measure of faith? (Romans 12:3) because the Bible says in (Hebrews 11:6). But without faith it is impossible to please God, for he that cometh to God, must believe that he is, and that he is a rewarder of them that "diligently seek him." (See Romans 10:17, John 20:29.)

I looked up the word *diligently*, and it simply means: (hardworking...steady at making an effort at...industrious...done with carefulness...being busy about the work of the Lord.) Some folks today don't even put out an effort to seek God, but to diligently work hard at it and putting out and making an effort. God blesses those folks. (Matt. 6:33) Seek ye first the kingdom of God and his righteousness, then all these other things shall be added unto you (Rom. 10:17) Faith comes by hearing and hearing by the Word of God. And this is why I like driving for a living for over thirty years of listening to the Bible on cassette tape, and on CD. I wore out several, rewinding them when I would hear something awesome, and replaying it sometimes over and over, and sometimes pulling off the road to write it down on a post note, and being a pastor back then, I got many sermons from God, just by driving out on the open country roads between towns all night, and on mountain roads hearing the Word of God, while building up my faith, and getting paid for it. HA.

And even putting in a Bible CD while showering or cooking... sure, many times some words get past ya. But when you know that Bible, you can say wait a minute, I missed...chapter 2 and hit rewind, and I'll give most of the credit of my Bible knowledge, to the Holy Ghost, for bringing it to my memory so many times. And to all those years of hearing it while driving and showering, and don't get me wrong I read as well, and one thing I've really enjoyed is when God gives you this Gold nugget, to research that blossoms into a beautiful sermon after you've studied it out.

And one thing that amazes me about God's Word is you read something this year and next year you read the same scripture and see something you never noticed last year (Luke 22:37) (Luke 8:10). This is one of God's great mysteries of God's Word. (Rom. 16:25, Col. 1:25–28, Eph. 3:2–6, Luke 8:10–11.) And it's also your most valuable weapon against the devil, and after learning it, then being able to quote the scriptures at the devil or at situations even as Jesus did in (Matthew 4). You may feel foolish but it works. (2 Cor. 5:7, 1 Cor. 1:18 to 27, Eph. 6:10 to 18, Heb. 4:12) And not just reading it, but studying and digesting, and absorbing it into your heart, mind, and soul. (2 Cor. 5:7, 1 Cor. 1:27, *Question?*) If quoting scriptures to the devil or at same ordeal, was really a God sent, and it is, don't you think the devil would definitely be trying with all his might to tell and make people feel foolish doing it…I mean, come on, folks, many places especially in the days of Jesus, like the time Jesus put a mud/clay spittal on the blind guy's eyes, then said go wash in the pool of Siloan in (John 9:7).

Hello, the dude is blind…wow, but preacher, there are keys of faith here, and obedience to God is one. Or like when Elisha told Naaman to go dip in muddy Jordan River seven times in (2 Kings 5:10–14), again obedience was the key to unlock the door of faith, no matter how foolish it may seem, sometimes God has to get rid of self will and stubborn pride. (Hello!) Yes! Read (Matthew 4:1–11) and if Jesus had to do it…wouldn't his followers have to also? (Yes!) And why does Jesus himself, and the Apostles tell us in so many scriptures that we need to learn the Bible, the Word of God, like (2 Timothy 2:15; Romans 10:17; Hebrews 4:12, 11–5, 6; Matthew 8:8, 8:16; Luke 4:36; James 1:21, John 1:1, John 12:48, John 15:3, 7; Acts 2:38–41; Matthew 24:35; John 8:47) Jesus was speaking here to the Jews, "He that is of God heareth God's words: ye therefore hear them not, because ye are not of God." So if we are truly of God we will hear and follow God's word. Amen. And there is also and many, many more, but the Word of God will help you to please God because the Bible says it is impossible to please him without faith, and the Bible says the way to get faith is by hearing the Bible.

How important is faith to you? Some people have to make notes while others have to read out loud. Faith, comes by hearing the word, it's impossible to please God without it. So get yourself a drink of prayer and bowl of faith and start your day with God. (Rom. 10:17; Heb. 11:1, 2, 3, 5, 6). And remember stay focused don't dose or day dream, get awake and alert first (Isa. 26:3).

When you have driven for a living, hauled oranges, grains, lumber, cranes, door slides, mail, etc., on the road up to sixteen hours. A day or all night, you learn you have to sike out your mind with what truckers call road games but staying alert and awake and focused is the key. But if you get tired you pull over, walk around your rig, check your load throw water in your face I usually carried a spray bottle of water, but nothing even coffee works after so, many hours nothing takes the place of rest, or sleep, but I was just using driving as an analogy, example: We have to stay spiritually focused in these last days. Don't neglect your souls. Remember I mentioned it earlier. (Matt. 25:1–14), the foolish virgins—these particular Christians wasn't even concerned enough about their own souls, to take extra oil to keep their lamp on which makes this preacher wonder do they really believe. But I was that way before I got saved, deep down I did believe, I just wasn't ready yet to make a commitment to God.

And my point again is, there is not a lot of time (Rom. 9:28) says, For he (God) will finish the work, and **cut it short** in righteousness, **because a short work** will the Lord make upon the earth. (Matt. 24:22, Rev. 12:12, Matt. 8:29) cause even the devil knows his day is coming to an end. (Matt. 8:29) cause when Jesus cast out a devil and the devil knew and ask about the end of time (Matt. 8:29) And I think that's pretty cool, and also (James 2:19) says, thou (you) believe that there is one God, thou (you) do well: "The devils also believes, and trembles." (Hallelujah.) Ha. I've used the analogy of the rich man in hell in Luke 16:19 to the devil, many times especially when going through some ordeal, and I'll slap him in the face with his future (so in my words) I replace the rich man burning, with the devil and I tell him while he's burning in the Lake of fire (Rev. 20:10)

He'll be looking up at me standing on the sea of Glass (Rev. 15:2) standing on water that He'll want to cool his burning tongue with, as in (Luke 16:24). And I also say, Jesus I ask in Jesus's name on that day, could I also have a cool drink of water in a dribble glass (HA...) Hey...it helps me, when I'm in a battle, okay, don't knock it, till ya try it.

And quote (Luke 10:19–20) Hey, if you were suffering, and you were chained up burning and you could see the biggest celebration of all time ever going on, with everyone standing on water, having the best time of their entire life (1 Cor. 2:9), and about to feast at the marriage supper of the Lamb (Rev. 19:7–9), while all the whole time you are burning and got a front row seat with the biggest one way window, or kinda like those two-way mirrors, where you see them, but all they see is there reflection or water. And for the devils people that give you a bad time and attack you on the Job, or other places cause they know you're a Christian, read (Rev. 3:9), it too gives me joy. "Behold I will make them of the synagogue of Satan, which say they are Jews, and are not, but do lie, behold, I will make them to come and worship before thy feet, and to know that I have loved thee." (Wow.) Please look up those last scriptures on time, please: And you tell me, when the devil knows that time is very, very short, and the Bible says, the Lord is gonna do a (quick work), he's gonna shorten the time: what? Or there won't be anyone left to save, wow (look 'em up...) I knew a couple of sweet godly ladies some years ago, Laura Liles and Peggy Peton, very, very anointed of God, and could sing the glory of heaven down, anyway this particular song, "Plenty of Time"...they sung...says, folks think they have plenty of time...and we all must make an effort to make it, according to prophecy events that scriptures point to Jesus's return. Yes, no one knows the exact, day, or hour (Again, but we will know it's close, even to the doors.) by the signs but remember, I mentioned earlier. (Matt. 24:33) notice the (s), which makes it plural (D-O-O-R-S). There is deep significance here, when you see things of this nature in prophecy.

There is one door to God and that's through Jesus, to have access to heaven (John 14:6, John 10:1–9) but my point of plural, is, this means many signs pointing you clues to Jesus's return are here, "Now!" But these lazy non-spiritual minded, carnal lukewarm in heart foolish virgin Christians in (Revelation 3:15–16, Matthew 25) wasn't even concerned about their own souls right up till Jesus's return, and scripture says, they didn't make it, because of no effort unlike what a lot of religions (and non-spiritual churches) that say and teach the opposite. Okay, another repeat). I've been trying my best to drill this in you. You need extra oil with God. The oil is what kept their lamps burning bright in the Old Days…but there is also a spiritual oil with God, that keeps your fire of God burning bright in your soul. In (Rev. 2:5), notice this scripture says three clues, remember when you fall is one and repent is two and do your first works over is three, now, this means when you first got saved and really repented good, cause you had the joy of the Lord, ad were all excited about doing God's work, but when you lose some oil your light starts flickering in your spiritual lamp, and your globe is smokie, and dark, your light is growing dim, loosen your desire to live for God, stuff in the world is catching your eye (you see my point) but those first works, your first spiritual true love is when you got saved and gave your heart to Jesus (read Rev. 2:4, 5; Rev. 3:15–16). When you first got saved (born again), there was an excitement in your walk with God, so when you lose your fire, seek God's desire and a fiery excitement for God, especially when you're not wanting to see souls get saved or other similar situations.

God gets angry (Rev. 2:4, God's wrath) because people has left their first love, plus, they forgot the hard crule torturous death Jesus died on the cross for their soul, this is why John said to remember when you fell, repent and get your joy back (Rev. 3:5, we need to get back to where we was spiritually, when we first got saved which only comes through true repentance.) Amen. (Ps. 51: 10 to 13, Acts 2:37, 38, 39, Matt. 5:15–16) So in these scriptures and all through the first three chapters of Revelation is a rebuke to those Lukewarm fence stratlers who are not on either side (They say they are Christians but are like (lukewarm) water. When I'm thirsty, I can't handle room temperature or warm water and many scriptures says God's no different, God wants us fired up…And filled with the Holy Ghost and fire, that purges, and purifies and he (God) inhabits the praises of his people, but I prefer cool or cold water to drink, and my coffee hot, so God is saying be hot or cold not lukewarm. Cold would represent a sinner, hot would be someone living for God with the in-filling of the Holy Ghost, and with everything in them, a fire shut up in his bones (Jer. 20:9) The word hot and fire, and candlestick (All represent the light of God, Matt. 5:16) Jesus said let your light so shine before men that they will see your good works, and glorify (God) your father which is in heaven. Now if the fuel oil for the lamp which represents us being the lamp or the candlestick, either one in those days was their only means of lighting up a room, but this analogy is saying, without light people can't see, God wants people to see God in you (with extra oil, you can keep that lamp that (you are) burning bright (wow) read the scripture again: people that say you are too religious or call you a fanatic, those are the lukewarm, that put out no effort, no holy ghost in filling, they are on the fence, well they say, "I'm not a sinner but I'm not an over board fanatic either." Okay, according to these scriptures, this guy on the fence does not have that extra oil, nor has he ever burned bright shining light for Jesus, doesn't witness, which that's why (Acts 1:8, Luke 10:19) was written (ok, movin on.) Pray.

God if this preacher is right. Fill up my lamp to overflow give it to me for this last day generation and evil day I live in, we need extra oil of God to keep our spiritual light burning bright cause we are in the last generation and in this evil day we need all of God we can get, people for years has misunderstood (Acts 1:8, Acts 2:17, Luke 10:19) and other prophecy scriptures, did Jesus return back and take all the Christian followers to heaven back then, followed up with the Tribulation and Great Tribulation Days? "NO"! "He did not"! or we wouldn't be here today! So having said that, so then Peter was just making his stand for Christ's Holy Ghost in Acts 2:17, about the Holy Ghost infilling (Luke 24:49, Acts 2:1–40) was a day to impower up the saints there then. (Read it.) They weren't the Last Generation! "We Are!" (Agree or disagree) it doesn't matter if you don't agree with me about the times we are in but you better take heed to the advice on having your soul ready for Jesus will come in an hour you think not. And if you don't believe that, you will probably get left behind for sure.

So many places in scripture Jesus says the kingdom of heaven will be like or as or when the son of man (Jesus) comes will he find faith (extra oil) the oil keeps our spiritual light on, hello but these five wise virgins (born-again Christians), in Matthew 25 (these smart (spiritual) Christians) took extra oil. And when it came down to it, when all hell is breaking loose, or an unreal, unnormal situation comes, that knocks you off your feet (Rom. 8:26) you will need that extra oil and you will be glad you let the holy spirit fill you up and pray through you, cause in many situations we don't know how to pray but the holy spirit prays through the extra oil servants, oh, they will call ya a holy roller. Who cares? Just get all you can from the Lord, and honest to God, you'll be glad you did.

Hope you're getting this, because it's all Biblical. Being ready for he comes in an hour you think not. (Matt. 25:13, Luke 12:40, Matt. 24:42, Luke 21:31–36, Luke 12:46, Mark 13:32–33) If you're not ready, and right with God in your heart, you'll get left behind to go through the Great Tribulation Days and then you'll have to refuse the mark of the Beast chip 666 (in) your hand, and then the Anti-Christ Dictator and his government will have you beheaded for disobeying the Anti-Christ, which then the only way to heaven will be to be beheaded after you accept Jesus you'll go to heaven, but if you take the mark of the Beast, you will go to hell. (2 Thess. 2:9–12, Rev. 20:4, Rev. 13:16–18, Rev. 14:9 to 12) and according to these scriptures if people that have turned back from following Jesus, their names that were in the Book of Life are now blotted out. (Revelation 3:5, read it.)

Okay, now when all this nightmare is going on (Luke 21:26) is now happening, and many will turn to booze, but then, that's why (1 Thess. 5:6–9) in all those prophecy scriptures say to watch and be sober (1 Pet. 4:7, 1 Pet. 5:8, 1 Thess. 5:6, 8). You're not watching if you're drunk, you soon become unconscious and pass out. I've been down that road before (1 Pet 4:7, Rev. 3:3, 5).

So if all these scriptures tell us, to watch and pray which is spiritually getting extra oil for our spiritual lamps, etc., there's a lot more

I could give but Hope you get the point. Where do we draw the line? Can we really get to much of God as in (Eph. 5:18, Acts 2:41). The same day three thousand souls were added cause we all see you've got people's attention, Lord (Matt. 24:22). Now help us to pray, and yield our hearts to you Lord, burn off the junk, and the dead dryness of my life, then send in that gushing living water and hose me out, help us Holy Spirit to repent ourselves, create a right spirit within me, in Jesus's name. (Ps. 51:10–13; Ps. 23:5; Acts 4:31–32) Notice, it says they were all filled, now, in order for this to happen, the people must lay aside their differences, because according to (Acts 2) there was a spirit of unity…In these last few weeks, I've seen people helping people of different races and of different religions all them, swallowing their different opinions, and pitched in and helped others, the sick, and the wounded.

If folks will just channel that attitude and tap into a spirit of love in the spirit, and yield ourselves to God and ask for forgiveness, together in unity, as the threads are woven together in a rope (read 2 Chron. 7:14, Ps. 133:1, Eph. 4:3 and 13, Amos. 3:3, Matt. 18:19–20) You see I believe, that God wants a revival service like before, in people's hearts, as it was on the day of Pentecost as in (Acts 2), when there was that spirit of one mind, in one accord, and in a spirit of forgiveness toward each other, a spirit of LOVE that causes each one to overlook each ones flaws faults, and not worry if they measure up to our expectations, but being focused on God, and having a spirit of thankfulness, being thankful to God that he spared us and died for us on the cross, and thankful he didn't send us straight to hell, but gave us many, many opportunities to get ourselves right with him. Then I'm thinking instead of having another upper room, those that had yielded hearts in that spirit of unity of love, and forgiveness, would just be ushered into heaven in the rapture, God's not taking a bunch of evil back stabbing unforgiving mean ugly in heart, people that could kill you, wow, have you been watching the news, and read our Bibles, the Lord said he's coming back when you see all this that's going on happening, so we need to love others and pray, not protest, not fight, Jesus is coming, ready or not! All of them were filled with the Holy Ghost because they were in a spirit of unity. You can't be in unity with hate and unforgiveness in your heart, no, so those that were filled with God's Holy Ghost were in a spirit of love and unity (Acts 2, Psalm 51:10–13, Mark 2:22). New wine must be put in new bottles (2 Cor. 5:17, Luke 14:23). God wants even his church house to be full as well as people's souls, Acts 2:4) it'll be the ones resisting the devil and the ones yielding to God that make it to heaven.

So all these scriptures say, "All of them were filled with the Holy Ghost" I've heard many over the years say you don't have to be, but I read in the Bible you do. And (Acts 11:24) says because there was a man full of the Holy Ghost, and there were added much people to the Lord. So we are the last generation, according to the way I understand this Bible prophecy…so why are there so many lukewarm, and so many people not full of the Holy Ghost in churches everywhere, because this is the Last Day Church of Apostasy as in (2 Timothy 3:5), good actors, and people that's not in all the way. For God. And the Days of Unbelief, cause if people would repent and turn to God, and read the first three chapters of Revelation and the whole chapter of (Rev. 18, 2 Chron. 7:14) and realize it's referring to us, and read the good and bad of (Det. 28) America was once a Christian nation; and even called the name after the Lord Jesus Christ (a Christian being Christ-like, 2 Chron. 7:14) but not anymore, "I'm not filling in space here"… Read these scriptures, please! Especially Deuteronomy 28 we *were* a blessed nation *because* we served God…but no more, and the only thing that has kept us from being nuked is the hand of God, that's been over the *few* that is born again and living for God," So was the virus a plague? Yes, now if God has power over plagues, then is this a wake-up call? Yes, it is! Then if it is, and people are just, sweeping it under the rug and not listening to God as in Deut. 28).

And yes, they are! So if that's true…then what's next? Because from the beginning of time, back in Egypt, did God stop at one? NO! No, God sure didn't, but God hit Egypt with ten plagues, and I ask you…did pharaoh listen? No, so the plagues continued on to hit Egypt, didn't they, yes, they did, from Exodus (chapter 7 to Exodus chapter 12) up to all the first born plague, God still warned pharaoh that all the first born would die in Egypt, and that's when God said to his people, to put the Lambs blood on their door posts, but Jesus

Christ in *our* Lamb today, cause Jesus shed his blood on the cross for the sins of the whole world (John 3:16–19) but the blood then, and now, must be applied. And again that comes by repenting of our sins (1 John 1:6–10, Acts 2:38–39) and by turning from our wicked ways and live for God. (2 Chron. 7:14) People today do not want to read anything that seems negative, or discouraging, but all of this is pure fact! It's real, and "AGAIN, HISTORY has come full circle," it's time to get our heads out of the sand, and wake-up and understand that God is trying to get people's attention"! Stop the fussing and bickering, and stop acting like a bunch of spoilt little brats, pray, get repented and get back to serving God with all your heart or you'll suffer more plagues! It's all in the Bible (especially about people who just don't believe).

Read (Revelations 21:8, Hebrews 4:6–11, 2 Peter 3:3–5, Revelations 2:4–5). Jesus said if these didn't repent of this, he would come and remove and take away their light. (In Revelations 2:5, says, Repent and do your first works) you must know if you don't already know, that when the Lord said if we didn't repent, he would come and remove the candlestick out of "His Place" (the Holy Spirit) that's in people, that saved them (he is that light that's inside them) that means God's spirit, God'll take out his spirit, we are in that day and hour, God is ready to remove out his spirit! Why God calls back his spirit back up to heaven (Rev. 4:1–2) Those that are born-again believers, will also be caught up! As in (Psalm 51:11 see verses 10 to 17 and Ps. 139:23–24); why is it some believe and receive the Holy Ghost infilling to the evidence of speaking in tongues, and they get mad at you cause you got it.

I don't understand that. They should desire it to, and want God's spirit inside them. Yet like in Jesus's Day instead of praying for it and asking God to create in them a right spirit and a clean heart, and give them a hunger and thirst for righteousness (Matt. 5:6). So because they don't believe or pray for it. They instead attack those that do (Acts 5:39, Acts 5:17, 18, 19). Isn't it funny, that these religious leaders in Jesus Christ day, was so puffed up in their own pride, they couldn't even see when they arrested the disciples and locked them in prison, that God sends them an angel to let them out. Read

(Acts 5:28) then the disciples are interrogated by those devils. Now go back to (Matt. 27:25) and notice, these same big shoot power gone to their head high Priest and Captain of the temple Leaders in (Acts 5:24–28) say, we commanded you not to teach in Jesus name, are you now trying to bring this man's = (Jesus)—blood upon us. Ha (in my words). Ha (they forgot). Now read (Matt. 27:25) they were so full of their self and all their power that gone to their head, that they forgot that they said, let his blood be on us (Jesus). And how about those same type wanting to kill Lazarus again, after Jesus resurrected him (John 12:9, 10, and 11), how blind can you be, didn't they know if Jesus raised up Lazarus once, he can do it again. Ha. Wow. (It sounds like jealousy, Joel 2:28, Acts 2:17, God is pouring out his spirit on mankind, but it's up to us to receive it.)

At any case, I'm gonna live for God, and do what the Bible says: if the Bible says, be filled with the Holy Ghost, then I'm gonna believe and pray too, until I got it. But we have to believe he is a rewarder of them that "diligently" = (having and putting out a constant effort) to seek him. (Heb. 11:6) and have faith…But the people that were jealous and came against the apostles and followers of Jesus (and there are those who even came against us today) their heart is not right with God who attack God's people to begin with. So that explains why God didn't fill their wicked unclean heart. And God also wants his church full, even as God wants us full of his spirit. He wants his church full of people to come and worship him, but as he told the woman at the well (John 4:21 to 24) The hour comes when you will neither worship God in the mountain or at Jerusalem. This is why the devil works on people with distractions, to keep people so distracted in their mind with so much stuff, that people can't focus on prayer and worship, but God wants us focused on him to where we can worship him in spirit and truth (John 4:24), not a performance or show. We were all out for dinner not long ago and this couple invited us with some other families, and this certain person yelled out let's all pray, with a very loud, thank you Lord prayer. Which is fine, but it was obviously a big show, to cover up their guilt because everyone knew they were shacking up together and there were before we got saved. Amen. Cause It's by grace, any of us is saved (Eph.

2:8) and I'm not their judge. I was just amazed at the performance, which reminded me of what Jesus taught in the four gospels about the Pharisees and in (John 4:7–24) and in (Matt. 2:3) and also in (1st Cor. 9:14) God wants us to be real folks and not putting on a big show, Hollywood's got that all covered. Amen. I just pray they get saved and married before Jesus comes, in Jesus name. Amen. (Isa. 26:3, Acts 2:4, Joel 2:28) Notice, the scriptures say, God poured out his spirit, on those followers that were yielding to God and waiting on the move of his spirit (Luke 24:49, Acts 1:14) with open and clean hearts after they tarried and repented, and thanked and worshipped God (which are secret keys to receive the Holy Ghost, Matt. 16:17, Matt. 6:33, Rom. 6:12–16, Matt. 16:18, 19) Notice (verse 18) not even the gates of hell can prevail against us (Matt. 6:33, Rom. 6:12–16) Again can anyone get too much of God…Notice (Acts 11:24) He was full of the Holy Ghost.

So can anyone get too much of God? No, but it will Help us be ready. And you will be so glad you were, as (Matt. 25:10–13) says, while the five foolish was not ready, and ran out of oil, this is representing, needing extra, where we will not run out but we need to be full (Acts 7:55) Wow, read verse 60 in our day and time, people that was stoned to death after working years for God, would have probably screamed "get 'em God they're stoning your anointed servant," but not Stephen, no, but, he cried with a loud voice, "Lord, lay not this sin to their charge…just before he died. Wow, now you news reporters want to print about a real hero (there's your man, Stephen, wow, or how about Paul and Silas in Acts 16:16–31 and won the guard and his family to the Lord. Now, these are real heros, to suffer for God and still pray with them. Wow.

So this is why we need to be full of God, so our flesh doesn't rise up to take out vengeance (2 Thess. 1:8, Rom. 12:19, Heb. 10:30, Luke 21:22–23) on their attackers, cause that's God's job. (Acts 4:8–13, Acts 4:31) so we are not detoured by the devil, cause when a Christian that's full of the spirit of God and running over, like a glass of water, that had dry leaves crumbled in the glass, representing stuff the devil tries to bring your way, running over with extra water, would keep the glass of water clean, drinkable, but a half-full, half-empty crumbled leaves, would still be in the glass, amen. So if the glass has a continual over flow, we're talking a clean full glass of drinkable water here. Let's not let the devil detour us from our Christian heritage and godly morals and Christlike values, that was handed down to us, And the Very most important part of being called an American Christian, that separates An evil terrorist on a Plane attempting to murder the whole group, versus that brave soldier that takes a stand, for truth, justice, love, family, and values of life, America can still get back to what America and the Christians once stood for. It starts with me and you. Our home, our church, our city, etc. (As for me and my house, we'll serve the Lord. (Josh. 24:15) that's the values that our Nation once stood for, And WAS Ready to die for, honoring those around him in respect and integrity even if it cost his life to SAVE, and to Spare All the others.

Unlike and totally opposite of the terrorist's way of thinking. This spirit and heart of love (the terrorist don't have) and this love of God seems to have leaked out of many of Americans hearts causing them to be vengeful or like the five foolish that ran out of fuel in Matthew 25 but there are still a mighty few when backed in a corner, that will still make that stand, When we as a nation all return to that frame of mind as this Nation once had, when it was founded, I believe with everything in me, we'll see God pour out his spirit and bless Our Land Again: It seems at Holiday time, and when people are shopping they get ugly in heart, tired, cranky, feeling the pressures of all they have to do and get to the different places they've got to get to and everyone's in everyone's way, pushing and shoving, trying to save a buck, developing a road rage spirit of aggravation versus the meek Christlike attitude of love and peace, unlike the lady in the elevator at the mall that had a ugly attitude while shopping for Christmas gifts, hanging on to bags full of gifts, and two screaming kids said angrily, I'd like to punch out the guy who invented Christmas, not thinking of what she said, a man's voice spoke up in the back of the elevator and said, you're too late lady, they crucified him two thousand years ago, and there was a hush in the elevator until the door opened.

Wow, and…at festive time of fellowship as we all are gathered around the table to give thanks to Our Lord who was born to Die on a cross, so we could live and make heaven, have we forgotten or laid these values ASIDE for the material T-h-i-n-g-s that give Pleasure (Luke 12:15), over happiness and joy full of Glory, And peace of mind that Passes all understanding (Luke 12:21, 34, Phil. 4:6–9), I don't know about you but I still get all teary eyed when I see a hero step out of a crowd stopping a bully, or one taken a stand for what's morally right according to the Bible verses (Romans 12:9–10; John 15:13; John 15:12, 13; John 13:34–35; and Romans 12:9–10; Romans 16:4), but today the new propaganda that's now being taught, as in (Galatians 1:6 to 10, 1 Timothy 4:1 and 2, 2 Timothy 4:3 and 4, Romans 16:17–18, which is not 1 Timothy 5:21), like Jesus Christ taught and lived. Yes, my brothers and sisters, there are still many still out there with biblical Christian family values…and yes my brothers and sisters, there are still a few good hearted people out there that have reached out to the prodigals, in prisons and rescue missions, etc. And I have had the pleasure of meeting many over the years that have sacrificed their family time and gave of their selves till it hurts, volunteering their time and money for the cause of Christ, and just making a difference and knowing (Heb. 11:39–40 and Jude 20–23).

"And these all having obtained a good report through faith, received not the promise. God having provided some better things for us, that they without us should not be made perfect" (Heb. 11:39–40). As the next chapter says, we need to get back to keeping our focus, and our eyes on Jesus and not on things of this life (Hebrews 12:2). Read (Luke 10:38 to 42) the one thing that is needful is Jesus, (see also Luke 12:15 to 21). Sure, we have to survive till the lord comes. While we are still on earth, but, as the scriptures teach we are in the world not of the world. I've been so proud of our troops and even as I said, about others that have taken a stand for what's right.

As I stood in anger, overlooking the casket, one of my right handman, in prison ministry, this dear brother that cancer took to heaven, but anger caused the family to X out Christ out of the word, saying X-mas, please don't X-out Christ, out of Christmas. He's the reason for the season (for Christ-mas). How could His family X-out God from his funeral, and talk only about His Mongol biker and gambler lifestyle, which was before he was saved. (2 Cor. 5:17) But all the years of his great work for God at my side, they never mentioned one word of the great work, so I say, Mike Hicks done a great work in prison ministry for God at my side, they never mentioned one word of the great work he did in prison ministry, at his funeral… And it really angered me, because "mike Hicks" was a changed man and shared how God changed his life to multitudes of prisoners…, Col. 2:8) To those who knew him, knew he was a changed man for God.

I was angry cause that man sacrificed his time and finances to get the gospel to all those prisoners, and knew this man should had some acknowledgment and been recognized for his labor of love and giving heart, like Mike Hicks had, yes, I know he'll get his reward in heaven, but this man really sacrificed his time and money for those prisoners and God, and yes so did Doc Peteon, Joe Avery, Rev. Wayne Blevins, those gone on to be with our Lord Jesus, but those still alive that had to quit due too bad health or situations, I want to acknowledge in my book, Rev. Ray Romeo is still going but the rest of us retired, including Rev. Art Alvedrez, Rev. Mike Maxodant, Rev. Gerald Eugene Rich, Steve Castleberry, Rev. Jim Peterson, Rev. Jim Walters and his wife Ruby, Dale and Linda Icoff, and my wife Brenda Davis by my side singing her heart out for Jesus and many others, that their names escape me that should be recognized for their great sacrifices of time and money to preach and sing the gospel story to rescue missions and prisoners, Juvenile hall, Jails, Prisons. Rev. Gibson, Chaplin Hooper Campbell back in our day taught us with Rev. Joe Avery, oh how we all learned from watching and hearing these men of God, leaving us a Christian heritage example to follow.

We weren't under some big organization like those on the radio that received huge donations. Like those great Gideons that also sacrificed their time (coming in the prisons and jails as we were leaving, done my heart, good to see the briefcases and boxes of New Testaments that they were also handing out. Thank God, sad to say I saw some prisoners use the pages to empty cigarette butts in to roll up a cigarette in, I wouldn't be in that guys shoes on Judgment Day for nothing. Worked with many over those eighteen years and sad to say, I'm bad with names and many since 1977 to 2006 have gone on to be with Jesus. And along with those I didn't mention and am sorry I couldn't remember. Will be rewarded according to scripture and like that wall for the soldiers that gave of their selves, I believe one will be erected for all those who were never acknowledged or recognized for all their labor. **"Please" don't misunderstand me, I know it wasn't done for the recognition.**

Plus, many more should always be at least thanked for their services even though these didn't receive pay since they were volunteer ministers. But those that did, they still risk their lives, but I want to say to all the ambulance and ER first responders, and paramedics, fireman, and all law enforcement, and all our troops, to all who serve and protect, thank you and may God bless you all. But the anger that came out of my soul back when I was at the funeral and nothing was said at the funeral except the old lifestyle type words, the wild life, etc. "These folks battled and sacrificed and gave their time, something should at least be said at the guy's funeral. My mother-in-law, used to say give me my flowers while I'm living (Tom and Rev. Lola Frost) and her daughter Diane Goulart.

Also done a prison ministry, in laws were pastors and convalescent hospital ministry. And my pastor Donahue Green, with Rev. Lori Aguirre and Dr. Debra Epps done reservation and retirement home ministry. And the choir and musicians and singers, wish I knew all their names, my wife Brenda Davis and Bro Mike Grayes and Sis. Martha Stroman, I don't attend them, these are done by my Pastor Donahue Green, and our church folks and I'm sure many more play and sing and preach, and I hate missing anyone but was mainly trying to recall those that passed on, when I was in that ministry with them in the prison ministry and rescue mission and Juvenile hall ministry. Not intending to take my long detour dirt roads or hurt anyone's feeling that I didn't mention, so many of these ministers were volunteers, that didn't receive no offerings or pay.

Even though these I'm mentioning and so many, many more great workers for God out there that have served our God, from out of their own heart and out of their own pockets will have great rewards, and here are a few scriptures on (good rewards) (Heb. 11:5

and 6, Matt. 10:42, 1 Tim. 5:18, and Ps. 58:11, Luke 6:35, Matt. 16:26, 27, Matt. 5:12) and there are "bad rewards" that will be given to the wicked and evil people…and those who reject Jesus Christ (Rev. 22:18, 19; Rev. 18:6; 2 Tim. 4:14; 2 Pet. 2:12, 13; Gal. 1:7, 8, 9; Gal. 5:14 to 22; 2 Pet. 3:3 to 17; Gal. 6:7, 8, 9), which is reaping and sowing on good and bad.) It was all strictly volunteer ministry, many paid their own gas, drove many miles bought tracts, Bibles, etc., out of their own pockets and hours that was out of their own pockets and hours on their feet that now I'm not able to do, but again they all have great rewards in heaven. Anyway, back to those who spent hours upon hours on their feet and knees for God, shall not lose their reward), they'll have great rewards in heaven.

Only God knows the sacrifices they all have done and others not mentioned, someone that you'd like to sit down and talk with is Pastor Donahue Green and minister James Johnson all the behind scenes all that goes on producing the ministry events, revival services, church magazines, etc., their writers and interviewers, all in all, someone like Bro. Don, Sis Frances, Bro Mike, Bro Malachi or Minister Snead, Donahue Jr., choir and worship team (and our soundman Bro. Juan working sound for Church and funerals and weddings), did some major times spending sacrificing and it's all for God, if it's music even in church or Jail, prison, convalescence home or rescue missions ministry. And all of these have a great reward from God for using their talents. And gifts, and taking out time to do a work for God. It's all for God, and no one ask me to mention them, and no I'm not out for Browny Points! I am my own person. I learned years ago after being under religious thumbs, trying to always be pleasing to them, please don't misunderstand, yes we should obey those that have the rule over us in the Lord but I'm talking about (1 Thess. 5:12), (Heb. 13:16, 17) (Col. 3:22–25), (Acts 5:29.)

Speaking of the religious organizations that want you to be in fear, if you mess up or fall short of their strict guidelines of measuring up to their standards, yes, I do believe in walking the straight and narrow way but according to God's Word, not a religious thumb. (Dirt road). Anyway, God's not having you to fear him or that you be under some power trip religious organization like I was in years ago, and thank God I'm under Living Christ Church, and Pastor Donahue Green (now) but some out there act like they are some cult dictator, that's not what the Gospel of Jesus Christ is all about. God never has wanted his ministers to have to walk on pins and needles in fear of the counsel. That's what I went through a few times with religious organizations, and watching these puffed up religious Pharisees look down their noses at you, acting like you are something they stepped in, and want to wipe you off, oh, how I have learned since then, and so many others have felt like God's even up their waiting with a baseball bat to club you when you fall short as minister Lt. Don Smith so well preached.

Good message (Minister Smith), cause he didn't know that he was confirming my book, and also Minister Smith and his wife Tina also are both ministers also and have also taken my grandson under their wing, and have really been ministering to him. Plus confirming my book, when I was in the middle of writing this book, when he preached that sermon (again) good job, and thank you for the conformation. Most ministers look for God to confirm a sermon or in my case this book, bishop Jakes did twice saying where do you draw the line to. Ha, I about jumped out of my chair, praising the Lord. (But back to my point) God is a loving God, and a forgiving God, and our mediator Jesus Christ that loved us enough and died for us and always goes to God as our mediator on our behalf of whatever the situation is, and he's our propitiation (which became a sacrifice of himself for us to God), for our sins and not us only, but also for the sins of the whole world (1 John 2:12, John 3:16–18). And God knows what we can stand and take, and he knows how much we can endure (Matt. 24:13, Matt. 10:22, James 1:12). (First Corinthians 10:13) says, there hath no temptation taken you but such is common to man; but God is faithful, who will not suffer (allow) you to be tempted above that ye are able, but will with the temptation also make a way to escape, that ye may be able to bear it.

God knows if we are able to handle a certain type struggle or situation, this is why you have teachers that can teach and exhort God's Word but don't have the patience with people or endurance, wisdom, and especially long suffering, which is what it takes to be a pastor, and sometimes, it's to be a good listener, to the one being counseled, and listening to God for answers, versus being a teacher or preacher. There are many good speakers and teachers but a God called pastor is very unique and a separated individual that has those certain qualities of a shepherd that takes on himself a spirit of humility and prefers others before hisself, and a pastor is able to counsel one-on-one, which is not really in teachers as much as pastors, that also sacrifices his time, and his comforts of his bed in the middle of the night to go to the hospital to pray and be with a parishioner, when a teacher rolls back over in his/her bed, both are called of God, but pastors spend more time studying, praying, visitation, funerals, weddings, counseling, etc. I remember when my dad died I also had a wedding. I was doing, I couldn't cancel it, there was no time, no way, the wedding was the next day I had to suck it up and just do it.

Everyone was so happy. I was crying inside, but I just put on a fake smile. That is when you really know your God called to be a pastor. Amen. Pastors are human too. They're not superman. So continually hold your pastor up in prayer because your prayers are definitely needed and the patience to counsel, etc., when your average speaker just isn't gifted in. These virtues and qualified individuals really do sacrifices more probably than others, but only God knows the in depth of it all and will reward all sacrifices made for him great and small. And believe me, you better be God called in taking that step! Most people just see that glamour of being in the spotlight so to speak, overlooking, the visitation, prayers, study, counseling, weddings, funeral (bottle sticking) "Oh did I say," yes even listening to baby Christians whine and complain over frivolous, petty, little minute ordeals that most would just say "grow up" instead, God gave pastors a spirit of long suffering and mentoring love in them like Pastor Donahue Green, preaches the word firm and straight. Yet also with love and don't sugarcoat it. Wow, and yes, with the power of the holy ghost anointing and in case ya. Didn't notice that man of God can be seen and heard at Living Christ Church. 2516 M. St. Tulare CA. 93274; 559 686-5838 (lcc2516@att.net) And on YouTube and Facebook or also (lcctulare.org).

No pastor didn't tell me to put in a plug for our church. I'm just a proud member that got a breath of fresh air when I visited, and stayed, ten years ago this Dec. and been a member since then. And it is a church of all races and nationalities. We are all God's children hearing God's Word, and Living Christ church lives what they preach, these folks has loved my wife and I like we were a member of their own immediate family, far and few from your average church. These folks and pastors demonstrate their mouth with their hearts that are full of love.

Thanks, pastors and Living Christ Church, for making us feel so welcome. And I say it with tears streaming down my face. Thank you everyone at Living Christ Church for when I had my wreck and surgery you brought us food, and Gail and her mom sis young's famous German choc. Cake, wow and the late Mike Smith mows my lawn and so much more, and the choir even came and sung to my wife and I, when I was in the hospital bed that sis. Young and the church gave me, and pastor and His brother Frank Green set it up at my home and Bro. Vance and Bro. Shawn even washed my truck. Love in power and demonstration as in 1 Corinthians 2:4. This church has went to the streets and parks putting their love and heart into it, not just saying words but demonstrating it by actions of love. Thanks church family for everything you've done and do. Just want to say thanks to so many of you that showed us so much love, I love you for all the extra special treatment, and thanks for the prayers and hugs, you'll never know how much you all touched my heart.

To give you an idea of the love I'm talking about, that they showed to us. I love you all. One particular example, Minister James Johnson was taking pictures for one of his magazines and this new preacher member namely me, didn't have a new robe yet, cause I just started going there, back then, which is soon-to-be Ten years ago. Anyway, they had preplanned the photo shoot, and all the ministers had bought themselves previously a new ministers robe for the photo that would go in the ministers voice magazine, and pastor Donahue Green said put my new robe on him...Wow, I cried...that touched me so, if ya look in that magazine, Pastor Green was the only one not wearing a robe...Wow...preferring your brother in action or what.

I was speechless, and said no, I couldn't do that, you all already had this planned out…No…and pastor insisted, wow, I was so impressed with his humility and he always gives the guest speaker his chair. Okay…back to…Well pastor said, put my robe on him and I cried and am still crying about it like the prodigal son. Pastor may never know how greatly touched I was.

Note: Pastor is a very humble man of God and does not like being fussed over but seeing this is my book I can, amen.

But seeing ministers, everyone with a robe on, Pastor Donahue Green preferred his brother in Christ (me) and said put my robe on the new minister Bro. Fred (wow) broke me up inside, wow). He was the only one in the picture without a robe on, and it was his new one he bought just for that occasion. And I've seen this humble man of God give up his seat to many visiting ministers, wow, I never saw this kind of humility till I came to Living Christ Church, where the spirit of God dwells, and where everybody is somebody. Wow, they've all made a super impression to me.

What that act of love did to me and making me feel so much part of the body of Christ, these people of this church and pastor and First Lady Evon Green, really demonstrates the love of God. So when you hear love being preached, I think of here, it's not just words as apostle Paul said in (1 Corinthians 2:4) and my speech and my preaching was not with enticing words of man's wisdom, but in demonstration of the spirit and of power. These folks really live it. This church draws the line away from all racial prejudice barriers of any kind, and if there was (any) church close to perfection this one's it, but I said (close to) but there's no perfect person, according to scripture and people makes the church so there is no perfect church… but I said close to, this would be it. Though we all know there is none righteous, no not one, the Bible says but I'm saying these folks are closer than any I've ever seen in my 70 years on this earth, but we know that when that spirit of the Lord manifests hisself in his saints of God, it's the quickening, of the Holy Spirit, that puts all this in his people, it's Jesus who makes us righteous, but I wanted to stress the fact that it's in full operation here at Living Christ Church.

And I must give the ultimate glory to God, even these willing vessels are willing and yielding and appliable in God's hands, he still gets the glory. Thought I should clarify that. The Bible says, (Romans 3:10), there's none righteous, no not one but what righteousness that is in any is that spirit of the Lord that makes any of us righteous and that spirit of the Lord is in these church folks and this pastor walks in the spirit. Again (Heb. 10:25) is probably the best scripture that tells believers and followers of Christ to go to church, and one good reason is, the pastor has lain before the Lord praying and fasting and studying to get a word from God to give to God's people.

It's getting them to church, that's the trick, no one these days seems to want to go (except on Sunday mornings) but I'm speaking of all churches in general to (The Church) (Rev. 2:7 and 29) The Bible does say in the end time, in the last days, there will be a great (2 Thess. 2:3 falling away...) we are seeing it and we are there, this is that same generation, and many are going for the wrong reasons, number 1 if you are calling yourself a Christian and are hoping to go to heaven, I must tell you, not everyone that says Lord, Lord will go to heaven. (Matt. 7:21–22, Luke 6:46, 2 Chron. 7:14) Some go as going to a social club, and some wise guy wrote a song years ago, "come as you are," so many people feel you can go in shorts or as one woman came in a bikini just to make a statement. "Now at our church," Thank God...

And I believe one day she will get her answer, and he (God) will not be the merciful God then as he is today (Matt. 25:41, Luke 13:27). And I already mentioned, about some award ceremony dinner's for celebrities, or presidential type black tie $100 plate dinners that no one in shorts in many fancy restaurants, you wouldn't even get in the door wearing shorts in many fancy restaurants, or the high dollar black tie dinners so why do people make such a big deal on dressing up and going to church? I wonder what those people will say on Judgment Day when God reads out of the Bible on those scriptures on stubbornness, and rebellion is the sin of witchcraft...or the scriptures on wearing The Right Proper Atire (Matt. 22:11, 12) (Notice verse 2, 1 Tim. 2:9) They won't have a prayer...and you go ahead and get mad, but there are functions and business meetings and even ceremonies, weddings funerals, Dinners in Award Ceremony type with high Officials…that it's black tie, only, some will even rent you a Dinner Jacket, etc., but it's more than just dressing appropriately for God's house versus looking your best at a black-tie dinner with the president at the White House or when you're invited to be on a TV talk show. Most people wouldn't go to either of those dressed just any ol' way like in shorts, no! We would look our best. But it's actually about having the right frame of mind as in Philippians 2:5 and thinking in a godly and holy way: WWJD = "What would Jesus do?" Number 1, you're representing your God and your church in public. Number 2, it's for visitors at church because you're not at the White House but at God's house. And know that on Judgement Day, how you conduct yourself now will be shown on God's big screen then on Judgement Day. If you went to the White House's black-tie dinner dressed up and looking your best in your wedding apparel (1 Cor. 10:22), for example, or even when applying for a job interview. Nowadays people dress better for a boss and to make a good first impression rather than dress nice for God and church. Wow. Read (1st Cor. 10:22) (2nd Cor. 5:11) (2nd Thess. 1:7–12) (Heb. 10:30–31)

Do you not know God's Word says his word will not return to him void, and God's a jealous God, and mankind thinks he/her can dress and act any ol' way and think because it's in a song God is gonna allow it…Many…Many people…will be shocked. When God reads (Matt. 22:11, 12, 13, 14) and does being tossed out into outer darkness sound like this guy made heaven to you, Ha. Don't think so I dare any one to stand before God on Judgement Day and say I'll wear what I want, and do what I want, you're not my Judge? Huh? Are people really that blind and stupid (read 2 Pet. 3:3 to 5) and there are people that reject God's Word and reject God, He'll reject you, also, (1 Sam. 15:23, James 4:17) No, I don't wear a suit every time I go to church, but when I'm preaching I do, even on Sundays, I do, and weekdays I usually dress casual dress, but always appropriate for church, I already mentioned I was an ex-hippy biker drug user, well even then, I knew better, and was taught as a child, proper ways to dress, and act, especially on going to church, we were poor when I was a kid, no we didn't have a suit, but mom would still dress us up in nice clean slacks and dress shirt, in church clothes, but I later rebelled and quit going to church and got in with the wrong crowd.

It took ten years to get back with God, wished I'd have stayed in church. It would have saved me a lot of trouble, but the Bible says, in (Philippians 2:5), "Let this mind be in you that was in Jesus" and to work out our own Salvation with fear and trembling (Phil. 2:12). A preacher once said How you live here and act here, will determine if you make it there, but you must be born again, and follow the Bible. But I'm seeing people that's supposed to be changed (2 Cor. 5:17) and saved, but they still look and act like a devil and are still following the ways of the world. (Matt. 7:16 to 23, Luke 6:46, 1 John 2:15, 2 to verse 17, Pet. 2:9) The Lord knows how to deliver the godly out of temptation, and to reserve the unjust to the day of judgment to be punished. Now, do you really want to disobey God, after reading God's word?

The Lord is not slack concerning his promise, as some men count slackness, but is longsuffering to us ward, not willing that any should perish, but that all should come to repentance (2 Pet. 3:9). On the DAY of Judgment Day, there will be no more time to get right with God.

My whole point on this is, when man's heart is 100 percent right with God, you will know what's right (James 4:17) and what's wrong, and when you read God's Word, you'll receive instruction down to the very core of your soul and you will want to build up your faith (Jude 20, Rom. 10:17) and you will want to please God and do what's right in the sight of God esp. if you know how powerful God really is, and knowing then he'll be damning souls to hell that were evil. (Rev. 2:8) (Heb. 11:5, 6: Heb. 11:24, 25) But evil people, hypocrites, thieves, liars, murderers, cons people who swindle you and trick you, and cheat you, these kind of people are deceiving their own selves, as in (2 Thessalonians 2:10, 11, 12; Eph. 4:14 to 32; 2 Tim. 3:13; Gal. 6:7, 8, 9), but according to the Bible, those that make heaven, will be those who have accepted Jesus Christ as Lord and have repented of all their sins, and read and follow the Bible to the best of their ability. Again, I hope people see and know God is way, way, more advanced in technology than man is, and man has progressed so much he feels he doesn't need God (1 John 2:22, 23) History of time has indeed came full circle back to the place, where God looked down and saw that man was continually wicked (Gen. 6:5, 6; verse 7; Prov. 15:3) and man feels he's okay and does not need to repent (1 John 1:5 to 10, Rev. 16:9 to 11, Rev. 9:20, 21). But that's the whole reason Jesus died on the cross, but man rebels and rejects him…and with man's technology he wants to be a god and create life with his hands by cloning and I just saw on the news, China is now making walking, talking femal robot and female sex dolls, and many of USA scientists have been cloning and experimenting with making test tube babies, etc. (even using aborted fetus's tissue cells in women's makeup and skin creams (called collagen) which again I have mentioned earlier already.

But man wants to take God's place (Isa. 14:12 to 16) and be God, which according to scripture is a spirit of anti-Christ, which reminds me of what Satan told Eve in (Gen. 3:1–6) (1st John 4:1–5) (Isa. 14) (see verse 5) or I should say the devil that has possessed these scientists and doctors which reminds me of the stairway to heaven in the Old Testament (in Gen. 11:1 to 9) called "The Tower of Babel" where men, said to each other, let us make bricks, and a city, and a tower that will reach up to heaven (see verses 3 and 4) and yes today, man is indeed way, way more advanced and way more intelligent than back then, but the evil spirit is still the same ol' devil, that causes man to rebel (Acts 28:25 to 28) and makes him want to rule and be like God. So my question is, what will God do next to man to show these (god wannabes, that he's the only God and the only real creator of life?)

This is that generation, that is ripe and ready for the dictator Anti-Christ, which again history has come full circle, the spirit of rebellion is so rapidly entering the youth today. They don't want God's spirit, just like in Moses Day when he took to long up on the mountain, so they make their own false god, a golden calf idol they made it with their own hands and then they worshipped it, this is why God gave Moses the Ten Commandments (Exod. 20) see (verse 2 and 3 and 4 and 5) Wow, I can understand that, so how come so many millions of intelligent college students, professors, and scientists, and people way more smarter than me don't see this? The Holy Spirit gives us understanding, when we get saved (spiritual understanding is from the Lord, Acts 28:25 to 31, Eph. 2:8, 1 Cor. 2:14) I don't mean to sound self-righteous (I'm not) cause it's by God's mercy and grace any of us is saved.

But the fact remains, that this is that generation that the Anti-Christ is about to reveal hisself in any time now, and people's minds and hearts are turned away from God. As the Bible says, so this tells me our Lord Jesus is about to come, cause before this dictator sets up his seat as the world dictator, as in (2 Thessalonians 2:3 to 13). Jesus will come, cause so many people want a leader, and instead of turning to Jesus, which means they'd have to straighten up and line up with the Bible, they'd rather sin and have fun and follow the devil's puppet the Anti-Christ, everything is now ready, computers, and the whole worlds system has been being changed to adapt over to a-one-world-government with a one world dictator leader that'll be the devil's puppet.

And will announce he's God. Where do we draw the line on who to follow, Jesus Christ, or the anti-Christ? But the world that follows the Anti-Christ, and takes his (Mark 666 chip), will be doomed to hell according to the Bible. And it's obvious they aren't saved. Because when you're saved, you'll follow Jesus (John 10:27) when people sear or override their conscience that God gives us to keep us in line with him (1st Tim. 4:1 and 2), then that is called giving place to the devil or you're yielding to the wrong voice. (Rom. 6:12 to 16, Eph. 4:27) instead of (Rom. 8:11) but if we yield ourselves to God, that same spirit of him that raised Jesus up from the dead would dwell in us, would also quicken us by his spirit (in my words) that means, God does the changing. God does the transforming (Rom. 12:1 and 2, 2 Cor. 5:17) in us, so many want to do the changing in others…It has to be God, or it will not last. Jesus taught these in parables in the four gospels.

But God wants our hearts to be repentive and moldable to him, and to be conformed to God and his word, and not to the world. (Rom. 12:1 and 2). So a sinner man will not follow God cause their heart is not right with God, because when the Heart is sold out and repented...that old man is crucified in the spirit with Jesus Christ, the Bible says the old things passes away, behold "All Things" are become new...Therefore if any man be in Christ, he is a new creature (we are become a new creation by our repented heart, we are changed inside the heart and soul as Jesus taught) once the inside of the cup gets clean the outside follows (in my words). and gets cleaned also (2 Cor. 5:17, Matt. 23:26) Apostle Paul, said in Romans 12:1 we must present our bodies a living sacrifice "Holy," and acceptable unto God, The renewing of the mind comes by studying the Bible and (2 Corinthians 4:16), which is your reasonable service. (it's our responsibility, And be not conformed to this world, but be ye "transformed" by the renewing of your mind (cause our mind and inward man is renewed day by day, as in 2 Corinthians 4:16, that ye may prove what is that good, and acceptable, and perfect, will of God., (Rom. 12:1 to 3, 1 Cor. 10:21), because you cannot drink of the cup of the Lord, and of the cup of devils ye cannot be partakers of the Lord's table, and of the table of devils.

Next (verse 22) says, DO we provoke the Lord to jealousy...Are we stronger than he? In (Luke 6:43, 44), Jesus said, "A tree is known by his fruit." On being real for God...Those who are truly born again and are real true repented Saints...will live forever in heaven John 6:51) When Jesus was stating at their communion, to eat his flesh, etc. Note: Jesus wasn't saying for people of God to become cannibals. No, but to receive his spirit into your heart, but it was definitely a misunderstood analogy, but he was trying to teach them that they need to receive him into their lives, but there were also unbelievers there as well, and they left, thinking he was teaching cannibalism. Now, those intellects religious Pharisees that were well studied in religions and full of the devil, which constantly attacked Jesus and trying to provoke him...and these next eighteen lines are saying, in those days they went to church daily), it kills people nowadays to go to church once a week, wow, but they went daily, and they went there to pray and ask forgiveness and repent of their sins, and they repented of their evil ways, and they followed Jesus, but when those religious Pharisees got up and left, because they thought Jesus was teaching cannibalism, Jesus turned to the twelve disciples, and said, will you also go away…and Peter says, to whom shall we go? You have the words of eternal life (John 6:64 to 70) but Jesus knew from the beginning who would believe on him (in my words).

Or seek him, and no, not just for clothes but the heart (Matt. 6:30–34). See (Matthew 6:33): "But see ye **first** rhe kingdom of God and his **God's righteousness** then all these things shall be added to you." Did you Google what his righteousness is? Study it, and you'll see God wants us to love on him; thank him for our health, food, shelter, etc.—for everything—and give him a hug, spiritually speaking. And yes, I have already discussed this, but following Jesus and seeking God is much more than praying for all your needs (Phil. 4:19). According to (Matthew 6:30–34). especially (verse 33), God wants us to show him and express that we love him first and not just with your mouth but out of your heart. So yes, everyone wants to go to heaven and have eternal life, but have you ever heard or saw in the flower shops the little card that says, "Just because I LOVE YOU"? I've heard this many times and have seen my two daughters do this to me and my wife even on a no-special-occasion day, just a "just because" day. Wow, did that make my day or what? Sometimes it's just a good day with a hug and saying, "Was just thinking about you," wow, don't you think that God melts when we do that to him? Or another good day could be when I get a little phone call from my daughters, both calling at different times and singing a jingle: "I just called to say I love you… I just called to say I care…" Wow, just a jingle with love, but that little two-minute call brightened up my day. And I don't know, for us to do that also to God, yes, he would love it too just like how you like having breakfast or coffee once a month with your two sweet sisters. It makes your day. But back to God's righteousness, he just basically wants us to have a yielding heart of thankfulness to him and not just for salvation, and I would like to challenge you to cross-reference all these words, such as *daily, forgive, repent, fruit, duty, study, hot, cold, lukewarm, filled, full, wise, foolish, vigilant, awake, sober*. I dare ya to look up these words in scriptures, oh sure, it'd take some time, so write them on a post note, and when you do your devotions, look them up, I promise ya, you'll receive some (spiritual) gold nuggets. You tell me, what does God have to do to get us on our knees? (2 Chron. 7:14).

Hebrews 10:25 (in my words) We should be going to church more, especially when you see how much closer the day of Jesus's return is…People's being chipped…With the prophecies in the Bible are unfolding right before our eyes, and now that virus (plague) has caused churches and places of business to be closed, maybe now people will want to go to church (Heb. 10:25) The more you see the day approaching. We are very close. The more you see the day approaching. Some churches are re-opening, yet, crowds are way, way, way down=(a great falling away) (1st Tim. 4:1 and 2nd Thess. 2:3). People are too scared to go, wow, we are getting so close to the Lord's return this is why (Rev. 3:18) says anoint your eyes to see, the end time is here esp. with churches on line now, it's becoming a lazy church. Staying at home because of fear, but we must be careful not to enter into a no effort to seek God attitude having a form (2nd Tim. 3:5)=a (spirit of complacity type attitude), we must always pray for a new desire and a new hunger and thirst for righteousness, according to the Bible. Look up in webster's dictionary the Laodicean Church, and it even gives you the scripture in the blooming dictionary.

Wow, so if you look up this one, the dictionary even gives us the scriptures, telling us to not be lukewarm, or complacent in our souls or we'll be spit out, if you spit out something that's soured, bitter etc. that means it's not welcome in your mouth to go into your belly, this analogy is in essence saying, if someone's bitter, cause of slackness or no desire or has a sour attitude, or ugly heart, etc. God will…differently according to (Rev. 3:16) not welcome you into his mouth=heaven, but will kick you out of heaven=spue=spit you out (Rev. 3:15–20) you need to stay ready.

Up till Jesus Christ's coming (Luke 21:27 and 28, 1st Thess. 4:13 to 18, 1st Cor. 15:50 to 58, Rev. 4:1 and 2) (Luke 4:16, Rapture, Notice in verse 16, it says, it was Jesus' custom to go to (the synagogue) church, Luke 4:16) Yes, Jesus went to church, the disciples also went to the temple "continually"…Oh preacher, you mean on Easter and Christmas, and Mother's Day? No, continually (Acts 2:46, Luke 24:53). Wow.

So our old man is crucified with Christ, then when your repented to a new creature, you will live forever, since I was a kid, I remember movies that spoke of a fountain of youth, that people wished they could find and drink, and live forever, yet, they have over looked what the Bible says, about being born again, and live forever, but they don't want to follow the rule book (called the Bible). (Matthew 4:4) says, "It is written; Man shall not live by bread alone, but by **every word=(Bible)** that proceeds out of the mouth of God." (Romans 15:4) and (1ˢᵗ Cor. 10:11) (2ⁿᵈ Tim. 3:14–17) and see (2ⁿᵈ Peter 1:20–21) Jesus then said this scripture to the devil, saying, **"Man must live by every word** that comes out of God's mouth." The Holy Bible is the authentic **Word of God**, but does the majority of the world live by it and follow it? No, but this is where you get the actors and those with a form of godliness (2 Tim. 3:5) but deny the power thereof. They look, dress, and act like, in my words, from such turn away. Wow. (Read Mark 7:6.) And it's all because they don't want to live right, which is living by every word that comes out of God's mouth, and it's all because they can't let go of sin! (John 6:58, 59). Note the word "ever" in (verse 58 in Romans 6:1 to 23, Romans 11:4, Romans 12:1 to 3).

(Matthew 26:55 to 56) (John 6:58, John 6:51) in (verse 58), these verses are not saying be a cannibal, but Jesus was giving his body—his flesh—on the cross. And if we receive Christ, the bread of life, in our hearts, we shall live forever, but not just Jesus alone but Jesus and the Word of God. Also see (John 1:1–2) again along with (Matthew 4:4 and John 6:63). The key word from (John 6:58) is "live forever," those who receive Jesus will live "for-ever"! And the keyword in (Matthew 26:55) is "daily" (many scriptures say they went "daily" to the temple (Acts 5:42) (Mark 14:49) (Luke 19:47) He (Jesus) taught daily in the temple) people then had more of a spiritual hunger and a deeper inside desire to worship and seek God. Maybe that's why they saw and received more miracles (Acts 4:30 and 31) they were all filled with the Holy Ghost. (Matt. 5:6, Blessed are those that hunger and thirst after righteousness, for they shall be filled.

Note: (And folks whine to go to church on Sundays what will they say to Jesus on Judgment Day. Oh, you died for nothing. Why would (Jesus) want to come and get you and take you to heaven for acting like that, we should say…"Thank you, Jesus, for the price you paid on the cross (1 Cor. 6:20), and for dying for our sins, so we could live forever with you in heaven," cause if people really deep down, really want to go to heaven, they would follow the roadmap, which is the Bible and the examples of the disciples and follow Jesus…and go to church as much as humanly possible. Sure, things come up…and yes, things happen, but most folks today just don't want to go, they "want to" rest, they "want to" watch the game.

They "want to" go shopping: my ol' pastor used to say they just need to get their ("want to") fixed…then God'll give you a new desire to "want to" ("seek ye first the kingdom of God," Matt. 6:33; John 14:6) Even in the Book of Psalms we read many, many scriptures of dwelling in the house of the Lord forever. (Ps. 23:6, Ps. 84:4, Ps. 42:4, Ps. 27:4, Ps. 122:1, Ps. 65:4) but I really like (Luke 24:53) says: were continually in the temple…wow, or (Hebrew 10:25), which is even better: "not forsaking the assembling of ourselves together, as the manner of some is, but exhorting one another, and so much more as ye see the day approaching…" "What Day?" (I believe it's saying the closer we get to the day of the coming of Jesus Christ) (Rapture). so we should gather together at church or…Hey we've had get togethers with the Lord and family and friends from church at home and brought out the guitar and everyone would sing and have church right at home. (At church or home, if God's in it, you'll be blessed because we've had church at home on times of barbecues and get-togethers, and singing those old gospel hymns that really touch my hearts, and so now that churches are closed down, we can do it again and we have been, at a safe distance of course, but maybe just maybe, God will burn it in people's hearts not to take the opportunity of going to church for granted anymore! Amen.

And when churches does start having services again, they'll probably be as it was in Bible days, because I believe what the Bible says, where Peter stood and said to the people gathered together, in (Acts 2:17), saying: "And it shall come to pass in the Last Days, saith

God, I will pour out of my spirit upon all flesh: and your sons and your daughters shall prophesy, and your young men shall see visions, and your old men shall dream dreams." And *now* you may see this done one more time before Jesus returns back to take his bride (the church) away (in the rapture) cause God has to have a prepared and ready people that's truly rapture ready=(a repented prayed up church.) I believe the Bible, and I believe that if all this virus plague stuff, that has happened, doesn't get people stirred up and prayed up, then what will, but I believe people's spiritual eyes are being opened, and many people are waking up spiritually in the spirit, and as scripture says, those that are gonna go, will be ready (Rev. 19:7, Luke 12:40) and those that aren't, will stay the way they are (Rev. 22:11) and they'll be left here to go through hell on Earth, in the three and a half years of Great Tribulation, when all hell of God's wrath is being poured out on a disobedient people cause people fail to read (2 Thessalonians 1:8 and 9 see verses 10, 11, 12, Ephesians 5:6). (John 3:36, 1 Thess. 1:10, Rom. 1:18, Rev. 22:6 to 12, Rev. 19:7 and 8, Rev. 6:16 and 17, Rev. 16:19; 1 Thess. 5:9, John 3:16 to 21.) Because if people really deep down, really want to go to heaven, they'd follow the road map that explains how to get there, which is (the Bible). John 3:16, 17, 18, John 14:6).

Mark 14:49 (daily)
Luke 19:47 (daily)
Acts 2:46–47 (daily)
Acts 17:11 (Search the scriptures daily)
Acts 14:1
Isaiah 2:3 (Many and many more)
Matthew 6:33 (Seek ye first)
Psalm 27:4: Key word (desire) and all the days of my life.
Psalm 23:6: I will dwell in God's house key word is "forever."
Psalm 84:4: Blessed are they that dwell in thy house.
Psalm 122:1: I was glad when they said unto me, let us go into the house of the Lord.
Psalm 134:1–2: Lift up your hands in the sanctuary.
Micah 4:2: Keyword is "he will teach us."
Luke 24:53: Keyword is "continually."

Look up these: The word *church* is spoke of in many different names...like "House of the Lord" or "Temple," or synagogue, sanctuary. And many times "church services" were where a bunch of people gathered together in an open meadow, etc. (or on the side of a mountain as in (Matthew 5:1, 2). Beach...Jesus would teach out in a boat and the people were gathered on the shore (Luke 5:3; Matt. 13:1, 2, 3; Luke 13:26; Matt. 5:1, 2, sermon on the mount).

(2nd Timothy 2:15) says to study, so here's you some homework. Google pleasing God or approved. Again, if we really plan on going to heaven we will study and follow the road map Bible (2 Tim. 2:15).

Note: A true sign of revival is seeing people wanting to go to church, the word, "Revival" means to revive and bring back to life. Yet so many say, you can't backslide, and yet, the Bible says God is married to the backslidder (Jer. 3:14, Rom. 1:20 and 21, Darkened is the opposite of light, in Heb. 4:1). Why would this text say any of you should seem to come short of? If Christians could never backslide? So this is why we need to study the Bible instead of studying-false religions that say you can't backslide when the Bible says you can, or again why does (Rev. 3:5) say, some names can be blotted out, unless they (repent, see verse 3) overcome! Or (Revelations 2:4 and 5), because you left your first love=backsliding...or again (Matt. 25) The five foolish got left behind. And why are there so many scriptures on repent if no one can backslide? Yes...I'm repeating-This repenting and backsliding topic (Heb. 4:13, all things are naked and open before God) and Prov. 15:3. The eyes of the Lord are in every place beholding the evil and the good. Honest to God, there will be no excuses excepted on Judgment Day (Rom. 1:20 and 21) according to (Luke 14, Heb. 9:27 Heb. 10:27, 1 Pet. 4:17 and 18, Jude 15, Rom. 1:20, 21, Luke 6:46, Heb. 2:3).

Okay, moving on, I want to point out (Romans 8:2, Ps. 37:37) mark the perfect man and behold the upright for the end of that man in peace.

Please note: (Romans 8:2, Romans 8:11) that our righteousness is that spirit of the Lord that dwells in our hearts when we have repented the Bible says, to let your light (God's righteousness) shine before men that they will see your good works and glorify your father which is in heaven. (Matt. 5:16). And that is my point, allowing the spirit to shine and flow through you and people see it like the glow that was on Moses, face and Stephen's (Acts 6:15, 2 Cor. 3:13, 14, 15, 16, 2 Cor. 3:7 and 1 Cor. 6:19, 20).

Again, I repeat myself. Because when you spend time with God, it shows on you. I have seen people with that Glow of God. Even though trouble may make you feel like you're in a lion's den, remember, Daniel was preferred above the others because of his excellent spirit in him, and that's because he prayed three times a day and I truly believe those lions even sensed it and saw it (Dan. 6:3 to 24).

When you spend quality time in God's presence it will definitely show, you won't have to try and show it. Others will see the glory of God on you. No…not of yourself. It's the gift of God, lest any man should boast (Eph. 2:8–9), I think of Moses when they put the vail over his face, when people are living in sin they want to cover your light of Jesus's glow on your face. And it bugs and convicts them, and makes them feel uncomfortable, and makes them uneasy, but (2 Cor. 4:3 and 4) says, if our Gospel be hid it is hid to them that are lost and under conviction (in my words) as in (John 8:9), (Romans 8:1). In (Exod. 34:35), the gift of God, from John 3:16 is the same Lord Jesus, who appeared as an angel, and that walked inside the fiery furnace with the three Hebrew children and in the fiery bush with Moses and was never burnt or singed, nor even smelt like smoke. (Wow, Exodus 3:2, Dan. 3:25, 27) People many times want to cover your light, I seen many devils in some that even try and provoke you, because they are so uncomfortable around the presence of God on your countenance. That's why they wanted to put a vail over Moses face and there's Stephen and Daniel also.

Stephen, just before his death in (Acts 6:15), says he had an angelic look in his face, it was the glory of God and in (Daniel 6:3), the Bible says Daniel was preferred above the presidents and princes because of an excellent spirit was in him.

Wow…so when someone appears righteous or holy, it's not their carnal flesh and blood that your seeing that makes them appear righteous and holy but the radiant force, of the spirit of God in them that was the same force shown out of that burning bush, that such a radiant force of power inside the bush and furnace of fire and light, so powerful to see and look with such amazement, yet notice. (The Bible says in Hebrews 12:29 God is a consuming fire.) Yet so gentle, because of being in God's presence and notice, fire that can burn, yet, when that force of God is present, his Spirit becomes like a force field of protection around his people, and God can deliver his people without them being burnt, like when God told Moses, you can look at my back, but you can't look at my face and live. (Exodus 33:20 to 23) but God told Moses I will protect you with my hand as I pass by you (Wow, what love) and a love that's so great, that God himself would leave heaven, and take on the form of a human man, to suffer and die on a rugged cross for the sins of us all (John 3:16) is that love, or what, cause if God wanted to be mean and awry, he could have said, I'm not gonna die on that cross. But a lot of these were done and written so people like us down through the years, later, could say God is the same yesterday. Today and forever (Heb. 13:8) He's still powerful, yet he's still full of love and compassion, still saves people out of their lion's dens and fiery furnaces, or get you a job or gets you out of jail or the hospital, etc.

And who can forget the three Hebrew children in the fire, yet also in the presence of the Lord and yet, the flame didn't hurt them as the lion's didn't hurt Daniel cause of the presence of the Lord that excellent spirit inside him. Don't you think otherwise for a minute that even animals' pick-up the presence of the Lord in you…oh yes, they do. If God allowed those lions to see that same type fire in Daniel as in the bush with Moses and allowed the lions to see the same "fiery Spirit." Come on, people. The holy ghost and fire in us (Heb. 1:7 and Ps. 104:4). I'm reminded of a funny story, I worked at an appliance factory years ago, I wanted to witness to them so at the smokers table I pulled up a chair, and right off, this smart mouth lady says, hey, you're a pastor why are you sitting at the smokers table, I said, you never read Hebrews 1:7 that God makes his ministers a flame of fire, and fills them with the Holy Ghost and Fire. Ha. It got so quiet, I don't think she said another word, HA. Anyways the Holy Ghost in us is gonna light you up. Hallelujah! As in (Matthew 5:16). Again, it's his glory not ours. We are just the candle and he is the flame. Wow. When you really think on this in depth. (Matthew 3:11–12). That Holy Ghost and fire, that fire if allowed will burn out the chaff (junk) the bad thinking (Heb. 12:1, 2). And God will help you lay those weights aside. The fire purifies your soul.

So many people agree when letting fire under the grill on for five hundred degrees or more for a while, agree that the fire kills, and burns off any bacteria and I've seen so many just throw their steak on, but as we need to let the fire on the grill burn off the germs and bacteria, then scrap it with a wire brush, then I go with a wet cloth, and wipe off the burnt charcoal dust, so the grill is clean and not on my steak, and God does this same type process, when the Holy Ghost and fire comes in people's lives and the Bible says, He burns off the Junk chaff. This is where I really question people that still live in sin, and still smoke, still get drunk, etc. No way. They are not even saved (2 Cor. 5:17). Cause the Holy Ghost Fire burns that stuff out of you, when you get saved, cause God's spirit will not dwell in an unclean temple (1 Cor. 3:16 and 17, 1 Cor. 6:14 to 20, 1 Cor. 10:20 and 21).

One said to me, the fire has purified and sterilized the grill, why do you wipe it and I say the wet wash cloth wipes off the ash excess, I don't want that on my meat and I truly believe God's that way with us as the holy ghost and fire burns off the chaff, sin and the junk out of our hearts. Purifying our minds in the spirit, then wipe us clean, removes all excess, (John 11:39). Removing all debris, (verse 40), and God will show us all when Jesus changes death to life on that met-a-mor-pho-sis type res-ur-rec-tion day, when Jesus raptures up all his saints (Rev. 4:1 and 2, 1st Thess. 4:13 to 18, 1st Cor. 15:50 to 58) (Please Note:) In the book of John's gospel, the 11 chapter, in (verse 39), Jesus first removed the obstacles in between Jesus and Lazarus=the bolder was blocking the way between Jesus and Lazarus, and Jesus said take away the stone, then Jesus thanks God for hearing him (verse 41) and in verse 43, he (Jesus) speaks life back into dead Lazarus (1 Pet. 3:22, Matt. 8:27, Col. 1:16, Eph. 3:9) calling him back from the dead, and he'll do it again to those who have called on him for salvation, many people think being a partier, or a drunk is really living, wrong, that's dying. But being ready and making it to heaven, that's living forever.

Again, Jesus purifies our minds, our hearts by his spirit, then you shine from the glory of God. Again it's like the barbecue grill… And it's gonna show on your countenance and if your using a wet white cloth to wipe off the grill's residue in front of company, that may be watching you clean your grill, then they to will be amazed at all of the residue ash that the hot purifying fire left, and it really shows good on a white wet cloth. Wow and I say that junk would have ended up in your belly and again, I believe God is like that and wants to not just purify us with his fire but God also removes all the residue. God told Moses that he would even protect him from himself with his own hand while he passed by him because God is a consuming fire (Heb. 12:29, Deut. 4:24, Deut. 9:3, Exod. 33:20, 21, 22, 23). And according to John 15, purging us clean. So we'll be clean and fill us full of joy.

So the fire purifies us, and in (John 15) through the word (verse 3), says we are clean through the word. And in (John 7:37, 38, 39) says, out of your belly shall flow rivers of living water.) (Spiritually speaking) Again this is why I don't like other versions, this scripture says out of your belly shall flow rivers (The Bible says) the devil comes to steal kill and destroy (John 10:10) so the word rivers, are usually a good heavy flow of water (look it up). one translation, NIV says streams, taking away from God's Word, a stream a trickle that won't hose anyone's soul out, but God's mighty rushing wind (Acts 2:2) and rivers of living water, will hose out your soul, and that Holy Ghost and fire will burn off the chaff. Hallelujah (John 7:37, 38, Matt. 3:11, 12). Remember in John 13:4–8, Jesus after supper, came to Peter and the disciples, Jesus humbling himself before the disciples and washes their feet. Wow, and Jesus came to Peter and Peter says. No, you're not gonna wash my feet, then Jesus said, if I don't wash you, you have no part with me. (Wow) so what's that saying to all these Mr. Cools, Mr. Attitudes with the cool walk, and the ear rings and the proud look, and the "Yo-dude" talk and still being Mr. Bad! No. Brother, No! You have to let the Master Potter (Jesus) take out those bad lumps out of your clay = life, brother, remember he's (God)

the Potter (Rom. 9:21–22, Jer. 18:2–6) we are the clay. And if you
don't let and allow him to remold and change you. As he said to Peter,
He'll say to you, either I wash you clean or you have no part with me,
there are even some church folks that have too much pride to humble
down and wash your feet. In (John 13:3–17), please read (verse 15)
very carefully, especially if you're into bodybuilding, full of pride for
yourself, and really into your physique and how you always look in
the mirror. Oh, sure, everyone shaves, combs their hair, etc., but I'm
referring to a constant over-the-extreme overall continually looking
and flexing to see where you have to get bigger muscles. It's no longer
just wanting to be in shape; it's now become a pride thing. And with
walking around shirtless, where you think you're so big and so bad,
and you're so full of yourself with what you've accomplished (1 Cor.
10:12; Prov. 21:4; 6:17) in addition to you thinking you're almost
indestructible—all of these types of thinking and acting is the wrong
spirit. It's a prideful way of thinking, which shows an Antichrist heart
and an Antichrist spirit, not a Christlike spirit (Phil. 2:5). Again,
there's nothing wrong with taking care of yourself in moderation. It's
the extreme—going overboard with it—that gets you in trouble with
God, and back in old Bible days, God destroyed such and even called
them a brute beast (read 2 Peter 2:12) because God wants us to be
more involved in him than ourselves (Matt. 6:33, Phil. 2:5–8, 1 Tim.
4:7–8). Again, pridefulness is the opposite of humility. I have never
in my life seen a bodybuilder that's humble, no, not ever. They are all
proud and arrogant, and think more highly of themselves (Romans
12:1–3, Gal. 5:15–22) than they should. Again, these human flesh-
and-blood bodies **are not** going to heaven but will be changed into
a heavenly body as it says in in (1st Corinthians 15:50–54.) (See
verse 50): "Flesh and blood **cannot inherit the kingdom of God**"!
Again, has any buffed-up dude ever read these scriptures? Probably
not (1 Tim. 4:7–8). Have you ever wondered why most real huge
buff bodybuilders die so young (you can Google it) (those extreme
ones especially)? Anyway, it's sad that they work at it so hard, only to
die so young, just to look good. But my main number one point in
this was the macho ego and the attitude these guys have. And those
that have that type of attitude **will not go to heaven**! Because that's

the opposite of humble (John 13:3–17 [see verses 15, 17, 34, and 35 specifically], 2 Chron. 7:14). That cool dude would never wash a brother's feet.

In the natural mind, we scratch our heads, but putting on the mind of Christ, we cast down our carnal imaginations.

In (2 Corinthians 10:3–6; Philippians 2:5; 1 Corinthians 2:14), our old man our old sinful nature, in no way, would come in, and stoop down and wash some other brothers feet (no way), but in the Christian world, the Christians follows Jesus Christ's examples in (John 13:15, John 13:4 to 8) because that's humbleness-a spirit of love-that only comes from God, but again the Mr. Joe cool can't, cause he's too cool, and being too proud to humble himself. That's why the Bible says those types "will not have no part with Jesus" in heaven! ("Read it"! John 13:8 through 15) Jesus gave us an example that we have to follow, and we have to learn how to humble ourselves before others, or we won't make heaven. In fact, when was the last time you saw a feet-washing service at a local church? I've been in some, many, many years ago, and those type services were awesome. But you hardly see them anymore. So are church people getting too prideful? Yes, many are. If you want to truly reflect the love of Jesus Christ, then try it. Yes, even church folks need to practice being humble, but there are little keys to the good ones. You start saying, "Lord, if I've offended this child of Gods in any way, please forgive me in Jesus's name," "Lord, bless this child of God up one side and down the other," etc. while washing their feet. At this one church I pastored, we used a fragrance soap with lotion afterward, making it special, and we had hymn music in the background. It was an awesome service. God really blessed us.

Wow…and that comes through prayer and reading and following the Bible, and we must allow the new man through repentance prayers to come in and let go of the old ways so the Holy Ghost can do the work in our heart, we just have to let him in and let the Holy Ghost do the work in our hearts, and give him the steering wheel of our life, and allow God to guide and direct our lives. God wants our hearts and minds to be on him, and not on sinful things (Isa. 26:3) then we'll have peace, and God wants to live and flow in us like a gushing Gyser, so let's review, I know it may sound crazy...but it's in the Bible...on one point. God wants to burn off all the chaff junk, crud that's not godly...then God wants to hose out your soul with the water of his word cleansing us and washing away our sins with the blood of Jesus (Rev. 1:5). This is why it's crucial to know God's Word as Psalm 119:11. Hide it in your heart so you won't sin against God, and the Holy Ghost will bring it back to your memory...checking you.

Our flesh, our old man, if we are not cutting away the old flesh from the new man in Christ. Being spiritual circumcised, (Colossians 2:11–15), it's called circumcise (spiritually speaking). We allow the holy spirit to cut away our old fleshly desires for the spirit man to be able to clean us up and put in new desires and we ask God (Ps. 51 from verse 1 to 13) and then once our lives are cleaned up then God can use us to win souls for God (verse 13). Read (Psalm 139:23 and 24). Wow, let's pray that psalm. So, so many times you see people that are not cleaned up in heart and they've not fully left the old life. I heard my pastor say once, you are either pregnant or you're not, you can't be half way. (Great Analogy Pastor Green) And this life with Christ in us is the same way (Matt. 12:30) we can't be half way. There is no lukewarm, it's either hot or cold.

In (Revelations 3:2 to 19, notice verse 15 and 16), a cold-hearted person God can still deal with and save and a hot hearted person has what they need in their soul but a lukewarm person that is not on either side is on dangerous ground of being spit out. "there is no middle ground with God, you are for him or you are against him (Luke 11:23) your either hot or cold. Hot born-again spirit-filled) is a participator, gets in and follows Jesus Christ all the way, and reads and lives like the Bible says. But the cold unsaved-sinner, that needs to be saved, that God can still deal with. But lukewarm is someone that just goes to church and doesn't sing, don't pray or listen, just daydreams and their very bored, They don't join in to the worship service...They are there in body...only. But wishing they were somewhere else. And they only go to the morning service like they are doing God a big favor by being there. That's lukewarm, half-heartedness (Ps. 57:7, Ps. 119:2). Seek the Lord with (your) whole heart.

(verse 10, Ps. 119:10). And some are worse, they'll perform a phony act...but it's obvious their hearts not in it. Read what Jesus told the Pharisees when they put on a phony act (Matt. 23:14). Isn't it strange that God is gonna punish the phonie actors, the non-real, the hypocrites that just act like their saved but really deep down aren't, but will burn hotter in hell than anyone else! Read it! But put 'em out at their favorite sports event.

It's written all through the word, yet there are so many false religions out there that don't want to be a fanatic, or someone extremely overboard, why? Have you ever noticed these are the same type at the football games, painting themselves for their team, supporting the morale and cheering on the game, A game (I don't get it.) People are dying and going to hell, we Christians are called fanatics cause we get excited when someone gets saved from going to hell, And we cheer and Praise God for saving their soul, cause we ourselves was also going there before we got saved...Our cheer and praise is real, and for God, and they are cheering for a guy running with a ball, for a game, or for a sport...painting themselves for their team, and they call spirit-filled Christians like me a fanatic and a extreme-ists... wow...I don't paint my body for Jesus, but I am considered worse than that. But isn't that being a football fanatic. Ouch. Please, don't misunderstand me, there's nothing wrong with the game. But don't you see, God wants us to be that tenacious and fanatical for him, then on Judgment Day.

When people stand before God an give an account of their life which of the two fanatics do you think he'll admire the most? (hmm) A game versus doing your all for God, winning souls for God, going to church, reading and studying the Bible, and following it to the letter with that loud bunch of fiery fanatics. Honey, if you don't like loud, as ol' Shambock used to say, you're not gonna want to go to hell. It will be loud screaming there, and the Bible says there's gonna be only thirty minutes of silence in heaven. Hey, then the hallelujahs roar. Hey, there's no in between. Man if you are that one that thinks like the lukewarm people, about going to heaven, that it's okay to be on the fence, and you think you are okay to be lukewarm, yet, your overboard in other things.

Friend, you have a big surprise coming. And frankly I hope you get right and I hope you make it. And please don't say. Don't judge me because I'm not, but the Bible is! Because, I know my Bible. And it says, God is a jealous God! And you're either a new creature in Christ and old things (your old ways) pass away, and you become a new creature (creation) in Jesus Christ. (Or you're not, 2 Cor. 5:17, Exod. 20:5, Deut. 5:9, 2 Cor. 11:2–3.) My brother Cpl. Alan E. Davis, that was killed in the Vietnam war, and he said back when we were kids, "Why, do you get in the water so slow. Just dive in, you'll get used to the water, quicker, he gave me fits over sticking my toe in rather than just get all the way in right away, and now I learned even living for God to just get in, all the way, so even on living for God, Hey, Dive in with all you got! The Bible says love God with all your heart (Matt. 22:35 through 40) with your whole heart, the psalmist even wrote my heart is fixed (Ps. 108:1; Ps. 57:7; Ps. 111:1; Ps. 119:2 and 10; Ps. 9:1; Ps. 14:2; Col. 3:1, 2; Jer. 29:13; Ps. 78:36, 37; Rev. 3:4 to 18).

Do any of you think that it says anywhere in the Bible, just live for God like you want, dress like a slut, act like a prostitute, show off your hooters to everyone in church, you're not at a club or a bar, you will answer to God for your loose looking inappropriate appearance in Church looking and having a Jezebel appearance. You're supposed to reflect God not the devil. And be separated from the world. No I'm not your judge, but I know my Bible. This is what I'm saying all through my book. "Where do you draw the line?" on living for God, I see so many hanging onto the old life, now as an experienced minister and Christian. I gave God my all, when I got saved. I let the old life of parting Go, no more women, etc. People that are Christians are supposed to have come out from the world and come away from our old lifestyles and be a separated people of God. (2nd Corinthians 6:17, 2 Corinthians 6:14) even tells you to stay away from the old crowds, and "not to be unequally yoked together (when this passage of scripture was written, they used "yokes" to team up a team of oxen, or horses together to plow a field.

But some, like a mule, would only work with a horse. You couldn't team up two mules together (they are too stubborn, Ps.

32:9). Don't you be stubborn like a mule! And this is why the scripture was taken from the same aspect as, two mules cannot be yoked
together, cause nothing would get done, so you yoke a horse with a
mule, and so the analogy goes, you don't be yoked up with unbelievers or sinners (2 Cor. 6:14 to 17), cause they will try to pull you back
out in to your old ways, and I speak from experience, four different
times, the devil sent old parting buddies, my way, but God had previously gave me some warning dreams, and in the dreams I died and
went to hell, so if the Bible says not to, then stay with God's people
and stay in church. And keep away from the Old partiers, cause two
mules would just duke it out. No work would get done, the same
way applies to the old partiers firen up a Doobie, and drinking a beer,
and witnessing to another partier nothing would be accomplished.
People that want to hang on to the worldly life and don't want to
leave their old partying lifestyle need to read (Luke 17:32, 9:62; 2
Corinthians 5:17, Hebrews 12:1–2, and Romans 12:1–2). A perfect
example is people are getting doctors to say it's okay for them to
smoke medical pot. Again, if it was sin in my day, it's still sin today. I
don't care who you are or how many doctors say it's okay! My cancer
doctor told me that pot and cigarettes both gave me cancer. Oh, you
really think that it's still okay? Well, what if I told you that you too
are gonna get cancer? Hello… (The Bible says we reap what we sow.)
Well, go ahead, you can have it all. (God made a believer out of me.)
Some folks have to learn the hard way (hee-haw). So you didn't really
read (Psalm 32:9)? The whole reason I write them down is to give
you proof and ammo against the devil, but if you're on a battlefield
with the enemy soldiers closing in on you fast and your gun is empty,
don't be like a child with your mouth and go, "Bang, bang, pow, pow,
you're dead." No, you'll be the one dead, so lock and load your spiritual gun with those ammo scriptures I gave you. They just my keep
your butt from going to hell. Amen. Sorry for my crude analogy, but
isn't it better for me to tell ya to not be like a mule than have God
tell ya when it's too late? (Please reread this page.) So, friend, why is
it that **no two donkeys can work together**?

Because no work'd get done, so you don't unequally yoke
together wrong animals, but Paul was using this analogy to show

us spiritually don't be unequally yoked with unbelievers (and that's no yoke! (Ha.) or two stubborn bull headed, donkeys, ha (Ps. 32:9). Because the day of Jesus's return has got to be soon, the crime and the evil in the world has escalated so much, okay, repeating myself (again.) But if people really want to make heaven, they will change, and allow God to remold them. But they are still committing adultery and fornicating, no change not even understanding scripture (2 Cor. 5:17) or (Mk 2:22). People going to church for years and still live like the devil himself. And some sinner going through hell wanting a change in his life, looks and sees a half-hearted hypocrite living a double life and thinks well if that's a Christian's life then I'm okay, so the devil plants the Judas's and the Ananias's and Achans in the lives of New Christians to lure them to a life of hypocrisy, but we are to pattern our life after Jesus Christ and even the apostles and disciples, and we can see that they were also human, I've stuck my foot in my mouth, like ol' Peter, many times, and in front of the whole church, I've repented with my shoe in my hand, saying this goes in my mouth, honest, and I ask your forgiveness, we must humble ourselves or the Bible says, either we humble ourselves or God will for us (see) (Luke 18:10 to 14) (James 4:10 see verse 6 to 10) (1st Pet. 5:5, 6) or for the macho fighters and bullies kinda people (read Matt. 18:23–35).

And believe you me, it's better on us, if we humble ourselves than God humble us (Matt. 23:12) (even Apostle Paul). we see he was angry and fell short with Barnabas and Johnmark, the contention was so sharp they had to part company (Acts 15:38 and 39) sometimes in order to keep the peace, it's best to humble ourselves and just walk away, as Apostle Paul did here, so everyone is human, and everyone falls short in some way or another. We just have to be the bigger Christian and have (Christlike love) and ask forgiveness from God and them, and go on. I've even repented to people, but they was the one that should have come to me, and they were the one at fault, and they never did admit they did wrong, but, my hearts clean, and the balls in their guilty conscience's court. You just gotta keep the monkey off your back, and keep your nose clean with God also. Amen. Just do what Jesus did, He forgave, and loved, you may have to cut all ties off to them, like Apostle Paul, and that's okay, pray for them.

I had to sever some that I associated with, but I will not fellowship with people who gossips about me to others after I helped them like Apostle Paul did and just love them from a distance. Some people just won't change (2 Cor. 11:13:15, verse 12, Acts. 5, Mark 14:21). The people that don't live it, shouldn't preach it, you've heard the old saying…practice what you preach…well it's pretty close to being biblical (1 Cor. 9:14, 1 Cor. 9:27, Luke 6:41 and 42 to 46, mote, means speck or splinter).

Anyone can say they are Christians. Anyone can go to church and act like one. I can stand in my garage with car parts hanging on strings all over my body, even making sounds like a car, sounds like, looks like, being in a garage does that really make me a car?

No…if God could get everyone that goes to church all the way in, we would see a move of God in our nation as never before as in (Acts 2), one mind and one accord as in (Matthew 18:19) or in (Philippians 2:5.)

Where do we draw the line in serving God, in living for God?

It's written in scripture, the so-called religious Pharisees, mocked those that were fanatics. Speaking in tongues (Acts 2:13) praising God, worshipping. They didn't understand because their hearts weren't right. (First Corinthians 2:14), they even wanted to kill Jesus and did. And Jesus said the time will come they'll think their doing God service by killing you (John 16:2). That's today friend. They don't want deliverance, you see when one is delivered and set free and changed, born again, and spirit-filled. They don't want to party and get drunk anymore, they tasted a new spiritual kind of wine, the holy ghost's wine. Once you've drunk out of Jesus's cup you don't want to drink anymore from the devil's cup (1 Cor. 10:21). That's pretty plain. Yet verse 9, they also over look God don't then nor now put up with it.

And verse 11, those things happen for our examples, and for our learning (Rom. 15:4) and (John 15:19, Rom. 11:4), God has seven thousand that have not bowed the knee to Ba-al, compare this meaning of the amount of people on the Earth. Seven thousand is just a few (now). In the last census took in 2017 there were reported to be 7.53 billion people on Earth, and you can figure a few more born in a couple more years now but, apostle Paul said the Lord had seven thousand that has not bowed the knee to Ba-al. (comparing the two, it sure looks like there are more people living for the devil) than for God, which also explains many are called but only a few are chosen as in (Matthew 22:14, John 10:16, Romans 9:25 to 28, John 14:2), (many mansions-many occupants) but I'm sure the amount of people on the earth was much, much less in apostle Paul's Day. But my point is again, it's the sin that blinds people, and the pleasure and, the world has come full circle.

The same evil and the same wickedness and corruptive spirit-in-man that was in Sodom, and in Noah's Day is back here again, and God is again about to pour out his wrath upon this evil world, and it will be according to what scripture says, which is the end of human existence on Earth (Matt. 24:37 to 39, 2 Thess. 1:7 to 10, 2 Pet. 2:1 to 14) but before the final destruction of earth, God has told man in his word, there will be three and a half years of Great Tribulation that those left behind, will go through plagues and horrible events, which is God's great wrath (of the last three and a half years) poured out on those who disobeyed him (God) but the first three and a half years of the seven years are called Tribulation, which is God's warnings' that the final destruction is coming, and for everyone to get ready, and to watch and pray (Luke 21:34, 35, 36, Matt. 24:15, Matt. 24:21, 22, Matt. 24:29, Rev. 2:22, Rev. 16:17 to 21) so the ones I would call the godly few the Christians, the righteous, the wise virgins, as in Matthew 25 will already be gone with Jesus (1 Thess. 5:9, Matt. 25:10 to 13) Wow, that's pretty plain to me, but it's only gonna be a few, it's not cause people say they are God's children and still cuss and party and get drunk, etc. (Matt. 24:44 to 51) but how many is a few to you? Again, comparing the whole world's population (to those ready) no not judging, just lining up with what the Bible says even how people are to live! Cause I'm seeing even some say that say they are Christians, but haven't circumcised their old ways and old lifestyles, we can't still live-in sin and I know no one's perfect, we all fall short, but I'm referring to literally continuing to LIVE IN SIN!

(1 Cor. 3:16 to 17, 1 Cor. 6:19). This is only just a few thousand, apostle Paul says in Romans 11:4 that doesn't bow or live like the rest of the world in sin! (1st John 2:15, 16) But a very few, the Bible says, many are called but a few are chosen (Matt. 20:16). (1st Corinthians 6:20), the price was paid for all. (John 3:16 yet read verses 17, 18), you always hear folks quote even children, quote verse 16. God so loved the world…but you never hear the next two verses, in (verse 17) For God sent not his son into the world to condemn the world, but that the world through him might be saved. In verse 18, He that believes on him is not condemned but he that believes not is condemned already, because he hath not believed in the name of the only begotten son of God, Jesus.

Read also (John 3:19) and (Romans 8:1) tells us that if we are in Christ and we don't go after our old fleshy desires, but we walk after the spirit of God, we won't be under guilt and condemnation. (In my words.) Look it up, read it. And this is the condemnation (also see Romans 8:1) that light is come into the world and Men loved darkness rather than light because their deeds were evil. (John 3:19) But this is why many don't get in all the way, they'd have to give up stuff. Repeating myself again, Hebrews 12:1. We must lay aside those weights and sins. (Try swimming across shark infested waters with some barbell weights tied around you. You'd drown plus be eaten.) So why do people think you can still hang on to things that will weight them down to hell. (Heb. 12:1, Matt. 16:26, Luke 6:46, Matt. 24:42–51, Matt. 11:12), which means if you are planning on making it to heaven with all the temptations in this evil world coming against you, you have to be strong in the Lord and in the power of his might (Eph. 6:10). But Matt. 11:12 is telling us to get violent in our spirit, **not in our flesh** like those road-rage wackos out there, no, but in the spirit—resisting your carnal, fleshly desires (Matt. 24:42–51, James 5:6–8) and yielding yourself to God. Nowadays, especially, you have to force yourselves to read the Bible, live for God, and resist the devil and the temptations of this life (Matt. 24:42–51). You must resist, and you have to just get violent in your soul against the devil (Matt. 11:12) (Luke 21:34, 35, 36). One way to do that is the same as when you were a kid: memorizing scriptures like you did the alphabet or, like when you got caught chewing gum or talking in class, writing it on the chalkboard a hundred times after staying after school or staying in at recess. Or how about the DMV test or that new phone number you had to memorize? Wow, I remember all that writing and studying over and over; reading, looking up, and thinking with your eyes closed; and having someone quiz you. Do you reeeemember? Ha, yes, you do… Well, why again do you think I repeat myself so much with the Bible to you? Oh, now you get it. Oh, and now you remember…right! and people that do those things in…a repeat or copying mode over and over we can and do memorize them this way esp. scriptures.

Everyone in the world should memorize (1ˢᵗ Corinthians 6:9 and 10 and Romans 10:13) and the Bible says in (Gal 5: 19, 20, 21), that you will not make heaven if your doing these things! So where does that leave ya? I even had a member of a cult tell me they believed they were not going to heaven, that's why they believed God made the new earth. Gonna be some very surprised people on judgment day. Especially those that do the suicide bombs, taken people's lives and killing their selves too. They need to read (Matthew 4). Okay, I won't repeat it. You'll get the point. But where do we draw the line between good and evil? Right and wrong between what's on God's side of the line and what's on the worlds to the devil's side of the line.

And the first three chapters of revelations are to the church, fourth chapter, note, the church is called up to heaven in verse 1 in Rev. 4. Then all hell is gonna break loose on earth. But God is still saving those who turn to him but to give your head when the mark of the Beast 666 (chip) is being now passed out, will be a nightmare, as in (Rev. 20:4) and being here when mountains are coming down and islands sinking, it'll be worth it to be ready ahead of time, before the rapture. (Now is the time) It's wrapping up folks, we can see identity chips are being made as I write, dogs and cats are already getting chipped. The Bible even says it's closer than when we believed. (Romans 13:11) **Notice (verse 12** of Romans 13): "The night is far spent, the day is at hand: **let us therefore cast off the works of darkness, and let us put on the armour of light**." Also see (Ephesians 6:10–18). It's plain; it's like when you're sweating, you take off your sweatshirt, or as the Bible puts it, cast off the works of darkness. The darkness here represents evil. Almost all of the youth in our world in today's day and time love dressing in black, which is equivalent to darkness, and they love the gothic look: anything that's evil looking such as skulls or crossbones, death metal music, etc. (Do you honestly think these types will make it to heaven?) You need to read (Matthew 24:22 and Romans 1:16–32). And let us put on (who is us? The one's going to heaven) the armor of light! Dressing in gothic, skulls, evil attire, crossbones, etc. and listening to music like death metal is not life but death. Heaven is life. Hell is death. Hell is outer darkness (Matt. 22:13, 8:12; Rom. 8:8). Also see (Romans 13:13): "Let us walk honestly, as in the day not in rioting and drunkenness." Wow, that sounds like today and sounds like new year's EVE party. Or nowadays, it's in the day time. And Mardi Gras seems to be held every day, not just at night anymore—many parties as verse 13 says. Are there gothic types casting off their evil ways and changing their attire to the light, as the scriptures say? No, they'll say, "You're not my boss," "Who are you to judge me?" etc. (Rev. 22:11). The evil will still be evil while the filthy will still be filthy when Jesus comes. That's this evil generation—rebellious and dark (and they will not change)! And they will riot in the daytime (2 Peter 2:13). Wow, these are actually real scriptures of the Last Days—end-time prophecies, wow. But you can't in no way tell these things to the stubborn, rebellious youth today (no way) (see Matthew 7:6 and Romans 8:8). So again, now you see why God sends destruction on to the earth in this evil generation. It's here as in (Matthew 24:33–34), and I ask you, don't you see that it's all prophesied already and written out in scripture? So now what? What else is God going to do? God will fulfill his word because he said his word will not return to him void (Isa. 55:11). (2 Corinthians 4:16, 17, 18) (Hebrews 4:1 through 8 see verse 11) said there'll be another day, a day of rest, a day of Jesus Christs return, a day of judgment and the first judgment will be at Jesus's return, you'll go if you're ready, but many say well I believe, but the Bible says in (James 2:19). So does devil's and they tremble but they didn't make it, but there's still time for you to call on the Lord, while it is still called today. Today is the day of salvation (Heb. 3:7, 13, 2 Cor. 6:2,

Right Now). Why wait, just bow your head and say, Jesus forgive me of all my sins and come into my heart and save me, I receive you Lord as my Lord and Savior. Thank you for saving my soul…in Jesus's name. Amen. (Simple but very effective.)

Two more crucial topics I want to ask where do you draw the line on competition, competitiveness has no place in the church, if you really study (Gal 5, verse 19 through 21) Study and look up those words, like in verse 20, emulations jealous, envious, want to be as equal as, or to be competitive (that's this generation today everyone wants or has to be in competition with each other). in the world you can understand, on the Job, and in school, in sports, but sad to say it's even crept in some churches out doing each other. The works of the flesh, competition is one, and there's a lot even in ministry and music, it's a spirit from hell and the Bible says ya won't make it To heaven with that in your heart, because in sports on a team against another to win the game, or on a salesman job where all the employees are in a contest to see whoever gets the most sales, wins a trip to Hawaii kinda thing is understandable, but not in church, yet you see it all the time, especially with musicians, and singers trying to out to do each other, God's not pleased with that (Hebrew 11:5–6), God does not bless that, but God will bless the humble heart, and God also anoints the sincere and humble hearts and those that have a repented heart, God is also will pleased with. (Psalms 51:17) (see 10 to 19) (Luke 15:10) (2nd Peter 3:9) what would it be like, for you or me to have such a testimony, (Heb. 11:5, 6) that we always kept such a repented heart, asking God (Jesus) to forgive us, as we also forgave other of their trespasses, (Mat. 6:14, 15) and in so doing, we please God so much that he (beamed) = or as the (KJV Bible says) (translated—us up to heaven) wow, (not dead but taken up alive) instantly in front of thousands, as Enoch (in Hebrews 11:5) or like the Prophet Elijah in (2nd Kings 2:1 to 12) (was taking up in a whirl wind in a chariot of fire) (wow) I love to fly, but what would that kind of flying be like? (Wow…in my words.)

I've mentioned already of some I've seen with so much pride they sometime are left standing there all alone, with God saying you don't give me the credit of your talent and you think you're doing a performance, instead of being like that little bird singing his heart out to God for the beautiful day…To God, To God, To God, It's for God, and To God, that it's in God we live and move and have our being (Acts 17:28). It's for God, and when it's truly to God and not because someone's in the spotlight. God puts his anointing on it, as to say I approve of your sincere heart, and I receive your worship.

And the other one is people in the church living together in adultery, and fornication, and start speaking in tongues and go right back to prostitution or back to their shacking up together. Yes, I used to live in sin as a sinner, as a hippy biker…pothead, but when I got saved and started going to church, I got married, and delivered, and God took the dope out of this dope. God's not ever gonna bless a fake, or a pretender, or some actor doing a performance putting on a phony show… They are asking to be cursed by God. But to hear a sinner speak in tongues and still be a sinner is an impossibility, because according to the Bible, in (1 Corinthians 3:16 and 17, 1 Corinthians 6:15 to 20, 2 Corinthians 13:5. God's spirit will not dwell in Mark 2:22, 2 Corinthians 5:17), an unclean temple (1 Tim. 4:1, 1 John 4:1 says don't believe every spirit) again, it's a counterfeit Spirit to believe any other doctrine except that of Jesus Christ and him crucified, any other is a cursed (see Gal. 1:6 to 10, 1 John 4:1 to 3, John 14:6) anything else is counterfeit and an anti-Christ spirit (2 John 7, 1 John 4:3, 1 John 2:18 and 22 and 1 Cor. 6:9, 10, 11) which the Bible tells us in many scriptures, people who do wrong will be punished and if they die in their sins, they don't go to heaven (John 8:21 and 24, Mark 14:21) no matter what some smooth talking false speaker says: you can't in no way, no how pray anyone out of hell after they die in their sins! As one lady at my work place said, it's an impossibility according to (Luke 16:19 to 31) if people don't follow the Bible and don't do what it says, they won't make it to heaven, you've got to get out of living in sin…sure everyone, sometime messes up and falls short, but we have to get up and repent asking God to forgive us…and keep going on living for God…but I'm referring to people continuing living in sin continually, Jesus himself said in the last part of (John 5:14), "Sin no more, lest a worse thing come unto thee." And in (John 8:11), Jesus said neither do I condemn thee, "Go and sin no more." (That's plain to me) I don't cheat on my wife since I got saved (adultery and fornication)! And I don't take drugs and don't smoke pot anymore since I got saved. No matter what those doctors being used by the devil to trick you say (2 Thess. 2:3) (Mat. 24:4) (Gal. 6:7, 8, 9) (Eph. 5:6) (Mat. 16:26), no! My soul is worth more than that. That's for just a moment, but after Judgement Day is eternity, which is forever, in heaven or hell! Second Corinthians 4:18 says, it's temporal, which means things in this life are just temporary, but in heaven or hell, it's for eternity. It's forever and ever (nonstop or infinity = no ending) (Heb. 10:26, Rev. 20:10). But do your best to stay away from sin. (James 4:17) so what was that speaking out of the prostitute in church? If it wasn't God…then it had to be the devil, yes, you heard right.

The devil, that anti-Christ, Jezebel Spirit, mimics and copycats the Holy Ghost, that's why Apostle John, and Paul said to Timothy. Try the spirits, to see if they are of God (1 Tim. 4:1 and 2, 1 John 4:1) he even comes as an angel of light. (2 Cor. 11:13, 14 and 15, see verse 3). Anyway, so if a devil possessed person tricks and fools people, then others, are deceived also, and this is how the anti-Christ will fool people and watch out for their literature also, many cults spreading lies and false doctrines out there. But we are warned of all this in all the New Testament. Even as the serpent beguiled Eve. (2nd Cor. 11:3) and lust of the eyes and heart. There's a lot of beautiful women out there and ladies, if I wanted to lust there are plenty walking the streets and on TV, etc. Cover up please, you'll answer to God for flashing your chest, that's a stumbling block, church is not a club, and church women don't need to look like hookers, so cover up. Pin up, sow up, I think all churches should offer and give away scarfs, clip-ons and pin on camisole lace covers is what their called those pin on type. And again, some do it deliberately, it's that anti-Christ jezebel spirit, to trap and seduce the man of God, and then some just get sucked into buying whatever those devil garment factory's put out.

If you're looking for a good business to go into godly garments could be the name, and selling women's appropriate church clothes would be the product, and it is well needed, you'd clean up on church folks. My wife has also had trouble finding dresses that aren't low cut, or ones that are too short. These clothing factories will answer to God, believe me, I know the Bible. And speaking of the devil beguiling Eve, ever since Adam and Eve's fall, the devil has still even today tricking (Matt. 4:1 to 11) people not just the women, but all kinds of people, men too. I am so amazed at how gullible an easily tricked people are today (2 Cor. 11:3, 2 Cor. 2:11, 2 Cor. 11:13–15) but it's even getting a hold of some church folks (magic, spells, witchcraft, false doctrine) and also those having a controlling spirit and those wanting everyone to bow to them, in politics, fortune readings (Acts 16:6–30) and in religions and even in marriages! (Col. 3:18) (Eph. 5:21–24) (1 Pet. 3:1) We all have to answer to God, if we don't obey God's Word. We were designed by God to be in unity and peaceful harmony in our marriage, not manipulating and controlling each other, that is a demon Jezebel Spirit from hell, and will cause you to miss heaven, and it's sad that these types are even in many churches, cause I've seen it, yes, even in church members, when the Bible says to be humble (Col. 3:16 to 25, verse 18) when you read it most women or a lot of them get mad (Eph. 5:23–25) (see verse 25), yes, men are to also submit and love your wives as Christ loved the church (true) but since (1 Kings 21:7, 1 Kings 18:4 and 1 Kings 19:1–2) is (dominating and controlling), this same evil spirit of control is in our land today, but God has gave us power to tread upon serpents and scorpions and over all the power of the enemy, and nothing shall by any means hurt us (in my words, read it, Luke 10:19–20, James 4:7).

If any of you think you can control your husband or wife, and still make heaven, I'm here to tell you, you friend are very deceived, you must first submit to God (James 4:7, 1 Pet. 5:5), then to your spouse (1 Pet. 3:1, Eph. 5:22, Col. 3:18) but a spirit of control is of the devil) like this, it's all in the Bible and the it's truth! And sad to say a lot of controlling Jezebels out there walking all over their spouses (1 Tim. 2:12, men and women) manipulating and controlling each other, this will make you miss heaven. (honest to God) and you go ahead and get mad, I didn't write the Bible, but if you follow these new agers, and this Jezebel spirit of control, and then go and read how she died, and then she was eaten by dogs, she also didn't read

(Psalm 105:15) and (1 Chronicles 16:22) when she came after the man of God to kill Elijah, she blew it…she touched God's anointed prophet and tried to get away with it, all through the Bible, especially in the New Testament, it tells us how to live and how to conduct ourselves. But again, there is definitely evil spirits in our day, spirits of deception again they are spirits of road rage anger, vengeance, lust, people deliberately trying to tempt you, and lure people, or provoke you, but seriously folks a man of God should not have to continue to turn his head and I do but in church this is so wrong. I was down praying at the altar, back when you got on both sides, this well-endowed sister knelt across. Just a glance and this gal was fallen out of her low top (1st Tim. 2:9) (1st Peter 3:1 to 7). The Bible speaks of (Rom. 14:13) putting a stumbling block and causing a brother to fall. Well, I got up and went to the other side of the church. The Bible also says we are not ignorant of the devil's devices (2 Cor. 2:11).

But this is definitely something for us all to pray about…and if you are blessed with a huge bank account, here is your golden opportunity to help women of God, because this is well needed. You could even have a table of Gospel tracts as in memory of me (HA) on the side. Just a thought.

Where Do You Draw the Line?"

And God even gave me a song on it. For me, and to me, on disciplining myself to look the other way, or get up and move. And I do. If you're really truly living for God, God will check you and speak to your heart. Get your eyes back in your head Fred. I think maybe why I look up and down so much. Someone's flashing and I don't want to be in trouble with God. I know his word, and it says if you look with lust, you already committed adultery with her in your heart (Matt. 5:28). Cause it's hard enough to stay focused on God without Lucy Goosee and Jezee D-bell flashing ya.

Anyway, I'm driving and look and see out the corner of my eye. Look on the road, and see the same thing on the left and on the right. (yeah hookers). They ain't hooking me.

> My song keeps your eyes on the Lord; the song kept ringing in my head.
>
> Keep your eyes and your mind on the Lord, keep your eyes and your mind on the Lord. Don't look left don't look right just keep Jesus in your sight. Keep your eyes and your mind on the Lord.
>
> Oh, there's trouble everywhere and there's heartaches every day but the Lord has said he'd bring us through. So when you come to the edge, just lift up your head, and keep your eyes and your mind on the Lord.
>
> (Repeat Chorus)

Don't allow your flesh to lead you but allow Jesus to direct your heart. Don't give place to the devil (Eph. 4:27). This means going through life we all see all sorts of things like picking up a smart phone after someone's been viewing those clip on cleavage covers…and start lusting and entertaining evil thoughts and drooling over women, you enter into sin… And don't get to judgmental ladies, I've seen many women checking out guys walking by in their tight-fitted blue jeans…oh and they didn't even know I saw them looking at him… No… Not me, I wear loose slacks… besides I'm a senior, I lost my looks years ago…anyway…the Bible says it's better to pluck out our eyes, and make heaven (that is if we can't discipline ourselves, Matt. 5:28, 29, 1 Tim. 2:9, James 4:17).

I come to the Lord in 1977 and started in prison ministry in 1978 but wasn't licensed yet and started a minister's chaplains study course, and in 1980, I started the study course to become a licensed minister and later became a pastor but did prison ministry for the first eighteen and a half years and took classes to be a criminal counselor, on-the-job training for about eleven months. But it was back in the 1980s. When I was studying to be a minister and just came out of the hippy biker pothead lifestyle and in those days would have used some choice words of a lady that exposed herself, but in church, you see it all the time (1 Tim. 2:9).

Come on, ladies, you're not hooking for Pete's sake. Cover yourself up. And yes, I know I mentioned this already, but I wanted to add that this is really a sad deal especially for new converts coming in, just getting saved, and yes, excuse me; it does go both ways. I've seen and known some guys that would go to church just looking for women; this is wrong too. You'd be surprised at the number I know of. Church is not a place of this sort. It's a house of prayer and worship. Yes, I believe God can send a lonely person a Christian mate but not in this fashion because if the spirit of God can't attract you the right one. Do you really want that type? That's looking in the fleshy manner, that kind of marriage won't last. Yet I've seen it time and time again, and I thank God my wife doesn't flash herself to other men. Thank God my wife loves me and submits to me and pleases me. No, I'm not looking, so you, ladies, that are desperate for attention be careful. "Touch not God's anointing and do God's prophet no harm (in my words)" (Ps. 105:15). I believe that means flashing yourself also. Try praying for God to help you. God is a good God (Ps. 84:11).

"Where Do You Draw the Line?" In Being Humble vs. Too Puffed Up To Exalt with Our Flesh

And question, do you wonder why God winked at us, or people as in (Acts 17:23–30) said, Paul was passing by an area in Athens, where he saw them doing their daily devotions, and noticed on their alter an inscription that said "to the unknown God"…and these igno-rant people didn't even know who or what they were worshipping… so God winks at man's ignorance, and either men or women has flirted with someone with a wink, but have you ever wondered why the Bible says God winked at man. My question is, was the wink at man, or at his stupidity of not knowing what he's worshipping? Well you can read it, as it says in (verse 30 of Acts 17:30) you have to read the whole text, God tells us of man creating and making graven images, and trying to capture the way God looks, etc., out of Gold, silver and stone, which is a sin against God, and is also one of the Ten Commandments (Exod. 20:3–5) wow…God took three whole verses to say, "It's wrong" to make them, or it's wrong to worship them, or even have them, yet they are all over the world. In every city, and in every state and every country, it's a big business in many countries, people are blind, stupid and gullible, God's people (perish) and are destroyed for their lack of knowledge in (Acts 17:30). God was saying man needs to repent of his ignorance, and maybe this is so we are not destroyed as in (Hosea 4:6). I, too, have repented many, many times because of some stupid things I did or, as I said earlier, because of something I didn't say just right. No one is perfect, according to scripture (Rom. 7:18–23), so when the Lord checks our heart, let's repent (Rev. 2:5). It won't hurt you but will help you stay humble (1 Cor. 10:12, 2 Chron. 17:14, James 4:6–8, 1 Pet. 5:5–7). Again, this is a command from God, but if you break man's laws, you'll go to jail (God's jail for man's rebellion and breaking God laws is called hell) This is a commandment, and a Law of God, no Idols, no graven images of a God like figurines. And people are stubborn and ignorant, the Bible says, God winked at the stupidity of man's ignorance...Now, blindness or illiteracy God may tolerate, but willfully premeditate-lying, when they know (Heb. 10:26). I laughed the first time I read (Acts. 19:24 to 35).

They were making big buck$ on making and selling those goddess idols, and today as well, but to lie and say it fell down from Jupiter. Ha and they call me dumb...Wow...People make them and then worship them...

Wow...so God...*winks*...I wonder if he laughed...can you picture them on Judgment Day...what will they say...I've watched idol worshippers on movies, and I have been amazed at the length of time they are down prostrated...for a false idol, you, no way could you get Christians to worship God like that...wow...God help us all. (moving on) But we must learn and be submissive to God, He wants our true worship in spirit and in truth (John 4:24) when we worship God, in other words don't put on a show but being real...and being thankful for a home, car, our health but most of all for God gave us his only Son, and Jesus saved our souls, and gave his life on the cross...so we need to always thank him for the price of his life he paid, for dying for our sins, and he died for us so we can make heaven (1 Cor. 6:20) Now that's something to thank God for, and that's real, and to thank God for, making a way for you and me to go to heaven.

But those who don't, I know many, that God has got their attention and gave them something big to thank God for...Some couldn't have kids my daughter Melanie was one, and was told by a doctor, due to radiation treatments she'd never have kids...was the doctor wrong No...God just gave her three little beautiful miracles, so now she can praise the Lord...Then there are others God has blessed with talents in music, and singing ability...and again we should always give God the glory and I already mention a pastor friend's wife that

410

was a beautiful singer, that God humbled her, by not anointing her, and letting her sing alone, without God's help (many of the great singers have) confessed that it was God anointing them, giving the honor and glory to God (Acts 12:21–23) which put a fear of God's wrath in people, who take the credit and fail to give God all the glory.

This pastor's wife even confessed and told the church, that's why she always gives God the glory because she loves God's anointing on her and that one time in front of three thousand people, God let her sing alone, with no anointing: we learn hard lessons the hard way. Me too. As OL. RW. Shambock says, I've had many apples out of that bag.

Every church in the world needs to study (Matt. 23). It amazes me how many singers, preachers and many that feel puffed up with their selves and have attitudes cause you can see they are thinking "you will never measure up to my knowledge, preaching, singing, or talents, or body, muscles, physique or figure, etc." cause it shows in their actions and attitude and countenance (Rom. 12:3, Col. 2:18, 1 Cor. 13:4, 5 and see verse 12, 1 Tim. 4:7 to 12, 1 Cor. 10:12, 1 Cor. 6:8 to 20, Prov. 16:18). And on singing or anything like I said some has fell on their face and stumbled all through it from beginning to end and repented and then confessed, to always give God 100 percent of the glory allowing God to get all the credit for anything I do!" "For God anointing them!" (Luke 4:18) This usually happens in the first few months to the first year or two, of getting saved. And some never get pass the new born baby stage of being newly born again, and becoming a new Christian when you first get saved…Some just never grow-up spiritually…Some quit and give up before God has a chance to mature them in the Bible, and in prayer and in learning how to self-discipline themselves in the basics. This is where the first three chapters of Revelation's is to the church esp. (Read) (Rev. 2:2 to 5) (Rev. 3:2 to 5 verses to 20) I remember not knowing any Bible, when the devil started messing with my mind, trying to make me think I wasn't really saved…and all the little aggravation kid-type stuff that just frustrated you…I felt like I was in the twilight zone.

Then as time went by I learnt that it's up to us to learn all those sneaky tactics of the devil…as in so many Bible verses (2 Cor.

2:11, 2 Cor. 11:3–15 see esp. verse 13 and 14 of 2 Cor. 11, Matt. 4:1–11) because if the Lord and the disciples learned and used the word = (Heb. 4:12) (Bible scriptures) as a sword against the devil (Eph. 6:10–18 see verses 10, 11 and 17), quoting them to him, and pleading the Blood of Jesus over (you and me and them) and rebuking the devil in Jesus's name, "then so do I!" You can also sing a hymn or spiritual song…as in (Colossians 3:16, Acts 16:25, 2 Chronicles 20:21 and 22). Not only will this minister to you and to God, but it also slaps the devil in the face but most people don't even believe there even is a real devil. And many people will take and look at things done by the devil in the carnal sense, which the Bible teaches this is not a flesh and blood battle with the devil…but it's spiritual (Eph. 6:12, 1 Cor. 2:14, Rom. 8:4–17, 2 Cor. 10:4–7). And how do you fight the devil, especially when he comes at our fleshly minds: it's by doing spiritual warfare, you plead the blood of Jesus over your mind, and you quote those Bible scriptures that applies to your situation, and always thank God for hearing your prayers that you pray and always pray in the name of Jesus.

And always rebuke the devil in Jesus's name, And there is also power in agreeing with someone in prayer (Matt. 18:19). And then the most power comes through fasting and prayer (Isa. 58:6, Matt. 17:21, Matt. 6:16–18) but don't look for these power scriptures in the NIV and other newer Bibles they took em out on using Bible scriptures as spiritual bullets to shoot at the devil…Your gun is your mouth but anyway when you just get saved, you have to grow up spiritually, and the Bible says we do that by drinking in the milk of the word, which are the pure basics, in (1 Corinthians 3:1 and 2, 1 Peter 2:2). That you may grow by it. One particular prisoner after he got out, couldn't read so he wanted me to write out some power scriptures to help him, and he'd have someone else read them on cassette tapes, and then he'd play them over and over to get them to memory, I was thrilled that a ex-prisoner wanted to memorize scriptures cause he couldn't read and It took a while, but we did…And the last time I saw him he was quoting most of them from memory… And the neat thing about having the Holy Ghost, he'll bring them back to your memory again, but something I forgot to write down, many times that's happened and the Holy Ghost brought it back to my memory each time.

Someone said that's called a senior moment when you forget something...and it was suggested I try this new herb vitamin that helps boost your memory, but when I went to the store...I forgot the name of it. HA. But when the Holy Ghost brings it back...it's a praise the Lord moment. Amen. But thank God we can read and write and like the exconvict wanting to, but his old life of booze and drugs kept calling him, so this guy was needing some real ammunition amo to fight against the devil with...And I loaded him for bear with bullets like (Isa. 40:31; Isa. 54:17; Isa. 55:11; Isa. 58:6; Isa. 59:19; Matt. 18:19; Luke 10:19; Acts 1:8; Phil. 4:13 and 19; Matt. 6:33; Rom. 10:9, 10, 13, 17; Heb. 11:6; Eph. 6:10 to 18; Luke 18:27; Jude 20; Rom. 8:26; Rom. 8:11; Rom. 8:31 to 39; Matt. 17:21; Phil. 4:6; Ps. 150:6, also some of my favorites, Prov. 3:5, 6; Ps. 124:1 to 8; Ps. 37:23, 24, 25; Ps. 34:7, 8; Ps. 84:11; Ps. 34:15 to 19; Ps. 23; Rom. 2:11; Eph. 6:9 to verse 18; Phil. 1:6; Heb. 13:5 and 8; 2 Chron. 20:15–25). (First Peter 4:1) says, to arm yourselves likewise with the same mind (Phil. 2:5, put on the mind of Christ, not to be in the flesh, but in the spirit, Rom. 8:5 to 26) And we need to have that Bible in our hearts (1 Peter 3:15) says always being ready to give an answer to anyone. A lot of times you hear on the news of some escaped prisoner on the loose and armed and dangerous... spiritually speaking, wouldn't it be cool...for us to hear the devils news broadcast to all his demons, be on the lookout, be alert, all local churches are in revival and are full of the Holy Ghost, and are armed and dangerous with the Word of God hid in their hearts, the Holy Ghost has armed them with spiritual machine guns to blast every demon back to hell.

And again remember, this is not a flesh and blood fight; it's spiritual (2 Cor. 10:4, 5). We must learn to walk and pray all the way and learn as we grow spiritually knowing and studying the word. Asking the Holy Spirit to lead, guide, and direct us, and give us understanding, as we do our very best, for him. We must always guard ourselves, especially when we have used our sword (Bible scriptures) and spiritual bullets victoriously against the devil through some trial of our faith, we must stay vigilant, again keeping your guard up especially after you've won your battle, and keep your armor on protecting yourself (Eph. 6:10 to 18, 1 Cor. 10:12) from becoming puffed up...and always give God the glory...remember...your just the gun...without God's bullets you'd fire blanks, then what good is a gun without Amo...Amen (1 Pet. 5:6, 7, 8, 9) stay vigilant (Heb. 4:12, 1 Pet. 1:7).

In fact, as I said earlier, giving God extra thanks with praise, followed up with several Gospel songs of thanks, and believe it or not, can be a weapon against the enemy of your soul. The devil don't like you thanking God...and it's very hard to do when you are going through a trial, or a physical battle. But remember (King Jehoshaphat, 2 Chron. 20:15 to verse 25, notice verse 22) and also Apostle Paul and Silas in (Acts 16:16 to 26) both sung songs to God thanking him (and God was so blessed he fought their battles. Wow...)

Jesus himself taught this, that the way we should conduct ourselves, and the way we should live and act. Because you can read the Bible and compare it with the six-o'clock news, the riots and protests and just getting out and going to the store, the way everyone is acting snapping at you like evil demons, this is just one area that I see we are definitely in the last days and it is time for Jesus Christ to come and get his people! Just yesterday my wife and I were doing our devotions over a cup of coffee and it was like (Matt. 25:8) leaped off the page, to me and I said wow, here's one of the problems with our world today, the verse reads (Matt. 25:8, and the foolish said unto the wise, give us of your oil, for our lamps are gone out). The text is speaking spiritually about peoples' hearts, souls and spirits are slack in no prayer life, no studying the Bible this biblical term of oil represents the salvation of your soul, it's the fuel that keeps the light on in your spiritual lamp (you) in other words, when your car runs out of gas while driving down the road, your engine will spit and sputter, jumps and kicks and some just dies in the middle of the road, leaving you stranded, all because you wasn't paying attention to the gas gauge, the car can't run on gas fumes, nor will none praying Christian people that's planning on going to heaven.

Go read all of Matthew 25:1–13 without light people are in darkness (John 3:19–21) out of fuel live in a evil world (Luke 18:1) Jesus said to pray least you faint, when you kill, steal, hate, have bitterness in your heart against someone, or your prejudice, these are signs you are out of fuel…a lamp can't give light without fuel or as in our day with electrical lamps, even so it is with you and me, if we're not plugged in to the source of power of being filled up with the Holy Ghost oil, as these five wise and five foolish virgins that represents ten spirit-filled saints of God (notice that after those five foolish stopped praying and reading their Bible, in my words, and in my interpretation), these foolish saints pure virgins—of God didn't make it into heaven (see verses 10 to 13) and the door of heaven was closed shut. (verse 10) and no matter how hard they screamed later it was too late, all because they ran out of oil backslide they got bitter and (Heb. 3:15) full of hate but while it's still called today cause today is the day of salvation, get ready, and call on Jesus, stay ready.

Because (2 Corinthians 4:16) says the inward man (our soul) is renewed day by day (2 Cor. 6:2). Now is the day of salvation, Jesus said daily take up your cross daily and follow him (Luke 9:23) we all have noticed when a car has been serviced, and gased up, and tuned up, it'll get you to where you're going…it's the same spiritually on making it up to heaven (Matt. 7:13, 14) (Rev. 12:27) (Rom. 6:23) (Matt. 7:21 to 23) (Rev. 21:8) (1 Cor. 6:9, 10, 11) (Gal. 5:19–21) (1 Jn. 1:9), sin will not enter heaven! (Heb. 12:1 and 2, Rom. 12:1 and 2, James 4:17, Matt. 6:33, Acts 2:38–39).

In (Titus 2:7), even showing yourself as a pattern of good works. When I was a kid my mom would get some material and a dress pattern and measure, and pin the dress pattern to the material, and cut out the dress by following the pattern. It's the same spiritually. We are to pattern our lives after the same example of Jesus Christ's life and follow the Bible. My old pastor Cleo Roberts said WWJD way before the T-shirts came out…what would Jesus do? (1 Tim. 1:16; 1 Pet. 5:5, 6; James 4:6, 10).

Our lives must be spiritually balanced, upright.

1. Balance of Priorities: lay aside every weights (Heb. 12:1, Matt. 6:33, Eph. 6:10 to 18, Eph. 4:27).

2. Self: read all through the four gospels especially "The Book of John, Christ taught and showed humbleness, when he came into town on a donkey (John 12:15) not a stallion, as you see at the rodeo on a cowboy's stallion horse doing a fancy side step, acting all proud of his award winning mare, strutting in the fairs parade. No Jesus came in town humble, on a blooming donkey...wow...what a difference between the two cause he served others, because most people want to be waited on, Jesus washed their feet and waited on them and served them (John 13:14–15) rather than, his disciples serving him as a king, but he was teaching and demonstrating to them, how to be humble, and prefer your brother-in the Lord before yourself.

Leaving us one powerful example (Rom. 12:10). I wanted to mention, our church once in a while every other year or so, goes to LA to the garment district. And so the brothers of our church would walk door to door, checking out all the men's suit shops, about a three-mile walk, anyway I bought me a couple of two nice suits and I'm using a cane to walk with after a hit and run car wreck, followed up with back surgery...anyway, I walk slow, and this big muscular brother named Keith Parker carried my two suits all day over those three miles of walking, and I tried several times to take them from him, but he refused to let me carry them, wow, a loving humble man of God, this is that true perfect example of a spirit of humility that Jesus Christ himself taught and lived. Wow...what an example of Christ's love, and what a sacrifice, that's some good seeds my brother planted. Wow, thanks brother Keith you are indeed a true man of God (Rom. 12:1–3). In (Matthew 25:40), Jesus said for such as you've done to the least of these you've done it to me. Wow.

Now some people are quick to learn all those things in the Bible on how to discipline their selves, in a lot of these things I've been discussing, and some folks are quick learners and pick stuff up right away. But I on the other hand was a slow learner, it took me a while after I got saved I was slow to grow up spiritually. I have really admired the spiritual maturity and love the folks at Living Christ Church in Tulare, California, has, and Pastor Donahue Green and Sis. Evon Green, and the reflections of love, and examples of Jesus

Christ, in power and demonstration in these church folks is truly a breath of fresh air.

But because of immaturity when I was a young Christian, I looked down on people that had lesser faith, or because they didn't measure up to my expectations. Now, I know this was wrong and it was spiritual immaturity or how about the one that had so much faith and he looks down on someone with a handicap, thinking, if you had any faith in you, you'd be healed, and it's happened to me, this is wrong thinking: Hey, I've even had preachers mock my handicap…This, too, is wrong…or the real smart high up the ladder intellects that looked down on people that's not so bright…Wow…This, too, is wrong…and I've had it happen to me by many…And like Paul's thorn in the flesh, that so many people try to say what it is… but don't know, so many times God gives people some type of thorn in the flesh to keep them humble, so we don't get to proud or puffed up with our high intelligence, Ouch…So some may be handicapped themselves in some way or another…and it may not always be physical, or some may have a child that is, or spouse or in my case, been in a bad car wreck followed by surgery with metal implants, then later having throat cancer surgery…and still cancer free praise God, so mine is a double handicap which I don't get because I've been faithful serving God (but Bishop Jakes said when you get higher up the ladder in serving God you fight the devil on another kind of level… new levels, new devils).

Something like that, I may not have said it exactly the same, but you get the point, God will keep us humble. Again, I've seen guys with muscles mock someone fat, or handicapped, and that's the reason I don't go to gyms, because it has happened many times to me as they pat your big belly, and laugh, or mock you using a cane. Yes, I've been there…but what these bully mockers you that are so full of their selves, don't realize is the Bible says…we all reap what we sow (Gal. 6:7, 8, 9) (read verse 7 carefully), and I'm living proof, and they evidently haven't ever read (1 Chronicles 16:22 or Psalm 105:15), that says, "Touch not my anointed, and do my prophets no harm. "watch out"…I've seen these types humbled by God the hard way. I saw two, one was turned into a paraplegic till he died, the other is in a wheel chair still. So don't ever mock people (Gal. 6:7, 8, 9). And I've seen a young preacher just starting out...praying for an older preacher and he had so much pride thinking this young guy isn't even up to my level in faith...I was the young preacher about thirty years ago...And later heard him preach and mentioned if these youngsters starting out, had been down the road as I've been down, they'd have as much faith as I got. Wow...yes...He died, not to long after that statement. No one has arrived, if we think we stand take heed lest we fall (1 Cor. 10:12) SO don't let no walls of thinking you've arrived go up...An old pastor used to say he believed even a child could pray the prayer of faith...we just have to believe God's Word, and heard another one say if God used a stick with Moses, and a donkey's mouth with Balaam, and a stone with David, and a donkey's jaw bone with Samson, then God can use a pen with me.

So back to the muscle body building guy that mocked me, that was so full of his self, and his own physique and didn't have a clue he was coming against and mocking God's anointed minister...No, nor many other people that I've worked on the job with. They all need to read (Matthew 25:40, Luke 23:31, John 15:19, 20, 21, John 16:2), so do we quit serving God because some self-centered egotistic muscular Pharisee jerk is hurting your feelings? "No"..."absolutely not!" Because serving God and making heaven will be worth it all! Oh yes, I'll take all of God I can get, even if it means, getting rid of my pride. And even if a little child wants to pray for me (lack of humbleness can rob you) Not realizing we all reap. But To portray ourselves in this fashion is wrong and again this was the rebuke of Jesus. And even Pharisees and Scribes and even to his disciples like he did to Peter in (Matthew 16:23), are we pleasing God or men (Gal. 1:10). Read these scriptures, and think, Jesus was really speaking to the devil that Peter was listening to. Many Bible scholars, and pastors believe Jesus was actually speaking to the devil that Peter was listening to.

Concerning (Peter) being rebuked time and time again for his carnal thinking: Yet we can apply this to ourselves in our walk with Christ (Rom. 6:13 and 16) so we don't give place to the devil (Eph. 4:27) nor mock God's people, nor listen to the devil's voice as Peter did and was rebuked (Matt. 16:23, John 21:20, 21, 22, 23. Matt. 17:5).

When Peter says in (John 21:20:22), well, what about John there. What's he gonna do? Ha. Jesus said to Peter, what's it to ya, you follow me, wow, how embarrassed he must have been, but sometimes when the foot gets in the mouth, we learn from the school of hard knocks, I had a few apples out of that bag myself. Remember no one has arrived yet! Jesus said those that are greatest (in my words or perfect in their own eyes will be your servant), and I think of my pastor, Donahue Green, always giving up his chair and would do anything for anyone, always going out of his way, preferring others first what a humble example he is. I've seen him do so much, and I've learned even after being in ministry for forty years, by watching this man of God, so you can't get to old to still learn, and this pastor doesn't act like those others I've known that think they've arrived, and think they are way up here and you are way, way down there and you could never, reach them. Not this pastor.

Okay, It's just, when you've seen so many Pharisees. And then you meet one of Jesus's right hand men. You go. Wow. Okay, Lord, I don't mean to put this man on a pedestal by no means. You know my heart, okay, getting back, the disciples were rebuked for trying to exalt themselves, like the time the two sons of thunder wanted to sit on the right and left of Jesus. Hey, I think everyone would desire that. And wouldn't it be great like when the police used to let someone do a ride-a-long, which was to inspire young folks to become police officers but you see the analogy here, maybe the Lord'll have a time that everyone'll get a-turn sitting on the throne next to Jesus for an hour or so. Wouldn't that be awesome. Do I sound like the kid that got to sit in the firetruck and blow the siren. Ha.

Just making it into heaven will be worth it all, cause this ol' world has definitely lost it's splendor, when I compare the two, heaven and earth, it just makes me want to see Jesus, and heaven. Like up in the high sierras, I hiked in with Richard, my brother-in-law, and Fred Hurley his brother, down into some canyons (This was in my younger days), and saw rivers, and meadows so beautiful, untouched by man, so if God in only six days created these beautiful sites we saw, how beautiful is heaven, cause Jesus has had two thousand years working on it. We saw waterfalls going into pools in this beautiful river, with beautiful green moss on the bolder rocks, and a funny story about the trout fishing, with these two fun loving brother-in laws, of mine, would catch a fish and move on upstream to the next pool laughing, well you could see these big rainbow trout, I wasn't catching nothing. So I would move up where they were and they left to go on up to the next pool laughing.

Weeks later, they told me if you can see the fish they can see you, and won't bite, Usually, you catch one and move to the next pool. Ha. (Well lesson learned the hard way.) And so it is when serving the Lord. Many things in our Christian walk with God we get our spiritual bumps and bruises, just like a toddler learning to walk, many falls, but the tenacious child continues to get back up an try it again. Unlike some baby Christians that are ready to throw in the towel, because they can't leave something alone, or lay down those cigarettes, that ruins their testimony and darkens their light, friend you weren't born with that and with God's help you can lay it down (Phil. 4:13, 1 Cor. 10:13, Isa. 54:17, Luke 18:27, I call these power scriptures). Like (Luke 10:19) Learn them, quote them, the Bible says you can pray and call upon the Lord, and ask him to fill you with his Holy Ghost (Holy Spirit). And fire, you see, it's like a man squirting a volcano with a squirt gun, or when fighting some temptation, or problem, that seems to high to get over, nothing is to big for God, no problem, no temptation is to much for the fire of the Holy Ghost that burns in our soul (Matt. 3:11, 12). So when God fills you with his spirit, he will burn off and kick the junk out, cigarettes, booze, etc., out of ya.

He takes away the desire for it and convicts your conscience to lay it down. Again, God don't play games...And will not allow you to try and make excuses to hang on to weights (Heb. 12:1 and 2) that ruins your witness, which we discussed already (Phil. 4:13, 1 Cor. 10:13) because people that try to hang on to stuff makes Christians and God look like fools cause God says with His help you can overcome anything. And this type turns into sin if he don't do right. (James 4:17) and again, this is explained in scripture, as rebel-

lion and those that rebel against God's Word don't make heaven...
And this is why everyone needs to be filled with the Holy Ghost fire
in your soul, to help you overcome the trials and temptations of this
life. And plead the blood of Jesus over you, and pray in Jesus's name,
and rebuke the thing and the devil in Jesus's name (Me and many
others has overcome these things, and so can you.) You must learn (1
Cor. 6:9–10, Gal. 5:15–22), learn the difference between the works
of the flesh and the fruit of the spirit. And keep repenting when you
feel you've fell short or messed up. Learn from it, and get up. And
get that spiritual fuel in your soul by hearing the word. On Bible
CD and in a good Bible study class. And remember, the disciples
were rebuked for trying to exalt their selves who'll sit next to Jesus in
heaven. (Matthew 20:20–27) if we are Christ-like Christians.

We must follow his examples, I see so many immature babies,
envying, jealous, looking at everyone else except at your own selves.
In (Matthew 7:3, 4, 5), how will you say to your brother, let me pull
out the mote speck of dust, splinter or tiny particle that is in your
brother's eye. Yet a beam is in your own eye (*Webster's Dictionary*)
quotes the definition meaning of a beam is a large piece of wood,
used as a support column, that supports the roof of a house, in Jesus's
analogy, he was pointing out, that we should first remove the huge
support beam Log, tree, etc., out of our own eye first, before trying to
remove a speck or splinter out of your brothers eye. Notice, in verse
5, Jesus says, after you pull the log out of your eye then you (thou)
will see clearly to pull the tiny speck out of your brothers eye...Wow.
I've often used this and other similar analogies to make a point.

People forget Jesus was a carpenter, some guy put in a song that
Jesus made the tree he was crucified on...wow (Brain teasers). or his
mother that birth him, had to also come to him for salvation: wow
(I worded these quotes in my words.) Okay...so it's not an exact
quote (Get over it.) HA. Just kidding: if the verse (Matt. 7:3, 4, 5)
says before you past judgment on me, try living the rough life I've
lived, or as the McKameys sung ("God on the mountain") song, that
says, you can talk of faith when you are up on the mountain, but life
comes so easy, when life's at its best, but it's down in the valley, of trials and temptations, that's where faith is really put to the test.) So my

point ten miles later is…The Bible says we are to examine ourselves, and first remove the beam out of our own eye before removing the speck or splinter out of your brother's eye. I preached an illustrated message on this topic years ago, where I took a couple volunteers to help me illustrate, by taping a splinter on a pair of eye goggles and the second guy had a plank board tied to his face, where he could not see a thing, and with a pair of tweezers he tried to remove the splinter, now, if the goggles was not there, that other poor guy would have probably been blinded by the tweezers, if you had a tiny speck in your eye, would you let a doctor or someone blindfolded take it out.

No way, so you see Jesus's point in Matthew 7:3, 4, 5. If the verse says, do not judge another, then that's what it means, and God wants everyone to make heaven, and the Bible says there is not anyone better than anyone else…There is not anyone righteous Holy. But President Thomas Jefferson said in 1776 when he was writing the Declaration of Independence, that "All men were created EQUAL," and in 1870 with The Fifteenth Amendment created equal and (in my words) in knowing, in God's eyes we are all equally loved…no big I's and no little u's even though many well to do wealthy people think they are better than others, and look down their noses at all of us poor folks, God looks down on them for not obeying his word (Matt. 25:40 to 45) and they really need to read these scriptures, so if anyone that this scripture is talking to and don't comply with it, and change, and repent (God will fry their butt…ouch…) Read it…oh yes, many will be shocked on Judgment Day, these are Jesus Christ's words in (Matthew 25).

Not mine, I'm just the messenger. Because all people are really created equal, cause Jesus and Paul, and John said so, and they are even equal for salvation (Luke 20:35, 36) says those that are accounted worthy to obtain that world those going into (heaven, in my words) are equal to the angels, wow the Bible says, Jesus died for all, for "the whole world" (John 3:16, 17, 18) for everyone who calls upon his name. "And there is no difference between the Greeks and the Jews who-so-ever, means anybody can call on Jesus and he's not prejudiced," even the thief on the cross who said "remember me," Jesus said today you will be with me in paradise, so even though he

WHERE DO WE DRAW THE LINE?

was a thief, because he called on Jesus with a repented heart, he was accepted, and forgiven (Luke 23:42–43). (Rom. 10:12, 13; Gal. 3:28; Rom. 2:11; Eph. 6:9, Col. 3:25 and God) even loved the prisoners (bond or free, Acts 10:34 and 1 Cor. 12:13) God loves all creeds, all races, the word who-so-ever means anyone, that will call on him and ask him (Jesus) for forgiveness he will forgive, "But"…God doesn't want any of us to act or think they are better than others (read James 3:14 to 18), check out that verse 17, "without partiality and without hypocrisy" (wow) or how about (James 2:1 to 10) wow…And there are many, many more, but the one that really gets me Is (Luke 16:19 to 31), This wealthy rich sucker passed by this poor beggar…every-day…And didn't do nothing for him.

It sounds like he sicked the dogs on him…Then in hell this rich chump has the nerve to ask for Lazuras to cool his tongue. Wow. So let's take a closer look in the mirror of self-examination first, and ask God to check us when we look down on others (Ps. 51:10 to 17). Yes, God has checked my heart many times…I like what one preacher said to another one, when the one pastor elbowed him and pointed at a drunk laying in the gutter, saying, isn't that a shame, and the older pastor said, "If not for the grace of God there we be." Wow (Eph. 2:8).

How Do We Draw the Line to Obstacles in Our Own Lives and Do We See Them?

No. 1, the Bible says in (Matthew 6:33), if we seek God first and his righteousness, all these other things will be added to you. (Philippians 4:19) says, God'll supply all our needs according to his riches in glory by Jesus Christ (and in my words, 1 Cor. 10:13) teaches us, that God will not allow more on us than what we can bear (God is able and he is a God of love) and he's faithful, and will make a way that you can escape it (many, many times in my own life, I didn't see know way out, but God raised and lifted up a barrier-wall against the situations that only God could fix (Read 1 Corinthians 2:9 and Isa. 54:17, Isa. 59:19) The last half of that verse 19 teaches us when the enemy (that ol' devil) comes in like a flood, the spirit of the Lord will lift up a standard, or a wall, or a shield against him (In my words). Just remember, God's Word is his promise to you (It's his bond and Isa. 55:11) says God's Word, it won't return to him void, but it'll accomplish that, which He pleases (in my words) you read these, and if you don't have the Holy Ghost, ask God in Jesus's name to fill you with his spirit because, Paul wrote in Romans 8:26, that we don't know how to pray as we ought to, but his spirit-itself'll pray through you, and make intercession for us with groanings (in my words and Jude 20) tells us to pray in the spirit and it'll build up your faith (in my words). And read (Romans 8:31 to 39). God's love is stronger than anything and nothing shall separate us from His love, that's in Jesus Christ (in my words) I really do try to be brief honest I do.

As the Ten Commandments clearly state in Exodus 20:3). The first commandment, says "not to have any other gods before me (God)." It's a command from God! But even Mary, that some religions pray to is wrong, cause the Bible says Jesus is our only mediator (1 Tim. 2:5) Because even though Mary was highly favored, and many saints, apostles, disciples, and prophets, and even angels were highly looked up to, but we are warned and told in scripture not to pray to anyone but (God-Jesus) because this angers God. They are not deity! Angels are not deity...one scripture says in (Revelations 19:10). John bowed before an angel and the angel rebuked him saying "See thou do it not" I am thy fellow-servant (Wow), I know many people that pray to family members that are gone on, and that pray to saints (this is religion) and it is wrong according to the Bible...and again...I didn't write the Bible, I'm just the messenger, so don't get mad at me. (Read Luke 16:19 to 31.) The rich man could see Lazarus in heaven, but notice he wasn't allowed to talk to him. Again, read the Ten Commandments and (Revelations 19:10 and 1 Timothy 2:5); we have (one mediator) between God and man (Jesus Christ, in my words). Mary give birth to Jesus, but that was it. That didn't make her a god. No...No way. (NOTE) if anyone in heaven could hear you pray this would alter scripture...then that would bring sorrow to that someone that has eternal life (Rev. 21:4). This is why (Matt. 24). Jesus warned of false preachers, false doctrines, etc. (Notice in (Luke 11:27), this lady was trying to praise Mary, Jesus's mother, saying "Blessed is the womb that bare thee, and the Paps which thou hast sucked." And Jesus replied (Luke 11:28), yeah rather, "blessed are they that hear the Word of God and keep it." (Notice, nowhere in scripture do you see people praying to Mary.) Again, this is religion, and is forbidden! All churches should do teachings on this and the Ten Commandments, and Jesus added two more (Matt. 22:36 to 40). I think it was Billy Graham or Shambock that once said, if you think that you are so important, put your hand in a bowl of water and take it out and look back to see your imprint on the water you made. God will use any vessel to carry his gospel but he wants us like the clay and pottery, clean, and appliable, ready to be used, moldable not molded but moldable. So he, the potter molds us, shapes us, and pours into us his spirit, and his life.

Once the disciples got passed the baby stage on not to be envious, or what about John stage and quit pointing their self-righteous finger at others and got in one mind and one accord and let the spirit of the molding Holy Ghost and fire burn off their fleshly chaff. Then they experienced the out pouring and infilling of the Holy Ghost. Notice when Jesus called back the dead, Jesus always fasted, putting his flesh under and he wasn't a whiny baby when he cried out, with authority, "Roll away the stone" (John 11:39) removing the obstacle. He spoke with authority...and again in verse 39; he commanded the stone to be taken away, and thanked God for hearing him in verse 41, then he spoke life into the dead man in verse 43 and spoke life back into a dead man in John 11:43 but notice in verse 41 Jesus thanked the father for hearing him. Wow and he (Jesus) commanded the huge stone out of the way. Are you saying there are keys, Yes, thanking God for hearing us is a key, as in (John 11:41), "And praying in Jesus's name is another one, (John 14:13, 14)" etc. I think I already mentioned earlier...but the secret keys, and techniques of quoting scriptures in your prayers come as you mature in God. Yes, Paul E. Billheimer says in his book *Techniques of Spiritual warfare* is like electric wires inside the wall that brings power to us, and all we have to do is flip the switch, and there's light. Someone else already fixed those wires, and done the work. Jesus paid the price (already) when we accept Jesus into our hearts, the switch has been flipped on.

Paul E. Bilhimer states in his book *The Techniques of Spiritual Warfare* says that like those wires inside the wall, you don't see them, but you can tap into the plug-in receptacle electric wall out let, just by putting in a plug and wa-la you have power to your hair dryer or appliance, the same with God, once you learn how to yield to him, and plug into the Holy Ghost and fire, you receive power after the Holy Ghost has come upon you (Acts 1:8). Then you can witness, lay down weights that beset you (Heb. 12:1–2). Using the name of Jesus, pleading the blood of Jesus, quoting Bible scripture, you think your puny, but mighty through Jesus (Eph. 6:10) like I said before, a little guy with a flame thrower can fry a guy in a tank, ouch. So stature doesn't matter in the spiritual realm, and this human life's only gonna exist maybe one hundred years old, at the most, or maybe in the eighties, etc., but the spirit life is forever and you'll enter it as you leave this mortal human body, but it all depends on how you live in this life, for Jesus or the devil, which destines your eternity in heaven or hell. You must be living by the Bible to make it to heaven.

Paul E. Billheimer, also said that the spirit of God in us, lets us know but, if we continually think with our natural mind, and continually walk in our flesh, we become an enemy of God (Rom. 8:6, 7, 8). Also see (vs. 11) but to walk in the spirit, and put on the mind of Christ. We become sons of God (Rom. 8:14 and 1 Cor. 2:14). And he states that spirits of evil are just outside the skin. As the wires are inside the wall and God has given us power to turn on that switch using the name of Jesus. Pleading the blood of Jesus (this is in my words) realizing and knowing that like those wires hid in the wall, the word and spirit of the Holy Ghost in the inner man, can be turned on by quoting scriptures, praying in Jesus's name, praying in the spirit (keys, tools, spiritual weapons, putting our flesh under subjection) and fasting with prayer. Probably one of the best two weapons the child of God has, are the main two, the devil's tried removing out of other version Bibles, which is removed in the NIV. That's why I read the KJV Bible and that's fasting and praying in the Holy Ghost (Jude 20, Rom. 8:26) our flesh don't like missing a few meals but the spirit of God arises stronger as we deny our flesh, and many times the Holy Spirit will pray through you, cause somethings in this life our fleshy man just don't know the right words to say to God. And then there's having a thankful heart, telling him, and making a big deal to him about things he's done. Sometimes I'll just kneel down by the toilet and say thank you, Lord, (I can go here) I'm not out on the mountain side, or going down the freeway, thanks for my eyes, and ears, and legs, and I can use the rest room without a machine or I don't have a colostomy bag on my gut, we are not in the hospital we are blessed, we are not in prison, we are blessed, our nation's not having bombs dropped in our city, we are blessed, we have a roofover our heads, shoes on our feet, food to eat, we should be thanking our Lord, every day, giving thanks not just at the table, but at the toilet, at the car, in the morning when you get up, for watching over you in the night. This thankful attitude will also give you favor with God. Just remember (Acts 16:16–25). Read it. They thanked God and sung him songs of thanks. And again in my opinion, you can't be spiritual if you are judging what others watch on TV, or with your nose in everyone else's business, gossiping about them to others, running down others cause they don't measure up to your standards, "What about John?" (John 21:20, 21, 22). Peter was jealous and envious that Jesus gave John more attention (this is carnal immaturity).

What's that to you, Jesus said, you follow me. You can't be spiritual if you're carnal.

Hello (Rom. 8:11, if the spirit that rose up Jesus, be in you).

3. If our life truly reflects Christ, others will see it, there is a definite difference in you when you are filled with the Holy Ghost and Fire (Matt. 5:14 to 16) and there are some that say, and don't do. Be a doer of the word. (James 1:19–22, verse 23) mentions about looking at yourself in the mirror, many times the Holy Spirit says, while looking when shaving, you better take care of you, don't worry about John, it's an all day job, just keeping my own life straight. Spend time with God, step away from the phones, TV, etc., get in your prayer closet, do some spiritual warfare, and take those things to Jesus.

Drawing the Line to Our Devotions with God

Note: Many people spend more time with their phone than a real true man or woman of God will have a time in his busy day, to spend with God, and pray and read the Bible (Ps. 91:1). He that dwells in the secret place of (God) the most high, shall abide under the shadow of the almighty. (Also, Matt. 6:33, Ps. 92:1–2, best time is when you first roll out of bed) before work, before phone's ringing, before someone's knocking at the door. (unless it's Jesus, We must discipline ourselves in order to be Jesus's disciple. Gee. That's what a disciple means. One who is self-disciplined. Seeking God, quality time, not depending on pastor or someone else to do my praying or feeding me…spiritually.

I said to a clerk (joking), while he was down on his knees stocking the shelf, hey…while your down there say one for me, I need the prayer and you need the practice. (and we both laughed). But that hit me back in the face. Many times my humor that just jumps out gets a big foot in my mouth along with a spanking, from the Lord. And try to get spiritual in prayer. Ha, ya…can't be spiritual and carnal but that's my beam. I got to work on myself the same as you do. Self-discipline means, being a disciple. We are all striving for the same goal: heaven. Let's grow up.

And those that you see are used by God, pray for them. I admire men of God. I've seen them humble themselves; Minister J. Johnson, like Pastor Green did at a big convention one night. He just said a couple words and got out of their way. Humble and yet, so anointed, lessons are learned by observing their sacrificed life, of prayer and dedication to God, busy for God. And you see that anointing just flows but it's the submitting to God, humbleness, putting God first, living it and giving of their selves is how these men of God are so anointed, a beautiful yard has someone spending time on it.

Straight is the gate, (Matthew 7:13–14) (note: just used part of scripture), but we all need to memorize this whole chapter (Matthew 7) (verse 21, "not everyone that says, Lord, Lord will enter into the kingdom of heaven...but he that does the will of my father in heaven" or verse 22 "not everyone that prophecies in thy name... or casts out devils in thy name...[partial scripture]). We all need to read verse 23 because these people don't make it in. Evidently, God's not impressed with a performance. Or maybe these folks had the real goods, but something happened that made them quit serving, praying, and following the Lord. But it plainly says they were doing things for God. Then at the end of time, at Judgement Day, he'll tell you that you "worked iniquity" (living in sin): in (Matthew 7:24), Jesus says, "I never knew you, depart from me, ye that worked iniquity." So there is your answer. Those that continue to live in sin don't make it into heaven (John 14:6, 10:1–27; Luke 6:46; Heb. 12:1–2; Rom. 12:1–3). So again, we must lay aside our fleshly lusts and the sins that separate us from God. Remember, we don't want to grieve the Holy Spirit (Eph. 4:30).

Which is very dangerous. So...read...and learn, and follow the Bible.

How Do We Draw the Line to What Prejudice Is Considered to God? Or What Does God Think about It?

No. 1. God doesn't like it. And it amazes me at some cults that think they can commit murder, which is breaking the Ten Commandments plus being prejudice is a sin, we must love everyone regardless of skin color or origin, etc. It amazed me when I read where Jesus used prejudice texts in the Bible like when He used the Samaritans and women as the Heros of his parables, which the Jews hated, because the Samaritans were half breeds and some Bible verses were real life events, such as the woman at the well in (John 4 or in Luke 10:25 to 37), The man that was a "Good Samaritan," that the Lord was making a Hero out of him to rebuke a lawyer, or how about the Syrophenician woman (which is a Greek) in (Mark 7:25 to 30 and in Matthew 15:21–28) that the Jews considered the Syrophenicans to be dogs of the human race, but if you'll notice, Jesus honored her tenaciousness and admired her faith, when we are persistent, and have perseverance to keep pressing in till we get an answer…Like the women with the issue of blood (Mat. 9:20, 21; Mark 5:24 to 34; Luke 8:43 to 48), notice in (Mark 5:28) she rehearsed the matter in her heart…saying "if I may touch but his clothes, I shall be whole" but, folks there is absolutely nowhere in scripture that says go touch Jesus's garment, and you can be healed…This was coming out of her heart and soul…so the Lord rewards Faith, determination and tenaciousness, someone being persistent with a made up mind, and the Lord sees and blesses them, no matter what race they are, it's the whosoever is a thirst come, and who-so-ever will, let him come and drink of the water of life freely (Rev. 22:17, in my words). "Folks… it's really…Just how bad do you want help? Do you give up to quick, keep knocking…keep pressing, my old pastor used to say if you haven't fasted while praying, you've not done all you can, then you let God have it: there are times we've seen in scripture where people got there miracles by being persistent (Luke 18:7 and 8) others, like King Jehoshaphat, the Lord told him the battle is not yours…I'll fight this one for you "just sing me a song"…wow (1 Pet. 5:7, 2 Chron. 20:15, 2 Chron. 20:22, Acts 16:25) And sometimes he wants you to sing your way out, with praise songs to God. Wow…To obey God's voice, when we are told to do something foolish or something that sounds stupid (1 Cor. 1:27).

The Bible says, obedience is better than sacrifice (1 Sam. 15:22) all through the Bible we read The Lord telling people to do stupid foolish things, and those who were obedient received their miracle, example, the blind man Jesus told to go wash in the Pool of Salome, the guys blind, hello, or God told Moses to throw a tree in the water to make the water not bitter anymore. Jesus told Peter, go fishing, and the first fish will have a piece of money in his mouth, go pay our taxes for you and me. Wow…or how about the time Jesus told the disciples to feed the five thousand people with five loaves of bread and 2 fishes…After he blessed it. Double wow, it was multiplied enough to feed the whole 5,000 and even had left over fragments… or how about when Elisha told Naaman to go dip seven times in the Jordan River, (2 Kings 5:14) and then God would heal his leprosy. Wow (2 Kings 5:14). Or how about dropping an (Iron Axe) in water and some preacher say…cut a stick, and put the stick in the water and the Iron Axe floated up to the top: (2 Kings 6:5, 6, 7) or (John 21:3 to 6) and (Luke 5:4 to 6), the disciples fished all night and caught no fish (I've been there) but the Lord says let down your nets, and they caught a full net, and that was after fishing all night for nothing… "A lot of times God wants us to exhaust all resources, to where we have to depend upon him. But you got to admit that sounded pretty foolish…hey…we fished all night, hello…but they obeyed and was shocked, at the amount of fish they caught. Praise the Lord. So when we obey God no matter how foolish it seems…we get results. And again this also applies to prejudism, God wants us all to get along, and Jesus made a statement to the disciples, in (John 13:34, 35). By this shall all men know that you're my disciples, IF you have "LOVE one to another" after Jesus washed their feet and showing them love, he said "love one another," as I have loved you…" And you have love one to another." Now, if you recall the upper room in (Acts 2:9, 10, 11) tells of all sorts of different nationalities speak in the other peoples own language, so God pours out his spirit on all flesh (nationalities, Acts 2:17). And I want to say to those that are prejudist, I'll give you all the scriptures you want, that you will not make it to heaven, if you have hate toward people of a different race, which is prejudism, and to you cult members, Jesus and Adam and Eve, were not white…wow…Study out the geographical maps of the Garden of Eden, the only place it could have been would have been Africa which is a giant jungle type garden…or an Amazon type area…but the rivers that flow through Africa tells us that this was indeed the Garden of Eden, and if so then the first man and woman was black, well that's what I believe, and I've heard so many say it's not…but there are many anti-Christ spirits in our world, and was also in Jesus's Day and ours… But there are bullies, even in churches and religions, and cults which hate black people and other races also which reminds me of "Ray Stevens song in the '50s and '70s era called "Everything is beautiful" and says Jesus loves the little children…Red and Yellow, black and white…but to be against others and hate them because of there skin color is so wrong, and again in my book, it's a bully spirit and an anti-Christ spirit, cause God so loved the world (John 3:16, the whole world.) Anyway…

A bully spirit or racist or bad attitude toward any human being is wrong. And God will Judge them for it on Judgment Day.

I cannot undue the past especially what has happened before I was born, but I will say again, what has been done to other races and cultures with every fiber of my being, I say forgive us, forgive my race, please forgive us with tears in my eyes, many, many from the black race to the Indians, Mexican, and Chinese laborers. To all that feel they have been misjudged, mistreated by the white man, in behalf of all my ancestors, I pray that somehow you find it in your heart to forgive us. (Revenge is God's and he will repay!) Many times I see especially in kids pay evil for evil, two wrongs does not make a right. The hero movies that do this just might send you to hell, if you follow those bad examples an take out vengeance on a bully, yes, bullying is wrong (Matt. 14:21 to 35, Luke 21:22, Rom. 12:19, 2 Thess. 1:8, Heb. 10:30) and there is a lot even in businesses, and on the job and in government officials, law enforcement, and even in churches sad to say that even some church leaders makes you wonder, especially those in the News that were arrested make you wonder don't they remember anything in the Bible especially (Rom. 13:1, 2, 3 and 2 Cor. 5:11) no. 1, cause power goes to people in authority's head.) No. 2, (because power belongs to God.) No. 3, unless you hired a guy like Daniel as in (Daniel 6:3). Daniel was preferred because of his excellent spirit. This guy you would love to work for…but a mean nasty ol' grouch, that thinks he's a drill sergeant no one wants to work under. That brings to mind the parable Jesus told in (Matthew 18:23–35); you need to read it. This guy owes the king thousands, and begs for forgiveness, so the king won't throw him in prison, nor sell his wife and kids as slaves. And the king had mercy on him, and forgave him but that same guy goes out and grabs a guy by the throat saying: Pay me the few money's you owe me, and the other guy, falls down and begs him to have mercy but he didn't but threw him in prison. And the king, representing God, heard, what this unforgiving unmerciful creep done after the king gave him mercy, and Jesus said and so will God do to you if you don't forgive others their (in my words) trespasses. (Wow, verse 35.) But a bully spirit God will send to hell. In my words-Read it My race, and my ancestors, were so wrong to hire and mistreat employees like dirt. From hundreds of years ago, even up to today, they were human beings, not dogs. One brother told me of having to drink out of different fountains or ride in the back of a bus. This is not right, in God's eyes and mine, in it all.

I pray that you forgive us, I pray we all get the love and forgiveness in our hearts, one for another and I do not mean to stir up anything but want forgiveness from all people again. I have seen the love of God, the true spirit of love, in Living Christ Church, a church where all races of people are and the spirit of God is on them, where they all come together and pray as a big family and I feel so, so proud to be accepted in this body. I cry. They'll never know how much they've touched my heart by their love, prayer and Christ-like spirit they have.

Again Jesus said they will know you are my disciples by the love you have one toward another. (John 13:34–35) in the verse 34, Jesus said I give you a new commandment a commandment is a command...hello, and He said, "To love one another as I have loved you." So this is the opposite of prejudism...to being...Christlike.

How Do We Draw the Line to What's Called Being Christ-Like?

So many I've seen over the years seem to draw a different line than what I read in scripture. In (Acts 8:26–39), Philip was not concerned that the eunuch was of another race, and Philip was so yielded to the Lord. He was directed by the Holy Spirit to join him on his chariot and witness to him, and lead him in prayer to Jesus. Many times I, too, have listened to an anointed singer like Vestal Goodman or, the late, great Mahalia Jackson, who sung, "Just a closer walk with thee," this morning. Wow, and I just lifted up my hands and said repeating words in the song… Yeah, me too, Lord. I just started yielding myself with a thank-you type of praise, and the tears began to flow. The Lord wants us all to yield to him and not be ashamed of tears because many times, folks are just too busy, but sometimes, when a good anointed singer is singing the glory down, you just yield yourself to it with a praise, asking for forgiveness first and then saying, "Thank you, Lord, for all you've done for me," especially for things that you are really grateful for. See if you don't get zapped by the Holy Ghost. Anyway, Philip wasn't concerned about this guy's culture, race, or background even though Scripture does indeed mention his duties as a eunuch in Acts 8:26–39); but notice that he heard the eunuch read out of (Isaiah 53:7) about Jesus being as a sheep before the shearers and a lamb before the slaughter. Philip preached unto him Jesus and how he died for the sins of the whole world (John 3:16–18). Not just this culture or that particular people but the whole world! And the word again teaches in Matthew 18. We must forgive and practice the Christ-like life as he forgave us. We also forgive others. Thank God don't know about you dear saint of God, but I was a real creep, a real vomit of the earth, and I just pray again with all my heart that anyone that I have offended even with this book, please forgive me. I know my past life as a hippy-biker pothead jerk that I was, I can't undo what I did. But ask for forgiveness and have asked many others also and will still walk in forgiveness because that's what Jesus Christ taught (you must forgive others.) I heard a pastor say once about throwing feathers from a pillow in the air then with a sack. He said go and gather all those feathers up, but you and I know that's impossible even as she said to the old pastor, and he replied, yes, and so is all the gossip that has gone out of your mouth. You can't get those words back, just like the wind carrying the feathers…the ol' devil runs with your evil gossip words that wound and hurt the hearts of people. Wow. And being fully 100 percent dedicated to God, are we really any different from the great heroes of the Bible? No, but they were fully 100 percent dedicated to God. (That's the only difference.) They were just obedient to God, some like old Peter, Samson, David had to learn things the hard way. But we are all God's children created in his image: we just need to walk close to God and keep a repented heart (daily, take up your cross and follow Jesus Christ). And Jesus taught us to walk in love and forgiveness, and Apostle Paul taught to forget the junk behind you…and press on forward (in my words, in Philippians 3:13, 14). In other words, live it, walk in love, and forgiveness. Jesus said forgive 490 times; that's a lot of cheek turning as Jesus taught and Peter said, "Am I supposed to forgive others seven times in a day?" Jesus said, I didn't say seven times, but seventy times seven = four hundred ninety times in a day (Matt. 18:22, Luke 6:46). Wow. Sounds like, as many times as we mess up and ask Jesus to forgive us…*again*. Huh…

How Do We Compare or Draw the Line of Our Lives to the Bible Heroes of Old?

Are we really spiritually any different maybe physically? But is there any difference between us than others. No, and even if you have a crooked face or bent nose or extra toes, or one long arm, longer than the other, if you have large blotches on your face, or your short, or your tall. You get the point. We are all some way different in character, but it doesn't matter to God, it's what's inside your heart and that is getting out the bitterness, ask Jesus to forgive us, and hose us out with the sweet Holy Ghost, and He took out that bitterness out of me and put in his self. Hallelujah and he can hose you out also, I read of all the human flaws of so, so many men of God, where Noah got drunk after the flood, does that permit me to party, no! (2 Pet. 3:17). But beware lest you also, be led away with the error of the wicked, fall from your own sted fastness (to be stable or fixed, or succored) as in (Psalm 108:1 or Hebrews 3:15–19, Hebrews 4:1)... Note: if our heart is fixed on serving God, then God will succour us, and keep us stable in him (Jesus) (Luke 6:46, John 6:67 and 68).

David and Moses committed murder, and David also committed adultery, but God forgave them...so does that mean that we can kill and fornicate, No, (Romans 6:12 to 17) we must follow God's commandments, but if we fall, or slip, we have an advocate with the Father. (Jesus, 1 John 2:1; Ps. 37:23–24; Rom. 6:1–2.) Now. I even read how that great man of faith, Elijah after killing and standing up to all those false prophets, turn and ran from one woman. (Human) They were in many ways like you and me. Humans had their own individual faults characteristics and failures as we also do, they were heroes of the faith and even you think because your little small amounts of what you do compared to what others may do, that they seem more important than you, not so, if we are doing what we feel God wants us to do, then we will be rewarded, hey, look at me, I've served the Lord over forty years, just now six years ago I started writing, wow, it took a car wreck to bring it out. And I have felt like a failure and a loser over half my life, but we know that the Bible says that voice is the devil, he is the accuser of the brethren, that's why you can't be prejudice, that's the devils voice. Those are anti-Christ spirits—opposites (2 Tim. 3:5). But as (Rev. 12:11) says, "They overcame him (the devil) by the blood of the Lamb (Jesus), and by the word of their testimony, and loved not their lives unto the death!" Little is much if God's in it. I heard just the other day a big famous preacher from back east say, he started out with just (I think he said seven) and his huge congregation now because of his faithfulness to God and was faithful over a little and did what he could with what he had. And boom, look at God. Don't you know saint of God that the obedience of the woman with the handful of meal that her sacrifice to that man of God Elijah, her reward will be like Elijah. Hey, she obeyed the man of God and was taken care of, we sow good we reap good hello... God still blesses faithfulness and giving hearts, show love reap love, sow hate reap hate it's a law of God that'll never change. I'm a product example.

I have seen whole hearted anointed saints of God...highly used—greatly used by God in saving souls.

In prison ministry, street ministry, shut in hospital convalescent retirement ministry, etc., know many that do ministry at Indian reservations, etc., that are all doing a great job and giving it their all. And every one of them will have great rewards in heaven and I am so proud of them all for hanging in there, especially when times were rough and tuff. And being tenacious for God. To the saving of souls, if even just one in your life time. It's worth it all, when we take a stand, and tap into the anointing of God, we'll see great results, sometimes later on in life and there's always some type of opposition, but like the prophets and apostles God'll help us too.

One TV preacher said new levels, new devils, so the higher in God you go, different types of oppositions, but (Rom. 8:31) says, if God's for you, who can be against you. Somethings we have to allow him to do the majority of the work, some he has us do, but I've seen a lot of people, get upset and try to change people, you can't, that's God job.

We plant and another one waters but God does the increase, the change of the heart, the deliverance of the soul of mankind is God's job, allow him to use you, to deliver his word to folks, the watering of the word and it'll fertilize the soul and heart and convict man when he errs. But to many times I've seen some say, if you walk away now, oh come on (1 Cor. 3:6, 7). God is long-suffering and you better thank God; he was with you. Amen.

The Time Will Come That When People Kill You, They Will Think They Are Doing God a Service

(John 16:2, Matthew 24:9–12)

We know we are close to the Lord's return, and folks, people should draw as close to God as possible, not walk further away but in today's world, the people are walking a far off, these are indeed the last day prophecies being fulfilled, that says in the last days there will be a great falling away (see verse 2 of 2 Thess. 2:3, Heb. 12:25, 2 Pet. 3:16–17) as the day of Christ is at hand = the return of our Lord Jesus Christ. It's here folks. We better pray like never before (2 Thess. 2:3 to 13) I saw on TV this CEO getting a microchip 666 (Rev. 13:14 to 17, Rev. 20:4) mark of the beast in his hand on the six-o'clock news, and I recorded it. And you'd think the churches would be packed full knowing we are close to Christ return, because this is prophecy being fulfilled. Hello, people. I see it, why doesn't others, people have lost their first love (Rev. 2:4 and 5), but you run and place an ad in the paper. Millionaire is giving away 100 thousand dollars at church next Sunday. It would be packed out. Why, people love money, more than God, ouch, am I telling the truth. You better believe it. We are in those last days, that people'll kill you for a dollar, or a dirty look, young girls, are being sold as sex slaves, in America?

What? This is the last generation. Get ready. It's time to get on the boat of God. We need to try our best to persevere, press and push on in our prayer life like never before myself included (1 Cor. 9:27). Pray and ask God to direct you, lead and guide you and teach you when you read and pray. Guess what, he will if you are really sincere in your heart. I would suggest starting in the New Testament in the four gospels work your way through it then go to the Old Testament. We taught this in the prison ministry. We also need in this day and evil time we're in, is to pray for God's spiritual discernment and the Bible says to try the spirits to see if they are of God, the world is getting to where they give place to the devil, which the Bible says not to. So we need 100 percent divine intervention in so many areas in this evil day.

But mostly stay ready and stay on guard (Luke 21:34:36). Don't get caught up about religion, follow the Bible to the best of your ability. The world is ripe and ready for the anti-Christ but the word says he can't come until he (the spirit of God) that's in you (2 Thess. 2:7 and 8) is taken out of the way. In other words, when Christ's spirit that saves us, that's in our heart is caught up. (1. Thess. 4:13:18, 2 Thess. 2:4:12.) we are not appointed to wrath = great tribulation— (1 Thessalonians 5:9), so be ready.

Soon It'll Be Ready or Not; Here Comes Jesus…

What does man give in exchange for our soul? (Matt. 16:26) Really… is there anything worth your soul being doomed to hell forever for? Stop it! don't start saying but I've been a good person all my life, living by the golden rule, etc. (Matt. 19:16 to 21, see verse 20, Rom. 3:10, Isa. 64:6) this type thinking is a lie, that I've been a good guy all my life and deserve to go to heaven, on my good merits either you believe the Bible or you don't and if you don't, your doomed, but if you believe the Bible, it says God's own people are destroyed for their lack of knowledge (Hosea 4:6) you can be good all your life and still miss heaven, you must be born again (John 3:3–5) and live for God, and read and following Jesus Christ and the Bible. I have worked beside many over the years, that really believe just because they do huge donations to poor needy organizations and children's hospital, etc. That the good deeds somehow win them entrance into heaven, and outweighs the bad, well, all that's nice, and needed, but none of that gets anyone into heaven, you have to live according to the Bible. And you have to be born again, repenting of your sins, receiving Jesus Christ into your heart (Acts. 2:38–39) And following the Bible. That's what'll get you in those pearly gates, hey, there are Atheist that do good deeds, and donate (but they live like the devil and they do not believe) the Bible says, you must believe (John 14:6, Rom. 10:9–10) Jesus Christ, was born of a virgin, and died on the cross for our sins, And Rose the third day, from the dead, and ascended back up (Acts 1:1 to 11, John 16:7–8) to God (then Jesus) sends back his spirit, "the Holy Ghost" that comes into us and saves our soul, and that is the rocket fuel that's gonna shoot you through the sky, up to

Jesus, when he comes back, he'll be above the earth, and call his spirit back that's in the Christians, taking (1 Thess. 4:16–18) us believers to heaven but if you don't have his spirit, you don't go (Rom. 8:9). (1 Thessalonians 4:1) Good people, and many good organizations, tons of them do good deeds and live like the devil, I know many. No again, I'm not the judge, just saying what I know, you wouldn't sell your soul to the devil for no amount of money would you? no, so why throw it away for a false belief. I'm telling you scriptures, and facts, that the Bible is lining up with the news today, events and things that the two-thousand-year-old, Bible says will happen in the Last Days. Yes, you still get unbelievers, but that to is also recorded in the Bible, in (2 Peter 3:3–5).

And you probably wouldn't hear this kind of talk at most churches today, because there are so many that are (Rom. 12:1, 2.) Conforming to the world, the Bible says, be ye transformed by the renewing of your mind (by reading and following scriptures in the Bible.) not by being conformed to the world and false religions, and doctrines of devils in (1 Timothy 4:1) (in my words) and dressing, and looking like those in the world, the church folks are supposed to be a separated group of people who follow Jesus Christ. One of the whole problems with many churches today is, you can't tell the difference between some church folks and the partiers in the bars, and many dress like hookers, wear shorts, live like the devil himself, okay. I'm repeating myself but you get my point. About the wild loose lifestyle today, but this is the opposite of what Jesus Christ taught and He said plainly in scriptures that the last generation would be like it was in Noah's day (2 Pet. 2:5, Matt. 24:37), when God destroyed the world with flooding the earth (Luke 17:26–32) but this next time it's gonna burn (Rev. 18:8, Rev. 16:8). So God's Word is telling us, not to be conformed to the world, but be ye transformed by the renewing of your mind (Rom. 12:2). Because the world has gotten into so many churches, because people quit putting the Bible in their mind which is renewing and transforming our minds, like Apostle Paul was saying, to be renewed after Christ. Because the church Jesus Christ needs to be in the hearts and minds of the people of the world, but they say, I'm as good as those church folks. This is why the Bible says the Christian must live a separated life (1 Cor. 9:27, Heb. 4:1, 1 John 3:20, 1 Pet. 4:2, Col. 3:5), so the sinners will see the change in you...which is Jesus (Matt. 5:16). When people see a real true Christian, they should see a reflection of Jesus Christ in us. Amen. But if for some reason you should miss the return of Jesus, you'll have seven years, three and a half tribulation and three and a half Great Tribulation, you don't want to be here then (during great tribulation) this is gonna be the time of beheading, and the mark of the beast, and men's hearts failing them for fear of looking after the things coming on the earth that is written in prophecies so pray you're ready to go in the rapture (1 Thess. 4:13 to 18; 1 Thess. 5:9; Luke 21:34, 35, 36, see vs. 16; Rev. 20:4; Rev. 9:18, 19; Rev. 16:18; Rev. 8:1 to 13; Luke 21:26; Rev. 16:1 to 4; Rev. 16:8, 9; Rev. 16:18 to 21) and many more on God's wrath, you can Google and look them up, and you will not want to miss the Rapture and be left behind while all this is going on, because God has been more than lenient with this generation, but the main number 1 reason God pours out his wrath and fierce anger on EARTH is because they rejected his son Jesus Christ. So they miss the Rapture, and go through seven years of hell on EARTH (God's wrath is the last three and a half years of the seven.) Man rejects God's plan of salvation, God has warned the world since the days Jesus Christ walked the earth. And we've had warnings since Noah's Day, but man is stubborn and wants to rebel and live and party, and do whatever he wants, and the prisons are full of them and more on the way. So where do you draw the line. Do you think all of God's laws and rules should be trashed? (NO WAY! Absolutely not! And yes, there has always been good and evil people) but after the Rapture, there will be no conscience in man. Those evil years of Great Tribulation will be the first years of the history of mankind that man has not had a conscience to convict him of his sins, it will be the evilest time ever. Things will happen. A spirit of offense is going all over the world that (Matt. 24:10) will cause man to turn against one another, and will trick and deceive you or have you to be put to death. (John 16:2; John 15:18), (Luke 6:22, 23; Luke 7:23), because people are offended everywhere (Matt. 24:10) And this is because God is taken his spirit back to heaven (1 Thess.

4:16; Acts 1:9 thru 11 see verse 11; John 14:3; Jn. 14:28; Jn. 14:18). Note: After the Rapture of the church, Jesus Christ calls back up his spirit (Rev. 4:1–2), which is the same spirit that comes into people's hearts when they repent of their sins and become born again. Now, God's Holy Spirit will convict us of sin, but when the Lord tells his spirit to come up here, that's what we call the Rapture of the church, being caught up, etc. Now, when God's spirit is gone from the earth, there will be complete evil; man will no longer have a conscience, according (1 John 3:20–21). And since there's no more conscience in man to convict his heart of sin and when he does wrong, then it will be like all of the prison walls fell flat. It will be hell on earth. (Rom. 1:18 to 32). And God's anger will be poured out on the earth, called God's wrath. Like you've never imagined. Worse than any horror movie you've ever seen, I guarantee it. And it will be God's wrath upon the earth, the day of God's vengeance on Earth (2 Thess. 1:8 to 10), and will be judged for rejecting Jesus Christ. You better draw your line of your life straight with God because if your eternal soul, depends on your choice why do you think your reading my book. Don't argue. There's not a whole lot of time left. Be sure, be ready… Jesus is coming, get ready ask for forgiveness of your sins.

God could really use someone like you, with your skills, talents, and expertise, time is short…you could reach your friends, and family that I can't. (Even with a tract, just hand 'em one.) So what are you waiting for? You agree with the majority of all this…so get moving, call (1-909-987-0771 or www.chick.com/samples) say Rev. Fred Davis sent you…say send me samples and price list, order and get busy.

(Acts 1:8) says, "Ye shall receive power after the holy ghost comes on you, and pray Jesus I believe you died on the cross for my sins and rose from the dead and I pray you come into my heart and soul." Save me from all my sins. Please forgive me of all my sins, and all my trespasses and all my iniquities. Have mercy on me, I receive you Jesus into my heart, I receive you as my Lord and Savior. And pray you teach me your word and help me to follow it and you, in Jesus's name I pray (Rom. 10:9, 10).

Confess with your mouth that I'm saved and born again to someone. Jesus saved my soul.

Now live for God, read the Bible to the best of your ability, go find you a church that preaches the 100 percent true Word of God, ask for a pamphlet on their beliefs. Don't just settle, keep looking. Ask, pray to God for a sign and to direct you to the right one. Remember that there are wrong ones out there, and cults, and false doctrines, and false religions, and false preachers everywhere, so be careful. And watch and pray (Heb. 10:31, Heb. 2:3).

I pray no one gets offended on my opinions.

My prayer: Father, in Jesus's name, direct these folks in their walk with you. Direct them to the right church, save them, and keep them, teach them not to be offended, explain to them. Holy Ghost, as you did to me, in Jesus's name, turn on the light in their soul. Amen.

Ending Closing Thought

(America...Earth...)

The Bible says it's not God's will that anyone perish, but that all come to repentance. (2 Pet. 3:9)

Draw the line straight to God through Jesus Christ.

If we really knew the one, the awesome one, the all-powerful, all knowing creator of the universe and creator of all living life. The real supernatural force behind creation of life that huge giant spiritual force we call God, Jesus, Holy Ghost (spirit). So big that he created the planets, earth, heaven, all the universe, yet so small he lives in our hearts. Can give us power, protect and bless our lives, give us the one wireless communication device called prayer. Yeah. I know, that's an old saying but I like it. And the Bible is a real road map to heaven, and it's the best GPS you could ever have. The Bible is our Road Map and the Holy Spirit is our guide, guarding angels around us.

Okay, I'm done.

God bless.

Dedication and Special Thanks to

My pastor Donahue Green and First Lady Evon Green, for their love and prayers and inspiration and Living Christ Church Family.

And church families and ministers and a special thanks to my wife for all her prayers and support through all my hideaway, quiet times, during corrections, and standing by my side and understanding through it all. And a special thanks to my daughter Mel on my last book and immediate family for prayers. God bless you all and thanks for your encouragement and prayers.

Special thanks to all those at Christian Faith Publishing. Special thanks to the editor, the photographer, artists, and Pastor Vincent Damino and Cassy Byham, and anyone else that I fail to mention. CFP has my consent to include their names there at this wonderful Christian Faith Publishing Co. God bless you all.

And a very special thanks to Sis Lanet and Bro and Sis Harris. I would also like to thank Sis Lanet at church and Bro. Sye Harris and Naomi Harris for taking off work, and Lanet for driving me to UCLA for my surgery, and the Harrises for driving me to my procedure and MRI at Standford. They really sacrificed their time and money for me. Real true friends. Thanks to all of you.

And special thanks to Lois Earles, a sweet neighbor. She has come to our rescue, many times babysitting our cats and brought food many times.

Also, Steve and Sheila Nelson, thank you for fixing our busted waterpipe. Thanks so much, our sweet neighbors.

And thanks to everyone for all their prayers and those that has confirmed this book.

And most of all, to my Lord and Savior Jesus Christ for inspiration and thoughts and making it all possible, for allowing me to write this book.

And to my readers, may God bless you in your walk with him.

I failed to say thanks to Deacon Vance McKinney and his wife Elsa who bought my diabetes medicine when I was out. God bless all these that have and blessed us.

I pray my book turns on a light in your hearts and mind and adds a fresh stirring in your soul that you'll see we are so close to Jesus Christ's coming and realize that we need to tell more people. Get ready. And stay ready. See you there. God bless, Fred Davis.

Draw your line straight to Jesus Christ.

About the Author

Reverend Fred Davis is, in most people's eyes, a fanatic last-days, end-time preacher. In Fred's eyes, he doesn't profess or consider himself to be an author—just a voice of a preacher sending out a warning to the world to get on God's boat that's about to sail. Fred loves people and don't want anyone left behind. Fred loves prophecy of the Bible ('cause you can see it unfolding) but also enjoys taking a bike ride on a pretty day, enjoys life, and loves listening to the old, southern gospel songs as well as the old gospel song book hymns. He loves watching old comedies and spending time with his grandkids. Fred was a prison minister for eighteen years and pastor for eight and a half years.

Reverend Fred Davis was not always a minister: He comes from a hippy biker lifestyle—drugs, booze, parties, etc. He was sent home with bad news from a local hospital—that he could die, without a miracle. He was raised in church as a child, had a praying mother and grandma that most people would call them type fanatics, but it was okay, because when you're dying that's who you want to pray for you. So the light came on when the doctor told him, He said, "Doc, I've been a bad person. I'll go to hell." And the doctor said, "It sounds like you need to talk to a preacher." Mr. Davis did, and a year or two later, he became a prison minister. Then years later a pastor…now author…who has lived in Tulare, CA, with his lovely wife, Brenda, of 51 years in-together on this Nov. 12 from 1971 and enjoy being very active in their church. They love to visit the beach now and then, and loves spending time with their grandkids. They enjoy playing games especially chess, and fishing was fun till his on the job car wreck, but still enjoy just getting out with them at the park.